Following Tradition

Also by Simon J. Bronner

American Folklore Studies: An Intellectual History

Popularizing Pennsylvania: Henry W. Shoemaker and the Progressive Uses of Folklore and History

Grasping Things: Folk Material Culture and Mass Society in America

The Carver's Art: Crafting Meaning from Wood

Old-Time Music Makers of New York State

Piled Higher and Deeper: The Folklore of Student Life

American Children's Folklore

Ethnic Ancestry in Pennsylvania: An Analysis of Self-Identification

Edited by Simon J. Bronner

Creativity and Tradition in Folklore: New Directions

Folklife Studies from the Gilded Age: Object, Rite, and Custom in Victorian America

American Material Culture and Folklife

Folk Art and Art Worlds

American Folk Art: A Guide to Sources

Consuming Visions: Accumulation and Display of Goods in America, 1880–1920

Following Tradition

FOLKLORE IN THE DISCOURSE
OF AMERICAN CULTURE

Simon J. Bronner

Utah State University Press
Logan, Utah

Utah State University Press
Logan, Utah 84322-7800

Typography by WolfPack
Cover Design by Barbara Yale-Read

Library of Congress Cataloging-in-Publication Data

Bronner, Simon J.
    Following tradition: folklore in the discourse of American
culture / by Simon J. Bronner.
        p.   cm.
    Includes bibliographical references and index.
    ISBN 0-87421-239-1
    1. Folklore—United States—History. 2. Oral tradition—United
States—History. 3. United States—Social life and customs.
I. Title
GR105.B67   1998
398'.0973—dc21   97-45342
                                                      CIP

for Robert Gunderson (1915–1996)

Contents

Illustrations

Acknowledgments

WHAT WOULD A BOOK ON TRADITION BE, IF I DID NOT ACKNOWLEDGE MY DEBT TO generations from the past into the present? First, my father reminded me before he died of the meaning of the long ethnic-religious tradition to which I belong. My mother strived to be ever modern, to be "American," uttered in her noticeable immigrant accent. My sister opened my eyes to the vantages of family and community, and my friends let me be different. Therein lies much of my inspiration.

I am indebted to Penn State University for granting me a sabbatical leave and research funds, and Harvard University and Osaka University, Japan, for providing me good teaching homes while I saw the work into publication. The Fulbright Program, Japan-United States Educational Commission, funded my stay in Japan, and the American Council of Learned Societies provided a grant for my work in England. I was fortunate to be around able staff and faculty at the various institutions, including William Mahar, Michael Barton, John Patterson, Alison Hirsch, Irwin Richman, Tim Evans, Matthew Wilson, Patricia Levin, Suren Lalvani, Sue Etter, Donna Horley, Ruth Runion, Kathy Ritter, Harold Shill, Greg Crawford, Henry Koretzky, Alan Mays, Fay Youngmark, Gloria Clouser, Joseph Harris, Deborah Foster, Lawrence Buell, Daniel Aaron, Werner Sollors, Laurel Thatcher Ulrich, Patrick Ford, Susan Countryman, Susan Hunt, Christine McFadden, Michael Wescoat, Daniel Long, Hisashi Ishida, Seisaku Kawakami, Yuichi Morioka, Chiyo Yoshii, and Kazumi Tanaguchi. At Penn State, graduate assistant Kenneth Patrick deserves special credit for his handling of computer and archive tasks. Other students who contributed include Margaret "Peggy" Reynolds, Douglas Manger, Elizabeth Sparks, Beth Summy, Patricia Meley, Brenda Beasley, Eri Sekiguchi, Keiko Hirose, Shoko Nakamura, and Eriko Tanaka.

I also benefitted from being on faculty in two summer folklore institutes at Utah State University. They were memorable occasions that included enlightening conversations with Barre Toelken, William Wilson, Steve Siporin, Barbara Walker, Patrick Mullen, Beverly Robinson, Chip Sullivan, David Hufford, Elliott Oring, Sylvia Grider, Carol Edison, Tom Carter, Austin Fife, Alta Fife, and many enthusiastic students. I gained admiration for Utah State Press there, and I valued the advice and encouragement that Linda Speth and John Alley of the Press provided.

I am grateful to many colleagues in American studies, history, and folklore who commented on my papers and ideas, especially Bill Nicolaisen, Jay Mechling, Don Yoder, Roberta Wollons, David Wilson, Sarah Emily Newton, Roger Abrahams, Patricia Turner, C. Kurt Dewhurst, Marsha MacDowell, Thomas Schlereth, Linda Dégh, Jeannie Thomas, Eleanor Wachs, Thomas Gallagher, Stephen Stern, John Vlach, William K. McNeil, Sandra Dolby, Ronald Sharps, Haya Bar-Itzhak, Daniel Long, Joseph Corn, Bradley Taylor, Donald Durnbaugh, Helen Bradley Foster, Carolyn Henry, Steve Roud, Gordon Ashman, Mark Skidmore, Wolfgang Mieder, Michael Owen Jones, Tsuguya Sasaki, Tetsuya Taguchi, Kazuko Miyashita, Hideyo Konagaya, and Misako Koike. I want to mention a few folks, family really, for staying close, even when I was away: Bill and Sue Aspinall, Ron and Cathy Baker, Ken and Anne Marie Thigpen, Ron and Manya Segal, Clare Luz, Joyce Kasman Valenza, Terry Feder Seplowitz, Eric Epstein, and Sally Jo Kahr.

I credit many tradition bearers for being teachers, although few of them recognized themselves as such. Stan Merzanis, Charles Rebuck, Beulah Rebuck, Philip Owen, and Bill Medlin especially gave of their time for my understanding of folk arts. Emma Schrock, Abner Beiler, and Stephen Scott guided me into the folklife of the Amish and Mennonite worlds. Other educators with more formal titles have given me long-lasting lessons, especially Bill Nicolaisen, H. L. Nieburg, Ronald Baker, Roderick Roberts, Roger Janelli, William Wiggins, Richard Dalfiume, Sam Chianis, Mary Ellen Brown, and Warren Roberts. While I am reflecting back, I know that Richard Dorson, Louis C. Jones, Mac Barrick, Samuel Bayard, Bruce Buckley, and Sue Samuelson would have wanted to comment on this work, and although they are now sadly departed, their admonishments to me still linger.

I am thankful for many curators, librarians, and archivists for access to special collections, including the Folklore Society Library in London (English folklorists); Utah State University (American Folklore Society); Pattee Library at Penn State University (Jacob and Wilhelm Grimm, Henry Shoemaker); Lilly Library at Indiana University (Richard Dorson); University of Nebraska (Benjamin Botkin); State Archives of Pennsylvania (Henry Shoemaker); Franklin and Marshall College (Alfred Shoemaker); Library of Congress (Allen Eaton); Abby Aldrich Rockefeller Folk Art Center (Holger Cahill and Abby Aldrich Rockefeller); Frederick R. Weisman Art Museum (Circles of Tradition exhibition); Albright-Knox Art Gallery (Arts and Crafts of the Homelands exhibition); Brooklyn Museum, Smithsonian Institution, National Anthropological Archives, and University of Pennsylvania Museum (Stewart Culin, Otis Mason, Frank Hamilton Cushing, Franz Boas); New York State Historical Association (Harold Thompson, Louis C. Jones); Vassar College and Mt. Holyoke College Archives (Martha Warren Beckwith); Hampton University (Hampton Folklore Society, Alice Bacon, Robert

Moton); and Harvard University Archives (Francis James Child, George Lyman Kittredge, Nathaniel Southgate Shaler, Richard Dorson, Committee on History of American Civilization).

I dedicate this book to the late Robert Gunderson, who left a deep impression on me as professor of history, speech communication, and American studies at Indiana University, Bloomington. Many years ago he urged me to look closely at rhetoric, politics, and history for their revelation of American beliefs, and I can only hope my work honors his memory.

Prologue

The Past and Present in Tradition

THIS BOOK IS ABOUT AN AMERICAN TRADITION—ARGUING ABOUT IT. AMERICANS through their history have stood up to claim tradition passionately, shape tradition, and break tradition to define their special status in the brave new world. The United States, an upstart nation of myriad communities, was assuredly a place to reevaluate tradition, and view it from various social angles. Americans have hailed their basic beliefs, customs, and myths—in short, their folklore—to epitomize this tradition. Basic indeed. Whatever this tradition was, it presumably beat at the heart of the society. As a point of social argument, "tradition" undoubtedly has been one of the most common as well as most contested terms in English language usage, and its intimate connection with another politically, indeed emotionally, charged keyword—culture—only added to its great significance in public exchanges.

Toward the present, invocations of "traditional values," "cultural tradition," "multiculturalism," "cultural diversity," and "culture wars" on the floors of legislatures, at school board meetings, in the popular press, and at many universities across the country proclaim the struggle of Americans to distinguish their nation and communities at a time when social and physical boundaries in a technological, mass society appear indistinct. Against this background many calls of tradition connote the ways that identity—national, social, individual—becomes expressed, and folklore and history, often compressed into our "culture" and "heritage," become key evidence to fashion a vision of the future that will clarify the meaning of living in mass society.

This book illuminates the debate on the character of American culture as a struggle to rationalize diverse American traditions into a coherent identity. It examines ways that the recovery of these traditions became translated into a conceptualization of American folklore. It brings into focus the prominent figures—often called folklorists—who have guided the translation of academic views into

1

public perceptions. It offers rhetorical and philosophical interpretations of folk-lore "talk" to provoke thinking about the significance of ideas of tradition in American intellectual history.

While sometimes bitter commentary on whether American culture can be, or should be, unified makes today's headlines, the issue is hardly new. In 1887, Lee J. Vance evoked heated responses by highlighting America's "composite" cultural character borne out by folklore that refused to fade from diverse immigrant and black communities in America. He asked readers of the popular magazine *Open Court*, "What have our American students of Folk-Lore done toward contributing their share to the History of Culture?" And being a popularized "subject of the day," folklore, he realized, had been central to magnifying views of culture, views that mattered so much to a nation struggling with rapid changes wrought by large-scale immigration, industrialization, and urbanization. In this book, I have altered Vance's question somewhat to ask about the contribution to the *discourse* of culture, especially in intellectual life. This includes the very invention and spread of the words "folklore" and "folklife" in the nineteenth century to represent the traditions—beliefs, customs, narratives, crafts—that compose and explain culture.

Vance recognized folklore as a buzzword for the kind of recoverable expression that offered "scientific" evidence of culture. In the new perspective he described, culture grew from roots deep in the gritty soil of past everyday life. It appeared to his readers as a kind of localized, even "vulgar" culture contrasted with civilized or "high" culture within a modernizing society. His readers were well aware that in Europe the Grimm brothers had sparked a movement to gather the folk literature of the unlettered and that this led to speculation on the relation of traditional life—defined then as a bottom layer to civilization—to ideas of a modern nation-state formed from a shared cultural root. It also led to a discourse on social and political issues ranging from nationalism to international socialism. Then, as now, mentioning "folklore" and "culture" raised differing attitudes toward the importance of individual will and collective authority. It can equally inspire argument over the significance of the past and the influence of one's surroundings on behavior. It can have associations with class, gender, age, and ethnicity. In America, it can raise voices taking stands on minority rights and education standards, among other issues that spin off from issues of American tradition.

The substance of the discourse on culture involves the relation of self and community to the nation. The ways that this discourse have been communicated, contested, and altered over the last century reveal historical struggles to declare sources for streams of the American experience. Spurred in the nineteenth century by industrialization, urbanization, and immigration, it has been renewed and heated in the late twentieth century by immigration again, in addition to perceptions of racial divides and social upheavals in the composition of family and community. Set against this social background, arguments over cultural identity today are colored by ideas that might be summarized as nationalist, pluralist, and behavioralist. Other terms can be heard for these ideas such as progressive, communitarian, multiculturalist, and universalist, and various shades of meaning can be drawn in, but consider some basic differences in outlook.

In the *nationalist* view, the American story is one of continual material and social progress, building a nation through cultural democracy with citizens accepting, even embracing, an American identity. As the story is variously related, American culture evolved from a few major sources into a national spirit involving core values of democracy and individual freedom. The narrative of America's traditions is tied into the surprising and glorious historical emergence of the nation, distanced from other cultures by huge oceans and an untamed land. Richard Dorson's words bear out one common view: "A new nation, born suddenly in a seventeenth-century wilderness, possessed neither cultural nor folk traditions to call its own. Yet in a relatively short span an American civilization has arisen on the naked earth, endowed with distinctive institutions, literature, behavior, and folklore" (Dorson 1959a, 7). For Dorson and many kindred spirits in American studies, American historical conditions were exceptional—or the combination of themes such as mobility, individualism, and democracy was distinctive—and gave rise to American traditions influencing a common culture that integrates immigrants and racial minorities.

The *pluralist* view values the diversity of local traditions in a nation that legitimizes the rights of social difference. In this view, America from its inception has been home to an array of persistent social heritages of language, religion, ethnicity, occupation, and region thriving in self-defining communities. Under the pluralist umbrella, reference can also be heard to communitarian and multiculturalist perspectives, to cite two special movements frequently invoking pluralist manifestoes of early twentieth-century critics Horace Kallen and Randolph Bourne. As the spin-off terms indicate, there can be dispute under the pluralist umbrella about political impositions upon distinctive communities and their ability to define themselves, especially when primary social categories in the American experience are presented as being broadly of race, class, and gender rather than more ethnographic concerns of ethnicity, religion, occupation, and region. More socially and geographically relative than historically progressive, the pluralist hand maps many continuities existing between traditions adapting to America and those abroad. This variety presumably gives America its vitality and ensures openness to new ideas. The nation is a political idea supporting a "pluralism" of communities rather than a cultural unity. In envisioning pluralism, there can be different opinions on the amount of intercultural connection as well as the level of national conflict and consensus that ensues from a diverse society. There can also be vigorous disagreement on the degree to which government should manage and encourage communal difference. This is especially true with the thorny matter of race and gender of special concern in multiculturalism. Yet there is a basic agreement that multiple identities are possible, even desirable, and traditions inherited as well as invented help perpetuate the varied social landscape.

Often overlooked is a "third force" that takes culture and its social aspects in a behavioral or psychological direction. It reflects on the emergence of mass society and conversely on individualism in the course of human experience. It is *behavioralist* or universalist in the sense that it views experience as less national or communitarian than based on individual intentions and responses to different social contexts. These contexts are changeful and relate to conditions of human making; humans are actors that have to adjust cultural roles in their daily performances on multiple stages. There is an implication that nation-states have reduced significance in cultural experience, and increased mobility across borders—political and social—suggests that communities are shifting and temporary: they are essentially intellectual constructions. Questions of cultural production are themselves objects of inquiry into relative (that is, without value judgments about hierarchies of art and culture) human urges to create, needs to express, and desires to organize experience. In this view, individuals belong less to groups or communities than to themselves. They respond to factors, such as age, gender, sexuality, and body presentation, that may not be a matter of community but of image and representation. Another issue that receives different interpretations among those working with the universalist idea is the systems of behavior that guide lives, such as organizations and living and working arrangements (i.e., families, friendship and professional networks, schools, stores, and institutions). Traditions do not carry the deep sense of a localized past as much as broad structural and aesthetic concepts that transcend group and national limits.

In assessing American cultural identity, folklorists, anthropologists, and now a growing number of historians and students of "cultural studies," have referred to the keyword of tradition. Folklorists, I will argue, have been primarily responsible for the use of tradition in the discourse of culture, and their rhetorical shifts over time are clues to shifting orientations toward American society. These shifts, I will show, are a result of political events, national and social movements, and some outstanding individuals from the late nineteenth century to the present. My title of *Following Tradition* has a double meaning, then, to refer to the *subject* of such concern—life and expression that responds to social precedent—and its *object*—consideration of the ways that modern existence builds on or breaks away from tradition, indeed defines tradition itself.

Working in a society that is often characterized as future-oriented, American folklorists have had a special problem. Working against a conventional view of tradition as comprising an ancient lineage and shared racial stock, American folklorists have fashioned ideas of tradition against the background of the country's relative youth among the world's nation-states and the diversity of peoples settling over a broad and varied landscape. The domain of Americans has dramatically changed from one coast to another and to areas outside the continent. All this commonly leads to a kind of apology in American culture studies for never really giving full account for the extent, socially and geographically, of the country's cultural

reach. While recognizing America's European, African, and native roots, many writers uncomfortably admitted that the nation did not neatly apply the idea of tradition from the Old World. Conventional wisdom holds that the United States, after
all, is all about a progressive, some may even say revolutionary, basis of seeking new
patterns to follow. America is often viewed as youth oriented, not responsive to the
inherited wisdom of old age or the past. Yet it is also home to longstanding "folk
cultures," such as the Amish or Cajuns, who are said to be authentically perpetuating "tradition." Further, political rhetoric in the country makes constant reference
to the plan of the "founding fathers" and the inspiration of the Mayflower. What
makes the United States so significant to contemplate is the special problem of joining tradition and modernity in a diverse, emergent social landscape to fashion a
distinct cultural identity.

In presenting the title *Following Tradition,* I offer that the philosophy of folklore
study and its relation to public ideas of culture reside in the keyword of tradition.
I am specially concerned with folklore studies because, more than other fields, it
centrally engages questions of tradition in its mission and has had in America a
notable public role in government, cultural agencies, museums, and historical
societies. To be sure, folklore is not alone in its concern for tradition. In the interdisciplinary mix I formed with historical American studies, the question of
national ramifications couples with the problem of tradition. My experience has
been that historical American studies tended to speak in broad abstract terms
about the basic ideas that characterize the United States, while folklore referred
often to local communities bound by traditions observed as specific practices.
Although folklore studies and American studies come at tradition from somewhat
different directions, they share thoughts on the way that tradition is "followed" as
idea and expression. Both studies, however, have often stopped short of discussing
a philosophy of tradition that becomes apparent from the emergence of so many
kinds of cultural practices. In bridging the studies of folklore and America with
philosophy, I needed to reassess the concept that they seemed to take for granted—
tradition—and the way it brings into its orbit other highly charged concepts in
American public discourse—identity, community, race, ethnicity, and art.

Many readers may think of my effort as "cultural studies," in which I explore the
ways that attempts to objectify culture from investigations of tradition have in fact
sprung from personal, social, and political agendas. I am viewing scholarship itself
as a significant cultural production and evidence of ideology in addition to a supposedly objective record of cultural practices. This book may well be used by folklorists as a way to look inward at the foundational matters that have concerned
them. For others, the essays will be a move outward toward questions of the
process of intellectually constructing society and culture. Overall, my book makes
the point that justification for an American tradition has been a cause, as well as a
study, for folklorists to show the special role of culture within the American experience. Various tensions exist over defining that role, especially between hopes for

a land of humane significance rooted in the face-to-face experience of diverse ethnic-regional communities and a nation transforming, indeed often escaping, the past, offering new opportunities to build a unified, mobile, progressive culture. Set against this background, talking about folklore is a discourse about belonging in America.

The first issue with which this book is concerned is the "problem of tradition." I do not mean to rehearse arguments for definition as much as I am interested in finding the perceptions of tradition for the purpose of persuasion in public and scholarly discourse. At moments when the terms of tradition become contested, when they become laden with values, when they reveal self-concept, they become political and historical artifacts worthy of interpretation. I begin with a discussion of the protean nature of "tradition" and attempts to objectify its meaning. In this effort, one of the contested moments to which I refer is apparent: the issue of the authority carried by tradition. Spilling over into public discourse, the problem of tradition is evident in different forms. To get at this usage, I examine applications of tradition in the press and its reflection of popular attitudes. Another reflection of popular attitude that I explore is the rhetoric of recent political campaigns, especially in constructions of "liberal" and "conservative" sides in the debate over "traditional values."

I then ponder the historical change in views from nineteenth-century intellectuals assessing modernism to twentieth-century scholars mulling over post-modernism. If this move implies a move from the mission of uncovering an ordered natural science of global civilization to understanding the capriciousness of individual human endeavor, then the history of folklore studies and its attention to "tradition" and other cynosures should be recognized for their contribution to this century's significant turns of thought. I examine the ideology, for example, implicit in the uses of folklore, as it reflected evolutionary doctrine in the politics of America's Gilded Age at the time folklore studies were being organized. In the era's exhibitions of "primitive" traditions at new museums dedicated to natural history, in the organization of a folklore congress at the Chicago World's Fair, and in the cultural recollection of slavery at black colleges will be found efforts to guide a dramatically changing nation.

In the chapters that follow, I interpret the conflict and convergence of two main strains on American cultural literacy, English and German, much as they represent two major ethnic movements to the United States. Apparently oppositional ideas of national progressivism and evolution of culture, I find, have been adapted from English anthropological methodology in the late nineteenth century, while similarly juxtaposed concepts of pluralism and romantic nationalism owe greatly to German *Volkskunde*. *Volkskunde* has had peculiarly American interpretations in folklife and material culture, especially in the receptive atmosphere of Pennsylvania, and I explore these interpretations in seeking explanation for the nationalization of community as a cultural concept. I argue in the sixth chapter that the ideological basis of folklife and material culture owes largely to the force of Alfred Shoemaker, who turned his devotion to Pennsylvania-German tradition into a national cause for appreciating America's diverse regional-ethnic folk cultures. Charges of political maneuvering (not to mention "madness") hurled at the outspoken Shoemaker are part of the story of representation of the ethnic scholar in America engaged in a social mission. The sometimes touchy issue of public representation of his Germanness is also there in the popularization of the Grimms, and I give particular attention in the fourth chapter to American uses of the famous brothers' fairy tales in popular culture and the rise of an origin legend tracing scientific views of folklore to the scholarly duo.

I am interested in the way folklore studies emerged to objectify tradition and the way scholars viewed its role in society. History is an issue in folklore studies because of disputes over the form that a retrospective on the field should take. In addition, folklorists and cultural historians in their studies have displayed an uneasiness that probably results from dealing with a past based on tradition and collective wholes rather than historic events and outstanding individuals. As the history discipline has increasingly embraced the rhetoric of narrative, memory, and tradition in the last decade, it has come closer to folkloristic concerns for culture and society and should join in the discourse on the past as well as historiography in folklore studies. To give an example of that intersection, I consider individuals who had "folklore firsts" and helped formulate influential outlooks on tradition. I begin with Martha Beckwith, America's first chair of folklore, who I credit with pragmatically emphasizing folklore as a distinctive study of multicultural tradition and women's roles within that study. I cover the dramatic career of Alfred Shoemaker, who founded America's first college department of folklore, organized America's largest folk festival and folklife society, and helped tradition take an ethnological turn in America. I devote a separate chapter to his nemesis, Henry Shoemaker, America's first state folklorist, and their fight over the ways that folklore would be conserved in the public sector to encourage a nationalist viewpoint.

Implicit in the phrase "American folklore" is the presence of a distinctive national identity, even as folklorists' collection of American traditions showed a decidedly international inheritance. This is the substance of the third issue I present. In nineteenth-century England and other nations of Europe, folklore had been used to rally nationalism and rationalize race. Could the same be said for twentieth-century America? This issue of the use of tradition has spilled over into controversies of the 1990s over "multiculturalism" and "cultural diversity." Invoking American studies, Richard Dorson set the debate during the 1950s with, first, the questions of identifying authenticity and variety in American tradition, evaluating social and political uses of folklore's popularization, and, finally, reconciling an international view of "folklore in America" and a nationalistic "American folklore." It is his polemic that I discuss in the chapter on "Richard Dorson and the

Great Debates," and moving beyond the university setting, I show other forms of the public debate in the last chapter on popular strategies of displaying American folk arts in galleries, festivals, and communities. The final discussion allows for a closing reflection on the contested interpretations of tradition in the modern present as art, performance, and praxis, and the translations of tradition for America's future.

It is admittedly a wide subject that I begin to probe here, and to encourage further inquiry I attach a bibliographic essay on the substantial contemporary literature of studying American traditions. My work should not be construed as an attempt for comprehensive historical coverage. Instead, it introduces the problems of tradition as a created object as much as a subject of inquiry. It raises critical issues and identifies key figures and moments in the conceptualization of tradition in America. It may begin to answer how American tradition came up for grabs.

1

The Problem of Tradition

THE CENTRAL PROBLEM OF TRADITION IS EXPLAINING THE WAYS THAT PEOPLE RELY on one another, with reference to precedent, for their wisdom, their expression, their identity. The problem may not be immediately evident from the mechanical sounding definition of tradition in most dictionaries as the "handing down" of lore from generation to generation, especially by oral means. In common usage, tradition can refer to an item dependent on this process, such as a story or custom, or to a precedent given the force of repeated practice, or to knowledge whose official source cannot be verified but is held widely, or to a concept—"a mode of thought or behavior"—characteristic of people generally.[1] As one goes down the list, more authority is ascribed to tradition. The suggestion of reverence due tradition means that people "follow" it, willingly or not, and may define themselves through its presence.

An emotional or even spiritual connotation to tradition exists that may belie objective chronologies or social inventories. To claim tradition, after all, is to bring into play the force, and guilt, of countless generations of ancestors, and perhaps the gaze of present-day neighbors. To follow tradition may be construed as keeping the faith; to break it a risk of apostasy. Hence, a vibrant legacy of writing on tradition exists from the view of how religion draws its meaning from continuities of shared ritual and belief and how individual expressions of art and literature respond to socially inherited aesthetics, symbols, and themes. That is not to say that attempts at clinically objectifying tradition do not exist. Tradition can be calculatedly viewed as a biological specimen and given the look of a genealogical chart. It may be stolidly recorded as a series of motions and minutely analyzed frame by frame. Traditions can be alternatively "collected" as empirical evidence of everyday practice or in the singular described as some conceptual, almost mystical whole, often outside the awareness of individuals. In both directions, scientific and humanistic, the problem of tradition questions the sources from which people draw the basis of actions and attitudes.

A problem *with* tradition, then, is its multiple meanings and conceptual soft-ness. Given to emotional usage, tradition can appear imprecise, inconsistent, and infuriatingly elusive. At the same time, therein lies its significance, for it offers something essential in the human condition. Tradition is a term we all hear and use, even if it defies crisp definition. As a basic component of life in need of under-standing, it seems to demand scholarship. Tradition, it is often assumed, is a source of basic learning, occurring even before formal education begins, and continuing through our lives. It is a font, therefore, for drawing a sense of the self from a social world. That font, that wisdom, has a sense of being part of a sequence of genera-tions that many view as desirable for a sense of belonging. Thus being *in* a tradi-tion suggests being a link in a social chain reaching well back in time.

The problem of tradition intensifies when value judgments intervene. Feelings about authority, about the virtue of the past, about the state of the present, shape the positive and negative value given tradition. Max Radin wryly remarked about tradition in the *Encyclopedia of Social Sciences* that "in all its aspects it retains enough of its primary characteristics of vagueness, remoteness of source, and wide ramification to make it seem peculiarly strong to those who have recourse to it and peculiarly weak to those who mean to reject it" (1935, 67). When celebrated writer Lafcadio Hearn described in the early twentieth century how in Japan "every act of domestic life" was "regulated by ... tradition," he suggested to Americans that this structure provided an admirable social model. He emphasized "the law of duty"— "obedience absolute to ... tradition" (Hearn [1904] 1984, 287). Vehement argument can arise whether *following* tradition means unconsciously following a severe form of cultural authority or *choosing* from tradition that which one finds appropriate.

In America, abundant examples serve to highlight both attitudes toward the authority of tradition and images of ambivalence toward it in mass media. Communal groups such as the Amish, among whom "tradition" presumably carries authority and preserves social harmony, are represented in media from tourist pre-sentations to mass-market movies such as *Witness* (1985) and are typically por-trayed as odd, a conspicuous "other" in American culture. Especially warning of the dangers of authority in tradition, the movie *Dead Poets Society*, a box-office smash of 1989, opened with students at an exclusive preparatory school carrying a lead banner of "Tradition." It announced a theme of the limitations of tradition placed on a creative individual by family and school. The movie would have its audiences believing that the severity of this tradition forced the suicide of the artistic boy wanting to define an identity for himself. Encouraged by an unconventional teacher, the boy is shown blissfully performing Shakespeare's comedy *A Midsummer's Night Dream* of man free in nature. He could also have invoked the resounding reminder of the authority of tradition in *Henry V*: "Will you mock an ancient tradition [begun] upon an honorable respect ... ?" (V, I, 70).

The *Oxford English Dictionary* impartially notes the value placed upon prac-tices or collective wisdom deemed worthy of "tradition." In the sense of practice, narrative, or wisdom passed through the generations, tradition can be found in print well back to the Middle Ages, but the more recent call of "traditionalism" rings harder with the air of harsh authority from the past. Putting together his widely known vocabulary of culture and society, Raymond Williams suggested that the "time-honored" process of inheritance from an older generation implies respect for elders and a certain duty to carry on the process. But he warned that persistence through time is not necessarily a mark of honor if it is enforced irrationally. From his progressive viewpoint, he thought of the labels of traditionalist and traditionalism as authoritarian enforcement, and therefore negative (R. Williams 1983, 318–20). Amitai Etzioni, another prominent scholar concerned with the charge of authority implicit in traditionalism, drew a contrast between modernity, associated with an emphasis on universal individual rights, and the unfortunately negative view of traditionalism that he thought conjures up the rigidity of the Middle Ages. In fashioning what he called a communitarian movement for the future, he hoped to recover the legitimacy of order and the claim of appropriate social virtues from traditionalism (Etzioni 1996, xvii).

Associated with precedent, continuity, and convention, tradition is commonly put forward to direct future action. Whether one wants the future to break with or continue the pattern of tradition dictates judgments of tradition as negative or positive. Especially common in the modernist literature of culture are statements emphasizing tradition as a guide or choice. Many contemporary writers take the tone that in the modern push toward novelty, choosing tradition, a social connection hearkening back to a past, is a threatened freedom allowed humans. Barry McDonald offered an example in a study of musicians: "I see tradition as founded upon personal choice. In the Archibalds' case, this translates as the conscious decision to engage in a certain sort of historical relationship, involving a network of people and a shared musical activity and repertoire" (B. McDonald 1997, 58). Hence, folk musicians, folk artists, and folk tradition bearers may appear to be touted as exemplars of free will in a mass society that applies pressure to conform to change. There is noticeable irony here in the invocation of tradition, a social connection to the past, as a sign of individualism. In political usage, as discussed later in this chapter, tradition may variously refer to individual autonomy and social authority. It can suggest a so-called conservative virtue in stability through continuity, and deference to previous authority, while supposedly liberal views may credit tradition for encouraging a constant reshaping to form new, or "progressive," directions.

Culture is often confused with tradition, but the related terms can mean different things, and perceptions of them have gone through historical shifts. Most persistently, tradition, especially when referred to in the plural, has carried the connotation of practices of a society, while culture has been considered an encompassing idea of the society. There is an implication that one can grasp traditions, participate in them, invoke them, more easily than the abstraction of culture.

Tradition connotes a social connection and historical precedent that underlie a cultural presence. Tradition frequently means continuity of a practice through time with which people are familiar, a way of doing things, while culture often suggests an unconsciously experienced existence, a way of thinking about things. Henry Glassie summarized culture, for example, as "intellectual, rational, and abstract; it cannot be material, but material can be cultural ... " (Glassie 1968, 2). Culture in the past was a reference to place, often to a language group bounded in space, whereas traditions were more variably social, possibly referring to family, age, and gender. In humanities, traditions can be more broadly defined than culture, as in the widely used singular use of the capitalized Western Tradition and its supposed opposite Eastern Tradition, which suggests "pattern" as a synonym for tradition. Culture now can be heard as easily applied to all kinds of associations as well as bounded groups, but often there still is a view that traditions define a culture, rather than the other way around. In European-American intellectual history, "the science of tradition," seeking to objectify and organize tradition, has been associated for better or for worse with folklore.

FOLKLORE AND THE STUDY OF TRADITION

You will not find "tradition science" or "traditionology" in an American university catalogue.[2] To be sure, courses in history, literature, art, music, religion, and philosophy, among others, will undoubtedly make reference to tradition. Frequently encountered interdisciplinary combinations of American studies, cultural studies, and ethnic studies use it, but I have yet to find "tradition studies" as a separate program. As close as you will come to the "science of tradition" is the study of folklore, where you will find professionals calling themselves "folklorists." As early as 1899, Englishman Edwin Sidney Hartland clarified, indeed encouraged, the professional pursuit of folklore as first the "study of tradition" and then the "science of tradition." (Hartland 1894–1896, [1899] 1968; G. Bennett 1994). Even as methods and theories changed drastically from the Victorians to modern-day Americans, the flag of tradition continued to be waved over the territory of folklore. During the 1970s, updates of "folkloristics" were frequently defined as "scientific in the study of human traditions" (Ketner 1973, 1976; Georges and Jones 1995).[3] If not always called a science, folklore studies is usually represented today as a "discipline" forming a bridge between humanities and social science, and American institutions such as Indiana University, UCLA, and the University of Pennsylvania offer the Ph.D. in it.

Folklore courses are most commonly found in English and anthropology departments and interdisciplinary programs. You can find folklore courses at over five hundred colleges in America, of which around eighty have some kind of folklore program (Baker 1986a). Reference to the study of "tradition" is a hallmark of these programs. Indiana University's Folklore Institute calls its newsletter

"Traditions" and describes the academic study of folklore as "focusing on recurrent traditional aspects of life." The brochure for graduate study in folklore at the University of Oregon advertises: "Students study the extent to which tradition continues to enrich and express the dynamics of human behavior throughout the world." The University of Pennsylvania explains the subject matter of its folklore and folklife department as "traditional arts and aspects of life." UCLA's program in folklore and mythology "examines the ways in which human traditions both reflect and contribute to continuity and consistency in thought and life." Harvard's program in folklore and mythology "takes up the world of tradition in its many forms."

The link of folklore and its emphasis on tradition to other disciplines affects many programs throughout the United States. The catalogue listing for the folklore program at the University of California at Berkeley explains: "Since it is a study of the humanist expression which is handed down by tradition rather than by writing, it is related to all departments that deal with literature, art, music. Since folklore also deals with the entire traditional culture of mankind as manifested in customs and beliefs, it has close affiliations with anthropology, design, history, linguistics, philosophy, psychology, and sociology." Folklore's primary connection with "tradition" and "traditional" is distinctive when compared to the general orientations of "the past" with history, "society" with sociology, or "culture" with anthropology. Indeed, the study of tradition through folklore may be in social sciences or humanities, and sometimes in behavioral sciences (see Nicolaisen 1983; Bronner 1984b; Zumwalt 1988; W. Wilson 1996; Bauman 1996; Mullen 1996).

When twenty-one authorities were asked during the late 1940s to define folklore for Funk and Wagnalls's *Standard Dictionary of Folklore, Mythology, and Legend* (1949), fifteen referred to "tradition" or "traditional" to explain the subject. Stith Thompson, arguably the dean of folklorists at that time, was especially direct in his usage of tradition: "The common idea present in all folklore is that of tradition, something handed down from one person to another and preserved either by memory or practice rather than written record" (403). Another leading light, Archer Taylor, similarly offered: "Folklore consists of materials that are handed on traditionally from generation to generation without a reliable ascription to an inventor or author" (402–3). While they construed tradition as a learning process of primarily oral transmission, others referred to it as a body of material familiar to a people. MacEdward Leach referred to traditions as "the accumulated knowledge of a homogeneous people" (401), and John Mish delineated this body as "fairy tales, myths, and legends, superstitions, festival rites, traditional games, folk songs, popular sayings, arts, crafts, folk dances, and the like" (401). Folklore had the appeal of giving *form* to the abstraction of tradition. As literature allowed for a range of forms, so folklore was varied in its content but had a conceptual unity under the tent of tradition.

It may well be that literary scholars were attracted to tradition to describe the list of folk items because it elevated them alongside a canon of classic arts. A folktale, or a ballad, emphasizing vernacular texts and social sources, had a dubious distinction within literature organized by acclaimed authors and unique compositions. Responding to a canon of great works created by valued artists, literary scholars frequently referred to "folk literature"—tales, epics, and ballads, and myths, for example—as worthy of attention because of their raw artistry, and their persistence through time. They often argued for an alternative view of literary art—that as traditions, these items were sources of great literature, high "culture," or classical civilization. Stith Thompson (1975), for instance, entitled his multivolume reference work on the folktale *The Motif-Index of Folk Literature* (1932–1936), and Francis Lee Utley highlighted tradition in his case for the legitimacy of "folk literature" (1961). They taught the analysis of individual tales much as a critic reading a text for motifs, types, and themes; with their indexes, they established a cultural canon of traditional stories. Both Thompson and Utley realized the higher esteem afforded folk material as tradition within the Western canon rather than as part of "primitive" culture. They also wanted to make a place for folk material within industrialized nations of Europe and America that connected appreciation of culture with works in modern languages. In other words, they joined the oral and written word under the broad heading of tradition in studies of English, French, German, Italian, Russian, and Spanish, among others.

In the prestigious area of classics, Milman Parry in his short life (1902–1935) revolutionized the criticism of Homeric texts by arguing that they were products of "oral tradition" that dated back into a preliterate age rather than the work of a great single artist. If it was "traditional," he argued, then forms of the epic could be investigated historically into the present with fieldwork, and he went to the Balkans to make recordings from which he formulated a lasting theory of oral composition (Parry 1971; Beye 1990). With his forceful argument, prominent position at Harvard, and the continuation of his project by Albert Bates Lord (1912-1991), "oral tradition" gained legitimacy (Lord 1960, 1991; Bynum 1974; Foley 1987, 1988; Finnegan 1977, 1991). Lord declared, for example, that "what is called oral tradition is as intricate and meaningful an art form as its derivative, 'literary tradition.' In the extended sense of the word, oral tradition is as 'literary' as literary tradition. It is not simply a less polished, more haphazard, or cruder second cousin twice removed, to literature. By the time the written techniques come onto the stage, the art forms have been long set and are already highly developed and ancient" (Lord 1962, 62). Oral tradition affected other hallmarks of "Western civilization," such as the works of Chaucer and Shakespeare, which received similar scrutiny for their "traditional" influences (see Lawrence 1911; R. Loomis 1927; Ashton 1957; Mandel and Rosenberg 1970). Attention to relationships between oral and literary tradition made its way into American letters with their inspiration from regional folklore and "local color" in the canonical writings of Nathaniel Hawthorne, Washington Irving, and Mark Twain (see Rourke [1931] 1959; Collins 1957; D. Hoffman 1961; C. Brown 1987).

The literary scholars working with folklore in the early twentieth century set a process in motion of expanding the limits of literature as imaginative tradition, and laid the groundwork for the present growth of American literature conceived as anti-canonical "textual studies" and "cultural studies." In light of folkloristic efforts with oral tradition to break down the privileging of published original prose and poetry in literature, it is more common now to hear of "narrative" and even "narrative diversity" to describe the scope of literature (Bercovitch 1995). The construction of tradition as conventional knowledge and a form of narrative apart from a written or elite record has been especially useful to describe cultural histories of marginal societies or everyday life in industrialized nations.

There can still be scholarly resistance when using tradition as an overarching concept for documenting majority cultures in contemporary societies. Overall, it can be argued that national traditions have been categorized as histories while marginal groups have often been described in terms of culture or tradition. There has been a pattern of treating publicized events recorded in print as having a national bearing, translated as "major proportions," while orally communicated matters of social importance were relegated to localized, and hence marginalized, existence. Michael Kammen, a president of the Organization of American Historians, spread notice, for example, of "the weakness with which *national* tradition—as opposed to particular ethnic, or religious, or regional traditions— has been felt, perceived, and perpetuated" (Kammen 1978, 4).

The perception of history as subjective tradition of national dimensions raises the nagging question of how to assess the kind of truth represented by tradition, especially the way tradition, thought of as inherited wisdom representing some social collectivity, relates historical events and social patterns. Bridging scientific history with its reverence for the documentary source and classifiable fact and folklore with its attention to belief and narrative, Richard Dorson recognized that "oral traditions may well exasperate the historian of a literate, or at least print-glutted society, with their quick-silver quality and chronological slipperiness. But they can be trapped, and they offer the chief available records for the beliefs and concerns and memories of larger groups of obscured Americans" (Dorson 1964b, 234). As a historian, he described documents of history and folklore as equally based on belief and narrative, and therefore most revealing of attitudes, biases, prejudices, and outlooks. Indeed, the scholarly avoidance of the issue of tradition as a kind of knowledge in need of recovery and interpretation may be explained by the scientific historical tendency to search for external reality and reject cognitive perception as evidence. In this kind of rigid categorization, tradition has been located most often in a shadowy region between positive fact and created fiction rather than conceived as everyday cultural behavior.

Anthropological authorities in the *Standard Dictionary of Folklore* mostly cited culture, custom, and belief as central terms beside or in place of tradition. In this rhetoric, the synchrony of ethnography as the observation of behavior in the context of place tended to be emphasized over the diachrony of chronological history, and hence tradition, arranged in time. One can find precedence for an anthropological uneasiness with tradition and preference for custom and belief. Influenced by evolutionary thinking, early anthropological citations of folklore found custom more scientific than tradition for generalizing about the universality of the civilizing process. When British antiquarian William J. Thoms coined the term "folklore" in 1846, he encouraged a study of "customs, observances, superstitions, ballads, proverbs … of the olden time" that he encapsulated as folklore and underscored as "the Lore of the People" (Thoms 1965). Custom had an appeal as a category of objects that could be classified into cultural types and species much as natural science, the center of scientific discourse at the time, had for higher and lower forms of life. Indeed, the common evolutionary classification of custom as a primitive predecessor of civilized "manners" connoted the irrationality of "lower stages of progress" and underscored the rude or crude otherness of the folk (Lang 1885).

Because of the interest in the nineteenth century in rationalizing racial types around the world and the evolution of civilization from primitive culture, anthropologists tended to favor custom because of the presumption that it was ritualized for a close-knit group of like-minded, or like-colored, participants. It tended to draw people together and it constituted generally public, collective statements of a race or society. Custom thus conceived referred to repeated rites and practices, often exotic in their nature. Custom was the documentable, observable material that could be classified, arranged, and "scientifically" compared. Tradition could hence be the process by which the material was unconsciously perpetuated. When referring to tradition, though, Victorians often implied an ancient body of knowledge. According to *The Handbook of Folklore* (1913) by Charlotte Burne, customs and beliefs were the "relics of an unrecorded past" that needed special documentation and were the focus of the folklorist's effort. Yet they were part of what could be loosely described as tradition. Burne pronounced: "the scientific study of folklore consists in bringing modern scientific methods of accurate observation and inductive reasoning to bear upon these varied forms of Tradition, just as they have been brought to bear upon other phenomena" (Burne 1913, 2). The capitalization of tradition suggested a universality to the body of knowledge.

To many of the early British anthropological folklorists particularly, the concept of a universal tradition was similar to the idea of culture as Edward Tylor defined it: "that complex whole which includes knowledge, belief, art, morals, law, custom, and any other capabilities and habits acquired by man as a member of society" (Tylor [1871] 1970, 1). Tradition, however, was especially associated with the process of "survivals," customs "which have been carried on by force of habit into a new state of society different from that in which they had their original home, and they thus remain as proofs and examples of an older condition of culture out of which a newer has been evolved" (Tylor [1871] 1970, 16). Tylor described tradition as some fixed cultural content endlessly perpetuated. Tradition as a form of learning most characteristic of a primitive stage would be viewed negatively, especially when contrasted to the association of "science" with advanced stages. Tylor's rhetorical use of "survivals" suggested that tradition could and should only be found in relic form in the contemporary, industrialized societies.

The relativistic idea of tradition in plural cultures as particular local knowledge adapting to change, rather than as an evolving whole, took hold in the twentieth century within anthropological thought. In his definition of folklore for the *Standard Dictionary of Folklore* (1949), Melville Herskovits made reference to this shift when he opened with the explanation: "Originally the study of cultural curiosities, and held to be the survivals of an earlier period in the history of 'civilized' literate peoples, folklore has come more and more to denote the study of the unwritten literature of any group, whether having writing or being without it" (400). He expressed the influence of Franz Boas on American anthropological thought and his reliance on folklore as an oral literary product that reflected the local social life, or culture, of a bounded group. Boas used tradition as a noun to describe shared practice or as an adjective to describe an oral and customary process of learning. In his chapter on mythology and folklore for the textbook *General Anthropology* (1938), Boas wrote: "The continuity of the ancient tradition and its gradual infiltration into popular belief can be proved. On the other hand, the belief in witches and the elaboration of the ideas underlying the trials of witches require for their understanding not only the traditional transmission of belief but also the current beliefs in witchcraft" (Boas 1938b, 621). What was significant to Boas, and the "school" of American anthropology he inspired, remained not so much in the transmission of belief as it did in the society which the belief reflects.

The kind of societies to which Boasian anthropologists were attracted were those that were "traditional" and therefore the products of that society were traditional. Especially in the United States, the Boasian anthropologists appeared preoccupied with recording endangered American Indian tribes and isolated African-American settlements. The use of folklore as it emerged from oral literature studies became increasingly attached, however, to traditional products in nontraditional societies. Crediting the study of folklore, especially the "oral tradition" work of Milman Parry for her inspiration, Ruth Finnegan in 1991 called for the reintegration of tradition into anthropology by emphasizing that changing practices function as tradition. Distancing herself from the "colonializing" view of primitive cultures held by early anthropology, she suggested attention to "traditional" societies as part of an updated strategy for anthropology. As she described them, such societies rely on face-to-face and oral communication and have collective norms, and their traditions can be observed to be functioning within the society. She stopped short, however, of views of tradition within what she called "modern"—"urban living within Western industrial civilization"—although other "urban" anthropologists had gone that route (Finnegan 1991, 107; Dundes 1980d).

She ultimately advocated "looking at tradition and traditional forms not as distinctive *things* nor as age-old products of the past but as researchable in living *practice*, and of taking a critical and searching—as well as comparatively oriented—approach to investigating the manifestations and uses of that intriguing and appealing and sometimes treacherous concept 'tradition'" (Finnegan 1991, 121).

A view owing to anthropology that went further in recognizing workings of tradition within America's industrial society was the "folklife" movement that had begun in the late nineteenth century and gained momentum in America after World War II. Even in the literary orientation of folklore, a social orientation toward living practice has been evident for some time. The continuous, variable quality of folklore as observable, authentic evidence of tradition's adaptation and change came through especially in 1968 in the title *Our Living Traditions: An Introduction to American Folklore* edited by Tristram Potter Coffin. With specific reference to the commercial culture with which American folk traditions often vie, the essays were gathered together, the editor wrote, to distinguish "moral, maudlin nonsense" packaged for the mass market and "genuine oral traditions through which ethnic, occupational, and regional groups maintain their individual cultures" (Coffin 1968, vii). Coffin thus identified the cultural link of folklore with a sense of authenticity deriving from a living connection to the traditions of specific social groups.

Surveys of folklore studies after the 1980s showed even more than they did during the 1940s a consensus about the emphasis on tradition. Dan Ben-Amos (1984, 124) declared: "*Tradition* has survived criticism and remained a symbol of and for folklore." Michael Owen Jones (1989, 263) concluded that "what appeals to folklorists is the study of traditions—something in which all people of every time and place engage." Richard Bauman (1992, 30) observed: "There is no single idea more central to conceptions of folklore than tradition." In a special issue of the *Journal of American Folklore* in 1995 on keywords used by folklorists, tradition appeared first in a list with art, text, group, performance, genre, and context. Tradition, Henry Glassie reflected in his lead essay for the issue, may have been relegated to folklore, but as a "continuous process of creating the future out of the past," it belongs widely in association with history and culture.

In fact, studies of history and culture took up the problem of tradition with new vigor after the 1980s. Attracted to the association of tradition to the continuous past that is understood in the present, Michael Kammen in *Mystic Chords of Memory: The Transformation of Tradition in American Culture* (1991) masterfully periodized trends in the ways that tradition as a collective memory has been invoked in American history. It included the Colonial Revival obsession of the early twentieth century with building a national culture based on the lessons of the founding fathers and the mid-century rediscovery of regional and ethnic folk and their integration into cultural democracy. Getting away from the historical task of reconstructing what happened in the past as an objective enterprise,

Kammen urged a realization of historical reconstructions as selective cultural and political acts. Once thought too soft to build an objective inventory of the past, tradition as a concept could be embraced to explore the social and intellectual creation of the present out of the past. Historian David Glassberg, for instance, incisively analyzed the ritualization of American history into patriotic pageants during the early twentieth century, and subtitled his study "The Uses of Tradition" (Glassberg 1990).

The problem of tradition in American history brought into focus the unsettled issue of locating America's cultural continuity with a past, *some* past, a *contested* past, not revealed easily by recording of events and biographies. Oscar Handlin had dramatically set out the problem in the mid-twentieth century by suggesting that the social history of immigration rather than the diplomatic facts of America's founding explained the history of American nationhood. But such a social history required an inquiry not only of the events of immigration, but an exploration of cultural baggage brought into, or discarded in, America. Handlin touched off a debate still raging about the character of immigrants and the influence of "ethnic" tradition in American culture. Immigrants were described prominently in terms of "tradition" because they represented a social movement, with connections to folk cultural legacies. Although noticeably evident in changes occurring to America, they were not well represented in the documentary record. Much of their story was in fact derived from their stories. Handlin presupposed a predominant "tradition" common to immigrants of European descent, a presumption for which he was taken to task by later historians of the ethnic experience (Bodnar 1985; Daniels 1990). He explained the stability of America in the adjustment necessary for traditions of the Old World to change for the New. He viewed immigration as an alienating experience encouraging envelopment within an altered American tradition. Tradition therefore lost its authority in the New World. He raised hackles as well as garnered awards for writing: "In this world then, as in the Old Country, the safest way was to look back to tradition as a guide. Lacking confidence in the individual's capacity for independent inquiry, the peasants preferred to rely upon the tested knowledge of the past. It was difficult of course to apply village experience to life in America, to stretch the ancient aphorisms so they would fit new conditions" (Handlin 1951, 109).

The frequent characterization in historical studies of tradition as a collective memory links historical and folk tradition, but distinctions frequently arise. In keeping with a concern for past events and figures causing change, historical tradition often implies the inherited narrative of what happened previously, what acted as a cause toward a present effect. Kammen, for instance, gives ample space to discussion of the "myth of the West," with reference to Frederick Jackson Turner's thesis of the movable frontier as a spur to democracy and individualism. Folk traditions typically refer less to causal events or movements and more to socially significant practices and lives. Folk tradition when it is used commonly refers to the process or result of oral transmission or imitation characteristic of the persistence of legends, tales, songs, and so on. Thus *American Folklore: An Encyclopedia* (1996), edited by Jan Harold Brunvand, does not have an entry for the frontier or Frederick Jackson Turner's frontier thesis. But the volume includes long entries for cowboys, rodeos, loggers, and Mormon folklore. Another example of the folkloristic usage of tradition as forms of expressive culture by social groups and localized contexts is Cecilia Conway's book on African-American influence in banjo performances in Appalachia plainly subtitled "A Study of Folk Traditions" (Conway 1995). And an exhibition of the early crafts within the round of life in the Susquehanna Valley of New York is baldly entitled *The Folk Tradition* (Barons 1982).

"Folk tradition" as a constructed category gives special attention to an "informal" transmission process through time and a social context that encourages group exchanges and identities. Kammen's historical, or popular, tradition could be conveyed through various media including schools, television, and newspapers, and does not necessarily require a basis in the social group. To underscore this distinction between folk and popular tradition, Jan Brunvand in his three editions of the popular textbook *The Study of American Folklore* (1968, 1978, 1986) drew a contrast between the formal records of a heritage or history of a people and the social inheritance of folklore. He wrote: "Folklore comprises the unrecorded traditions of a people; it includes both the form and content of these traditions and their style or technique of communication from person to person. The study of folklore (or 'folkloristics') attempts to analyze these traditions (both content and process) so as to reveal the common life of the human mind apart from what is contained in the formal records of culture that compose the heritage of a people" (Brunvand 1986b, 1).

Brunvand speaks for many folklorists in applying tradition as evidence of practice which reveals mind. He is ambiguous about the element of time required or the extent of social participation necessary for constituting tradition. The appeal of tradition is apparently its location in the everyday, outside of "history." There is continuity of this view with the earliest proponents of attention to America's "traditions." From his base in Philadelphia, John Fanning Watson from the 1820s to the 1850s promoted the collection of "traditionary lore," composed of legends, artifacts, beliefs, and sayings from aged informants to recover an unwritten record of everyday "olden life" (Watson [1830] 1857). He imagined that rapid changes in American life had threatened to obliterate appreciation for traditional ways of doing things, and histories of the time were preoccupied with biographies of the nation's leading figures. Washington Irving, a renowned novelist creating an American fiction out of this kind of tradition, credited Watson with "multiplying the local association of ideas, and the strong but invisible *ties of the mind and of the heart* which bind the native to the paternal soil" (Watson 1857, vi–vii). Expressing a positivist tone permeating much of later folklore research, Watson honored the motto, "If any man were to form a book, of *what he had seen or heard himself*, it must, *in whatever hands*, prove a most useful and interesting one," and added, "I am of the same opinion from numerous facts known to me in my researches among the aged for reminiscences and traditions" (Watson 1857, 12). More than imitating Sir Walter Scott or the Grimm brothers, Watson differentiated American research of traditions because of America's future orientation, its progressivism. He wrote: "A single life in this rapidly growing country witnesses such changes in the progress of society, and in the embellishments of the arts, as would require a term of centuries to witness in full grown Europe" (Watson 1857, 2).

Thoms's coinage of "folklore" won out over Watson's lengthier "traditionary lore," but references to tradition and folk tradition remained. If folk refers to the process of tradition, is "folk tradition" redundant? Not necessarily. "Folk tradition" usually connotes local, expressive knowledge especially among members of a bounded group identified as ethnic, religious, regional, occupational, or familial, which lends a certain "authenticity" to the cultural product (see D. Evans-Pritchard 1987; Hansen 1996). It may even be as small as two friends who create lore to identify themselves or perhaps a relationship between a person and pet, although these examples are typically seen as stretching the perception of authenticity (see Oring 1984a; Mechling 1989a). A recent trend has been to call forms of local knowledge "cultural tradition," perhaps to stress the functionality and universality of tradition. "Cultural tradition" indicates a changing attitude toward the understanding of tradition in cultural theory. Robert Winthrop, citing tradition as a concept worthy of discussion in cultural anthropology, noted the break away from an earlier view of tradition as inflexible and irrational. "More recent culture theory," he wrote, "recognizes tradition to be relatively fluid, capable of being invoked to justify or guide innovation, while conferring a sense of continuity with the past" (Winthrop 1991, 302). This view allows less reliance on the assumption of objectivity toward an exotic other who presumably has stable tradition as opposed to the modern researcher who is progressive and somehow culture-free. In this revision of culture theory, traditions describe all classes and situations, but are still associated with social interaction, most notably within small groups (see Jain 1977).

Tradition in such new clothing answers a vigorous scholarly concern for the basis of cultural production—the small group—rather than the bounded nation-state or boundless civilization. It can be argued, then, that "tradition studies" did not separately arise earlier because of the precedence of culture, literature, and history in American intellectual trends. Yet there has been a steady recognition that the materials of tradition called "folklore" constituted the interstices, sometimes the foundations, of culture, literature, and history. "Folklore" as a study moved, in the nineteenth century, from various antiquarian and linguistic concerns increasingly toward claiming tradition as its polestar. That did not mean, however, that "tradition" threatened to crowd out "folklore" as a name for a field of inquiry. Folklore, as I will show later, remained on the masthead partly out of historical accident, partly out of the appeal of "folk" as a cultural category, and partly because it had an attraction by objectifying tradition, hardening it, into classifiable units that could be materialized, manipulated, classified—indeed rationalized.

FOLK AND TRADITION IN POPULAR DISCOURSE

Since the nineteenth century, use of tradition as a keyword in popular discourse and in several disciplines has surged at moments of perceived rapid change, often thought of as modernization. The growth of folklore studies, in fact, reflects this historical trend. The Grimm brothers in Germany and Thoms in England commented on the disappearance of folklore or what they perceived as agrarian expressive traditions in the wake of European industrialization. Similarly, from the 1880s to the end of the century, the groundbreaking work of William Wells Newell, first editor of the *Journal of American Folklore*, was bolstered by his conviction that "to save precious traditions from perishing ... appeals to the support of the American public" (Newell 1889, 2). He defined folklore as "the study of popular traditions" and insisted on its importance to show continuities between the rapidly changing present and the distant past. Although he opined that popular traditions were often vulgar, rude, and backward, they were invaluable in explaining the rise of an industrial civilization. Speaking to "modern men and women of science," he justified attention to tradition by offering the "recognized principle, that higher forms can only be comprehended by the help of the lower forms, out [of] which they grew" (Newell 1889, 1). He associated tradition with "ancient stock" and he hoped to allay the fears of the public that the world was created anew by showing in the pages of the journal that modern industrialization, invention, transportation, and urbanization evolved naturally out of the traditions of primitive culture.

When the journal shifted to the editorship of anthropologist Franz Boas in 1908, the contents featured less of Newell's evolutionary tone, but they still used "traditions" to respond to issues of modernity. Particularly after World War I, authors moved folklore closer to the American present. In 1923, Martha Warren Beckwith published a startling account for the time of superstitions held by supposedly modern college students to show that they rely on folk beliefs for unpredictable human issues that concern them: courtship, marriage, future prosperity. In 1920, Emelyn Gardner published a collection of play-party games in Michigan that revealed adaptation and creativity rather than blind repetition of past musical forms. Her materials were hardly from the exotic folk of anthropological usage; they were from ordinary residents of Michigan. Toward the end of the turbulent 1920s, Boas prepared a guide to the layman called *Anthropology and Modern Life* (1928). From his research on folklore, he referred to the lessons of traditions for the present day: "Notwithstanding the rapid changes in many aspects of our modern life we may observe in other respects a marked stability. Characteristics of our civilization are conflicts between the inertia of conservative tradition and the radicalism which has not respect for the past but attempts to reconstruct the future on the basis of rational considerations intended to further its ideals" (Boas [1928] 1986, 136–37). He assured readers that even in a rapidly changing society such as the United States, "the old and the new live side by side" (Boas [1928] 1986, 137). In folklore, tradition could be a source to invigorate modern culture, and even became celebrated in many folk festivals, such as the National, White Top, and Pennsylvania, which drew big crowds and media interest during the 1930s. The kinds of tradition especially at issue in the push toward modernization and nationalism were those from the multiple European immigrant groups that had come in a huge wave between 1880 and 1920; from descendants of slaves in the South, some of whom had migrated to northern cities; and from persistent regional folk cultures in Appalachia, Pennsylvania, the Ozarks, and elsewhere.

The post-World War II period through the 1970s is often described as a special period of interest in folk tradition. The simultaneous dominance of mass culture and individualism, which was associated with modernism in America's prosperous industrial nation-state, led to many references in the press and other forms of public discourse to "folk revivals," "rediscovery of folklife," and "getting back to tradition" (Cantwell 1988). At the same time, a counterculture movement was accused of breaking popular traditions in a form of youth rebellion. The perception of increased interest in traditional cultures at the same time as countermovements looked to new cultural formulas is not necessarily a contradiction. Both movements drew ideas from so-called folk cultural traits of plain living and social harmony (see Shi 1985). They both sought restoration of a spiritual quality to life that had been lost or had been allowed to suffer in the postwar consumer society. Folklore again offered a sense of authenticity associated with the traditions of ethnic and regional communities.

The revealing moment in this folk revival discovery of tradition was the 1963 Newport Folk Festival. The Newport festival was not the earliest folk festival in what has been called the folk revival of the 1960s; but it was the best known, and it came to symbolize boom years of national publicity for traditional music and performers (Jackson 1993). The festival, featuring folk songs of struggling workers, repressed blacks, and forgotten heroes, attracted scores of thousands to the New England city known for its wealth and elite prestige, and this contrast became the keynote for press coverage across the country (see Brauner 1983). Appearances in Newport of aging black blues singers from the poor South, who were described as newly "discovered," became in the words of blues historian Jeff Todd Titon, "media events" (Titon 1993, 225). In addition to this sign that the media noticed racial integration in a setting engineered by northern youth, the introduction of Appalachian singers, Cajun musicians, and Ozark balladeers suggested redefinition of American views of modernization. It had been assumed that postwar America held a future-orientation that gave little account to its rustic roots. While the importance of

Newport to popular acceptance of regional-ethnic musical traditions still implied a northeastern commercial establishment, it also signaled an alternative to the mass-marketed blandness of the recording industry.

Many of the new stars put on record during the 1960s, such as Joan Baez, Bob Dylan, Judy Collins, and Tom Paxton, forced a reconsideration of labels such as folk and traditional in public usage. These artists were called folk singers even though they had little connection to oral transmission of songs in America's familiar folk cultures. They brandished acoustic instruments and occasionally sang songs taken from American oral tradition. They were identified with nonrustic locales such as Ivy League schools and Washington Square Park in New York City. They sometimes attracted derisive labels such as "folkies," "folkniks," or "urban folk." The singers from Appalachia and the Ozarks meanwhile were designated "traditional" to make the separation between an air of historical or ethnic authenticity around them and the construed folky manner of the commercial youth artists. Reflecting on the Newport festivals during the 1960s, one prominent participant gave this accounting of the urban-traditional split: "In 1963, there were around twice as many urban as traditional and ethnic performers; in 1967 and 1968, it was just the other way around" (Jackson 1993, 77). Reviewing "Folk Music" on October 9, 1964, *Time* anchored the list with Bob Dylan and the New Christy Minstrels while noting "Traditional Songs and Ballads" from seventeenth and eighteenth century Scotland performed by Ewan MacColl. While folklorists such as Richard Dorson disparaged the folk revival movement and this kind of juxtaposition for tainting the understanding of folk as an oral transmission process within a bounded group, the movement's rhetoric significantly brought the concept of tradition in a modernizing country into a public forum. The meaning of tradition as a visceral, hazy category of authenticity came to the fore.

The organizers of the Newport festival brought together "traditional" performers—many from ethnic and disenfranchised groups—and "folky" artists connected to a dominant commercial culture in a celebration of a new integrated social vision. In 1964, the crowd at Newport mushroomed to an impressive seventy thousand and witnessed, in the words of critic Stacey Williams who covered the event, "all this wonderful variety adding up to a feeling of one brotherhood, as hard to define as it is easy to sense" (S. Williams 1965; see also R. Cohen 1995). This integrative idealism bred use of tradition to express sympathy for neglected or abused groups, but the media had a field day reporting the intolerance of the crowd for Bob Dylan's 1965 appearance with electric guitar and an accompanying rock band. By 1969 media attention had shifted to the stinging electricity, and alienation, of Woodstock. Folk festivals with powerless old-timers on homemade instruments were characterized as corny and passive compared to the charged atmosphere of youth rebellion at Woodstock. A participant in the folk revival recalled, "The romantic idealism so much a part of the folk festivals was, I think, inappropriate in the climate of continually escalating violence. For many individuals who had formed a large part of the festival audiences, singing about social and political problems was no longer adequate" (Jackson 1993, 78). Nonetheless, many festivals, often recast as folk arts or folklife programming with professional folklorists as watchdogs for the authenticity of tradition continued or reemerged. While Newport became history, as the same participant commented, "The nice thing about the folksong revival is how much of it survived and became part of the general culture, how much of it is still accessible. I doubt that rock music would have developed the way it has were it not for the folksong revival. More folk festivals go on now than ever went on during the 1950s and 1960s, and many of them reflect real sensitivity and sophistication in programming. Many are directed by graduates of folklore Ph.D. programs—men and women who themselves had often been in the audiences of the folk festivals of the 1960s" (Jackson 1993, 79–80).

During the early and mid 1960s, the Newport festivals were central to the folk song revival. Many who could not be at the festivals could listen in on the events through popular recordings put out on the commercial label of Vanguard, or re-create the atmosphere in a host of festivals and tours based on Newport's success. The 1964 Newport Folk Festival alone spawned seven anthology albums putting together big-name stars and "traditional" ethnic and regional performers.[4] Fans could even see some of the folk stars on a prime-time television show with the folky title of "Hootenanny." Robert Cantwell described the special significance of the 1963 festival this way:

> While "thousands of fans milled in the darkened streets outside, listening to the music drift over the stone walls of the arena," Pete Seeger, Bob Dylan, Joan Baez, and Peter, Paul and Mary linked arms with the Student Nonviolent Coordinating Committee's Freedom singers to sing the festival's closing songs of freedom, peace, and hope. It was a moment in which, like a celestial syzygy, many independent forces of tradition and culture, some of them in historical deep space and others only transient displays in the contemporary cultural atmosphere, briefly converged to reveal, though inscrutably, the truth of our national life. (Cantwell 1988, 190)

That truth was one of tension between the disturbing undercurrents of racial prejudice, social class conflict, and "sheer money working to carry the influences of the northeastern cultural establishment into broad circulation in the wider republic" and an idealistic hope for a tolerant, plural society where a rigid nation had stood (Cantwell 1988, 190). Tradition offered more than a sense of a stable past to give identity to a baby-boom generation entering a disposable, plastic world. It marked the recovery of group life and everyday expression in modern society. With tradition, the rhetoric suggested, the man in the grey flannel suit got a face and was able to express his inner self.

This intensity of experience was attainable not only through discovery of folk songs emphasizing communal participation, but also by dirtying one's hands with traditional crafts and practices. The tremendous popularity of *The Foxfire*

Book (1972) and its many sequels (nine between 1973 and 1993), edited by Eliot Wigginton and published by the commercial house of Doubleday, is attributable to the appeal of a rural southern connection with authentic historical tradition.[5] Plain and earthy in its design, it bucked the marketing formula of glitzy appearance to become a huge commercial success. The book sold over three million copies, more than any book in the company's publishing history (Wigginton 1989, 285). It began in 1967 as journalistic work by high school students in an English class who collected descriptions of rural crafts, skills, narratives, and beliefs from old-timers in Rabun County, Georgia. It turned, in Wigginton's words, into "an investment that linked the public school curriculum and the area's traditions and culture together in powerful and magical ways" (Wigginton 1989, 285). In the first volume in the series, Eliot Wigginton bemoaned the loss of folk wisdom because of the advent of electronic civilization. He especially thought that ethnic and regional contributions to American culture would suffer. Originally intended as a teaching tool, Foxfire, as it became a mass culture phenomenon in a Broadway stage play and movie, expressed the emotional vitality of life in tradition. The books became manuals for lost skills and practices of a simpler, and apparently wiser, day. By encouraging his students to collect the stories and crafts from older people who lived this way, Wigginton offered that they "gain an invaluable, unique knowledge about their own roots, heritage, and culture. Suddenly they discover their families—previously people to be ignored in the face of the seventies—as pre-television, pre-automobile, pre-flight individuals who endured and survived the incredible task of total self-sufficiency, and came out of it all with a perspective on ourselves as a country that we are not likely to see again. They have something to tell us about self-reliance, human interdependence, and the human spirit that we would do well to listen to" (Wigginton 1972, 13). Foxfire became a national movement and spawned numerous local imitations such as Salt in Maine and Bittersweet in Missouri (see Clements 1996). It became a symbol for the association of tradition with old, rural living.

There were other "moments" that exemplify the reorientation of tradition during the 1960s and 1970s. One such moment often labeled a "phenomenon" was the publication of Alex Haley's *Roots* in 1976 and its production as a television miniseries (Kammen 1991, 641–45). *Roots* appeared as a twelve-hour adaptation in January 1977, and besides breaking television audience records for a miniseries, it won nine Emmy awards and spawned a fourteen-hour sequel, *Roots: The Next Generations,* in 1978. Nielsen estimated that an incredible 130 million Americans—representing eighty-five percent of all the television-equipped homes—watched at least part of the original twelve-hour miniseries. The final episode riveted the attention of a staggering 80 million viewers (H. Waters 1977). In fact, seven of the ten most-watched television shows in United States history were episodes of *Roots* (D. Moore 1994, 6). The book sold over a million copies within a year of its publication and was quickly adopted as a text in over 250 college courses. It held the top spot of the *New York Times* nonfiction best-seller list for an amazing run of five months beginning in November 1976. Its success landed Alex Haley on the cover of *Time* (February 14, 1977) and brought him coverage in a host of mass-market magazines. In *Newsweek* (February 14, 1977), columnist Meg Greenfield reflected that the last publishing event in America comparable to the phenomenon of *Roots* was the publication of *Uncle Tom's Cabin* in 1852.

Like *Uncle Tom's Cabin*, *Roots* was a narrative of slavery, but its distinguishing features were its sources and the mass appeal of an African-American writer. Haley recovered his family's saga from Africa to the New World through oral tradition. He wrote that much of it came from elder family members who related "snatches and patches of what later I'd learn was the long, cumulative narrative that had been passed down across generations" (Haley 1976, 566). He added to this material oral chronicles regarding his ancestors he received from an African *griot* in Juffure. Calling his work a "novelized amalgam" woven from family tradition, Haley challenged conventional categories of fact and fiction (Gerber 1977; Mills 1981). At first Haley defended his work as "carefully preserved oral history, much of which I have been able conventionally to corroborate with documents" (Haley 1976, 584). Faced with caustic questions about the historical accuracy of his account, Haley increasingly used the rhetoric of saga and symbol (McFadden 1977; Gerber 1977; Courlander 1986; Puschmann-Nalenz 1987; D. Moore 1994). He admitted, in fact, that he had lifted sections of folklorist Harold Courlander's *The African* (1967) for his narrative (A. Johnson 1984, 467–69). Although promoted as a history by the publisher, *Roots* was given a special category award by the National Book Awards committee. Coming to the defense of the use of tradition in *Roots*, columnist Meg Greenfield offered the impact of its "emotional truth." She wrote: "'Roots' is romantic and melodramatic, its characters are in many ways unconvincing and unreal. But none of that disturbs its larger human truth…. Overnight, it has become part of the national folklore, this saga with its enormous power to move, and we all seem mystified by that" (Greenfield 1977).

While Greenfield observed that the popularity of *Roots* was "an unexpected and unaccountable wildfire thing," Haley and others gave explanations revolving around the search for a sense of tradition and group belonging at a time when those associations, especially to rooted family and immigrant bonds appeared to be dissolving. Few argued for its impact on the basis of artistic merit, especially of the television series ("Why 'Roots'" 1977; Gerber 1977; Fiedler 1979, 71–85). Many reviews that appeared when the series was aired related the phenomenon to a new, benign period of race relations which created new sympathy and interest in a black saga ("Why 'Roots'" 1977; H. Waters 1977). Nancy Reagan, for one, disagreed, and was widely quoted in her criticism of the show as racially inflammatory (D. Moore 1994, 6–7). Haley dodged the issue of race and told interviewers that the appeal of *Roots* was based on the lure of an antimodernist theme at a time of mass cultural alienation. Haley generalized that he had tapped into "the average American's longing for a sense of heritage" (Marmon 1977). Blaming television for alienating youth from its elders and cutting off the tradition of storytelling, Haley said: "In this country, we are young, brash and technologically oriented. We are all trying to build machines so that we can push a button and get things done a millisecond faster. But as a consequence, we are drawing away from one of the most priceless things we have—where we came from and how we got to be where we are. The young are drawing away from older people" (Marmon 1977, 72). In a commencement address at Xavier University, he elaborated further on family tradition as a source of identity for Americans: "every family on earth has some ancestry and goes back into some native land and that, fundamentally is what *Roots* dealt with" (Haley 1982, 70).

In the years that followed the publication of *Roots*, family sagas drawn from oral tradition, guides to collecting ethnic oral history and folklore, and advisers on genealogies came out in record numbers (Hijiya 1978). The *Roots* phenomenon turned from a reference to race to ethnicity and family. Often remembered in the *Roots* story is the protagonist's (Kunta Kinte) insistence on maintaining ethnic African identity in the face of adversity (Courlander 1986; Haley 1982). Coincident with the appearance of *Roots*, Irving Howe's *World of Our Fathers* (1976) climbed the *New York Times* best-seller list and won a National Book Award. A social and cultural history of East European Jews who came to America, its narrative tone and attention to family and community as social cynosures drew popular notice. Its hefty sales meant that many non-Jews were reading it for its message of ethnic cultural connection to the American experience, much as many nonblacks were consuming *Roots* for its narrative of identity search.

To encourage ordinary Americans further in the pursuit of heritage, popular advisers such as Jeane E. Westin's *Finding Your Roots* (1977) hit the market in abundant supply. On Independence Day, 1977, *Newsweek* devoted its cover story to "Everybody's Search for Roots." To feel the authenticity of tradition, which was presumably emotional and positive, the magazine suggested, meant attaching to a group, especially ethnic or familial. This challenged a cherished American notion of individualism built around a myth of separation from Europe ("the fresh start") and self-reliance ("the self-made man"). As James Hijiya reported with a tone of surprise in 1978, "To an unaccustomed degree, Americans are conceiving themselves as products of groups" (Hijiya 1978, 549). Since Haley's work had been based on the story of his family as he had heard it from "tradition," public discourse associated interviewing older family members with finding social centeredness in an overly mobile, overly faceless society. Tradition, especially family and ethnic tradition, it could be argued, provided one a sense of roots. To quantify America's growing sense of ethnic belonging, the United States Census in 1980 added an ethnic ancestry question for the first time that requested ethnic self-identification from Americans. It reported an impressive ninety percent response rate to the

question. The 1990 count repeated the question and census publicity drew attention to this kind of question with the message: "Our families, our communities,
our culture—these are the things we cherish" (see Bronner 1996b).[6]

While the census carried national significance, folkloristic activity tapped into
the *Roots* phenomenon, especially at the community level. I took notice in 1981,
for example, of a newspaper article on a folklore professor I had at the State
University of New York. His community activities had been cited as a new kind of
cultural "fieldwork" during my stay at Binghamton in the early 1970s. Still at it in
1981, his work was recast then in a headline, "SUNY Prof. Helps Others Explore
'Roots'" (Mittelstadt 1981). Calling a folk-artists-in-education program "Roots
and Wings," folklorist Roger Abrahams argued that the benefits of this roots
awareness can be tremendous, "not only in keeping traditions alive and putting
students in touch with the past, but also in fostering a sense of local pride"
(Abrahams 1987, 80). Nationally and locally, cultural or folk tradition in public
discourse at the time especially described the attachment to subnational and
small social groups.

With so much emphasis in "cultural" and "folk" tradition on local and ethnic
placements of culture, it is easy to overlook the concomitant movement to
describe a common national tradition around World War II. During and after
the war that had urged the nation intellectually to stand together against fascism, a number of popular works such as B. A. Botkin's bestselling *Treasury of
American Folklore* (1944) touted national folk heroes representing the spirit of
democracy. He especially spread the fame of the legendary Paul Bunyan, portrayed as a gigantic, yet kindly workingman, as a sign of a vibrant national folklore. Bunyan entered, or was promoted, in popular culture in film, literature, and
music as a typically boisterous American folk hero, along with the likes of
Johnny Appleseed and Pecos Bill ("King of the Cowboys"). A television series
playing on the legends of Davy Crockett (dubbed the "King of the Wild
Frontier") during the mid-1950s became a sensation and spurred sales of coon-
skin hats and other frontier garb. "The Ballad of Davy Crockett," a song from the
show, became a number-one hit in the nation for thirteen weeks in 1954. The
post office issued a series of stamps featuring "national" folk heroes such as
Crockett, Johnny Appleseed, and Pecos Bill and called it the "American Folklore
Series." Thousands of newspapers and magazines carried notice of national folk
heroes of mythological proportions and recovered or invented tall tales about
them. Remarking on the popularity of Paul Bunyan in particular, Richard
Dorson offered that "professors and critics and composers swallowed the myth
as eagerly as the man in the street. The explanation for this phenomenon lies
largely in the staple reading fare of the country and the century, the newspaper,
whose reporters had found a lusty, 100 percent American symbol in Paul
Bunyan" (Dorson [1956] 1976c, 336). Brandishing one of the first degrees ever
offered in "American civilization," Dorson observed after the war that "the

maturing of American society and the crystallization of American nationalism have generated the desire for a New World Thor or Hercules or Gargantua, with no taint of foreign genesis" (Dorson [1956] 1976c, 336).

Some commentators after the war noticed a connection of the new cultural nationalism to more than American victory of democracy over Nazism and competition with communism. They frequently pointed fingers at the boom of commercial mass culture or celebration of industrial progress (D. Hoffman 1952). Richard Hofstadter voiced distress at the public's "ravenous appetite for Americana" in his landmark book *The American Political Tradition* (1948). In his work he recognized the cultural impact of inherited narratives about American political heroes such as Jefferson and Lincoln. He attributed the nostalgic search for national traditions, what he called "the most common vision of national life, in its fondness for the panoramic backward gaze," to a keen feeling of insecurity. It was a response, he thought, to a profoundly shaken confidence caused by the Great Depression and war. Sounding a note of realism, he wrote, "If the future seems dark, the past by contrast looks rosier than ever; but it is used far less to locate and guide the present than to give reassurance" (Hofstadter [1948] 1989, xxxiv). Hofstadter differed with Dorson as to the root of the Americana craze, since Dorson considered it a sign of postwar bravado that "in the era of world eminence, Americans should proudly unfurl their folk heritage" (Dorson 1959a, 3). Coming from the same generation, indeed both born in 1916, Dorson and Hofstadter gained prominence for reevaluating national traditions after the war, and they trumpeted similar calls for a rationalism rather than nostalgia in this quest. Equally concerned for the authenticity of national heroes in oral tradition and a valued role for intellectuals in public life, they agreed that the popular, commercial notice of national folk themes after the war was a remarkable "phenomenon."

The postwar "phenomenon" was a climax to an effort coming out of a certain cultural inferiority complex. Americans turned the characterizations of their lack of refinement into a virtue and their ordinariness into civic art. A canon of American literary treasures from Hawthorne, Cooper, Irving, and Twain that owed to folk traditions became identified. Some intellectuals looking to the cachet of Europe were skeptical. Even though American arts were supposedly "coming of age" in the early decades of the twentieth century, Van Wyck Brooks's plaint that "old American things are old as nothing else anywhere in the world is old, old without majesty, old without mellowness, old without pathos, just shabby and bloodless and worn out" laid doubt about the cultural results (Brooks [1918] 1958, 94). The charge was that America had age, but lacked tradition. The impediments to the dream of a "national culture," he wrote, were individualism without creativity and the industrial worship of size, mass, quantity, and numbers that fostered a commercial shallowness (Brooks [1918] 1958, 101–2). In answer to his attack that American society lacked "the indwelling spirit of continuity," many proponents of a national culture worthy of scholarly interpretation constructed an artistic legacy that built on a distinctive American vernacular as the ennobling stuff of native tradition. With impetus from new programs at Yale and Harvard, an intellectual movement took shape by the 1930s, making claims for the rise of a new glorious civilization, an American civilization. It distinguished a national culture that would change the way hallmarks of Old World civilizations were viewed, and indeed esteemed.

The movement to rationalize American civilization especially gathered steam during the post-World War II period. Much of its purpose seemed to lie in identifying historical and folk traditions that could broadly define a national character (T. McDowell 1948; Dorson 1976a; Gleason 1984). In the absence of an ancient stock or geographical unity, some analysts in the movement wondered whether an equivalent could be found to the mythologies that bind other nation-states (see H. Smith 1950). Admitting that America lacked the culturally shared sacred narratives conceptualized by folklorists as myths, postwar Americanists nonetheless located a national tradition that they attributed to beliefs—interpreted as having "mythic" qualities—arising from perceptions and experiences of settlers in the new nation (see Tate 1973). The national tradition usually described involved special historical events or movements affecting all Americans. Louis Hacker in 1947 produced a commonly used textbook called *The Shaping of the American Tradition* (1947) in which he identified historical patterns unique to the American experience that led to formation of an American tradition. The patterns he offered were the conquest of a movable wilderness frontier, freedom from church authority, weakness of the state, strength of the middle class, promise of opportunity, installation of democratic institutions, and a system of parties and pressure groups. He presented the traditional American "as a type," as an individualist, a democrat, an equalitarian, and a utilitarian.

To Hacker and many other intellectuals of the period, the American type and its traditions fulfilled the promise of building a new, great contemporary civilization in America that would take its place alongside the classical Greeks and Romans. As they had their heroes, gods, and myths that united and characterized a proud civilization, so America could make its claim to such traditions. Henry Nash Smith in *Virgin Land* (1950) offered the backwoodsman and frontiersman as national heroes that exemplified the distinctive American "myth of the garden." By this he meant not so much a narrative, but an idea imaginatively expressed in literature, arts, and institutions that America was a place of abundance whose resources could be cultivated by pioneers willing to develop the land. Other myths and heroes followed. Richard Dorson located Davy Crockett and Mike Fink in the "pantheon of American folk heroes" as epitomes of American boastfulness and optimism (Dorson 1959a, 1973a). R. W. B. Lewis examined the archetype of the American Adam who established the tradition of the country as the place of the fresh start, a locale to shed the European past and start anew (R. Lewis 1955). These traditions, then, were popular ideas rather than cultural expressions as they were described for small folk societies.

Potential conflicts between the rise of national and plural visions of American tradition culminated in the bicentennial celebration of American independence in 1976. It was a national celebration, but many localities used the occasion to celebrate what they associated with the nation's admirable past—its sense of plural community. Many local celebrations in their sponsorship of "vernacular themes" were markedly different from the centennial celebration of 1876 with its strong promotion of sweeping nationalism and industrial progressivism (Bodnar 1992, 238–43). In 1976, Chicago organizations sponsored demonstrations of local pioneer spinning, weaving, and cooking; Jasper, Alabama, had a log cabin reconstructed; Ellettsville, Indiana, restored a one-room schoolhouse; some hearty residents of Galesburg, Illinois, retraced the route the earliest settlers of the town took from New York State; and Lock Haven, Pennsylvania, floated a lumbering raft down the hazardous West Branch of the Susquehanna River. The Illinois State Museum's bicentennial exhibition showcased folk arts and artifacts of everyday life. The catalogue explained: "There has been an attempt to go beyond amply recorded political history, well-known personalities, and events in order to focus on the geographical and folk history of Illinois. Hopefully, the activities of hundreds of unsung individuals who made the true 'history' of the state will be brought to light" (Madden 1974, xii). It was a sign of alienation in the post-Vietnam and post-Civil-Rights years from the politics of national leadership, and a reaffirmation of community within the superficiality of a growing mass culture.

The widespread use of local traditions and folk arts to bring out America's plural communities during the bicentennial was offset by several splashy attempts to show the unity of the nation's traditions. The New York State Historical Association installed "Outward Signs of Inner Beliefs: Symbols of American Patriotism" to highlight a tradition of shared pride in the nation. Director emeritus Louis C. Jones hoped that the message coming from displays of historic patriotic objects made and used by everyday people showed a continuity, indeed a love of country, from the beginnings of the country to the troubled 1970s torn by racial, gender, and age conflicts. Reflecting on the spirit of the folk objects, he wrote of his wish that "some of the ebullience, some of the confidence in the future, some of the belief in ourselves can be a useful elixir in today's dark and threatened world" (L. Jones 1975, 9). Philip Morris Incorporated sponsored an even larger show using "folk art" at the Whitney Museum of American Art and several other prominent locations. Called *The Flowering of American Folk Art, 1776–1876* and curated by American art historians Jean Lipman and Alice Winchester, the show made reference to the Declaration of Independence as the beginning of the seeds of a "native folk tradition" (Lipman and Winchester 1974). The show's nationalized folk art in the form of weather vanes, decoys, needlework, portraits, and wall decorations diminished the ethnic diversity of the country and emphasized the mostly middle-class character of America's New England roots. The curators used the timing of the bicentennial to highlight the spirit of democracy in the nation's founding. The "unconventional side of the American tradition in the fine arts," the folk arts to the curators "have always been an integral part of American life" (Winchester 1974, 14). Introducing the massive summer-long Festival of American Folklife on the Mall in Washington, D.C., during the bicentennial, the director of the National Park Service tried to steer a middle course between the use of vernacular themes of tradition for promoting the nation and its divided communities. He wrote: "The Festival of American Folklife is an expression of these beliefs that we are different in many ways, but we are still one nation, one people whose individual differences helped shape a great nation" (Everhardt 1976).

The popular moment that probably more than any other put the keyword of tradition on the lips of Americans was the staging and later filming of *Fiddler on the Roof.* It may seem to be an odd choice for influencing American culture. Indeed, the producers of the show worried before its 1964 premier that the play's depiction of Jewish shtetl life in Russia was too esoteric for American mass cultural tastes. Its backdrop of frustrating poverty, painful prejudice, and violent pogroms hardly seemed the stuff of musical comedy. It turned out to be a theatrical wonder, breaking records for the longest-running show on Broadway, garnering nine Tony awards including one for best musical, and enjoying huge sales of soundtracks, books, and sheet music. It was among the most popular shows for repertory companies and community theaters across the country to produce, even in podunks without a Jewish presence. Playbills for subsequent productions of the play carried the tag "World's Most Acclaimed Musical." Metro-Goldwyn-Mayer produced in 1971 a film version, faithful to the Broadway production, that earned eight Academy Award nominations and won three Oscars. The movie earned 25 million dollars, ranking it among the top grossing musicals of all time. In fact, more people saw the movie that year than any other, except for another memorable film with ethnic-family tradition as a strong theme, *The Godfather. Fiddler on the Roof* reached more audiences in 1994 with the release of the film on home video. The most prominent word and binding concept in the movie is tradition.

The song "Tradition" opens the play, and in the script the word "tradition" appears thirty times in ten pages (Stein 1966). Audiences hear from the beginning of the play that tradition provides stability in people's lives. "And, how do we keep our balance?" the main character, the patriarchal Tevye, asks. He answers his own question, "That I can tell you in a word—tradition!" If that exclamation wasn't enough to convince the audience, villagers enter the stage and sing,

> Tradition, tradition—Tradition.
> Tradition, tradition—Tradition.

"Tradition," Tevye reflects. "Without our traditions, our lives would be as shaky— as a fiddler on the roof!" He explains that traditions provide identity to people in this world. "Because of our traditions," he says, "everyone knows who he is and what God expects him to do."

In the prologue, Tevye defines traditions as both time-honored guides to behavior and expressions of them. He relates to the audience: "Because of our traditions, we've kept our balance for many, many years. Here in Anatevka we have traditions for everything—how to eat, how to sleep, how to wear clothes. For instance, we always keep our heads covered and always wear a little prayer shawl. This shows our constant devotion to God." To hear Tevye talk, tradition in this community seems to be a given of life, an unanalyzable faith: "You may ask, how did this tradition start? I'll tell you—I don't know!"

After the prologue, Tevye's cherished traditions are subject to challenge and change. Listening to the radical teacher of his children, he hears "strange ideas about turning the world upside down." "Times are changing," his daughter Motel tells her father. "The world is changing," Chava, another daughter, tells him. "Where does it stop?" he sighs. Going against the custom of arranging marriages through a "matchmaker," Hodel makes her own decision about who she will marry and a reprise of "Tradition" can be heard. Tevye sings:

> Tradition!
> They're not even asking permission
> From the papa.
> What's happening to the tradition?
> One little time I pulled out a thread
> And where has it led?

Tevye eventually draws the line when Chava wants to marry outside their faith and community. "Can I deny everything I believe in?" Tevye ponders, as the refrain "Tradition, tradition—Tradition" wafts in the background. Whereas the Broadway play with mass appeal allows the interfaith couple to remain united and hints at eventual reconciliation with Tevye, the earlier Yiddish-language dramatic movie *Tevye* (1939), which aimed at Jewish audiences, would have none of that. The distraught Chava, abused by her husband's gentile family, abandons the unhappy union and begs forgiveness from her father. For American audiences of the 1960s watching the Broadway play, the struggles of the couple for acceptance implied the need for integration and tolerance as a break with traditional social divisions of the past. The American translation of tradition on the stage was to be faithful to one's ethnic identity while joining in a diverse, progressive society. The play much more than the Yiddish movie offered that tradition could indeed be chosen and adapted rather than religiously followed.

Another difference between the Broadway play absorbed into American culture and the Yiddish work on which it was originally based is the explanation for Tevye's removal from his home. In the Yiddish movie, the gentile town council invidiously orders him out. In the Broadway play, the culprit is the state, represented by the police loyal to the czar. The anti-authoritarian theme must have appeared easier to swallow for Americans than representation of inherent vindictiveness of Christian neighbors. In the work on which the play was based, writer Sholem Aleichem made reference to a senseless persecution causing the endless wandering of the Jews waiting for a Messiah. That is their tradition. In the story, Tevye resignedly says,

> For since they taught me the lesson—*Lech-lecho*, Get thee out—I have been wandering about constantly. I have never been able to say to myself, "Here, Tevye, you shall remain." Tevye asks no questions. When he is told to go, he goes. Today you [speaking to the writer Sholem Aleichem] and I meet here on this train, tomorrow we might see each other in Yehupetz, next year I might be swept along to Odessa or to Warsaw or maybe even to America. Unless the Almighty, the Ancient God of Israel, should look about him suddenly and say to us, "Do you know what, my children? I shall send the Messiah down to you." (Aleichem 1973, 103)

In the Yiddish-language movie and the earlier Yiddish theater play named *Tevye der Milkhiker* (1919), Tevye makes a choice. Rather than wait for the Messiah, he takes the initiative to go to the Holy Land so that he can live a traditional life basic to his beliefs (Wolitz 1988). But in the Broadway play, and later in the popular English-language movie, his destination is America, and what he will face there is uncertain and worrisome. It is an omen of further pressures on tradition he might expect that his wife berates the children: "Stop that! Behave yourself! We're not in America yet!" In the last line, Tevye turns to the younger generation and quietly commands, "Come, children. Let's go."

Through its long run on Broadway (3,242 performances), *Fiddler* instigated public discourse about the raw nerve in America that the play's theme of tradition touched. The strongest character, indeed the central character of the play, is Tevye boisterously played originally by a rabbi's son and veteran Broadway actor Zero Mostel (born Samuel Joel Mostel) with connections to East European traditions. *Newsweek* put Mostel in his role as Tevye on its cover on October 19, 1964. After noting the portrayal of Tevye's fatherly role in defense of tradition, the author made the comment, "The sentiment is one which a great many Americans in need of replenishment are coming to understand" ("Hail" 1964, 98). From the first notice of the play's run in Detroit on August 8, 1964, to the two months after its Broadway opening on September 22, no less than eight articles in the *New York Times* reported the show's tremendous resonance with audiences. Howard Taubman in his column of October 4 asked: "Who would have guessed that the stories of Sholem Aleichem would be suitable for the musical stage? Who could have predicted that such a work could play fair with the mood, color and characters of these tender and comic tales of poor Jews in Russia's villages in the early years of the century? Who would have thought that a yarn describing poverty, anti-Semitic brutality and the Diaspora could be transformed into a sunny and heartfelt musical?" (sec. 2, 1). Implying a parallel to black struggles for civil rights, he interpreted the appeal in the pathos of those forced to live uneasily amidst prejudice, antagonism, and the peril of violence.

Prominent Yiddish novelist Isaac Bashevis Singer pointed out to readers of the *Times* that the adaptation of Sholem Aleichem's nineteenth-century Russian stories offered two themes that were timely during the American 1960s (Singer 1964). One was the continuity of everyday folklife, even while great, potentially cataclysmic events of the day raged on. But when traditions change, he argued, that is the really great change in life, and many audiences, whether or not they were Jewish, realized that. Related to this stabilizing factor of everyday tradition is the other theme of impending revolution caused by new ideas and old prejudices. The comfort of following tradition and feeling complacent in one's home and society is weighed against action forced by the injustices of the nation and the inevitability of social change.

Multiple interpretations of the play could be heard from reference to the Holocaust to ethnic disintegration, but it was difficult to get away from the keynote of tradition presented in the production. Modern life "without traditions," the play warned, was as "shaky as a fiddler on the roof." And at the same time, traditions had to change to be effective in modern life. The closing of the play leaves the question unanswered of the integration of tradition and modernity. As the curtain falls, the fiddler follows Tevye and his family to America but he stops playing his music.

When the show was revived on Broadway in 1977, critic Jack Kroll in *Newsweek* jumped on the connection of tradition as a haven from mass and urban culture. He wrote: "The very first number, 'Tradition,' may be pure showbiz, but it immediately invokes a social and even spiritual quality that's in short supply in the mean streets of our cities." And he added, "We don't have folk art any more—not in the plastic, big-deal urbanized popular arts of our mass culture. But we have, on very rare occasions, a *Fiddler on the Roof*" (Kroll 1977). Tevye comes closer to modern American sensibility in *Fiddler* by moving from Sholem Aleichem's original countryside to the play's town or *shtetl*. Audiences saw community bonds dissolving, yet providing a source of ethnic strength.

In the transition from the ethnic *Tevye* to the American *Fiddler*, an American rhetoric of rights entered into the dialogue, replacing the class conflicts of Sholem Aleichem's Yiddish. Explaining her revolutionary lover Perchik to Tevye, Hodel says, "He cares nothing for himself. Everything he does is for humanity." In the play, however, Perchik's most radical gesture was to observe gender relations: "Our ways are changing all over but here. Here men and women must keep apart. Men study. Women in the kitchen. Boys and girls must not touch, should not even look at each other." When Perchik tells of "our ways" as a collective statement of tradition, he is not so much the Bolshevik revolutionary as the American moralist calling for adaptability to modern conditions. Seth Wolitz incisively commented on this kind of dialogue: "A gigantic substitution occurred in the musical. American ideals of individual rights, progress, and freedom of association are assimilated into the Judaic tradition which is presented as a cultural tradition parallel to the American. The class conflicts, which riddled the *shtetl* and which Sholem Aleichem considered destructive of Jewish communal interests, are sidestepped in the musical" (Wolitz 1988, 527).

If *Fiddler* gave new life to use of tradition in public discourse, it did not necessarily clarify its meaning. It lent recognition to tradition as a fragile and threatened, yet indispensable part of modern life. It pointed to the rituals and marks of tradition in folklife that distinguish ethnic groups. In the chant of "Tradition, tradition—Tradition," it suggested tradition as a key concept, even a haunting one, for modern audiences. It implied the peculiar condition of America as the symbol of the fresh start, the progressive future hostile to tradition. And in the questioning climate of the 1960s it seemed to pose a challenge for reintegration of tradition—ethnic, family, regional—into contemporary life.

In another major production playing on the separation of tradition and modernity, the movie *Witness* (1985) offered the Amish as an American anomaly of a tradition-oriented, communal society in the midst of modernism. It made 28 million dollars and generated millions more for the tourist industry of Lancaster County, Pennsylvania, "the Amish Country," where the film was shot. The movie was the first by Australian director Peter Weir to be filmed in America. He had previously drawn on the theme of tradition and modernity with a film called *The Last Wave* about rural Aborigines practicing their rites in an Australian city. The Amish, like the Aborigines, may be romanticized from a distance but close up might be scorned for their stubborn, unreasonable hold onto tradition.

The story in *Witness* concerns a tough city detective coldly called "Book" who finds refuge among the cozily named "Lapps" in the nearby serene environs of rural Pennsylvania. Book has been forced to flee because he knows too much about corruption, violence, and drugs within the city police department. Capable of brutality, he honestly "goes by the book," as his name implies, and his life is therefore in danger. In contrast to Book's background in the dark, noisy city with its pressure-cooker stress, vice, and filth, the Amish rural way of life is pictured with unforced peacefulness and clean morality. Wounded in the city, Book recuperates in the country among the Amish, and he finds value in unselfish traditions of plain dress and communal activity. He rediscovers long-neglected craft skills, emphasizing construction rather than destruction, and he begins to mesh with the communal Amish way of life. But his difference is revealed when he cannot hold his temper in response to mean-spirited taunting in town by non-Amish for the group's plain, passive ways. Word of the hostile incident attracts the notice of the corrupted cops from the city who come to the country to hunt him down. Gunfire erupts on the bucolic Amish farm, and Book is on the defensive without his gun. There are symbolic overtures such as Book's triumph over one bulky gunman by drowning him in harvest grain. In a powerful scene showing the moral power of community, the last surviving gunman finally surrenders his weapon in front of hundreds of unarmed Amishmen who look incredulously at the violent scene unfolding before them. Book has learned an ethical lesson, but he cannot stay. Surrounded in an epilogue by the imposing lights and machinery of police cars, Book signals his identity with a puff of a cigarette. He is seen driving toward the city, while a young Amishman walks on foot toward the farm, wheat gently, peacefully waving in the background.

Even before *Witness* came out, Lancaster County, Pennsylvania, laid claim to being among America's favorite tourist destinations. The movie added to the popular image of the region as home to Amish tradition, and compounded views of the Amish as a conservative folk culture. In reality, Lancaster County does not boast America's largest Amish population. Holmes County, Ohio, holds that distinction. It is not the area with the most conservative Amish communities either. Mifflin County, Pennsylvania, may hold that designation. The perception of Lancaster as home to Amish tradition is related to the idea of its being among the oldest Amish settlements, having been established in the eighteenth century. But more significant is its seemingly defiant location near urban centers. Within easy reach of major metropolitan areas of New York, Philadelphia, and Baltimore, Lancaster County had been promoted as a therapeutic escape from modernity, even though tourists rarely encountered authentic Amish community members or stayed in rural surroundings. The immense popularity of tourist attractions such as the Amish country in Pennsylvania is based on the recreational lure of a pastoral group life associated with tradition. Other such promoted draws exist in America—Ozark mountaineers in Arkansas, Cajuns in Louisiana, Navajo in the Southwest, for example—but arguably the Amish, maybe because of their close proximity to America's most bustling, cosmopolitan cities, most often epitomize American tradition. Asked to name a folk group, students I have surveyed consistently put the Amish at the top of their lists.

The prominence of the Amish in public notice is not a position they have sought, and the success of the tourist industry in Lancaster County has in fact diminished the pastoral landscape with which their "folk tradition" has been associated (Black 1992, 1993). Yet it is also among the factors encouraging Amish population growth and economic prosperity (Kraybill and Nolt 1995). The *Wall Street Journal* took notice, for example, of the entrance of Amish women into entrepreneurial businesses and the *New York Times* noticed the financial security of Amish farm families at a time when considerable press was being given to the failure of American family farms (Aeppel 1996; Schneider 1986). Responding to the image of traditional rural groups as impoverished and hard-hit by government social program cuts, the *Journal* reported the addition of 160 new industries and the operation of communal self-help traditions among the Old Order Amish that had made them impervious to cuts in government benefits (Ingersoll 1995).

The *Washington Post* appeared particularly surprised by the opening of commercial Amish markets in six mid-Atlantic locations, including some in malls within the cities of Philadelphia and Annapolis (Argetsinger 1997). Once almost exclusively agricultural, the Amish are no longer restricted to farm labor and have been mostly successful in the move to small businesses (W. Roberts 1995; Veigle 1990). Even in agriculture, change is apparent. Many Amish communities have allowed more tractors and mechanical assistance than in the past ("Some Amish" 1995). The popular press often delights in reporting such changes, especially when they appear inconsistent. Examples are reports in *USA Today* on the use of stereo "boom boxes" in Amish buggies, and in the *New York Times* on the use of trendy in-line skates while old bicycles are prohibited (S. Marshall 1996; Chen 1996). The *Chicago Tribune* highlighted the consumer consciousness of an Amish carriage shop that offered options of steel wheels, solid rubber tires, vinyl roofs, canvas tops, tinted windshields, and slide-across doors (T. Jones 1997).

While such anomalies make news, the dominant image in tourist literature is the unchanging serenity of Amish tradition. The same *Tribune* gave the headlines that touring Amish country was taking "A Step Back in Time," with a glimpse of "The Simple Life" (P. Moore 1995; Ammerman 1989). The *Detroit News* touted in its travel section the way that the Amish "still value life's simple ways" and the *Houston Chronicle* praised the way the "Amish Community Takes Visitors Back" ("Modern-Day" 1991; Racine 1995). "Old-time" values placed on family coherence, reliance on the land, and simplicity are highlighted in reports such as "Family is First for Devout 'Plain People'" and "In Amish Country, the Scenery and Food are Good and Plenty" (Grossman 1992; R. Cutting 1992). Lancaster's Amish attract national, indeed international, press for their hold on the past amidst supposedly future-oriented America.

Despite dire warnings by cultural critics and several notable folklorists of the demise of the Amish because of modernity and tourism, the population of the Old Order Amish in Lancaster County has more than doubled to over 16,000 from 1970 to 1990, a figure fifteen times greater than it was in 1910 (Glassie 1968, 4; Bronner 1996b, 33–34). Nonetheless, in keeping with the image of a communal folk, the Amish are misleadingly portrayed in countless brochures as an inscrutable, monolithic sect, soberly noncommercial, and generally noncommunicative. The apparent riddle of Amish culture thriving on rural tradition within a modern urban setting has turned them into a symbolic text in which everything they do—craft, dress, and eat—becomes anachronistically traditional and ethnically unique, so as to force reflection on mass cultural traits of individualism, technology, and progress. Tourism, however, tends to direct visitors away from Amish life into commercial zones with attractions based on symbolic narratives of Amish traditionality (Buck 1978; Brandt 1993–1994). The narratives appear especially distorted when one realizes that the major attraction of Amish country in the last decade has been factory outlet malls with romantic names invoking Pennsylvania-German tradition where Amish farms once stood.

There is also scholarship, supposedly the voice of reason, that has contributed to the notoriety of the Amish. Some of it could be faulted just as well for presenting the Amish as an endangered species that desperately needed to be protected from their non-Amish neighbors. This tendency in early scholarship on the Amish reveals an association of folk tradition with passivity and isolation as well as stability. It suggests that traditional societies cannot hold power in a modern state and need cultural brokers, often in the guise of outsiders "close" to the group, who will look out for their interests. To be sure, the Amish exhibit, as one aptly titled book called it, "A Struggle with Modernity" (Kraybill and Olshan 1994). But there are also signs that the Amish are in fact thriving and have been more vocal in recent decades in managing their affairs with the non-Amish "English" as well as the state (Kraybill 1993). In Lancaster, the Amish successfully blocked a highway expansion project through their farmlands, lobbied for maintenance of their midwife birth tradition, and exerted considerable pressure on local zoning boards for protective regulations (Levin 1996).

In light of a legacy of preservationist scholarship and popular uses of Amish tradition to spur consumerism and recreational therapy, many modern scholars of Amish tradition insist that social change and individual creativity, albeit cautious, are part of the cultural dynamics of Amish life (Kraybill 1989; see also Kraybill and Olshan 1994; Hostetler 1963). There is a reassessment of the assumption that a traditional society cannot thrive within a modernizing mass culture. Consider the centrality of tradition as described by a young Amish minister:

> The Amish outlook on tradition is somewhat different than other churches. We consider tradition as being spiritually helpful. Tradition can blind you if you adhere only to tradition and not the meanings of the tradition, but we really maintain a tradition. I've heard one of our members say that if you start changing some things, it won't stop at some things, it will keep on changing and there won't be an end to it. We have some traditions, that some people question and I sometimes myself question, that are being maintained just because they are a tradition. This can be adverse, but it can also be a benefit. Tradition always looks bad if you're comparing one month to the next or one year to the next, but when you are talking fifty years or more, tradition looks more favorable. Don't get me wrong, I don't feel that everybody who is traditional is okay. But there still is a lot of value in tradition and we realize that. (Kraybill 1989, 41–42)

From the Amish minister's perspective, tradition as the precedent of the past does not have to be separable from the present. The Amish value tradition for the social stability and coherence it provides; they maintain it more than their neighbors. Yet that does not mean that tradition is unchanging or consistent.

While tourism has been blistered for fantasizing the Amish, even racializing them apart from the Pennsylvania-German heritage of which they are a part, it has prodded several efforts for studied self-presentation of the varied regional-ethnic traditions of Southcentral Pennsylvania. In the heart of Amish country, the non-Amish Landis brothers—George and Henry—notably began during the 1940s what they called a "folk museum" to record the craft and agricultural traditions of the region. Its folk label was as much a reference to the modest general-store background of the Landis brothers as it was to the record they amassed of small-town everyday life made into relics by industrialization. But they drew scholarly interest as an early example of presenting material culture in a regional environment. It was an effort repeated in many outdoor museums emerging after World War II such as the Farmer's Museum in Cooperstown, New York, Old Sturbridge Village in Sturbridge, Massachusetts, and Old Salem in Winston-Salem, North Carolina. Old was the operative word. Captured as a moment in time, the buildings and artifacts of the Landis Valley Museum (later the State Farm Museum when it was taken over by the state) were celebrated as prime antiques, old things to be experienced amidst the modern environment of novelty. This was never more evident than at the Shelburne Museum in Shelburne, Vermont, where Electra Havemeyer Webb, a wealthy New York heiress, located her antique Americana collections in Colonial buildings that served as galleries. As histories of the museum note, it was a visiting experience that strangely had viewers give a materialistic eye toward overstocked cabinets of glorious objects in a demonstration of a supposedly simple past.

Museums such as the Landis Valley Museum engaged in education programs to insist on the relevance of relic collections for living viewers. The programs frequently showed the continuity of activities such as gardening and children's play in present-day communities. The Lancaster Heritage Center emphasized craft activities in education programs as the common traditions of the old city that transcended ethnic and religious divisions. Such traditions presented as old activities nonetheless appeared distant, separated in the past from the present. At a time when the loss of community was bemoaned because of apparently inevitable modernization, a noticeable rise was evident in presentations—in tourism, education, and art—of traditions as reminders of a sense of social connection that might still be recovered. What the efforts of the Landis brothers, Electra Havemeyer Webb, and others to declare local tradition not tied to religious separation reveal is a tendency to turn tradition into a form of history, a distant past remembered for its dislocation from the present.

TRADITION IN SCHOLARLY DISCOURSE

Seen as a common human inheritance, tradition especially in American scholarly interpretations did not need the homogeneity of a group or an ancient reference to qualify it as part of culture. The most frequently cited definition of this type is Alan Dundes's explanation of the term "folk" during the 1960s. To apply tradition in the modern, and especially plural American contexts, he reconfigured "folk" to refer to "*any group of people whatsoever* who share at least one common factor." Folklore, the logical, functional outcome of such a common grouping, becomes a popular, necessary commodity instead of a rare find or survival. Apparently fundamental to social life, folklore according to this definition persists for its significant purpose of expressing the cultural reality of a group.

Dundes expounded on tradition emerging from social interaction: "It does not matter what the linking factor is—it could be a common occupation, language, or religion—but what is important is that a group, formed for whatever reason, has some expressive traditions which it calls its own. In theory a group must consist of at least two persons, but generally most groups consist of many individuals. A member of the group may not know all other members, but he will probably know the common core of traditions belonging to the group, traditions which help the group have a sense of group identity" (Dundes 1965, 2). A person can simultaneously be a member of multiple groups and share many different kinds of traditions as a result. In this view, the repetition and variation of that shared knowledge, such as jokes, nicknames, and sayings, designate the material as traditions. The traditions have functions that are rationally interpreted—they lend an identity to the group.

Dundes replaced the conventional association of culture with locality, growing organically from roots in a place, with a modernistic connotation of social interaction and situational context giving rise to expression of traditions. Following this line of thinking, one can theoretically have traditions introduced and "invented" in a group as small as two people or as large as a nation. One can, generally speaking, experience traditions that emerge from any social encounter. The implication is that even educated "folk" such as professors or doctors have cultural traditions; use of traditions is not relegated to a level of society. Traditions do not have to be transmitted orally through generations either but can owe their multiple existence to short-lived social, typically unofficial, uses of photocopiers, faxes, videos, and the Internet (see Dundes and Pagter 1978; Tucker 1992; M. Preston 1994; Bronner 1995, 232–46). An identifying "folk" can be temporary, such as a group of friends, rather than being rooted in a region. The key in Dundes's definition was that people *needed* to express, indeed vary (often updating and customizing), traditions recordable as folklore in their formation of a group. Folklore as a basis of identity-formation and social existence gained a rationale and a living, even dynamic quality in its image of continually responding and adapting to shifting social encounters in contexts of different times and places.

Considering the close connection of folklore to tradition in scholarly as well as public discourse, one would expect more exploration of tradition than there has been in folklore studies. The *Standard Dictionary of Folklore, Mythology, and Legend* lacks an entry for tradition. The 100-year index to the *Journal of American Folklore* contains only one citation to "tradition"; references to "folk" cover hundreds of citations extending over four pages. Highly regarded reference works such as *Encyclopedia Britannica, International Encyclopedia of the Social Sciences, Encyclopedia of Philosophy*, and *Dictionary of the History of Ideas* have no entries on "tradition." Tradition, as Dan Ben-Amos has aptly pointed out, has been a term to think *with*, not to think *about* (Ben-Amos 1984, 1). It is often treated as a given of discourse, a term whose meaning is taken for granted probably because it seems so fundamental to the human condition. Within scholarship, it becomes a "problem" mostly within humanities and social sciences when evaluation of it is forced in relation to controversial keywords in scholarly discourse such as modernity, innovation, and creativity (see Acton 1953; Popper 1965; Zaretzke 1982; Kristeller 1983; Mieder 1987; Gustavsson 1989; Oliver 1989; Rapoport 1989; Tuan 1989; Bruns 1991; Hammer 1992).

One can find abundant entries on specific traditions rather than to the idea of tradition. In one of the few books philosophically exploring the meaning of tradition generally, Edward Shils observed: "There are books about tradition in Islamic theology and law; there are books about tradition in Judaism; books about tradition in Roman Catholic and Protestant Christianity. There are books about particular traditions in literature and art and law. There is however no book about tradition which tries to see the common ground and elements of tradition and which analyzes what difference tradition makes in human life" (Shils 1981, vii). Shils's extensive effort to describe tradition emphasized the social aspect of tradition as a universal trait. Tradition, he argued, is basic to the ways that societies function. He viewed tradition emerging from the need to direct action with things, works, words, and modes of conduct created in the past. Reflecting on the tendencies of social sciences, he blamed the progressive thinking of the Enlightenment for minimizing the evaluation of traditions in assessments of the present and future. He explained: "A mistake of great historical significance has been made in modern times in the construction of a doctrine which treated traditions as the detritus of the forward movement of society" (Shils 1981, 330).

An implication of revising this Enlightenment doctrine is a challenge to assumptions that Western civilization is more creative or progressive whereas non-Western or nonindustrialized societies are primarily "traditional." Toward the social scientific goal of predicting and suggesting social patterns, Shils treated traditions positively as "constituents of a worthwhile life." Yet in emphasizing the basic social function of tradition, he sought a universal model for a process of tradition rather than grounding it in specific histories and cultures and evaluation of expressive traditions as many folklorists and ethnic scholars had done (see Gailey 1989; Bronner 1992b; M. Roth 1995, 177–85). Shils's concern was not so much with evaluating traditions as it was with integrating them into the functionalism of society (Shils 1971). He was joined in this concern by S. N. Eisenstadt, who offered the idea of a "dynamics" of tradition. In this view, the stronghold of tradition as a human need for rootedness explained the use of the past to control, but not impede, social change (Eisenstadt 1969).

Although Shils and Eisenstadt were faulted for not adequately particularizing traditions within groups in the context of time and place, they had an important role during a period of shift in cultural theory toward relativizing assumptions of progress and modernity. The separation of "literature" from "narrative," "art" from "craft," "civilization" from "culture," all came under closer scrutiny for fallacies of elitist thinking. Questioning the "genius" of Western art, Shils in fact pointed out the ways that innovations are dependent on traditions in any cultural setting. Dundes's "dynamic" definition of a folk group and its use of traditions that may indeed be "new" is an example of relativizing culture. In 1972, S. N. Eisenstadt argued that intellectuals noted for their individuality and supposedly wedded to innovation are not above "tradition." Intellectuals in a society, he surmised, are influenced by, and themselves influence, the construction of traditions. Tradition, he agreed, is a framework for creativity. Intellectuals may indeed through their critical stance toward tradition, serve "in modernity ... to create some new tradition" (Eisenstadt 1972, 3). Countering the progressive criticism of tradition, Eisenstadt shared with Shils a perspective on tradition "as the reservoir of the most central social and cultural experiences prevalent in a society, as the most enduring element in the collective social and cultural construction of reality" (Eisenstadt 1972, 3). Basic to this intellectual turn from the progressivist perspective is the reconfiguration of tradition and its oppositional pairing with "creativity."

If tradition and creativity are thought of working interdependently, "dynamically," since any present action takes into account the past, as well as individual preference and social influence, then tradition appears as an active rather than relic force in people's lives. Folklore as the expression of this dynamic adapts readily to different situations and needs. Folklore becomes manipulated knowledge; it is expressed as a blend of personal and social influence. The linking of creativity and tradition suggests the modern philosophy that "the ability to create is not limited to artists or writers but extends to many more, and perhaps to all, areas of human activity and endeavor" (Kristeller 1983, 106). This ideal succeeds the romantic notion of art as the sole domain of exceptional cultivated minds as existing free of tradition, as an expression of originality or genius that can create something where nothing existed previously. A celebrated artist such as T. S. Eliot in 1919 complained indeed that "in English writing we seldom speak of tradition, though we occasionally apply its name in deploring its absence. We cannot refer to 'the tradition' or to 'a tradition'; at most we employ the adjective in saying that the poetry of So-and-so is 'traditional' or even 'too traditional.' Seldom, perhaps, does the word appear except in a phrase of censure" (Eliot 1960, 3). Eliot's protest was that the so-called fine arts had overemphasized the individual to the detriment of his or her art.

By 1983 when philosopher Paul Oskar Kristeller surveyed uses of creativity and tradition, a change in thinking was apparent. Kristeller observed: "Perhaps the concept of genius has been less widely used in recent decades since it is definitely an 'elitist' notion, whereas in an egalitarian age such as ours it is claimed and believed that everybody, not only some gifted and talented artists, is original and creative" (Kristeller 1983, 108). Although thought of as a post-1960s phenomenon, the concept of the interdependence of creativity and tradition in folklore studies has been in formation at least since the 1910s, when Franz Boas, for one, questioned a West European tendency in folklore studies of viewing folktales as intact, uniform units and tellers as passive repeaters of texts (Boas 1940, 403). In fieldwork among Native Americans, Boas found varying levels of originality in the performance of folklore and he explained differences with reference to personality and social context. He underscored his view by referring to tale tellers as "individual artists" (Boas 1940, 451–90). Later Daniel Crowley addressed the problem in folklore of reconciling anthropological attention to dynamics and literary concern for stability in "Tradition and Creativity," the introduction to *I Could Talk Old-Story Good* (1966; reprinted 1983). In this study of Bahamian folk narratives, he observed that "no tale, no matter how sacred or traditional, can be told twice in exactly the same way without improbable feats of memory," and therefore, "variation both intentional and accidental confuses the problem of studying diffusion patterns, and threatens the validity of anticipated results" (Crowley 1966, 1). Narrators are not merely receptacles for tradition, he concluded, but rather are choosers, arrangers, and performers. He added a relativistic swipe: "The pattern of creative activity within the forms of one's own society is valid not only in such folk arts as pottery or storytelling, but equally in the most extreme forms of personal self-expression in modern European painting" (Crowley 1966, 136).

The prevalence in folkloristic inquiry of tradition with creativity and innovation is demonstrated by the appearance of thirty-seven entries between 1981 and 1996 in the Modern Language Association's (MLA) bibliographic database, a standard reference of the humanities. Almost seventy-five percent of the titles belonged to authors engaged in folklore research. The combination of folklore and creativity brought up about as many titles as a search for tradition and creativity. These terms showed up rarely in combination before the 1970s. The association of "tradition" with "innovation" was more common in literary study (193 hits), while folklore and innovation showed up rarely. Innovation rhetorically implied more of a break with tradition, whereas creativity suggested a process involving tradition (see Bronner 1992b). One could find reference to integration in titles such as "The Creativity of Tradition" (Peacock 1986; C. Briggs 1988), "Folklore Function in the Development of Creativity" (Voigt 1983), and "Folklore as a Special Form of Creativity" (Jakobson and Bogatyrev 1980).

The ideas expressed during the 1980s about the linkage of tradition and creativity speak to the modern redefinition of the arts and to the emphasis on change and variation in contemporary societies. Creativity, a term gaining currency in the twentieth century, has a rhetorical significance over the older use of "creation" or bringing something into being where nothing had been before. The latter view applied to art, which has occupied a dominant position in Western history, makes reference to the idea of Biblical creation as a new stroke of genius or miraculousness (J. Mason 1988). "Creation" implies unity, stability, order, and harmony; it is the work of a "creator."

"Creativity," linked in form to the physics of "relativity," implies less of a superhuman model. It exists more at the level of an artisan's work; in myths, it is the tool of tricksters and smiths rather than deities. Thus creativity implies multiplicity, change, conflict, and physicality. Creativity emerges from everyday struggles and actions of people considering the tensions between old and new, individual and society.

Use of the MLA database, which especially represents works on language and literature, not only reveals a growth of a linkage in scholarly discourse between tradition and creativity, it also shows striking interrelationships between tradition and keywords of culture and society such as folk and modern. Searching keywords in titles of works indexed for the period 1981 to 1996, one finds that folk is among the most frequently found terms in the database with 31,080 appearances; added to the number of hits for "folklore," the figure climbs to 40,591. "Modern," as I have pointed out, shows a parallelism with folk. It shows up in the database 48,172 times; modern and folk appear together, however, only 526 times. "Culture" (15,756) and "society" (10,261) are major terms in the database, although they appear less often than folk and modern. Probably the most numerically significant pairing of folk is with tradition or traditional (1,442) and culture (5,726). Comparing the results of the MLA search with another database such as UnCover, which represents a wide range of scholarly journals beyond language and literature, I found comparable results. A keyword search for the first six months of 1996 revealed 4,800 appearances of "tradition" and 8,207 hits of "traditional" for a combined total of 13,007, which is comparable to the 15,562 appearances of "modern." "Folk" and "modern" appeared in combination only 22 times, while "tradition" and "modern" appeared 180 times. There were no hits of "tradition," "modern," and "folk" together, while "folk" and "tradition" accounted for 47 titles.

It is difficult to determine from this statistical evidence, however, whether the uses of "tradition" or "folk" are consistent in the works that appear. In fact, the meanings probably vary, although recent culture theory has emphasized the relativistic idea of the "dynamics" of tradition (see Eisenstadt 1969; Toelken 1979; Wagner 1981; Thompson, Ellis, and Wildavsky 1990). Reflecting on this shift, Dan Ben-Amos summarized seven strands of tradition used in American folklore studies from an early view of "tradition as lore" to "tradition as performance." In between he offers "tradition as [cultural] canon" (especially the valued texts in a folk society), "tradition as process" (especially oral transmission), "tradition as [transmitted] mass" (or a "load" carried by exceptional tradition bearers), "tradition as culture" (from the anthropological view of tradition as a defining and identifying aspect of social life), and "tradition as *langue*" (from the linguistic distinction between the language system of *langue* that guides the expression of a *parole* or "word") (Ben-Amos 1984).

One can fit, from the previous discussion, Herskovits's construction of tradition as custom or culture or Dundes's view of the folk group in "tradition as culture." There are rhetorical clues within scholarly discourse to some of these categories.

The use of "folk culture" signals tradition as culture, "oral tradition" suggests tradition as a process, "folk literature" (and sometimes "folk traditions") implies tradition as a canon, "verbal art" stands for tradition as performance, and "folk expressions" or "expressive folklore" for tradition as *langue*. Sometimes the distinctions are not so neat. While Thompson in *The Standard Dictionary of Folklore* emphasized the transmission of folklore by oral means from generation to generation, he also wanted to identify a literary canon for folk society in his formulation of a global tale-type index (see also Pentikäinen 1978). Ben-Amos also suggested that while in theory Herskovits epitomized anthropologists who construe tradition as synonymous with culture, in practice he actually conceived of tradition as a canon of folk society because of his method of identifying traditions within a society that gain acceptance or get rejected.

Unlike Shils, Ben-Amos as a folklorist was especially concerned with the expressive dimension to traditions. He referred to the "literary" folklorists who wanted to establish a historical canon comparable to those identified as "classical," "great," "popular," or "Western." The ethnographic-linguistic concern for the guiding structures of *langue* and dramaturgical metaphor of performance may both involve tradition as an abstract system of rules that generates the enactment of folklore. Ben-Amos cited Kay Cothran's performance-oriented proposal to redefine folklore as "tradition—not antiquity and orality, but 'our ways, our means, our categories, our system'" (Cothran 1979, 445). Furthermore, the idea that tradition is a process of transmission and hence of learning and action is central to perspectives on tradition as a situated performance. Ben-Amos, who in 1972 fashioned a definition of folklore without reference to historic tradition as "artistic communication in small groups," favored a perspective of tradition as performance and its attention to communication in dynamic situations (Ben-Amos 1972; see also Ben-Amos 1977, 1993). Yet he pointed out an often overlooked difference in "dynamic" views of tradition. Someone like Roger Abrahams, he felt, epitomized the approach that *langue*, like folklore, represents the stable, preexisting system of rules and symbols that produces *parole* or performed expressions (Abrahams 1977). Someone like Barre Toelken in his popular textbook *The Dynamics of Folklore* implied that tradition is performance itself:

> … we might characterize or describe the materials of folklore as "tradition-based communicative units informally exchanged in dynamic variation through space and time." *Tradition* is here understood to mean not some static, immutable force from the past, but those pre-existing culture-specific materials and options that bear upon the performer more heavily than do his or her own personal tastes and talents. We recognize in the use of *tradition* that such matters as content and style have been for the most part passed on but not invented by the performer. *Dynamic* recognizes, on the other hand, that in the processing of these contents and styles in performance, the artist's own unique talents of inventiveness *within* the tradition are highly valued and are expected to operate strongly. (Toelken 1979, 32)

If "dynamic processes" characterize both tradition and performance, rather than being a related contrastive pair, tradition and performance appear integrated.

In summary, most evident in folkloristic scholarship from the nineteenth century through the twentieth are ideas of tradition as (1) an everyday past, often ancient, represented as stable and immutable, (2) learning as a kind of custom or process usually described as being outside formal institutions and involving older generations passing on "lore" to younger ones, (3) tradition as a shared body of knowledge and belief, a conventional wisdom, existing outside of formal records, (4) a repeated, variable expression or performance emerging from social interaction, and (5) a symbol or mode of thought characteristic of a group's identity. These orientations have emerged in parallel development with concepts of modernity, nationality, and creativity describing human progress and identity. The combination of social and historical influences in the meaning of tradition implies a configuration of some basic human relations: among individual, group, society, and nation; between thought or idea and action or expression; between the contexts of time and space; and between perceptions of self and other. Largely defining the problem of tradition, with its suggestion of identity and existence, folklorists may well have provided the lasting lesson that meaning resides in the ways people express themselves through shared, local knowledge.

Tradition in the Press

One test of the relation of scholarly constructions of tradition to the public discourse is to examine uses of tradition communicated through the popular press. If scholarship has evaluated traditions as memories of the past, processes of informal learning, and types of collective wisdom, popular media has reflected, and contributed, public notions of the significance of tradition in the events of daily life. The news that is reported and discussed daily constitutes a clue to the visibility of tradition in society. News, as many critics have pointed out, more than reporting facts, reveals forms of public consensus (Fowler 1991, 46–65). Headlines assume that readers have a sense of the normative state of affairs, for headlines often draw attention by blaring "breaking" stories that often involve change, action, disaster, novelty. With common uses of slang and puns to engage readers in many daily headlines, there can be a feeling of clever conversation, as if a lively story was being narrated to a listening audience. Since newspaper space is normally at a premium, headline writers select words carefully, and the frequent appearance of tradition with various modifiers in headlines attests to forms of its public meaning.

Press databases such as Newspaper Abstracts and Periodical Abstracts showed that "tradition" turned up in headlines 2,173 and 2,613 times, respectively, in one six-month period of 1994. Scanning the list of titles, one can detect strong associations in the popular press between tradition and family, sport, ethnic, and local (often appearing as "small-town" or "neighborhood") activities. The phrase

"American tradition" appeared surprisingly rarely. In national newspapers, it occurred only twenty-two times. "Japan-bashing," "bilking consumers," "baseball," "victory at the Olympics," "splashy marketing," "abuse between fans and athletes," "Greek Revival style," were the kind of patterns branded as national in city dailies. Periodical Abstracts revealed more references to national traditions, presumably because magazines such as *Time* and *Newsweek* in the database appealed to a mass market. Another reason is that they had many more book reviews with headlines often making reference to national literary and artistic trends. Yet I still expected more than the 312 citations I found. A scan of the list revealed that "American tradition" was mostly used in magazines to discuss ethnic, local, and family contexts.

To get a closer look at the public use of "tradition" in the press, I collected examples of headlines using "tradition" in one city daily over a period of two years (1994–1996). Monitoring the *Harrisburg Patriot-News*, which claims the largest circulation in central Pennsylvania, I counted fifty-five occurrences of "tradition" or "traditional" used in headlines. All but two of the headlines counted had "tradition" as its keyword. Many more articles concerned tradition in the texts of articles, but I was mainly following examples of the newspaper using tradition as a rhetoric of public engagement in its headline placement. The simplest headline was a one-word banner "Tradition." Below appeared a picture and caption describing a ranger at Independence National Historical Park reading a draft of the Declaration of Independence in Philadelphia. "Congress approved the document on July 4, 1776, and the first draft was read in public four days later, beginning a tradition that has been followed ever since," the paper explained (July 9, 1994). Headlines tend to be short and snappy, but some referring to traditions, such as the following front-page news stories, extended over two lines: "Midstaters Join in Holiday Tradition: All Forms of Transit Jammed on Busiest Travel Day" (December 23, 1995) or "To Keep Tradition, Hunters Return for Annual Rite of Fall" (November 28, 1995).

On two occasions, the newspaper used "tradition" in three headlines in a single issue (June 24, 1994, and November 25, 1994). The first was divided between coverage of Jubilee Day, a community festival in Mechanicsburg, Pennsylvania, and a sports story. The second drew attention to local Thanksgiving traditions including a charitable custom of giving free meals on the holiday, and playing of a high school alumni football game. Uses of tradition in headlines tended to cluster around holidays, especially the winter season stretching from Thanksgiving to New Year's Day. In a busy, mobile society, the paper suggested holidays were rare occasions for togetherness and sharing associated with tradition. Many stories that involved localities also included a quotation about the loss of community and the added significance of traditions in the present as a reminder of social connection and historical continuity. On thirteen occasions, "tradition" was prominent on the front page of the newspaper, usually to refer to a repeated local event such as Jubilee Day (Patch Town Day in the coal region was another event referencing tradition) or local ritual connected with the start of hunting season. Indeed, the newspaper's headlines frequently linked "tradition" with community events. "Tradition" was prominent thirteen times on the front page of the State/Local section of the newspaper. Counting the references to local events in the top World/Nation section, local connections to tradition accounted for most of the headlines with tradition, forty-four percent of the total.

When a "local" story appeared in reference to "tradition," it tended to celebrate a repeated community gathering or a dislodging of community and its bonds of familiarity. It did not have to be old to be "tradition" in this context. For example, a report on an annual community dinner in Fairview Township announced, "32 Year Old Tradition Continues" (December 7, 1994). Explaining why Jubilee Day had significance, the newspaper brandished the headline, "Celebrating a Tradition." It quoted a participant who said of the sixty-six-year-old festival, "It's just a tradition. I came back to see the people I know." Elaborating on the comment, the reporter observed that there's "something deeper and more meaningful" than lemonade and funnel cakes. "Yesterday, on the streets of Mechanicsburg, a community came together. People who grew up together, then drifted apart, met once again under the hot sun" (June 24, 1994). It was news, then, when "Tradition Ends on 50th Anniversary" of a Lawnton community dinner (December 26, 1995) or "Another Tradition Canceled: 'Living Creche' Has No Director" (December 13, 1995). One headline about community was unusual because it crammed innovation and tradition as a contrastive pair into a single headline: "Halifax to Mark 200 Years in Traditional, Original Style" (July 14, 1994). The traditional part of the bicentennial celebration, the paper reported, was a community barbecue, parade, fireworks, and carnival. It also had an "original" musical, a pony express ride, and an antique car show. The organizers hoped the celebration would be an annual event "bringing people together." In another reference to a community's presentation of traditions as a demonstration of its social self, the newspaper (with overdone alliteration) emphasized the intention of the town in its banner headline, "Dillsburg Marches Out Traditional Festivities to Fete Farmers' Fare" (October 21, 1995).

I found few references to national traditions, but the rare instance stands out. In the middle of the crisis in former Yugoslavia, the paper editorialized about "Clinton's Gamble." Specifically it was that he was banking on "American Tradition for Support of Bosnia Peacekeeping Role" (November 29, 1995). It suggested a popular outlook consistent through history that is shared nationally. Reviewing his speech to the nation, the paper reported that the president "sought to appeal to the traditional American repugnance toward bullies who take their wrath out on the innocent and defenseless." The paper credited the president with appealing to this "tradition" to win acceptance for what would likely be an otherwise unpopular decision to send troops. It implied that tradition was based on belief and emotion rather than rationality. The other reference to national tradition was also political.

Reporting the unconventional approach of Steve Forbes during the early presidential primary campaign, the paper blurted on its front page, "Millionaire Undermines a Tradition" (February 12, 1996). Referring to the "mythology of presidential politics," the paper noted Forbes's use of saturation media advertising over the "traditional" personal contact tour. The "tradition" not only had the ring of convention, but it also carried an association with the backwater reputation of Iowa and New Hampshire. The paper stated, for example, "Some experts claim the Forbes strategy is spoiling the quaintly bucolic political traditions of both states." The implication is that politics, often resisted in humanistic scholarship as too formal and hegemonic to be expressive, has a cultural dimension and therefore can be described in terms of traditions (see Thompson, Ellis, Wildavsky 1990).

A survey of the newspaper shows a strong association of tradition, in fact, with humanistic pursuits. The second largest category of headlines using "tradition" appeared in sections covering Arts and Leisure, Living, and Food (issued only on Wednesdays by the newspaper). Each of these sections accounted for five headlines. If I count in the single appearances of tradition in Religion (issued only on Saturday), Environment, Real Estate, and special sections (weddings, Christmas), the total for art and daily living references to tradition comes to thirty-six percent of the total. Many of the references concerned holiday customs. On April 3, 1996, the headline "Holiday Food Traditions Preserved by Families" referred to Polish Easter practices. The front of the Food section for December 7, 1994, offered "Here Are Recipes for New Tradition." In this case, tradition was meant to be something that would be annually repeated rather than something necessarily old. The article suggested that "family favorites" for holiday cookies such as baked truffle treasures and lemon pecan stars sent in by area residents could be taken up by readers. Another article entitled "Retiring of Some Traditions Sought" (December 18, 1994) discussed choices made by couples for the rituals used in their weddings. It also implied that traditions in a modern context could be managed rather than followed slavishly.

When "tradition" appeared in combination with another word, it was likely to be "holiday," "local," or "family." "Folk" did not appear with "tradition" in the newspaper, and "folk" occurred much less than "tradition." When "folk" appeared, it referred to one of many "folk festivals" in the region, to "folk art" on display in museums or for sale at auctions, to contemporary "folk musicians" performing on the stage, or to "folk heroes" (especially used in stories on General Colin Powell after the Gulf War). Unlike the scholarly practice of linking "folk" or "cultural" with tradition in popular discourse, if the newspaper is an indication, the main rhetoric is one of custom, community, and especially family. A report on strawberry picking season had the headline "Pick-Your-Own-Patches, A Sweet Family Tradition" (June 18, 1996). Commenting on the rise of tree farms engaging in Christmas trade, the newspaper reported, "Family Traditions Helpful to Tree Farms" (November 27, 1995), and explaining American card exchange, the headline playfully read, "Family Traditions Are in the Cards" (December 22, 1994). Recounting the accomplishments of an outgoing college president, the paper carried the banner "Retiring President Kept Family Tradition at Messiah College" (June 27, 1994). The repeated use of "family" with "tradition" suggested an intimacy and stability of one's most immediate social group. Even more than following tradition, the coverage of family sharing in the newspaper suggested that families more than other groups traditionalize their activities (see Kotkin and Zeitlin 1983).

Ethnic connections were also apparent in headlines using "tradition" in the arts and living sections. The paper referred to "Traditional Symbols" in Native American art and characterized it as "Art Strongly Rooted in Past." Another essay on Native Americans on the techniques used by the Carlisle Indian School was accompanied by a photograph of boys and girls with fresh haircuts and uniforms in front of the school. It carried the caption "Shorn of Their Hair and Traditions." Found in the Perspective section, it was a retrospective on the experiment to "civilize" Native Americans by breaking their cultural traditions of dress and appearance (February 12, 1995). In addition to this historical example, references to tradition as a political issue also appeared in the editorials or Nation/World section of the newspaper. During this period, the paper noted court battles about gender equality at military colleges that culminated in the headline "Citadel Ends Its Long Males-Only Tradition" (June 25, 1996). This headline made tradition sound like a historical custom that had taken on the authority of a rule before it became rightly challenged. The newspaper also editorialized about eliminating the "tradition" of the Hegins Pigeon Shoot because the "blood sport" was not surviving in the face of animal rights protests (September 7, 1994).

Sports in general was a special area for mention of tradition in the newspaper. I found this consequential because folkloristic scholarship has tended to neglect sports as too formally organized for evaluation of cultural tradition (see, however, Peterson 1983; G. Fine 1987b). In the public discourse of the press, sports teams were the most recognizable location of groupness in modern life. If one specially goes to "see the Amish" for tradition, one understands teams as organized groups that foster traditions. Moreover, there is a kind of functional assumption that players fit roles on teams, or players are supposed to sacrifice their individualities for the sake of the team. Many articles in reference to Celtic tradition, or even Berwick High School tradition, suggest that players come and go, but the traditions of the team continue.

In sports coverage, teams tend to formalize links to locality. Rivalries, often touted as traditions, pit comparably sized schools or towns in the same region against each other. "Tradition, Rivalries Fuel Women's Event," the paper trumpeted on March 16, 1995. Because Tennessee had repeatedly been in the NCAA tournament, the paper ran the headline, "Tradition Spurs Lady Vols Ahead." On a local level, because Lebanon Catholic High School had played in the state finals before, whereas their rival had not, the paper announced that Lebanon Catholic had tradition on its side (March 26, 1995). Tradition in sports can also be interpreted in public discourse as an attitude or fate—grittiness, luck, winning, losing. Announcing "New Coach is Part of Flyers' Tradition," the *Patriot* remarked on the "essence" of team tradition, "hard work, dedication and defense" (June 24, 1994). Surprised by the success of the Cleveland Indians during the 1994 baseball season, the paper carried the headline, "Indians Break Losing Tradition." The story connected the rise of the perennial doormats to the league with the renaissance of the reputedly dowdy city as an attraction. Tradition was used as custom suggesting a role in relation to other teams or communities.

Occasionally, reports referred to specific "traditions" in sport as expressive customs. Because sport is commonly construed as "play" in America, it is often given to ritual references in the press. It is reported that teams and their coaches have routes they superstitiously follow to big games, they insist on routines for game preparations, and they break tension with outrageous practical jokes. Implying this playfulness to sport, the *Patriot* included the headline in its Sports section for October 27, 1995, "A Tradition with Meaning." As the paper explained, "Since Hershey High grad Vince Pantalone became a member of the Lower Dauphin coaching staff in the mid-1980s, either he or Hershey head coach Bob 'Gump' May has been the recipient of a cigar depending on which team won their annual game. It is not the midstate's best-known tradition—possibly because the exchange of a tobacco product among high school coaches defies the current swell of political correctness—but it has meaning. It was started by Pantalone's father, Emil, and has been carried on by both coaches since Emil died in 1987." If the previous example brought out the theme of modern sensitivity to a tradition from the past, another article tried to bring the clash of old and young generations in baseball, and by extension, in society. On July 15, 1994, the paper carried a long story about the argument of "tradition-abiding keeper of the game" ("or an old fogey at 38," the paper stated) manager Buck Showalter of the Seattle Mariners with his star player Ken Griffey, Jr., over a hat. To Showalter's chagrin, Griffey was following the "new" tradition among youth of wearing the baseball cap backwards. As these reports indicate, coverage of sports tends to bring out family linkage, community spirit, historical precedent, and ritualized activity as the stuff of tradition.

Going back to the 1980s, American sports coverage can be credited for creating a dramatic moment of defining American tradition. Ostensibly a contest for a basketball championship, the playoff series between the Boston Celtics and Los Angeles Lakers became translated in the press as a tussle for the national character. The Celtics and Lakers battled for the National Basketball Association championship three out of four years between 1984 and 1987. To heat up the rivalry, the press portrayed the Celtics as the team of old, playing in the antiquated, dark and dingy Boston Garden in the traditional setting of old New England. It harped on the social virtues of the Celtics' teamwork, work ethic, and naturally a winning tradition. The dowdy digs of the Boston Garden and the plebeian reputation of

Boston fans roused feelings of heartiness and pride in old-fashioned values. The Lakers, on the other hand, "Never ... anybody's blue-collar baby," as *Sports Illustrated* observed, attracted a strikingly modern image (McCallum 1987b, 15). The team was located in the glitz of booming Los Angeles, and came to represent the "well-lighted" future of easy street and consumer culture. It had individual superstars on its team and Hollywood stars in its audience. The press featured the "showtime" of the Lakers, given to egotistical theatrics and stylish futuristic garb and cool sunglasses of the fun, if shallow, life. "Legend has it that the Lakers are into style," a *New York Times* columnist sneered, and "a five-game victory in the Garden ... would be so much more stylish for them than having to go back home and work on the weekend" (Vecsey 1987). In contrast, a *Newsweek* report beamed, "The Celtics are a strikingly old-fashioned team, from their unselfish playing style right down to their dark green high-top sneakers" (Leehrsen 1984). The dapper coach of the Lakers, Pat Riley, announced "concern that his team's reputation was wasting away in Celebrityville." He protested the press's portrayals of his team, in his words, as "a bunch of glitter-group, superficial laid-backs." "This is the hardest-working team I've ever had," Coach Riley declared, "but regardless of what we do we're minimized ... we're empty people ... and most of us aren't even from California" (Kirpatrick 1987, 24–25). George Vecsey, the renowned sports columnist for the *New York Times*, distinguished the slickness of Los Angeles fans from the homely old Boston loyalists, where most people "look like they ought to have a nickname. Spike. Lefty. Knuckles" (1987).

The protests of the players and coaches that the championship was not a culture war, but a game among players with much in common, did not lessen the tone of the press's puffed-up narrative of a street fight over American tradition. "Laker Talent, Celtic Team," a headline from *Time* blared in 1984 (June 25), indicating an American identity crisis. "When East Meets West," "The Toast of Both Coasts," and "Playing It Tough in the East," were typical headlines contrasting the working-class ethic of the old industrial Northeast and the laid-back lifestyle in the California Dream (Simpson 1984: Newman 1984b; McCallum 1987a). To read the papers was to believe that much more was at stake than a trophy, and the unfolding plot of the rivalry attracted many new adherents to the sport as basketball fever rose in America. The narrative plot of cultural confrontation of old and new America peaked with public anticipation of the climactic 1987 series. The television broadcast of the decisive sixth game was the highest-rated basketball game ever shown on television. The introduction of that game on television built up the "mystique of Celtic tradition," in "ancient Boston Garden" against the "jubilant Laker Express" and "bright lights of Los Angeles." At a time of rapid mobility when economic shift from manufacturing to service and information translated into an image of decline for the East and boom for the West, the press found a story other than the outcome of the games.

In its typical location on the back page, American sports coverage raises signs of social significance. Running stories on the reverse side of the usually political slant of the front page, sports coverage has allowed readers to imagine dramas involving defense of fragile traditions. Commenting frequently on the development and disappearance of "traditions" naturally arising from communal activity, the press was often inclined to make team accomplishment a test of social virtues. Reporting individual achievement in relation to the needs of the group, fan loyalty at a time of loss, and community support for the team as public representative, the press kept watch over sports as a barometer of American conditions.

In other news behind the front page, especially of community events and human features, tradition is a frequently encountered prompt to readers and listeners. It reminds them of the malleable social values in everyday life that are seemingly in flux. It comes out as a keyword to measure the stability of an American sense of community, especially at moments when the cultural landscape is shifting. In coverage of national holidays and community festivals, in the "human features" of locality, family, religion, and ethnicity, the American press creates texts of tradition to follow.

THE POLITICS OF TRADITION

To read the entry on "tradition" in the erudite *Companion to American Thought* (1995) is to see the term through a political lens. Look through it and it appears that conservatism holds claims on the merits of tradition while liberalism eschews them. Uses of tradition are attached, after all, to household names of the resurgent conservative politics of the 1980s and 1990s such as Ronald Reagan, George Bush, Dan Quayle, Pat Robertson, and William Bennett. The author of the entry, Russell L. Hanson, connects "tradition" with a sense of the past toward solutions for the future. The past is the source for selected social virtues known best in the 1990s as "traditional values." Waving tradition as the banner of a national culture, a sensible mode of thinking, and a moral way of acting, several figures gained prominence by tainting liberalism with being against tradition in political campaigns of the 1980s and 1990s.

Meanwhile liberals regarded the conservatives as being stuck on tradition to the point of wearing blinders to modern-day social realities. Or they assailed the conservatives for misleadingly offering one kind of tradition as the only worthy kind, rather than allowing for many different traditions of separate communities, all legitimately American. Different sides argued over who would be the proper guardian of a reemerging American tradition, variously defined of course. And as I will discuss, folklore has been right there in the fray.

In 1996, slogans collided as presidential hopeful Robert Dole promised to use the traditional values of the past as a bridge to the present, and Clinton answered by offering the present as a bridge to the future. Dole played out the platform of what Hanson refers to as "the party of the past," often called conservative, or the voice of the "right." On the other side of this scenario is the party of the future, given to labels of liberal, leftist, and progressive. In this head-to-head matchup, the party of the past warns of a breakdown of a sense of order and a loss of decency in society. It seeks a return to "traditional values" that have presumably sustained the greatness of assimilating America—among them, the nuclear family, community, and religion. There is a nationalistic, or nativist, connection because of the frequent assumption that the assimilation is to a version of values held by white Christian America at the nation's founding. It implies a social good in seeking national unity based on this "mainstream," encouraging free enterprise, and maintaining beneficial hierarchies of leadership (Sigler 1969; Kirk 1982; Aughey, Jones, and Riches 1992; Sobnosky 1993; Dunn and Woodard 1996). In education, a major battleground in the square off between the parties of the past and future, the concern from the party of the past is that "students who have not absorbed traditional lessons will not become a part of America, nor will they conduct themselves in ways that continue its greatness in years to come" (Hanson 1995, 681). Extolling individual rights, the party of the past often seeks less government intervention in managing social problems and more efforts to strengthen social institutions of family, church, and school that build moral character and social responsibility.

The party of the future looks forward to breaks with the institutionalization of conservative social views it associates with racism and sexism. It often accuses an elite of wealth and power of controlling society and discourages groups marginalized because of difference of color, gender, and class from participation in the polity. At worst, it may accuse the elite of repressing dissent and encouraging discrimination. It seeks to build tolerance through establishment of new traditions recognizing the integrity of plural groups, many with alternative values, within the polity, and through special consideration for those at a disadvantage in a racially divided society (Abbott and Levy 1985; McElvaine 1987; Garry 1992; Tomasky 1996). It "condemns the self-aggrandizing tendencies of the so-called dominant tradition or cultural mainstream," and will commonly offer critical narratives of the past to warrant new directions for building a more benevolent future (Hanson 1995, 681). It will encourage multiple perspectives for social solutions, insisting on participation of, and models drawn from, traditions of marginalized groups. Or it will expound on the need to avoid value judgment in education, family planning, immigration policy, and public welfare, and, in keeping with an unfulfilled American tradition of egalitarianism, will call for wider social inclusion in a renewed cultural democracy. In the spirit of tolerance, it would allow citizens to make decisions for themselves about their social and moral identity and use government to manage this diversity.

Hanson realized the danger of a facile split between the party of the past and future, typically seen as a polar opposition of the right and left. The separation of vision is misleading if it suggests that one side wants to do away with tradition, while the other wants to hang onto it. The party of the future, Hanson pointed out, has always been careful to maintain its affiliation with the past, and the party of the past typically makes efforts to make its stands sound progressive (Hanson 1995, 681). A hero of the party of the past like Ronald Reagan, for example, harped on America's future-orientation, in his words its "tradition of progress," in his second inaugural address (1985). He explained his position this way:

> When I took this oath four years ago, I did so in a time of economic stress. Voices were raised saying we had to look to our past for the greatness and glory. *But we, the present-day Americans, are not given to looking backward. In this blessed land, there is always a better tomorrow.* Four years ago, I spoke to you of a new beginning and we have accomplished that. But in another sense, our new beginning is a continuation of that beginning created two centuries ago when, for the first time in history, government, the people said, was not our master, it is our servant: its only power that which we the people allow it to have. (emphasis added)

Bill Clinton in his first inaugural address also referred to the ideals of the nation's past, its noble traditions, in calling for "a spring reborn in the world's oldest democracy, that brings forth the vision and courage to reinvent America" (1993). He built his position on the tradition that "when our founders boldly declared America's independence to the world and our purposes to the Almighty, they knew that America, to endure, would have to change."

Differences in the inaugural addresses over the intentions of the nation's founders probably excited Americans less than the furor ignited by Vice President Dan Quayle over "traditional values" in 1992. It was a phrase that had floated around political circles through the 1980s, but it erupted on the national scene after Quayle used it as a crusade for the 1990s (see Lasch 1986; Sobnobsky 1993; Smith 1995). Quayle's opening salvo came shortly after rioting exploded in Los Angeles. The disturbing riot scenes after a police beating of an African American, Rodney King, were very much on the minds of Americans as television beamed across the nation dramatic live footage of random violence. Speaking to the Commonwealth Club of California in San Francisco on May 19, Quayle blamed the kind of "lawless social anarchy" in the riots on "the breakdown of family structure, personal responsibility and social order in too many areas of our society." As an example of this breakdown, he cited displeasure at the choice of the professional woman on the television show *Murphy Brown* to raise a child out of wedlock. His comments about the television show made national news, and raised a hail of points and counterpoints around the country (J. Smith 1992; Greenfield 1992; Canada 1992). In fact, the issue of the riots, racism, and police brutality seem to drift away as the press mainly picked up Quayle's family choice issue. The response aired as the opening segment of *Murphy Brown* in the new fall season on September 21 attracted an incredible forty-one percent of all viewers or 70 million Americans. Despite being portrayed in many media outlets as a dolt, Quayle had successfully set the tone for the Republican campaign of 1992, and the theme kept being hammered by others through the next election (Harwood 1992a; D. Williams

1992; Sobnosky 1993). While hot-button issues of prayer in the schools, prohibition of flag burning, censorship of obscenity, and gun control had inspired headlines of "culture wars," Quayle effectively turned the discourse of the campaigns toward the sanctity provided by tradition for the nuclear, heterosexual family (Steven Roberts 1990, 1994; Herbert 1996). His rallying cry for the family was a tip to policies restricting gay rights, abortion rights, and welfare assistance to single mothers (Quayle 1994).[7]

In the 1992 and 1996 elections, Democrats Bill Clinton and Al Gore refused to be set up opposing "traditional values." Although they may have differed with Bush and Quayle on the policies necessary to preserve "traditional values," they insisted that the matter was at the heart of their platform. Thus the *Wall Street Journal* blared the headline in 1992, "Clinton and Bush Stress Initiatives to Foster Traditional Family Values" (Harwood 1992b). Clinton tied the demise in family not to moral decay fostered by the party of the future, as Bush and Quayle insinuated, but to inaction by the party of the past that caused economic crisis. Clinton and Gore went on the offensive for "traditional values," trying to replace the Republican emphasis on family with a Democratic keynote of "community." At the first campaign rally as running mates, they appeared at the county courthouse in Carthage, Tennessee, and extolled the traditional virtues of small-town life as the essence of plural America (Suro 1992). After the election, Clinton proposed new taxes on the social elite to pay for tax breaks for low-income families. Thus would the poor preserve their families and the middle-class have less stress on theirs, he offered. The move inspired the somewhat scoffing headline in the *Los Angeles Times* replacing "family" with "Democratic," "Traditional Democratic Values Having a Rebirth" (Lauter 1993). Both Clinton and Bush avoided being tagged as organizational men, however. Even if party differences arose between them, they were equally enthusiastic about speaking for the values of the common people as the basis of American tradition. Bush especially tried to lose his patrician background, and Clinton played up his childhood struggles. It just did not pay to appear elite in America, rhetorically speaking, and invoking tradition lent a hearty populist ring to political stumping.

The use of traditional values became more complicated when religion was thrown into the mix of American tradition. The subject of religion was extremely sensitive, especially in a political system that held to separation of church and state, and a society given to extensive denominationalism. Perhaps in response to the headway that Clinton had made with the criticisms of economic policies that disrupted families, Bush and Quayle observed that religious faith kept families together through time, and government should respect this need in allowing policies such as prayer in the schools. Countering liberal criticism of a hegemonic social elite, Quayle revived the charge that an irreligious "cultural elite" primarily in the media and academe conspired to spread a radical liberalism, and contributed to the dissolution of basic American moral guides (see Medved 1992; C.

Smith 1995; F. McDonald 1994). He addressed conventions for Southern Baptists and the National Right to Life Committee in the weeks following the California address, and picked up his advocacy for a "commitment to Judeo-Christian values." He cited one example of a cultural elitist organization undermining traditional values in the case of Time-Warner's production of rap singer Ice-T, known for antipolice lyrics. He added to his criticism of the relativism and multiculturalism of public schools, which he connected to a loss of "moral bearing" (Quayle 1992, 1995).

New associations such as the Coalition for Traditional Values, Toward Tradition, and Concerned Citizens for Traditional Values took on the "traditional values" label to represent conservative religious groups in lobbying for prayer and religious programming in the schools, public support for parochial institutions, and school voucher programs (Yoachum 1993). Although sounding secular and broad-based, "traditional" in the organizational titles came to stand for an orthodox morality upholding the centrality of religion in public life. It invoked the merit of "traditional" describing "values" proven worthy by time and by popular usage. In 1997, the Christian Coalition announced that there would be no issue higher on the organization's agenda than passing a proposal by Rep. Ernest Istook (R-Oklahoma) for a constitutional amendment to insure "the right to pray or acknowledge religious belief, *heritage or tradition* on public property, including public schools" (emphasis added; "Stoll Report" 1997). Taking exception to the Coalition's conservative representation of Christians in this campaign, a less publicized religious left countered with keywords of community and "dignity of the individual."[8] James Davison Hunter in *Culture Wars* (1991) made his mark on the national scene by observing these trends and interpreting the alignment of religious groups advocating for public policy at the heart of "culture wars" that preceded shooting wars (Hunter 1994, 4–5).

In answer to the insistence that traditional values of white Christian America carried the nation to its greatness, or at least gave it a clear moral basis, many writers answered that the harmonious, religious "way we were" was really the troubled "way we never were" (Gordon 1972; Miller and Nowak 1977; Cowan 1983; Coontz 1992). The past as a basis for American tradition became disputed territory especially when academics, led by distinguished historian Gary Nash at UCLA, drafted national standards for history that outraged many stalwarts of "traditional values" (Nash 1995a, 1995b). The critics assaulted the turn away from the conventional narrative of America's progress and national heroes. Lynne Cheney, director of the National Endowment for the Humanities in the Bush Administration, barked that American history had been shamelessly twisted and blasted the report for the nonsensical extremes to which it went to represent minorities over the contributions of America's great leaders (see Cheney 1990, 1995). The report gave culture more due in attention to the experience of ordinary Native Americans, African Americans, and Hispanic Americans, with little reference to an overarching

Christian religious influence and some defiance of chronicles of the great figures, mostly white, and events of American history.

Alarmed at what she thought was an ignorance of the unified narrative of America's past, Cheney sought to restore a proper sense of a publicly shared tradition oriented toward the rebuilding of national culture with extensive "American Memory" projects (Cheney 1987). She set up battle lines of underdog critics speaking in common-sense terms to protect an unsuspecting national public against "tyrannical" academics on a mission to fragment and thereby undermine the nation. The historians put on the defensive answered that they hoped to widen history by making it more socially inclusive. In an answer to the plaint that America's shared memory was quickly fading, they gave the decentering rejoinder that "every American is, indeed, his or her own historian" (Rosenzweig 1997).

The sides in the American memory debates both tended to view social disarray in the present, but they disagreed on the narratives appropriate for redeeming contemporary society and culture. The facts on the social realignment of family, community, and nation were these for the 1990s: the marriage rate in 1993 was the lowest in thirty years; after reaching a peak around 1980, the divorce rate declined to 4.7 divorces per 1,000 between 1988 and 1993 (National Center for Health Statistics). Still, it stood among the highest in the world. In 1994, nearly one out of three births were to unmarried women, and the percentage of single-parent households had more than doubled since 1970 (NCHS). Nonetheless, Americans reported preferring stronger traditional family ties and stepping back from sexual freedom ("Faith" 1989). Although church and synagogue membership was the lowest ever recorded going into the 1990s, Americans also told pollsters that organized religion remained their most trusted institution ("Faith" 1989; Wattenberg 1995, 129). Opinion polls gauged that Americans most feared the scourge of crime and drugs, had declining confidence in their schools, and were concerned about a deterioration in public civility. They appeared less optimistic in the early 1990s about the economy, and they often voiced the opinion that life had become overly complex and treacherous (Wattenberg 1995, 117–24).

At least one scholarly sociological survey reported the finding that Americans when closely questioned were really not as politically polarized as the venomous discourse frequently aired indicated. Regardless, public spokespersons widely held the perception that America was in the midst of a "culture war" with battles on several fronts of education, censorship, affirmative action, and social policy (DiMaggio, Evans, and Bryson 1996; Hunter 1991; Scott 1997). While the culture wars originally were declared by defenders of traditional values to rally troops to the cause, the term was also picked up by sentries for multiculturalism, who announced that they were really the embattled ones. In the construction of culture war rhetoric, it was an advantage to proclaim you were losing. Another strategy was to make the "public" the voice of tradition and the artificial institutions of education, media, and government the organs of transformation. Set up in this way, the contest invited crowning a winner, even though the wars were part of a longstanding struggle in the definition of American culture. During a lull in news of culture-war standoffs in 1997, a year without national elections to galvanize opinion, the *New York Times* offered the consensus that the "conservatives" won the hearts of the public in the battle of ideas, and "liberals" triumphed in the "battle of institutions," especially in academia (Scott 1997). Although anxious to have an end to the story, such press accounts of an Appomattox in the culture wars typically missed the historical significance of the battles over American "tradition" and the uncertain alliances they represented.

Although a narrative emerged in the culture wars pitting right against left, the rhetoric drew attention to issues that did not easily fall into diametrically opposed camps. Debates over abortion, censorship, and affirmative action, for example, often crossed party lines. With the double-figure percentage results for Ross Perot in the 1992 election, more speculation turned toward the potential emergence of a major third party. In 1995, for the first time, more Americans identified themselves as independent than Democratic or Republican (Wattenberg 1995, 118). Special interest organizations such as the Christian Coalition wielded power in both parties. The emerging Communitarian movement expressed dissatisfaction with the conservative-liberal split in America, and in a pitch to the moderate majority of Americans proposed a blend of tradition and modernity, individual autonomy, and social order. Backed by the academic prestige of Amitai Etzioni, former president of the American Sociological Association, the Communitarian platform insisted that "the American moral and legal tradition has always acknowledged the need to balance individual rights with the need to protect the safety and health of the public" (Communitarian Network Home Page; Etzioni 1996). It sought to strengthen normative institutions, what it called "foundations of civil society"— families, schools, and neighborhoods. From another angle, the Institute for Cultural Conservatism sought ways to instill "a government that recognizes traditional culture's vital role" (Lind and Marshner 1987). Its advertisement boasted that its agenda was hailed by conservatives and liberals alike. Taking notice of such trends, *U.S. News and World Report* in 1994 proclaimed in a special report that "politicians of all stripes are painting themselves as guardians of old-fashioned values as Americans seek a way out of a cultural recession" (Steven Roberts 1994).

A major theme connecting many of the fronts of the culture war was "multiculturalism" and its implications for American tradition. Even Quayle admitted that "it sounded nice," and Nathan Glazer quipped that in the political atmosphere of the 1990s, inescapably, "we are all multiculturalists" (Quayle 1995; Glazer 1997). Open to many interpretations, multiculturalism became at least in part equated with tolerance of difference from the mainstream, especially in matters of race and ethnicity. Women, as a large, but arguably "historically underrepresented" group, became prominent in the multicultural picture (see Banfield 1979; Nieto 1996; Glazer 1997). In the wake of tumultuous political protests for civil rights during the 1960s and 1970s, multiculturalism promised to quiet the shouting by more inclusive racial and gender representation in the institutions, such as schools, responsible for setting American society's norms. As African-American writer Clarence Page observed, "'Multiculturalism' need not be a dirty word. It can simply be a better way to keep our ethnic mulligan stew from boiling over" (C. Page 1997). Jesse Jackson as a presidential candidate similarly sounded a multicultural call for an inclusive "Rainbow Coalition" brilliantly forming a peaceable unity from many colors and recognizing the integrity of each hue. As calming as these images were, however, they did not halt the shrills. In multiethnic New York City, the proposal for "A Curriculum of Inclusion" drew flak for sounding antiwhite in its effort to build black self-esteem. It made what many considered dubious claims of African primacy in various fields, and railed angrily against prejudicial legacies of white America. Many avowed liberals who had supported the movement for curriculum reform signed a public statement skewering the report (Glazer 1997, 24–25). Hardly reactionaries, the critics took aim at the way the report "viewed division into racial groups as the basic analytical framework for an understanding of American history." Although supporting "diversity," the protest reasserted that "we are after all a nation—as Walt Whitman said, 'a teeming nation of nations'" (Glazer 1997, 24).

The New York City case was only one of many skirmishes that sought to question the primacy of race in multicultural reorientations, at a time when Americans generally believed that racial attitudes had improved and race needed to be deinstitutionalized (Wattenberg 1995, 130–31, 210–13). The most rancorous response was probably to the pronouncement in 1996 by the Oakland School Board that Ebonics, a reference to speech of its inner city black youth, derived from West African languages and would be recognized as a separate language. The school board understandably suffered a great deal of public ridicule for its faddish claims. Unfortunately escaping notice was the sore of educating culturally isolated "minorities" who had become an economically depressed majority in many inner cities (Katz-Fishman and Scott 1994). That sore continued to fester. In recasting America's integration of ethnic heritage into a racial divide, several forms of multiculturalism drew resistance for increasing social tensions rather than alleviating them, as had been their original promise. Nathan Glazer sagely observed that "multiculturalism is the price America is paying for its inability or unwillingness to incorporate into its society African Americans, in the same way and to the same degree it has incorporated so many groups" and hoped to moderate some extreme reactions to multiculturalism that altogether rejected the pluralist mission (Glazer 1997, 147; see also Spencer 1994).

The debates over multicultural curricula at the center of the culture wars came at a time when views of America balanced losses of ethnic expression in the wake of an enveloping mass culture against the introduction of ethnic folkways brought by a new wave of immigrants. The search was on again for metaphors to replace the melting pot—salad, stew, mosaic, to name a few—and it revealed the ambiguity inherent in modern American identity at a time of global migration. A record high of 19.8 million foreign-born residents lived in the United States in 1990, and they were more likely to be from Asia and Latin America than ever before in American history. Although many of the new metaphors emphasized ethnic multiplicity, a case emerged for a prevailing black and white split. Spike Lee's movie *Do The Right Thing*, a surprise hit of 1989, climaxed in disturbing scenes of a race riot and prompted audiences and reviewers to talk about lingering sources of racial hostility. Mass-scale reporting of the Los Angeles riots and O. J. Simpson trials through the 1990s featured a host of opinions on the roles of race in American justice.

Contributing to the social and political confusion between race and ethnicity, claims for America often fluctuated between the polar extremes of multiculturalist fragmentation or melting-pot unity. Despite frequently heard boasts such as "There is no other place in the world as diverse as ours," on a widely cited international scale of ethnic composition called "the homogeneity index," the United States is divided between homogeneity and diversity factors at a square fifty percent (Dresser 1996, 95; Kurian 1984, 43–44). It ranks in the lower middle of the world's nations. Ethnic diversity is actually most marked in Africa, where many nation-states inherited arbitrary colonial boundaries and tribal loyalties. Of the thirty-one nation-states ranking lowest in homogeneity, all but seven are African. Canada, often cited as the source of the multiculturalist movement, is among those seven. Two others that are there, to the delight of multicultural critics who point out the dangers of cultural fragmentation, are the former Soviet Union and Yugoslavia. But except for Belgium, European countries carry more weight of homogeneity than the United States, thus setting up a scenario of America distancing itself from the traditions of Europe and in light of immigration and social changes opening its perspectives to those of the Third World.

The simultaneous tendencies toward diversity and union in the discourse of the 1990s do not represent a new struggle in America, which has redefined its nationhood several times in relation to social changes within its leaky borders, and proclaimed its unity, in various degrees of looseness, out of its plurality (Kammen 1991; Barone 1994; Glazer 1997). Although there has been a prevailing belief that the new nation was culturally homogeneous at its inception, comparison of foreign-born populations and racial composition feeds an argument that diversity was greater two hundred years ago than it is now (Parillo 1994). That notwithstanding, several explanations can be posited for the tension felt today over America's fragmentation. First of all, the number, if not the percentage, of foreign-born is at an all-time high in America. Second, the increased array of nationalities and ethnicities present in America, especially with new Third World immigration thrown in, appears staggering. That by itself may not present an immediate problem, but coupled with the perception that the new groups are not assimilating, indeed do not need to, in multicultural America, questions arise about the management of this diversity. In some widely noticed cities—Los Angeles, New York City, and Miami—new immigration has contributed to the rise of foreign-language communities, seemingly self-contained, within metropolitan areas. That, too, adds to the sense of diversity today. A final consideration is the publicity for predictions that the percentage of racial minorities will likely increase into the new century, which adds to a sense of social upheaval (Wattenberg 1995, 209; Sam Roberts 1995, 71; M. Spencer 1994).

With the promotion of ethnic, sexual, and racial consciousness in multiculturalism, it is worth contemplating whether other forms of identity have been displaced. The most striking contrast between American cultural studies of the 1950s, for example, and the present is the diminishing presentation of region as an American cultural priority. The *Journal of American Folklore* featured five articles indexed under regionalism in the postwar decade, and not another one for twenty-seven years. In contrast, sixteen were indexed under "ethnicity" or "ethnic identity" during that gap, while only one article appeared during the 1950s (Jackson, Taft, and Axlerod 1988). There is indeed evidence for an American vagueness about the "homeplace" as a social root. The U.S. Census estimated in 1990 that about one in six Americans, more than 40 million people, moved from one residence to another in a single year, and one in six of those moved to another state. Most moved to suburban areas that had a tenuous hold on community tradition between the firm historical and literary realms of city and country. Americans lived increasingly at the edge of communities, figuratively and literally. In fact, in 1990 for the first time, half the nation's population lived in the orbit of thirty-nine metropolises of 1 million or more persons (Sam Roberts 1995, 122). With major population shifts occurring during the 1980s toward the West and South, more than half the residents of eight states were born in other states. Nevada claimed an extraordinary seventy-five percent of its population born elsewhere. As one census expert acknowledged, "this degree of mobility is unique in the developed world" (Sam Roberts 1995, 144).

Since Tocqueville made his classic observations of American society in the early nineteenth century, Americans' loose grip on place has been an often-sounded theme. For his part, Tocqueville wrote that Americans "broke the ties of attachment to their native soil long ago, and have not formed new ones since" (Sam Roberts 1995, 147). Nonetheless, regional loyalties, particularly in the South and New England, remained lodged in the literary imagination through American history, and the mythology of America's small towns as its backbone raises its head every political campaign. And one function of folklore scholarship has been to recognize locations, such as Appalachia or the Ozarks, where place matters. In the burst of regional romanticism in the early to mid-twentieth century, town and region provided a desirable folk sensibility of a social identity below the nation (see Allen 1996; Allen and Schlereth 1990). More socially intimate than the political nation, the region was itself a model for *E Pluribus Unum*. The region apparently tolerated, and integrated, myriad ethnic, religious, and occupational traditions into a sense of place and gave America a lasting image of diversity (see Dorson 1964a; Jones 1976). As I have shown, the press and political institutions especially exploited connections between locality and tradition. A search for, as well as a sense of, place did not go away, and yet they gave way in the culture wars to other combatants for American social priorities. What became crucial for views expressed during the 1990s was that cultural critics and educators promoted ethnicity and race as the most mobile, and symbolic, marker of identity for citizens on the move. Set against the background of unstable institutions of family, company, church, and community, Americans increasingly turned to ethnicity and race as ways for individuals to be counted in mass culture.

America's divided legacy of union and diversity prompted Robert Wiebe (1975) to quip in *The Segmented Society* that Americans were held together by their capacity for living apart, and Michael Kammen to astutely discern Americans as *A People of Paradox* (1972). The view of the ethnic cup as half full, or multicultural, or half empty, or integrating, depends largely on how diversity is gauged—as percentages or total population, as matters of a few races or an array of ethnicities, or as cultural observations or changes in consciousness. To be sure, since the 1970s it has been apparent that thinking has shifted from an outlook of cultural pluralism formed from groups that move toward consensus to a multicultural politics of identity that stands for group solidarity and separation. The cultural pluralism of much of the twentieth century hailed a polity drawn from the social inheritance of many countries through European immigration and assuredly predicted integration within American society. It often was guilty, however, of leaving out blacks, Asians, and Native Americans from the mix. Compensating for such omissions, multicultural politics could be more inclusive but has also been interpreted to bring out racial victimization or ethnocentrism. In its well-meaning intention to increase tolerance, many of its forms have risked instilling division. Recounting the furious battles over multicultural curricula in the 1990s that showed a deep racial divide, Nathan Glazer finally had to ask, "Can We Be Brought Together?" Sounding a hope that many felt had become elusive, he thought Americans could, calling upon the tradition, "the common American way," of respect for identity in the context of a common culture.

Whether or not the rush to multiculturalism had peaked by the end of the 1990s, as Glazer thought, its key feature of representing Americans by various social identities appears to be here to stay (see Scott 1997). "It is certainly true that in much of the culture, the image of America seems permanently changed," the *New York Times* affirmed for the world to hear. "It will never again be monochromatic. P.C. [Politically Correct] or not, the accepted standards for representing gender, race, ethnicity, sexual orientation, disability have irreversibly shifted" (Scott 1997). What still remains to be worked out in the discourse is the mapping of those identities and the locating of their bridges and boundaries. Especially urgent is explaining their uses—personal, social, cultural, political—in the post-modern, post-ethnic, post-whatever society.

I have not mentioned many folklorists, or anthropologists, or sociologists in the discussion of multiculturalism because they increasingly felt banished to the sidelines during this politicized discourse. Although the fields represented by these authorities had long dealt with models of ethnic-religious-racial identity, they scrambled to be consulted in the growing curricular debates (see Stern 1991; Roseberry 1992; Mechling 1993; T. Turner 1993; Fuchs 1994). The identity politics of the 1990s largely relied upon a dialogue between educators, politicians, and community leaders. To be sure, folklorists had increasingly begun using "multi-cultural" in their presentations to draw attention to their experience in ethnic cultural issues. Speaking to the California Folklore Society for its prestigious Archer Taylor Memorial Lecture in 1994, Norine Dresser wryly dubbed her talk "The 'M' Word." That special, or dirty, word of course was multiculturalism. Citing precedents for multiculturalism in the first issues of the *Journal of American Folklore* of the late nineteenth century, she recognized that "in those days we didn't use the term multicultural to describe our diverse society. Nonetheless, even then we concerned ourselves with the folklore of what appeared to be groups of 'others' among us. Depending on the decade, we gave them different names—'immigrants,' 'folk groups,' 'ethnic groups'" (Dresser 1996, 96). Folklorists in public agencies such as arts and humanities councils often justified their purpose as serving multicultural needs of the society and its public institutions. Private nonprofit organizations run and staffed by folklorists also offered multicultural resources and services (see M. Jones 1994). They signaled a direction for folklorists and anthropologists involved in diversity training and multicultural awareness programs. Many folklore Ph.D.'s came into university employment in multicultural programming rather than academic folklore instruction. Often vocal that educators invoking cultural theories were out of their league, many folklorists and anthropologists through the 1990s sported claims to multiculturalism (Sharrow 1992; T. Turner 1993; Fuchs 1994).

The rhetoric of folklore had a significant role to play in the politics of tradition during the 1990s. It can be understood at "ground zero" in the culture wars. That spot is where precious children dwell, for it is there that the public believes the morality of the future is determined. And folklore, long hailed as an educational repository for moral lessons conveyed to generations of American children, came under the multicultural magnifying glass. The underlying question in the new scrutiny given to childhood texts was, as stated by *U.S. News and World Report*, "How to raise decent kids when traditional ties to church, school and community are badly frayed"? (Herbert 1996). The battleground of the schools reopened during the 1990s because of the dependence of American society, even expanded, on them to shape the values of impressionable American children. The lessons gained came into dispute when they altered the inherited narratives of the past and in the process challenged the values of many parents.

It had been widely accepted in American education that reading of folk and fairy tales provided engaging education and moral lessons in the early grades and at home. This transmission of folklore was not only elementary in the schools, but fundamental to the growth of cultural literacy in children. In *The Dictionary of Cultural Literacy* (1988) Edward D. Hirsch, Joseph F. Kett, and James Trefil placed folklore first before art, history, and philosophy in recognition of its place at the foundation of culture (see also Hirsch 1987, 1989). Classic mythology and European folktales are there—familiar figures such as Zeus, Snow White, and Cinderella. They are the hallmarks of civilization, and for America's part, one used to find that every schoolchild knew textbook legends of Davy Crockett, Johnny Appleseed, and John Henry.

Things began to change in the 1980s with the rise of sensitivity to ethnic and religious representation, a kind of relativism that would encourage tolerance of alternative lifestyles, and a multiculturalism that would enhance wide social inclusion (La Belle and Ward 1994; Glazer 1997). Multiculturalists encouraged teachers to avoid authoritatively drumming the legacy of Western civilization into children's heads. In keeping with a relativistic perspective, teachers opened awareness to an array of moral codes and cultural identities from a number of legitimate alternatives—Eastern civilization, African societies, and possibly even "new age" philosophies. Often accompanying this self-determination of identity is a cultural criticism of Western "isms"—racism, sexism, classism. Many of the tales of the Brothers Grimm were scornfully reevaluated as presenting female roles in a bad light, or being too violent, or irreligious, or privileging European ancestry (Katz 1991). A nationally carried wire story in 1993 about the banning of Snow White in Jacksonville, Florida, led to the realization in many localities of formerly revered folktales that had now been condemned. Customs and stories of Halloween came increasingly under attack from religious groups for encouraging Satanism, and many schools forbade traditional decorations of ghosts and goblins as well as trick-or-treating (Marlow 1994). At least one folklorist stood up to publicly question, "Can't We Pass on Fairy Tales without Being Accused of Satanism?" (Bulger 1992).

Many of the new children's books of the 1990s recast folk and fairy tales to serve multicultural purposes. A report coming out of the 1993 American Library Association made the observation that using folktales of Native Americans, African Americans, Hispanic Americans, and Asian Americans to represent multiculturalism was the key to new books that were appealing to libraries and schools (Webb 1993; see also McCarthy 1993). And why not? Many of the groups underrepresented in history and literature textbooks were known more for their oral traditions than documentary records. The richness of folklore was a way to show the dignity of their cultures. With its association of providing roots, folklore could lend legitimacy and authenticity to claims for cultural continuity. Better assertive role models were also sought for women, and a spate of books appeared that boosted female heroines (San Souci 1993). Others used folktales to emphasize progressive values of social justice and international peace (Brody 1992). To be able to comment on this outpouring of new children's books using folklore, the Children's Folklore Section of the American Folklore Society initiated an annual competition for the Aesop Prize to recognize excellence in folklore presentations for children. It gave its prize in 1995 to one of the progressive titles, *Fair is Fair: World Folktales of Justice* (1994) by Sharon Creeden.

Most of these books drew praise for giving children of various backgrounds more topics they could relate to and increasing cultural awareness. But when Home Box Office in 1995 announced it was adapting some of the best-known European-American folktales to a multicultural message for television, it created another skirmish in the culture wars. Produced as colorful cartoons, HBO's *Fairy Tales* took the basic plots of classic European folktales and adapted them for non-European ethnic and racial groups. It also changed the roles of the female characters to be aggressive and independent. While some reviewers appreciated the "kick of diversity" and "multicultural twist" to the old tales, others protested that the result was "anti-white washes" that encouraged racial animosity among children (Heffley 1995; Koch 1995; Fumento 1995). In reference to the reversal of roles in a classic like Cinderella, the *Detroit News* warned, "Time's Up for Wimpy Cinderellas" (Bondi 1995). Shortly after this media brouhaha, another multicultural adaptation of fairy tales drew the publicized ire of a Michigan lawmaker when he learned that a state arts agency had given money to a group to create "rap" versions of fairy tales for presentation to inner-city black youth (Hornbeck 1996).

Conservative advocates of "traditional values" answered the rush to mine folktales for multicultural ore with adaptations of their own. Spreading the message that schools and libraries had been stormed by irreligious multicultural agendas, some writers reached out to parents to use folktales to teach moral lessons at home. Christine Allison published a "parent's guide" she called *Teach Your Children Well* (1993). It included fables and tales meant to "instill traditional values" and bolster a "moral imagination" (see Guroian 1996). The biggest surprise in the publishing world may have been the success of William Bennett's *Book of Virtues,* also released in 1993. The unwieldy 832-page anthology of re-tread material appeared to many literary pundits an unlikely choice for a pivotal book of fin-de-siècle America, but it enjoyed a spectacular run at the top of the *New York Times* best-seller list. An audio version, children's edition, wall calendar—and a host of parodies—followed. The original book was a compilation of stories, including many European-American folktales meant to teach moral virtues of compassion, responsibility, self-discipline, courage, honesty, friendship, and faith. Bennett bemoaned the erosion of traditional values of family and faith, and called for renewing a tradition of storytelling drawn from the moral lessons of Western civilization. He culled stories from classic folklore collections of the Grimm brothers, Andrew Lang, and Joseph Jacobs, and gave his own brief ethical commentaries. The huge success of the book spawned a television series, *Adventures from the Book of Virtues* on the Public Broadcasting System (PBS). The choice of PBS for a conservative answer to the controversial HBO multicultural series had its ironies, since the beleaguered system supported with public funds had been accused by some lawmakers in budget hearings of being too liberal in its programming.

One need go no further than look at the furor over popular uses of folktales to find political divisions over the character of American tradition. Sides in the culture wars found it essential to locate a folklore that would legitimize a claim to an authentic tradition at the heart of an American culture. It would provide a foundation of the past for the constructed edifice of the future. Whether right or left, conservative or liberal, party of the past or future, folklore had been shaped to goals of an imagined society.

THE CHARACTER OF TRADITION

Scholarly and public discourses of tradition vary in their content, but noticeable among intellectuals is the special concern for the *emergence* of tradition and its relation to creativity. With this emergence the basis of identity, culture, and performance is often rhetorically prominent. Public discourse, as scholarly discourse in many instances, tends to question the *continuity* of tradition as a category for community, locality, and religion. At issue in both discourses, especially in America associated historically with rapid progress and future-orientation, is the effect of change (see Dundes 1969b). Various forms of change lay in the background of the discourse of tradition—physical displacement, social fragmentation, and historical modernization. Change in various rhetorical guises—progress, modernity, movement, fashion, invention—appears as the assumed constant of a normal life. Tradition is often seen as a balancing concept in America, often applied to a constructed social other, and more recently applied to a personal self in search of identity and community.

Tradition can be invoked to lend support to public causes as well as scholarly interpretations. With its connotations of respect and duty it has been used to suggest the urgency of retaining a path of action. The perception of tradition as a matter of a continuous past and collective social relations means that it can invoke a persistent force driving the future. In the United States, tradition has especially been a publicly contested term for viewing different priorities of building national unity and multicultural community. "Tradition" rarely stands alone. Modifiers to tradition such as "national," "ethnic," "religious," "folk," "cultural," "family," and "local" have implied a need to place a feeling of social connectedness, a collective memory, in an identifiable niche within mass society. The association of tradition with folk especially brings out the perception of tradition's strength in locality, in small (often marginal) groups, in everyday life. The social conflicts between ideas of a technological mass culture of convenience and uniformity exist against that of a spiritual folk society with its bonds of intimacy and identity. The scholarship and the rhetoric of tradition points to values held and the selective valuation of history and culture. At a basic level, the problem of tradition in the last few decades has posed challenges to individuals about finding the meaning of their cultural inheritance and the choices they make in their lives.

The problem of tradition in America brings into question the assumptions of national individualism and progressivism. Tradition and its expression in folklore bring out group associations and feelings of belonging to past patterns. The "freedom of choice" that Americans have prided themselves on is based on the idea that the separation that individuals make from their background groups—ancestral, regional, national—leads them to progress. There have been cultural "riddles" raised, however, about societies such as the Amish or American Indians emphasizing tradition as a basis of society within the supposedly progressive American context. And there have been politicized questions about whether some social structures for blacks, homosexuals, or women foster traditions because of repression rather than free will (see Fry 1975; Goodwin 1989; Davis 1996; Hollis, Pershing, Young 1993). One can understand the cultural and political influence of the "dynamics" of tradition on modern everyday life, for ordinary people, as a reflection on the meaning of tradition in a future-oriented society. If modernization has brought an idea of free association through extended communication, transportation, and commerce, then identities and their social bases may as a result tend to expand and fragment. Yet the authenticity of these bases may appear doubtful and in need of reinforcement through the power of ritual, custom, narrative—folklore. That reinforcement suggests one kind of future where tradition is not assumed to devolve, as many Victorians thought, but may be selectively revitalized and invented. Transnational movements, often charismatic, of fundamentalism, orthodoxy, and religious revival, for example, bring into focus the interpretation of tradition as a stabilizing, spiritual, and moral force. In such cases, tradition may be perceived as a mode, an order, to be *in* as well as an observable item to *do*. Constructed rituals adapted for new conditions such as the "mid-life crisis" at turning forty, African-American initiation into adulthood, or same-sex marriages indicate a self-consciousness about invoking the power of tradition to urge continuation and legitimate community (Brandes 1985; Nelson 1992). Rituals and objects designed for holidays and celebrations can also be spread by consumerism and tourism to "traditionalize" mass-mediated events, blurring the lines of authenticity and artifice, popular and folk culture (see Jones 1980b; Handler and Linnekin 1984; Mechling 1989b; Dégh 1994; Santino 1996).

In addition to the conditions of industrialization seen as the cynosure for modern society during the nineteenth century, twentieth century self-awareness of anomie, disaster, genocide, incorporation, and computerization have led to consideration of continuous tradition in a post-modern state of discontinuity. Many post-modern critics have argued further the problem of tradition set against the future by examining the expansion of choices and performances (Dorst 1988; Workman 1989; Dobruskin 1990; Warshaver 1991; Anttonen 1993). Accounting of human "performances" rather than "lives" or "societies" suggests post-modern views of the heterogeneity and simultaneity, indeed discontinuity, of an existence that, on one hand, appears to have infinite, often uneasy choices available without the guidance of tradition, and then on the other, seems to have restrictions created by cybernetic, artificial dependence. To be sure, there are apparently post-modern definitions of action that make little or no reference to tradition and emphasize any moment of communication as potentially a cultural event (see Ben-Amos 1972). Yet overall, tradition has grown in significance as a concept to think more *about*, to derive the meaning of the present as well as past, to apply to historical and social artifacts, to interpret as a process of thought and behavior. It has been appealing particularly for its suggestion of removing absolutes of a supposedly objective history. It has helped contextualize perceptions of reality as relative viewpoints influenced by social associations and historical precedents.

Folklore as a study of tradition has contributed to making the cultural challenges before societies and individuals more explicit. It has especially examined the social landscape growing out of the past and the need for social expression of the ways that people relate to one another. Set against the background of change, tradition's role in the way that people live and view the world commands renewed attention as new forms of communication arise. As industrialization and urbanization of the late nineteenth century in America brought folklore prominently into view as the new century approached, trends of computerization and reorganization in the late twentieth century have raised thorny questions about the future of tradition. Observing the startling changes to life brought by the "electronic revolution" in 1989, Alan Gailey philosophized: "A future for tradition seems assured. So long as people need rules and categories by which to live, and they cannot on the spur of the moment develop them for themselves in a manner acceptable to their fellows, they will adhere to traditions, to past ways of doing and thinking about things, which they have inherited as useful, tried responses to the vagaries of their existence" (159). Commenting on the ramifications of the videotape boom on the creative storytelling of children, tomorrow's adults, Libby Tucker thought in 1992 that "if the mouth can hold its own while ideas continue to proliferate, oral tales should continue to thrive well into the twenty-first century" (Tucker 1992, 31). Seen as a process fundamental to social existence, tradition is guaranteed a future, but viewed as a formulation of the past, as a type of knowledge or memory, doubts set in, and it opens the door for calls of preservation, memorialization, manipulation, and invention.

The essays that follow discuss the problem of tradition as a critical point of controversy about the character of American culture or cultures. As this controversy has been greatly informed by the work of folklorists, I select several key figures, significant texts, and pivotal moments from the tangled narrative of tradition. I discuss the ways that folklorists became authorities for tradition and how their contributions have been interpreted in scholarly, public, and commercial realms. I record the ways they spoke as moderns who became followers—that is, preservers, critics, and adaptors—of tradition. I also explore the ways they became concerned with those who follow or live with tradition to advise moderns and assist traditional (or marginal) societies in the context of social and political change. I am interested in how they have identified who has followed tradition in society and attempted to answer what follows tradition for the future. I find their intellectual wrestling with the concept of tradition significant for its balance against public perceptions of the present human condition. And I particularly record their dialogue on, and in, American culture as telling for interpretations of intellectual constructions of America.

2

Folklore and Ideology during the Gilded Age

THE NINETEENTH CENTURY HAD NOT EVEN DRAWN TO A CLOSE BEFORE E. Benjamin Andrews, President of Brown University, self-assuredly declared in his massive history of post-Reconstruction America that "few quarter-centuries in the world's life bristle with salient events as does that following the year 1870" (Andrews 1896, vii). As speculation turned to the order of the new century, he and many other intellectuals offered justification for the "progress of civilization in the United States" in a brand of cultural history promoted by folklorists and anthropologists. This progress was an industrial vision of expansive empire and unfettered enterprise. It was an imprint of progress designed along the lines of rational science and with the promise of Utopian peace and pleasure.

My purpose here is to interpret the rhetoric established by writers on folklore to this dominant theme in American ideology between 1880 and 1900, and consider the philosophical reasons for its rise and fall. I do not propose another exercise in the ways in which scholars produced work reflecting the temper of the times, but rather suggest that in this formative period for professional studies, writers self-consciously prepared a menu of culture which fed the appetite of policymakers and opinion molders. Borrowing the topics of the industrialist William Washington's influential book *Progress and Prosperity* (1911), I might summarize the menu as "The Old World and Its Remaking into the New—The Story of the Mediums of Development—The Building of Empires in America, the World's Wonderland." It includes concerns for the advancement of industry, the modern role of women, and the integrity of the American nation-state. It is, as Washington noted, built on the theories of cultural evolution provided by scholars following Darwin and Spencer, scholars who Washington said "are vitally concerned in the healthful condition and expansion of their own and the nation's industries" (Washington 1911, 1–5).

This statement appears ironic at the very least, since folklorists during the late nineteenth century were hailed as preservers of tradition. But, while many folklorists recorded "survivals" of ancient tradition for a modernizing audience, they were not necessarily advocates of preindustrial life. From his station in the nation's capital at the Bureau of American Ethnology, John Wesley Powell urged the study of American Indian folklore to help control the Indian lands and railed against the scourge of superstition, and Captain John Bourke of the army called for the colonization of Mexico and referred to the "abomination" of its native folkways (Hinsley 1981, 147–51; Bourke [1895] 1987; Porter 1986). There were some figures such as Cornell University's T. F. Crane, one of the founders of the American Folklore Society, who pointed out the aesthetic power and intrinsic value of folklore. As I will discuss later, the special situations of blacks and Jews in American society complicated matters for folklorists, but they did not deter the charting of an inexorable "progress toward civilization."

The dominant tide of evolutionary doctrine was given impetus by the first great chronicler of American folklore studies, Lee J. Vance. In 1896 he offered the view that the end of the nineteenth century

> will be marked by the rise and growth of a new science—the science which studies mankind from the time when the earth and the human family were young down to the present time. This science (whether called Anthropology or Comparative Folk-Lore) studies the progress of man in culture. It reveals the evolution of modern culture from the beliefs and usages of savages and simple-minded folk. Now folk-lore is concerned more particularly with the "survival" of primitive or ancient ideas and customs in modern civilization: that is to say, our study traces the development of tribal custom into national law; of pagan custom into Christian ecclesiastical usage and popular festivals; of sorcery and magic into astrology, and finally into astronomical science; of song and dance into Greek drama and poetry; of nursery tales and Märchen into the epic and the modern novel. Again, the end of the nineteenth century is remarkable for the immense number of books devoted to the Folk—to people who have shared least in the general advance. These people are, first, the backward races, as the natives of Australia and our Indian tribes; then the European peasantry, Southern negroes, and others out of touch with towns and schools and railroads. (Vance 1896/1897, 249)

With the "immense number of books devoted to the Folk," as Vance stated, the path to culture could be diverted from the established one charted in classical education. The discovery, or invention, of "the Folk" in the nineteenth century shook the elite pillars of Greek and Roman civilizations as the source of valued modern arts. In widely discussed works tracing culture "scientifically" to the savage folk, such as *The Golden Bough* (1890) by J. G. Frazer, even classical religion received challenge as the wellspring for human destiny (Ackerman 1990). Locating origins of modern culture in the customs of the folk allowed for expansion of civilization to include the popular practices associated with growing middle class existence.

Slow and steady progress could be charted from narrow native roots to an expansive foliage of the rational present. In decentering civilization toward the present, the evolutionary concept of the folk opened possibilities of global connections to advanced industrial developments, even for upstart social experiments like the United States.

Folklore was a popular "modern" subject at a time of change when the "modern" seemed more distanced from "tradition." By 1893, the American society outnumbered its European counterparts, and branched out into local organizations in New York, Philadelphia, Boston, and other major cities. In 1895, according to press reports of the day, folklore stole the show at the Congress of American Scientists, which featured seven learned societies, including highly touted organizations for psychology, mathematics, and anatomy. "Scientists Make Great Progress, Folk-Lore is Discussed," the *Philadelphia Inquirer* announced with a special regard for the significance of industrial progress. "Important Papers on Many Subjects Read by Men Well-Known in All Professions," the headline continued, but it was the folklore society's doings that led the story. The story of folklore, told in evolutionary fashion, confirmed the Victorians' lofty opinion of themselves. Folklore delved into exotic customs and rites and measured the advancement of the present day. It titillated the senses and it offered explanation on a grand scale.

MUSEUMS IN THE ADVANCE OF CIVILIZATION

Folklorists were men and women who had a stake in advancement of "progress" as it was perceived in the late nineteenth century. It was led by industry, invention, and transportation and involved an adoption of rational science to understand and improve the world. The American Folklore Society, one of the many new "scientific" societies of the late nineteenth century, was founded in 1888 and boasted a membership mostly of physicians, lawyers, writers, military officers, and museum officials. Like other learned societies formed at the time, the American Folklore Society appealed to middle-class professionals who sought new intellectual pursuits outside the classical university curriculum (Bledstein 1976, 80–128; Bronner 1986a, 17–19). The study of folklore and ethnology arose outside of the academy, which was slow to give up its classical curriculum. If the experts on the new subject wanted a full-time occupation, they found homes in museums. By storehousing relics of preindustrial ages and exotic cultures, many new museums of the day praised material and scientific progress of the Gilded Age. With museum exhibits emphasizing the interpretation of clues to the ancient past excavated from belowground sites or collected from exotic cultures, often in arrangements that drew comparisons to the allure of world's fairs and department store displays, many ethnologists and folklorists were able to find influential platforms from which to proclaim their principles. The Museum of Natural History opened in 1869, the United States National Museum in 1879, the University of Pennsylvania Museum

Stewart Culin, c. 1905. (Brooklyn Museum)

in 1887, and the Brooklyn Institute Museum and the Field Museum in 1893. Each of these added ethnological sections to their collections. From this vantage, many ethnologists had rare opportunities to reach the public with their ideas, and the ethnologists also benefitted from private and governmental funding of great collecting trips, especially to Indian lands out west. Between 1890 and 1903, ten presidents of the American Folklore Society, when they took office, held professional affiliations with ethnological museums. Frederic Ward Putnam, head of the Anthropology Department at the Chicago World's Fair, was director of the Peabody Museum. Otis Mason was head curator of ethnology at the United States National Museum and worked closely there with Frank Hamilton Cushing. Cushing also did work for the University of Pennsylvania Museum, the home base of Daniel Brinton and Stewart Culin.

To get a profile of the Gilded Age museum man using folklore to respond to issues of his day, I point to the life of Stewart Culin, who became president and curator of the American Folklore Society. Born in Philadelphia in 1858 to merchant-class parents who had roots in America's colonial settlement, Culin graduated from Nazareth Hall, where he fondly recalled being regaled with American Indian tales by an influential teacher. At the age of seventeen, Culin entered his father's merchant business in Philadelphia, where he conducted business with Chinese immigrants and learned their language. Versed in the early studies of anthropology, he recorded the "exotic" customs of the Chinese in the city. He collected their medicines, games, arts, and religious objects. With the merchant's care for detail and accurate record keeping, he expanded his collections and interests to cover the entire Orient. He joined and later became secretary of the Numismatic and Antiquarian Society of Philadelphia. He was influenced there by fellow member Daniel Brinton, who attracted international acclaim for his prolific writings in archaeology, linguistics, mythology, and religion. Brinton, later to become the first university professor of anthropology, published Culin's article on medical practices of the Chinese in 1887 and encouraged him to make a career of his studies.

Brinton envisioned a museum at the University of Pennsylvania which would undertake the collection, display, and study of cultural objects. Plans went ahead for the museum in 1887, and Culin left his business to become the first secretary for the Oriental Section in 1890. That same year he publicized his innovative plans for a "folk-lore museum." Such a museum, he wrote, "would have an extended field, and might embrace a vast number of objects which do not ordinarily come within the domain of the collector, and yet are most valuable as illustrating customs, myths, and superstitions." He gave as an example the rabbit's foot to bring good luck and the potato and the horse chestnut carried to prevent rheumatism. They are "often quite interesting in themselves," he said, and "if properly arranged and labeled with their special story or signification, would form a vastly entertaining collection and a valuable aid in the study to which the Folklore Society is devoted" (Culin 1890, 312–13).

Frank Hamilton Cushing working on Southwestern Indian pottery for the Smithsonian Institution, 1890s. (National Anthropological Archives, Smithsonian Institution)

In 1892, Culin put together a ballyhooed exhibition of religious objects of the world at the University of Pennsylvania Museum. Largely as a result of the show's success, he was appointed secretary of the American Historical Commission to the World's Exposition in Madrid in 1892. He then rose to the position of director of archaeology and paleontology for the university museum. He followed in 1893 with a display of "folklore objects," many garnered from American Folklore Society members, for the Chicago World's Fair. Visitors to the fair marveled at the exhibit he had assembled in eye catching arrangements. "Folklore most intimately connects this age with the greatest antiquity," exclaimed the *Chicago Record*, "and of folklore no branch so directly informs of our relation to the people of most ancient days than the games for the different stages in the history of the world."

At the fair Culin met Frank Hamilton Cushing of the Bureau of American Ethnology, who took great interest in Culin's exhibit and offered to collaborate on a study of Indian games. The exhibit showed an evolution of religious objects giving way to games. Besides this concern for custom, Culin noticed the ornamental features of his objects. "When we examine the products of man's handicraft," he reflected, "we everywhere find evidences of an aesthetic sense, of an effort, not only at mere utility, but at decoration and ornament, analogous to that which is universal among cultivated people at the present day." His explanation? Ornament stemmed from religion, magic, and superstition—"of the reasoning which led many to attempt through magic to control or influence the forces of nature" (Culin 1900a).

In 1899 and 1900, Culin grieved over the deaths of his two greatest influences: Daniel Brinton and Frank Hamilton Cushing. To Culin was left the goal of advancing his mentors' evolutionary studies. He replaced Brinton as lecturer in anthropology and continued Cushing's study of Indian games. In 1900, he left the comforts of his Gilded Age house in Philadelphia to travel west with the Wanamaker Expedition into the Indian territories, sponsored by the famous department store mogul. The first stop was Tama, Iowa, where he visited the Sac and Fox nations. Observing a tribal feast, his eyes turned to the old men sitting on platforms in the longhouses, their medicine bags hanging from rafters above them. Culin was deeply moved by what he witnessed. He passionately wrote in his journal, "These feeble creatures, with strangely wrinkled faces, expressive of patience and suffering and more of life's experience than falls to all the collected multitude of our modern towns, were once the tribal leaders and are still the repositories of the tribal secrets and traditions. One by one, they will be carried to the little graveyard on the hillside and buried with their precious packs, and all their wealth of curious knowledge will be lost to the world forever" (Culin 1901, 2). Culin vowed to rededicate himself to recovering the traditions of the natives and especially their rites and objects.

In 1907, Culin published his magnum opus of 846 pages, *Games of the North American Indians*. In the book, Culin classified and illustrated American Indian gaming implements in American and European museums according to activity and called upon field observation to document and compare the games across cultures. Culin penned a letter to the chief of the Bureau of American Ethnology explaining the significance of the work: "I might suggest that this is the first serious attempt to compare and study the games of more than one tribe. It is by far the largest collection of data about aboriginal games, whether in the Old World or the New. It is, too, the largest collection of data existing on any particular subject referring to the objective culture of the Indian."[1] The term *objective* appealed to Culin because of its inclusion of "objects," the center of study, and its objectivity, reflecting the stress on a detached "scientific" approach. By this he meant "science which embraces the examination of all man's activities…. Like modern science generally it is based upon multitudes of more or less minute and widely extended observations, but unlike those sciences such as mathematics and chemistry which we know as exact its formulations are less definite, although no less alluring" (Culin 1924, 93). With his reference to the singular *Indian*, rather than the plural *Indians*

Otis Mason, c. 1890s. (National Anthropological Archives, Smithsonian Institution)

or *Indian cultures*, he shows the racial classification commonly used to mark cultural division in evolutionary writing.

Culin argued for the practical use of folklore collecting among "lower" races to benefit American industry. He had a guiding hand in the commercial packaging of the traditional game Parcheesi by Selchow and Righter. Almost thirty years after his triumphant exhibit of toys and games at the World's Columbian Exposition, the commercial magazine *Playthings* interviewed Culin about the exhibit and his suggestions for better-designed toys. He told the magazine that "I constantly think of the possibilities of the practical adoption of games which I encountered in remote places to the requirements of our own American industry" ("World's" 1920, 105–10). Culin wrote columns for *Men's Wear*, *Women's Wear*, and the *New York Times* on good fashion based on the history of textiles and primitive design, and he served as a judge for window display contests. He organized a series of lectures at the Brooklyn Museum on decorative objects such as "portable boxes and containers employed in conserving and transporting merchandise and household gear, bearing in mind the primitive and oriental objects I describe supply unnumbered suggestions of value to our manufactures."[2]

Culin as merchant used the museum as an adviser to industry and an educator of the public. As curator and ethnologist, he sought purposes and themes for objects and for his age. Seated in a Paris bistro in 1920, Culin questioned how far the age had actually progressed according to his evolutionary belief. He watched a drunken display of jazz playing and dancing and entered the scene in his journal. "I have been among the savages, but a display like this I have never seen." This was not, in his view, social progress. Walking through his museum gallery for one of the last times, he reflected, "It has been my habit as an ethnologist devoted to the study of the material culture of mankind to think of the races of antiquity as younger and not older than the people of our own age; to refresh myself with such contacts as I have had with their minds to feel myself younger and more vital. I have realized my dreams among savages in whose lives and thoughts I have had glimpses of the dawn of the world" (Culin 1927, 43).

While Culin gained prominence in museum positions in leading commercial cities of Philadelphia and New York, Otis Mason (1838–1908) iterated the message in the country's "national" museum at the Smithsonian Institution in Washington, D.C. Both figures used exhibitions of folk artifacts organized on the basis of evolutionary doctrine to address the remarkable material progress of America as a culmination of the civilization process. Born in Maine and raised in Virginia, Mason went to Columbian College (now the George Washington University) in Washington, D.C., receiving, in the tradition of college education at the time, a general knowledge of biblical and classical studies, literature and philosophy. After graduation in 1861, he stayed on to teach natural history, classics, history, English, mathematics, and geography. During the 1870s, he championed "general principles of Natural Science" at the school. By 1880 he was instructor of English and history.

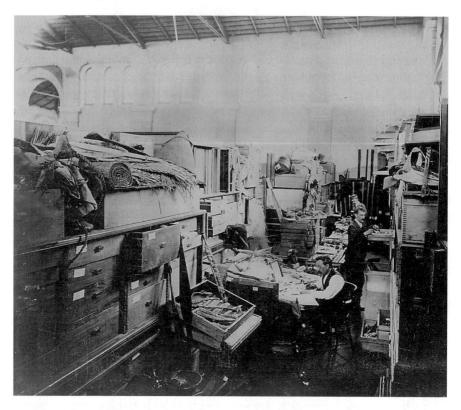

Workers at the United States National Museum, Smithsonian Institution, sorting ethnological collections, c. 1890s. (National Anthropological Archives, Smithsonian
Institution)

When he left in 1884 for the United States National Museum of the Smithsonian
Institution, he was listed as professor of anthropology. Among the courses he
taught were "Races of Man," "History of Culture," and "History of the Past as
Revealed in the Sciences of Archaeology and Folk-Lore." In folklore he found the
ancient "artifacts" of civilization and the "specimens" for its cultural history. To
organize the growing study of folklore, he became a founder of the American
Folklore Society, its president in 1891, and host of its meetings in 1891 and 1894.
Reflecting on the appeal of this study, Mason said, "In the last decade of the
nineteenth century, when the world was looking forward, it was a relief to vary
this mental attitude by occasionally glancing backward, and considering the past
as it appeared by its survival in the present." And Mason found many present-
day labels to attach to cultural survivals. "Without doubt," he offered, "there is
also a folk-speech, folk-trades and practices, folk fine art, folk-amusement, folk-
festival, folk-ceremonies, folk-customs, folk-government, folk-society, folk-his-
tory, folk-poetry, folk-maxims, folk-philosophy, folk-science, and myths or

folk-theology. Everything that we have, they have,—they are the back numbers of us" (Mason 1891).

As head curator of the ethnological collections at the United States National Museum in the Smithsonian Institution, Mason took on the enormous task of sorting the museum's cultural collections. He used the objects in the collections to establish a cultural history based on the evolutionary principles of natural science. He categorized by technological type and arranged them from primitive to industrial. As cultural history, Mason's studies were intimately connected to issues of the day which were being hotly discussed in the nation's capital. Students of primitive and folk culture were naturally involved with such issues, he observed, because they participated in the search for the hidden "secrets of man's origin, progress, and destiny." "Folk-lore," he said in 1891 in a manifesto of evolutionary folklore studies, "stands for the hereditable part of our activity; invention is the creative, originating part of our action. Folk-lore is crystalloid; invention and science are colloidal. Folk-lore is kept alive by public opinion, and is opposed to progress; invention and science are centrifugal, venturesome, individual. This ability to act in common has itself had a historic growth, beginning with such savage acts as beating time to a rude dance, and rising to a grand chorus, a great battle, or a modern industrial establishment employing thousands of men marking time to one master spirit" (Mason 1891).

In 1894, Mason published *Primitive Travel and Transportation*, a 350-page combination of a detailed catalogue of objects in the museum's collection and of the reconstruction of the development of modern transportation industries from "primitive" cultures, mostly American Indian. According to Mason's study, rail and steam travel were the culmination of thousands of years of development and provided the direct route to enlightenment. In the same year that his study of transportation appeared, Mason's *Woman's Share in Primitive Culture* was published. He noted that the moving, socially aspiring "new woman" of the late nineteenth century had raised pressing political and cultural questions. What effect would changes in her traditional roles have on the family and society? Would she be industrious or leisurely, scientific or sentimental? Mason defended the modern woman of leisure by pointing out that women had been the first industrialists. In primitive cultures, they had manufactured the shelters, clothes, containers, and foods for domestic and community use. If middle-class Victorian women now appeared to be idle, it was no wonder, Mason thought, because they had earned that right from their taxing early industrial efforts. In 1911, social critic Anna Spencer, writing in *Forum*, used Mason's ideas to make an argument for women's adaptability to industrial work. Women, she opined, first "attained the discipline of a 'steady job.' The biological hints of the busy bee, the industrious beaver, the ant, to whose example the human sluggard was long ago commended, all seem to have been taken lightly by the primitive man" (Spencer 1911, 546–48). She argued that women therefore embodied the character of modernity. Olive Schreiner's

Women and Labor, which in 1912 was one of the ten best sellers in America, warned, however, that "in a strange new world" women could became a race of "laboring and virile" women, the equals of their ancient ancestors.

In *The Origins of Invention* (1895) Otis Mason expanded his arguments for the explanation and justification of modern industrial advancement in the hidden past of tradition. The labeling by folklorists of primitive and folk activities commonly stressed modernist terms such as "industry" and "invention." Besides Mason, who used the terms widely, Alexander Chamberlain, the first American Ph.D. in anthropology in 1892, wrote on "Mythology and Folklore of Invention" for the *Journal of American Folklore* (1904); Thomas Wilson published "Primitive Industry" for the *Smithsonian Institution Annual* (1893). Mason and these authors helped to fashion a distinctive social rhetoric. By connecting manual labor to "primitive industry," no conflict was implied. The development from handicrafts to industry seemed natural. The progressive present set the standard for the primitive past. The lack of conflict is noteworthy, because America during the 1890s was plagued by strikes from hand trades, which were protesting against the "unnatural" industrialization of their work and consequent dehumanization of their activity. A depression in 1893 brought criticisms that industries had grown out of touch with society and its patterns by overproducing and speculating. But, in the same year, the Anthropology Building at the Chicago World's Fair featured exhibits on "labor-saving devices, illustrating generally the progress of the amelioration of the condition of life and labor" (Truman 1893, 260–61).

From their positions in museums, folklorists actively wrote and exhibited on divisions of culture: the past and present, industry and craft, men and women. Their writing was spread in popular magazines of the day as the voices of scientific authority on social and cultural change. Besides writing on Indian crafts and foodways, Frank Hamilton Cushing of the Smithsonian wrote on "primitive motherhood" (1897). Stewart Culin of the University of Pennsylvania Museum, meanwhile, regularly wrote in the For Woman's Entertainment section of the *Philadelphia Record* and contributed to *Women's Home Companion* with articles on folk toys and games, religion, tables, and decoration. "There is no more amusing game," Culin satirically wrote, than "picking out people and objects and then arranging them properly."[3] To Culin, the division of men and women's roles in primitive cultures suggested explanation for the rise of the "new woman." George Wharton James argued in "Primitive Inventions" (1903) that if women were not active in invention for the industrial age, it was because their period of invention had passed. He had collected among Southwest Indians, and he credited basketry, weaving, pottery, house building, and food customs to woman's predominance in primitive culture, and hence to an earlier stage of modern civilization. Some intellectuals such as Thorstein Veblen in "The Barbarian Status of Women" (1899), William Thomas in "Sex in Primitive Industry" (1899), and Lester Frank Ward in "Our Better Halves" (1888) argued that women, like their children, were still treated like primitives.

Folklore exhibit in the Anthropology Building, World's Columbian Exposition, Chicago, 1893.

Rather than viewing the modern age as one of rest from their previous labor, they viewed the present as a repression of their march to progress.

Elsie Clews Parsons (1875–1941), president of the American Folklore Society in 1919 and 1920, signaled the end of feminist reliance on evolution and the idea of a primitive matriarchal age. Downplaying the empiricism of evolutionism, she proposed a psychological argument for the reality of perception. In "Femininity and Conventionality," published in 1914, she used the relativistic argument that it is "apprehension of difference rather than actual difference which bulks so large now and always in the social regulation of sex. It is fear of the unlike rather than the fact of it" (Parsons 1914, 47–53). She argued that as the Victorian preoccupation with a usable past had subsided, so, too, would studies emphasizing evolution give way to the examination of social function within specific societies.

Folklore at the Fair

The Chicago World's Fair of 1893 was probably the high-water mark for the American ideology of industry and enterprise as well as for evolutionary folklore studies. At the fair America's corporate vision of grandeur was forcefully put on display, and folklorists played leading roles. The midway of the fair, with its exhibits of people "who have shared least in the general advance," was put under the charge of the anthropology department. The department was also responsible for what turned out to be among the most popular exhibits of the fair, a gold-medal-winning display

FLETCHER S. BASSETT.

Fletcher S. Bassett, founder of the Chicago Folk-Lore Society and organizer of the Third International World's Folklore Congress at the Chicago World's Fair, 1893.

of "folk-lore objects" consisting of gaming artifacts shown to evolve from religious rites, prepared by Stewart Culin. In the Manufactures Hall, the university museum exhibited "a very complete series of objects illustrating the customs of the Chinese laborers in the United States." Elsewhere, "George F. Kunz displayed under the name of the New York Branch of the American Folk-Lore society a collection of gems and minerals having a folk-lore significance which were of peculiar interest and value." The Chicago World's Fair, Stewart Culin observed, "afforded the greatest opportunity to the student and collector of folk-lore that has ever been presented upon this continent" (Culin 1894, 51–59).

As part of the fair's educational mission, learned congresses served to honor the pressing issues at the end of the nineteenth century. The task of organizing a folklore congress was given to a former navy officer, Fletcher S. Bassett (1847–1893), founder of the Chicago Folk-lore Society. The society was formed in December 1891, and saw as its special field the collection of "traditional literature" west of the Alleghenies. The significance of the section, according to the society's credo in its second publication, *The Folk-Lorist* in July 1892, was that "its progress so far has been encouraging, and it is now established on a footing that insures its usefulness" ("Chicago" 1892, 1). The first publication was a manual of folklore collection that carried a logo showing an American Indian engaged in a mystical ritual to cure disease and insure

CHICAGO FOLK-LORE SOCIETY'S PUBLICATIONS

No. 1.

The Folk-Lore Manual

BY

Lieutenant FLETCHER S. BASSETT, U. S. N.

Secretary of the Society.

CHICAGO, ILL., 1892.

Cover of the Chicago Folk-Lore Society's publication *The Folk-Lore Manual*. The seal was drawn by Frederick W. Gookin and, according to the society publication, depicted a "Navajo *'akáán ndeinilii,* or meal sprinkler—a courier sent by the singer, or chanter, during the ceremonial known as *Dziłk'ijí,* or Mountain Chant." The motto is a verse from Longfellow's "Hiawatha."

prosperity. The motto on the logo was taken from Longfellow's *Hiawatha*, "Whence These Legends and Traditions?" The motto invoked the search for hidden, ancient origins of exotic lore, and it also implied applying the lessons gained from this search to American polity and culture. "There is abundant traditional lore to be gathered in the Western country," the introduction to *The Folk-Lorist* announced, "and much that is fast disappearing." It emphasized that "this Society encourages the collection of such material, important to the study of the history of mankind, and in its bearings upon the many problems of life" ("Chicago" 1892, 1).

The Chicago Folk-lore Society proclaimed its purposes in its major public event, the "Third International Folk-Lore Congress" at the Chicago World's Fair in July 1893. It was the first such congress to be held in the United States after previous meetings in prestigious locations of London and Paris. Bassett organized an advisory committee of two hundred scholars from around the world and received promises for one hundred papers on the program. The subject matter of folklore made the program "the center of attraction" among several congresses held at the fair, according to the *Chicago Tribune* (McNeil 1985, 13). Newspapers carried notices of several of the presentations, especially accounts of exotic American Indian rites and customs. One headline expressed amazement at a demonstration of sign language by several members of the Sioux nation and a Lieutenant Scott to "Converse without the Use of Words." According to the paper, "Lieutenant Scott's expert use of the sign language met with the unqualified approval of the warriors, who rewarded every speech with greasy grins. The audience applauded the performance vigorously and wanted more, but the length of the program wouldn't permit more to be given" ("In a Sign" 1893). Public attendance and interest reached a height at the folklore congress with the arrival of eminent "scientific authorities" and "a monster twin concert held in the Hall of Washington and the Hall of Columbus" consisting of highly arranged folk music held at the Chicago Art Institute. The *Tribune* reported it on July 15 as the fair's main "event of the day."

When the congress in Chicago opened, Bassett gushed when speaking of the growth of folklore studies in the previous few years: "Publications, annual, quarterly, monthly and weekly, appear in our own city, in Boston, in London, in Ghent, in Antwerp, in Liège, in Helsingfors, in Copenhagen, in Berlin, in Leipzig, in Leyden, in Paris, in Palermo, in Vienna, in Warsaw, in Bombay and in other cities, devoted to this study, besides others whose columns are largely devoted to Folk-Lore" (Bassett 1898, 20; see also McNeil 1985). Bassett then went on to note the special role of folklore studies in American society. "Folk-Lore societies encourage the collection, publication and study of this important and beneficent information and serve an important purpose in our civilization," he explained. "The labors of the eminent scholars of America in this direction," he offered, "demonstrate that Folk-Lore is far advanced in our midst, in spite of the youth of our existence. Folk-Lore," he emphasized, "has become a subject of the day" (Bassett 1898, 20).

Indeed it had. In studies of folklore, writers described unusual "manners" of "ruder ages" and "removed lands," judged by the rigid moral standards of the day. The accounts dwelled on sensuality and emotional bonding in customs and tales and the deep attachments and meanings apparent in ritual and decorative objects. Folklore showed the closeness of humans to nature and the plight of the toiling hand. The sweep of tradition was broad, but Victorians drew three special lines of inquiry related to rapid changes in the social life of the late nineteenth century. Related to the Victorians' concern for the secularization of modern culture, the displacement of religion by science as a formula for living, was their search for the meaning and development of spiritual belief. Related to their concern for the rapid industrialization of everyday life was their uncovering of primitive "invention," "industry," and "technology." And, linked to their concern for the utilitarianism of the rational order brought by industrialization, many Victorians sought out the character of art and expression in folk tradition. For expansive nations like England and America, where folklore was especially popular, evolutionary folklore studies opened the world for cultural judgment.

What, then, was the message provided by the evolutionary folklorists of the fair? Perched before the turn of the century and the momentous change it represented, University of Chicago professor and president of the Chicago Folk-lore Society William I. Knapp chimed the idea that folklore showed the transformation of the past into the civilized present. It was a movement of progress, with science replacing superstition. And what better place to show this than Chicago, America's symbol of rapid growth—social and material? "Chicago is to-day the centripetal maelstrom toward which the tidal wave is rolling and from which the centrifugal reaction will be world-wide," Knapp bellowed (Knapp 1898, 24–25). The triumph of cultural evolution theory at the time of the fair capped fifty years of Victorian scientific advances which benefitted the public, according to W. J. McGee. "The main movements," he announced, meant that

> the sources of aesthetics and ethics have been successfully sought, the early steps in the course of industrial development have been traced, the beginnings of law have been analysed, and the course of human development has been brought to light; and it is now known that the lines of human progress in the arts and industries, in sociology, in language, and in thought are convergent, rather than divergent like the lines of development among beasts and plants, and that the unification of ideas by telegraph and telephone and press is but a ripple marking the course of the great stream of human activity. (McGee 1898, 319)

This grandiloquent rhetoric with its declaration of modern American social dominance also marked the opening of the International Folklore Congress at the Chicago World's Fair. "The crowning principle of the nineteenth century," Knapp's keynote addressed emphasized, "is the brotherhood of man." "For forty years," he continued, "the peaceful procession has moved on from the remotest corners of the earth to a few common centers. Quaint faces, strange costumes, unintelligible tongues, have blended with the dominant civilizations of Western Europe and the New World beyond, while venerable races have made obeisance to the material prosperity of younger and novel institutions" (Knapp 1898, 24–25).

To the Victorians, the tradition of the primitive past represented collective repetition while the present fostered individual creativity. When he spoke in Chicago at the World's Fair, Otis Mason praised the city as the epitome of creativity. He observed that Chicago, the most rapidly growing city rightly situated in the heart of the world's most quickly developing nation, had an air of experiment, invention, and expansion. Mason told the folklore congress at the Chicago World's Fair that the student of folklore "deals chiefly with those who follow suit. He does not require patent offices, but places of assembly, and listens to the repetition of things that have been done often and often before." From this basis he outlined five evolutionary climbs which explained the rise of invention in modern society. The first is "the creation of new desires with progress and the greater complexity of each want as it became more exacting." Summarized, this evolution is a progress, he said, from naturalism to artificialism. The second evolution is in "the mental change involved in the act of invention," that is, from the assumedly simple observations of nature to the complex uses of a controlled laboratory. The third evolution is the improvement of implements, and the fourth evolution is the growth of public rewards for the inventor. The final evolution is vaguer than the rest; it refers to the organizational development in a society. In Mason's words, it is "the unfolding of that national, or tribal, or family genius which constitutes the mark by which they have become known." Each family of mankind in its native home, Mason concluded, "has invented a series of arts, the relics of which lie buried in their tombs and place of business. The history of their industries is written in these things. At the same time, by frequent trials and failures, they have invented languages and social structures, philosophies and mythologies, the history of which is written in the sayings and doings of the folk." Taken together, this evidence provides the all-important "evolution of thought in the world" (Mason 1898).

The rhetoric of evolutionary doctrine was evident at the Chicago fair in justifications of spreading empire of industrialized countries to "backward" countries. The United States stood divided on the question of annexing the Philippines after the Spanish-American War because of the conflict with the nation's revolutionary past against colonialism. Invoking evolutionary rhetoric, President McKinley supported territorial acquisition, reasoning that the Filipinos were not ready for self-government. His mission as representative of an advanced civilization was "to educate the Filipinos, and uplift and civilize and Christianize them" (Cashman 1988, 331). At the 1904 World's Fair, called the Louisiana Purchase Exposition, the United States government organized the Philippines Reservation to showcase the association of "primitives," as they were called, with unexploited natural resources. In its use of reservation—some twelve hundred Filipinos demonstrated their culture in the center of the fairgrounds—organizers of the exhibition drew comparison to America's control of "savage" Indians through the reservation system. It became the most popular exhibit of the fair, and as Robert Rydell explained, it "exalted imperial prowess." "Depicted as resource rich and lacking the material goods that anthropologists equated with civilization, 'primitive' cultures on display had the effect of underwriting the predictions of a bountiful future for the 'culture of abundance' and expansion of overseas markets forecast at the fair" (Rydell 1989, 196–97).

At previous fairs, anthropological exhibits appealed to American voyeurism about "primitive peoples" and their folkways—on the Midway Plaisance, which stood well behind the central "Court of Honor" with its main feature of the Manufactures Hall. The Midway Plaisance consisted of numerous small exhibitions giving the impression of the variety of races in the world. The Manufactures Hall was the largest single building of the fair and it culminated a trip through the fair by representing the unity and progress of industrial advancement. The president of the Chicago Folk-Lore Society welcomed participants to the World's Fair by declaring, "So all this gathering of human races and faces from the four winds of heaven, contains a lesson that will soon be incarnated into a purpose. We are transforming, almost transformed" (Knapp 1898, 24–25). President Cleveland's symbolic evolutionary procession to open the Chicago World's Fair began with "the uncouth aliens of the Midway Plaisance," in E. Benjamin Andrews's words, and ended at the Manufactures Hall. Making reference to the traditions lying behind him as foundation for the "stupendous results of American enterprise and activity," the president announced, "We stand to-day in the presence of the oldest nations of the world, and point to the great achievements we here exhibit, asking no allowance on the score of youth. It is an exalted mission in which we and our guests from other lands are engaged as we co-operate in the inauguration of an enterprise devoted to human enlightenment" (Andrews 1896, 244).

THE IDEOLOGY OF EVOLUTION

Viewing primitive customs and rites, Victorians felt reassured that they had risen above what they assumed to be their ancient ancestors. Yet while feeling superior in thought and behavior, they sensed emotional loss. Industrial advancement had its price, so it seemed, and many cultural critics thought that a spiritual vitality apparent in primitive rites and customs was traded in for the march of civilization. Some social advisers sought to refine primitive rituals for modern application so as to invigorate the sensibilities of modern cosmopolitans. Often borrowing from the example of masked rites, masquerade events enjoyed a vogue in Victorian society; secret and fraternal societies arose invoking elaborate rituals and codes; and cosmetics and bodily ornaments grew in popularity with the suggestion that they provided primitive sensuality. Game manufacturer Selchow and Righter copyrighted the Asian game of Parcheesi in the 1870s, and the "primitive" game caught on as a Victorian parlor game. Books of peasant fairy tales, savage myths, and Indian legends were among the best sellers of the Victorian period, and their redactors, men like Andrew Lang, Hans Christian Andersen, and of course the Grimm brothers, became world renowned.

In American literature, Mark Twain (a member of the American Folklore Society) is celebrated perhaps above all other fiction writers for his use of folklore to represent the piquancy of American vernacular characters and settings. He also is noteworthy for his attention to evolutionary theory used to interpret folklore. In his preface to *Connecticut Yankee in King Arthur's Court* (1889), Twain declared that the customs touched on in the tale were "survivals" found at a later time, which can be assumed to have been practiced during the sixth century. But Twain satirically concluded, "One is quite justified in inferring that wherever one of these laws and customs was lacking in that remote time, its place was competently filled by a worse one" (Twain [1889] 1979, 45). In an unpublished preface, he addressed the ethnological rhetoric of progress more explicitly: "The strange laws which one encounters here and there in this book, are not known to have existed in King Arthur's time, of course, but it is fair to presume that they did then exist, since they still existed in Christian lands in far later times—times customarily called, with unconscious sarcasm, 'civilized and enlightened'" (Twain [1889] 1979, 518). Writing at a time when he invested in as many as a hundred new gadgets and manufacturing schemes, particularly an ill-starred typesetting machine, Twain sketched the central character, Hank Morgan, as the bourgeois Yankee, practical and free of "sentiment." One of Morgan's workers, who carries the mythical name Hercules, knocks Morgan unconscious in a factory squabble. Morgan wakes up in medieval England, but rather than becoming despondent over his fate, he decides to take commercial advantage of the situation. He embarks on a campaign for industrial development, on the one hand, and for the destruction of traditional life on the other. At different times he calls King Arthur's subjects "this folk," "white Indians," "modified savages," "pigmies," "big children," and "great simple-hearted creatures." His plan to have a modern industrial establishment mark time to a master spirit finally clashes with the forces of tradition in a great nihilistic war. He destroys his "civilization-factories," and with a band of fifty-two boys indoctrinated into his industrial system, creates a destructive automated battlefield against hundreds of thousands of noble, but hopeless, barbaric Englishmen.

In the disturbing battle scene, the comic tone of the early part of the novel is gone, and the narrative turns grimly dark. Many critics have attributed Twain's change in mood to frustration in his own life with his failing investments in technological gadgetry and his subsequent questioning of popular confidence in the progress of industrial civilization. The spin put on the book by the publisher for the Gilded Age audience, however, was to promote Twain's ideological defense of American democracy. "The book answers the Godly slurs that have been cast at us for generations by the titled gentry of England," the advertisement copy stated. It implied that the book was an affirmation of the superiority of American progressivism and the benevolence of a government of the people trying to deal with rising industrial labor movements that were making a case for an American working class consciousness. Appealing to national "patriotism," the publisher's announcement further blurted, "Without knowing it the Yankee is constantly answering modern English criticism of America, and pointing out the weakness and injustice of government by a privileged class often mentally and physically far inferior to the masses of the people over whom they rule. At the same time the Yankee illustrates in a practical way the advantages of a Republican government like that of America" (Twain [1889] 1979, 540).

Twain used materials of an English medieval age that in the American popular imagination dripped with folklore. Volumes of medieval English fairy tales compiled by Andrew Lang and Joseph Jacobs, among others, well captured an American market, and they often noted the English coinage of the very term "folklore." Such tales, canonized as the textual core of tradition, had come under the name of "folklore" since 1846, when Britisher William John Thoms (1803–1885) proposed a "good Saxon compound" for what had previously been referred to in English as popular antiquities and literature. In a letter to *Athenaeum*, a leading weekly review of literature, science, and the arts, Thoms described folklore both as a connected whole—"the Lore of the People"— and as separable parts—"manners, customs, observances, superstitions, ballads, proverbs." In the next issue of the weekly magazine, a department of folklore was established, with Thoms in charge. During the 1850s, English books began to appear using "folklore" in their titles: Thomas Sternberg's *The Dialect and Folklore of Northamptonshire* (1851), Jabez Allies's *On the Ancient British, Roman and Saxon Antiquities and Folk-Lore of Worcestershire* (1852), and Thoms's *Choice Notes from "Notes and Queries": Folk Lore* (1858). By 1876, Thoms was signing himself "An Old Folk-Lorist," giving a name to the student of the subject. The next year, the term was given sanction by the formation in England of the Folk-Lore Society.

Thoms's goal was to accomplish for the British what the Grimm brothers had done for Germany. He claimed that "the present century has scarcely produced a more remarkable book, imperfect as its learned author confesses it to be, than the second edition of the *Deutsche Mythologie* and, what is it?—a mass of minute facts, many of which, when separately considered, appear trifling and insignificant,— but, when taken in connection with the system into which his master-mind has woven them, assume a value that he who first recorded them never dream of attributing to them" (Thoms [1846] 1965, 5). His description of the appearance of folklore as a collection of discrete parts that when brought together take on a great value provides a metaphor for nationalism during the mid-nineteenth century. Emerging nation-states sought to justify their boundaries by pointing to the varied folklore of many communities that have at their heart common themes. The

Grimms contributed to the mid-nineteenth-century push to unite German-speaking regions of central Europe into a united Germany. As lore, parts of tradition could be separated more easily from the communities of which they are a part, and connected to a greater whole.

Some writers who distinguished folk "life" from folklore during the nineteenth century argued for the integrity of communities and ethnic minorities within regions. William Wells, writing on "Folk-Life in German By-Ways" in *Scribner's Monthly* in 1873, for example, pointed out that "the German peasants form the most conservative communities in the world. Within a stone's throw of all the habits and customs of modern civilization, they will persistently maintain their speech, their costume, and their notions, both at work and at play. These differ also greatly in different regions, so that one can stand on a mountain summit, and look into valleys right and left, whose inhabitants wear different garbs, speak different dialects, and who, quite likely, may be of opposite faiths" (Wells 1873, 590). Despite a scattering of folklife references, citation of folklore as the survival of ancient customs dominated English-language periodical literature during the Gilded Age.

In Europe, and increasingly in America, folklore could be heard to invoke a sense of peoplehood that justified national aspirations. No less a political figure than Theodore Roosevelt urged the collection from the folkloric "treasure-house of literature ... of a buried past" in the United States to stir nationalism. He especially praised the "expressions of that valor of soul" as the wellspring of a serious national art and literature found in the national folklore in Ireland. Citing the collecting of Ireland's Lady Gregory, he called for an American effort to represent the country's uniqueness through "all the local features of our composite nationality." "American work must smack of our own soil, mental and moral, no less than physical, or it will have little of permanent value," and "Americans must in some degree express the distinctive characteristics of our own national soul," he emphasized (Roosevelt 1926b, 334, 336). Answering the call were volumes such as the popular *Myths and Legends of Our Own Land* by Charles Skinner in 1896 and *American Myths and Legends* in 1903. In his placement of "our own land" in the title, Skinner indicated the association of mythology with countries outside of the United States, especially in Europe. Skinner's strategy was to promote a national mythology for the United States around the mystery of the American land. He showed wondrous narratives inspired by a fabulous wilderness and remarkable deserts that transformed Europeans into Americans.

In his efforts to hail in folklore an enlivened American spirit as well as celebrate a stupendous land, Roosevelt was especially excited by the appearance of *Cowboy Songs and Other Frontier Ballads* collected by folklorist John Lomax (1910). Roosevelt sent a letter of congratulations which was printed in the volume, and Lomax in turn dedicated the volume to the president "who while President was not too busy to turn aside—cheerfully and effectively—and aid workers in the field of American balladry." In his letter Roosevelt drew comparisons of the inspiration for the material in "the conditions of ballad-growth which obtained in medieval England," but pointed out the distinctive American condition of the frontier West that contributed to folk literary composition. During America's Gilded Age, the cowboy, the lumberjack, and the raftsman became exalted into zesty American folk types that characterized national traits of ruggedness and independence born of the mythic wilderness.

Concerned for the absence of a native peasantry inspiring a national "soul," a host of writers around the turn of the century focused their primitivist attention on American Indians and various groups perceived to be rich in tradition, such as European immigrants, African Americans, French Canadians, Appalachians and isolated mountain or maritime groups, and children. For notable journalists like Roosevelt's conservationist colleagues George Bird Grinnell, editor of *Field and Stream*, and Henry W. Shoemaker, who published over two hundred books and pamphlets on regional folklore and natural history of America's forests and mountains, folklore showed America's "medley of races" and the sacredness of America's natural surroundings. All three were founding members of the Boone and Crockett Club in New York City, named after rough-and-ready folk heroes personifying the wilderness mettle of America.

Collecting folklore took place in the "field" much as Darwin collected specimens in the wild for his grand natural history. As Victorians became more and more "worldly" in the search for empire, they ventured out on collecting trips to gather exotic flora and fauna, as well as customs and objects, and arranged them on parlor furniture and museum shelves. In countless evening lectures that were part entertainment, part education, Victorians heard that their collections were like mosaics revealing wondrous hidden worlds in the small pieces and offering a pattern or "object lesson" when looked at from the lofty vantage of civilization. The placement of folklore as a layer covered over by civilization came out in several definitions of folklore that followed Thoms's. The British *Handbook of Folklore* (1914) explained that folklore "has established itself as the generic term under which the traditional Beliefs, Customs, Stories, Songs, and Sayings current among backward peoples, or retained by the uncultured classes of more advanced peoples, are comprehended and included" (Burne 1914, 1). George Laurence Gomme in *Ethnology in Folklore* (1892) offered that "the essential characteristic of folklore is that it consists of beliefs, customs, and traditions which are far behind civilisation in their intrinsic value to man, though they exist under the cover of a civilised nationality" (Gomme 1892, 2).

A range of writing, academic and popular, saluted natural history in the wake of Charles Darwin's explosive evolutionary theories. Natural history at the time worshiped a version of science that rewarded a new faith in knowable, minute facts, "links" as one writer explained "in a great chain of development from primitive to advanced forms" (Merrill 1989, 260). Reacting to religious reliance on the unknowable, natural history offered keywords stressing observable objectivity: specimens, collections, cabinets. It used an arrangement of globally scattered facts shaped by humans into an ordered whole emphasizing advancement through time. "The nineteenth century made the mistake of worshiping the Muse of History as a goddess," Noel Annan reflected. "Truth, they believed, was revealed in History, not in the Bible—but like every revelation it required interpretation" (Annan 1966, 151). Truth was based on empirically verifiable facts, but faith could still be interpreted from sentimental virtues of nature, lore, and literature.

In a secularizing and industrializing age, a sense of lore associated with nature became apparent in new studies that suggested that folklore held a special spiritual appeal. It was consequential for a growing middle class to temper the "nervousness," the popular term for a kind of anxiety over change, engendered by the new cult of business and science (Lears 1981). In George Miller Beard's widely circulated book *American Nervousness* (1881), for example, the author invoked the traditional past to understand the present, for "the moderns differ from the ancient civilizations mainly in these five elements—steam power, the periodical press, the telegraph, the sciences, and the mental activity of women. When civilization, plus these five factors, invades any nation, it must carry nervousness and nervous diseases along with it" (Beard 1970, 238). In the perception of the period, nature and lore—"the old log cabins, shady groves, giant trees, old fords, ferries, beaver dams, and reed-grown pools" and "the legends, the folklore, the ghosts that lingered about these survivals"—represented a simpler day that had been left behind because of the inevitable march of civilization (H. Shoemaker 1916, 187).

Among Darwin's revelations to his Victorian audience was that the past extended far longer than had been proposed by religious leaders, advanced species of life evolved from "lower" forms, and natural laws controlled the evolution. Opening up the long history of nature by collecting, classifying, and arranging specimens into an evolutionary order suggested that creation might be similarly defined for humanity, and hence for culture. In culture, however, survivals collected by folklorists implied a convergence toward unity from bottom to the top rather than diverging to a variety of species as in nature. With the past apparently remote, specialized practitioners with esoteric "scientific" skills became necessary to uncover the past for the public. The social side effects of such changes in thinking were significant. For one, a shortened theological past which had been part of the older wisdom meant that changes in nature and man were necessarily large leaps. The opening of the evolutionary past suggested that the world's beginning was not a literal wholesale creation, but was a metaphor for slow and constant change. While Victorians frequently expressed the belief that transformative changes were occurring during their time, the new world view provided the security that their era was not a cataclysm, but a natural climax of steady growth. The narrative of history, natural and culture, was progressive, one layer of life building on and over another that will not accept change. Darwin himself commented in *The Descent of Man* (1874) that "it is apparently a truer and more cheerful view that progress has been much more general than retrogression; that man has risen, though by slow and interrupted steps, from a lowly condition to the highest standard as yet attained by him in knowledge, morals and religion." At the conclusion of the book, he endorsed the view of progress that was common to his age: "Man may be excused for feeling some pride at having risen, though not through his own exertions, to the very summit of the organic scale; and the fact of his having thus risen, instead of having been aboriginally placed there, may give him hope for a still higher destiny in the distant future" (Darwin 1874, 162–65). Edward Tylor, a leading authority on the new cultural evolutionism, emphasized the relation of collecting folklore survivals to dealing with issues of the day when he wrote, "not merely as a matter of curious research, but as an important practical guide to the understanding of the present and the shaping of the future, the investigation into the origin and early development of civilization must be pushed on zealously" (Tylor 1970, 24).

Victorians prescribed healthy doses of fantasy and exoticism in folklore to balance the nervousness and monotony of public industrial life. Building on the groundbreaking collections of the Brothers Grimm, Victorian writers anthologized and created new fairy tales of enchanted forests and magical animals. European folklore, especially, was popularly collected and presented to satisfy the public hunger for mysticism, and even nationalism, while a small circle of "scientific men and women" insisted on keeping its study on "sound" evolutionary principles. In popular magazines such as *Harper's Monthly, Atlantic Monthly, Scribner's Monthly, Century, Nation, Open Court, Outlook, Popular Science Monthly*, and *Overland Monthly*, readers found essays on, among other subjects, primitive invention and industry, women's roles in primitive society, beliefs and customs having to do with the supernatural, and the evolution of folk religious objects into play items.

Further evidence of the folklore "vogue" during the Gilded Age is that the two main guides to popular periodicals at the time, *Poole's Index to Periodical Literature* and the *Reader's Guide*, indexed the *Journal of American Folklore*. The number of articles cited under "folklore" reveals a pattern from the founding of the American Folklore Society into the first decade of the twentieth century. *Poole's Index* listed fourteen articles on folklore (folk song was listed separately) from 1887 to 1892; from 1892 to 1896, the number jumped to seventy-seven, but dropped down to seven from 1902 to 1905, when *Poole's* ceased publication. The *Reader's Guide* listed a whopping 177 articles for folklore between 1890 and 1909, not counting entries for the *Journal of American Folklore*. In 1905, however, the *Reader's Guide* ceased indexing the journal. In the ensuing years, the *Reader's Guide* doubled the number of periodicals that it indexed, but between 1910 and 1924, the guide listed only fifty-eight articles on folklore. The last decades of the nineteenth century not only have the claim, then, to the Gilded Age, but also the title of the Ethnological Period, full of folkloristic forays far from the beaten path to answer questions close to home.

W. J. McGee, writing in *Atlantic Monthly* in 1898, boasted of the particularly favorable response to evolutionary folklore doctrine in America. "The earliest and strongest apostles were Americans," he claimed, and "the free, vigorous and trenchant American mind was peculiarly hospitable to the tenets of the new law; and it was accepted here as the foundation for the cult of science years before it was similarly accepted in Great Britain." While industrial advances ushered in the greatest revolution in the history of civilization, according to McGee, Darwin's ideas on evolution triggered "the most profound revolution in the history of human thought" (McGee 1898).

Americans gave a particularly hospitable reception to the social Darwinism of the Englishman Herbert Spencer, who made a case for industrial progress and laissez-faire economics on the grounds of Darwin's natural selection. By 1903 more than 368,000 volumes of Spencer's works had been sold in the United States. The popular American writings of John Fiske, author of *Myths and Mythmakers* (1900), and William Graham Sumner, author of *Folkways* (1906), applied Spencer liberally in their work. Preacher Henry Ward Beecher wrote Spencer with this observation on the American embrace of his work: "The peculiar condition of American society has made your writings far more fruitful and quickening here than in Europe." Beecher thought that although industrialization and its social effects came to the United States later than to Europe, it spread more quickly and with greater ripples through the diversity of cultural groups living on America's soil.

Fiske and Sumner likened America to Darwin's Galapagos Islands because of its rich variety of cultural species and settings. John Sterling Kingsley followed this line of thinking by attributing American uniqueness, and greatness, to its blend of races. He wrote in *The Standard Natural History* published in Boston in 1885: "Instance after instance could be cited, were it desirable, to show that intercourse between nation and nation, mixture of blood between race and race, lies at the root of growth, development, progress, and culture; that offered by our own country is all that need be mentioned. Here there has been mixture almost beyond precedent; here the most different elements have been amalgamated, and the result is one which fully confirms the law" (Kingsley 1885, 472). He assumed, however, that the "amalgamation" tended toward the progress set by a dominant white English race.

Lewis Henry Morgan, influential author of *Ancient Society: Or Researches in the Lines of Human Progress from Savagery through Barbarism to Civilization* (1877) opined that "rich as the American continent is known to be in material wealth, it is also the richest of all the continents in ethnological, philological, and archaeological materials, illustrative of the great period of barbarism" (Morgan 1974, iii). On American soil, where native tribes provided an authentic layer of primitive culture below "American civilization," Morgan's evolutionary lens brought into focus a unified orderly outline from savagery to barbarism to civilization to enlightenment. Using natural history metaphors inspired by Darwin and Spencer, Morgan offered that "these circumstances appeal strongly to Americans to enter this great field and gather its abundant harvest" (Morgan 1974, iv).

The natural history model of a cultural ladder from savagery to enlightenment was the organizing principle for the Bureau of American Ethnology, established by the United States government in 1879. The Bureau sought out folklore, language, architecture, and customs in its field collecting trips as a key to uncovering the nation's savage past among its Indians. It had fashioned, W. J. McGee said, "a New Ethnology, in which men are classified by mind rather than by body, by culture rather than by color." In a popular view of cultural evolution, McGee classified all the world's peoples into stages of development, "namely: (1) savagery, with a social organization resting on kinship reckoned in the female line; (2) barbarism, in which the social organization is based on kinship reckoned in the male line; (3) civilization, in which the organization has a territorial basis; and (4) enlightenment, in which the laws and customs are based on intellectual rights." Again pointing to American conditions to explain the intellectual fervor for this scheme, McGee wrote: "Our physical progress has been great because invention is encouraged by free institutions; our progress in geology has been rapid by reason of intellectual freedom and a vast domain; while our progress in anthropology has been marvelous because of the elevated point of view and an incomparable range of types both of blood and of activity" (McGee 1898, 318–19).

McGee and his fellow evolutionists at the Bureau of American Ethnology especially sought rites and customs to illustrate the "mind" of culture. Such "specimens" often appeared unusual or exotic and suggested to the Victorians backward and progressive levels of beliefs about man in relation to his environment. At lower levels, rites represented control of the world by supernatural and natural forces, and later in advanced stages, by human, technological forces. The progression of items, many evolutionists believed, worked from superstition to science, from primitive rites to refined manners, from exotic customs to rational observances. They held that while societies advance, many folk items persist in practice, although they lose their original significance and intimate connection with the group. In evolutionary theory, the persistence of such customs was analogous to survival of the culturally unfit. The survivals could be collected often in remnant form among civilized folk and could be seen in full flowering among existing "savage" groups such as American Indians. Thus, many writers offered to give the piquant original meanings of curious sayings and objects that once had significance in primitive customs, while others gave a glimpse of the similar ways of thinking among different primitive groups.

BLACK FOLKLORE AND "PROGRESS OF THE RACE"

American writers viewed Indians as the nation's main "primitives" during the Gilded Age. Government policy treated them as a conquered nation, isolated from whites who presumably gave the nation its culture. Removed to reservations, Indians were considered remote and tribal, comparable to "aboriginal" groups stuck in a savage state around the globe. In keeping with the natural science model, many folklorists and anthropologists connected to the Bureau of American Ethnology (BAE) and various museums viewed American Indians as a pure, ancient species in danger of extinction, and they scurried to the reservations to record an array of exotic tribal languages, myths, songs, and crafts before they inevitably disappeared. The museums were typically natural history museums which included the native Indians in the natural realm. Natives appeared to be in commune with flora and fauna, maintained the virgin land before whites came, and made productive use of it. Folklore was especially important evidence in the salvage work done by the BAE and natural history museums. Folklore collected from Indians documented uses of language and history, since most tribes rarely kept written records. Overall, this material constituted for many of the museum anthropologists the "spiritual" side of culture, offering the beliefs, indeed the character, of the "race." Hence, the early leadership at the BAE justified the "scientific" expeditions as a national cause to help guide Indian policy toward management of the reservations.

The "Negroes" or "Afro-Americans," as they were sometimes called at that time, presented a special problem in American culture during the Gilded Age. While they often were isolated, especially in sections of the South, they were lodged, if precariously, within American society. They were not on native, or virgin land. They were less remote than the Indians, more numerous, and more geographically spread. Many American writers differentiated, as well as stigmatized, them in America because of their origin in Africa and history of enslavement. While they were recognized for a distinctive patois, they mostly spoke English, and were forced to adopt the former masters' manners, so conventional wisdom held. They did not seem comparable as the Indians were to natives on other continents. Yet their racial difference also suggested cultural contrast, and in evolutionary thinking their darkness was a gauge of their backwardness. While they resided in view of the advancements of the age, in evolutionary doctrine they had lagged well behind in progress toward civilization. The progress that was possible, or acceptable, after emancipation became closely watched. In this view, folklore could be a measure of how far blacks had come or could go. Folklore of the former slaves was late in being collected compared to that of American Indians. As Reconstruction ended and the Gilded Age began, black folklore was more likely to be comically distorted on the stage than analytically reported in print. As the harvesting of black folklore proceeded, the intentions of the reapers were naturally questioned. They attracted close scrutiny, arguably even closer than for the Indians, to check for suggestions of challenge to the social order, especially as segregation became deeply entrenched.

The main evidence for cultural difference of African Americans that entered popular discourse during the Gilded Age was in spirituals, superstitions, and folktales. The recognition of a distinctive American "Negro" spiritual by whites opened the black folklore field for inspection. It also contained enough ambiguity of meaning to allow a range of opinions on "the Negro problem." That problem was essentially a way to forge a future for blacks as free citizens after a history of white control. For if Negroes in the South were no longer slaves during the Gilded Age, they nonetheless were regarded, as many social critics noted, as something of a created serf class, even a caste, without the poetic suggestions it had in some places in Europe of serving as the ethnic backbone of a nation (see Fry 1975; Levine 1977). Even after emancipation, they were long tied to the rural Southland by various measures that recognized their economic value as cheap agricultural labor, while resisting social equality, capitalist development, and educational advancement (see Steinberg 1981, 24–31).

References to spirituals sung by slaves as symbols of the desire for freedom appeared in several pre-Civil War autobiographies, most notably Frederick Douglass's *Narrative* (1845). Douglass asserted that the traditionally learned and emotionally performed songs gave him his "first glimmering conceptions of the dehumanizing character of slavery" (Sundquist 1995, 322). From the viewpoint of the ex-slave writers, they were also an introduction to literacy—intellectual and cultural (Sundquist 1995, 323–24). By learning an extensive repertoire traditionally, expanding upon the songs and elaborating them, all in apparent defiance of masters' restrictions on education and expression, the spirituals seemed to be a communally shared language of hope as well as frustration.

Ex-slave narratives often described spirituals as a communicative code and an ethnic marker during slavery, and hinted at their therapeutic value after emancipation (Levine 1977; O'Connor 1995; Peters 1996). Songs could be heard, such as the famous "Go Down Moses," making an analogy between the biblical bondage of the Israelites in Egypt and blacks in the South. A symbolic link was also possible between heaven and the North, as fugitive Harriet Jacobs indicated in her *Incidents in the Life of a Slave Girl* (1861): "Ole Satan's church is here below/Up to God's free church I wish to go" (Peters 1996, 682). Other songs supposedly could be used to signal that a way was safe for escape, or offered warnings. Lyrics intoned the sorrow of bondage and the promise of deliverance. The music sounded familiarly close to white Protestant hymns, but showed differences, presumably from African influences and American black creativity, performed in a style more emotionally rendered than whites considered usual.

If narratives written by former slaves pointed to the symbolic meaning of spirituals, it was a trio of whites who brought spirituals as an American black cultural trove to wide public attention. Only two years after the end of the Civil War, William Francis Allen, Lucy McKim Garrison, and Charles Pickard Ware published a collection entitled *Slave Songs of the United States* (1867). Allen, the main force behind the volume, was a Latin and classics teacher from Massachusetts who spent two years in the South with the Freedmen's and Sanitary commissions. He began collecting the songs in South Carolina and Arkansas and upon meeting

Ware and Garrison, who had transcribed some spirituals, led the collaboration to prepare a substantial volume. It stood as the first extensive collection of black folklore published, and in the words of W. K. McNeil, "whetted the interest in collecting, analyzing, and performing Negro folk music that has never since abated" (McNeil 1996a, 18).

Slave Songs contained 136 examples of songs taken from oral tradition and accompanied with commentaries. Some of the most memorable that were frequently picked as literary references included "Go Down Moses," "Roll Jordan Roll," "Nobody Knows the Trouble I've Seen," and "Swing Low Sweet Chariot" (Sundquist 1995, 318–23). Black music was not unknown in the period—it was mimicked in hokey minstrel shows—but Allen and his collaborators gave the songs as the genuine article of slave life. In keeping with evolutionary thinking, the collectors used white church music as a standard and typically judged the level of "barbarism" evident in the black folk songs. Intent on presenting the civilized dignity of the spirituals, famous black choirs from Fisk University and Hampton Institute usually formally performed the songs with sanitized arrangements (Marsh 1876; Fenner et al., 1901). In such settings, the spirituals could be alternatively heard as signs of black adoption of white ways or of a new cultural creation.

Popular acceptance of the spirituals may have owed to their recognizable Christian forms and reorientation of African-American performance toward white audiences. To be sure, many reviews of black choirs praised the emotion of the songs conveyed in performance. Mark Twain seemed to have been especially affected, and his endorsement for the Fisk singers may have helped spread their fame. He wrote for the group's publicity in 1897: "I think these gentlemen and ladies make eloquent music—and what is as much to the point, they reproduce the true melody of the plantations, and are the only persons I ever heard accomplish this on the public platform. The so-called 'negro minstrels' simply mis-represent the thing; I do not think they ever saw a plantation or heard a slave sing. I was reared in the South, and my father owned slaves, and I do not know when anything has so moved me as did the plaintive melodies of the Jubilee Singers" (Fishkin 1993, 150). Twain may have been slyly ambiguous in justifying on the one hand the cultural difference of blacks and on the other giving a muffled reference to the pain of slavery expressed in the songs when he observed, "It was the first time for twenty-five or thirty years that I heard such songs, or heard them sung in the genuine old way—and it is a way, I think, that white people cannot imitate—and never can, for that matter, for one must have been a slave himself in order to feel what that life was and so convey the pathos of it in the music" (Fishkin 1993, 150).

As spirituals were performed through the Gilded Age by the choirs, they were commonly introduced as a legacy of slavery, well past, and not taken as a threat for the present. They could be reassuringly heard as signifying the promise of black adoption of white religious virtues rather than the cry for protest. They became symbols of plantation and cabin, and of rural Negroes who had not strayed far from home. Secular songs, many of them from urban locales, were late in being recorded compared to spirituals, and aroused more controversy. When the often irreligious content of the secular work songs, hollers, and laments began to be published, often alongside accounts of magical practices, they revealed hardy, boastful singers capable of resistance.

The location of New Orleans as the main stage of the drama ensuing over the black secular material is not coincidental. The city was different enough culturally from other southern cities to attract attention for its exoticism, and similar enough for its common race prejudices to be familiar. The contrasting backgrounds of the main characters in the morality play—George Washington Cable and Lafcadio Hearn—thickened the plot. Unlike the English domination common in the other major eastern cities, the French established New Orleans, and the city took in many ethnic influences in its subsequent history. The city had a decided French flavor, even after the Spanish came in.

Many writers described the "easy intermingling" of ethnic groups within the city, and the intermarriage of Spanish and French settlers, who shared a Catholic affiliation, producing a new American group called Creoles. Added to the mix were black Creoles who retained many Caribbean and African characteristics, including religious practices sometimes called "voodoo." They, too, circulated in the city, and the resulting mixtures were given names such as quadroons (one-quarter black) and octaroons (one-eighth black). New Orleans carried a reputation for social and cultural miscegenation that at the time made it morally loathsome, and exotically alluring, in American consciousness. White Americans had entered the wide-open city even before the United States had completed the Louisiana Purchase in 1803. New Orleans showed more diversity by taking in German, Irish, and Italian immigrants through the nineteenth century. By 1860, it became the largest city in the South, and it had a sizable black population, including many freedmen.

George Washington Cable (1844–1925) is credited for first bringing national attention in fiction and folklore to the Louisiana Creoles, black and white. And through this work, he viewed the problem of race relations as central to the decline of the South as a sectional society. He was born in New Orleans, but was neither Creole nor Catholic. His parents came to the city from the North, and most accounts credit the mother with passing on to the writer son a strong streak of New England Puritanism (Butcher 1962). Cable fought for the Confederacy during the Civil War, but came to question southern secession and the institution of slavery.

After the war, Cable wrote for the New Orleans *Picayune* where he had a regular column on city events. Tired of factual reporting, he became attracted to a form of writing called "local color" that was increasingly featured in national magazines. It was a prose sketch of the compelling geographical and cultural aspects of a region. Folklore that brought out the charming peculiarities of local residents and their relationships to the distinctive environment was regularly featured in this journalism. Local color writing gained popularity at a time when the nation achieved its "manifest destiny" and spread its population from coast to coast. Editors at the magazines boosted an interest in the dazzling variety of American community life in the geographically spread nation.

Cable first tried his hand at some local color fiction based on Creole life in New Orleans, for *Scribner's Monthly* during the 1870s. The New York editors were eager to arouse readers with the reputation of New Orleans for exoticism. Encouraged by the response to his stories, Cable brought his magazine stories together in 1879 as a book entitled *Old Creole Days,* and it was quickly followed by *The Grandissimes: A Story of Creole Life* (1880). Cable offered a good amount of picturesqueness in his scenes and characterizations, and lent realism to his narrative with convincing details of folk sayings and customs.

While Cable gained national notice for uncovering Creole life, he garnered resentment at home. He could not be dismissed easily as a mere parochial writer offering gentle nostalgia for a bygone day. For as his writing gained national currency, it brought out in the rise and fall of Creole life the problem of institutionalized race prejudice that undermined the future of the South. The aristocratic white Creoles at first recoiled from the suggestion that they were formed from intercourse not just between the French and Spanish, but also with blacks and Indians. They were further incensed when Cable connected them to convicts who had settled in the old colony, and insinuated their patronage of prostitutes. Rather than blame the loss of the war for their troubles, Cable fingered a racial mindset that kept them from progressing socially. He flattered black characters and intimated the need for social agitation. In *The Grandissimes,* a white character tells the quadroon Honore Grandissime, who appears to be Cable's surrogate, "I can imagine a man in your place, going about among his people, stirring up their minds to a noble discontent, laying out his means, sparingly here and bountifully there, as in each case might seem wisest, for their enlightenment, their moral elevation, their training in skilled work; going, too, among the people of the prouder caste, among such as have a spirit of fairness, and seeking to prevail with them for a public recognition of the rights of all; using all his cunning to show them the double damage of all oppression, both great and petty—" (Butcher 1962, 83).

As Cable became more forcefully political through the 1880s, reviewers from corners of the white South outside of New Orleans castigated his fiction. Cable published stormy essays advocating government-sponsored education programs for blacks and attacking the convict-lease system, which primarily used black labor. He especially raised a row in the South by unequivocally demanding social equality for the races in "The Freedman's Case in Equity" (Cable 1885). Denial of freedmen's civil rights as American citizens, Cable righteously proclaimed, degraded blacks and corrupted whites. When Cable published an opinion piece on southern race relations in *Century* magazine in 1885, it brought an avalanche of letters to the editor and a ferocious rebuttal from the editor of the *Atlanta Constitution,* a southern ideologue reasserting the inferior status of blacks and their needs for white control (Grady 1885). A biting rejoinder by Cable answered that change could be made, had to be made, if it were not for "the Silent South," composed of whites who would grant blacks fair treatment but who were intimidated into silence. Cable offered moral justification from his religion for altering the social order and political reasoning for further reconstructing southern state govern-ments. Backed by the American Missionary Society, Cable republished his editori-als and attempted to blanket the South with them (Cable 1885). Cable's opinions made residence increasingly difficult for him in the South, and he moved north to Massachusetts in 1885.

Cable gained prominence in 1884 by joining Mark Twain in a tour featuring their readings of fiction about the South. Yet the pair never appeared south of Kentucky. He performed black Creole songs on the tour, and by all accounts they roused the loudest audience reaction. A survey of reviews written during the tour reveals more mention of encores for the songs than for any other part of the pro-gram. Introduced originally as an impromptu variation from the program, the songs became an anxiously awaited feature of Cable's performance. The *Buffalo Express* for December 11, 1884, noted that Cable had "varied the printed pro-gramme by an African Creole song, which he rendered very finely. It was a peculiar bit of plaintive minor music, and the light soft voice of the novelist was well adapt-ed to it. Responding to the encore he sang a short bit representing the wail of a Creole mother for her lost child." The next month, the *Chicago Tribune* delighted at the sight of the "dignified," "refined," and "graceful" dandy (Twain was not, so most of the reviews read) Cable rendering gutty black songs in his sweet, high-pitched voice. The reviewer observed: "His third number consisted of Creole-negro songs in the French patois used by that race in their weird dances and incantations." Twain, according to the memoirs of the tour's manager, encouraged Cable's performance of the songs and gave renditions privately of "plantation songs and Mississippi River chanties of the negro." Around the same time that the songs became a regular feature of the tour, Twain added a reading of a new section from *Huckleberry Finn* in which Tom Sawyer and Huck Finn free the slave Jim. Twain integrated the songs into the reading, as he explained to his wife, Olivia: "To-night I read the new piece … & it's the biggest card I've got in my whole reper-toire. I always thought so. It went a-booming; & Cable's praises are not merely loud, they are boisterous…. It took me 45 minutes to recite it, (didn't use any notes) & it hadn't a doubtful place in it, or a silent spot … I make 2 separate read-ings of it, & Cable sings a couple of songs in the middle" (December 29, 1884, Pittsburgh). Reflections on the injustices of slavery were evident thereafter. From Chicago, Cable excitedly wrote his wife: "Ah! What an effect we did have tonight. Clemens's story of Huck Finn and Tom Sawyer liberating runaway [Jim] was received with a continual tempest of merriment, and when I gave 'A Sound of Drums' I saw persons in tears all over the house. I was called back twice after my Creole songs and twice after 'Mary's Night Ride.'" (January 17, 1885).[4] With this favor for the songs and their protest themes probably in mind, Cable in 1886 published a groundbreaking collection for the popular magazine *Century* entitled "Creole Slave Songs." He then went on to encourage more literary attention to the songs by opening a Department of Negro Folk Song in the Chicago Folk-Lore Society, later known as the International Folklore Association.

The secular songs were important to Cable in his cause for racial equality because they affirmed the living tradition of southern blacks. In attaching a marked African influence to the songs, Cable suggested an independence, a dignity, that comes with a separate cultural continuity. It was a music not controlled by whites, he intimated, and furthermore showed an enlivening process of racial creolization. In presenting what he had collected and realizing the sensitivity of the material, he hoped to encourage blacks to research their own cultural history. Contributing "A Negro Folk-Song" (a transcription of a game song, "Susan Gay") to *The Folk-Lorist* (published by the Chicago Folk-Lore Society), he wrote: "There is a kind of folk-song in the Southern States which it might be found very interesting to consider, if only some one would give it some research. Doubtless there are educated negroes in the South who might do this, and who would have facilities for such a labor of love, which others would hardly command" (Cable 1892). In advocating educational programs at black industrial schools, to which he contributed generously, he had in mind this kind of collection that could lead to progressive social and literary results. In his call for intellectual advancement and the priority of social equality, he parted company with former ally Booker T. Washington about the educational needs of southern blacks (Butcher 1948). By the turn of the century, his uncompromising stance lost him supporters, both black and white.

Cable apparently lost his missionary zeal for the campaign, for his published work after 1892 hardly makes mention of "The Negro Question" (Cable 1888). His biographer, Philip Butcher, thought that Cable had his idealism dashed that "the South would listen to dispassionate debate on controversial subjects and would heed the advice of high-minded men who urged the adoption of a course of action based on principle rather than on expediency" (Butcher 1962, 110–11). It is also true that his disillusionment coincided with the end of his religious writing and distance from the South. Prominent black figures such as Booker T. Washington, Charles Chesnutt, and W. E. B. DuBois who had once lauded him barely mentioned him after the turn of the century (Butcher 1962, 177). Nonetheless, activists in the Civil Rights movement of the 1950s revived his political writing with an important volume called *The Negro Question* (Turner 1958). The reception for Cable's political writing may lead to the conclusion that during the Gilded Age he was either too late as a postbellum abolitionist or too early as a southern civil rights advocate.

Lafcadio Hearn (1850–1904), Cable's street-wise companion in the search for black Creole folk songs in New Orleans, could not be said to have shared Cable's puritanical motivation. But he bore Cable's sense of outrage at social injustice to blacks and even more than Cable penetrated the hidden African-American realms of the city. He also fired away at the hypocrisy of a city that claimed racial separation even though abundant evidence could be found of social and cultural miscegenation (Hearn 1926). Cable and Hearn had both covered local events for New Orleans newspapers and incorporated black folklore into their fiction. Hearn was even more of an outsider to the city, having been born in Greece, raised in Britain, and schooled in France. But to his advantage within New Orleans, Hearn was fluent in French and had lived closely with blacks. Forced into homelessness, he lived for a time on the street where he learned of the city's underside and its cast of haunting characters.

Hearn came to New Orleans from Cincinnati in 1877 after establishing himself as a journalist sensationally exploring uncharted cultural territory on the other side of the tracks. Instead of bringing back stories on crime, he narrated the life of criminals; rather than reporting the degradation of underclass blacks, he gave their artistic expressions of spirited hope in song and story. More than a decade before Cable gained fame for his collection of secular slave songs, Hearn had published a riveting series of essays on black folklife in Cincinnati. It exposed the present, maybe the future, of black life uprooted from the staid countryside and flourishing in the rising cities. He wrote incredible reading material for the time—lurid descriptions of scarred roustabouts and their toughened expressions of hardscrabble lives and boisterous surroundings. Along the docks of a black section called Bucktown, he recorded for city readers the rough-hewn lyrics, "I went down to Bucktown, Nebber was dar before, Great big niggah knocked me down, But Katy barred the door" (Cott 1992, 101; see also Hearn 1957). In 1876, he brought out the racial protest of lines like "Nigger an' a white man playing seven-up, White man played an ace; an' Nigger feared to take it up, White man played ace an' Nigger played a nine, White man died, an' Nigger went blind" (Cott 1992, 103). It was hardly like anything dripping with plantation nostalgia or the wholesomeness of the spirituals. He did not see acquiescence in this churning urban setting. "There is an intense uniqueness about all this pariah existence," Hearn engrossingly wrote of the city's black section: "its boundaries are most definitely fixed; its enjoyments are wholly sensual, and many of them are marked by peculiarities of a strictly local character" (Cott 1992, 100). He avowed the African origins of the melodies he heard, and applauded the creative exuberance of the singers teasing effusive narratives out of their bustling city scenes.

Hearn had personal reasons for his interest in black life. In defiance of antimiscegenation laws, he married a black woman in Cincinnati who had been born a slave, and his employers at the *Commercial* unceremoniously fired him when the union was discovered. Moreover, he expressed sympathy with the plight of a racial outcast out of his experience in Britain, where he felt ostracized for his dark looks gained from a Greek Gypsy mother. His father was of Irish birth and experienced a variety of exotic cultures at various military stations for the British Empire. Lafcadio came into the care of an elderly great aunt, who attempted to instill strict Catholicism into the boy and opened her library to him to keep him from wandering. He learned languages, devoured books, and explored the countryside. Compensating for an eye blinded in an accident, he took notes on the minutest details of natural life. He was drawn to mysticism and talked of being hounded by ghosts. Lafcadio ended up being abandoned by his family and, with his strange ways and swarthy appearance, was shipped off, not by his choice, to America. He took to journalistic writing to support himself and built a reputation in the United States as an accomplished prose stylist. He became so intimately associated with absorbed reporting of African-American life that the black editor of the *Colored American* swore that Hearn must have been at least partly black (Murray 1904).

In the different places in America that Hearn worked, he became lured to the world respectable America rarely encountered and hardly understood. In his naturalist essays, he waxed poetic on the complexity of the small insect, and in cultural forays he glorified the "little people." In an America grabbing after material wealth and industrial strength, Hearn followed those not sharing in national progress. He offered their traditions as spiritual advances and showed that they had myriad aspirations, complex lives, and longstanding traditions.

More than Cable, Hearn dug at the roots of New Orleans black life to show their long reach. He devoted extensive literary efforts to traditional sources of New Orleans black culture in the West Indies and Africa (Hearn 1890a, 1890b). Cable helped Hearn place his pieces in national magazines, and the two worked together collecting songs with Cable transcribing the music while Hearn recorded the lyrics. After the gentlemanly Cable left the flattering light of New Orleans's main quarter, the rumpled Hearn continued to explore the dingy back streets deep into the night. Following his experience in Cincinnati, Hearn took quickly to the inner life of the black Creole community and became enthralled with the mystery of its traditions. Hearn assiduously studied the language of the black Creoles, and besides gathering songs he feverishly recorded foodways, beliefs, customs, tales, and proverbs (Hearn 1885a, 1885b, 1924, 1964; see also Fortier 1895). He wanted to show black tradition as more than entertainment; he billed it as a robust way of life.

At a time when the local press tarred Cable as a despicable traitor to southern tradition, Hearn stood alone in defense of Cable in columns for the *Times-Democrat*. Distance grew between the writers, however, as Hearn affronted Cable's puritan sensibilities by making it known that he was a regular customer at the brothels. It also must have been shocking for Cable to read of Hearn's deep involvement in the city's voodoo world. It was Hearn's journalism that helped boost the legends of Marie Laveau (the Queen of Voodoo) and Jean Montanet (the King of Hoodoo). He described them as agents of enormous power, proud of their African origins and commercially successful. He wrote, for example, "Jean, in short, possessed the mysterious *obi* power, the existence of which has been recognized in most slave-holding communities, and with which many a West-Indian planter has been compelled by force of circumstances to effect a compromise" (Cott 1992, 142). Here were prideful blacks to be feared and respected, Hearn brassily reported.

Other Gilded Age folklorists who delved into the voodoo world saw a different implication. Mary Alicia Owen in *Voodoo Tales* (1893) considered the tradition a confirmation of the superstitious nature of blacks, which represented a lower state of advancement toward civilization. The collection of the magical aspects of "Negro superstition" was indeed sensitive work, because of the path it suggested away from Christian sensibilities (see Puckett 1926). In the minds of many readers, it confirmed a primitive irrationality indicative of an ignorant race and the necessity of guidance from the higher vantage of white civilization. Voodoo particularly was a far cry from the spirituals, which could be more easily accepted as signs of moral accommodation to white Christian ways. Hence the special significance of the relativistic view given by African-American writer Zora Neale Hurston in "Hoodoo in America" (Hurston 1931). Influenced by the antiracist anthropology of Franz Boas, who wrote an introduction to her *Mules and Men*, Hurston carried further Hearn's implications of voodoo being a religious cultural system in its own right based on ethnic continuity (Hurston 1935, 1938).

Hearn left the problems of race relations in New Orleans behind and immersed himself in the homogeneous society of Japan. He extolled the serenity of well-preserved tradition in Japan and uttered his disgust at the materialistic West that lost its soul in the crusade for industrial progress. He continued to write (and took teaching posts) on folklore as a location for antimodern values and gained considerable renown for collections of Japanese ancient myths and ghostly legends. Yet the very same enrapturement with old Japan that made him interesting to American readers also made him seem all the more bizarre, blind to the promise of Western modernization. Embracing the mystical traditions of Buddhism in Japan, Hearn alienated himself further from American outlooks. Considering Western advances in Asia to be a harmful intrusion, he chided evolutionary folklorists for their support of industrial progress that spurred imperialism.

Despite the efforts of Cable and Hearn to expose the unrestrained urban possibilities of postbellum black life and cultural miscegenation, literary uses of black folklore during the Gilded Age remained primarily attached to the romanticized antebellum plantation. The images of spiritual song and superstition appeared in relation to control of whites and a static rural environment. They fed an ideology of accommodation necessary, so the thinking went, for a people cut off from a native culture and dependent on whites for guidance. In "Shadowy Memories of Negro-Lore" written for *The Folk-Lorist* in 1892 by a former slave owner, the author affirmed the importance of "attempting to trace to their origin the superstitions of the race" (Barron 1892, 46). Yet as "backward" as Negro folklore appeared to him, he noted that it was decidedly different from the "aboriginal state," presumably because of the civilizing effect of the plantation. He emphasized that, "the

Illustration by Edward Windsor Kemble of slavery from *Daddy Jake, The Runaway and Short Stories Told after Dark* by "Uncle Remus" (1889), by Joel Chandler Harris. The caption read, "The Field-Hands Were Singing as They Picked the Opening Cotton."

Southern negroes had in antebellum days many notions, beliefs, traditions and superstitions similar to those set down as peculiar to English, French, or Norse countries. You will at once declare this to be likely enough, the thing indeed to be expected, considering the mixed condition of the society in which they were held in slavery. Americans being a heterogeneous people, assembled from all parts of the world, it is naturally to be supposed that their slaves would pick up and assimilate the multifarious folk-lore of the household" (Barron 1892, 47–48). From the view of this author, blacks received rather than created traditions under the institution of plantation slavery. Indeed they were served culturally by the plantation system and, in a portent of the future, seemed to operate best within it.

Within the discourse of the Gilded Age, the constructed, and contested, images of folklore from the southern plantation are especially evident in the awesome popular response to Brer Rabbit tales proffered by Joel Chandler Harris (1848–1908). Born in Eatonton, Georgia, to a struggling, fatherless family, he apprenticed at the tender age of fourteen to a weekly plantation newspaper, *The Countryman*, where he absorbed the concerns and events of the South through the Civil War. He bounced around newspapers in New Orleans and various towns in Georgia until landing an editing position in 1876 at the major daily *Atlanta Constitution*, where he stayed for twenty-four years. The editorial tone of the

Constitution resisted northern pressure to reconstruct the South. It was the editor of the *Constitution*, in fact, that howled the loudest in rebuttals of George Washington Cable's editorials for social equality of the races in the 1880s. Literary pieces placed in the paper often tendered reassuring nostalgia for the Old South before the Civil War.

In line with the Old South theme, Harris developed humorous sketches in dialect that he drew from the everyday life he knew as a child in Georgia. In 1879, the paper published his tale of the rabbit outwitting a threatening fox as told by a genial old slave named Uncle Remus. While it might have seemed a shift to give a black voice in the newspaper, the story's setting on a plantation, exuding a natural pleasantness and stable social order, was in keeping with the images commonly set before its readers. The sensation the story created took the author and his paper aback, especially when over a thousand requests came in for reprintings shortly after the piece appeared. A little over a year after the first story was published in the newspaper, Harris hurriedly collected his material into the first book presenting Uncle Remus's tales. The illustrations of the Remus character added to the text by Frederick Church and James Moser in the early editions set an endearing and lasting portrait of Remus, smiling, bespectacled, and bearded, spinning his tales to a wide-eyed white boy on the antebellum plantation.

With the creation of the Uncle Remus storytelling character and the popularization of his Brer Rabbit stories set on the old plantation, Harris fixed an image of slavery times in American consciousness of black folklore and brought the ideology of accommodation into view. Harris made sure to indicate the benevolence of the slave plantation system in his introduction to the first set of Uncle Remus stories. His parting words in the essay were: "If the reader not familiar with plantation life will imagine that the myth-stories of Uncle Remus are told night after night to a little boy by an old Negro who appears to be venerable enough to have lived during the period which he describes—who has nothing but pleasant memories of the discipline of slavery—and who has all the prejudices of caste and pride of family that were the natural result of the system." These words flew up at William Francis Allen, the groundbreaking compiler of black spirituals. Allen angrily wrote in his review of the book for *Dial* of the "moral for those who cannot see how the freed slaves should ever act politically with their old masters." Allen complained of this attitude in favor of an "unaccountable servility of spirit" that formed a main obstacle to necessary reconstruction of the South. While another reviewer eleven years later in *Dial* admitted the "great wrong" of slavery, he saw in Harris's volume a case for preserving the best qualities of blacks during that period into freedom: "full of quaint good sense, full of affection, of good humor, and of natural courtesy."[5]

Folklorists meanwhile jumped on the issue of the tales' origin to test evolutionary ideas about cultural survivals in America. Harris invited commentary on the matter by affirming that animal stories he heard and faithfully rendered in dialect assuredly came from Africa. Lest this view sound overly sympathetic to a case for

Illustration by A. B. Frost from *Uncle Remus: His Songs and Sayings* (1880), by Joel Chandler Harris. The caption was "Brer Rabbit ain't see no peace w'atsumever."

Illustration by Milo Winter of Brer Rabbit as a trickster figure outwitting Brer Fox, from the story "Brer Rabbit's Riddle" in *Tales from Uncle Remus,* by Joel Chandler Harris (copyright 1911 and 1935 by Esther La Rose Harris). The caption read "Brer Rabbit Turnt 'Er Aloose, En Down She Come—*Ker-Swosh!*" The story originally appeared in *Nights with Uncle Remus: Myths and Legends of the Old Plantation* (1883). (Reprinted by permission of Houghton Mifflin Company. All rights reserved.)

black cultural continuity, Harris hedged his bets by noting unexplainable parallels to the story outside of black influence and speculated on a pre-African origin. He contrasted the Uncle Remus character, who owed his good manner to whites and told his stories to a white boy, with a later invention, African Jack, who spoke Gullah dialect and seemed primitive and more dangerous by comparison. In subsequent volumes of Remus's tales, Harris tired of evolutionary speculation and emphasized the literary value of what he offered while maintaining that he genuinely rendered the stories from oral tradition. In the years after Harris's tales were published, hundreds of collections of animal stories from southern blacks collaborated his claims to oral tradition and a frenzy for finding variations and origins ensued to locations as remote as India and Japan (Griffis 1893).

If Harris sounded like an unreconstructed Southerner in the 1881 edition of *Uncle Remus,* his proposal for the function of the trickster rabbit in many of the stories anticipated later interpretations and retellings of black resistance in the performance of the animal stories (see Levine 1977; Lester 1987, 1989). He swore "it needs no scientific investigation to show why he [the Negro] selects as his hero the weakest and most harmless of all animals, and brings him out victorious in contests with the bear, the wolf, and the fox. It is not virtue that triumphs, but helplessness; it is not malice, but mischievousness." Yet softening the blow of this revelation, Harris took the position that an interpretation of the stories as "allegorical … may be unreasonable."

As the Uncle Remus stories became nationally and then internationally known, Harris took the part of children's entertainer rather than southern interpreter. He changed much of his tune by singing the praises of universal moral themes in the stories such as avoiding stinginess or being honest rather than referencing social struggles in the South. In the 1892 edition of *Uncle Remus and His Friends,* Harris retreated from his earlier "serious" intentions by quipping, "I knew a good deal more about comparative folk-lore then than I know now." He avoided functional, or political, commentary, proclaiming that "the stories … were written simply and solely because of my interest in the stories themselves, in the first place, and in the second place, because of the unadulterated human nature that might be found in them." He deflated the impact of the stories by juvenilizing them, turning them into entertainment for children, especially white children, rather than an expression of black subversion. He explained: "As I wrote them with my own children around me, or with their voices sounding not far away, I seemed to see other children laughing as the homely stories were read to them" (Harris 1892).

In the Gilded Age discourse on the status of black culture in America generated by an outpouring of titles on Brer Rabbit stories particularly and songs and superstitions generally, opinions of blacks themselves on their folklore appeared conspicuously absent. But an organized movement at Hampton Institute changed that. The school founded in 1868 in Hampton, Virginia, had featured black choirs singing spirituals and folk songs since the 1870s. Its publication, the *Southern Workman,* founded in 1872, featured essays on slave life and lore. Guiding a student body made up of 537 blacks and 135 Indians, the newly appointed principal in 1893, the Reverend Hollis B. Frissell, intended to expand the school's efforts in folklore to mark racial progress from the uneducated state of slavery to the present. Thinking of the Indians in his school who had what he considered a developed sense of their rich cultural tradition, Frissell worried that blacks "would stand as an anomaly among civilized races, as a people having no distinct traditions, beliefs or ideas from which a history of their growth may be traced" (Sharps 1991, 30). He fretted that in the educated black tendency to repress the memory of slavery almost thirty years after emancipation, a valuable cultural inheritance was slipping away. From that cultural inheritance, he argued, the "progress of the race" could be held up to inspire black achievement and white support. The person who became primarily responsible for launching a movement for blacks to interpret themselves turned out to be a white teacher at the school named Alice Mabel Bacon (1858–1918).

The daughter of an abolitionist Congregationalist minister, Bacon had come from New Haven, Connecticut, in 1883 to Hampton to teach and help with the operation of the school. It was a return trip actually, since she had spent a year there in her childhood residing with her sister Rebecca, then assistant principal of the newly established school. She attended classes with blacks and developed a fascination with their spirituals. A member of the American Folklore Society, Bacon knew several founders from their philanthropic and administrative connections to Hampton. Alice Cunningham Fletcher, who made her fame in collections of Omaha tribal folklore, was a Hampton teacher and administrator, and Thomas Wentworth Higginson, who wrote on black folk song, was a Hampton trustee. Bacon was named an editor of the school's journal, *Southern Workman*, and initiated a "Folklore and Ethnology Department." With many of her duties focused on training of teachers for service in black schools, she saw folklore as a connection that the educated blacks could make to their students and environments in the rural South.

Bacon came up with the idea of forming a folklore society at Hampton after reading "Science and the African Problem" by eminent Harvard educator Nathaniel Southgate Shaler (1841-1906) in *Atlantic Monthly* for July 1890 (see also Shaler 1884, 1886, 1895, 1900). Bacon was so impressed with the article she reprinted it the same year in the *Workman*. Shaler had been born into a slaveholding family in Kentucky, and many family members joined the Confederate forces during the Civil War; but he fought on the Union side. He referred to himself as an "ex-Southerner" concerned for the future progress of the region if it did not adequately deal with its racial divide. In the annals of science, he became renowned as an early American proponent of evolutionary theory, breaking away from his famous naturalist mentor, Louis Agassiz. A regular contributor to the popular magazines *Atlantic Monthly*, *Popular Science Monthly*, and *Arena*, Shaler frequently applied the rising evolutionary theories to social issues of immigration and race (see

Alice M. Bacon at Hampton University. (Hampton University Archives)

Shaler 1893, 1895). Primarily known as a naturalist and geologist (he also wrote books on government and philosophy), he suggested a "scientific" organization for recording the cultural history of blacks according to natural science principles, in an effort to solve their social problems (Shaler 1890). He argued that the data would be invaluable in establishing black "progress in civilization," which was a prerequisite for equal participation in modern industrial society. Putting his faith in science for providing a social solution, he declared the goal that the collecting work "would give to all who are interested in him [the Negro], data from which to *reason* toward more efficient work" (Sharps 1991, 33; emphasis added).

Principal Frissell and teacher Bacon became enthusiastic about Hampton, translating Shaler's call into a focus on folklore work because it helped build the ideological case for the school's approach to the "Negro question." The school was devoted to vocational training that would economically uplift blacks before social equality could be achieved. It would join blacks to the drive for materialism as a mark of success during the Gilded Age. Toward this end, it encouraged development of an economically viable yeomanry composed of black masses serving the South. It presumed a need for slow and steady social progress and the secondary importance of intellectual pursuits as signs of advancement (Warren 1996). It was a doctrine publicized by Booker T. Washington, Hampton's best-known student and the driving force at the industrial school at Tuskegee Institute. Underscoring the connection of awareness of black traditions and industrial progress at Hampton and Tuskegee, Washington bragged that the schools had "done more good, and, in the true sense of the word, been more cultural than all the Greek and Latin that have ever been studied by all Negroes in all the colleges in the country" (Sharps 1991, 149).

At the same Atlanta Exposition where Washington made his famous speech calling for economic preparedness before social equality could be achieved, Hampton had a featured exhibition on black material progress staffed by members of the Hampton Folklore Society and documented in a book by Alice Bacon (Bacon 1896). The book, in fact, reprinted the text of Washington's speech. Washington understood the value of her folklore project in supporting his accommodationist ideology and expressed the hope that such an enterprise would reveal "the true history of the race." He additionally proposed to collect "in some museum the relics that mark its [the race's] progress" (Verney 1996, 148). That evolutionary history tended to view the antebellum plantation as a "civilizing school" for blacks, tearing them away from African savagery and in Washington's words giving them "a stronger and more hopeful condition, materially, intellectually, morally and religiously, than is true of an equal number of black people in any other portion of the globe" (Sharps 1991, 138). The collection of antebellum black folklore, joined to plantation life, could establish a tradition for blacks that rationalized commitment to, rather than departure from, the South. Echoing Frissell's cry for recovering a cultural tradition to mark racial progress, Washington advised his black brethren: "We must have pride of race. We must be as proud of being a Negro as the Japanese is of being a Japanese" (Verney 1996, 147). Washington's comparison raises the possibility that he had indeed Bacon's other major project at a national tradition in mind, for she spent several years at work in Japan on folklore, and Washington for all his overseas travel never visited Asia (Bacon 1894, 1905; Verney 1996, 148).

Following attendance at the Chicago World's Fair, where Hampton had an exhibition of "Negro progress" and a folklore congress had been held, Bacon prepared a circular letter to graduates of Hampton in 1893 encouraging the formation of a folklore society that would have as its object "the education of the colored people to do their own observing and collecting; to watch the little things peculiar to their own race, and to record them and place them where they can be made of permanent value" (Bacon 1898, 17). Attached to the letter were testimonials of support for the project from luminaries Booker T. Washington, George Washington Cable, Thomas Wentworth Higginson, William Wells Newell, Alexander Crummell, and Nathaniel Southgate Shaler. The letter warned that if preservation of the lore was not undertaken, then the common school system and loss of memory would combine to eradicate any sense of a distinct American black tradition. The letter insisted on the responsibility of educated blacks to appreciate the heritage of the largely uneducated masses and implied that this task was made all the more pressing by the misinterpretation of black folklore by white literati. Bacon wrote that the work

> must be done by observers who enter into the homes and lives of the more ignorant colored people and who see in their beliefs and customs no occasion for scorn or contempt or laughter, but only the showing forth of the first child-like but still reasoning philosophy of a race reaching after some interpretation of its surroundings and its antecedents. To such observers every custom, belief, or superstition, foolish and empty to others, will be of value and will be worth careful preservation. This work cannot be done by white people, much as many of them would enjoy the opportunity of doing it, but must be done by the intelligent and educated colored people who are at work all through the South among the more ignorant of their race, teaching, preaching, practicing medicine, carrying on business of any kind that brings them into close contact with the simple, old-time ways of their own people. (Bacon 1893, 306)

If the call for racial pride, and appreciation for the southern black tradition, suggested bonds to the masses that hinted at black nationalism, another side to the appeal was confirmation that Hampton graduates represented the most likely elite to lead them to integration with whites. In the words of prominent Hampton graduate and folklorist Robert Moton, "I know of no institution that inculcated more throughly, and I believe more successfully, the missionary idea—that every student is trained not alone that he may make a better citizen but that he may devote himself to the elevation of his people" (Sharps 1991, 104). It did not escape the notice of Principal Frissell that showing the backwardness of southern blacks reinforced the

Robert R. Moton as a student at Hampton University. (Hampton University Archives)

Robert R. Moton as principal of Tuskegee Institute. (Hampton University Archives)

value of Hampton's approach to education (Sharps 1991, 30). This set up a potentially damaging admission, as historian Kenneth Warren has described it, that "whatever its intent, uplift necessarily presumed some degree of depravity, incapacity, backwardness, and general unfitness as being prevalent among the black population" (Warren 1996, 1595). Calhoun School in Alabama, founded by Hampton faculty, for instance, accomplished cultural and economic progress because it was set in the "midst of a small cabin population of ignorant and degraded black people," so *Southern Workman* reported in 1894 ("Report" 1894). The backwardness attributed to black folk culture could be checked, however, by the reminders of pride of tradition it provided and the promise of joining the material progress of the age.

Washington and Frissell rhetorically expressed tradition and progress as social virtues especially enjoyed by whites. Washington thus rallied members of the Negro Business League by references to folklore of slavery and then proclaimed, "Let us go from this great meeting filled with a spirit of race pride; rejoicing in the fact that we belong to a race that has made greater progress within fifty years than any race in history" (Verney 1996, 147). Another example of this "check" on the perceived black "folk" class came from Bacon in 1897. Reflecting on the work of the society, she simultaneously noted efforts to "preserve a record of customs and beliefs *now happily passing away*, but which connect the negro's African and American *past with his present*" (Bacon 1898, 18; emphasis added). Her view was that black folklore emanating primarily from the plantation provided a valued identity, "a racial pride," which would impel contemporary efforts toward material progress.

In Bacon's rhetoric, the Hampton Folklore Society represented a black-led "movement." It was motivated less by scientific interest than social needs. She told the American Folklore Society in 1897 that "it arose, to begin with not in enthusiasm for the collection of folklore, but from a strong desire on the part of some of those connected with the Hampton work to bridge over, if possible, the great gulf fixed between the minds of the educated and the uneducated, the civilized and the uncivilized,—to enter more deeply into the daily life of the common people, and to understand more thoroughly their ideas and motives" (Bacon 1898, 17). The Folklore Society, she underscored in the same address, was designed to understand "present conditions," translated as social problems. The first public meeting was held the day after the college's commencement ceremony in 1894 and featured an encouraging address by William Wells Newell of the American Folklore Society. Blacks from the onset led the group's organization and held monthly meetings for those close to Hampton. Bacon left for Japan in 1899 and did not return to the school after her return to the United States in 1902.

The zealous devotion to Hampton exhibited by its graduates sustained the Hampton Folklore Society for many years. The society maintained a broad network of correspondents, who would often gather at reunions and school anniversaries. It forged links to folklore projects at Hampton's affiliated schools, including first and foremost Calhoun Colored School (Calhoun, Alabama) followed by Tuskegee Institute (Tuskegee, Alabama), People's Village School (Mt. Meigs, Alabama), Penn School (St. Helena, South Carolina), and Gloucester Agricultural and Industrial School (Cappahoosie, Virginia). It had communication with other fledgling organizations devoted to black folklore study such as the Washington Negro Folklore Society and the Asheville Folklore Society. Hampton thus became a flagship for a fleet of folklore projects to collect American black folklore. William Wells Newell, secretary of the American Folklore Society, urged the Hampton folklorists to form a Virginia or Negro branch of the national society, but they insisted on keeping the Hampton label as a symbol of the society's driving ideology. It publicized the society's "scientific" folklore work in the name of the institution's educational mission. Although Alice Bacon became a member of the American Folklore Society's executive council, the Hampton Society always remained independent from the national organization.

Southern Workman enthusiastically published notices of the Hampton group's projects and meetings. Bacon's editorial hand in reporting the society's collections avoided alterations and value judgments. Most of the material consisted of beliefs and folktales connected to the plantation South, which were occasionally reprinted in the *Journal of American Folklore*. In the avoidance of African traditions and the emphasis on plantation material was indeed an implication of acculturation, if not positive moral effects, during the slavery era.

In answer to white retellings of black folklore by the likes of Joel Chandler Harris, Hampton folklorists demanded exacting transcriptions of Brer Rabbit stories and supernatural accounts from tradition-bearers (see Bolden 1899; Washington 1895; see also Waters 1983). Although encouraging uses of southern plantation folklore by black writers such as Charles Chesnutt and Paul Laurence Dunbar, Hampton folklorists could also be critical of their black brethren as much as white authors for taking liberties with oral tradition or appearing insensitive to Hampton's ideology. They harshly reviewed Chesnutt's *Conjure Woman* (1899) for misrepresenting the conjuring tradition, which they had faithfully recorded, and they took Paul Laurence Dunbar to task for "a lack of appreciation of the character of the best South" (Sharps 1991, 198–99).

In keeping with their doctrine of fidelity to tradition, the Hampton folklorists avoided reporting folk songs. As Bacon explained, "The Hampton School has already done much work in the line of collecting, arranging for our system of musical notation, and publishing, the negro spirituals, but that is not the kind of work our Society wishes to do. Our desire is, not to obtain any song in a more or less changed or mangled condition, as you surely do when you take it out of its foreordained and appropriate setting in some part of the complicated negro religious ritual, and adapt it to be sung as a regular four-part song by a choir or congregation, either white or black" (Bacon 1898, 19–20). As laid out in the original circular letter, the Society's priorities were first the folktales, including the well-known animal tales, and second, customs, "especially in connection with birth, marriage, and death, that are different from those of whites." Bacon explained that "the old nurse, who first takes the little baby in her arms, has great store of old-fashioned learning about what to do and what not to do to start the child auspiciously upon the voyage of life" (Bacon 1894, 306). The society's emphasis on oral literacy and folk medical practices could be tied to vocational interests at Hampton. In addition to its teacher training program, Bacon had initiated a drive for the "Dixie Hospital" that opened in 1891 to provide nursing education and scientific medical care.

Among the black leadership of the Hampton Society emerged several figures such as Robert Russa Moton and Frank Dean Banks who attended American Folklore Society meetings and published folklore scholarship. Cementing the connection of Hampton to Tuskegee, Robert Moton (1867–1940) became Tuskegee's second principal after Washington died, while Banks, vice president and treasurer of the Hampton Folklore Society, was a Tuskegee board member (Moton 1921). Long-time president of the Hampton Folklore Society Frederick Douglass Wheelock had been a librarian at Tuskegee. While organized folklore collecting by these black educators became centered at Tuskegee in Alabama and Hampton in Virginia, the efforts of the group ranged beyond the South. In 1902 Hampton folklorists drew wide notice with the organization of a folklore concert at Carnegie Hall in New York City (Sharps 1991, 63–64). The rhetoric for the concert iterated the theme of promoting "race pride [of Negroes] by giving ... more respect for their customs and traditions" (Sharps 1991, 63–64). Moton particularly espoused the importance of the movement for interpretations by blacks of their own past and future. In the title of his book *What the Negro Thinks*, he gave notice that indeed blacks could intellectualize their own situation (Moton 1929).

While the collectors became a close-knit group tied with their folklore interest and allegiance to Hampton, the generation of Moton (class of 1889), Banks (class of 1876), and Wheelock (class of 1888) did not effectively sustain the organized work of the Hampton Folklore Society past World War I, although folklore studies persisted at Hampton. One factor affecting the attitude toward the original group's mission was that Hampton's vocational curriculum and accommodationist ideology underwent a sea change with the succession of principal Frissell by James Gregg in 1918. Yet the society's work came back into national notice through publications of unpublished material after World War I by Elsie Clews Parsons and Calhoun School graduate Portia Smiley. The editors framed the works, however, as raw data without comment on the organizing principles of "progress of the race" (see Bacon and Parsons 1922; Smiley 1919). By the time the groundbreaking collections found new audiences, a rethinking of the role of folklore in African-American life, particularly traditions of the old plantation, was evident among notable black leaders. The result was several directions that recast folklore in light of ideologies that challenged the Hampton movement.

In December 1896 Alexander Crummell, who had sent in a letter of support to the Hampton Folklore Society three years before, invited distinguished college-educated men to Washington, D.C. Crummell differed from the leaders of the Hampton movement in being a northerner, born in New York in 1819 to a family of free blacks. He had studied in England and was a missionary to Liberia. He had collected his learned essays into a volume called *Africa and America* in 1892. He expressed devotion to "preservation of traditions, folklore, ancestral remembrances, etc." that would reveal the ancestral "derivation of the American Negroes" in Africa (Sharps 1991, 158; Bacon 1894, 307). Beyond his irritation at the lack of attention to African origins and uncritical portrayal of plantation slavery by the Hampton folklorists, he increasingly felt discomfort with the ideology behind their effort to promote industrial education and emphasize the drive for material progress over the urgency of political rights.

A coterie of eighteen young learned men, many of whom taught classics in American universities, answered the call from the elderly luminary in 1897 and formed the American Negro Academy (ANA). Crummell explained its purpose to advance their race toward civilization by embracing the spirituality of Christianity and "the life of the mind" (Moss 1981, 39–40). He urged the group to find a different voice from Washington's to lead blacks to social progress in the new century. According to a chronicler of Hampton's relationship to the ANA, the

> ANA objection to the Hampton plan was broader and deeper than the mere cause of classical versus industrial education. The issue centered on the concept of civilization and Negro character. The academy creed asserted a belief "that the Negro people, as a race, have a contribution to make to civilization and humanity, which no other race can make," and that race identity must be maintained until that mission was accomplished and "the ideal of human brotherhood has become a practical possibility." Folklore was significant to an understanding of both the processes of civilization and the raising of race consciousness. (Sharps 1991, 165–66)

Among those processes of civilization in dispute were the uniqueness of black cultural expressions and ability of blacks to master intellectual pursuits. ANA publicist Anna Julia Cooper explained "the fact that the Negro's ability to work had never been called in question, while his ability to learn Latin and construe Greek syntax needed to be proved to sneering critics" (Cooper 1969, 260).

Cooper had endorsed the work of the Hampton Folklore Society but later urged it to change its tack. She along with another ANA member, William Scarborough, who addressed the Hampton Folklore Conferences of 1896 and 1899, wanted folklore used as a basis of a black intellectual renaissance emphasizing artistic uses. They understood such an effort to involve the rise of a distinct civilization, not tied to whites and led by black elites. Referring to folklore and classics together, Cooper said poetically, "if one had the insight and simplicity to gather together, to digest and assimilate these original lispings of an unsophisticated people while they were yet close—so close—to nature and to nature's God, there is material here, one might almost believe, as rich, as unhackneyed, as original and distinctive as ever inspired a Homer, or a Caedmon or other simple genius of a people's infancy and lisping childhood" (Sharps 1991, 173). Scarborough, born a slave in Georgia, was one of many classics teachers in the academy. He assaulted the cultural destruction to the race in slavery and iterated the call to creative uses of African-American tradition and intellect in an editorial for the academy in 1903. The encouragement of achievement in the arts, he insisted, kept "before the world the fact that the Negro possesses intellect; that he is both able and capable, and that through this possession and training the race proposes to develop its civilization" (Scarborough 1903, 3).

Another teacher of Greek and Latin who took on the leadership of the academy, indeed of the dissident movement for black intellectual development and political rights, was W. E. B. DuBois (1868–1963). At the first meeting of the academy, DuBois stirred the audience with a reading of "The Conservation of the Races." Referring to his intellectual audience as "the advance guard" of the black masses, he unabashedly argued that their destiny is "*not* absorption by the white Americans." Critical of the "immorality, crime and laziness" among the black masses, which he blamed on "a heritage of slavery," he urged leadership of the intellectual elite in the effort for the uplifting of American blacks. His rhetoric for racial pride was similar to the Hampton movement at the time, but his goal appeared to be separation rather than integration of the black masses.

DuBois's platform was to push for aggressive political agitation and artistic applications of black contributions. In another call for renaissance, he emphatically pronounced, "that if in America it is to be proven for the first time in the modern world that not only Negroes are capable of evolving individual men like Toussaint, the Saviour, but are a nation stored with wonderful possibilities of culture, then their destiny is not a servile imitation of Anglo-Saxon culture, but a stalwart originality which shall unswervingly follow Negro ideals" (DuBois 1986, 820). With Crummell's death a year after the first meeting of the ANA, DuBois became president of the group, serving for the next five years. In 1905, DuBois issued a redoubled civil rights call "for organized determination and aggressive action on the part of men who believe in Negro freedom and growth" (DuBois 1986, 618). Meeting near Buffalo, New York, the group declared themselves the Niagara Movement, openly hostile to what DuBois called the "Hampton-Tuskegee machine" of Booker T. Washington.

DuBois, like Crummell, was a northerner, born in Great Barrington, Massachusetts, in 1868, but he attended Fisk University in Nashville, Tennessee, before going to Harvard for a second B.A. in 1890, and Ph.D. in 1895. He described the black South as foreign to his existence; it was in his mind "the South of slavery, rebellion and black folk" where he was "thrilled to be for the first time among so many people of my own color … which I had only glimpsed before, but who it seemed were bound to me by new and exciting and eternal ties" (DuBois 1986, 569).

While still north, he had an emotional response to a symbol of the South, which he referred to often as a life-changing moment for him. He heard for the first time "Negro folk songs" performed by the Hampton Quartet. He recalled the moment as fixing his attention to black tradition: "I was thrilled and moved to tears and seemed to recognize something inherently and deeply my own" (DuBois 1986, 570).

Connecting the urban North to the rural South, DuBois undertook an ambitious sociological study of black Philadelphia and its sources in rural Virginia when Crummell issued his invitation to the ANA. He then went south to join the faculty of Atlanta University but defiantly refused to patronize segregated facilities or transportation. He left Atlanta for New York, where he edited *The Crisis* for the National Association for the Advancement of Colored People (NAACP). His reputation grew as an unrelenting critic of American racism and a forceful advocate for civil rights. Toward these ends he promoted projects showcasing the history of American blacks reaching back to Africa. In 1913, he staged a history pageant called "The Star of Ethiopa" in New York, followed two years later by publication of *The Negro*, an overview of black history and culture. Realization of a racial tradition going back to Africa served DuBois's cause by proclaiming a cultural vitality deserving of black self-pride as well as American intellectual and social respect.

The role of folklore in DuBois's rhetoric can be seen in his classic work, *The Souls of Black Folk* (1903). Every chapter heading was emblazoned with a bar of a spiritual, which he emphasized in his introduction as "Sorrow Songs." The book culminated in the last chapter with a case for the spiritual as a metaphor for black experience. Its emotion and sacredness provided the "soul" of a resistant enslaved culture, and its singers were the "primitive folk," capable of expressing vibrant beauty despite their bondage. The sorrow of the songs was for the cruelty of slavery and the destruction of cultural integrity. Rather than gaining civilization in slavery and finding new roots in the rural South, DuBois found civilization prior to America and implied a remigration to find cultural renewal. He read in the lyrics of the folk songs hope as well as faith in social justice that would allow blacks to be themselves. "Persistently mistaken and misunderstood," the black folk song to DuBois constituted the only "spiritual heritage of the nation" and was the greatest gift of African heritage to the world.

In declaring a struggle to establish a racially egalitarian society in America, DuBois beheld black strength above all in its sacred traditions. He insisted on rebuilding black culture on its distinctive features, rather than imitating the legacy of whites. Referring to evolutionary theories of progress, DuBois reinterpreted the role of American blacks on the ladder of civilization. "Like all primitive folk, the slave stood near to Nature's heart," DuBois wrote (DuBois 1989, 210). From the path taken from there to the present, DuBois drew a different conclusion. Instead of concluding that the "backward races of today are of proven inefficiency and not worth the saving," DuBois saw sometimes greater virtue in the original. Seeing in the classics a lesson for the priority of an enlightenment previous to modern industrialism, DuBois asked "Why should Aeschylus have sung two thousand years before Shakespeare was born?" In fact, he saw in ancient civilizations on the African and Asian continents a counterargument to the "dogmatism" of the "blond races" leading civilization. His version of civilization provided a basis in his mind for commanding wisdom and justice through classical pursuits in need of being regained. It implied an antimaterialist construction of culture in need of renewal. He posed haunting questions from the plantation folk song: "Sometime, somewhere, men will judge men by their souls and not by their skins. Is such a hope justified? Do the Sorrow Songs sing true?" (DuBois 1989).

For DuBois as well as many critics of evolutionary doctrine, the "barbarism" of World War I was a severe blow to a model of European-American industrial enlightenment promised by the ideology of cultural evolution. Indeed, commentators on the "Great War" often viewed it as a terminus for the Gilded Age that crushed the self-confidence in the evolutionary progress of the West (Kern 1983). With the brutal reality of the mechanized war made vividly clear in the world press, DuBois wrote, "The day of camouflage is past." His harshest indictment came in "An Essay Toward a History of the Black Man in the Great War" originally appearing in *Crisis* in 1919 (DuBois 1986, 879–922). "To everyone war is, and, thank God, must be, disillusion," DuBois baldly wrote. He explained that "this war has disillusioned millions of fighting white men—disillusioned them with its frank truth of dirt, disease, cold, wet and discomfort; murder, maiming and hatred.... But the story of stories is that of the American Negro" (DuBois 1986, 880). He caustically observed that "we gained the right to fight for civilization at the cost of being 'Jim-Crowed' and insulted; we were segregated in the draft; we were segregated in the first officers' training camp; and we were allowed to volunteer only as servants in the Navy and as common laborers in the Army, outside of four regular Negro regiments" (DuBois 1986, 881).

DuBois exposed racist policies practiced by the American army and concluded that no longer could the United States claim to be on the highest rungs of civilization when it possessed starkly vicious social attitudes. To DuBois and other critics, the carnage of the war discredited any claims Europeans had to a superior civilization. Instead of seeing race as a natural state suggested by the evolutionary anthropologists, DuBois argued for race as a phenomenon of the modern era and its intersection with capitalist class formation engineered by European whites (Holt 1995, 189). Increasingly calling for black separatism and embracing communist support, he split with the NAACP over the board's integrationist policies and became more estranged from reigning black leadership. Before he left *The Crisis* in 1934 in a bitter dispute with the NAACP, DuBois used the magazine to foster one of his goals of ushering a renaissance of black self-expression by publishing many black writers who drew on folklore, such as Langston Hughes, Jean Toomer, and Countee Cullen.

While DuBois became painted by his opponents as a dangerous radical after World War I, other leaders emerged with him who also used folklore in their rhetoric for social change. Charles S. Johnson (1893–1956) fought in France during the Great War, and upon his return became distressed by urban race riots in the North, especially during the bloody "Red Summer" of 1919. He subsequently decided on an academic career pursuing the social bases of racial conflicts. He became convinced that races could be integrated if historical and economic barriers were lifted. Like DuBois, he used the rhetoric of civilization to show that blacks have had a beneficial contribution to make to American culture (Johnson 1930). In contrast to DuBois's spiritual and aesthetic campaign for black self-expression, Johnson established *Opportunity* for the Urban League in 1923 to "scientifically" address social problems for blacks and whites in a common cause against traditions of prejudice.

Trained in sociology at the University of Chicago, Johnson undertook wide-ranging empirical research of the rural South at Fisk University that helped form an argument for integration. Ascending to the position of Fisk's first black president, he became widely recognized in the ranks of the nation's educational leaders. Earning the respect of white racial reform leaders, he provided heaps of social statistics to discount the reality of an inherent biological racial difference between blacks and whites. He posited the idea of a constructed "folk Negro" to describe the isolation of the rural black put in that position by historical and economic forces (Johnson 1930, 1934, 1967).

Johnson's studies were further ammunition against the evolutionary conception of the biological inferiority of darker races. He railed against stereotypes perpetuated by "the subtle handicap of tradition ... a sort of conspiracy of the ages" (Sharps 1991, 270). He found folklore significant for its psychological effect on both blacks and whites as a "vague and intangible world of feeling" (Sharps 1991, 273). In the first volume of *Opportunity*, Johnson penned an editorial called "Romulus and Uncle Remus," in which he viewed the way that traditions of the old-time Negro could be perpetuated by whites through a master narrative that clouded over actual changes in the black population. He wrote that "in these rapidly shifting scenes, when all classes are breaking with traditions and old moorings are being swept away, one is too apt to overlook the fact that Negroes themselves are subject to these same influences" (Johnson 1923, 195). In underscoring the need for social causation, he could be critical of DuBois's narrative of African priority as well as Joel Chandler Harris's image of the pleasant plantation.

With reference to Johnson's social scientific efforts to detail the "folk Negro," Alain Locke (1886–1954) pronounced a construction of the "New Negro" apparently removed from Gilded Age folklore of the Old South. In 1925, he wrote that "in the last decade something beyond the watch and guard of statistics has happened in the life of the American Negro.... The Sociologist, the Philanthropist, the Race leader are not unaware of the New Negro, but they are at a loss to account for him"

(Locke 1994, 22). Spotlighting a great migration of blacks to northern cities, Locke predicted a great divide between the folk tradition of the black South and a new "Twentieth Century civilization" being created in the North. Hailing from Philadelphia, Locke in 1907 had the distinction after his undergraduate study at Harvard of being the first black to be awarded the prestigious Rhodes Scholarship. He returned to Harvard to earn his doctorate in philosophy and taught at Howard University and City College of New York.

Locke used the model of Jews who had been able to form a distinct artistic consciousness out of prejudice heaped upon them. He saw in their urban experience on the Lower East Side of New York a dramatic shift from repressed village life of the Old World to New York intellectuals and artists in a single generation. Harlem to him was the new beginning, "the home of the Negro's 'Zionism'" (Locke 1994, 30). Setting a tone for a movement called the Harlem Renaissance, Locke declared that blacks could no longer be seen as peasant folk artists, but instead as modern cosmopolitans of a fresh period of history.

Although participants in the renaissance such as Zora Neale Hurston, Langston Hughes, and Arna Bontemps made artistic usage of folklore, they had a new urban audience and experimented with novel forms. Apparently less concerned for argument over the historical character of slavery or origin of folktales, they set a future course for innovative black expression in a new environment that joined a modern cultural democracy. The creative "pulse of the Negro world has begun to beat in Harlem," Locke enthusiastically announced. He drew attention to a new "second crop" of literary contributions separate from the first crop of the South's folk music and art. Setting the jazzed excitement of Harlem as the symbol for the new-fashioned vibrancy of black life, he scanned how the Negro "now becomes a conscious contributor and lays aside the status of a beneficiary and ward for that of a collaborator and participant in American civilization" (Locke 1994, 31). While black cosmopolitans might be inspired by the rhythm and emotion of southern black tradition, Locke believed that ultimately "the American mind must reckon with a fundamentally changed Negro" and, with that reckoning, different kinds of racial relationships in a plural American culture (Locke 1994, 25). Locke's manifesto had a major intellectual effect of loosening allegiance to southern tradition and its attachment to folklore. He foresaw in the swirling northern city a creative independence, indeed, "a spiritual Coming of Age." He obscured the Gilded Age priority of "making material headway and progress" for the race in favor of the cosmopolitan ideal of creative "self-expression and spiritual development" (Locke 1994, 31).

RELATIVISM AND THE DIVERSITY OF AMERICAN CULTURE

Not far from Harlem, Franz Boas (1858–1942) at Columbia used the lessons of American black and Indian folklore to encourage replacement of evolutionary

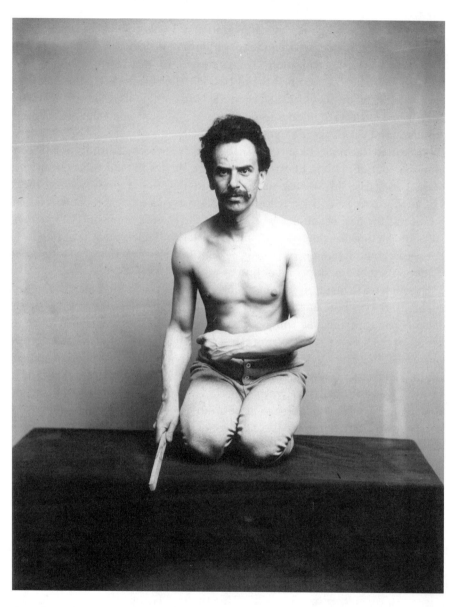

Franz Boas demonstrating a Northwest Indian ritual for the Bureau of American Ethnology. (National Anthropological Archives, Smithsonian Institution)

"progress of the race" with a relativism of plural cultures. That relativism, he noted, countered a racist undertone in evolutionary thought of connecting biological differences to a cultural hierarchy from dark to white peoples. He had worked on the evolutionary exhibitions for the Chicago World's Fair and had been hired by the Smithsonian's Otis Mason in 1894 to collect Northwest Indian ritual objects. But in the multiethnic atmosphere of New York City toward the turn of the century, his writing increasingly showed skepticism of evolutionary claims. After assaulting in print the methods of evolutionary anthropologists and folklorists, he severed his ties with institutions that promoted cultural evolutionary doctrine (Boas 1896). He resigned from the Museum of Natural History and criticized the powerful Bureau of American Ethnology. He opposed American entrance into World War I, which earned him censure from the American Anthropological Association. Facing resistance in the association to his demands for a relativist agenda, he used the American Folklore Society and the *Journal of American Folklore*, which he controlled as editor, to expand on his vision of culture as holistic, relativistic, and pluralistic (Liss 1995).

Boas established an academic program in anthropology at Columbia University and advanced a way of thinking about cultures applying the new idea of relativity known in physics. Relativity assumed that one's view, one's cultural patterns, depended on the time and space one occupied. If that was the case, then cultures were relative to one another rather than arranged in hierarchies. Cultures were not united into a march to civilization but ranged widely in their histories, locations, and social structures. Boas sketched distinctive patterns for each culture and came up with a level ethnographic map of many whole cultures around the world instead of an outline of a converging ladder with succeeding rungs of savagery, barbarism, and civilization.

Boas explained cultural similarities by the diffusion of ideas between cultures rather than an evolutionary rise, and he introduced ideas of individual psychology into the evaluation of styles of cultural expression. He embraced folklore as primary cultural evidence to reveal the particular character of a group and the ways that cultural ideas move. Folklore for Boas comprised the tales and myths that revealed the specific values and history within a bounded group. Using folklore even more than linguistics or physical anthropology, he described cultures by their geographical spread and special conditions rather than by their level and type (Reichard 1943; Jacobs 1959b).

In Boas's view, the world was varied, heterogeneous, and simultaneous. Its cultures needed mapping and observing in their totalities, rather than what he thought of as the purging of their cultural specimens. From his position of power at Columbia University, Boas and his students controlled the American Folklore Society after the turn of the century, and offered the intellectual foundations for twentieth-century views of race and society that supplanted Victorian ideas of cultural evolution. At the same time, Boas pushed the study of folklore into academe, isolating it from the center of public consumption it had enjoyed in the late nineteenth century. As editor of the *Journal of American Folklore* from 1908 to 1924, Boas published many dissertations and studies completed under his direction at Columbia University that emphasized the distinctiveness of cultures. The distinctiveness could be measured by the use of folklore as a reflection of a group's special social and historical conditions.

After Boas stepped down as editor, his influence continued at the journal because his students Ruth Benedict and Gladys Reichard maintained the editorial helm until 1941. A new generation weary of the previous generation's dubious grand claims took the place of the older "scientific men and women" who had touted evolution as rational explanation of cultural variety and industrial advancement. The first editor of the *Journal of American Folklore,* William Wells Newell, recognized that evolutionary doctrine, apparently so well suited to the nineteenth century, would not last in the new century. In 1901 he wrote in the journal: "From the small body of anthropological students in America during the last decade have been removed many names, some of world-wide reputation, others beloved and admired in their own circle, and the places of these laborers have not as yet been filled" (Newell 1901, 56). Gone by 1901, for example, were leading Victorian lights such as Daniel Brinton, Frank Hamilton Cushing, Fletcher S. Bassett, and John G. Bourke, and six years later Newell himself died. The year 1900 was a turning point in the direction of folklore studies, for it also marked Franz Boas's ascent, at the age of forty-two, to the presidency of the American Folklore Society (McNeil 1980, 866–926).

Boas had emigrated from Germany to the United States in 1887, apparently because he felt frustrated by anti-Semitism and organizational restrictions on his work (Herskovits 1953, 12). Familiar with the role of a minority culture considered inferior in Europe because of his German-Jewish background (in America he joined the Society for Ethical Culture), Boas attacked racial classifications and assumptions of inferiority based on theories of natural science (Glick 1982; Hyatt 1990). His social conviction for the future was to eliminate racial stereotypes, and indeed to eliminate race as an objective category. He wrote, "The identification of an individual with a class because of his bodily appearance, language, or manners has always seemed to me a survival of barbaric, or rather of primitive, habits of mind.... Groups as they exist among us are all too often subjective constructions; those assigned to a group often do not feel themselves to be members of it, and the injustice done them is one of the blots on our civilization. Too few among us are willing to forget completely that a particular person is a Negro, or a Jew, or a member of some nationality for which we have no sympathy and to judge him as an individual." His contention was that "it must be the object of education to make the individual as free as may be of automatic adhesion to the group in which he is born or into which he is brought by social pressure" (Boas 1938a, 203).

If individual freedom—the basis of civil rights movements beginning in the early twentieth century for blacks, women, and Jews—became a touchstone for Boas's ideas, then tradition became a central concept to explain the attachment of individuals to groups. He announced, "My whole outlook upon social life is determined, by the question: how can we recognize the shackles that tradition has laid upon us? For when we recognize them, we are also able to break them" (Boas 1938a, 202). Boas, then, was also not calling for the preservation of tradition, as much as using its knowledge to enhance intellectual freedom. He used his father's example to make his point: "My father had retained an emotional affection for the ceremonial of his parental home without allowing it to influence his intellectual freedom. Thus I was spared the struggle against religious dogma that besets the lives of so many young people…. As I remember it now, my first shock came when one of my student friends, a theologian, declared his belief in the authority of tradition and his conviction that one had not the right to doubt what the past had transmitted to us. The shock that this outright abandonment of freedom of thought gave me is one of the unforgettable moments of my life" (Boas 1938a, 201). For others, Boas's stands sounded revolutionary, and indeed, Boas had publicly mentioned that he had been conditioned by "a German home in which the ideals of the revolution of 1848 were a living force," referring to unsuccessful protests of noble privilege and efforts to guarantee civil liberties for Jews and other minorities.

As a result of his social and political stands, Boas frequently suffered anti-Semitic as well as ideological attacks in America. Working in the same city as Boas, Stewart Culin unleashed some of the most vitriolic rhetoric against the Columbia professor. Embittered in the 1920s because of the decline of museum evolutionism and fired up with Henry Ford's support of anti-Semitic tracts such as *The International Jew*, Stewart Culin implied that Boas's scholarship was a brand of radical socialism inspired by a conspiracy of international Jewry. He observed at a council meeting of the American Anthropological Association in Philadelphia that members "were aligned, divided into two parties, who separated and seated themselves on opposite sides of the room. On one side were the Jews and their converts and supporters, mostly students of Franz Boas of Columbia University, and on the opposite side, their opponents. The Jews stood for Internationalism, and so proclaimed themselves. They had succeeded in securing possession of this important association and used it for their personal and political ends."[6] Some old-line scholars associated Jews, especially from Russia, with revolutionary activity, and apparently feared a consequence of world diasporization that would be implied from the diffusionist and relativistic arguments of anthropologists with Jewish backgrounds such as Franz Boas, Melville Herskovits, Joseph Jacobs, and Moses Gaster. Although most anthropologists were not Jewish, this fact did not stop some critics from blaming Jewish influence on the rise of the new "radical" theories, especially because of Columbia's location in New York City.

Staunch evolutionist Adolph F. A. Bandelier (1840–1914), who had done field-work in the Southwest and Central America for the American Museum of Natural History, was especially vocal in anti-Semitic criticism of Boas. He wrote to Culin in 1912 that

> since the Jewish elements has [sic] loomed up in Mexico, the Mexicans have become practical for the Israelites (worthily represented by Seler, Boas and soon, by Capitan) are manipulating the Mexican Government for scientific use to their heart's content, and getting "monish," where the children of the soil never could…. I see clearly the game. If the thing lasts, Boas will soon declare, indigenous assistance useless and then, he will forcibly and generously be compelled—to import TRUE scientific help from the out-side, which help, the children of Abraham, Isaac and Jacob will furnish…. He rummages about the country in quest of linguistics. What he says he is in search of is, the Morphology of the idioms. How he gets that in such a short time, now here, now there, without a system or definite plan, I fail to understand. His doings seem to me "all in the eye." It is the JEW speculating on the ignorance of others.

Bandalier closed with a reference to the privilege that Boas's presence seemed to threaten: "Until now his influence is not to be dreaded, because he cannot penetrate the circles in which we move, what he may attempt to do in the United States we cannot foresee."[7] In another letter, he invoked a conspiracy theory to explain Boas's ascendancy: "In the United States, I am told—he is very unpopular, but feared owing to his influence with wealthy Jews…. His school of archeology is again repre-sented by some blooming youngsters and by a Sheeny from Russia…."[8]

Beyond the evidence of ethnic prejudice in Bandelier's letters, there was an intellectual problem in the discourse on evolution posed by the presence of sup-posedly "superstitious" Jews in the advance of rational science, indeed the very persistence of ancient Judaism in modern industrial civilization. The progress and mobility of Jews, indeed the recurring reference to an ascribed Jewish scientific "genius," challenged the consistency of evolutionary racial doctrine (Efron 1995; Gilman 1996). According to Sander Gilman, "The anxiety about the meaning of Jewish superior intelligence haunts the American scene at the beginning of the century" (Gilman 1996, 80). Joseph Jacobs (1854–1916), a Jewish scholar known for his diffusionist folklore studies, presented results of an elaborate social study defy-ing evolutionary predictions of cultural backwardness. In works such as "The Comparative Distribution of Jewish Ability" (1891) that built a case for the claim of Jews as being "civilized," expressed ultimately in *Jewish Contributions to Civilization* (1919), he found that Jews have shown a higher rate of intellectual abil-ity than evolutionary doctrine predicted. In his prideful phrase, "'Tis a little peo-ple, but it has done great things" (Gilman 1996, 71).

Jacobs understood the Jewish record of achievement historically in their urban experience, reliance on multilingualism, emphasis on children's education, and tradition of resistance to prejudice. He infuriated the evolutionists with his closing rhetorical flourish in the form of a mocking explanation. He turned the evolution-ary assumption of the natural progression from Jewish to Christian civilization on its head. He accounted for Jewish persistence by a natural selection where the weaker members of the race unable to weather persecution embraced Christianity. He daringly wrote: "Jewish reason has never been in fetters, and finally the weaker members of each generation have been weeded out by persecution which tempted or forced them to embrace Christianity, and thus contemporary Jews are the sur-vival of a long process of unnatural selection which has seemingly fitted them excellently for the struggle for intellectual existence" (Jacobs 1891, lv). Whether or not Jacobs was serious, Franz Boas emphatically recoiled as much from the case for Jewish genius as the one for Christian superiority because of their problematic biological bases. In *The Mind of Primitive Man* (1911), he dismissed a relationship between cultural achievement and mental ability generally as a fallacy produced by racial typology (Gilman 1996, 79–80). This relationship had been prejudicially used in evolutionary tracts to judge fitness for social leadership of nation-states. It was especially a problem in America, he observed, because it provided an ideolog-ical impediment to democracy, the kind of representative democracy that allowed for cultural and political participation of plural groups in society (Boas 1945).

Presenting a case for racial typology in cultural evolution, John Sterling Kingsley in *The Standard Natural History* insisted on Jews as a race at a "low stage of culture" characterized by ignorance, fanaticism, and superstition (Kingsley 1885, 472). Yet if an evolutionary racial classification based on English Christian superi-ority categorized Jews in a primitive cultural rung, Kingsley had to explain the renown of highly regarded Jewish scientists, intellectuals, and leaders such as English prime minister Benjamin Disraeli, who was of Jewish heritage. "A Jew, it is true," Kingsley admitted, "can rise to be the premier of the British empire, but this is the exception noted; here there was contact with other people. To see the Jew in all his purity and the accompanying degradation, we must visit those places, like southern Russia, where they form whole communities" (Kingsley 1885, 472).

As a degraded "race" and an ancient religion functioning successfully in urban-industrial society, Jews provided a puzzle of civilization for evolutionists to solve. In "Present-Day Survivals of Ancient Jewish Customs," published in the *Journal of American Folklore*, one writer summarized the perplexing "two-sidedness" of Jews this way: "For nearly three thousand years they have been hurled from one end of the earth to the other; and yet, in spite of degradation and indignity … they have lived by adapting themselves to their environment, although they have also always persisted in retaining their individuality in spite of change" (Yoffie 1916, 413). The author underscored that Jews were "indeed a 'peculiar people.'" Minimizing the challenge of Jews to evolutionary theory, she isolated them as an unexplainable exception by calling them "a miracle of history" (Yoffie 1916, 413).

Whether example or exception, the Jewish experience tested the doctrinaire works of Spencer, Frazer, Gomme, and Lang because of their confidence that

The "racial type" of the Jew depicted in *The Standard Natural History* (1885), edited by John Sterling Kingsley, p. 471.

enlightened Christianity replaced superstitious Judaism as assuredly as civilization succeeded barbarism. In evolutionary thinking, religion was supposedly more rational than superstition in its approach to explaining natural phenomena. In this view, a better system "naturally" succeeded a primitive one. It can then be conceived that Jewish belief hung on as survivals, and Jews, supposedly set against "progress," would accept the "new covenant" and convert. But this scenario did not materialize from theory to practice. Responding to Edward Clodd's concern for the "exception" of the three-thousand-year-old Jews or "Hebrew race" to evolutionary assumptions, Edwin Sidney Hartland admitted that "science has not yet solved every question in connection with the history of Hebrew myths and customs," but predicted that "researches in Hebrew civilization will at no distant day be brought into line with those in other departments of the Science of Man" (Hartland [1899] 1968, 249).

Andrew Lang compensated for an apparent lack of consistency in the evolution of religion by suggesting that the origins of Christianity did not lie in Judaism at all, but rather derived from Babylonia and Persian customs. He argued that those practices constituted savage survivals in Christianity (Lang 1901, 76–81; see also Clodd 1885, 131–36). Although skeptical of Lang's historical facts, Joseph Jacobs pointedly chose the word "conversion" to describe Lang's statements on diffusion (Dorson 1968, 502; see also Maidment 1975). Reflecting the Jewish experience of diasporization, Jacobs's view of folklore was that it spread from social movements and could be created in contemporary situations (Fine 1987a). Resisting racial stereotypes, Jacobs characterized the "folk" not as primitives, but as social segments of societies, "many-headed … and often many-minded" (Jacobs 1893, 234). Instead of a hierarchy of folk and modern, Jacobs declared the relativistic concept, "we are the Folk as well as the rustic, though their lore may be other than ours, as ours will be different from that of those that follow us" (Jacobs 1893, 237).

But asking, "Are Jews a Race?" Karl Kautsky reiterated the centrality of race to cultural evolutionism by trying to show that Jews in advanced European societies naturally seek progress, hence explaining their involvement in science, but the bonds of Judaism to the ancient superstitious past ultimately worked against evolution and kept Jews from advancing culturally. Franz Boas in championing cultural relativity referred much less than one would expect to the Jewish situation, although he often gave the example of American blacks, whose status of a persecuted group he related to that of East European Jews (Herskovits 1953, 110–14; Glick 1982). His strong voice opposing the ideas of Kautsky and Bandalier can be heard in addresses such as "Race and Progress" published in 1931. Boas maintained his barrage on the emphasis of evolutionism on biological determinism, by insisting on a turn toward cultural explanations. "Ethnological evidence," he said, "is all in favor of the assumption that hereditary racial traits are unimportant as compared to cultural conditions" (Boas 1940, 13).

If Boas tried to point out the deleterious social consequences of cultural evolutionism, the old-line scholars reverted back to the Utopian promises of its ideology.

William Knapp had optimistically announced at the folklore congress at the Chicago World's Fair, for example, that "the weapons of war shall be transformed into the innocent implements of joyful harmony, and the recognition of the old God of the ages shall convert hatred and ambition into a vague tradition, only known to the annals of a long-past history" (Knapp 1898, 25). With the experience of World War I, it became apparent that technological advance brought more destruction, rather than, as many writers had predicted, the obsolescence of war. In a rational evolutionary order, nations would realize the "superstition" or "uselessness" of war to reach sociopolitical ends; civilization supposedly harnessed technological power for practical purposes and encouraged negotiation to settle disputes. But in the aftermath of the Great War, the world seemed more divided than united, more barbaric than enlightened.

A growing bookshelf of works published after the Great War, such as *The Decline of the West* (1918) by Oswald Spengler, painted a gloomy picture and challenged the assumption that Western civilization is the pinnacle of progress. Instead of echoing the evolutionary argument that America would be the next great civilization in a steady western march from Asia to Europe to America, Spengler predicted that an abundance of social and economic resources will place power in Asia and Russia. Many new scholars took pains to disavow the evolutionary scheme for culture because of its disregard for existing social conditions. In France after the war, Arnold van Gennep contrasted folklore according to natural history, which is the study of "dead facts," with biology, the study of living lore in a specific environment (van Gennep [1924] 1985). In Germany and Scandinavia intellectual fervor for geography and physical sciences provided encouragement for application of new models to explain cultural reformulations as once isolated peoples migrated in massive waves from Europe to North America.

The denouncement of indisputable "natural laws" suggested by evolution and a search for social flexibility in new approaches was a way to ward off the gloomy outlook that had been brought by the ills of modern warfare and industrial capitalism. Meanwhile, the reign of laissez-faire economics in governmental policy, which depended on "natural laws" in evolutionary theory for justification, was under attack. Dissatisfaction grew from unregulated cycles of booms and depressions that caused economic and social instability during the 1890s. Critics went after laissez-faire economics for aiding the rise of exploitative monopolies and stagnating society, instead of encouraging progress and competition, as a social process of natural selection promised. One prominent critic, Lester Frank Ward, arose to stress the rationality of primitive culture and propose a model of social intervention contrary to evolutionary thinking. He denied that uniform natural laws somehow mysteriously moved the social economy toward progress and insisted that rational bases of social planning, drawing on a physics of causes and reactive effects, were needed to insure growth in the public interest (Commager 1950, 199–226).

The splashing flow of immigration at the turn of the century reminded Americans of the influence that a movement of people could bring to another culture. Lee Vance acknowledged in 1897, "Our folk-lore is highly composite, resulting from the great tides of immigration which have rolled over our shores and formed our present strange commingling of races" (Vance 1896/1897, 251). For some evolutionists, anthropology provided evidence for making cultural judgment about the fitness of immigrants, judged by their primitive "racial" characteristics, for entry into progressive American civilization. George Dorsey, for example, wrote Stewart Culin, "I have come to the conclusion that Italians are undesirable immigrants. … They are either better than we are and we should turn the whole country over to them, or they are rotten and we should stop the flow. I hold to the latter opinion." In another letter, he worried about what East European immigrants "take with them of blood and brain to the United States" and the ways they "will affect American ideals."[9]

Suggesting a more supportive view of immigration, ideas of diffusion introduced into folklore studies implied that immigration was a natural cultural process. Countering the evolutionary assumption of biological inheritance of depravity and criminality among the immigrants, Franz Boas undertook a massive statistical study entitled *Changes in Bodily Forms of Descendants of Immigrants* (1911) to show that the physical characteristics of the foreign-born could not be used to predict their intelligence or personality. The ability of immigrants to continue folk cultures within industrialized, urban societies challenged assumptions of modernization. Apparently contradicting evolutionary doctrine's emphasis on the irrationality of old traditions and the inevitability of progress, the "survivals" of these cultures appeared to function rationally to serve social ends. Global comparison of a level of culture became less convincing because the functions and contexts of the traditions seemed more different than similar upon close ethnographic examination.

A major event that raised doubts about the cultural ladder from savagery to civilization was the Russian Revolution. Russia had skipped a step, or moved back one, depending on the point of view, moving from a peasant economy to a communistic society. Around the same time, a new feeling of isolationism swept America. After seeking its place in a global community, America sought exclusiveness, shunning the League of Nations and stressing America's cultural distinctiveness. Accordingly, in 1893, Frederick Jackson Turner caused a stir with a paper about the influence that the settlement of the West had on American culture. More mobile, more aware of space, Americans brought attention, in their leisure and in their theories, to movement across the landscape.

Despite fundamental differences in social views and approaches, some provocative parallels exist between folklore study in the late nineteenth and late twentieth centuries. During the 1890s and the 1990s, popular discussion of "materialism" and rapid technological change translated into a surge of folklore in the popular press.

Changes in roles of women and ethnic minorities gave rise to soul-searching stud-ies, encompassing folklore, of problems in American society. During the 1990s, discussion centered far less on origin and evolution from so-called primitives; and the "dynamics" (to quote an oft-used metaphor taken from physics common in today's folklore studies) of behavior among people in all walks of life in the present typically holds the attention of folklorists rather than history of remote, "ruder ages." The dire consequences of some forms of technology have led to a reassess-ment of folk culture on its own terms for what material, social, and psychological benefits it provides. A preservationist fervor has been evident in folklore studies; often contemporary folklorists appear to be advocates for the folk, rather than for "industrial progress." Rarely today are folk practices examples of primitive "indus-try" or "invention"; rather they are "folk arts" in need of "cultural conservation."

The value of culture has been equally in dispute in the late twentieth century, but its translation was much more as everyday experience rather than an exotic hidden past. Indeed, a contribution of folklore studies, once it made a break with the cultural anthropology of "primitives," was to emphasize the workings of expressive tradition in everyday life close to home—in factories, cities, and camps, and among ethnic groups as well as groups of friends. Questions arising from bureaucratic life, humanistic questions of a person's social function, role, and pur-pose, often within a large organization, typically took center stage, with nods toward modern concerns of psychological adjustment provided by traditional expression. To be sure, the precedents that nineteenth-century scholars set for col-lection, classification, and display continue into the present, not only in the exhibi-tionistic treatment of artifacts of tradition, but also in the artifactual treatment of oral traditions. The empirical bias of folklore studies to *observe and collect exam-ples of culture* in fieldwork remains at the core of the folkloristic enterprise. Indeed, it can be argued that Victorian anthropology and folklore established culture in public discourse as the expressive property of groups.

In addition to the elite notion of culture as a sign of lofty, "civilized" taste—culture with a capital C, so to speak—there emerged a notion of culture that aris-es from universal social existence. This is the kind of culture associated with shared local knowledge and performed expression. As rhetoric associated with descrip-tion of "folk" and "primitive" traditions, this vogue of vernacular culture during the Gilded Age influenced interpretations of the advance of industrialization and incorporation. Ironically, discussions of social and technological innovation typi-cally had a reference to cultural tradition as if the connection to "folk" tradition could temper the impact of change on American "nervousness." "Folk-Lore," Fletcher Bassett constantly reminded his audiences, "has become a subject of the day" (1898, 20). Its organization into professional and public discourse in support of ideological positions on industrial and social progress stood as one of the "salient events" of the Gilded Age.

3

The English Connection,
from Cultural Survivals
to Cultural Studies

Considering that the settlement and language of America owe so much to Great Britain, one would expect more communion of folklore studies between the domains. This is not to say that great achievements have not been made. Receiving persistent use in the twentieth century are Francis James Child's catalogue of British ballads, Cecil Sharp's harvest of British folk songs in the southern Appalachians of the United States, Ernest Baughman's type and motif index of English-American folktales, and Richard Dorson's encyclopedic narrative of the Victorian British folklorists.[1] The assumption in these works was that American culture and cultural scholarship both relied primarily on English precedents. The English inheritance appeared to be outside of America's "ethnic" traditions, and particularly after the 1980s a strong intellectual movement arose to show a multicultural society that did not have a single dominant influence. Bibliographies of American ethnic folklore, for example, often leave out an English category (although they include Irish, Scottish, Welsh, and Cornish), suggesting that English influence pervades national culture (see Georges and Stern 1982).

Although it is possible to point to a flurry of research activity across the Atlantic before the turn of the century, and again after World War II, until recently Americans like their English cousins in folklore studies mostly turned their lenses on peoples they considered more exotic—American Indians, East and South European immigrants, Africans, and Asians. Richard Dorson generalized that "in the twentieth century the links between English and American folklorists (exclusive of folksong devotees) have snapped, while ties between the United States and the continent have grown stronger" (Dorson 1973b, 16). In this chapter I explain the transatlantic rift set against the background of intellectual history. I view the way that Americans separated in the direction of pluralist and behavioral agendas to design a discourse of culture that allowed for individual choice and creation of traditions. Finally, I consider whether the development of "cultural studies" in England has forced the paths to cross once again.

American folklorists had the best intentions for English-American study. After all, they organized the American Folklore Society in 1888 on the model the English society formed ten years earlier, whose stated object was "the preservation and publication of Popular Traditions, Legendary Ballads, Local Proverbial Sayings, Superstitions and Old Customs (British and foreign), and all subjects relating to them." The title page of the English society's journal showed the society's view of folklore as remnants of the past by carrying the banner of "The Folk-Lore Society for Collecting and Printing Relics of Popular Antiquities, &c." In a nod to the mission of the Folk-Lore (later Folklore) Society, the founders of the American society announced that their purpose was to encourage the "collection of the fast-vanishing remains of folk-lore in America." Several examples of these remains were given including the lore of French Canada, Indian tribes in North America, and "Negroes" in the southern states, but listed first if not foremost were "relics of old English folk-lore (ballads, tales, superstitions, etc.)" (Newell 1888d). At the International Folk-Lore Congress, sponsored by the English society, three representatives of the American society participated, and two years later at the International Folk-Lore Congress in Chicago, three English society folklorists offered papers on mythology and primitive custom in Europe (Dorson 1973b, 16). The prevalent mission of applying ideas of evolution to culture in the early years of both societies fostered the attitude that folklorists revealed a natural history of civilization with attention to "folk" on the lower rungs of the ladder of progress. In short, their "folk" were exoticized, typically racialized, others, rather than familiarized selves.

RATIONALITY AND MORALITY

The most cited definition of culture used by the society folklorists was Edward Tylor's statement drawing on natural science that "culture or civilization … is that complex whole which includes knowledge, belief, art, morals, law, custom, and any other capabilities and habits acquired by man as a member of society" (Tylor [1871] 1970, 1). As Darwin explained the origin of species, so he took as his task to explain the origin of civilization, especially its most revered feature of religion. He devoted most of his magnum opus *Primitive Culture* (1871), in fact, to matters of the origin of religion viewed in myths, superstitions, rites, and ceremonies. In broadly conceived culture as inherited social skills and institutions, he also suggested finding the origins of other contemporary features such as art, invention, and industry. Culture was a constant of existence as much as nature, he argued, and it equally carried authority. Tylor's call for comparative study of the traditions that made up culture was akin to finding laws of nature. It was, he said, "a subject apt for the study of laws of human thought and action."

Tylor had a conception of culture divided into "stages of development or evolution, each the outcome of previous history, and about to do its proper part in shaping the history of the future." Within the stages, Tylor suggested that great uniformity existed, and he rationally ascribed this condition "to the uniform action of uniform causes" (Tylor [1871] 1970, 1). Tylor's ideas had been shaped by travels to "primitive" Mexico in 1855, in which he found comparisons of institutions there to modern-day England, although the two were not ethnically connected. An additional influence was his Quaker faith, which had lost much of its sectarianism and had become open to liberal currents of thought.

Tylor was swept up by the English-Scottish philosophy of Hume, Locke, and Mill that emphasized empiricism of observed evidence and logical assumptions (Radin 1970, xii). He credited "our modern investigators in the sciences of inorganic nature" who "are foremost to recognize, both within and without their special fields of work, the unity of nature, the fixity of its laws, the definite sequence of cause and effect through which every fact depends on what has gone before it, and acts upon what is to come after it" (Tylor [1871] 1970, 2). The "acts that come after" in a study of culture he assumed to be an improvement over what came before. The "facts" of arts, beliefs, customs, and myths are arranged in upward evolution from the simple to the more complex much as laws of development for nature. He even made the claim that the study of traditions in culture was more on a scientific basis than natural history, because "it is an open question whether a theory of development from species to species is a record of transitions which actually took place, or a mere ideal scheme serviceable in the classification of species whose origin was really independent. But among ethnographers there is no such question as to the possibility of species of implements or habits or beliefs being developed one out of another, for development in Culture is recognized by our most familiar knowledge" (Tylor [1871] 1970, 14–15).

Evolutionary doctrine reigned in the intellectual life of late nineteenth-century Britain, and in folklore study it especially supported a search for a long-hidden past where the origins of modern institutions in pagan rituals could be unearthed. For the Victorians, the related genres of custom and belief, and their symbolic ascent from superstition to science, from rude existence to genteel manners, from the spiritual to the material, became the standard of study. Stressing the rationality of a science of culture and the global vantage of imperial Britain, they advocated a method that would be globally comparative and minutely systematic. Andrew Lang, a leading British proponent of the science, summarized its method as "when an apparently irrational and anomalous custom is found in any country, to look for a country where a similar practice is found, and where the practice is no longer irrational and anomalous, but in harmony with the manners and ideas of the people among

Henry Balfour, first curator of the Pitt-Rivers Museum in Oxford, England, examines, c. 1890, an ethnological exhibit of war implements arranged to show evolution to modern technology. (Pitt-Rivers Museum)

whom it prevails.... Our method, then, is to compare the seemingly meaningless customs or manners of civilised races with the similar customs and manners which exist among the uncivilised and still retain their meaning" (Lang 1885, 21). In this line of thinking, "The European may find among the Greenlanders or Maoris many a trait for reconstructing the picture of his own primitive ancestors" (Cox 1895, 33).

Moral judgment pervaded much of the evolutionary scholarship. The background for such judgment was the question of responsibility that higher civilization represented by England had for uplifting as well as controlling primitive cultures. Even among "civilized" nations there were judgments made about the character they showed as a result of cultural development. Charlotte Burne offered that the comparative folklore method allowed for tracing "lines of development of the several systems of civilized nations from their source, and to fathom the reasons of their strength and weakness." She counseled, "Eventually we may hope to adjust the balance between circumstance and character, and to arrive at the causes which retain some races in a state of arrested progress while others develop a highly-organized civilization" (Burne 1913, 3). Arthur Mitchell writing in *The Past in the Present* (1881) added the warning that the comparative study of beliefs and customs isolated items that should be eradicated from modern culture, so as to maintain the power of the British Empire. He observed, "It will scarcely, I think, be saying too much, if I say that the British Empire stands now very much where the Roman Empire stood then, and occupies a like dangerous place of breadth and prominence" (233). Britain needed to represent the model of strength and enlightenment for the world, for according to his view of cultural evolutionary theory, "in every civilized society there must be the strong and the weak, the clever and the stupid, the cultured and the uncultured, but they all share in the state of civilization and benefit by it" (Mitchell 1881, 196). British folklore study served to point out the differences from top to bottom.

Folklore study had social and political applications, for British folklorists often mentioned the need for use of folklore scholarship by religious missionaries and government officials, especially colonial governors to better administrate their subjects (Hartland [1899] 1968, 243–50; see also Brewster 1943; Asad 1975; Huizer and Mannheim 1979). Edwin Sidney Hartland proclaimed, for example, that "it requires but little insight to be assured that we might enormously strengthen our hold upon India if our Government were to take a different line, and were to encourage, instead of discouraging, civil and military officials to inquire systematically into and report upon the ideas and practices of the races of that vast continent" (Hartland [1899] 1968, 246). He considered colonialism an application of anthropological work because of its culturally modernizing and morally uplifting influence on "backward" races stuck in a lower stage of progress (see Barkan 1992, 34–37). He promoted folklore collection as a way to respond better to attitudes and practices based on native beliefs and to determine areas for administrating progress. He further urged missionaries and moralistic businessmen to take up education in folklore because it "is not less necessary to Christian enterprise than to good government and successful commercial intercourse" (Hartland [1899] 1968, 244).

The British anthropological experts in race and culture used scholarship as a pulpit from which to moralize. Their great questioning of the role of religion as a controlling influence in their daily lives, especially as science became touted as a rational formula for modern living, led them to intensely scrutinize primitive custom and belief and its replacement by religion as precedents for a late-nineteenth-century shift from religion to science. Finding order in the evolution of civilization, indeed a plan to the world's social mysteries, carried on religious goals of explaining existence. "There is on present lines a whole world of thought between science and religion, although they both have the same object. They both seek the great unknown," Edwin Hartland wrote, for example (1908, 138). Many cultural evolutionists proclaimed that Christian belief properly remained in the evolution of science, and justified moral judgments of those left behind by the "advance of civilization" (Clodd 1885, 222–36; Lang 1885, 11–14; Lubbock 1978, 256).

At the center of world empire, England looked upon the world as its subject and the lack of a regional modifier for the "Folklore Society" reflected this bias. The

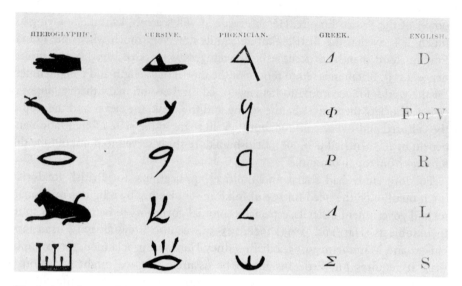

HIEROGLYPHIC.	CURSIVE.	PHOENICIAN.	GREEK.	ENGLISH.
			Δ	D
			Φ	F or V
			P	R
			Λ	L
			Σ	S

"Evolution of Letters" from *The Standard Natural History* (1885), edited by John Sterling Kingsley, p. 17.

cultures of the world were collected for the English to evaluate and interpret on a global scale. Coining the title of the American Folklore Society, founders implied that their society held to the goals of the Folklore Society within America. Even within the nation, the idea of layers of culture arranged by achievement of progress had applications. In England, the reference was often to the intersection of race and *class*. Englishman Edwin Sidney Hartland wrote that "the conflict of the classes and the masses about which we hear so much today is all the bitterer because of the chasm which education has opened between high and low." Hartland opined that "the more completely you can identify yourselves with their modes of thought, the greater your influence for good upon them" (Hartland [1899] 1968, 247). As a result of the thinking that suggested social organization by class found in English society, folklore could be perceived as a distinct geological layer of culture associated with the unlettered and uncivilized. The organization also contributed to the view of ethnic groups or "races" within such layers as isolable "strains" based on visible features, including physical attributes and traditional customs (see Kingsley 1885, 1–4). The idea of folklore as an expressive process that every individual possesses as a member of overlapping and interacting groups had few advocates in England, and they, like Jewish scholar Joseph Jacobs, tended to be from marginalized ethnic backgrounds (Jacobs 1893; Fine 1987a; Maidment 1975).

Evolutionary study of folklore was particularly suited to English and American ideas of civilization during the Gilded Age. According to the predominant philosophy, the civilizing process was a moral and technological uplifting of peoples into nations and empires. In the best-selling works of Englishman Herbert Spencer, who applied Darwin's natural history precepts to the civilizing process, and similarly minded scholar-writers in America such as John Sterling Kingsley, John Fiske, Lewis Henry Morgan, and William Graham Sumner, Victorians read of language and folklore as key evidence of the rise of civilization from savage and barbaric stages. Kingsley in his *The Standard Natural History* (1885) created an "evolution of letters" among other examples of "inventions" that showed English as the natural culmination of cultural progress. "The art of expressing words in written characters belongs to a late stage of civilization," Kingsley presumed, "and it is from this fact that we are able to trace more or less clearly and distinctly its development" (Kingsley 1885, 15). The unveiling of evolutionary connections from inventions in the industrial centers of England and America back to primitive, lower forms suggested to the Victorians a right to prominence in the world. The social ladders that civilizations climbed assured rising national powers in the West of their superiority, for they stood on the top of the ladder proud that their technology, expansiveness, and rationality marked the height of civilization.

British folklorists such as George Laurence Gomme and Andrew Lang insisted on building a "science of folklore" that would prove assertions of the evolution of nations much as Darwin's science of natural history showed the development of species. The terminology of the new science borrowed heavily from natural history as it referred to "development," "specimens," and "field collection" (Gomme 1884). Gomme's book *Ethnology in Folklore* (1892), in the series on "Modern Science" edited by John Lubbock, stood prominently among titles in natural history and botany. Gomme wrote that "the essential characteristic of folklore is that it consists of beliefs, customs, and traditions which are far behind civilisation in their intrinsic value to man, though they exist under the cover of a civilised nationality. This estimate of the position of folklore with reference to civilisation suggests that its constituent elements are survivals of a condition of human thought more backward, and therefore more ancient, than that in which they are discovered" (Gomme 1892, 2).

With so much attention to ancient relics in the folklore journals, one would expect close ties with archaeology, but folklore, its students declared, uncovers the *spiritual* side of culture. Especially in England, where archaeologists unearthed Roman and Saxon remains of societies replaced by imperial England, folklorists sought to mark their place in a mystery of the past that reveals the present. Writing on "The Method of Folklore," Lang made the distinction that "there is a science, Archaeology, which collects and compares the material relics of old races, the axes and arrow-heads. There is a form of study, Folklore, which collects and compares the similar but immaterial relics of old races, the surviving superstitions and stories, the ideas which are in our time but not of it. Properly speaking, folklore is only concerned with the legends, customs, beliefs, of the Folk, of the people, of the classes which have least been altered by education, which have shared least in progress" (Lang 1885, 11). *The Handbook of Folklore* published by the Folklore

Society established the scope of folklore as "the mental equipment of the folk as distinguished from their technical skill. It is not the form of the plough which excites the folklorist, but the rites practised by the ploughman when putting it into the soil … " (Burne 1913, 1).

The separation that had occurred in England between oral and material genres in the scope of folklore also found its way into the American conception of folklore. "Lore" as the "unwritten history," the "spiritual side" of culture, offered the literary remains set against a modernizing background, as opposed to the use of "life" which assumed more integration between people and their being. Lore suggested the archaeology of past traditions while life referred to the sociology of living practice. The materials of lore were collected as specimens and classified into genres and lines of development. Evolutionary folklorists presumed that the genres could be categorized by English divisions of narrative and custom—such as myth, tale, and legend—rather than using native categories that would be culture-specific. And they supposed that the genres as well as items were comparable and part of a general theory of cultural development. This approach to organizing genres had a few detractors such as diffusionist Moses Gaster (1856–1934), a Rumanian-born Rabbi who came to England in 1885. He accepted the categorization of analytical genres but questioned the assumptions of comparability and antiquity. He wrote that

> The fault inherent in every new undertaking, viz., of mixing the elements promiscuously, and attributing to every branch of the new study the same origin, was conspicuously felt in the new study of folk-lore. Once a theory was adopted, say for customs or myths, it was immediately applied to superstitions, tales, or charms, as if these were all of the same age, and derived from the same source. This *general* explanation is still in force, although, as I think each branch of folk-lore should be studied separately, endeavouring to prove the origin of each independently from the other; afterwards we may try to ascertain the relationship which exists between each. (Gaster 1887, 339)

He emphasized that "the knowledge of the *illiterate* is not a homogeneous element, but one which has been acquired during centuries, and it only appears to us to form one indivisible unity. There may be elements in folk-lore of hoar antiquity, and there may be on the other hand other elements relatively modern, which we can trace even to our own time, growing, so to say, under own eyes, as, for instance, all the *popular etymologies* and the stories invented *afterwards* to explain them" (Gaster 1887, 339). Gaster's proposal was blasphemous to the evolutionists such as Andrew Lang, Edwin Sidney Hartland, and Edward Clodd whose evolutionary writings looking for origins in the hidden past held sway in English scholarship (Dorson 1968, 273–76; Newall 1975).

The stress on analytical genre, and classification by text, rather than social group had a lasting influence in English-American scholarship. It was spread by George Laurence Gomme's standard-setting *Handbook of Folklore* published in

1890, and expanded by Charlotte Burne in 1913. Gomme's influence can be seen, for example, in *The Folk-Lore Manual* of 1892 in which its American author, Fletcher Bassett, admits that its essential contents were pulled from Gomme's work. The very name of "folk-lore" with its delineated examples of "customs, observances, superstitions, ballads, proverbs" taken from William John Thoms's coining in 1846 lent itself to textual interpretation of the materials of tradition and their classification into analytical genres.

A progression similar to the one from Thoms to Gomme and others in England can also be found in the United States. John Fanning Watson, a Philadelphia merchant, saw industrialization and urbanization taking away what he called "traditionary lore" during the 1820s, and moved by Sir Walter Scott's gleanings of folklore in Scotland, made a collection which he titled *Annals of the Olden Time in Philadelphia* (1830). Although striking for its dig in the backyard for local customs, Watson's antiquarian efforts, like Thoms's, were co-opted by the rush for an anthropological science of folklore. William Wells Newell, organizer of the American Folklore Society, claimed in 1892 that "American students will prefer ... to consider the comparative examination of this material as a part of anthropological science" (Newell 1892).

Folklorists working in archaeological and natural history museums, especially, flocked to the society. Serious about the study of folklore but lacking university status, the American society sought to convey a professional image. Later, when folklorists in anthropology, language, and literature managed to establish footholds in American universities, the society became more academic. In this development is an essential difference between the American and English societies. The English society could not carry over its serious image into the universities, and instead it fostered the noble stature of the enthusiastic amateur. The emphasis on survival and custom in English folklore study continued well into the twentieth century. With this concern the English society retained an international, cross-cultural scope, owing to the days of global empire. The American society meanwhile focused more and more on its own turf, increasingly perceived as a nation of nations.

American study diverged from its British precedent largely at the behest of Franz Boas, a German-American professor at Columbia University who became president of the American Folklore Society in 1900 and served as editor of its journal from 1908 to 1924. Boas moved folklore study from its natural science model to a physical system of relativity inspired by Albert Einstein's theories. Thus the evolutionary assumption that survivals found in a culture of the present could be connected to a different culture of another time did not hold up in a perception of time and space that was heterogeneous rather than homogeneous. Boas's cultural relativism stressed the integrity of individual cultures and, often, the individual within the culture. Such a move meant a drift away from national comparisons, such as between England and America, and a move toward smaller segments of

Proceedings of the American Folklore Society meeting in Baltimore, from *Baltimore American,* December 29, 1897.

culture studied in depth. A resurgence of literary interest in folklore after World War II coupled with the simple fact that many Americans spent time in the British Isles during and after the war ushered in a wave of studies seeking British-American connections. Samuel Bayard studied American fiddle tunes of British origin, MacEdward Leach and D. K. Wilgus asked questions anew about British ballads, and Francis Lee Utley and Louis C. Jones looked at other examples of lore traveling across the ocean.

FUNCTION AND THE ROLE OF TRADITION

While America had its Boas, England had its Bronislaw Malinowski (1884–1942), who espoused a social anthropology revolving around the functional uses of traditions. Skeptical of evolutionary doctrine, he considered the rational system of custom in a culture and insisted on studying societies as bounded units rather than as a global development. Malinowski was educated in physics and mathematics at the University of Cracow, but during a period of ill health he set aside his science studies to read the original English version of James Frazer's *Golden Bough* (1900), then in three volumes. He completed his Ph.D. in science but came to the London School of Economics and Political Science in 1910 to study anthropology. There he became influenced by Charles G. Seligman, one of the few anthropologists of the early period with training in psychology (Barkan 1992, 30–34). In addition, Seligman espoused diffusionism and sharply disputed racial ideas prevalent among the evolutionists, which culminated in his public outcry against Nazi uses of anthropological ideas during the 1930s.

Malinowski had an opportunity for cultural fieldwork when he became secretary to Robert Marett, former president of the Folklore Society and a colleague of Seligman who was traveling to Australia for a meeting, on an expedition to the Torres Straits near New Guinea. Malinowski carried out research in New Guinea and concentrated two one-year stays in the Trobriand Islands off the northwest coast. His experience contributed to the idea of an intensive method of field research in a single culture for an extended stay. He published his work as *Argonauts of the Western Pacific* (1922) with a preface by the same James Frazer who had inspired him toward anthropological studies. Glimpsing through Malinowski's narrative another exotic life in the story of global culture, Frazer complimented Malinowski's detailed account of the whole round of Trobriand life: "Dr. Malinowski lived as a native among the natives for many months together, watching them daily at work and at play, conversing with them in their own tongue, and deriving all his information from the surest sources—personal observation and statements made to him directly by the natives in their own language without the intervention of an interpreter. In this way he has accumulated a mass of materials, of high scientific values, bearing on the social, religious, and economic or industrial life of Trobriand Islanders" (Frazer 1961, vii–viii). Although the evolutionist in Frazer realized that Malinowski suggested "a new vision of savage humanity" by studying "the totality of all social, cultural, and psychological aspects of the community, for they are so interwoven that none can be understood without taking into consideration all the others," Frazer still thought that Malinowski could be productively read for showing evolutionary concern for "conspicuous predominance" of magic before a stage of religion, "even in the culture of a people so comparatively high in the scale of savagery as the Trobriand Islanders" (Malinowski 1961, xvi; Frazer 1961, xiv).

Malinowski responded to evolutionary doctrine by concentrating on a traditional system of exchange and trade. Showing his concern for the rationality of economics in a society, Malinowski found that customs and "institutions" were based on rational thinking of needs and outcomes. Customs also could be understood in light of the society's particular circumstances—its islands and peoples—and interconnection with other distinctive features of the culture including "social organisation, the power of magic, to mythology and folklore, and indeed to all other aspects as well as the main one" (Malinowski 1961, xvi). Malinowski considered the problem under study to be "sociological and geographical," thus corresponding to the grounding of social conditions in space, which was common among Boas's ethnographies in America. The economic theme that was the center of his study was the *Kula* (the Trobrianders' name for exchange and trade). Looked at as a structured system, the exchange forms a ring among the islanders. The result is that the bonds form among the often scattered islanders; their boundaries as a tribe are measured by participation in the *Kula*. The system of exchange had the function of maintaining the society. It persisted, not as an anomalous "superstition," but as a functioning enterprise in an integrated whole.

What set Malinowski's ethnography apart was its emphasis, not on origin and diffusion, but on the function of customs working within a system of culture (Malinowski 1944, 67–74). He saw customs as "a blend of utilitarian anxiety about the most necessary objects of his surroundings, with some preoccupation in those which strike his imagination and attract his attention" (Malinowski 1954, 21). In contrast to the hidden past of origin and the great extent of diffusion, Malinowski's consideration of "institutions" moved ethnography to its modern meaning of the immediate present and he signaled a British social anthropological move away from preoccupations with race and civilization to society and culture (see Barkan 1992, 124–27). He called for more use of behavioral observation and less of a judgment about the superiority of civilized society. Indeed, he was especially concerned for learning primitive "wisdom" and appreciating different "worldviews" rather than levels of culture. Especially considering what he regarded as the impractical uses of modern warfare in World War I, he wrote that

we cannot possibly reach the final Socratic wisdom of knowing ourselves if we never leave the narrow confinement of the customs, beliefs and prejudices into which every man is born. Nothing can teach us a better lesson in this matter of ultimate importance than the habit of mind which allows us to treat the beliefs and values of another man from his point of view. Nor has civilised humanity ever needed such tolerance more than now, when prejudice, ill will and vindictiveness are dividing each European nation from another, when all the ideals, cherished and proclaimed as the highest achievements of civilisation, science and religion, have been thrown to the winds. (Malinowski [1922] 1961, 518)

Further influenced by post World War I nationalism based on the determination of cultural boundaries, Malinowski's functionalism stressed the direct observation of how a specific culture relates to society in a present time and over a limited space.

Malinowski became the first chair in anthropology at the University of London in 1920 and as Edward Evans-Pritchard recalled, Malinowski taught most of the social anthropologists who subsequently held chairs in Great Britain and the Dominions (Evans-Pritchard 1981, 153–69). Malinowski's prominence was a mixed blessing for English folklore studies, which did not have a university foothold. Malinowski and others espousing social anthropology, such as A. R. Radcliffe-Brown, had little to offer on English folklore. Although Malinowski had much to say on native categories of narrative, particularly myths, he rarely referred to folklore after 1926, and his concerns became more on the sociological aspects of exotic cultures in establishing his branch of social anthropology. As a result, the goal of a systematic survey of English folklore, hoped for by the anthropologically minded Victorian folklorists who issued a bookshelf of "county" studies of folklore in the English countryside, did not materialize. In contrast to the American Folklore Society, the English Folklore Society in 1959 reported that anthropologists were a "dwindling minority" and "possibly doomed to extinction" (Simpson 1989, 3). Gillian Bennett, editor of the Folklore Society's journal, reflected that had folklore established itself as an academic subject in England or had it aligned itself more closely to the social anthropology that emerged prominently in English universities, English folklore studies would have developed well beyond the evolutionism with which it has been associated (Bennett 1994, 34–35).

Malinowski had a profound impact on the development of functional approaches in American folklore scholarship, which had a strong tie to cultural anthropology. William Bascom, an anthropologist at the University of California who had been president of the American Folklore Society, declared that Malinowski was "the most important single influence on my own study of folklore; witness my articles 'Four Functions of Folklore' and 'The Forms of Folklore: Prose Narratives'" (Bascom 1983, 163). Attempting to reconcile humanistic and anthropological perspectives prevalent in the American Folklore Society, Bascom proposed that functionalism provided a general framework for interpreting folklore in both culture and literature. Assuming that folklore maintains the stability of a culture, he presented four ways in which folklore generally persists by fulfilling roles. Through the first function of amusement, a person finds escape from the repressions imposed by the society. Thus the system continues by means of the built-in safety valve of folklore. Second, folklore validates cultural activities such as rituals and institutions for those who perform and observe them. Third, folklore educates persons in the values of the society. Fourth, folklore maintains conformity to accepted patterns of behavior. Folklore can apply social pressure and even social control, in forms such as lullabies or proverbs. A fifth function overarches the others. Folklore, Bascom summarized, integrates society and makes it cohere (Bascom 1965).

Bascom's proposal may have been appealing because of the harmony it offered of culture and text, anthropology and literature, rather than its explanatory power (Zumwalt 1988). Historian of anthropology Fred Voget speculated that Americans, working in an open society, had become skeptical of the closed system that European anthropologists had drawn. Americans tended to view cultures through the careers of typical individuals, while Bascom's functionalism described a social life that was dominated by an orderly arrangement of statuses (Voget 1975, 462). American folklorists typically replaced assumptions of a closed society with a looser social definition of community or a psychological focus on the individual. Some folklorists such as Elliott Oring further loosened the priority of social maintenance in explaining cultural production by arguing that function is logically a consequence, not a cause, of folklore's generation (Oring 1976). Unintended effects of a cultural item cannot account for its origin, he insisted. Moreover he warned that functions that allegedly generate effects may be falsely generalized as causing all instances in which certain conditions are present.

If the line of function as explanation slackened in the United States, the reputation of Malinowski as pivotal in relativizing culture, if anything, rose. As keywords of "performance" and "context" became appealing to American scholars concerned for building a behavioral model emphasizing free will to enact traditions in an individualistic, open society, Malinowski above all became a prominent intellectual precedent (Abrahams 1968; Bauman and Paredes 1972; Ben-Amos and Goldstein 1975). An oft-quoted statement found in *Myth in Primitive Psychology* (1926) is that "the text, of course, is extremely important, but without the context it remains lifeless. As we have seen, the interest of the story is vastly enhanced and it is given its proper character by the manner in which it is told. The whole nature of the performance, the voice and the mimicry, the stimulus and the response of the audience mean as much to the natives as the text; and the sociologist should take his cue from the natives" (Malinowski 1926, 29–30; see also Bascom 1977, 13). While bristling at Malinowski's "English" tendency to generalize and pointing out that he did not fully develop the contextualist line of thinking, Bascom thought Malinowski's brand of ethnography offered an important foundation for later American efforts to describe the cultural participation of individuals in multiple communities and the rational use of traditions for social purpose.

If Malinowski and Bascom did not emphasize studying one's own culture in the "large" context of nationality, then Richard Dorson (1916–1981) at Indiana University did. He was the great catalyst to realizing the British inheritance in scholarship as well as lore. Trained in history and literature within American civilization, Dorson disagreed with anthropologists who disavowed the cultural reality of national societies. He agreed that folklorists could no longer talk of an absolute culture as did the Victorians. But his study of American folklore made the case for a distinctive national culture built on the foundation of European and especially British sources. Stumbling upon the library of the Folklore Society in London in 1948, Dorson devoted many years afterward convincing scholars, as he said, "that familiarity with the brilliant history of folklore science in England was as indispensable for the American, and indeed for the European, Asian, or African student of folklore, as for the British" (Dorson 1968, v). His monumental influence training students devoted to a separate discipline of folklore helped spread his message of nationality and cross-cultural connections. His Folklore Institute at Indiana sponsored an "Anglo-American" conference in 1969, and his students through the years were required to put *The British Folklorists* (1968) to memory (Dorson 1970). Dorson enabled the writings of the British folklorists prominently to come back into print with his two-volume anthology *Peasant Customs and Savage Myths* (1968). Greatly owing to his efforts, more university courses on British folklore sprang up in America than in Great Britain.

English-American folklore study could grow because of the kind environment to interdisciplinary study the postwar American university provided. The growth of American studies, including folklore, followed from the growth of American power and attention to the recent past. In the landscape of national knowledge, folklore was a sign of the cultural strength of a new nation derived, but also separated, from Europe. In addition, the influx of new kinds of students—immigrants, workers, women, Appalachians, Jews, blacks—created a demand for representation of their own history and culture. Faced with an intellectual legacy alien to their roots, such students turned to oral and artifactual records for verifying their cultural integrity and found folklore to be a socially and politically significant area of exploration.

Some other conditions peculiar to the American experience fostered yet another movement in American folklore studies, the embrace of folklore as performance and communication. Although not in the vanguard of the performance studies movement, Dorson as a student of American civilization recognized that the great mobility of Americans, their staunch individualism and mix of identities, called for approaches that were different from European study of rooted, homogeneous groups. Dorson himself contributed essays on the narrative style of outstanding tale-tellers, and assessed how identities were conveyed differently by individuals as they traveled in various circles (Dorson 1972e). Later articulated in the works of Roger Abrahams and Richard Bauman, among others, performance analysis centered on the small, often temporary, group and on symbolic events which typically defied cross-cultural comparison.

Intellectual history, then, shows that American and British strands of study developed differently. The American strand went through several changes, most notably the development into an academic discipline devoted to national traditions, and came to emphasize American conditions of individuality, mobility, and communication. Although itself experiencing change, the Folklore Society did not stray far from its original mission (Bennett 1996). The opportunities for English and American cooperation were limited by the cross-purposes of the different organizations. In addition, the English inheritance representing the dominant cultural source of America was often passed over in folklore study in a search for the subcultural diversity of American life.

Americans appeared to view the stuff of folklore at the local level as a counter to the nationalization of history. Folklore was the evidence that confirmed an American pluralism, in region, ethnicity, race, and occupation. When English inheritance was noticed, it was typically in relation to regional subculture, as in Appalachia or the Ozarks. Otherwise, English influence formed the master narrative of nation-building, from old New England to the American Revolution. Emphasizing a heterogeneous conception of America open to subcultural diversity, American folklorists after World War II often looked beyond the survivals of English folklore to the living traditions of communities encompassing a folk*life* in Scotland, Wales, and Ireland. Instead of claiming a lineage back to Thoms, the folklife group cited *Volkskunde* perspectives of Germany and Scandinavia (Hines 1972). Alfred Shoemaker and Don Yoder made calls for American folklife study that reintegrates oral with material and social traditions in the consideration of the totality of traditions in ethnic-regional subcultures (Yoder 1976b). Resisting English models that implied assimilation of ethnic cultures into a dominant political system, folklife advocates in Scotland, Wales, and Ireland magnified the integrity, as well as creativity, of regional cultures, especially manifested in crafts and architecture necessary for daily living (Hines 1972; Ballard 1994).

The movement away from English models became apparent in the reintegration of material and social traditions after the 1960s. A convergence seemed to have occurred between post-1960s consideration of performance of tales and creativity in craft. Scotland's Alexander Fenton, one of the more influential figures in the folklife movement of the British Isles, observed that "just as the contextualising of a song, musical performance or tale within its social setting came to be important, so was it also with objects. The questions asked ceased to be mainly about points of origin, diffusion and continuity. They now touched on the role within a regional or local community, the function of elements of popular culture in marking social differentiation within a community, and the effects of external influences. In other words, social spread was added to geographical spread, and the present was added to the past" (Fenton 1993, 9). Showing a range of arts and their integration in a local community underscored the vitality, indeed differentiation, of a variety of cultures as they moved, adapted, and changed across the Atlantic.

ANALYZING TRADITION ACROSS THE ATLANTIC

If the English influence receives a cold shoulder in cultural study and a warm reception as national history, then what is it that students justly need to know about the English-American connection in folklore and folklife? Henry Glassie in his important work *Pattern in the Material Folk Culture of the Eastern United States* (1968) tried to give balance to the portrayal of America by charting infusion of various European ideas into the formation of American regional cultures. Locating four major "cultural hearths" opened on the Eastern Seaboard by different European groups, Glassie showed that America's regional development owed to the nature of original ethnic settlement and spread.

In Glassie's overview of varied cultural diffusion, he responded to the historical and political emphasis on the spread of a unified "American spirit" from Puritan New England roots to the rest of the country. He helped to answer nagging questions about the persistence of regional cultures derived from the British cultural inheritance. Unlike historical documents that were used to emphasize change over periods and the unity of a literate class, folk materials seemed especially useful to provide cultural answers because they tended to be variable over space and stable over time and represented a wider range of people. Folk materials could be used to trace longstanding cultural traditions. Folk houses, which stood in place on the landscape, offered visible proofs of diffusion and adaptation to the new environment (Kniffen [1965] 1986). Behind this effort are basic issues of the effect on regional and national character as cultures separate, spread, integrate, settle, adapt, and change. It is essentially a search for symbols of a common and divergent heritage, an exploration for roots of a complex and diverse nation.

Maybe the hesitation to draw English-American connections in oral lore additionally stems from the international nature of many verbal forms. Indeed, the English scholarly emphasis on folklore as oral narrative had an international reach and complemented the evolutionary consideration of global convergence. The job of transporting material culture is slower and more cumbersome than diffusing oral tradition; architecture and art are often presumed to better represent cross-national, rather than broad cross-cultural, movement. These assumptions are based on the English emphasis on classifying genre according to natural history typology, and the split between material and oral genres, for the analysis is based on the separation rather than integration of forms in cultural patterning. Material traditions are expected to stabilize and harden on the landscape in a region or community. Oral traditions, being fleetingly spoken, are expected to vary and move quickly. As the experience of English settlement became more distant, American folklorists turned to the development of a distinctive

American civilization, shown in traditions peculiarly suited to the American experience. This was "American folklore," Richard Dorson claimed, as opposed to a derivative "folklore in America" (Dorson 1959a, 1978c, 1980a). Taking the idea of context influencing the generation of culture even further, many "performance-oriented" folklorists of the 1970s appeared to take the issue of national culture out of the analytic picture in favor of consideration of immediate conditions and social interactions that made the question of English-American continuities a moot point.

Another kind of question looks for continuities rather than dichotomies. Questions of structure and aesthetics, which are more common in American than English folklore studies, ask about the underlying guiding principles that direct the creation and performance of cultural traditions. Such traditions, it is often assumed, are not as subject to national histories as social and psychological patterns that influence individual choices of traditions made in certain environments. Such principles imply more personal volition in the choices of tradition and less textual fixity in the forms that tradition take than evolutionary perspectives assume. If forms emerge from individually developed aesthetics and traditional structures, then folklore is constantly being re-created rather than "surviving." The examination of culture thus necessarily de-emphasizes the historical dimension and stresses more ethnographic views of changeable cultural "scenes." Behavior accommodates the variable backdrops and actors on stages of life.

Looking at structure and aesthetics of expressions within some significant scenes—in houses, fiddle tunes, and stories—integration appears possible, indeed crucial, in the analysis of contemporary American folklore and folklife. Here I will offer some perspectives on this kind of examination by tracing base concepts of linear order, binary construction, and rectangular foundation in American traditions owing to English influence.

It is on the basis of structure, in fact, that the American argument for expanding the definition of folklore to include nonverbal forms was made. Alan Dundes in "On Game Morphology: A Study of the Structure of Non-Verbal Folklore" (1964) contended that children's games follow a linear sequence similar to one followed in most folktales. Dundes's example was the English-American game of Hare and Hounds, which he found followed Vladimir Propp's "syntagmatic" structural scheme of folktales (Propp 1968, 1984). The game contains a protagonist (hare) and antagonist (hounds), and it moves sequentially from a lack (for the hare, wanting to go home) to the elimination of a lack (returning home) with intervening moves of an interdiction (without being caught by hounds) and violation (being caught by hounds). The game then is visually shaped rectangularly with a binary pair forming the action which moves linearly through four (two pairs) moves. The rectangular shape is indeed a fundamental building block of English-American folk housing and other material forms. If the structures of games and tales, or games and houses, are similar, they can be analyzed as part of a unified whole, that of tradition in culture.

Differences in structure are apparent in various cultures. The Western fondness for three divisions cited by Axel Olrik in his epic laws for folk narrative, and by Henry Glassie for the design of folk art, contrasts with many American Indian uses of four or Chinese uses of five. Three is a symbol of human control representing the shape of the human head in relation to two arms (Glassie 1972, 269, 273–74). Studies of American Indians have shown that the number four is often used as a natural symbol relating to four cardinal points. Many Asian cultures add one more for the self (Dundes 1980b). In these assumptions are contained different attitudes toward the landscape. Western embrace of technological progress and control of the environment are offered in the very structure of tradition based on human power (Stilgoe 1982). Similarly, the communal circle as a basis for housing is a natural symbol used in many African and American Indian cultures, but the rectangle, a technological symbol, is the primary base concept of individual expansion in Western tradition.

Structural patterns arranged geographically are used to answer the puzzle over why more British construction techniques did not cross over the Atlantic with the original settlers. Adapting to the new environment, English Americans used local forms and devised new ones based on the structuring patterns they learned as part of their culture (Bronner 1989a). Although an occasional English half-timber or wattle-and-daub house exists in America, Americans mostly constructed in log, brick, and stone. The abundance of wood and land in America, especially, made a difference in the cultural look of the countryside. Following the route of human control, the sequence in the early days of the Republic followed the clearing of the wilderness to announce ownership of property through the erection of linear fences and private outbuildings to the establishment of a new classic civilization with application of Greek Revival ornamentation. Despite the feeling of creating a new material civilization, American folk architecture owed much to the sense of eighteenth-century geometric order popularized by British thinkers and designers (Glassie 1975). The order was influenced by the spread of literacy during the period. Writing, the ultimate statement of rational human control, produced neat rows and tabular forms. Geometric order announced rational human control over nature, again well suited to American designs on its future.

The binary pair in folk architecture is an example of the structuring power of geometric order and goes beyond national boundaries of England and America (Glassie 1973). The layout of the single pen unit, the basic unit of the home, consisted of four sides, or two squared. The proportions of the room were typically four squared, or sixteen feet square. The rectangular base concept then was formed with two such units. The bodily shape represented by threes took form when the binary pair was situated around a central door. The bodily image became social in the house with the suggestion that the one to one structure of the binary pair in the house formed from the union of man and woman. Often, in fact, two trees were planted, one on either side of the house to reinforce the visual image of union.

The so-called "English barn" is not unique to, or predominant, in England, but its typological name extended the idea of rectangular proportion associated with English form (Glassie 1974). Its doors centrally located on the non-gable end, its plan arranged in an even ratio of two-to-one, the English barn was the utilitarian extension of the social house's structure. The grammar of construction continued to use binary pairs when the need for space increased. Rather than extend the house with three pens, builders arranged the house to rise upward with two rooms over two rooms. An indication of the persistence of this aesthetic is in the harsh conditions of the Great Plains of the American West where in the absence of trees settlers turned to sod for their building material (Welsch 1968; Barns 1930). Although circular and dugout designs might have actually proved more pragmatic, the settlers insisted on the rectangular base concept reminiscent of forms back east.

Houses are not the only keys to identifying base concepts. Gravestones, especially in New England, borrow heavily from British iconography. Cemetery design retained the ordered, linear format of British churchyards and stood in stark contrast to the nature of American Indian burying grounds. The Indian grounds fitted the cosmology of returning to the earth and establishing a cycle to life. The rectangular emphasis is a cosmological statement as well, giving emphasis to the material life spent on earth. The stones themselves showed a sense of permanence to the individual, and were shaped like the top of a body with a head and shoulders forming a binary pair around a central unit (Deetz and Dethlefsen 1982).

Perhaps most noticeable in tracing a British-American connection is the fiddled dance tune. My fieldwork in upstate New York uncovered many fiddlers who learned the tunes with transatlantic roots such as "Soldier's Joy," "Lamplighter's Hornpipe," and "McLeod's Reel" (Bronner 1987b). These tunes have the "endless" repetitive quality arising out of an *aabb* form, two sets of binary pairs. In performance, the solo fiddler dominated, although I occasionally witnessed twin fiddle arrangements. I most commonly beheld an aesthetic placing value on precision and repetition in the ability to play in unison rather than in harmony. New England is associated today with the preponderance of the English line dance, and the South is especially well known for development of the basic "square" dance. The make-up of these squares is of two-by-two-by-two-by-two or four sides containing two persons on each side. In performance, the squares are arranged in lines, typically two, although it is significant to note that contextual studies have pointed out stylistic differences between southern and northern dancers and fiddlers. Bill Malone has hypothesized that the southern country music tradition—allowing for more improvisation, emotional expression, and *aab* lyrical forms than in the North—owes greatly to the pronounced African-American presence in the South (Malone 1968). Another explanation may be in the development of a predominant Baptist religion among southerners that fostered an affective performance orientation in some contrast to the Congregationalism of the North (Ellison 1995; Bronner 1987b). In addition, the popular social dance known as the "square dance" accompanied by a caller (shouting rhymed instructions) with fiddle, banjo, and guitar, varied from South to North (and later East to West with the introduction of "swing jazz" beats) especially because of southern African-American adaptations (in rhymed calling, syncopation of fiddle tunes, and instrumentation of the five-string banjo) (see Winslow 1972; Feintuch 1981; Bronner 1987b; Abrahams 1992b, 197–98; Bluestein 1994, 66–74). The point of delineating these contexts is to draw attention to the complex regional-ethnic-religious mix of the United States that frequently raises more questions of adaptation and syncretism rather than transplantation.

To be sure, a case for transplantation and eventual dominance of English tradition over American culture had its hardy advocates. Its high point may have been a period called the Colonial Revival beginning in the late nineteenth century when references to styles of colonial New England and Virginia came into fashion in architecture, music, and dance. Enthusiasts for the Colonial Revival played up the appeal of stability and solidness of old English forms and encouraged the search for signs of English persistence in America. Led by descendants of the original settlers who feared the transformation of white Anglo-Saxon Protestant culture by waves of immigrants from southern and eastern Europe, the Colonial Revival used the ready observation by Victorian scholars that American song, tune, and dance stemmed largely from English tradition (see Axelrod 1985).

To cite some examples of efforts to reconstruct America on an English foundation: the popular magazine *Harper's* launched a series of articles on the cultural emergence of America as "An English Nation" toward the century's close, immigrant youngsters from southern and eastern Europe were taught English-American folk songs and dances in schools to encourage assimilation, and the New England (sometimes called the "Old Tyme" to reinforce its traditionality in American culture) Kitchen exhibit became a fixture of American tradition at World's Fairs through the Gilded Age (Higginson 1883; Rhoads 1985; Roth 1985). Responding to social changes caused by massive immigration from eastern and southern Europe, and expressing a perceived need for national unity based on the founding principles and English-derived culture of the young Republic, some authors located Appalachian singers of British ballads as America's "genuine ancestors" (see Frost [1899] 1989). As if to reinforce the bond of a common language, oral tradition drew special consideration in most of these studies on the survival of English culture in America.

THE PROBLEM OF CHILDHOOD

Several leaders of the American Folklore Society, most of whom came from New England and Eastern Seaboard cities, made much of the social connection of childhood to the shared oral tradition of England and America. In their evolutionary way of thinking, childhood as the beginning of cultural life became prominent to understand the English inheritance as the foundation from which American culture emerged. Two notable contributions to children's game study in Britain and America published within a few years of each other in the late nineteenth century became classics and continued to appear in print in numerous editions through the twentieth century. Alice Bertha Gomme, wife of prominent English evolutionary folklorist George Laurence Gomme, published her first volume of *The Traditional Games of England, Scotland, and Ireland* in 1894, and William Wells Newell, a Unitarian minister and schoolmaster from the Boston area, came out with *Games and Songs of American Children* in 1883. In their evolutionary thinking, children represented an early stage of cultural development of adults much as savages related to the civilized. The origin of line games, for example, Gomme attributed to a hidden past rather than the structural or aesthetic needs of present-day children. Considering the prevalence of line games, she wrote that "it is obvious that we have elements of custom and usage which would not primarily originate in a game, but in condition of local or tribal life which has long since passed away. It is a life of contest, a life, therefore, which existed before the days of settled politics, when villages or tribal territories had their own customs differing from each other, and when not only matters of political relationship were settled by the arbitrament of the sword, but matters not considered to be of purely personal relationship, namely, marriage" (Gomme 1964, 2:489). Games played by British children represented to Gomme survivals of customs that led to the development of modern drama and even religious practice. Alice Gomme intended to bring the classification of games together with those beliefs and folk institutions investigated by her husband George to give a complete picture of layers of British historical development in a grand dictionary of British folklore (Dorson 1968, 277).

From his New England base, Newell thought that America was an even better place than Britain to view the survivals of ancient customs in game because "the New World has preserved what the Old World has forgotten; and the amusements of children to-day picture to us the dances which delighted the court as well as the people of the Old England before the settlement of the New" (Newell [1884] 1992, 3–4). He saw in games the remains of customs found among the elite that had filtered or corrupted down to folk usage. He viewed religious practice and courtly amusement in games that had been preserved in the countryside and diffused from there, rather than the evolution from peasant and savage to higher levels. "If these usages seem rustic, it is only because the country retained what the city forgot, in consequence of the change of manners to which it was sooner exposed," he wrote, and he sentimentally commented that "now that our country towns are become mere outlying suburbs of cities, these remarks may read with a smile at the rude simplicity of old-fashioned American life" (Newell [1884] 1992, 6). There was something of an American democratic ideology implied in Newell's comments because of his opinion that unlike England, Americans rich and poor, rural and

Cover of the first edition of *Games and Songs of American Children* (1883), by William Wells Newell, showing "London Bridge Is Falling Down," in his view a prime example of a "cultural survival."

urban, share in the same folklore. American schools offer a "mighty engine of equalization," he wrote, and he observed that "the English-speaking population, which imposes on all new-comers its language, imposes also its traditions, even the traditions of children" (Newell [1884] 1992, 2).

Pointing to the dramatic changes in the "motion and novelty" of industrial American life, Newell felt that the conditions of preindustrial America removed from "the currents of thought circulating in Europe" maintained the predominance of the old English traditions into the modern age, despite introductions of other ethnic influences. Although laying claims to represent American tradition widely, his sources of New England schoolchildren undoubtedly influenced his declaration that the typical games of Americans, or "usages of play" as he put it, "are almost entirely of old English origin."[2] Newell inferred a national gaming tradition in America emerging from English origin and a separateness of childhood from adulthood borne out by the prevalence of gaming folklore (Abrahams 1988). American children's games showed a uniformity across regions, he wrote, because "the extension of intercourse between the States has tended to diffuse them, so that petty rhymes, lately invented, have sometimes gained currency from Maine to Georgia" (Newell [1884] 1992, 3). Newell encouraged collection of English-American children's folklore from his post as editor of the *Journal of American Folklore* and calls for investigation continued from his successor Alexander Chamberlain (1865–1914), editor from 1900 to 1907, who published *The Child and Childhood in Folk-Thought* (1896).

Chamberlain fixed on what he called the "child-idea" in culture, the view that children represent through folklore the vitality of a culture. Chamberlain took the vantage of "elders" who pass tradition to children and evaluate them. "Everywhere throughout the world," Chamberlain wrote, "the activities of childhood have been appealed to, and the race has wonderfully profited by its wisdom, its naiveté, its ingenuity, and its touch of divinity" (Chamberlain 1896, 403). In keeping with the evolution from simple childhood to complex adulthood, Chamberlain's impressive tome and Newell's collection give the impression that children in America primarily knew simple rhymes, games, and beliefs crafted ages before, probably by English adults. Neither Newell nor Chamberlain offered much in the way of narrative behavior given by children. Four brief paragraphs in Chamberlain's study describe "story-telling" *to* children, but none gives an account of what children do with this knowledge, much less recognize narrative creativity (Chamberlain 1896, 204–5).

The influences of English Darwinian philosophy and modern aesthetic values should be apparent in the assumptions of many studies of children's folklore from the nineteenth century to the present. Although Newell and Gomme argued about the direction of cultural survival and the diffusion of its forms, Darwinian influence is still present in the evolutionary premise of the "natural" movement from simple to complex forms, from children's rhymes to adult narratives. Although

Newell recognized the inventiveness of children, he and others nonetheless selected the "traditional" forms showing stability and distribution over generations for
comparison. Scholars well after Newell chose specimens that had a completed
quality to them and drew attention to themselves because of their customary or
literary characteristics. Such arrangements and choices resulted in a picture of
cultural stability over an extended time. Another result was a map of cultural
space in which isolable groups expressed their differences through lore. Within
this map, children and adults, women and men, to name some divisions, inhabit-
ed separate spheres.

In a departure from Chamberlain's concern for "folk thought," one can examine
a process rather than form, of thinking rather than thought. One does not collect
specimens so much as recognize interactions that employ "stories," many of which
may be unique but follow recognizable structures (Goodwin 1990). The questioning is not about lines from "yesterday" into "tomorrow," but rather about the ways
people express themselves taking cues from any number of simultaneous influences, and indeed create themselves through expression. The breaks that this questioning of expression make with English-American evolutionary approaches are
evident in the emphasis placed today on the keywords of development, learning,
and communication. By using development, many researchers since the 1980s
drew attention to varying rates of growth and varieties of expression among children. It is granted that children strive toward the maturity of adulthood, but one
also recognizes that children have distinctive behaviors that do not necessarily
carry over into adulthood.

Within the broad neutral native category of "kids" lies an implication of
change, physical and social—and cultural. Through the life course, individuals
learn from a variety of sources about responding to different situations. The perception of physical difference between children and adults, however, not to mention the social clustering of children in school, tempt Europeans and Americans to
categorize childhood as a social unit separate from adulthood. Yet contextualizing
aging with the life course as a process of structuring experience and aestheticizing
expression in the investigation of children's lives offers a closer look at the ways
children use lore to respond to developmental and social changes (Bronner
1990b). Addition of visual and oral recording devices, in contrast to the literary
methods of Gilded Age folklorists, suggests more multidimensional consideration
of movement, voice, and surroundings—recordable elements of interaction—
than the one-dimensional treatment of the written page. Indeed, the activities
through the life course become visual frames to be individually analyzed rather
than specimens to be classified.

The notable children's folklore collecting of Peter and Iona Opie in Britain half
a century after Newell and Gomme retained most of the evolutionary classificatory emphasis on custom and text. As Newell had done years before, the Opies marveled at the conservative retention of ancient tradition and the simultaneous

inventiveness with which children can improvise language and play. From a glance at the English-American folkloristic bookshelf from Newell to the Opies, it appears that children's folklore has been the most persistent reminder of British folkloric connections next to folk music and architecture. Perhaps the area of children's folklore most vividly reminds Americans (and Australians, judging from children's folklore work there) of the English connection because of the emphasis in children's expression on textual form (Cansler 1968). Just listen to American children singing "London Bridge Is Falling Down," which you can almost every day, or counting out "One, two, three, four, Mary's at the kitchen door." Listed and indexed in the antiquarian manner of noting anachronistic items, texts invite comparison of stability across the ocean, and the Opies were especially concerned for categorizing them and finding their provenance.

Yet a tradition such as hand-clapping games that involves performance and integration of different expressive behaviors defies easy typology. Such games combine gestures, music, and words creatively arranged in rhyme. Socially, they vary according to ethnicity and region, and, significantly, age. Typically played between two girls, each using two hands, the hand-clapping games involve speaking four-line verses usually with alternate lines rhyming. In performance, the number of verses remembered is usually two, three, or four. One common game begins "My mother gave me a nickel, My father gave me a dime, My sister gave me a lover boy, Who loved me all the time." It continues: "My mother took her nickel, My father took his dime, My sister took her lover boy, and gave me Frankenstein. He made me do the dishes, He made me mop the floor, I got so sick and tired of him, I kicked him out the door" (Bronner 1988a, 62–63; Opie and Opie 1985; Rutherford 1971, 76). Often, however, the action of giving and returning, and characterizations of mother and father, offer other binary pairs: "My mother gave me peaches, My father gave me pears, My boyfriend gave me fifty cents, And kissed me up the stairs. My mother took my peaches, My father took his pears, My boyfriend took his fifty cents, So I kicked him down the stairs." This is the contemporary form of an old skipping rhyme: "Nine (or twelve, or seven) o'clock is striking, Mother may I go out? All the boys are waiting, For to take me out. One will give me an apple, One will give me a pear, One will give me fifty cents, To kiss behind the stair." Even in the skipping version, performed between two holders of a single rope, the stress is on the construction of a rectangular base concept from the use of binary pairs.

Identifying such base concepts and the aesthetics arising from them helps to put emergent forms in cultural perspective. Culture becomes less of a form and more of a process available to individuals to enact. The identity of an American child does not refer to English precedent in this view, although questions may arise as to why the choices available to the child derive from English sources. In preadolescent play, a strong element of improvisation and fantasy that uses structures of tradition rather than texts to form play behaviors are at work (Dargan

and Zeitlin 1990). The strength of American popular culture brings new characters and commonplaces into children's folklore. The influence, then, is moving
back across the Atlantic and into other English-speaking cultures such as
Australia and New Zealand. One that has attracted notice in Australia as well as
the United States and England is "Ronald McDonald," the clown character in
McDonald's advertising. In Harrisburg, Pennsylvania, I have collected children
clapping to the words: "Ronald McDonald, a biscuit oh McDonald, A biscuit oh
she she wa wa, A biscuit I got a boyfriend" (Bronner 1988a, 65–68; see also Grider
1976, 752–53; Langstaff and Langstaff 1973; "Clapping" 1985). The second verse is:
"A biscuit she's so sweet, A biscuit like a cherry tree, Baby down the roller coaster,
Sweet sweet babe I never let you go." And the third verse is: "Shimmy shimmy
coco pop, Shimmy shimmy pal, Shimmy coco pop, Shimmy shimmy pow!"
Showing the mark of post-World War II rhythm and blues music, the clapping
game is syncopated when compared to older English-American rhymes, but the
routines that accompany these jive clapping verses still retain some binary base
concepts. The movements are first clapping, then snapping fingers, one hand up
and the other down, hitting the other person, right-hand thumb over shoulder
and then left, make a fist, hug the other person, imitate a gun with hand and point
at other person (at "pow"). These examples remind us that while the content and
performance of lore adapt readily, the structures underlying them are slow to
change (see Fine 1980a; Maranda and Maranda 1971). When they do change, signs
of significant cultural shift are usually evident.

During the late nineteenth century, evolutionary doctrine led some scholars to
imagine that literacy and technology naturally replace oral forms of learning. Yet it
became evident that people surrounded by technology still relied on the kind of
learning usually associated with folklore—by word of mouth, imitation and
demonstration, custom. Indeed, literacy and technology often became tools to
engage narrative behavior and make syncretic combinations of traditional structures and popular messages, as children's parodies of television jingles or personal-
ized retellings of fairy tales indicate (Roemer 1977, 214–28; Bronner 1988a; Tucker
1992). Other examples might be the use of photocopiers for passing traditional
humor and computers for folk games. The important lesson is that people use
folklore for the kind of powerful learning and communication it offers and are
willing to adjust it to new technology so as to engage its qualities. This lesson leads
to an awareness of children's marked complexity and ability, such as the remarkable rapidity with which children learn language and the distinctiveness of the first
few years of life. Within their first year, children become aware quickly of
sequences of words that carry meaning and evoke responses from adults (Brown
1973). In multilingual households, children can quickly select different codes of
speech and often exaggerate their styles. All too little recognized are the culturally
variable developments of ordered "baby talk" and the creative uses of play languages by children (Sherzer 1976; Sanches and Kirshenblatt-Gimblett 1976).

Children do not simply graduate from rhymes to narrative, but employ a range of expression that in fact relies upon narrative competence early in their lives.

Explaining the mechanisms by which children recognize some word sequences as "stories" and find ways to strategically use them essentially challenges scholars to question social interaction and development (Fischer 1960; Edmonson 1971; Rayfield 1972; Nicolaisen 1990; Friel 1995). Even before language is acquired, children became aware of culturally defined spaces that suggest narrative structures in that they have directions and boundaries. In American culture, the rectangle—in the crib, the room, the play block—is a particularly ubiquitous model. In many cultures, circular spaces dominate and may be investigated for a relation to narrative structure. In one study of the Mescalero Apache, for example, Claire Farrer found that houses, dances, and children's games such as Tag showed strong circularity in contrast to English-American linearity (Farrer 1976).

Reading in lines reinforces the aesthetics of linearity in English-American societies (Sullivan 1992; Toelken 1979). Even before adults read to children, they typically use play to enumerate objects on the body as points of reference for narrative sequencing. Among the first playful performances recalled from tradition offered by adults to children are finger or toe formulas. They engage the child and repeat linguistic references—metaphors often relating the child's body to family members or animals—in a memorable way. In French a formula uses the structure of the family in a sequence from the thumb to the little finger:

> Voici le père
> Voici la mère
> Voici la demoiselle
> Voici le fils
> Voici le petit rincouincouin. (Shiver 1941, 223)

And in English a similar sequence can be heard:

> This is my father (hold up thumb)
> This is my mother (hold up index finger)
> This is my brother (hold up middle finger)
> This is my sister (hold up ring finger)
> This is the baby (hold up little finger)
> Oh! How we love them all (clasp hands together).
> (see Welsch 1966, 191; Barrick 1968, 45)

Some of my Pennsylvania-German neighbors recall a formula using the occupations on the farm:

> Der is der Bauer [farmer]
> Der ist die Bauerin [farmer's wife]
> Der ist der Knecht [farmhand]

Der ist die Dein'rn [farmhand's wife]
Und dies kleine wutzlein in der wiegen [piglet in a cradle].
(see Stoudt 1915, 32–33)

And compare it to the sequence of:

Des iss der douma
Der shittelt de blouma
Der laist se oof
Der drawgt se hame
Oon der glay shellem fresst se oll dahame
[This one is the thumb, this one shakes the tree on which grows the plum, this one
   picks them up, this one carries them home, and this little rascal eats them all up].
   (See Shoemaker 1951, 3)

The most common sequence played on the toes in English and American culture is:

This little piggy went to market
This little piggy stayed home
This little piggy had roast beef
This little piggy had none
And this little piggy went (cried) wee, wee, wee (all the way home; I can't find my way
   home; give me some).
(see Barrick 1968, 45; Brewster et al. 1952, 185–87; Opie and Opie 1952, 348–50;
   Northall 1892, 420)[3]

Or one I have frequently collected is an improvisation on the formula for the
body:

What's this? [Is this your nose?] (touches nose)
And what's this? [Is this your chin?] (tickles chin)
And do you know what this is? [Is this your chest?] (touches chest)
For this I'll have to come in for a closer look (looks down at navel or "bellybutton"
   and then presses mouth to it and blows, making a fluttering noise).

Predominant interest in "This Little Piggy," among the others, has been its origin in eighteenth-century English verse and its spread in American usage (see Opie
and Opie 1952, 348–50), but the reference to historical precedent does not explain
the transatlantic selection or adaptation of the tradition. It does not account either
for its function and meaning, since today's parents do not make reference to its
English background as a reason for its enactment. Sometimes known one-dimen-
sionally as "rhymes," the gestural and verbal expressions offered by adults, usually
performed before the child is of reading age, are more in the way of verbal formulas accompanied by physical action that make the infant aware of itself. Because of

the playful context of the sequential activity and the often musical performance of the text, the expressions may also be generically referred to as games (Welsch 1966; Barrick 1968). The verbal stress and elongation in the conclusion accompanying the grabbing of toes or fingers give the sense of an ending that relies on what preceded it. After the routines, finger formulas are introduced to children. They will commonly later demonstrate command of the routine on themselves, essentially narrating themselves (Brunvand 1986b, 113–14).

Are the expressions early in the child's life recognized as stories, then? In some German sources, they are called *Fingermärchen*, or "finger tales" (Shiver 1941). If American children do not recognize them as stories, then they may employ their structures in their own playful expressions using repetition and rhythm. The formulaic rhythm of "This Little Piggy," for instance, relates closely to the youthful narrative told in England and America, and identified as "In A Dark, Dark Wood"[4]:

> Okay, you walk down this long, black road and there's this big, um, black house and you go in this big black room and there's—(speeds up) In the big black room there's a big black closet, in the big black closet there's a big black tuxedo, in the big black tuxedo there's a big black pocket, in the big black pocket is a big black box, in the big black box is a red jelly bean [a genie; dark, dark ghost, whooo!; little tiny mouse eating cheese]. (laughs) (Tucker 1977, 209, 483, 495, 497, 502; Opie and Opie 1959, 36)

Even later in childhood, the rhythm and repetition characterizing this narrative form appears in ghost stories often given at camps and slumber parties (distinctive American institutions). One such story is sometimes identified as a subunit under the heading "Johnny, I Want My Liver" (a subtype, as it has been categorized by European-American folklorists, of Aarne-Thompson Tale-Type 366), although the narrative technique repeats in many stories used by children.

> This lady gave this boy named Johnny a dollar to go to the store to get some liver. But he spent it on something else before he got the liver, and he had to bring this lady her liver. So he saw this graveyard right next to the store. So he unburied a guy, and he got the guy's liver and brought it to the lady. The lady said, "this is a real good liver." But that night they heard, *"I want my liver back, I want my liver back, I want my liver back."* Then *they hear, "I'm on your first step, I want my liver back, I want my liver back, I want my liver back. I'm in the bedroom, I want my liver back, I want my liver back, I want my ..."* (teller grabs listener in abdomen in expectation of third repetition of "liver back") "*LIVER BACK!*" (Bronner 1988a, 158; see also Opie and Opie 1959, 36; Tucker 1977, 370–73, 495–96; Grider 1976, 197–210; Virtanen 1978, 76)

Much of children's narration does not conform to "type" but contains familiar incremental structures in apparently spontaneous compositions. A six-year-old boy, for example, told this "routine" in a play setting at which several children offered "stories":

Once upon a time there was this girl named Lisa, and every night when she went to bed she heard this voice saying like "Lisa I'm at the first stair of the staircase," and on the second night she heard "Lisa I'm in the hall," and the next night she heard "Lisa I'm in your bedroom," and the NEXT night she heard "Lisa I'm right beside you." GOTCHA! (grabs hold of another child) (Roemer 1977, 210)

In so-called spontaneous or invented stories, one can discern similar structures and rhythms, such as this one told repeatedly by a girl from two to three years old that employs the familiar family structure along with the repetition of actions leading to a conclusion:

2/22/75

The man stayed home
the children went out
then a Cookie Monster came
then the Cookie Monster went away
and the mommy was angry
and then the father was angry
and then the children went out again
then the father went out
then the mother went out
they went to the park
then they went home
and then the father was doing work
and then it was getting late
the children went to sleep
and the mommy and the father went to sleep.

8/13/75

The mother went out
then the father went out
then the mother went out again
and then the father went out
then the children went out
then policeman came
the mother came back from the meeting
then the father came back from the meeting
then a Cookie Monster came
and the policeman came again
then the Cookie Monster went away. (Sutton-Smith 1981, 53)

With these "texts" reproduced on the printed page, the analyst of cultural "frames" longs to know the social interactions and cues that gave rise to them. One has to wonder how participants understood their meaning. When these texts are construed as narrative, there is an assumption that they are in themselves part of a sequence. An additional assumption is that while the story draws attention to the text, "narrative" directs inquiry to the performance, some of which may be out of the awareness of the "storyteller." The sequence around the narrative may involve conversation, or play, signals that aid in the recognition of the beginning and ending of "story" and its different meanings in various situations (Rayfield 1972; Scheub 1977; Toelken 1979; Bauman 1986; Haut 1992). And narrative construed in this way is not a separable level of culture, but a necessary, everyday behavior (or "cultural register") in social interaction (Nicolaisen 1990). Narrative is a human way of knowing and expressing meaning.

The use of "narrative" to describe stories is more characteristic of scholarship in an electronic age than that of turn-of-the-century English-American scholarship on children. Narrative has become a technical term that refers to the result of a process (narrating in context) rather than the form of relating information in an organized way. "Narrative" is conspicuously absent in folkloristic dictionaries such as the *Standard Dictionary of Folklore, Mythology and Legend* (1950) and *General Ethnological Concepts* (1960). American folklorist Elliott Oring, however, made the term central in his chapter on "Folk Narratives" in the textbook *Folk Groups and Folklore Genres* (1986). "Narrative," he declared "is another word for story." Then why not use the more familiar "story"? The answer lies in the suggestion of the process of "narrating" in narrative and its implication of behavioral interpretation (Georges 1976). Oring invoked a behavioral perspective when he proclaimed that "narrating is a method by which an experience is transformed into verbal account" (Oring 1986a, 121). The rhetoric of narrative creates a distance with "history" and the past, with which "story" has traditionally been aligned (Nicolaisen 1990). In another American source, the *Dictionary of Concepts in Cultural Anthropology* (1991), Robert Winthrop claimed that "one trend discernible, in both anthropology and folklore studies, is a concern for understanding narrative as a communicative performance, 'a totality encompassing not only the verbal story but the entire narrative experience, auditory and visual, of spectator and actor.'" Winthrop argued that narrative essentially brings out the "expressive dimension of culture"; that is, culture is realized, and even constructed, by narrative communication (Winthrop 1991, 126; see also Edmonson 1971; Ben-Amos and Goldstein 1975; Scheub 1977; Abrahams 1977).

By insisting on processual "narrative" over the English generic distinctions of tale and custom, American researchers have favored native categories and blurred the lines between the verbal and nonverbal dimensions of culture by emphasizing the behavior of communication (Herskovits 1958; Ben-Amos 1972; Ben-Amos and Goldstein 1975; Georges 1976; Scheub 1977; Brady 1984; Stahl 1989). Narrative suggests the organization of communicated experience in a number of ways (Abrahams 1986). How, for example, does the parent's playing of "Peek-a-boo (I see you)," one of the first traditional forms of play experienced between adult and child in American culture, affect an understanding of narrative sequence? The structure moves repeatedly from the hidden face to the face revealed, accompanied by a rhyme, "Peek-a-boo, I see you!" or "Now I see you, now I don't." This frame around the repeated play activity causes delight in the child. Then among the first organized games played by children among themselves is Hide-and-Go-Seek (Bronner 1988a, 176–78). One can also notice that a number of spontaneously "invented" fantasies in children's story composition or pretend play involve the dramatic tension of disappearance and recovery. These examples suggest attention to a process of creativity rather than one of creations (see Crowley 1966; Briggs 1988; Jones 1989; Bronner 1992b).

Creativity is employed to bring old and new elements, as well as individual and social concerns, together in response to social situations and personal needs (Toelken 1979; Evans 1982). The "creation" of concern to Chamberlain and Newell implied the separation of folklore from new inventions. As Chamberlain and Newell used folklore research to reflect on the hierarchical industrial age rising in their Gilded Age society, so the trend represented by "narrative" contemplates the swirling social currents of an electronic era that crosses national boundaries and defies isolable levels of culture. There is a reflection with "narrative" on the tasks of being human as well as the identities that people culturally construct. Especially in the American field, one can discern more of a willingness to document the researcher's experience as well as the subject, to blur genres with attention to the framed "event," and to bring out the spontaneity and profundity of everyday behavior (Georges 1969).

THE FOLKLORE OF MODERNISM

In a frequently encountered perspective on everyday behavior, American folk-lorists look for folkloric responses to similar conditions of electronic communication. The emphasis on human control and progress seen in the structure of tradition, it can be argued, is reduced or enhanced by technological change, and cultural analysts often comment on the ways that people regain or restructure lore to establish their human and group identity. American folklorists have especially commented on the process of folkloric response to technological change in new expressive forms such as photocopied cartoons and memos that declare emergent folkloric processes (Dundes and Pagter 1978, 1987; Bronner 1984c; Smith 1985, 1986; M. Preston 1996a). Much of it understated, and denying what is seen with what is said, the forms follow structural and grammatical rules. Using the standard size of paper as the base, the illustrations and satirical memos follow the rational geometric models of office communication. But oppositions and incongruities emerge from the conflict between the text and illustrations on the parodies. In "The Job Isn't Finished until the Paperwork is Done," a child is usually depicted sitting on a toilet with a large roll of bathroom tissue beside him or her. Here nature conflicts with the organization, the child with the adult message, the informal circular roll with the official rectangular paper. Analyzing the conflicts expressed in these forms, folklorists have difficulty assessing the national origins of texts. Rather, they are faced with the character of human responses to a modernizing, organizational world. Often replacing national culture is the reference to "corporate culture," which is assumed to be multinational.

"As a folkloric mode of cultural production," Danielle Roemer wrote of photocopy traditions, "alternative to and subversive of that produced by official corporate culture, they, like their less bawdy counterparts, are available for wider interpretation" (Roemer 1994, 121–22). The folklore of photocopying restores individuality to organizational life in her outlook: "Unofficial photocopy practice returns to the individual some sense of the authenticity of a maker. It does so through encouraging action—the duplication of a sheet—and through encouraging interpretation—the use of the sheet by employees to contextualize themselves within the workplace" (Roemer 1994, 136). The small worlds of "context" in contrast to the large global view of evolution thus often invoke human control within a mass society.

Leaving the nineteenth century behind, British evolutionary folklorists sought to comprehend the primitive roots of humankind as a way to justify and explain imperial expansion and industrial advancement centered in British experience. While heavily influenced by this view, American folklorists, "looking ahead" during the twentieth century, explored the varied American experience and expanded it into at first a national and then a contextual model of analysis that emphasized individual will in a mass society, and questioned the role of aesthetics within traditional structures. As the twenty-first century approached, folklorists depicted cultures as the humane element carved by people in an inevitable technological society.

Indeed the questioning of folklore, as several studies have suggested, refers to the qualities of "being human" (Wilson 1982a, 1982b). William Wilson expressed the humane hope that folklore studies "in a world challenged by polluted air, disappearing natural resources, a depleted ozone layer, unchecked diseases, crowded highways and airways, burgeoning crime rates, killing drugs, and rapidly shifting geo-political borders and alliances" offers "courage to face the future by learning to celebrate ourselves" (Wilson 1991, 129). Senior folklorist Archie Green reflected that he strives "for a future that is humane, a future that is small in scale, a future that is manageable, a future in which, if we cannot stop progress, we can at least retard it" (Green 1984). Others do not take a stand *against* progress, but for *cultural conservation,* and announce that folklore has an application for reform (Feintuch 1988; Baron and Spitzer 1992; Hufford 1994). Michael Owen Jones, for instance, proclaimed in a special issue on future prospects for folklore research that, "I consider some of the benefits of including organization in folkloristics, especially those of increasing the understanding of organizations and behavior in them and of improving the conditions under which their members labor" (Jones 1991, 31).

During a sabbatical stay in England in 1987–1988, I sought out the organizational character of English folklorists as well as connections to American architecture and folk arts. I found energetic and devoted folklorists not connected to universities, but engaged in libraries, museums, and professions. The indexes and bibliographies sponsored by the English society are as numerous and detailed, maybe more so, than those for any other folklore society I have ever encountered. Indeed, the society's journal editor emphasized that "to collect and categorise is an essential activity" and, in keeping with English intellectual history from Tylor to Malinowski, she noted that interest has shifted from speculations about origins to investigations of functions (Simpson 1989, 6). The society's meetings appeared to be more social occasions than American conferences, and they were centered in London, rather than moving about from city to city, as occurs on the North American continent. English meetings occur frequently during the year and often have the feel of a club rather than an association. I vividly recall my presentation to the society in one of those semiannual meetings that occurred above a pub. It reminded me of Victorian clubs that met for evening lectures. I detected a serious commitment to collection and a willingness, even more so than in the United States, to engage in collaborative projects. And if American folklorists are characterized as ethnographic in their approach to the present, English papers I heard typically had an historical dimension to them. Jacqueline Simpson commented that much of the historical interest concerns folk memory of famous personages such as Cromwell or Nell Gwynn as well as local characters. She also hoped for more connection to oral history, especially "working class history," of special concern in class-conscious England (Simpson 1989, 5).

Although English folklore as a discipline does not have the organizational cohesion of its American counterpart, it boasts great scattered enthusiasm for the location of evidence toward a historical record of folklore. English folklorists still tend to divide their subject into textual types. Study groups had developed for material culture, legend, and music and dance apart from folklore. Beliefs and children's folklore, two areas that have been specialties in English folklore studies, continue to have strong adherents within the organization. Surveying the society journal's contents for the thirty years since 1959, Jacqueline Simpson commented that examination of modern folklore and the ways that "folklore is ever an active force affecting all levels of the community and functioning through many channels" came late to the journal's pages (Simpson 1989, 4). The continuity with the past lies with a still-steady stream of studies of customs, tales, and religion. Although the representation from the outer boundaries of the former British Empire in Africa, Asia, Polynesia, and the Middle East has been reduced, as well as relations with European peasant folklore, Simpson still noted that social studies of English folklore have not necessarily filled the gap. "Much work remains to be done," she observed, "on the sociology of British folklore, whether in relation to class, to occupations, or to regional, racial, and religious groupings" (Simpson 1989, 5).

In the areas of song, dance, and drama, English folklorists have had special contributions to make that have attracted attention beyond England. In summarizing folklore studies in her country, Simpson pointed to the importance of "social" as approach and the "present" as perspective, although she is unwilling to abandon evolutionism altogether. In her words,

> I see in our Journal a steady broadening of the scope of the subject, a growing preference for precise documentation rather than far-flung theorizing, a more realistic appraisal of historical and social factors, a greater diversity both of the genres and of the social groups studied. Above all, I see a shifting of the time-scale. The first two or three generations of folklorists were greatly concerned with origins—generally set in the remote past—and worked from a definition of "tradition" which stressed almost exclusively the handing on of information or custom over many generations. These are valid concerns, which should not be discarded. But they need to be balanced, as they now are, by an equally strong concern with the present, as exemplified by the emergence of new genres, the updating of customs and oral lore to meet new conditions, the circulation of traditions among contemporaries and peer groups, the use of new channels of transmission, the interconnexions with other levels of culture. (Simpson 1989, 8)

The very same journal which carried Simpson's essay featured eight articles on historic phenomena and two that were historiographical. The subjects? Dance and drama (mumming, Morris dance), supernatural belief (house charms on the Isle of Man, witchcraft in the Balkans, old superstitious uses of horse skulls), and narrative (medieval love allegory, legend of Christ's visit to Britain, Norse Grail legends). The comparable volume for that year in the *Journal of American Folklore* featured a special issue on folklore of the Vietnam War and articles on tourism and cultural display, UFO abduction reports, the use of computers to organize ritual food exchange at the Jewish holiday of Purim by contemporary orthodox women in New York City, contemporary Romanian jokes, jazz and American culture, and a performance analysis of an emerging form of riddling in America. The American journal's emphasis is decidedly contemporary and concerned with emerging or adapting, even "invented" (e.g., in tourism) forms of tradition. The problem with the self-assuredness of pronouncements in many of these articles on the state of theory oriented toward performance, communication, and process is that it purports to be international when it is decidedly American.

If the story of English folklorists has been one of "grand theorizing" on an imperial scale, and an overstatement of "survivals," have the claims of American theorizers been equally grand and more nationalistic, even as they appear multicultural? In a plea for more internationalism, or transnational and cultural studies, Sweden's

Barbro Klein decried in the American society's newsletter "myopic Amerocentrism" that is "unreflected." Echoing Henry Glassie's declaration that "this world is one of peasants," Klein recognized the predominant interest of folklorists in Asia and Africa in "arts and traditions of the large peasant groups in their own countries" (Klein 1995). Whether it is a response to an absence of an analytical category for peasants in America or the relativistic turning away from studies of primitive and peasant survivals in the English evolutionary school, American folkloristics—as its journal contents show—tends to take as its subject contemporary performances in modernizing, multicultural society. Yet it is also true that "more folkloristic research traditions are represented in the United States than in any other single country," making easy categorization of an American perspective problematic. Moreover, the discourse on culture involving folklore has often been a heated dialogue on the role of the past, nation, and creativity in the formation of tradition.

Because of the intensity of the national discourse in the American Century, or the expectation that "North American folklore study is so interesting that there is little need to fetch inspiration elsewhere," the flow of theory, and the dialogue on it, Klein complained, is expected to move from the United States outward. When she referred to "American hegemony," she implied that this expectation of theory flow also applied to production of popular culture from movies to music disseminated from the United States to the world. "Theorizing folklore," she summarized, "unabashedly means 'theorizing American folklore'" (Klein 1995, 13). Perhaps this can be explained by noting that the small frames of ethnography employed in performance theory can sometimes minimize the political and social context of nation and state. Or the relatively large American land mass, for a nation-state, widespread use of English, and emergence of a folkloristic discipline with a number of centers has indeed convinced many American students that America is the world. Maybe Dorson's use of his impressive history of British folklorists after its publication in 1968 helped persuade American students that they were set to embark on another golden age. He implied that as England had its day of world leadership in the late nineteenth century, so America would in the late twentieth (Dorson 1980b).

To be sure, Americans have not generally had the European experience of multinational exchange, although American folklore studies have been greatly shaped by scholars born and educated abroad, including figures such as Franz Boas, Linda Dégh, Dan Ben-Amos, and W. F. H. Nicolaisen. And there has been a substantial history of foreign scholars seriously studying American folk expressions (e.g., blues music) before Americans had fully appreciated them (see Oliver 1970). Evidence for American internationalism is in the folklife movement that openly credits comparative work in Germany, Scandinavia, and the British Isles (see Yoder 1990). Revising international comparative methods, few studies anywhere can match the insights on process and symbol drawn from British social anthropology and folklife studies provided by Paul Oliver's *Dwellings: The House*

Across the World (1987). From his position at Oxford Brookes University, Oliver joined American folklorists with anthropologists, geographers, and architectural historians in other continents for the ambitious, and suggestive, *Encyclopedia of Vernacular Architecture of the World* (1997). Oliver's work shows a special concern for African and Asian cultures that are on the one hand often neglected in Eurocentric historical studies, and on the other, have become more significant as Pacific Rim and Middle East countries take increasingly forceful roles in world economy and politics.

Moving beyond ethnic studies that concentrated on European groups, many American folklorists have worked on new acculturation and identity patterns apparent among immigrants from Asia, Africa, the Middle East, and the Caribbean and Latin America (Almeida 1995; Koltyk 1993; Blair 1991; see also Santoli 1988). Because of the emphasis on contemporary multiculturalism, in fact, English traditions as well as scholars may be neglected. The practice of multiculturalism often involves examination of supposedly victimized racial and ethnic groups whose cultures have been dominated by hegemonic elites, associated with English colonialism (Davies 1995, 23–24; see also Feintuch 1992; Kurin 1993). Another factor in the decline of the English connection is that despite the preponderant English presence in early America (estimated at 83.5 percent of the white population and 64.2 of the total in 1790), most Americans today lack an attachment to English ancestry. Ancestry is a revealing census category because it refers to the way people identify their background. The 1990 census reported that at 11 percent of the total, English trailed well behind German (19.6) and Irish (13.1) as the most frequently reported ancestry. This statistic means that many Americans of English descent do not consider themselves as such (Waters 1990; Bronner 1996d).

One scholarly direction from England has since the 1980s taken a critical stance toward English cultural influence. "Cultural studies," so named to differentiate it from the positivist "culture studies" of social science, often theorizes ways that cultural practices, including the study of culture, involve relations of power. British cultural studies presumably held an appeal because of its revision of contemporary consciousness for a postcolonial world that looked to break the limitations of primitivism on the one hand and aristocratic control on the other. It especially assaulted the design of culture for fostering romantic nationalism and hierarchical social division. A prime example from this movement is an analysis of the "manufacture," as one author put it, of British folk song to serve interests of an elite (see Harker 1985).[5] Other English perspectives on folklore using cultural studies have examined the colonizing "invention" and "marketing" of tradition in festival and tourism (Hobsbawm and Ranger 1983; Brewer 1994).

The consideration of ways that scholarship on cultural traditions has encouraged nostalgia and nationalism in popular culture, and altered the shape of the original traditions, attracted many American intellectuals during the 1990s who sought ways to turn the popularization of cultural heritage into a subject of inquiry. They invoked cultural studies in an effort to alter the academic separation of American popular and folk culture so as to view the political process of traditionalizing throughout contemporary culture (see Bluestein 1994). It could examine fashion as well as festival as cultural production, and cover "cultural texts" from advertisements to zoos as examples of marketing and consuming tradition.

Although cultural studies takes in an assortment of approaches and subjects under its wide umbrella, one significant contribution with ties to American folkloristics has been to demonstrate how, and interpret why, cultural images have been produced, organized, and disseminated. The term received a substantial entry by Cathy Lynn Preston in *American Folklore: An Encyclopedia* (1996), edited by Jan Harold Brunvand. "Folkloristics intersects with cultural studies," she proclaimed, "when folklorists position folklore within the politics of cultural production—in other words, when folklorists address how folklore is shaped by, and in turn shapes, sociocultural power relations" (C. Preston 1996, 183). She recognized the development of cultural studies from British interest in class-based power relations within "modern industrialized societies," but suggested expansion to such relations for gender, ethnicity, race, nation, and sexuality. Preston confidently predicted wider adoption of British cultural studies, "disclosing folkloristics as a politics of culture." She cited several prominent examples of cultural studies within the theorizing of contemporary folklore studies (Stewart 1991; Briggs and Shuman 1993; Babcock 1993). She also could have shown ways that perspectives in cultural studies had long been anticipated in earlier American folklore studies (Wilson 1976; Dorson 1976a, 1978b; Oinas 1978). The converging trajectories of British cultural studies and American folklore studies, she thought, were constructions of "the dominant culture's 'quintessential others,' the 'folk,'" the evaluations of "socioeconomic politics" of folklore's supporting institutions—universities, arts councils, and historical societies—and attention to contemporary labeling of cultural difference (C. Preston 1996, 184).

American folklorist Barbara Kirshenblatt-Gimblett jumped on the preoccupation in British cultural studies with the "contemporary" as an ocean-wide divide from that of American folklore studies. There is truth in her keen observation that folklore's "canonical subject" is the "contemporaneous—that which is in the present, but not fully of the present" (Kirshenblatt-Gimblett 1996b, 251). In a presidential address to the American Folklore Society and widely noticed essays in the *Journal of American Folklore* and *Journal of Folklore Research*, she avowed the resistance of American folklore studies to bedding with British cultural studies (Kirshenblatt-Gimblett 1994, 1996b). She considered cultural studies to be more politically critical of tradition, or even nihilistic, while "not surprisingly, folklore is the champion of conservation."

In its tendency to rationalize "culture," American folklore studies appeared to her less cynical than British cultural studies. Much folkloristic effort had been to amass aggregate data of tradition—objectified "hard facts" that made a case for the reality and artistry of subcultures. With a reorientation toward cultural studies, these collected facts, taken to be the untampered knowledge of folk groups, were threatened with charges of being power-serving illusions broadcast by scholars and elites. Indeed, the very name of tradition as "folklore" could appear suspect because it provided an invented, distorted lens on culture. The making of "culture" over into "cultural" itself was a rhetorical turn that made writers question those things that are *of* or like culture, rather than *in* it. "Cultural" suggested "devising" culture with some societal goal in mind rather than "constituting" it for localized identity, community, and tradition. Folkloristic approaches to the hard facts of expressive "folklore" as revelations of culture still summoned the social, rather than virtual, reality of tradition as a spontaneously generated event (see Oring 1994).

Although the term "cultural" should direct attention to the functioning of diverse local cultures, Kirshenblatt-Gimblett beheld its preponderant use by industrialized nations producing mass-marketed arts. While appreciating the shared sympathies of British cultural studies and American folklore studies for the postcolonial politics of difference—racial, sexual, cultural, transnational—Kirshenblatt-Gimblett argued that in the theorizing of difference, folklore and cultural studies part ways, "even as their trajectories increasingly converge." Her argument was that cultural studies deliberated largely on the inequitable allocations of *difference* while folklore worked mainly on the relativism of *diversity*— "that is, on community, solidarity, and tradition" (Kirshenblatt-Gimblett 1996b, 251). In the stormy political climate of America in the 1990s she saw "difference" proclaimed by cultural studies as the ready shelter to which humanists carrying the burden of social inequality ran. Whether they stayed there was in doubt. Even though American folklore scholarship had long been a haven to locate issues of cultural identity, diversity, and construction, the worry was that down the road it would have to compete rather than ally with cultural studies for the favor of scholarship.

To be sure, the work of British cultural studies engaged many American folklorists along with other students of culture during the 1990s. In 1996, the Internet buzzed with a long thread at the American studies site concerning the "Americanization of [British] Cultural Studies" (see Pfister 1991). If there was consensus from the hailstorm of messages, it was that the American interest in cultural studies reflected a renewed effort in the United States to relocate the significance of class in American culture. In positing an "underclass," many socially minded scholars suggested that cultural characteristics arose from *imposed* conditions of social degradation and economic restriction (see J. Wilson 1996). The argument could be more loudly heard that although there may not be a sharp class consciousness in America, there is nonetheless an awareness of barriers and distinctions from culturally constructed, and often peculiar, perceptions of class in America. Moving away from the view of culture as naturally preexisting, cultural studies encouraged views of traditions being organized and generated to maintain boundaries of class in emergent settings such as suburbia, corporations, clubs, and revived regions (see Burnett 1978; Oliver, Davis, and Bentley 1981; During 1993). If class was not publicly acknowledged, whether it was nonetheless implicit, and determinative, might be asked, as well as how it intersected with public conceptualizations of race and gender.

While the questions of class raised by British cultural studies have understandably been more evident in American scholarship, they nonetheless have had to wait for response. As Nathan Glazer has sharply discerned, the multicultural movement that dominated American scholarship of the 1990s prioritized factors in cultural production first as race, ethnicity, and gender, and lastly class (Glazer 1997). In an analysis of traditional blues and bluegrass music as "tough arts of the underclass," Joe Wilson admitted that "it is jarring to speak of an American underclass." He pleaded his case: "We like to pretend that we have only one socio-economic group ('middle') structured like ancient Egypt, with upper and lower parts. This odd egalitarian myopia distorts our artistic perception and confuses understanding of why our popular culture is so strong" (J. Wilson 1996, 82). Americans have been more likely to assert organization or community than class in the production of culture. Proponents of British cultural studies might answer that the fact that citizens negate class does not mean it is not significant in power relations. The identification and role of elites, the place of occupational identity, and the influence of poverty, among other frequently raised issues of socially based class, are surely significant to an analysis of an organized American culture, but have not been easily integrated into an American conception of temporarily, and ethnically, situated tradition in which "we are all the folk."

Since a common presumption of cultural studies has been that elites manufacture traditions in their best interests for the masses to accept, then emphasis often has been placed on popular, nationwide forms. Although American folklorists have shown that their scholarship long had been concerned with political uses of culture to induce nationalism and counternationalism, indeed predated concerns of cultural studies for cultural construction, their bibliography appeared strangely absent from major British volumes defining the field. An argument could be made that the study of American folklore since the 1930s, especially by students of American civilization such as Richard Dorson, has had to consider the ways that folklore, and the folk, in America were "discovered," "invented," and "popularized." Since the United States did not have an ancient history, united racial stock, and peasant folk, which were associated with folklore in British anthropological thought, American folklorists early on had to defend the emergence of a folklore deserving the label "American." They raised folk culture to point to people who had control of their own traditions in the face of mass culture. American folklorists had to further account for the legitimacy of tradition in a mobile and industrializing society in their claims to the authenticity of folk cultures. The nation's mass communication has often translated to concern for "presentation" and "persuasion" of folklore in public consciousness.

As an expansion of the emergent concept of folklore as a strategically designed event, a major American folkloristic concern for the process of traditionalizing behavior has translated into closer questioning of ways that formal organizations create culture and organize symbols (see Jones 1991; Jones, Moore, and Snyder 1988). Thus folklore as staged expressions came across in interpretations of the rhetoric of tradition in the press, records, film, and stage as well as government, museum, corporation, and community. Whether looking at World's Fairs, the New Deal, or a local festival, folklorists have brought out ways that organizations manage images of folklore for various publics as part of a politics of culture. It has often been presumed to be a special problem in a changeful, diverse nation like the United States where traditions often appeared sought and promoted rather than inherited and shared. In their efforts to find times and places where folklore sincerely functioned or somehow served organizational purposes, folklorists necessarily confronted perceptions of genuine and spurious traditions to clarify kinds of culture appropriate, and appropriated, for America.

Sewing organizational and political threads into the weave of American folklore work may have obviated the need for the kind of reflexive design offered by British cultural studies. Without making reference to cultural studies, the entry on politics and folklore in *American Folklore: An Encyclopedia*, for example, identified attention to "folk political organization and alternative social institutions," "politics of applied folklore and folklore policy," "politics of folklore," and "folklore of politics" in the interest of American folklore scholarship (Westerman 1996). If convergence of American and British cultural studies with reference to folklore occurs, it probably will be along these lines. One thing for sure, the influence of British cultural studies has been more evident since the 1990s in rhetorical consideration of "invention of traditions," "social empowerment," and "cultural production" in settings in and out of the United States.

In keeping with trends in cultural studies generally in the United States, American folklorists have expanded from being experts on texts to analysts of social and artistic behavior, and have been more attracted to the scholasticism of the European continent. Since Richard Dorson declared that "links between English and American folklorists (exclusive of folksong devotees) have snapped," English folklore studies have continued, but have had to deal with the tainted image of antiquarianism (Dorson 1973b, 16). Venetia Newall, a prominent present-day English folklorist, complained that "too often, I am afraid, the English folklorist has been regarded as an antiquarian romantic, who has turned his back on the contemporary situation, escaping from its pressures and its problems into an idealised Merry England filled with May poles, thatched cottages, and country folk in handmade smocks, perpetually smiling" (Newall 1973, 95). Jacqueline Simpson, a longtime editor of the Folklore Society's journal, wondered whether "a suspicion lingers in some quarters that this Journal is obsessed with fertility rites and secret witch-cults, or with starry-eyed idealizations of 'Merrie England'" (Simpson 1989, 4).

Another editor of the Folklore Society's journal, Gillian Bennett, announced that perception of British folklore work had improved, ironically "largely owing to the influence of the *American* approaches … " (Bennett 1991, 26). She saw the focus of many English folklorists adopting the American lead of analyzing "'the 'lore' part of 'folklore' as a body of beliefs, activities, ways of making, saying and doing things and interacting with others that are acquired through informal, unofficial channels by the processes of socialising in family-, occupational-, or activity-related groups. In other words, they considered folklore as a 'cultural register'—as W. F. H. Nicolaisen working on both sides of the ocean conceptualized it on the analogy of a linguistic register—one of several options available to members of a cultural grouping for thought, activity and interaction" (Bennett 1991, 26). She blamed the persistence of antiquarianism and evolutionism in English cultural scholarship on the maintenance of a national identity that stresses picturesque rurality and the glory of a distant past. She characterized evolutionism and antiquarianism as perpetuating the English belief in the wholesomeness provided by the bucolic past. Bennett emphatically added that "what perhaps now bedevils folkloristics in Britain is the result of the founders' successes and failures put together. Their success lay in establishing a theory of culture so comprehensive, elegant and satisfying that it became assimilated not only into the culture of the FLS [Folklore Society], but into everyday popular conceptions of culture and society" (Bennett 1994, 34).

The discourse of culture arising from American scholarship on folklore separated from the English pattern by stressing contemporary social conditions—urban, ethnic, and occupational. With the development of an academic base after World War II, folkloristic commentary on American culture tended to record the present for social relevance rather than digging deep in the past for origins of civilization. Its concern for the local stages on which Americans enacted their values diverged from English views of authority carried by class as well as tradition. America was not so much rooted in place or a "common heritage" as it was shifting, redefined, constructed—according to social movements and technological changes. In the United States, folklorists influenced the discourse of culture generally, and American culture particularly, by joining intellectual movements to conceive of individuals empowered to create traditions and thereby express their identities.

4

The Americanization of
the Brothers Grimm

WHEN FAIRY TALES ARE MENTIONED IN EVERYDAY CONVERSATION OR SCHOLARLY forums, reference is probably being made to the remarkable legacy of Jacob and Wilhelm Grimm (1785–1863, 1786–1859, respectively), known popularly as the Brothers Grimm. The work of the Grimms has gone through a complicated history of interpretation and application. Since the Grimms made a giant splash with their folklore collections in the nineteenth century, their successors have credited them with establishing often opposing positions in debates over the character of tradition. They have been commended for defining folklore romantically and scientifically, internationally and nationally, historically and contemporaneously. References thus abound to the Grimms, for alternately espousing fragmentation and unity, international diffusion and romantic nationalism, historical reconstruction and cultural fieldwork, blatant literary license and fidelity to tradition.

The Grimm connection to America needs sorting. In America the Grimm legacy has gone in two directions, between the popular consciousness of the Grimms for their juvenile fairy tales and the scholarly awareness of them for their national theories. It has been something of a given in popular culture that their authentic German tales have spontaneously had universal appeal, and in scholarship that the Grimms intentionally began scientific folklore study that spread globally. Much of this impression has been a combination of manipulated fact and created fiction, and I want to not so much debunk as explore reasons for the perpetuation of these impressions. By way of prologue, I open the pages of *German Life* (March 1996), a slick new American magazine aimed at a popular audience, and I see the contents raise the keywords and themes of unity and fragmentation—and their cultural associations. The first article, naturally, is on the folkloristic legacy of the Grimms

184

Jacob and Wilhelm Grimm drawn by Ludwig Emil Grimm. (Staatsbibliothek Berlin)

in extending German fascination with its unity, its past, to the world. The second reflects on the 125th anniversary of the German Empire and asks "What Price Unity?" The third looks at "How Germany Was" while the fourth looks ahead to how German telecommunications "Sets a New Tone." As if to note German-American fragmentation and the need for unity, the United German-American Committee calls in the magazine for a National German-American Heritage Museum and Cultural Center in the nation's capital. Folklore, one quickly learns, is central to the group's concept of heritage and culture. The folk, one ascertains, is a lasting reference from German to English, from Europe to America, from tradition to groupness.

The Grimm connection to folklore in American cultural discourse is evident first in the popularity of the fairy tale as a public reference for entertaining fantasy and wish fulfillment. Second is the idea that folk traditions representing the character of nature provide renewing spiritual or poetic powers for modern existence. Third is the juxtaposition of folklore's international spread with its use for building a romantic sense of nation and peoplehood. Each of these connections brings up the centrality of tradition taking organic form and drawing on the past in references to the Grimms' influence on American uses of folklore. I will show varying German and American perceptions of cultural unity and difference evident through scholarly and popular interpretations of Grimms' tales, and answer why

GERMAN POPULAR STORIES,

Translated from the

Kinder und Haus Märchen,

COLLECTED BY

M. M. GRIMM,

From Oral Tradition.

JAMES ROBINS & Cº LONDON.

AND

JOSEPH ROBINS JUNᴿ & Cº DUBLIN.

MDCCCXIV.

Title page of *German Popular Stories* (1825), the first translation of the
Grimms' tales to appear in English. (Rare Books Collection, Pattee Library,
Pennsylvania State University)

uses of the Grimm legacy in American discourse have often been at odds with each other.

The Grimms are my starting point because for many Americans, they are equated with folklore. Yet a peculiar version of folklore centered in the "fairy tale" apparently far removed from American experience becomes evident. Americans especially know Grimms' stories of Snow White and Cinderella as "Grimms' Fairy Tales" through movie and video adaptations, and a host of colorful children's books. As if their names were not associated enough with the tales, a mass market movie in 1962 underscored their global reach in the title of the movie as *Wonderful World of the Brothers Grimm*. The Grimms' tales have been translated into 140 languages and are indeed known worldwide, but they have a special American impact because of Hollywood's recontextualization of Grimms' tales into mass culture. As Walt Disney and countless children's authors re-created Grimms' fairy tale figures for popular consumption, the German quality of the original has given way to media fantasy. They have become stylized vehicles for popular entertainment of romance, music, and comedy rendered gleefully through cineramic animation. Indeed, they have become Americanized, given a cheery message and romantic core, and thereby globalized. If there is a German connection within mass culture, it is in the Grimm reference to the German peasantry as the quintessential folk. Assumed to be old and of earthy appearance, isolated and communally rural, poor yet socially content, peasants are depicted as unusually telling stories, often for children, and being fairy tales unto themselves.

The popularity of the fairy tale as folklore and the peasantry as folk owes to *Kinder-und Hausmärchen* (Children's and Household Tales), published by the Grimm brothers first in 1812. Despite the common belief that it was an overnight success, in reality it struggled until it became available in illustrated editions aimed at children, first in 1823 translated into English by lawyer and student of medieval literature Edgar Taylor (with help from a friend, David Jardine) as *German Popular Stories* and then in German in 1825 as *Kleine Ausgabe* (Small Edition). A publisher in Boston quickly issued an American version of *German Popular Stories* in 1826 and another soon followed in 1828. The original German edition had a scholarly intention of presenting the significance of the tales interpreted as *Naturpoesie*, the language and natural expression of common folk instilled in the present with the poetic spirit of a past golden age. Addressing "adults and serious people," Jacob and Wilhelm confronted the uses of tradition, defined in the narrative reminders of the stability of past country life, for invigorating modern existence defined by mechanistic advances. The brothers contrasted the "devotion to tradition" of such folk "who always adhere to the same way of life" to "we (who tend to want change)" (Tatar 1987, 212).

Arguing for the aesthetic, spiritual quality of the folk's narrative expressions, the Grimms offered in the first edition that the *Märchen*, "which have stood the test of time, have a certain intimacy and inner effectiveness that other things, which may on the surface seem far more dazzling, rarely attain. The epic basis of folk poetry resembles the color green as one finds it throughout nature in various shades; each satisfies and soothes without ever becoming tiresome" (Tatar 1987, 212–13). The rhetoric of the brothers was in response to French Enlightenment rationality which extolled the supposedly progressive virtues of objective science and fine arts. They were aware that in many literary circles glorifying a modernism of reasoned elitism the attitude prevailed that such tales of common folk were vulgar and backward. In a later edition, the brothers alluded to the attitude when they elaborated on the spiritual aspect of the act of folklore performance: "Telling these tales is so extraordinary a living custom—and this too the tales share with all that is immortal—that one must like it no matter what others say. At any rate, one can quickly see that the custom persists only in places where one finds a warm receptivity to poetry or where there are imaginations not yet warped by the perversities of life" (Tatar 1987, 216).

The brothers did not delineate the perversities they had in mind, but their preface made it clear that they went hand in hand with "modern," supposedly progressive conditions of urbanization and mechanization. In a letter to his teacher Friedrich Savigny, Wilhelm explained: "What is most depressing is the thought that if industrial development and striving for commercial success everywhere get out of hand, then an ever greater contempt for higher, spiritual, and scientific development will take hold and a splendid barbarism, such as prevails in America, will predominate" (Peppard 1971, 91).

THE GERMAN GRIMMS

The Grimms singled out the rural German state of Hesse in what is now southwest Germany as a special place where a "warm receptivity" to tradition existed among the populace. It had its natural splendors and was a region removed from Slavic influences on German culture to the east, but it had changed rapidly with the stress of war and a changing economy. It had lost much of its homogeneity and sheltered innocence as its borders were traversed by a host of European armies and industrial trade came into view. Within this climate of change, the Grimms were part of an emerging educated middle class engaged in professional careers. In favor of a democracy that empowered the middle and lower class, the Grimm brothers resented the privilege and obstruction of the aristocracy that prevented them from opportunities. They sympathized with the peasants, for they supposedly represented the will of the people and a tradition of social inclusion.

The Grimm family had deep roots in Hesse as clerks, lawyers, and clergy, and the brothers appeared to follow a similar path using education and religion, rather than wealth or family title, to maintain their social position. The family followed the Reformed faith associated with the German surroundings. It likely influenced the Grimms in at least two significant ways: its nationalistic overtones with use of the German language and the movement for union of German Reformed and Lutheran divisions during the Napoleonic period. From accounts of the time, it appears that ministers regularly preached on the presence of God in nature, religion as an inward spiritual experience, and the spiritual glory of simplicity (Craig 1982, 88–90). Although biographers often neglect the religious background of the Grimms, the messages they were hearing apparently had a bearing on their attitudes toward spirituality and nature they later expressed. Jacob Grimm assumed that "through the Reformation and Protestantism intellectual culture has been furthered," and with a swipe against Catholicism, he commented that New High German was a "Protestant dialect" with a "liberating nature" (Peppard 1971, 6).

Devoted to ideals of the German Reformation, the brothers reportedly considered a life in the pulpit, but seemed to have taken a worldly turn after the death of their father in 1796 left the family of six children with diminished means (Peppard 1971, 7). With help from an aunt, in 1798 the adolescent brothers moved from the small medieval town of Steinau to the principal city of Kassel in Hesse to attend Lyceum in preparation for university study in law. The brothers saluted Hessian sources in the preface to the second edition of *Kinder- und Hausmärchen*:

> Hesse, being a mountainous region off the major thoroughfares and principally oriented toward agriculture, has the advantage of preserving old traditions and customs more carefully. A certain seriousness, a healthy, sturdy, and stalwart character, which is sure to go down in history, even the tall, handsome physique of the men in those regions that were once the home of the Chatti have been preserved in this way, and they all make the lack of comfort and elegance, which one notices quickly by contrast to other states (coming from Saxony, for example) appear as an advantage. One begins to feel that the rather rough-hewn but often truly splendid regions are, like the stern and stoic way of life, part of a whole. The Hessians in general must be counted among the people in our fatherland who have, through the changing times, held fast to their original homelands as well as to their own special character. (Tatar 1987, 219–20)

The Grimms thus offered, some say even invented, a distinctive and apparently romantic image of German tradition and indeed tradition generally. It consisted of isolated, illiterate pastoral people, untampered by alien influences, living simply and roughly, and adhering to the ways of the past. They possessed a quiet but profound wisdom exhibited in their oral treasures of tales, songs, and proverbs. Being close to nature, these people and their folklore expressed a human vitality and social cohesion, the brothers thought. Implying the therapeutic use of folk expression as a palliative to modern existence, the brothers wrote: "Everything that is natural can also be healthy, and that is what we should be after" (Tatar 1987, 214). The contrasting contemporary backdrop for this image of harmony, peace, and unity as the Grimms wrote was the fragmentation and weakness of German-speaking states, the conflict of the Napoleonic wars, and intellectually, the spread of French Enlightenment ideas of progress and rational reasoning. In his autobiography,

Wilhelm talked of his "spiritual depression" in "days of the collapse of all previously existing establishments" for Germany during the early nineteenth century. He
remarked: "Undoubtedly the world situation and the necessity of withdrawing in
the peacefulness of scholarship contributed to the reawakening of the long-forgot-
ten literature; but we did not only seek consolation in the past, but we hoped naturally that this course of ours would contribute somewhat to the return of a better
day" (Peppard 1971, 40). The brothers embraced a patriotic Romantic movement
that emphasized a medieval poetic vision of a golden mythopoeic age of
humankind that could still inspirit and reform the present. Inspired by the German
Romantic philosophy of Johann Gottfried Herder, the brothers along with literary
comrades Clemens Brentano and Achim von Arnim found special virtues in
ancient folk poetry retained in folk songs and folktales surviving in the present.
During the late eighteenth century, Herder extolled *Volkslieder* (folk songs) as the
spiritual "voice" of the folk (*Stimmen der Völker*, 1778–1779; see Herder 1911, 1975).

The connected concepts of folk and tradition were central to Herder's views of
knowledge, history, politics, and culture. He explained: "It must be evident by now
that the principles underlying this philosophy of history are as simple and unmis-
takable as those underlying the natural history of man. They are *tradition* and
organic powers. All education arises from imitation and exercise, by means of which
the model passes into the copy. What better word is there for this transmission than
tradition?" (Barnard 1969, 313). In this view, tradition varies across societies, which
represent different unities of social relations, customs, and language, and therefore
is the basis of political organization (Barnard 1965, 54–87; Barnard 1969, 317–26).
Herder argued that the Enlightenment was short-sighted because it assumed that
its inventions broke with tradition of the primitive. Comparing the "civilized"
European with "primitive man," he found more of the poetic, viewed abstractly as a
spiritual force gained from closeness to nature (Herder 1993, 141–200). He wrote:

> Primitive man in his narrower sphere knows how to think for himself and how to
> express himself with more truth, precision and force. Within this sphere of activity he
> knows how to employ his mental and physical powers and his few implements, with
> skill, practical understanding and an instant presence of mind. Man for man, he is pal-
> pably more educated than the erudite, politically suave European, that machine of a
> man, or should I say child, that sits perched on a lofty edifice erected by the hands of
> others, by the labours of preceding generations. The man of nature, to be sure, is more
> limited in his accomplishments, but he is sounder and stands more firmly on the
> ground. (Barnard 1969, 316)

He contended that for the sake of progress, modern society needed more than
inventions. It needed the inventiveness, the pure and natural tradition, of the folk.

The Grimms invoked Herder's ideas in promoting the collection and preservation of German folk poetry as spiritual and aesthetic reminders that they considered to be endangered in "pure" and "natural" places like the Hessian countryside.

In fact, the Grimms had at first collected the poetry of folk songs but their friend Clemens Brentano encouraged them to focus their effort on the often overlooked artistic font of folktales to round out an anthology he planned to publish (Kamenetsky 1992, 39). After 1806, the brothers took up the collection of tales in earnest. The preface to the first edition made it clear that they had other interests in language and literature, but they indicated an almost mystical attraction to the living quality of the tales, and a preservationist mission to save and pass them on before they die. They wrote: "It is probably just the right time to collect these tales, since those who have been preserving them are becoming ever harder to find (to be sure, those who still know them know a great deal, because people may die, but the stories live on). The custom of telling tales is ever on the wane, just as all the cozy corners in homes and in gardens are giving way to an empty splendor that resembles the smile with which one speaks of these tales—a smile that looks elegant but costs so little" (Tatar 1987, 205). Referring to intellectual condescension and moralistic judgment toward expressions of the folk, the brothers defended their excitement for the stories: "Where they still exist, the tales live on in such a way that no one thinks about whether they are good or bad, poetic or vulgar. We know them and we love them just because we happen to have heard them in a certain way, and we like them without reflecting why" (Tatar 1987, 205).

The brothers were, however, reflective in the preface to the first edition of *Kinder- und Hausmärchen* about the grounding of the tales in the benevolent cycle of nature—its spontaneity, primitive beauty, and wholesomeness. Their opening paragraph made the connection of ancient poetry and tradition in folk songs and tales to spiritual renewal:

> When a storm or some other mishap sent by heaven destroys an entire crop, it is reassuring to find that a small spot on a path lined by low hedges or bushes has been spared and that a few stalks remain standing. If the sun favors them with light, they continue to grow, alone and unobserved, and no scythe comes along to cut them prematurely for huge storage bins. But at the end of the summer, once they have ripened and become full, poor devout hands come to seek them out; ear upon ear, carefully bound and esteemed more highly than entire sheaves, they are carried home, and for the entire winter they provide nourishment, perhaps the only seed for the future. That is how it all seems to us when we review the riches of German poetry from olden times and discover that nothing of it has been kept alive, even the memory of it is lost—folk songs and these innocent household tales are all that remain. The places by the stove, the hearth in the kitchen, attic stairs, holidays still celebrated, meadows and forests in their solitude, and above all the untrammeled imagination have functioned as hedges preserving them and passing them on from one generation to the next. (Tatar 1987, 204–5)

If the brothers gave the impression that they had salvaged all that was left of tradition, in a later edition they sounded more hopeful for spreading the collection of folktales. "These folktales," they expounded, "have kept intact German myths that were thought to be lost, and we are firmly convinced that if a search was conducted in all the hallowed regions of our fatherland, long neglected treasures would transform themselves into fabulous treasures and help to found the study of the origins of our poetry" (Tatar 1987, 213).

Before the Grimms published their annotated collection, European folktales had received literary notice most notably from the work of Charles Perrault in France (1697) and Giambattista Basile (1637) in Italy. Among the tales given in both were Cinderella, Sleeping Beauty, and Puss in Boots. The French volume drew attention to Little Red Riding Hood, Bluebeard, and Hop o' My Thumb, while the Italian included Snow White and Beauty and the Beast. The Grimms considered the unannotated stories of Perrault to be *Kunstmärchen*, or artistic compositions of individuals, as opposed to their *Volksmärchen*, collected from oral tradition and representative of collective creation (Hunt 1884, 2:489–90). Basile, the brothers thought, had captured the Neapolitan dialect in which the fifty stories were told, although he "abounds too much in picturesque and proverbial forms of speech" (Hunt 1884, 2:483; see Basile 1927, [1637] 1976; Cocchiara 1981, 513–15). The Grimms distinguished themselves by announcing their transcription of the stories as they were told. They bragged that their sources were genuine tradition bearers, or "voices of the folk." This did not mean that alterations were not made in the stories by the brothers, but they insisted that they were loyal to the spirit of the orally transmitted tradition. In the first edition, they proclaimed that they "tried to collect these tales in as pure a form as possible.... No details have been added or embellished or changed, for we would have been reluctant to expand stories already so rich by adding analogies and allusions; they cannot be invented" (Tatar 1987, 210). The Grimms pointed to this feature as the unique quality of the collection.

In the preface to the second edition, the brothers confessed that the collection had been reworked. They removed phrases they thought inappropriate for children, they "improved" stories by relating them "more directly and simply," and they expanded "fragments" or combined versions into full-blown tales. Yet they defended their loyalty to tradition by claiming: "We did not add anything from our own resources, nor did we embellish any events and features of the story itself. Instead we tried to relate the content just as we had heard it; we hardly need emphasize that the phrasing and filling in of details were mainly our work, but we did try to preserve every particularity that we noticed so that in this respect the collection would reflect the diversity of nature" (Tatar 1987, 220). The Grimms left latitude for the presentation of their texts (how much is still a matter of dispute), and it became even wider in English editions (see Ellis 1983; Dundes 1985; Kamenetsky 1992, 151–77).

The brothers followed the call to action by literati Achim von Arnim and Clemens Brentano, who urged contributors to their *Des Knaben Wunderhorn: Alte Deutsche Lieder* (The Boy's Magic Horn, 1805) to record authentic folk songs and tales. The folk were essential to their vision, and the message carried well to a

German audience in the critically acclaimed volume. Expanding Herder's ideas of a spiritual power in ancient folk poetry, Arnim entitled his interpretative essay *Von Volksliedern* (On Folk Songs) at the conclusion of the collections in the first volume of *Des Knaben Wunderhorn*, wherein appears the term *Volkskunde* (folklore) for the first time (Cocchiara 1981, 205). While Herder had found the unifying soul of folk poetry for artistic and national renewal in several cultural sources, Arnim called for concentrating on German roots (see Herder [1778–1779] 1911; Ergang 1931, 234–37; Wilson 1973; Cocchiara 1981, 168–207; Bluestein 1994, 28–45; Weissman 1991). In his call for *Des Knaben Wunderhorn* in 1805, Arnim solicited "ancient orally-transmitted legends and tales" "in the name of the fatherland." "Thus," he envisioned, "we will be able to gather many threads of the vast cloth on which our history is embroidered and which it is our duty to continue to embellish" (Cocchiara 1981, 203–4). In his social philosophy, the enfeebled middle class that had risen to prominence in German modern life needed the healthy instinctive force of ancient poetry drawn from the tales and songs of the folk to regain a spiritual and artistic sense of mission. To Arnim and his group of Romantics working against the tide of French Enlightenment elitist reasoning, *Das Volk* was a specific class of peasants and artisans who had been the core of German vitality and peoplehood (Cocchiara 1981, 205).

The Grimms collected fifty-three tales for Arnim's collaborator, Clemens Brentano, who planned to "embellish" them for new literary compositions. After Brentano misplaced the manuscript and then lost interest in the project, the Grimms decided to publish the tales as they recorded them under their own name.[1] Resisting the literary impulses of Brentano to convert the tales, the brothers saw a precedent for their presentation of the collection in a publication of two folktales ("The Fisherman and His Wife" and "The Juniper Tree") rendered in their original Plattdeutsch dialect by Romantic painter Philipp Otto Runge in Arnim and Brentano's *Zeitung für Einsiedler* (Journal for Hermits) (Peppard 1971, 45). Runge used the tales to call for a broader collection of such stories directly from oral tradition that would reap spiritual rewards for a German nation, and the Grimms incorporated his tales into their collection. When the Grimms' first edition appeared, it drew attention because of its relatively large number of tales (Perrault had published only eight), German sources, dialect style in which they were presented, and the new wrinkle of extensive comparative notes. As a collection claiming to represent the character of the folk, *Kinder- und Hausmärchen* attracted some criticism. Even their supporter Arnim observed that the Grimms had overlooked or intentionally censored the great mass of popular tales that were erotically tinged (Peppard 1971, 58). Arnim especially worried that in emphasizing the collective nature of folk composition the brothers had presented the tales as impersonal, generic units rather than the varying expressions of individual taletellers (Cocchiara 1981, 228–29).

The brothers exercised editorial license in eliminating horror stories and tales they considered to have "arisen on foreign ground" (see McGlathery 1993, 37, 49).

While they were well aware that the stories had counterparts in other countries, they underscored the special German quality of the tales in their collection. They closed the preface to the second volume of the first edition with the declaration: "Everything that has been collected here from oral traditions is ... purely German in its origins as well as in its development and has not been borrowed from any sources, as can easily be proved on the basis of externals if one wanted to dispute that fact for individual tales" (Tatar 1987, 215). In the original edition, the brothers accordingly attached notes comparing the tales with counterparts in other countries for forty-nine tales, twenty-two of which had been contributed by the Grimms as gems of antiquarian interest taken directly from the oral tradition of contemporary speakers. They issued a second volume with additional tales in 1815. In 1819, they enlarged the corpus of tales into two volumes with 161 tales, and in 1822, added a separate third volume devoted to notes and folkloristic commentary.

The Grimms were not the first to refer to German *Märchen*, but they innovatively included notes on the tales that described their sources and listed analogues toward the goal of showing possible origins, development, and diffusion of the tales (Cocchiara 1981, 187–200; see also Musäus 1782–1787). The notes provided the "basis of externals" they used to show the German quality of folktales and their spread through Europe. Later they would use comparison of motifs and language to argue that the tales stemmed from an old, probably Indo-European common origin in the mythopoeic age (Peppard 1971, 49–50). The notes also established the authenticity of the tales by giving locations and tellers of the collected tales. Not only did they find references to comparable tales outside of German-speaking regions, but they also insightfully recognized parallel themes and motifs in proverbs, beliefs, games, legends, and myths. The Grimms were able to find such references in rare old manuscripts as well as oral tradition they collected and remembered. For a time a royal librarian after attending the University of Marburg, Jacob Grimm had access to ancient literature, and used his training in several languages and self-taught ability in deciphering medieval manuscripts to take notes on folktales in printed sources. Together with Wilhelm, Jacob studied law and philosophy at Marburg, and there used the medieval manuscript collection of professor Friedrich Carl von Savigny, who encouraged the understanding of society and customs toward knowledge of the law. Marburg recognized their scholarship by awarding them honorary doctoral degrees in 1819, and they stayed close to libraries and lecture halls with posts associated with Göttingen University (1830–1836) and Berlin University (1841–1863).

The English Grimms

The Grimms' German volumes of 1819 received appreciative scholarly notice, but that hardly helped the books become a popular success. They had sold less than a thousand copies before Edgar Taylor aroused popular interest in the Grimms' work with his English edition. Taylor loosely translated twenty-nine of the tales in his first edition and another twenty-two in his second volume of 1826. Taylor replaced the original preface of the Grimms with one of his own. The first volume included stories now considered classics in fairy tale literature: Snow Drop (White), The Elves and the Shoemaker, Hansel and Gretel, The Frog-Prince, The Golden Goose, and Rumpel-Stilts-kin. The second volume added such stories as Ashputtel (Cinderella), The Robber Bridegroom, and The Goose Girl. He romanticized the sources of the tales as "the mouths of German peasants," although in fact the Grimms had relied on educated middle-class neighbors in Kassel as well as their own recollections. Neither were the tales all from the nursery or old wives. A major source was Johann Friedrich Krause, a retired soldier. While resorting to High German, the Grimms made an effort in their editing to preserve the idiomatic rendering of oral tradition centered in the peasant folk. They represented at least ten dialects in the tales. Taylor apparently was attracted to the work because he knew students at Göttingen who enjoyed reading the stories aloud (Michaelis-Jena 1970, 175). He noted "the eager relish with which a few of the tales were received by the young friends to whom they were narrated" (Grimm and Grimm 1823, iii).

Taylor added illustrations in the first edition of the translation, including one on the title page showing a group of old and young men and women listening to a man reading a book aloud. The illustration was keyed into Taylor's comment that the stories were "ostensibly brought forth to tickle the palate of the young, but are often received with as keen an appetite by those of graver years" (Grimm and Grimm 1823, iii). In the second edition, Taylor made the juvenile audience more central. The illustration on the title page showed an old woman orally relating a story to children gathered around a hearth. Taylor made the book more accessible by cutting down the notes, and explained to the Grimms that he intended the "work less as antiquarian Man [than] as one who meant to amuse" (Kamenetsky 1992, 198). Although Jacob the linguist and Wilhelm the literary scholar had resisted aiming the collection at a popular juvenile audience, Taylor's effort apparently made them reconsider their stand and their *Kleine Ausgabe*, essentially a juvenile storybook without notes, successfully tapped into the Christmas gift season. The small, inexpensive paperback greatly outpaced sales of the original editions, and by 1886 another thirty-five editions had appeared (Kamenetsky 1992, 49). Eight editions of the original *Kinder- und Hausmärchen* appeared in German during the Grimms' lifetime, and another twenty-one appeared between 1864 and 1886 (see McGlathery 1993, 97–98). By one estimate, the Grimms' collection became the second most popular book in German, and during the last 150 years only the Bible has exceeded it in sales (Zipes 1986b, 275). The brothers vied, however, for a time with J. G. Büsching, who published *Sagen und Volksmärchen* (German Legends and Wonder Tales) in 1812, and Friedrich Gottschalk, who used the same title for a collection in 1814. "A real fashion for folk tales has arisen," Jacob wrote Wilhelm in 1814, and he added "the poor collections will harm and hurt the good ones"

(Peppard 1971, 94). At midcentury, sales of *Kinder- und Hausmärchen* lagged behind Ludwig Bechstein's *Deutsches Märchenbuch* (German Wonder Tales, 1845), which became available in English translation (Bechstein 1872; Bottigheimer 1988, 198–99). Outside of Germany, the Grimms were credited with spurring folktale collections in areas seeking nationalistic renewal such as Norway and Ireland (Michaelis-Jena 1970, 183–85; Hennig 1946; Kamenetsky 1992, 202–9). The renown of the Grimms had the effect of motivating others in and out of Germany to produce authoritative, and entertaining, folktale collections.

As Taylor had taken liberties in his translation to combine versions of texts, render the tales into language appealing to children, and emphasize the English elements of the fairy tales, Wilhelm Grimm in his popular editions exercised editorial license, elaborating on the dialogue and drama. Judge the changes in translation, for instance, to Grimms' 1812 edition of Snow White. Grimm 1812:

> When Snow White awoke, they asked her who she was and how she happened to get into the house. Then she told them how her mother had wanted to have her put to death, but the hunter had spared her life, and how she had run the entire day and finally arrived at their house. So the dwarfs took pity on her and said, "If you keep house for us and cook, sew, make the beds, wash and knit, and keep everything tidy and clean, you may stay with us, and you will have everything you want. In the evening, when we come home, dinner must be ready. During the day, we are in the mines and dig for gold, so you will be alone. Beware of the queen and let no one into the house." (Zipes 1987, xxvi)

Taylor 1823:

> In the morning, Snow-drop told them all her story; and they pitied her, and said if she would keep all things in order, and cook and wash, and knit and spin for them, she might stay where she was, and they would take good care of her. Then they went out all day long to their work, seeking for gold and silver in the mountains; and Snow-drop remained at home; and they warned her, and said, "The queen will soon find out where you are, so take care and let no one in." (Grimm and Grimm 1823, 132)

Grimm 1857:

> When it was morning little Snow-white awoke, and was frightened when she saw the seven dwarfs. But they were friendly and asked her what her name was. "My name is Snow-white," she answered. "How have you come to our house?" said the dwarfs. Then she told them that her step-mother had wished to have her killed, but that the huntsman had spared her life, and that she had run for the whole day, until at last she had found their dwelling. The dwarfs said, "If you will take care of our house, cook, make the beds, wash, sew, and knit, and if you will keep everything neat and clean, you can stay with us and you shall want for nothing." "Yes," said Snow-white, "with all my heart," and she stayed with them. She kept the house in order for them; in the mornings they went to the mountains and looked for copper and gold, in the evenings they came back, and then their supper had to be ready. The girl was alone the whole day, so the good dwarfs

warned her and said, "Beware of your step-mother, she will soon know that you are here; be sure to let no one come in." (Hunt 1884, 1:210)

In addition to emphasizing the action of the tales, Taylor had changed the story of Snow White by eliminating narrative details that he felt English readers might have found gruesome. Absent from his translation, for example, is a part of the Grimms' story where the queen orders her servant to bring back Snow White's heart as proof of her death. In the original scene, the servant covers up his evasion by offering her the heart of a boar he had killed. The queen takes it, salts it, and then voraciously devours the bloody organ. "To avoid offence" in other stories, Taylor used "giant" instead of the devil and "cave" rather than hell (Grimm and Grimm 1823, 236).

In his preface, Taylor had recontextualized German traditions for English audiences. He included a quote on the frontispiece from a 1621 English edition of "Tom Thumbe the Little": "Now you must imagine me to sit by a good fire, amongst a companye of good fellowes, over a well spiced wassel bowle of Christmas ale, telling of these merrie tales which hereafter followe." Appealing to racial theories of a common northern European ancestry that had come into vogue in the early nineteenth century, Taylor wrote in the preface that the Grimms' collection "ought to be peculiarly interesting to English readers, inasmuch as many of their national tales are proved to be of the highest Northern antiquity, and common to the parallel classes of society in countries whose populations have been long and widely disjointed" (Grimm and Grimm 1823, vi). Although acknowledging the Grimms' intention to present the tales as evidence of "the pure and primitive mythology of the Teutons" underlying a German cultural bond, in the second edition Taylor chose stories having "more of the general character of fairy tales, and less of German peculiarity." He added notes, in fact, pointing out connections of the stories to traditions in the British Isles. He had the effect of emphasizing the fairy tradition in the stories that were familiar to English readers from their knowledge of Shakespeare, Chaucer, and other authors (Briggs 1967). Taylor essentially turned Grimms' household stories into children's fairy tales.

Taylor insisted on the value of the tales for youth who had been deprived of flights of fancy by moralists of what he called his "arithmetical age" who considered tradition to be vulgar and antiprogressive (Kamenetsky 1992, 200). Taylor attached a testimonial in the second edition from the esteemed writer Sir Walter Scott that the "wild fairy interest" in the tales are "better adapted to awaken the imagination and soften the heart of childhood than the good-boy stories which have been in later years composed for them. In the latter case, their minds are as if they were put into the stocks…." Taylor reoriented the collection of German tales to represent a common human imaginativeness that would be appealing to English readers who should recognize Jack the Giant-killer and Tom Thumb as their own. "The rich collection from which the following tales are selected," he stressed, "is very interesting in a literary point of view, as affording a new proof of the wide and early diffusion of these gay creations of the imagination, apparently flowing from some great and mysterious fountain head, whence Calmuck, Russian, Celt, Scandinavian and German, in their various ramifications, have imbibed earliest lessons of moral instruction … " (Michaelis-Jena 1970, 176). In America and England, then, the tales entered popular culture as a literary product and suggested further revision for purposes of children's amusement and "moral instruction."

The moralistic themes became especially pronounced in the popular multicolored "Fairy Books" edited by renowned literary critic and self-declared folklorist Andrew Lang toward the end of the century. In the *Green Fairy Book* (1892), he observed that fairy tales as the oldest stories in the world, "were made, no doubt, not only to amuse, but to teach goodness. You see, in the tales, how the boy who is kind to beasts, and polite, and generous, and brave, always comes best through his trials, and no doubt these tales were meant to make their hearers kind, unselfish, courteous, and courageous. This is the moral of them" (Lang [1892] 1965, x). Lang, like Taylor, acknowledged his debt to the Grimms, but he equally popularized the varied stories into the generic form of "fairy tales," universal products of the imagination that were especially delightful to children of a dulling industrialized society removed from the spirituality and morality of the folk.

Taylor in 1823 had translated the Grimms' concern for *Das Volk* as "popular." In English usage during the early nineteenth century, popular had the connotation of common people, and in the class consciousness of the country, was associated with those of lowly birth. Yet as the *Oxford English Dictionary* indicates, as the nineteenth century wore on, the plebeian association with popular became obsolete in favor of meanings pointing to a wider, "ordinary" public. Taylor also gave a lasting cast to *Märchen* as "fairy tales," although the German word had a wider meaning as an embellished narrative that could include fable and anecdote and is typically translated in scholarly discourse as a "wonder" or "magic" tale (Bødker 1965, 184–88). Editions of Taylor's translation during the 1840s in fact carried new titles with direct reference to fairy tales: *Gammer Grethel, or, German Fairy Tales, and Popular Stories* (1839) and then *German Fairy Tales and Popular Stories* (1846). Jacob Grimm had been discerning in his use of *Märchen* as a poetic form in distinction to *Sagen,* which he considered historical, attached to known places and names. He thought that the *Sagen* were older and may indeed have published them first if it had not been for his belief that the *Märchen* were more poetic and Arnim's advice that they held more popular appeal.

The significance of the *Sagen* to the Grimms was their historical priority. The brothers wrote their teacher Friedrich Savigny in 1808: "We both agree that a history of poetry is not possible until one has before him the *Sagen* out of which our poetry has developed, for all its ramifications go back to a *Sage* root, just as a stream may flow through the country in many branches. We are also convinced that one must treat poetry the way one does mythology, namely by giving back to each country that which is its particular property and then determining the modifications which it has undergone in each nation" (Peppard 1971, 93). Whereas Grimms' "fairy tales" caught on to an English-reading public in innumerable translations and editions, the Grimms' legends, originally published as *Deutsche Sagen* (1816–1818) were not available in English until 1981, and then in a scholarly edition (Ward 1981). Toward the close of the nineteenth century, prominent British folklorist Joseph Jacobs offered "the nearest approach to an English Grimm that we can hope to obtain in these latter days" (Jacobs 1895, iii). He used "fairy tales" in the titles of his well-selling collections, even though he observed that few of the tales included fairies. Nonetheless, he bowed to English children's generic usage of fairy tales for narratives that had any extraordinary motifs such as speaking animals or giants (Jacobs [1898] 1967).

THE AMERICAN GRIMMS

In nineteenth-century American editions, Taylor's translations of fairy tales reigned supreme. The early American editions were cheaper versions of the English books. Whereas the London house of C. Baldwyn issued *German Popular Stories* in a calf binding with gold tooling, the Boston company of Cummings, Hilliard, published the book in 1826 with a plain cloth cover. Instead of using the fancy calligraphy on the title page of the London edition, the American publisher employed a serif type and removed the English illustration of the hearth scene. Apparently unable to decipher German lettering used on the title page of the London edition, the Boston company rendered the subtitle of the work as *Translated from the Rinder Und Hans Marchen*. Maybe the publisher thought that the opening story of "Hans in Luck" set the tone for the rest of the work, hence the title "Hans Marchen." Two years later when two different American publishers, one in New York and another in Boston, took on the work, they did not correct the error. Later editions avoided the German altogether by referring to the Grimms' work as "the Household Stories" or "Fairy Tales." One change from the 1826 to the 1828 edition was a new frontispiece image of a giant holding a club in one hand and an elf in the other while a peasant plows in the background. Picked up by advertisers for "Green Giant Foods" in the era of television, the image obviated criticism that the tales could be harmful to children by offering a benevolent pastoral scene. The prevalent pattern in American versions of Grimms' tales through the nineteenth century was to produce cheap editions, increase the number of illustrations, and emphasize the juvenile audience.

A close relationship existed between English and American editions of Grimms' tales until early in the twentieth century. Even after Edgar Taylor died, his cousin John Edward Taylor published *The Fairy Ring* (1846) in London with illustrations by *Punch* comic artist Richard Doyle. In America, the same text appeared with the addition of color to the illustrations in *Stray Leaves from Fairy Land for Boys and Girls* (1854). Although the preface in the American version is taken directly from

Frontispiece to *Gammer Grethel, or German Fairy Tales and Popular Stories, from the Collection of M. M. Grimm, and Other Sources,* published in London (1839). (Rare Books Collection, Pattee Library, Pennsylvania State University)

the English version penned in London, it is signed with a Philadelphia dateline. The American version replaced the classic looking calf binding and marbled end papers (it also had cords on the binding and dentel edges) of the English version with a bright red cloth cover emblazoned with cherubs and a woman on a pedestal. The American publisher included an endorsement from Charles Dickens and drew attention to the visual quality of the book by proclaiming "Splendidly Illustrated" on the title page.

Some versions of Grimms' tales found in England and America introduced an imaginary storytelling scene. This was especially evident when J. Green put out Edgar Taylor's translations in *Gammer Grethel* in 1839. A year later, James Munroe, one of the companies that published the 1828 version of *German Popular Stories*, issued an American version. The book was divided into twelve "evenings" of tales and each evening was preceded by an illustration. The volume associated fairy tales with the Christmas season, since the "twelve merry evenings" were during the twelve days of Christmas. It probably was a recontextualization of the organizing principle of a classic sixteenth-century Italian collection of folktales bearing the title *Thirteen Delightful Nights* by Giovanni Straparola (Hunt 1884, 477–81; Straparola 1894). Among the tales related in *Gammer Grethel*'s "evenings" were "Rumpelstiltskin," "The Golden Goose," and "King of the Golden Mountain." The edition created the impression that a peasant, "an honest good-humored farmer's wife," dubbed Gammer Grethel by Taylor, related the stories to young folk. Taylor associated her with a rustic, homey past in his reference to her storytelling "a while ago" in a "far off" place. There and then, she had "strange stories" to tell to "the boys and girls of the neighborhood." The engraving by Ludwig Grimm used on the frontispiece was Grimms' "Bäuerin von Zwehrn" (peasant woman of Zwehrn) Dorothea Viehmann, a tailor's wife in her fifties who lived near the Grimms in Zwehrn and came to Kassel to sell produce. Relating the stories to the Grimms in their apartment, she had contributed close to one-third of the tales in the first edition of *Kinder- und Hausmärchen.*

Despite the image created by Taylor and to some extent by the Grimms of Grethel as an illiterate German peasant woman, the epitome of a traditional storyteller, most researchers are convinced that she was in fact of French Huguenot extraction and associated with the urban middle class (Kamenetsky 1992, 116–20; Dégh 1981, 25–26).[2] If not exactly a peasant, the figure of Gammer Grethel nonetheless became a symbol of the ancestor who had lived in closeness to God and nature, marked by a simplicity and naiveté of spirit that seemed to become more precious in the contemporary experience of English and German urbanization and industrialization (Kamenetsky 1992, 117). Critic Christa Kamenetsky offers that the Grimms thought that this "pure and naive state of mind" was a "treasure beyond comparison—the very precondition for traditional storytelling—as it favored an intuitive power of vision needed to make contact with the 'core' of tradition" (1992, 117).

Grethel appeared again in *Grimm's Goblins* (1867), which had been first issued in "penny parts" for popular consumption before being repackaged as a single volume. The book took several forms and titles and continued to be published into the early twentieth century. In the turn of the century edition, the subtitle changed from "selected from the Household stories of the Brothers Grimm" to "a collection of fairy tales *for the young.*" The size of the volume expanded from Taylor's pocket editions. The Boston publisher added color illustrations and a brilliant red and brown cover embossed with a scene from the story "The Fox's Brush." Color illustrations rendered in a Currier and Ives style had earlier appeared in "a story book for holiday hours" with the title *The King of the Swans, and Other Tales* (1854). This book was an early entry in a long list of works that featured one tale in the title. The English publisher Cundall and Addey commissioned E. H. Wehnert to extensively illustrate a series of Grimm tales in nine monthly parts in 1853. It became the basis for the ten-volume "Grimm library" published simultaneously in New York and London in 1878. The British Library estimated that the series was the most widely read English translation in the nineteenth century (British Library 1985).

The popularity of the Grimm library owed to the appeal of the cover design and color illustrations rather than the stilted translation. The anonymous culprit who did the translation woodenly narrates Snow White with lines like "while she was thus engaged" and a dialogue such as "You shall want for nothing" and "Be careful of your step-mother, who will soon know of your being here; therefore let nobody enter the cottage" (Grimm and Grimm 1878, 23). Yet, as artifacts the books were handy and handsome. Featuring an attractive embossed cover design of a leafy plant divided into dark and light diagonal sections, the popular series of thin books included "The Goose Girl," "The Almond Tree," "The Donkey Cabbages," "The Golden Bird," "Snow White and Rose Red," "The House in the Wood," and "The Old Woman in the Wood." A rival illustrated set of books called "Grimms Fairy Tale Series" published in New York by McLoughlin Brothers emerged during the 1880s. It featured books revolving around stories such as "The Twelve Brothers" and "The Six Swans." McLoughlin also issued adaptations of the Grimms' tales into rhymed verses with romanticized titles such as *Hours in Fairy Land* (1883) during this era (Pollard 1883; see also Mieder 1985). This was followed by dramatic adaptations, including a musical for Snow White and the Seven Dwarfs by Jessie Braham White in 1913 (see also Abbott 1913, 9–30).

American households bought up editions of the Grimms with renewed enthusiasm around the turn of the century. They were encouraged by revolutionary institutions of consumerism such as the department store and mail order catalogue that gave new life to sales of fairy tale volumes. Books were among the major commodities of the age made available to dramatically wider circles of Americans than before. Catalogues from Sears and Montgomery Ward featured book sections and regularly peddled fairy tale volumes. Between 1876 and 1910, Kamenetsky estimated, the number of new American editions ranged from seven to fourteen every five years, and in 1902 forty-five editions were available. The jubilee celebration in 1912 of the Grimms' groundbreaking publication spurred production of even more versions. By 1928 the number of Grimms' editions rose to ninety (Kamenetsky 1992, 235). The rise in sales owed more to households before the turn of the century than they did to school orders. Grimms' tales had not been widely used in American schools the way they had been in Germany to instill social and nationalistic awareness.

While American school readers typically included speeches, essays, and patriotic legends, German textbooks, even those appearing in America, prominently featured the Grimms' tales. Charles Otis's school edition of *Kinder- und Hausmärchen* (1887), for example, taught the tales as "a product of German soil," "representing man in his most essential and general relations" (Otis 1887, viii; see also Guerber

1896; Kern and Kern 1907). By this latter comment Otis meant that they outlined social types of peasant and noble stock, and characteristics of kindness and charity, obedience, and shrewdness associated with German character. He added: "The stories, moreover, which in every German home are a constant delight of the old as well as young, commend themselves to the student of German as being an essential part of German life and literature" (Otis 1887, iii). While Andrew Lang in his fairy tale readers dropped references to the German loyalty of the Grimms and presented fairy tales as universal instructive tales with moral lessons, American readers shied away from moral or religious statements common in English editions. They tended toward pragmatic uses of information and realistic renderings of the recent past (Kamenetsky 1992, 231–36). With a view of America as pragmatically modern and Europe as romantically medieval, some critics went after the image in the Grimms of "the entire medieval worldview and culture with all its stark prejudice, its crudeness and barbarities as they are so characteristic for those dark times" (Kamenetsky 1992, 233). They questioned whether children should read about outdated savage customs that taught neither ethics nor provided a sense of social reality appropriate to America (Kamenetsky 1992, 233).

But outside of the schools after 1900, story hours spread rapidly in libraries with readings from editions of the Grimms meant to captivate children's attention and inspire virtues. Inspired by this trend and applying new educational emphasis on recovering creativity and imagination for an industrial age, new advisers appeared calling for uses of imagination-building storytelling in the classrooms. Hamilton Wright Mabie's introduction to *Fairy Tales from Grimm* (1909) sounded the educational keyword of "imagination" in expanding industrial society. Noticing that education had become "more practical and exacting," he urged the classroom use of Grimms' folktales, "as legitimate and important a place in the training of the child as the arithmetic or the textbook of science; for the child has not only a faculty of observation and aptitudes for work of all kinds, he has also the great gift of imagination—the master workman which directs all human activities when they become constructive on a great scale; when they build colossal bridges, extensive canals and railroads that climb mountains, as well as when they take the forms of art" (Mabie 1909, 15). Mabie attempted to centralize fairy tales, particularly the Grimms' tales, as part of an American cultural literacy by entitling a volume published by the prominent commercial house of Doubleday, Page, and Company, *Fairy Tales Every Child Should Know* (1905, 1915, 1923).

Uneasy with the narrow practicality of American education, many reformers during the early twentieth century promoted use of fairy tales in public schools to stimulate "imagination" and "aspiration" in a democracy. One report suggesting "progressive" policies to stimulate American democracy claimed that tales as part of literature embodied civilization's "funded and accumulating wisdom." "Without the literature and the arts which keep alive imagination and aspiration, which reflect taste and give enjoyment, industry would be on a low level and government

Cover of *Grimm's Fairy Tales*, published in Philadelphia and Chicago by John C. Winston Company (1922). The cover art and the sixty illustrations in the book, which was aimed at children, were by Edwin John Prittie.

would partake of the culture of the barracks," the report concluded (Educational Policies Commission 1937, 79). Based on his work at the Demonstration Play School of the University of California, Clark W. Hetherington advised in the introduction to Katherine Dunlap Cather's *Educating by Story-Telling* (1918) that reciting stories such as those by the Grimms advanced democracy because they developed the "imagination in mental terms that will function in life today" (Cather 1918, xiv). Tapping into pragmatic attitudes, Cather understood that folktales convey "facts" as well as having the potential of stirring the imagination. Cather suggested the Grimms' folktales for illuminating standard classroom subjects and teaching ethics. The most common American classroom use right up to the present is still for pragmatically teaching communication skills of reading, writing, and listening (Bosma 1987). Rarely were the Grimms' tales mentioned for teaching cultural awareness.

Part of the reason for the attachment of the Grimms' tales to language skills in early childhood is the steady juvenilization and visualization of the tales through the twentieth century. Fairy tales drew younger audiences, and then were justified because the animation of the drama engaged them for primary development of listening and reading skills. The fantasy in the tales was a touchy subject, since educational goals emphasized the need for children to acquire "training" more than enrichment. According to this thinking, children in an industrial society needed a realistic awareness of their surroundings and a pragmatic view of their future. But fantasy could be incorporated into these goals as an encouragement of primary values presumably helpful in an industrial democracy. The fantasy, and accompanying animation, of fairy tales became attached to an early childhood stage of development, often outside of "schooling."

Ultimately after many years of rising use in the schools, Bruno Bettelheim's controversial, and highly publicized, book *The Uses of Enchantment* (1977) was less noteworthy for its unoriginal Freudian interpretations, than for its suggestion that fairy tales could be instrumental in education for helping the child, as he said, "come to grips with reality." Growing up on fairy tales, he concluded, "a person will gain happiness for himself and his life's partner and, with it, happiness also for his parents. He will be at peace with himself and the world. This is one of the manifold truths revealed by fairy tales, which can guide our lives; it is a truth as valid today as it was once upon a time" (Bettelheim 1977, 310; see also Heisig 1977; Zipes 1979, 160–82; Dundes 1991; Tatar 1992, 76–80).

Although Bettelheim's popular psychology caused some reexamination of the therapeutic uses of folktales, the pragmatist trend, as he noted, was well entrenched in America. The children's fairy tale book by midcentury had become a primary book, usually with few words on an oversize page accompanied by brilliant color illustrations. The Grimms' collection became fragmented into separate pictured tales. In the brief five-year period covered by the *Index to Fairy Tales, 1987–1992* (1994), for example, compiler Joseph Sprug lists nine children's editions devoted to the Frog Prince, ten for Little Red Riding Hood, fourteen for Sleeping

Beauty (Little Briar Rose), and sixteen for Cinderella. The illustrations in the single-tale books typically have stereotyped German peasant surroundings of thatched cottages, deep forests, and distant castles. But child characters in the books often have a contemporary reference by sporting a fashionable hairstyle or artistic design. Jean Lee Latham's *The Brave Little Tailor* (1962) shows the page-boy cut and abstract designs of the 1960s while Maurice Sendak's celebrated illustrations in *Dear Mili* (by Ralph Manheim, 1988), an adaptation of a Grimm tale discovered in 1983, has a ribboned natural child of the 1980s amidst a heavy wondrous background of medieval forest and foliage (see Tatar 1992, 70–93; Zipes 1994, 143–46). In 1983, a Caldecott Award went to Trina Schart Hyman's *Little Red Riding Hood*, which stayed true to the plot if not the language of the Grimm tale, but was put in a Victorian country setting, apparently a cross between American picket fence and German forest, calico dresses and buckskin jacket.

Kees Moerbeek's *Little Red Riding Hood* (1990) was a pop-up book with "action characters" set in contemporary America. The mother appears in curlers and tells her blonde-haired daughter to take a "health food hamper" to Grandma. She adds the warning "Don't stop to talk to strangers." The daughter protests having to wear the red hood, but her mother insists she does because "it is chilly in the woods." Toning down the violence of the original Grimms' tale, Moerbeek shows the wolf shutting Grandma in the bathroom rather than eating her. The woodcutter, smoking a pipe and dressed in a green German feathered hat, "knocks out" rather than kills the wolf. In the aftermath of this scene, Red Riding Hood admits that she learned not to talk to strangers. The woodcutter suggests that he could share the "health food lunch" with Grandma and Red Riding Hood, but Red answers, "I am sorry, Sir, but you are a stranger, too. And you should give up smoking. It is bad for you." Moerbeek's visual tale is one, therefore, about learning to obey and behave, and about maintaining good habits.

While Little Red Riding Hood, Cinderella, and Snow White have international variations, and indeed were reported prior to the Grimm's collections, the Grimms still provide the most common reference for American children's consumption of fairy tales (see S. Jones 1983; Bottigheimer 1988; McGlathery 1993, 66–71, 76–77). Renditions of Snow White set up expectations of Disney animation, and while many children's books have taken up that style to appeal to generations raised on television, Josephine Poole's *Snow White* (1991) for later elementary grades provides a contrast to Disney's Snow White because of the dark realism of its illustrations and the starkness of its prose: "Snow White was very frightened next morning when she went into the kitchen and saw seven little men sitting around the table. But they were polite and friendly, and when she had told them her story, they said, 'If you will keep house for us, cook and clean and wash and sew and knit, you may stay with us, and we will look after you always.'"

Snow White and the Seven Dwarfs was not especially evident in many nineteenth-century English editions or school readers of the Grimms' tales, but it arguably became with Cinderella and Little Red Riding Hood in the twentieth century one of America's favorite Grimm tales. Even before Walt Disney chose Snow White for the subject of his first feature-length animation in 1937 and Cinderella for blockbuster adaptation in 1950, American publishers had begun the process of animating these characters.[3] Wanda Gág had nine American printings by 1938 of her "freely translated and illustrated," colorful children's book *Snow White and the Seven Dwarfs.* "Pop-up" color books that featured figures that folded up as the pages turned appeared during the 1930s for Cinderella, Sleeping Beauty, and Little Red Riding Hood. Pop-ups were available for Mickey and Minnie Mouse, already suggesting a connection between Hollywood versions of old fairy tale and new cartoon characters. Later Mickey would star in juvenile adaptations of Grimm tales such as *Mickey and the Beanstalk* (1947). Children's books in size and visual appeal were meant to be looked at by children even more than to be read by adults to children (see Hearne 1988). Disney quickly adapted visual movie techniques to book versions of Snow White in standard, "Big Golden Book," and pop-up formats (Wehr 1945; Stearns 1946; Grant and Werner 1952; Intervisual 1981).

The drastic change in the text of Snow White announced that the film would provide a radically different experience of the fairy tale. In the passage of Snow White's awakening, one reads:

> "Wh-wat is it?" whispered one.
> "It's might purty," said another.
> "Why, bless my soul, I think it's a girl!" said a third. And then Snow White woke up.
> "Why, you're not children," she exclaimed. "You're little men. Let me see if I can guess your names." And she did—Doc and Bashful, Happy, Sleepy, and Sneezy, and last of all Dopey and Grumpy, too.
> "Supper is not quite ready," said Snow White.
> "You'll have just time to wash."
> "Wash!" cried the little men with horror in their tones. They hadn't washed for oh, it seemed hundreds of years. But out they marched, when Snow White insisted. And it was worth it in the end. For such a supper they had never tasted. Nor had they ever had such an evening of fun. All the forest folk gathered around the cottage windows to watch them play and dance and sing. (Grant and Werner 1952)

With dialogue mimicking American vernacular delivered by recontextualized characters in technicolor wizardry, Disney had created a fairy tale he would call his, and America's own. He gave the impression of a folktale without reference to the folk. It became *Walt Disney's Snow White and the Seven Dwarfs.*

Disney made a short animated film of the fairy tale *Three Little Pigs* in 1933 and, buoyed by its tremendous success, applied a fantasy formula of brilliant color and kinetic motion to an adaptation of Snow White in three years of production from 1934 to 1937. He held to his faith in the appeal of a Grimm tale as a feature-length feature despite the skepticism of his advisers. In addition to receiving acclaim for

Scene from *Snow White and the Seven Dwarfs* (1937), produced by Walt Disney.
(© Disney Enterprises, Inc.)

Three Little Pigs and *The Big Bad Wolf* that immediately followed, he recalled fairy-tale adaptations of several Grimm tales including Cinderella, Little Red Riding Hood, and Jack and the Beanstalk as early as 1922 (Zipes 1994, 76). He first viewed a silent version of Snow White in 1915, one of the first films he had ever seen. When Disney saw a short animated version of the fairy tale in 1933 made by the Fleischer studio using its popular female character Betty Boop, he thought an adaptation could be more effective with more time for the story. Concerned that many theaters during the Depression were dropping use of short features to cut costs, he hatched the idea of a full-length movie. But industry insiders questioned whether audiences would sit through more than a five- or ten-minute cartoon. Disney apparently thought he could score a hit during the Depression by combining the name recognition for Grimms' tales with characterizations suggesting movie stars of the day. He left notes advising that Janet Gaynor could provide a model for the character of Snow White, and Douglas Fairbanks for the prince (Stone 1988, 59). Disney required the creative team working on Snow White to watch Charlie Chaplin films to imitate movements in the animation (Eliot 1993, 94).

With a cross of literary folktale and mass-marketed movie, Disney hoped to create a film first with the animated feature that would engage adults along with their children. In this regard, one might understand the debate among the Disney staff over whether the dwarfs should exude adult sentimentality or child-like, comic entertainment, and the animators ended up trying to work both in to their characterization. Disney individualized the dwarfs with names representing different traits such as Bashful, Happy, and Grumpy. Disney writers also narrowed potentially disturbing evil to the queen, and recast the mirror and the huntsman as unwilling, unsuspecting pawns (Stone 1988, 59). Two large changes motivated by the shift from printed to visual medium are evident in the film. While the original has the queen disguising herself as a peasant, Disney splashed a magical transformation into a hag. In addition, she plunges dramatically over a cliff to her death rather than using Taylor's translation of her simply choking "with passion," or following the Grimms' version of the queen dancing to death in iron shoes (Stone 1988, 60). In addition, Disney eliminated the father and death of the mother found in the original, and reduced Snow White to more menial labor than she had done in the original, thus accentuating a rags to riches rise. He also heightened the romantic interest by adding a courtship song by the prince at the beginning and substituting a loving princely kiss to awaken Snow White rather than the clumsy drop of the coffin by a dwarf in the Grimms' version.

Snow White played to an audience of more than twenty million ticket buyers in its first run. Disney added to the healthy profits of the film by licensing a line of Snow White souvenirs that quickly outdistanced the line he began for *Three Little Pigs*. In all, Disney contracted with 117 toy manufacturers to use characters from Snow White. The *New York Times* and other newspapers ran stories admiring this marketing of the film for the employment and production it produced in the midst of the Great Depression ("Prosperity" 1938). At the 1939 Academy ceremonies, Disney was given a special award (a full-size Oscar and seven small ones) for the film's "significant screen innovation." By emphasizing the innovativeness of the film, critics suggested that the Grimms' story had become America's, and reported the film as another American invention for the world. Frank Nugent in his review for the *New York Times* acknowledged that the story was a "Grimm fairy tale," but the headline assured that it was "Walt Disney's Delightful Fantasy." Nugent saw the film's importance in its technical features and "comic Disneyesque patterns." "Nothing quite like it has been done before," he raved (Nugent 1938).

Following its American opening, the film was dubbed into ten languages and distributed to forty-six countries. It ran into a slight snag when priggish British censors restricted children from the film because some violent scenes could cause nightmares ("British" 1938). Once adjustments were made and the bluenosed censors conceded that children could sleep easy, the film became a smash. The *New York Times* editorialized that this international appeal was remarkable considering the sensitivity of nations to depictions of "races or national boundaries, opposing systems of government, wars or threats of war" ("Folk Film" 1938). It also may have been the case that the fantasy was viewed as an escape from tensions of war and

Scene from Cinderella (1949). The caption included with the still when the movie was re-released stated "'BIBBIDI BOBBIDI BOO' and a magic wand are all it takes for the Fairy Godmother to transform rags into ballgowns and pumpkins into coaches in this enchanting scene from Walt Disney's animated classic, 'Cinderella.'" (© Disney Enterprises, Inc.)

various interpretations of the triumph of innocence over "dark forces of evil." Reinterpreting the oral vitality of European folktale with reference to American technology, the *Times* made a case for the film as a form of folklore born in America. The editorial proclaimed, "Snow White and company are basic folklore. In the long time to come there may be more films than there are now that have this appeal—and with living actors as well as cartoons. As folktales were once passed from tribe to tribe and nation to nation, so that few societies have lacked something resembling the Cinderella story, or the Aladdin story, so we may have folk-films. Television and the radio may carry the trend farther" ("Folk Film" 1938). The newspaper made Disney into an American Grimm who would create folklore as well as adapt it.

Many critics have commented that audiences found escape during the Depression in the happy musical spirit and wholesome optimism of the animated features (Mast 1976, 290–91; Zipes 1979, 113–15; Eliot 1993, 75; Zipes 1994, 85–86). Snow White adjusts to hardscrabble surroundings and is able to "live happily ever after." *Cinderella* even topped the popularity of *Snow White*, becoming one of Disney's most profitable films. With *Cinderella*, the attraction of wealth and status as prevalent Hollywood themes came to the fore. Some critics have noted the relation of Disney's emphasis of the rags to riches formula with Algeresque American children's fiction (Yolen 1977, 296–97; Zipes 1994, 89–90). This fairy tale reference is still evident in Hollywood films and mass media. A down-on-her-luck American woman who lands by accident in a wealthy household in a film such as *Mrs. Winterbourne* (1996) is introduced as "a Cinderella" and the trailer opens with "Once upon a time." The movie was advertised as a "story of a girl who is going from filthy to rich." In sports coverage, American broadcasters look for a "Cinderella" team in every tournament to get the big prize. The team is the underdog who Americans cheer for overcoming the odds against the favorites. Headlines in the sports pages such as "Midnight Strikes for Mocs [University of Tennessee-Chattanooga]; Providence Still Dancing," which appeared on ESPN News in the 1997 NCAA basketball tournament, ran without explanation of the Cinderella reference (March 23). It did not need one because of the understood search for a Cinderella in the drama of an American tournament. Indeed, for the sake of claiming an American egalitarianism, and creating good theater, broadcasters bemoaned the lack of a Cinderella team in the Final Four for the 1990s. They intimated that the tournament needed a Cinderella to affirm its Americanness.

In addition to inspiring subsequent references to fairy tale transformation, Disney also commodified animation of the Grimms' tales in an American mode of showing off technological wizardry and organizational prowess. Disney's advertising touted the "dazzling color and brilliant color" that brings the tales to "magical life." In repackaging *Snow White and the Seven Dwarfs* in 1995 for video, Disney Enterprises proclaimed the feature as "the definitive Disney masterpiece" and "a landmark in the history of animation." Inside the packages, the company offered free "mirror image" stickers and an array of products for sale with help from fairy-tale characters, including magazine subscriptions, bakery products, and videocassettes. For many critics, Disney's display of technical mastery, creative control, and mass consumption overshadowed the story or any discernible message. Critic Jack Zipes observed in Disney's films a thematic emphasis on cleanliness, control, and organized industry reinforcing the technology of the film: "the clean frames with attention paid to every detail; the precise drawing and manipulation of the characters as real people; the careful plotting of the events that focus on salvation through the male hero" (Zipes 1994, 94). It is a long stretch to come to Zipes's conclusion from this observation of Disney's commodification, but it is also true that Disney globalized the special themes of romance and material wealth bringing happiness, and technological manipulation offering passive, unreflective pleasure. Disney understood that the movie could be the beginning of a larger material fantasy, and he pioneered merchandising of movie images in a wide range of consumable goods. Disney had the effect of imbuing fairy tales with commercial magic and thereafter tied consumption to the wish fulfillment of a "fairy tale" life.

The continued popularity of Snow White and Cinderella in American culture is at least partly attributable to the relation of children to the coming-of-age heroines of the films. Coming of age in these mass-mediated fairy tales is defined in terms of a blushing first romance, and the happy outcome of maturity (see McGlathery 1991). Disney's Snow White has a speech and appearance that exudes American cuteness, and brings her from being with nature to the arms of a suitor. In mass-mediated fairy tales, beauties come of age from viewing their pursuers as beasts to embracing them as princes, often replacing their fathers, although in a tale such as Little Red Riding Hood, a warning about intimacy outside the family is held up to the naive, virginal youth (Tatar 1988; McGlathery 1991, 55–86; Warner 1993; see also Bettelheim 1977, 283–309; Mieder 1982). The "wolf" in Little Red Riding Hood has become a common English metaphor for the lusting male, while the girl on the way to Grandma's house often appears pubescent (Bettleheim 1989; Dundes 1989b; Zipes 1993).

Cinderella's connections to pubescence seem especially strong because of her depiction as a virginal girl prevented from going to the ball, but who enters eventually into union with the prince because her foot fits into a glass slipper (Bettleheim 1977, 268–71). Her "rags" literally turn into a rich gown in many tellings. The contrast is not only between rags and riches, but also between domestic passivity in the house and courtship activity at the ball. Cinderella's connotations of erotic awakening come into play in American jump rope rhymes, in which girls use the sexually suggestive lines, "Cinderella dressed in yella, Went upstairs to meet a fella, Made a mistake, kissed a snake, And came down with a bellyache" (Bronner 1988a, 70–71). She also enters into a joke popular with teenagers that has a reference to the coming-of-age symbolism of menstruation. The fairy godmother turns pumpkins into a tampon and a coach to accommodate the menstruating Cinderella. At midnight she tries to pull away from the prince, who begs for her name. After she tells him "Cinderella," he responds that his is "Peter Peter Pumpkin Eater," and she sighs with relief, "Thank God!" (C. Preston 1994). Snow White meanwhile took on overtones of racial imagery regarding sexual desirability in at least one harsh joke circulating in America during the 1980s. The narrator describes a black girl looking into a magic mirror repeating the lines "Mirror, mirror on the wall, who's the fairest of them all?" The answer comes back, "Snow White, you black bitch, and don't you forget it!"

In addition to entering contemporary folklore, the characters and settings of the Grimms' tales became common allusions in popular speech and commercial advertising after World War II. Proverbial comments such as "you have to kiss a lot of frogs to find your prince" and "I'm waiting for prince charming" attest to the strong romantic reference to the tales in popular culture. "Living a fairy tale" in common usage often meant luckily finding wealth as well as romance. As Linda Dégh noted, "In modern society, tale particles divorced from the book assume a life of their own. They become symbols for reference, capable of describing feelings, arguing for right and wrong, and summarizing conditions in delicate situations" (1995, 280). Increasingly those symbols become visual through children's books that have become showcases of color illustrators with simplified texts, an explosion of video products adapting Grimms' tales, and greeting cards and other ephemera with icons of a frog prince or fairy godmother. Hallmark not only includes fairy tale characters in many of its products, but also produced a line of videos entitled *Timeless Tales from Hallmark.* The advertising for Hallmark's "Rapunzel" (1990) announced, "You and your family are transported to a brilliantly animated, whimsically updated realm of classic storytelling."

Frog princes and fairy godmothers were regulars in comic cartoons aimed at children, such as "Fractured Fairy Tales," which depended on a knowledge of common Grimm plots to make twists that usually brought crass modern realism into the make-believe stories. During the 1980s, producer Shelly Duvall also made reference to modern social issues in her adaptation of Grimms' fairy tale plots into comic family television theater in her series, *Faerie Tale Theatre,* containing updated dialogue and showcasing prominent Hollywood actors.[4] As a shared public reference, fairy tale images frequently appear in commercial culture, and Snow White and Cinderella again seem to be American favorites for parody as well as representation on American advertisements. Snow White appeared in an advertisement for Palmolive Rapid Shave in which her prince charming is unable to awaken her with a kiss until he shaves. A Mr. Clean promotion showed Cinderella scrubbing the floor until her fairy godmother hands her a bottle of the product which makes the job easier (Dégh 1994, 38; Zipes 1979, 106). Fairy tale references become significant because they represent a realm contrary to the gritty realism and frustration of modern life.

The fairy tale became less innocent in American discourse during the late twentieth century as more moral and social concerns about the appropriateness of relating Grimms' tales to American children became highly vocal. Complaints that the tales were disturbingly violent and irreligious go back well into the nineteenth century (Tatar 1987, 3–38; Kamenetsky 1992, 192–95). Yet the discourse became especially heated in the middle third of the twentieth century because of ideological uses of the Grimms by the Nazis. The Nazis made special use of folklore in schools and youth organizations to promote national unity and cultural superiority, and their propaganda especially touted the Grimms' tales for showing morals that "the strongest one always wins" and "might is always right" (Kamenetsky 1972, 1977, 1984). Nazi textbooks used the Grimms as examples idealizing authoritarianism, militarism, enforcement of discipline, and violence toward the outsider (Snyder 1959; Zipes 1988b, 134–69). Nazi use of Grimms' folktales to teach the presence of a German master race and inferiority of folk types such as Jews and

Gypsies drew outrage from American folklorists, including Ben Botkin, who organized his *Treasury of American Folklore* (1944) with examples of American hero tales to counter fascist uses of the Grimms. Nazi bureaucrats instructed teachers and youth leaders in Hitler's Germany to recontextualize the Grimms as prophets of Nazism and ignore their democratic principles and Christian faith (Kamenetsky 1992, 242–43).

From the 1940s on, memory of Nazi manipulation of Grimms' tales invited closer scrutiny of fairy tales in schools and libraries. In his foreword to *Folktales of Germany* (1966a), Richard Dorson took the Grimms to task for altering the tales with the effect of castigating stepmothers, merchants, and Jews as outsiders in society. He was especially alarmed at the Grimms' handling of *Der Jude im Dorn* (no. 110, reported in Hunt 1884, 2:97–101; translated in different editions as "The Jew in the Bush," "The Jew among Thorns," "Jew in the Brambles," and "Jew in the Hawthorn Hedge"). With the Holocaust in mind, Dorson criticized the treatment of the story as one that "not only pictures the Jew as a miser and skinflint but finds amusement in having him dance on thorns and be strung on the gallows" (Dorson 1966a, xix).

Feminist criticisms of the tales as reinforcing social submission of women, especially in the romantic core of Snow White and Cinderella, came to the fore during the 1970s (Minard 1975; Rowe 1979; Stone 1986; Bottigheimer 1986). The image of Snow White cooking, cleaning, and knitting in exchange for male protection did not sit well with modern representations of the liberated woman. It was not only a scholarly complaint. Suzie Bogguss hit the top of the country charts in 1993 with the song "Hey Cinderella," which implied that modern women had been deceived by fairy tales. Her chorus resounded for many women listeners: "Hey Cinderella, what's the story all about/I got a funny feeling we missed a page or two somehow/Ooh, Cinderella maybe you could help us out/Does the shoe fit you now?" Two years later, singer Garth Brooks scored a smash success with a similar plaint in "It's Midnight Cinderella": "I guess your prince charming/Wasn't after all/'Cause he sure seemed different/Right after the ball/I guess more than horses/Are turnin' into rats/And by the way he's walkin'/I can guess where your slipper's at." For adult American listeners, it was clear, as Brooks sang on his platinum-selling recording invoking Cinderella, "There's gonna be some changes in the way this story goes."

Writer Jane Yolen complained that in children's fiction American Cinderellas, who usually are more forgiving and passive than the Grimms' Aschenputtel, have "presented the majority of American children with the wrong dream," and she blamed the mass market for perpetuating an "insipid beauty waiting for Prince Charming" (Yolen 1977, 303). She has tried to provide an alternative for children by publishing revised traditional tales to produce unpredictable endings and assertive, independent heroines (see Yolen 1981, 1983, 1989; see also Riordan 1985). Jack Zipes meanwhile provided a reader of contemporary feminist fairy tales for adult reading to counter the Grimms' tendency to provide "for rational cohesion and a reward system that justified male domination within the bourgeois sphere" (Zipes 1986a, 1988b, 73). With the implication that the Grimms altered texts and perpetuated an ideology that supported their middle-class self-interests, this criticism added to charges against the Grimms issues from "cultural studies" of class to multicultural plaints of gender and race bias (Zipes 1988a, 1988b). Inspired in his criticism of fairy tales by the lessons of the Holocaust, Zipes has recast tales in a more egalitarian light. Intending to challenge stereotypes and encourage "seeing the world in a different light," his "Little Red Riding Hood lives in London and outwits the wolf, not once, but every Sunday, as she crosses town to visit Granny for afternoon tea" (Evans 1997, 8).

A common critical stance in popular discourse is to assault the effect of the popularity of the Grimms' tales for privileging an ideal type of the international fairy tale, which is Eurocentric (see Lüthi 1970, 1982; Dundes 1986, 263–64). The fairy tale, many folklorists have found, is neither exclusively European nor of one type (Dundes 1986). Yet the Grimm formula calls for an ordered sequence and symmetry between the "once upon a time" opening to the "happily ever after" closing. This fairy tale type has kings and queens, peasants and princesses, apparently out of touch with contemporary sensibilities of complexity to life and relativistic definition of values. One alternative trend has been to create "post-modern" fairy tales of simultaneous, even chaotic action and uncertain, even multiple meanings (Zipes 1994, 157–61; see also Bacchilega 1989). In post-modern fairy tales directed at children such as *Cinderella: The Untold Story* (1990) by Russell Shorto and *The Frog Prince Continued* (1991) by Jon Scieszka, expectations are reversed, closure is not achieved, and absolutes of truth or goodness do not exist (Cox 1994). Jane Yolen in *Here There Be Dragons* (1993) offers a fantasy tale narrated from the perspective of the dragon roaming the gray area of good and evil, and evoking mixed sympathies by the story's abrupt end.

Beginning in the 1980s, critics attached the keyword of "multicultural" to revisions of the canonical status of the Grimms. Instead of universalizing the themes of the Grimms' tales, folktales in a multicultural perspective could be used to show the reflection of different societies and cultural traditions that produced the tales. These traditions did not necessarily follow national lines, but emphasized the multiple ethnic traditions that make up a multicolored, multivocal world. Indeed, multicultural advisers emphasized that folktales, the products of ordinary people often left out of the historic and literary record, countered a supposedly elitist privileging of "dead white men" belonging to the upper class who attempt to unify culture in their image. Calls for diversifying the folktale canon in the schools to include African, Asian, and Hispanic traditions went out, and while one response has been more children's editions of non-European tales, another has been to present these diverse traditions in classical fairy tale style rather than presenting living traditions (DeSpain 1994). Stories drawn from exotic or historical ethnic locales with "heroes of color" were meant in some cases to expand global cultural awareness, in others to build self-esteem by relating traditions heard in folktales to children's ethnic experience, especially in schools dominated by "minorities," usually defined as Americans of African, Spanish, Native, and Asian background.

The social theory behind multicultural applications suggested that by signifying the distinctiveness of a group's cultural traditions, folktales would teach toleration of ethnic differences in children's social development (see Grant 1995). They could also relativistically show a variety of moral imaginations possible in America, instead of privileging the virtues of Western civilization. Yet some critics worried that this usage would fragment an already strained society or create moral confusion (Schlesinger 1992; Guroian 1996). There were those that suggested that replacing the Cinderella and Snow White of the Grimms, or Anansi the Spider (African) and Coyote (Southwest Indian) with Davy Crockett and Paul Bunyan in storytelling to children might help bring unity to the culture (see Studer 1962; Zorn 1992). The use of Grimms' fairy tales and multicultural alternates became a public dispute over a social vision of America, startlingly referred to as a choice of whether "To Buy or To Burn" in one conference held in 1996 and explained as "Children's Literature in the Age of Political Correctness." The driving question was "What do librarians and teachers do with books that some find offensive, yet are considered classics by others?"[5]

One subject that especially brings out a public clash of beliefs of reality and supernatural, diversity and unity, is religion. While public schools generally avoid the issue, especially in the choice of folktales, critics get riled over religious affirmation in the canonical folk fantasies. Because of the supernatural qualities of many Grimms' tales, questions occasionally arose about the appropriateness of religious symbolism in the classroom at a time when right and left clashed over school prayer and religious subjects in the schools. One school adviser on using folk literature in the classroom in 1994 warned teachers: "Today, diverse groups ranging from fundamental religious groups to witches and warlocks question the use of folk literature selections. Religious groups object to the supernatural elements found in the selections, while others question their authentic portrayal in tales and poetry. It is likely these groups will continue to object to the use of folk literature in the classroom. Wise teachers will attempt to circumvent such censorship by knowing the literature used with students and determining whether the selection will comply with the beliefs of the families in their classrooms and schools" (Goforth and Spillman 1994, 8). Like other advisers, this one avoided imposition of values in the classroom and pragmatically insisted that folktales such as the Grimms hold student interest and therefore can be used to encourage reading comprehension and creative writing (see also Bosma 1987).

In the adult market, revisionist versions of Grimms' tales equally tout and parody modern sensitivities. Robert Bly had a best seller with *Iron John* (1991) in which he reinterpreted the folktale to pronounce a spiritual renewal for embattled men in the 1990s (see Zipes 1994, 96–118). Allan Chinen, M.D., offered baby boomers "classic stories and mythic tales to illuminate the middle years" in *Once Upon a Midlife* (1992). Altering Grimm classics involving aging workers such as The Elves and the Shoemaker, it provided therapeutic perspectives on women's emancipation and midlife role reversals. Poking fun at multicultural righteousness rampant during the 1990s, James Finn Garner scored a hit with *Politically Correct Bedtime Stories* (1994). He rewrote American Grimm favorites such as Snow White, Cinderella, Rumpelstiltskin, and the Frog Prince, he said, "so they reflect more enlightened times." They had to be revised to correct "insensitivity to womyn's issues, minority cultures, and the environment." The passage from Snow White quoted earlier becomes: "When she awoke several hours later, she saw the faces of seven bearded, vertically challenged men surrounding the bed…. 'My name is Snow White,' she began, 'and I've already told you: My mother-of-step, the queen, ordered a woodperson to take me in the forest and kill me, but he took pity and told me to run away into the woods as far as I could" (Garner 1994, 46–48). For children and adults alike in American popular culture today, the Grimms' tales have been once again recontextualized to discuss changes, and problems, in society.

THE ACADEMIC GRIMMS

In addition to the public Grimms of fantasy and entertainment in the fairy tale canon, there are also the academic Grimms, who have been invoked to impress folk, folklore, and romantic nationalism into scholarly discourse. In a kind of origin legend, the Grimms are typically credited in annals of scholarship with founding the study of folklore. Yet the basis of that study in romantic or scientific terms can cause ambiguity in the scholarly contextualization of the Grimms' legacy. The *Standard Dictionary of Folklore, Mythology and Legend* (1949) unequivocally stated that the Grimms were "German philologists and mythologists, the founders of scientific folklore study" (Leach, Maria 1949, 1:466). Writing on "The Scholarly Study of Folklore," Louise Pound wrote with certainty that "conscious interest in what we now call 'folklore' arose early in the nineteenth century in the wake of the Romantic Movement. Its foundation was laid by the eminent German scholar Jacob Grimm, helped by his brother Wilhelm" (Pound [1959] 1987, 223). In making the case for the patriarchy of the Grimms, American folklorists pointed to the brothers' use of comparative notes that implied a method of historic-geographic comparison to arrive at statements of origin and diffusion. Because their comparisons went beyond a specific literary genre to consider games, songs, proverbs, and speech, they bound the study of folktales to a consideration of oral tradition generally. It implied crossing the disciplinary boundaries of the day in philology, literature, religion, and history.

If a new scholarship depends on a community of researchers, then the Grimms' correspondence with scholars throughout Europe on the folktale is another key to their priority. They were not unique in these points, although their success with *Kinder- und Hausmärchen* and university position drew attention to their scholarly efforts. One skeptic objecting to the crowning of the Grimms came from Giuseppe Cocchiara in his sweeping history of folklore in Europe, originally published in Italian in 1952. He resented the priority placed on German academics and took as his uphill struggle the interpretation of the discovery and invention of the folk in the nineteenth century as a culmination of humanistic forces throughout Europe concerned with the primitive, rather than the organizing power of the brothers. Yet he acknowledged the prevalence of allegiance to the German Grimms as the sources from which folklore studies sprang.

The origin legend of the Brothers Grimm has had several lasting effects in folkloristic discourse. It established the significance of field collected evidence as authentic texts that could be classified into literary types and compared, or "scientifically" analyzed. It began special pleading for gathering traditional material before it inevitably disappears. It pointed to folklore as an international phenomenon and it contributed to the organization of its study along national lines. It laid the foundation for constructing tradition from the materials of oral literature. Toward this end, the fantasy of the fairy tale and myth that preoccupied the brothers remained primary in a hierarchy of scholarly genres for many years. "Folk Literature" remains the first listed and largest category in the Modern Language Association bibliography for folklore. Ethnomusicology, folk belief systems, and folk rituals follow, and material culture is last. My university's catalogue lists a whopping 613 citations under "fairy tales," while myth is the next largest category with 319 entries. Legends, meanwhile, can muster forty-nine book titles, while ballads and proverbs boast thirty-four and sixty-three, respectively. Indeed, there are almost as many entries for the Grimm brothers as there are for folklore.

Some movements, apparently at odds, simultaneously invoke the Grimms' precedents. Because the Grimms used their collected texts to show survivals of a medieval past, they contributed to a search in folklore studies for medieval origins of ballads, tales, and epics (Lindahl and Brady 1980). With the view of folklore as dependent on an ancient peasant ancestry, many folklorists doubted that America as a nation could indeed have a folklore of its own. German-trained Alexander Krappe (1894–1947), who wrote *The Science of Folklore* (1930), insisted that "there exists no such thing as American folklore, but only European (or African, or Far Eastern) folklore on the American continent, for the excellent reason that there is no American 'folk'" (Krappe 1930, 291). Whatever traditions existed in America, Krappe asserted, had been reduced radically by "a ruthless standardization" (Krappe [1930] 1964, xviii). Krappe was American-born but attended Berlin University, where his interest in *Märchen* was sparked. He taught at Columbia and several Big Ten universities, and translated the complete Grimms' tales for an American edition (Grimm and Grimm 1960). He organized his guide to the science of folklore according to literary genres and gave first priority to "The Fairy

Tale" followed by "The Merry Tale" and "The Animal Tale." Down on the list are "Custom and Ritual" and "Folk-Dance and Folk-Drama." Krappe venerated Jacob Grimm for laying "the scientific foundations of our discipline" in developing a historical method (Krappe [1930] 1964, xix; see also Burson 1982). He credited British folklorists with expanding Grimm's ideas on historical survival even as German folklorists neglected a legacy of their own.

The Grimms could also be invoked by folklorists developing a functional approach to uses of tradition in contemporary society. Explaining the adaptation of the tales to different historical periods, the Grimms offered that the tales "were forever being created anew as time went on" (Tatar 1987, 208). The tales could therefore be used to reflect social conditions in various periods. Noting modern references to apprentices, pipes, and cannons in the telling of "old" folktales, the Grimms explained that "these things, like the words of our spoken language, are just what was refashioned by the lips of each storyteller, and you can be sure that sixteenth-century storytellers spoke of mercenaries and muskets rather than of soldiers and cannons, just as the hat that makes its wearer invisible was in the age of knights a magic helmet" (Tatar 1987, 215). Showing their awareness of community and individual differences in performance, they pronounced that "every region tells a story in its own way and that every teller narrates differently" (Tatar 1987, 221). To be sure, they did not give many details of taletelling sessions or community contexts, and they combined versions to present the collective form of the tale. In their concern for reconstructing the history of folk poetry, they rarely went into the villages to record the cultural background of narrating. American folklorist William Bascom in proposing functions of folklore that explain its persistence in and relevance to contemporary life, used the changes in the course of retelling observed by the Grimms to suggest a causal link between the instrumental ends of folklore performance and the stability of culture (Bascom [1954] 1965, 286).

If the Grimms' theoretical principles of a disease of language and mythopoeic origin of tales held less sway in the twentieth century, their ghosts still linger in the very use of "folklore." In 1846 William Thoms wrote a letter to *The Athenaeum* proposing "a good Saxon compound, Folklore,—*the Lore of the People*" to replace popular antiquities and popular literature. The inspiration for this shift was the Grimms' *Deutsche Mythologie* (Teutonic Mythology, 1835), which extended to four thick volumes. This work was regarded as more scholarly than the *Household Tales*, and it provided a sweeping examination of folktales, rituals, customs, beliefs, songs, and proverbs as survivals of German-Norse mythological concepts. The Grimms had applied their philological method of comparing the forms of language and arranging them historically to infer a devolution of tradition from the mythopoeic age into the present, and attempted to show that Christianity had triumphantly taken up mythological beliefs. Writing the preface to the second edition, Jacob admitted that he used the work to exalt his "native land." Yet he

William John Thoms in his study, as he was depicted in *The Academy,* November 11, 1899.

suggested an international study in applying the idea that "history teaches us to recognise in language, the farther we are able to follow it up, a higher perfection of form, which declines as culture advances." Further, he offered the premise that "natural science bears witness, that the smallest may be an index to the greatest; and the reason is discoverable, why in our antiquities, while the main features were effaced, petty and apparently accidental ones have been preserved" (Grimm and Grimm [1844] 1966, 3:vi–vii). Jacob suggested a unifying theory of tradition, then, that followed the devolution of language from the medieval ages, from East to West, and implied "a fundamental unity of the European nations, a mighty influence which is seen working through long ages, alike in language, legend and religion" (Grimm and Grimm [1844] 1966, 3:vii; see also Dundes 1969a).

Thoms imagined an intimate relationship between the folklore of Germany and the British Isles, and sought to create a common mission in the study of "manners, customs, observances, superstitions, ballads, proverbs." He admired the systematic order and contemporary significance that the Grimms brought to the items previously recorded randomly by antiquarians. Reviewing *Deutsche Mythologie,* Thoms called the work "a mass of minute facts, many of which, when separately considered, appear trifling and insignificant,—but, when taken in connection with the system into which his master-mind has woven them, assume a value that he who first recorded them never dreamed of attributing to them" (Thoms 1965, 5). The

"Anglo-Saxon" word folklore was an approximation of the German *Volkskunde*, the traditional knowledge of the people. The terms were not equivalent, since Thoms had more in mind a conception of folk material inspiring a search for evolutionary origin and history (Tokofsky 1996, 208). Linguistic evidence suggests that the German word connoted knowledge about peoples more than Thoms's notion of traditional knowledge of the folk (Tokofsky 1996, 208). A recontextualization of *Volkskunde* as the preferred German word to describe the study of tradition, however, did not occur until Wilhelm Riehl (1823–1897) promoted it at midcentury and published a volume entitled *Volkskunde als Wissenschaft* (Folklore as Science, 1858). It was this usage that British folklorists George Gomme and Charlotte Burne in *The Handbook of Folk-Lore* (1913) emphasized when they defined folklore as "literally, *'the learning of the people'*" (Burne 1913, 1) and credited Thoms with its conception (see Bennett 1996).

In redefining "popular antiquities," Thoms signaled a rhetorical shift for use of popular and antique. As popular had moved in meaning from the numerically predominant lower or peasant class to everyone in a society, folk offered the sense of ordinariness with the connotation of primitiveness. The lore expanded the essentially archaeological core of finding local historical remains to recovering elusive "spiritual" and "intellectual" specimens such as beliefs, customs, rituals, and myths. The lore was the non-artistic material associated with high culture that marked local knowledge. The "people" then, were subgroupings within a national society, and those subgroupings were typically at the margins of the country. As a special singular category, folk implied comparison across localities and nations, a type that carried tradition, defined as the kind of cultural stability maintained through oral and customary transmission. Following Grimm, Thoms could envision that the folk were left behind by progress, but provided a spiritual foundation for cultural development. Even more than the Grimms, Thoms and the English folklorists emphasized the antiquarian survival of traditions in a natural science model. And they followed the beliefs of the folk in their empire to connect primitive customs globally in imagining the unity of the folk mind and creating a natural history of civilization.

Thoms and the Grimms had not taken seriously the contribution of America to the folkloristic enterprise. Although the primitiveness of American Indians was of interest, the nation in their view lacked the authenticity provided by a peasant class and ancient history. Nineteenth-century American folklore scholars, many from New England, took up the Thoms-Grimm connection, not so much in tales, as in ballads. The first president of the American Folklore Society, Francis James Child (1825–1896), had heard the Grimms lecture in Germany from 1849 to 1851. According to Edson Richmond, "when he was in Germany Child became a great admirer of the brothers Grimm and was thoroughly imbued with the scholarly techniques of the German philologists, whose methods, relatively new to the United States, he adhered to for the rest of his life" (Richmond 1996a). Following

Francis James Child as a student in Germany. (Harvard University Archives)

the influence of the Grimms, Child became concerned with separating authentic ballads *of* the people (the Grimms' *Volkspoesie*) and "artificial" literary ballads *for* the people (*Volksthumliche Poesie*) (Rieuwerts 1996). Child's categorizations of authenticity, his distinction of folk and popular, his search for origin and distribution, and his admiration for a medieval golden age of orality, became more widespread in America through his teaching (Bell 1988). Child wielded great academic clout as Harvard's first professor of English and was followed by his prize student George Lyman Kittredge, once called the "dominant force in the humanities in America from the turn of the century to World War II" (Harris 1996). It was Kittredge who completed Child's final volume of *The English and Scottish Popular Ballads* (1898) and stimulated further interest in medieval English and early American folklore. Kittredge mentored many leading lights in American folklore studies, including Stith Thompson, Francis Gummere, Phillips Barry, Duncan Emrich, and Samuel Bayard (Birdsall 1973; Thompson 1996, 56–62).

Following the Grimms' lament for the passing of folk tradition, Child assumed poetic ballad singing to be extinct, and drew on historical literary texts to produce a typology of all known English and Scottish ballads. The result was *The English and Scottish Popular Ballads* (1882–1898), which became a standard reference for later collection in America. Child resisted Grimms' ideas of communal origin in the peasantry, but adopted their emphasis on comparative notes and organization of texts into types (Wilgus 1959, 6–9). Francis Gummere (1855–1919) at Haverford College followed the Grimms' interest in poetic origins and forcefully advocated that ballads, studied as survivals of ancient poetry, had origins in spontaneous communal compositions at public social occasions (Gummere [1901] 1973, [1907] 1959). Gummere's theory was his interpretation of a statement that Gummere attributed to the brothers, "*das Volk dichtet*," which he took to mean the folk collectively compose poetry (Richmond 1996b). His view sparked a debate that engaged many American folklorists for years between those taking the "romantic" communal view of the origin of expressive tradition and those emphasizing individual composition (Wilgus 1959, 9–32). It heated up when collectors such as Cecil Sharp, John Harrington Cox, Mellinger Henry, and Phillips Barry located American singers who still performed the ballads assumed to be extinct. Particularly in rural New England and Appalachia, the presence of songs that followed Child's types raised questions about the ability of the American environment to preserve tradition, rather than destroy it, as many European folklorists had assumed. So entrenched had the Child emphasis on text inherited from the Grimms been, however, that the songs and ballads of the singers were mostly recorded as remnants of ancient types rather than examples of living performances.

With this early emphasis in the scholarly discourse of American folklorists on ballad origins and perpetuation of tradition, attention shifted to transmission across the Atlantic from England to America. Within English departments it was

Francis James Child as a Harvard professor. (Harvard University Archives)

George Lyman Kittredge lecturing at Harvard. (Harvard University Archives)

possible to concentrate on English-language materials of relevance to American conditions. Indeed, it was a way that many American scholars of English literature made a case for studying American texts through courses on the ballad. Apropos of this position, Gummere led other American scholars in questioning the "hard and fast line" between folklore and literature (Wilgus 1959, 10). It became possible to view isolated pockets of tradition in Appalachia and New England as a shared American ancestry with a "poetic" as well as a "folk" tradition. Famed English critic Andrew Lang singled out work on ballads as the "most valuable" contribution of Americans, and, noting his comment, American chronicler Martha Warren Beckwith worried that "it sometimes seems, indeed, as if folklore societies existed today, for the literary enthusiast, for this cause alone" (Beckwith 1931b, 58).

While the Grimms had invented a folk with their presentation of the German quality of fairy tales, apparently in short supply in the United States, American scholars in the early twentieth century found a comparable folk tradition largely in songs and ballads circulating among descendants of pioneer settlers. The ballad as a "special point of departure for American folklorists," according to Beckwith, writing in the 1920s and 1930s, made the cultural leap from traditions "orally preserved by the British colonizers of our country" to "that which is native American" (Beckwith 1931b, 58). Typically, the "Child" ballad of supposed British origin was presented first in collections followed by songs and ballads of the type on American subjects, thus giving the impression that native songs had arisen out of, but were distinguished from, the ancient ballad tradition. The collectors implied the presence of an American canon that could be separated from European content.

Louise Pound in *American Ballads and Songs* (1922) made the case for a folk song tradition separable from popular culture. She defined "popular" as having "universal" currency and preserving forms fixed by the printed page. She wrote that folk songs "are the property … of the folk in certain sections and groups" and are "handed on orally from mouth to mouth" (Pound 1922, xviii). She held the devolutionary view that American conditions tended to move from the supernatural to the real. "The characters and manners of the American ballads betray their varying origins and the divergent social groups among which they have lingered," Pound wrote. She explained that although some American ballads retain references to Old World titles, "more often, if such pieces have been long in the New World, the characters, localities, and stories are accommodated to a New World setting. There is loss of romantic features and disappearance of many archaic literary touches in expression" (Pound 1922, xxiv). She began her survey with "English and Scottish Ballads in America" and moved to "Native Ballads and Songs," "Ballads of Criminals and Outlaws," "Western Ballads and Songs," and "Dialogue, Nursery and Game Songs." She excluded black folk songs, feeling that they deserved separate consideration, and without comment, she omitted immigrant traditions of non-English speakers. The categorization of an American song type based on the English ballad became especially evident after World War II with the publication of *Native American Balladry* (1950) by G. Malcolm Laws. He summarized: "Thanks to the tireless work of regional collectors of folksong during the past few decades, American literature has been enriched by the printed texts of hundreds of songs previously preserved in the memories of folk singers.... The large number of ballads thus garnered as well as the wide distribution of many of them offers convincing evidence that the United States has a vigorous tradition of balladry based on native themes" (Laws 1950, xi).

The regional folk song collections inspired a search for a parallel body of folktales showing ancient deposits of European poetry in America. Richard Chase opened *The Jack Tales* (1943) with the comment "Anglo-American folk music has had much attention in recent years. We are beginning to discover and to recognize the rich heritage of our people in songs and ballads, folk hymns and carols, country dance tunes and figures—living traditions that are known and loved wherever these people have pioneered" (Chase 1943, vii). He provided eighteen tales collected from oral sources in the Appalachians, and he provided comparative notes that recognized the connection of these tales to the collections of the Grimms in Germany and others in the British Isles. He even made reference to the way that the tales reflect "a highly spiritual folk" (Chase 1943, xii). Nonetheless, he made the claim for the Americanness of Jack's "fantastic adventures." He wrote: "*Reynard* is a one-sided rogue, the heroes of European collections of tales are many; other central characters are supermen or gods ... *Jack*, however, is thoroughly human, the unassuming representative of a very large part of the American people" (Chase 1943, xii).

Leonard Roberts in another popular collection of folktales from Appalachia, *South from Hell-fer-Sartin* (1955) specified the American conditions for the loss of tradition—industrialization. He argued that many generations in the eastern Kentucky mountains had kept alive oral tradition, associated with America as a whole, because of isolation and reliance on social entertainment into the twentieth century. "The old ways of entertainment have been almost forgotten," he observed, however. "The haunting tunes of the folk songs have given way to whining hillbilly music, and the barn dance has replaced party games. People no longer gather for an evening of storytelling" (Roberts 1955, 11). As if to show the range of lore representing the preindustrial way of life, he added sections of "Jokes and Anecdotes" and "Myths and Local Legends" in addition to the folktales. Yet even in eastern Kentucky, he predicted, "in another ten years this area, too, will have lost its distinctive folk culture" (Roberts 1955, 11). His statement sounded a Grimm-like warning for the spiritual future of America in its headlong rush to industrial progress. He admired the social meaning of storytelling as a sign of harmony in community, of "hill folk" living "peacefully with each other" (Roberts 1955, 10).

Vance Randolph presented folktales of the Ozarks in a number of books as reflecting the "pioneer way of life" associated with the American spirit. Making reference to an opposition of tradition and modernity, he observed, "The early settlers had little of our modern enthusiasm for novelty. They did not feel, as we do, that a new song or a new story is better than an old one" (Randolph 1952, xv). He invoked the Grimms in his pronouncement of the fidelity of his published texts to oral tradition, although he also allowed himself the right to make alterations while retaining the "Ozark idiom" (Randolph 1958, xv–xvii). He enlisted the help of folklorists who provided comparative notes showing sources and parallels to the stories following the model of the Grimms. One of those was Ernest Baughman, who eventually codified the English-American connection in a *Type and Motif Index of the Folktales of England and North America* (1966). While Randolph recognized the analogues of the Ozark tales in "the great European collections," he used his collections to focus attention on the specialness of the Ozarks as a place of tradition, a reminder of what America once was. Calling on the Grimm fairy tale image of an earthy folk bound to unspoiled nature and endowed with a cultural vitality, he called the Ozark country "an enchanted land" (Randolph 1958, xvii). As Chase and Roberts had done for the Appalachians, Randolph offered the tradition-toting residents of the storied Ozarks as America's primitive ancestors drawn from British stock. The isolated mountain settlers of America had become America's folk much as the Grimms had used Hesse.

Richard Dorson was a major American folklorist who drew on the romantic impulse suggested in the popular collections of Appalachian and Ozark ballads and folktales, but his nationalism was based more on the adaptive formation of new folklore from the events and conditions of American history. Befitting the modern existence of the American republic, origins concerned him less than the physical and social use of tradition to fit American needs and values. He averred that the European inheritance often remained in American tradition but became transformed by it. And more so than other regional collectors, he devoted attention to the American consensus of diverse influences, including African and American Indian, urban and industrial. He promoted attention to the American hero and local legend rather than the transplanted European tale or ballad as an especially telling indication of an American tradition emerging from varied sources. Often set in the recent rather than ancient past, not as internationally comparable as the ballad and folktale but sharply reflective of local values and attitudes, the legend seemed to stress the interpretation in narrative of new experiences appropriate to a strange new world like the United States. Whereas the localized legend collections of the Grimms had been secondary in European scholarship, with Dorson's insistence the connections to an American historical experience and value systems in legends became a primary scholarly concern in the United States.

The philosophical continuity between Dorson and Grimm lies in the organization of folklore by nationality. This approach was based on the idea that cultures were created by nature and history. Drawing on Herder's philosophy, it held that the physical environment provided natural boundaries for cultures and history gave them a distinctive sense of peoplehood. The argument is that history is divided into ages, each of which evolves naturally out of the preceding age, and each age possesses distinctive cultural features (Wilson 1973, 821; Berlin 1976, 59–67).[6] A nation's cultural history shows a natural development from a poetic, then heroic age, which influences its sense of self. By this thinking, nations achieve a progressive organic unity by building on a cultural foundation, a national soul that can be recovered primarily through folklore conceived as the expression of ordinary, natural people. Dorson, in fact, argued for the distinctiveness of American culture, young as it was, by an organization of its experience into successive cultural ages—religious, democratic, economic, and humane (Dorson 1973a). He posited an American heroic age, not in the medieval period, but in the preindustrial nineteenth century. America lacked a fairy tale tradition, he argued, but it had its tall tales and legends of mythic heroes such as the "down-to-earth" Davy Crockett and Mike Fink. If America did not have an ethnic unity, it managed a democratic consensus. He located evidence for interethnic relations in dialect stories, personal narratives, and jokes. In each he identified an American transformative process reconstituting the supernatural or subcultural element into forms reflecting the language and conditions of American surroundings. He Americanized romantic nationalism by making it appear less romantic and poetic and more realistic and pragmatic. He reported the prosaic legends as ways for people to comment on historical changes and conditions affecting their lives.

Dorson's new nationalism sparked rancorous debate, which I cover in more depth later. What is significant to this discussion is the way he applied the philosophy of Grimm and Herder to deal with the question of "folklore in a new nation" (Dorson 1966b). Folklore, he found, did not have to be connected to ancient poetry to form "a large component of emergent nationalism" (Dorson 1966b, 21). He was against the fabrication of a cultural foundation that would appear chauvinistic, even though he was accused of perpetuating that very image. He looked for the authentic, or natural, expressions of regions and groups that suggested national values. Although Dorson harped on the need for international comparison and comparative notes in the Grimm tradition to folklore scholars, he time and again divided folklore nationally and saw in folklore the essence of national values (Dorson 1973c). In opening his introduction of the apparently internationalist *Folklore and Folklife* (1972) with the origin legend of the Grimms' founding of folklore studies and connecting them to America through the coining of folklore by the Englishman Thoms and subsequent American revision, Dorson recontemporized tradition for American purposes. In keeping with his outline from the Grimms to the Americans, Dorson structured his survey of folkloristic concepts with the "historical-geographical" viewpoint first and made the claim for its outdated dominance over folkloristic practice. Dorson presented it as the method of international comparativism, and drew a line of its influence from Germany and Finland to American scholars Stith Thompson, Warren Roberts, and Archer

Taylor. Yet in Dorson's survey, they would be eclipsed by young American upstarts, many his own students, brandishing keywords of structure, context, and performance to build a modernistic conception of American tradition.

The connection to the Grimms is from Finnish scholars Kaarle Krohn and Antti Aarne, who extended the work of *Märchen* typology suggested by the German brothers (Krohn 1971). Much of their analysis mined the *Kinder- und Hausmärchen* for evidence of full-blown folktale types and premises about origin and diffusion. Aarne proceeded "from the assumption that folk fairy tales are stories which have arisen in a definite area and at a definite time, and have spread through borrowing from one land to another, from one people to another, and in doing so have changed and been recast" (Aarne 1907, iii). The goal, then, of comparing texts was to arrange the tales in geographic placement and determine their relative age so as to arrive at the origin of the story in time and place. To achieve this kind of global enterprise, texts were fixed in form and made comparable by arranging them into motifs and types. Aarne produced a tale-type index in 1910, and in America Stith Thompson translated, revised, and enlarged it in 1928 as *The Types of the Folktale*. It became a standard reference along with Thompson's *Motif-Index of Folk-Literature* (1955). The typology was based mostly on the Grimms' canon and drew on their commentaries of origin and diffusion in their comparative notes. But Aarne and Thompson reconfigured the Grimms' nationalistic concerns toward the search for distant origins, and suggested a monogenesis for many European tales in India because of the antiquity of Sanksrit texts and the historical migration of Indo-European languages. In drawing this line, another Grimm assumption came through of the decay of language from complex original forms to surviving remnants in recently collected texts.

Thompson added American interest in the largely Eurocentric method by applying it to North American Indian tales ([1953] 1965). He began with an introduction crediting the Grimms with the premises of "historical and comparative study of tales," but criticized them for simultaneously, and prematurely, trying to answer questions of folktale origin and meaning. Thompson systematized folktales for literary analysis and lent a degree of international scholarly credence to the enterprise. He backpedaled, however, from explaining the uses of folklore, which the Grimms had interpreted through the lens of romantic nationalism, and insisted that first individual tales needed to be studied for origin and distribution. The examination of specific texts tended to avoid issues of national culture; it traced migrations of texts as if they moved themselves. It separated folk from lore; it envisioned a seamless globe unmarked by social conflict. An example is the alternative treatment of Appalachian folktales provided in *Tales from the Cloud Walking Country* (1958) by Marie Campbell. She dedicated the book to Stith Thompson, and explained that she recorded examples of *Märchen* in eastern Kentucky following his attention to analysis of texts. Her organizing principle was that they are European tales that can be related to the Grimm collection and the tale types found in Aarne-Thompson's index. The purpose was to identify international types that have lodged in America but have their origin elsewhere. Although she explained the isolation and social occasions that influenced the retention of these tales, she resisted comment on a connection to regional or national culture. And she avoided value judgments about the passing of tradition. The burden of her analysis was on the annotation to connect what she found to tale types and European sources.

Archer Taylor (1890–1973) and Wayland Hand (1907–1986) were two prominent American folklorists who brought an international comparativist perspective to their studies from their training in German language and literature. Taylor was the only American contributing to the scholarly *Handwörterbuch des deutschen Märchens* (Dictionary of German Wonder Tales, 1930), edited by Johannes Bolte and Lutz MacKensen. He regularly traveled to Europe after World War I and met, among others, with Johannes Bolte in Germany, who was working on annotating the Grimms' collection, and Kaarle Krohn, who was refining the historic-geographic method in Finland (Ward 1994, 6; Bolte and Polívka [1913–1932] 1963; Krohn [1926] 1971). Taylor set up the Grimms as central to a folklore canon in his article "The Classics of Folklore" (Taylor 1972, 9–20). To establish an American presence in the field, he drew a connection of the Grimms to Child and Thompson. He proclaimed the great advance of folklore scholarship with the monographs of the historic-geographic school. He announced in 1964: "Folklore is now in a most fortunate situation. The available resources surpass anything ever imagined by the Brothers Grimm, Svend Grundtvig, Francis James Child.... There is abundant interest waiting to be aroused" (Taylor 1972, 20).

Taylor's contribution was to expand historic-geographic classifications and analysis of distribution from tales to proverbs and riddles. Hand, associated for over forty years with UCLA, meanwhile set up elaborate comparative classifications and annotations for beliefs, and wrote on the Grimms in German (Hand 1961, 1963). He established archives based on European classifications in a Center for Comparative Folklore and Mythology. In his introduction to his classification of an Ohio belief collection, he made explicit the connection between the philosophical ideas of the brothers and the search for international origin and distribution. He cited the duality of *Kultur* and *Natur*, and the medieval sources for folklore. He cautioned, however, that "in considering these important matters of the origin and dissemination of folk beliefs and superstitions, one should avoid the pitfalls and excesses of folktale scholars in trying to account for the wide distribution of folk tales that was discovered in researches dealing with the Brothers Grimm's *Children and Household Tales* and their congeners" (Hand 1981, xxvii).

Hand and Taylor translated the Grimm legacy to a comparative analysis of types and consideration of distribution. They also maintained an eye to European sources for American traditions, and centered folklore scholarship in Europe generally and in Germany and Scandinavia particularly. Surveying the "German connection" of folklore in the United States in 1994, Donald Ward added other patterns from the Grimms brought to historic-geographic scholarship: command of global bibliography and special attention to textual organization (Ward 1994, 7). As translator of the Grimms' *Deutsche Sagen* and active in the folklore and mythology program at UCLA, Ward placed himself (along with Wolfgang Mieder, heir to Taylor's devotion to the proverb) in an academic genealogy including Taylor and Hand, "with just four links in the chain between myself and the Brothers Grimm" (Ward 1994, 6). To Ward, it was a lineage worthy of pride because these forebears exposed in their extensive annotations a "meticulous scholarship."

The extensive annotations, classifications, and maps of the historic-geographic school appeared thoroughly scholarly and esoteric, apparently scientific, even if the method was modest in its goals. Thompson admired biologists who "have long since labeled their flora and fauna by a universal system and by using this method have published thousands of inventories of the animal and plant life of all parts of the world." He argued that "in like manner it should be possible to make available for study the entire body of collected folk-narrative in the world" (Thompson [1946] 1977, 413–14). The classificatory method left itself open to the criticism of ignoring human factors that influence the composition of the tales, bypassing native distinctions for narrative, and working on the basis of incomplete evidence that may indeed not be comparable. Setting up a case for an anthropological approach to studying specific cultures through folklore recorded in social context, Alan Dundes attacked Thompson's method for its reliance on written texts, constructed "types," and bias toward monogenesis (Dundes 1989a, 69–71). He worried that the method, which calls for comprehensively documenting all facts on individual tales before getting at meaning, avoided psychological and anthropological interpretation because it is impossible to discover *all* the facts about a given folktale "for the written record goes back only so far and oral tales clearly antedate written languages" (Dundes 1989a, 72).

Discovering "all the facts" for Thompson and Taylor led to a stated goal that could appear political although it was in the name of science. In calling for a systematic method that decided in advance its result, the location of a source or "archetype" for the international spread of traditional expression, the historic-geographic method as Thompson and Taylor perceived it avoided uses of folklore for nationalistic purposes. Speaking at the Midcentury International Folklore Conference five years after the end of World War II, Thompson went on the offensive against speakers who advocated social analysis and application of folklore. He declared, "If one begins to study the journals of folklore in 1925 and comes down to 1941 or 1942 and notices the kind of folklore used, one can see that the collected material sent out to the public is heavily weighted by the regime in charge. And it seems to me that this is a bad thing—folklore as propaganda, whatever the propaganda is used for" (Thompson 1953, 220). Aili Johnson answered that the historic-geographic method is a form of positive propaganda: "I wonder if Dean

Thompson doesn't feel that teaching the world heritage of our national background helps keep us from becoming too nationalistic, when, for example, you recognize that there are many things in common in the folk tales from many lands" (Thompson 1953, 226). It became apparent that the scientific aura of the historic-geographic method defused the national politics of the Grimms in an elevation of texts to universal and untamperable status. Indeed, it may have been appealing in the war-torn mid-twentieth century because of its suggestion that a common folklore source connected people everywhere and the spread of folklore is not affected by the nationalistic causes of military conflicts.

Some folkloristic voices decried the rosy global idealism of the historic-geographic method by invoking the social reality of a world fragmented into localities, regions, and nations. Especially concerned for locating national and subcultural meaning in folklore, Dorson leveled the charge against historical-geographical comparativists that "considerations of style and artistry, of the mysterious processes of creation and alterations, of the influences of national cultures, the social context, the individual genius, are out of order among percentage tables and plot summaries" (Dorson 1972b, 12). In separating himself from the method associated with Stith Thompson and the line back to Francis James Child and the Grimms, Dorson argued for the creation of a new American discipline based on special concerns of individualism and nationalism, and emergent traditions in modern contexts. Other critics outside of the United States also worried that tradition wrongly appeared as a petrified text rather than a continuous social process. Carl von Sydow in Sweden was especially vocal: "We must build our research on the life and laws of the tradition, not on dry and lifeless extracts. The flesh which research puts on such dry lifeless bones is, and remains, dead, without connection with a living reality, and therefore without value" (von Sydow 1948, 59). His call was often cited in the move toward an American contextual approach that described the observable social reality of traditions as they were created and enacted (Dundes 1964b).

Sounding the American keynote of realism, many folklorists increasingly called upon fieldwork for observations of folklore as part of the contemporaneity of specific cultures. Melville Jacobs in his presidential address of 1964 to the American Folklore Society undermined Thompson's influence by harshly calling the historic-geographic method an "unsophisticated worldwide grab-bag procedure." He complained that reverence given to the Grimm-Finnish comparativist legacy meant that "the foundations of folklore are not merely feeble, they are … antiquatedly historiogeographical about the wrong macro-units" (Jacobs 1966, 414, 427). Following the influence of Franz Boas, Jacobs favored the examination of a particular oral literature in a local culture, and called for resistance of imposing West European values onto non-Western folktales (Jacobs 1959b; Thompson 1978). For taking this stance and using dramaturgical references to folklore as "recitals," "scenes," and "acts," he has been called a precursor of performance theory in American folklore studies (Zumwalt 1988, 83).

Anthropologically oriented folklorists critical of Thompson's method, such as Alan Dundes, still saw value in cross-cultural comparison, although not the kind of comparison that lifts texts from culture (Dundes 1989a, 57–82). He wrote: "What we may conclude is that while the Finnish method is the most refined and sophisticated technique yet devised for investigating the distribution patterns of folklore cognates, it should not be identified as 'the' comparative method. And it is a form of the comparative method that could be of great assistance to the anthropologist anxious to isolate peculiarities or unique characteristics of people" (Dundes 1989a, 74). Dundes sought a middle ground in folklore studies between the reaction of cultural relativism that insisted on the uniqueness and noncomparability of different societies and the literary defense of textual typology. It is a middle ground between the Grimms' nationalism and internationalism and their extremes of fragmentation and unity.

The extreme of fragmentation to which Dundes referred is represented by a brand of performance-oriented ethnography that arose in American folkloristics during the 1970s. It was marked by the key phrase of "situational context" that pointed to anthropological models of Franz Boas and Bronislaw Malinowski rather than the literary precedent of the Grimms. Dan Ben-Amos's influential essay "Toward a Definition of Folklore in Context" (1972) bypassed the Grimms as did Richard Bauman in his survey of folklore for his "communications-centered handbook" of cultural performances (Bauman 1992, 29–40). It is noteworthy that a textbook of this approach, *The Dynamics of Folklore* (1979) by Barre Toelken, contained only one reference to the Grimms buried in the bibliographic notes. Toelken separated the earliest "schools" of folklore as errantly "antiquarian" from enlightened conceptions stressing the contemporaneity of group, performance, and context. Toelken responded to the supposedly antiquarian inclination toward the text by insisting that "contextual perspectives are demanded of all folklorists today" (Toelken 1979, 8). Context, as opposed to the texts of the Grimms, he asserted, "sets modern folklore scholarship apart from that of the late 1800s and early 1900s" (Toelken 1979, 9).

Elliott Oring in his major textbook *Folk Groups and Folklore Genres* (1986) explained the differences between present and past approaches with less certainty. He noted the influence of the Grimms in originally presenting folklore as ancient material that is the property of peasants. He recognized that the updating of folklore created contrasts of new with old, urban with rural. He ultimately arrived at the social understanding that "for something to be folklore in an urban society, it must be touched and transformed by common experience—ordinary humans living their everyday lives. As the romantics heard in peasant songs and tales the echoes of an ancestral folk, and the antiquarians attended to the manners and customs of the common classes, many contemporary folklorists still seem to see in folklore the reflection of an intangible, ordinary man. In other words, folklore is often regarded as a mode of expression which emphasizes the human and personal as opposed to the formal and institutional" (Oring 1986b, 16).

Toelken's and Oring's statements signify the difficulty that contextual folklorists have had with reconciling the tainted nineteenth-century foundations of folklore study represented by the Grimms and twentieth-century ethnographic emphasis on everyday experience. The connecting tissue between the two appears to be on attention to "fieldwork" as the recording of authentic expression. Yet in localizing fieldwork on human behavior wherever it is found, a reorientation of communal concerns has been evident toward a universal conception of tradition as the result of individual needs and urges. Reflecting on the ascendancy of performance and context-oriented studies in folklore scholarship, Roger Abrahams has lamented that the reorientation away from antiquarian and communal foundations has resulted in a neglect of "local manifestations of power, much less to the development of a national sense of consciousness" (Abrahams 1993, 25). His answer was to suggest a new construction of "reflexive folkloristics," relating "folklore to broader landscapes and larger social formations in a way that takes national movements into consideration even while criticizing them" (Abrahams 1993, 27). He called for retaining an ethnographic emphasis on specific performances while being able to identify forces that suggest kinds of national consciousness. It is a middle ground that relativizes folklore studies as well as the materials of folklore. He implies that one can get around the problem of choosing unity and fragmentation by realizing the issue itself as a cultural construction.

One manifestation of this resolution between past and present, local and national, is the suddenly recent recognition of "identity" as a keyword of tradition that allows for a simultaneous consciousness of personal, local, and national expression in a multicultural society (Carpenter and Vidutis 1984; Smith and Stannard 1989; Mechling 1993; Oring 1994). Essays appeared with increasing frequency in the 1980s observing that despite the particularity of performance orientations, comparison of identities, and indeed of texts, is still evident in their scholarly interpretations (see Georges 1986; Honko 1986; Dundes 1989a; Goldberg 1996). In 1986, Linda Dégh at Indiana University reported the results of a symposium on "The Comparative Method in Folklore" in *Journal of Folklore Research*. She summarized: "It may well be that the time is ripe for a new era of cross-cultural folklore study.... Old problems still have not been resolved, but we can start afresh" (Dégh 1986, 83).

If comparativism had returned to the table for discussion, the *Märchen* as a primary subject for American analysis arguably did not.[7] The *Journal of American Folklore* contained only five references to the genre during the 1970s and the number decreased to two during the 1980s. This count was surprising, considering a number of special events revolving around the two-hundredth anniversary of the Grimm brothers' births in 1985 and 1986. The largest reported celebration was the International Bicentenary Symposium on the Brothers Grimm at the University of Illinois in April 1986 (McGlathery 1988). The principal host was the Department of Germanic Languages and Literatures, perhaps explaining why the opening line of introduction to the book that reported the conference drew primary attention to the literary quality of the Grimms' work: "*Grimms' Fairy Tales* is a classic of world literature and will remain so" (McGlathery 1988, ix). The Grimms' tales appeared to be forms to read and view, rather than collect. Their significance as folk tradition diminished compared to their role in popular culture and mass media. Discourse turned to the artifice of folktale writers and editors rather than the nature of oral tradition or folk culture. It had become evident that literary critics, psychologists, and educator critics had become prominent in the American discourse of fairy tale meaning. An indication of this dominance is the lack of American folklorists in *Fairy Tales and Society* (1986) edited by Ruth B. Bottigheimer, which came out of a conference at Princeton University in 1984. That Alan Dundes entitled his essay "Fairy Tales from a Folkloristic Perspective" was a sign that taking the viewpoint of a folklorist deserved special notice. Only three of the twenty contributors had professional affiliations or education in folklore.

In the elementary classroom where controversy raged over the use of folk and fairy tales, folklorists were noticeably absent. The bulk of advisers for folklore in basic education concerned techniques of documenting contemporary local cultures (Belanus 1985; MacDowell 1987; Sharrow 1992). Folklorists in public projects mostly advised teachers to organize ethnographic programs or folk-artists-in schools that emphasized ethnic diversity and living community traditions (Nusz 1991; Haut 1994). While the volume *Teaching Folklore* (1984) edited by Bruce Jackson was solely devoted to university education, most advisers for folklore in elementary education were written by education specialists, not folklorists (see Bosma 1987; Goforth and Spillman 1994).

The upshot is that the Grimms' legacy has taken startling divergent public and professional routes in America. In the public direction, the Grimms' tales have spawned attention to romantic and moral uses of the fairy tale and its applications in education and media. On the scholarly path, the Grimms' annotations have inspired an orientation toward a bibliographic and typological scholarship. During the late nineteenth century, the two directions had been joined as English folklorists debated the public lessons of the tales for English children and the scholarly riddles of origin and diffusion. The post-World War II push to adjust folklore study to the realism of American conditions—the characteristics of a pragmatic "new nation" without an ancient peasant stock or homogeneous population—has had an effect on spreading interest in ethnographic studies of regions and ethnic groups with reference to legends, customs, and material culture. The association of the Grimms in America with a historic-geographic method—which was interpreted by critics as past-oriented, analytically flawed, and lacking human factors—led to a rewriting of the foundations of folklore studies for an ethnographic orientation stressing the contemporaneity of tradition. Academicians still viewed folklore as an international pursuit, but increasingly framed it within local and national boundaries, and later within situational frames.

Romantic nationalism with its connotations of ideological manipulation caused further revision to insure a positivist approach to culture that would transcend either national chauvinism or international idealism. The hierarchy of evidence for folklore changed. Although concern for oral tradition remained primary, the juvenilization and commercialization of Grimms' fairy tales through the twentieth century tainted the cultural authenticity of the genre and subverted the effort to elevate folklore study to academic respectability. American folklorists by and large cast folklore as an emergent rather than historic form; they sought to imbue its study with contemporary social relevance. Still, the emphasis on Grimm-Herder ideas of the "natural" spontaneity of tradition and the organic unity of culture is evident in their study, and indeed, separated it from consideration of the artifice of Grimms' tales as a mass cultural phenomenon.

In public discourse, the Grimms' tales became an issue of values, both ethical and commercial, and folklorists devoted to the search for the authentic and "natural" use in culture appeared to avoid discussion of both. Increasingly, the Grimms' tales in America became a children's genre, a visual medium and form of entertainment. The discourse over their use heatedly engaged parents and teachers because of the image of children's innocence altered by vivid romance, violence, and prejudice—depending on the moral position taken. The tales became the center of a tension between the unity, the hope, of Western tradition in American civilization and the fragmentation of ethnic diversity in an American social reality. They became simultaneously a sign of Eurocentrism and commercial Americanization. The tales in their various consumed forms were part and parcel of mass culture, and drew attention to the Hollywood recontextualization from America to a global audience. Educators and moralists, and later psychologists, argued over the messages, the uses, and misuses, of the Grimms' tales in American books and movies, in the home and school. Literary critics became more involved than folklorists in the public discourse because of the literary inclination to address the artifice—original and derivative—of artists and authors.

The Grimms became recast toward the close of the twentieth century as literary artists and inspirations, who presented problems of cultural constructions. If folklorists mused about tales as experienced "narratives," as socially real traditions of the informal and noninstitutional, public rhetoric focused on therapeutic uses of fantasy in institutional settings. That difference in rhetoric reflected the need of a public to commodify the Grimm legacy as products for modern consumption serving different ends of unity and fragmentation, while academic practice called for recovering objective ways of knowing, and following, tradition.

5

Martha Warren Beckwith and the Rise of Academic Authority

If the "folklorist" was to be looked to as the expert and adviser on America's traditions, then the folklorist label needed professional recognition in a society that increasingly valued institutional authority. While folklore as a field commenting on American culture had made substantial headway in museums and some notable Ivy League universities, its supporters did not necessarily identify themselves as folklorists. Franz Boas at Columbia, for many years editor of the *Journal of American Folklore*, called himself an anthropologist with an interest in the subject of folklore. The legendary Harvard professor George Lyman Kittredge billed himself a literary scholar who pursued ballad and belief in folklore. When Stewart Culin, president and curator of the American Folklore Society, had his portrait painted by the famed artist Thomas Eakins, he captioned it "The Archaeologist." Even British leading light Edwin Sidney Hartland, who boldly declared the study of folklore as having special issues that set it apart as "the science of tradition," admitted folklore as a "portion of Anthropology," or "the science of man" (Hartland [1899] 1968, 231).

One sign of the rise of the folklorist as a discrete academic type interpreting traditions for modernizing society is the first chair of folklore in the United States. It was held by Martha Warren Beckwith (1871–1959) and her story deserves attention for portending the growth of a publicly recognized academic discipline out of the subject of tradition. Her vision of an American cultural field that was ethnically complex, contemporary, and borderless offered a major counter to historical and literary uses of folklore and issued a social agenda that confirmed the exceptional identity of the folklorist. She conceived folklore as an umbrella term for many forms of traditional practice worthy of focused study such as dance, music, narrative, art, and belief.

237

Beckwith may at first seem an unlikely candidate for breaking new ground. She did not fit the profile of the young, dashing firebrand, often given in academic hero stories, when she started her cause. Maybe that explains why she has often been overlooked as a founding mother of academic folklore and folklife scholarship. Advanced in years and associated with Victorian propriety when she proposed a foundation for folklore studies, she perceived the relation of tradition with the understanding, even the support, of modernity. Shortly before she served as president of the American Folklore Society, she produced a standard guide to American folklore methodology and had a grand vision for a widening scope and potential of folklore to serve the public interest in social reform. Her writing produced six books, twelve monographs, and over fifty essays and reviews. Her publications mainly reported field research among Native Hawaiians, Jamaican Blacks, and Native Americans in the West, but she also collected among peoples as far-flung as Portuguese Indians, Dutch Americans in New York State, and Vassar College women. More dissatisfied as her career developed with the scattered analysis of surviving tales and songs, she prophesized an intellectual movement toward conceptualizing tradition belonging to and emerging from social groupings. She encouraged use of folklife terminology and proposed mapping America's ethnic-regional folk cultures in their totality.

In 1920, when she took her chair in folklore at Vassar College, she blazed a path of her own. She took the bold move of declaring herself in academe neither anthropologist nor literary scholar, but rather a professional folklorist. Beginning her career studying folk dance, she went on to cover a wide spectrum of folk arts, especially narrative genres such as myth, legend, and tale, and she made significant contributions to the study of beliefs, customs, festivals, games, songs, riddles, proverbs, religion, and folklife generally. But it was not the material she studied as much as her insistence on the ethnic complexity of American culture that set her apart. Folklore was her hard evidence of ethnic cross-fertilization in a diverse American society. Her devotion to work among many ethnic influences bore out her cause. And she could appear mighty feisty when exclaiming the use of her studies for social reform. As much as she established a university foothold for folklore studies, she did not restrict her work to the ivory tower. She went out on the festival stage and inside the museum laboratory to spread the mission of folklore studies.[1] Her teaching and advising encouraged the professional folklore research of many young scholars, particularly women, including notables such as Dorothy D. Lee, Katharine Luomala, Elisabeth Greenleaf, Laura Green, Constance Varney Ring, Margaret Treadwell, Mary Pukui, Elaine Lambert Lewis, and Helen H. Roberts.[2]

Beckwith's saga offers insight into the emergence of American folklore studies and women's roles within it, and the broadening of its subject to examine the function of tradition in everyday life. Her story also takes folklore from New York to California and into the Pacific, reflecting the expansion of transnational views of

American culture. To invite an interpretation of Beckwith's vision and her achievements, I will tell her story with special consideration to the circumstances that led to the formation of her chair in folklore and her activities while at Vassar.

Martha Warren Beckwith was born on January 19, 1871, in Wellesley Hills, Massachusetts, west of Boston, to schoolteacher parents George Ely and Harriet Winslow (Goodale) Beckwith. Harriet's mother was the great niece of a pioneer missionary to Hawaii, and Harriet was raised in the mission home at Kailua. George also had been on the islands as a teacher and met Harriet there in 1861. Two years after their meeting, Harriet and George were married. In 1867 the family moved to California, and a few years later to Massachusetts. Three years after Martha's birth, the Beckwiths returned to Hawaii. In addition to teaching at Royal School and Punahou College, Martha's father developed the Haiku Sugar Plantation on Maui that was eventually managed by the large shipping company of Alexander and Baldwin. While on Maui, Martha befriended Anne M. Alexander, who had family ties to the company. As youths, they were among the few English-speaking white children at Haiku, and thus learned the Hawaiian language and participated in many native festivals and customs.

Martha Beckwith eloquently described her interest in native folklore "grown out of a childhood and youth spent within sound of the hula drum at the foot of the domelike House of the Sun on the windy island of Maui. There, wandering along its rocky coast and sandy beaches, exploring its windward gorges, riding above the cliffs by moonlight when the surf was high or into the deep forests at midday, we were aware always of a life just out of reach of us late comers but lived intensely by the kindly, generous race who had chanced so many centuries ago upon its shores" (Beckwith 1970, xxxi). As there was no school for white children on the island, Martha's parents educated her and her sister Mary at home and insisted on their special attention to language and botany. As one chronicler recalled, "Mr. Beckwith often took the girls on long trips. Together they climbed Haiku Hill, and rode to the top of Piiholo, and into the woods to collect land shells and rare ferns. Mr. Beckwith loved nature, with ardor and enthusiasm that were contagious. His sense of humor was keen, enlivening even the rudiments of Latin grammar." While Martha's father explored the island with his children and drilled them on French and Latin, her mother, "an expert teacher and a wise counselor," instilled in the girls a love of folk narrative. Fleming recalls that Martha's mother was a gifted storyteller: "'Please Mother, tell us a story' was the prelude to many hours of entertainment."[3]

Martha returned to Massachusetts for her higher education at Mount Holyoke College, a pioneering liberal arts college for women and her mother's alma mater. Martha graduated with a B.S. degree in 1893, having taken a "Scientific Course" of study. This track included study in French, German, art, rhetoric, and Bible, in addition to studies in psychology, geometry, trigonometry, botany, zoology, astronomy, and physics. Reminiscing in 1928 on her college days, Beckwith wrote,

Martha Beckwith, c. 1900. (Archives, Mt. Holyoke College Library)

"I know now that it was folk-lore I sought after when I chased butterflies for Miss Clapp, dried flowers for Miss Hooker, and attended to Oriental Literature under that pretty woman the magic of whose interests sent me far afield to India to stand on the famous old battle-field of the Bharata." Reflecting back, Beckwith connected this quest for human origins and its scientific discipline to her later endeavors in folklore and folklife. In her words,

> A museum record of intangible things, that is the business of the folk-lorist to provide…. Our first dictum then of scientific method is the purely detached and objective gathering of the actual facts about folk thought, either direct from the field of folk life today, or from literary records (as Homer, Herodotus, or the Vedas) where folk ideas may be distinguished from their literary form. These facts furnish the specimens on our museum shelves, and for their sorting and arrangement and the clarifying of their relations to each other and to the whole field of kindred ideas the scientific folklorist is responsible. (Beckwith 1928a, 281, 278)

After graduating from Mt. Holyoke, Beckwith returned to Hawaii to teach in Honolulu elementary schools, but came back to the mainland in 1896 to take courses in English and anthropology at the University of Chicago. The following year she accepted an appointment as instructor of English at Elmira College in New York State. Her father died in 1898, and the following year, looking to advance her linguistic knowledge, Martha pursued language study in Europe. She studied Old English at Cambridge and French and German at the University of Halle an der Saale. Returning to the United States, she obtained an instructorship of English, this time at Mt. Holyoke College. The folk customs and literature she adored, particularly from Hawaii, seemed to have little place in the English curriculum at the time, however, and she searched for a disciplinary home that would be hospitable to her folk cultural interests. She thought she found it in the blossoming study of anthropology, and in 1905 went to Columbia University in New York City to work toward the master's degree, which she received in 1906. Under Franz Boas's direction, Beckwith completed her thesis on the traditional dances of the Moqui and Kwakiutl Indians, and he helped arrange to have it published (Beckwith 1907).

In addition to being informed by anthropologists with interests in folklore and folk arts, Beckwith also came under the influence of William Witherle Lawrence, a scholarly dynamo who excitedly lectured on relations between folklore and literature, particularly for English epics during the medieval period. Lawrence looked to folklore to reveal the sociocultural influences on literature, and published studies of Chaucer and Shakespeare in which he brassily pointed out the common folklore sources of so-called "original" or "great" works.[4] Beckwith quoted him extensively in her *Folklore in America* (1931) for developing the important "social value" thesis that "the point of view of the audience for which the artist writes determines the form which his narrative takes, and that when a popular tale is the source, the story

Photograph by Henry W. Henshaw captioned "A Hawaiian Paddler" from The *Hawaiian Romance of Laieikawai*, by Martha Warren Beckwith, Thirty-third Annual Report of the Bureau of American Ethnology, 1911-1912 (published 1919).

will be shaped, not after the current conception of reality and good taste, but after the traditional form familiar to his hearers" (Beckwith 1931b, 63–64).

Lawrence had a kindred spirit in Laura Johnson Wylie, who had published *Social Studies in English Literature* and chaired the English department at Vassar (Wylie 1916; Morris 1934). With Lawrence's recommendation, in 1909 Beckwith joined the faculty at Vassar, a liberal arts college for women, as instructor of English. Beckwith taught courses on the "Development of English Literature from Beowulf to Johnson" and "Exposition." Also on the small English faculty at the time was Constance Rourke, who later gained fame for her view of national folklore, although at odds with Beckwith's anthropological views of cultural diversity in America (Rourke 1942, 1959; Beckwith 1931c, 1943). The claims of America to a native folklore justifying its national character was a hot topic of debate at Vassar, and the two professors were not shy about grabbing the podium to express their views.

Beckwith firmly held to a heterogeneous view of America formed of many ethnic-regional communities adapting to one another, while the irascible Constance Rourke insisted on a master narrative arising from an American historical experience (Beckwith 1931b, 64). While allowing that the "whole story of pioneer colonization is one of extraordinary importance for our understanding of American folklore, as of American literature itself, so far as it is a native product," Beckwith warned of overstating "national aspirations" of "the high-powered mechanical culture" and passing over existing communities constituting folk cultures (Beckwith 1931b, 55). She agreed that American literature could reflect folk sources but should not be confused as the real stuff of folklore. Beckwith thought that Rourke's argument for a national tradition was more applicable to "European cultures with their long history of folk imagination" but granted that "even here in America a native folklore is discoverable whose pattern dominated the imaginative conceptions and the style of American *writers*" (Beckwith 1931b, 64; emphasis added). With her multilingual background and reading in Hawaiian and German writing as part of the United States experience, Beckwith additionally worried that Rourke had privileged the English tradition in conceiving an evolving American culture naturally moving toward unity.

In 1913, Beckwith returned to her beloved Hawaiian Islands and stayed until 1915 when she took another appointment in English at Smith College. During this stay, she began to intensively collect the native folklore and mythology of Hawaii. Hawaii wielded a great influence on Beckwith's thinking about American cultural formation. She saw in her experience there a complex process of ethnic displacement, fusion in some cases, separation in others, and often adaptation to changing conditions. As she reflected in *Folklore in America* (1931), "Our new primitive race, the Hawaiian, has shared American culture now for almost a hundred years and although it has lost much that was native and primitive in its highly developed prehistoric art, there are signs that *living forces are still at work* shaping the composite race cultures, native and foreign, into fresh forms of fantasy" (Beckwith

1931b, 55; emphasis added). She first appeared in the pages of the *Journal of American Folklore* in 1916 with an essay on the Hawaiian Hula dance. She built on the work of Nathaniel Emerson, who took the evolutionary stand of the dance as a tradition that "survived into modern time." But she called for a view of performance, style, and function in the dance. She speculated that the dance was "like a sign-alphabet, of conventionalized physiological reactions to special emotional suggestions, perhaps to the excitation of rhythmic beats. Added to this, the ready play of metaphor in the Polynesian fancy, stimulated by the desire to aggrandize social rank, has imposed the literary form of the accompanying song, and no doubt modified both gesture and symbolism" (Beckwith 1916, 412).

Also in 1916, Franz Boas's *Tsimshian Mythology* appeared, and its reliance on folklore to describe the essence of a historical culture propelled Beckwith deeper into Hawaiian mythology. The close study she made of the work is indicated by her eleven-page review in the *Journal of English and Germanic Philology* (1918). Her opening line anticipated her case for the intercourse of anthropology and literature to form a new hybrid of folklore study. She wrote: "Important to students of medieval literature who are interested in comparing their conclusions with the findings of modern ethnologists is this monograph on Tsimshian mythology, in which Dr. Franz Boas establishes certain principles for the diffusion of story material, by observing what actually happens among a distinct group of North American Indian tribes whose mythology has assumed marked individuality" (Beckwith 1918, 460). Rhetorically, she connected the "distinct group" with the "individuality" of its folklore. Folklore, in other words, was a "mirror of culture," relativized to represent the uniqueness of separate cultural histories. Following this relativist thinking, the search for folklore required fieldwork to find native viewpoints, "going to the myth-makers themselves for their terms of thought" (Beckwith 1918, 465). She became most excited about the process of folklore's formation and performance suggested by Boas as a direction for the professional folklorist. Emphasizing the professional label, she proclaimed that the work helped "start the folklorist on the right road towards a critical analysis of his particular problem" (Beckwith 1918, 467).

Inspired by *Tsimshian Mythology*, Beckwith completed her anthropology dissertation in 1918 at Columbia University on the Hawaiian romance of Laieikawai, but not without irritating Franz Boas (Beckwith 1919). Beckwith bucked Boas's purist tendencies to seek out the relic forms of primitive tradition untainted by modern society. She took as her subject a nineteenth-century newspaper serial based on an oral narrative which Haleole, a native Hawaiian writer, reinterpreted in the hope of instilling "old ideals of racial glory" on the islands. Another significant detail of the romance, and a source of Beckwith's interest in gender roles, was the fact that it centered on the actions of a *heroine*. Boas would have preferred that she continue her work in salvaging the tribal lore and language of Native Americans, and he questioned her preoccupation with modern literary texts. Beckwith was less interested in the "pure" forms of untainted tradition that Boas sought than the process of cultural production, in her words, "the single composition of a Polynesian mind working upon the material of an old legend and eager to create a genuine national literature" (Beckwith 1919, 294). She sought to sift the creation of a Hawaiian epic from its complex Polynesian sources "a common stock of tradition." "A close comparative study of the tales from each group should reveal local characteristics," she wrote, "but for our purpose the Polynesian race is one, and its common stock of tradition, which at the dispersal and during the subsequent periods of migration was carried as common treasure-trove of the imagination as far as New Zealand on the south and Hawaii on the north, and from the western Figi to the Marquesas on the east, repeats the same adventures among similar surroundings and colored by the same interests and desires" (Beckwith 1919, 297). More than a study of a literary text, her dissertation used fieldwork to analyze a creative process of cultural formation set against the background of ethnic migration and localization.

Although working in anthropology, Beckwith had already begun making a break toward folklore by studying literary traditions in contemporary society. As Katharine Luomala pointed out, "At the beginning of this century, when Miss Beckwith was starting out in anthropology, the emphasis was more on recovering or reconstructing the pre-European culture of natives than on what the natives had done with European culture. Alien European influences were weeded out of source materials to reveal the old. Miss Beckwith, it appears, early realized the significance of studying the post-European period in itself, of describing it as it existed, and of valuing it, first and foremost, regardless of what alien influences blended with the old, as still the culture of the natives" (Luomala 1970, xv).

From Boas, Beckwith adopted the idea of folklore as a reflection of culture, and especially the proposal of artistry as a relative concept explored historically within a culture (Beckwith 1918). In *The Hawaiian Romance of Laieikawai*, Beckwith devoted a section to the story "as a reflection of aristocratic social life." "In humanizing the gods," she wrote, "the action presents a lively picture of the ordinary course of Polynesian life." She went beyond a simple equation, however, by asserting social distinctions, and especially gender roles, particular to the romance form of tradition. She wrote: "Polynesian romance reflects its own social world—a world based upon the fundamental conception of social rank. The family tie and the inherited rights and titles derived from it determine a man's place in the community" (Beckwith 1919, 308). She in fact identified the priority of women in the social order. Breaking with the line of previous male ethnographers of Hawaiian culture, she argued that "even a successful warrior, to insure his family title, sought a wife from a superior rank. For this reason women held a comparatively important position in the social framework, and this place is reflected in the folk tales" (Beckwith 1919, 309).

The first sentence of Beckwith's *Hawaiian Mythology* (1940) amply demonstrated Boas's influence: "How traditional narrative art develops orally among a nature-worshiping people like the Polynesians can be best illustrated by surveying the whole body of such art among a single isolated group like the Hawaiian with reference to the historical background reflected in the stories and to similar traditions among allied groups in the South Seas" (1970, 1).[5] But arguably her attention to style and performance inspired by literary study questioned more than Boas did the creative process of folklore forms. In *The Hawaiian Romance of Laieikawai*, she devoted a chapter to "The Art of Composition," and anticipated later oral-formulaic explanations set forth by Milman Parry of storytellers' abilities to perform long recitations. She observed: "Counting-out formulae reappear in story-telling in such repetitive series of incidents as those following the action of the five sisters of the unsuccessful wooer in the *Laieikawai* story.... The story-teller, moreover, varies the incident; he does not exactly follow his formula, which, however, it is interesting to note, is more fixed in the evidently old dialogue part of the story than in the explanatory action" (Beckwith 1919, 321). This is probably what she had in mind when she mentioned that her study "claims a kind of classic interest" with connections to European epics.

Beckwith used Boas's phrase for artistic process, "perfection of form," to describe Polynesian ideas of beauty, and she viewed them relatively (See Boas [1927] 1955; M. Jones 1980a). She explained that Polynesians attribute beauty to divine influence made visible in nature. She read the intersection of aesthetics and social function in the folktale. She thus cited the examples of

> Dreaming of the beauty of Laieikawai, the young chief feels his heart glow with passion for this "red blossom of Puna" as the fiery volcano scorches the wind that fans across its bosom. A divine hero must select a bride of faultless beauty; the heroine chooses her lover for his physical perfections. Now we can hardly fail to see that in all these cases the delight is intensified by the belief that beauty is godlike and betrays divine rank in its possessor. Rank is tested by perfection of face and form. The recognition of beauty thus becomes regulated by express rules of symmetry and surface. Color, too, is admired according to its social value. (Beckwith 1919, 322)

With these observations Beckwith suggested that folklore more than reflects culture, it structures social relations.

In *Hawaiian Mythology*, Beckwith declared the converging influences of anthropology and literature in her folklore study with a dedication to Professors Franz Boas from anthropology and William Witherle Lawrence from literature (Beckwith 1970, xxxii). The convergence resulted, Beckwith began to realize, as a separate study of folklore. Yet until the 1920s no distinct curricula or professorial chairs existed for folklore, although students could study folklore as part of English, anthropology, German, and Spanish (Boggs 1940). Students of Franz Boas such as Alfred Kroeber and Melville Herskovits prominently taught folklore, but shared with Boas the relation of folklore to anthropology as field to discipline (Boas 1938b). Luomala observed that "despite the training the students of Boas got in folklore and the work many of them have done in it, Martha Beckwith was one of the few to become better known as folklorist than anthropologist although she also contributed to the ethnography of Hawaii, Jamaica, and Dakota Indians. Ethnography and oral narrative art are united in her work; one illuminates the other" (Luomala 1970, xvi). The common thread for Beckwith was the way tradition brought groups and their arts together, and this view deserved special attention and special methods, she argued (Beckwith 1931b, 1–10). Her focus on *tradition that bound groups* provided an answer to the problem of reconciling the diversity of subjects in folkloristic work (e.g, narrative, belief, art, speech) with the conceptual unity of a discipline (see Oring 1996b).

Beckwith credited Franz Boas with planting the idea of her teaching folklore "in connection with my college work." For Boas it was a practical suggestion to accommodate her anthropological training within the English department at Smith. Beckwith had grander ideas for the future of folklore studies as an intellectual pursuit. Meanwhile Beckwith had many conversations with her friend Anne Alexander about their mutual concern for "the fast disappearing customs and tales of the Hawaiian natives," as well as her uncertainty as a woman setting on a new academic path at the age of forty-eight.[6] In November of 1919, Alexander responded with a proposal to endow a folklore research position, specifically at a women's college, with the stipulation that Beckwith would hold the position for five years. Alexander insisted on making the gift anonymously.[7] Alexander had scholarly interests and previously had founded the department of paleontology at the University of California at Berkeley. Vassar apparently was the first choice for the folklore position from the beginning of the conversations.

Vassar did not have an anthropology department, and the social work pursuit of many of its graduates appealed to Beckwith's sense of the way that folklore study in America could be applied. Because of the opportunities afforded her at women's colleges, she asked to position the folklore foundation at a small women's institution such as Vassar. More than gratitude was on her mind. She thought that women cooperating in a team approach to field research, under her direction, in that environment, could specially develop folklore as a separate field. Encouraged by Ruth Benedict, probably the school's most famous folkloristic alumna, Beckwith anticipated that she could be a major force there and could get students to respond to her cause. She envisioned calling upon the loyal extended alumnae network of the school and creating folklore correspondents around the country. C. B. Bourland of the Smith faculty lamented to Henry Noble MacCracken, President of Vassar, that "my first reaction on hearing of it, was regret that Miss Beckwith had not offered the opportunity to Smith College." Yet Bourland graciously supported Beckwith's decision to leave Smith to pursue folklore: "Certainly she should be a competent person to direct studies in Folk Lore since she is so whole-heartedly interested in the subject, and has devoted so much time to research in that field…. And if, as I believe, people are most effective and useful when their heart is in their task, Miss Beckwith as a teacher of Folk-Lore ought to be a real addition to your faculty."[8]

A letter from Elizabeth Hanscom to President MacCracken offers further clues to Beckwith's choice of Vassar. She wrote, "She values Vassar highly and would, I think, be ready to find society and college congenial. I think that she has found the routine of her position at Smith irksome; and I know that she has been disappointed in not having the opportunity to teach folk lore, to which she looked forwards." Hanscom commented openly on Beckwith's tendency to march to a different drummer: "She is so marked an individualist that she would probably be happier in a somewhat indefinite position than as a regular member of a department where she might have to share work with others. Throughout her connection at Smith I have felt that she had power that was not brought out; at Vassar it might be exerted, and then you would have a unique addition to your staff."[9]

Despite Hanscom's portrayal of Beckwith as stubbornly going her own way, letters show faculty members at Vassar shared her interest in folklore, and that, along with the strong women's liberal arts tradition at Vassar, swayed Beckwith. Laura Wylie from English, who had previously influenced the cultural studies of Vassar graduates Ruth Benedict and Constance Rourke, and Grace Waverly from Greek wrote MacCracken to extend their enthusiasm. Indeed, Gertrude Loomis from English taught folklore previously at the University of Illinois and wrote Beckwith, "I have always wished I might begin my education all over again to be a pupil of Dr. Boas. So you are my more fortunate self, and you may be sure that I am interested in your work at Vassar. I gave a course in Folk Lore at Illinois but I see from your outline that you are presenting the material far more effectively. We shall enjoy talking over our variant ways. My work was more particularly Folklore in literature."[10] Boas recognized Loomis's folkloristic interest and commented to Vassar's president that the combined efforts of Loomis and Beckwith "will interest your students in a field that has been altogether too much neglected." For Boas, Beckwith's "strong side lies in the literary aspect of the study of folk-lore" and he observed that she was particularly "devoted to investigations of folk-lore."[11]

While Boas praised Beckwith's literary expertise, her literary mentor W. W. Lawrence drew out her ethnological work for special praise. He thought that in establishing a chair in folklore combining ethnology and literature Vassar would have "the honor of initiating a movement which might well be imitated by other institutions."[12] Columbia English professor A. Thorndike added in a letter to the president of Vassar, himself a professor of English and literature, that folklore "is a field in which, I think, we all ought to plan to do much more in the future."[13]

According to the terms of the fund, a "Research Professorship on the Folklore Foundation shall be established at Vassar College for five years," "the incumbent of this Chair shall have rank not less than that of Associate Professor," and "the work done by the incumbent of this chair shall be divided between research and teaching."[14] The chair was reserved for Beckwith, and by agreement she would not teach more than one course in any semester and devote her remaining time to research, publication, and management of the Folk-Lore Foundation. A brochure published on the foundation baldly stated that "The Folk-Lore Foundation is not established primarily as a teaching post. Its aim is to furnish a center at Vassar College for scientific research in the field of Folk-Lore."

Beckwith balanced her passion for a "scientific" approach to folklore with a recognition of its appreciation as art. "Anyone today will admit the value of folklore to art," she wrote with something of a challenge to the canon of great works. "The drama battens upon it. Since Gauguin and Matisse, especially since the amazing animal paintings of prehistoric man have come to light, carvings of the Eskimo and the elaborate art of alien civilizations like the Japanese, it has been borne in upon us that western civilization has scarcely reached the point where early art left off. Our dance shows nothing so good as the extraordinary muscular flexibility and control of primitive rhythms" (Beckwith 1928a, 277).

With folklore conceived as a new "modern" study out of art and science, literature and anthropology, history and psychology, geography and sociology, Beckwith embraced the Folk-Lore Foundation as an opportunity to establish a disciplinary tradition. As she told the press, "It is the hope of the donor that similar foundations may be established which will add the science of folklore to those of anthropology and ethnology in bringing the whole subject of man's primitive life into the range of the curriculum of modern science."[15] Charles Peabody, secretary of the American Folklore Society, recognized the implication of the post for the scientific pursuit of folklore. He wrote Beckwith to "offer you my congratulations, and at the same time to offer them to ourselves; for many years it has been an unfulfilled wish to see our science recognized in this way."[16] Henry MacCracken, president of Vassar, reported an orally circulating anecdote that exemplifies Beckwith's seriousness in her endeavor:

> Sometimes the unexpected self-assertion of women professors came from the same dynamic that makes professors absent-minded—devotion to truth in one's special field. Among my best friends on the faculty was Miss Martha Beckwith, who held at Vassar the chair of Folklore, a rare if not unique position. In her researches she had lived with the Hawaiians of the older stock, Negroes in Jamaica highlands and reservation Indians.
>
> "Come, Miss Monnier," she said one day; "the paper advertises a genuine Hawaiian hula at the theatre. I want you to see it. A car just went by with a big poster, too. Genuine hula, think of it!" …
>
> "This is unscholarly," said Miss Beckwith. "I must protest."
>
> "Please, Martha, don't make a scene. What is the use?"
>
> Martha rose and addressed the audience. "In the interest of truth," she said, "I must denounce this performance. It has nothing about it that in any way represents the true hula, except the skirt, and even that is artificial. You are being taken in."
>
> The theatre was in an uproar. "Go ahead, old lady. Speak your mind. Tell us about the hula!" "Sit down!" Miss Martha did not sit down. She told them what the true hula was, until the petrified manager came to life and started off the hula once more.

"Come, Mathilde," said the scholar; "we will not stay for such an unscholarly performance." Miss Monnier followed Miss Beckwith's stately withdrawal while the customers cheered. (Luomala 1970, xxiv–xxv)

The anecdote showed that Beckwith was hardly shy about publicly airing her views as a professorial authority on tradition, and she had more to say about the popular staging of folklore. In a review of the National Folk Festival in the nation's capital, she bluntly announced, "It is probably impossible to reproduce a pure folk art under such artificial conditions." Yet she recognized its value for promoting a pluralistic American culture and artistic appreciation of folk tradition. She asserted: "A folk art brought to high perfection by the people to whom it belongs does bring aesthetic delight to the great mass of our American people and hence has a very real function to perform in awakening our interest in and appreciation of the varied strains of folk life which make up our whole American culture. It is by extending perception of those traditional forms which are a part of folk memory among different groups of our people, and by reviving and perfecting them, that we may ... enrich our national art and add to our range of aesthetic enjoyment" (Beckwith 1938, 443). She warned that folklorists as a profession still needed to find their materials "among the folk in their own setting." But toward the building of a nation, she declared, "Let us amend to perfect a living art upon the old native tradition" (Beckwith 1938, 443; see also Beckwith 1933).

Beckwith came to Vassar in the fall of 1920 as research professor of the Folk-Lore Foundation and associate professor of comparative literature. The first course she taught was "Folk-lore" and it carried the following description in 1920: "The art of oral tradition. A study of folk-tales and other forms of oral art, their origin, distribution, and variations in the type; and of folk thought as reflected in oral tradition." She also submitted a longer description of the course with special attention to the special theme of individual creativity and group tradition in cultural expression:

The course aims to study folk-stories with a view to determining their origin, their distribution, and variations in the type. The development of literary forms will be considered, and an attempt made to characterize the body of oral tradition belonging to particular areas and to relate it to the whole culture of the group. Well-known European folk themes and typical European folk characters will first be studied in relation to their analogues in the oral tradition of other races and to the customs which may throw light upon the meaning or origin of the story. The question of independent origin or of historical dissemination will give an opportunity for fixing attention upon the geographical distribution of particular themes. The beginnings of such literary forms as the epic, drama, lyric, hymn, romance, as well as of the fable, proverb, riddle, and ballad, are to be traced in oral tradition. The influence is to be tested of symbolism or realism in determining the art form, and of group or individual production. The social value of storytelling is emphasized, and its dependence as an art upon social activities. Finally the attempt will be made to distinguish in the folk-lore of a group the distinguishing characteristics of that group, and if possible to discover the part which individual initiative plays in the variation from a typical form.[17]

Beckwith tinkered with the description of the course several times in the years she held the chair. In the catalogue copy for 1925–1926, the listing referred to the subject matter of "folk art": "The first semester will be occupied with the consideration of those beliefs which lie at the basis of folk tales and of other forms of oral art.... The second semester will be devoted to the survey of popular literature as it appears in written records of the past and in the folk art of primitive people today. Some attention will be paid to field work." In each version of the course, she stressed folklore as art, its study as science, and in later versions increasingly emphasized collections in the field. Here is how she described the class's activities in 1928:

> In the folk-lore study in the tower of the Vassar library, liberally loaned to us by the department of philosophy, we labor our texts from Hawaii, endless notes from the negroes of the British West Indies, Urdu songs from the East Indians of Jamaica, proverbs from Urdu and Marathi of India, texts in Konkani and in Portuguese from New Goa, stories from the Dakota Sioux and Dutch songs from our own Hudson Valley. One student brings a Chinese ghost story collected in Chinatown. Another has Porto Rican connections, another Czech. Ballad songs come from ex-Grenfell workers in Newfoundland and this summer an expedition thither is financed which Mrs. Greenleaf of Middlebury will conduct to gather folk material from that island. (Beckwith 1928a, 280–81)

Beckwith meanwhile sought to strengthen the visibility of folklore at the college. At Vassar, Beckwith resisted the listing of folklore under the heading of Comparative Literature. Although her title as professor of comparative literature was dropped in 1929, Beckwith's courses continued to be listed under Comparative Literature in the college catalogue. Beckwith protested in a memorandum she called "Folklore: A Statement for the Course in Advancement of Learning" (November 24, 1933). She cited the uniqueness of folklore studies and suggested a curriculum of related classes.

> The courses listed under Comparative Literature do not constitute correlated subjects making up a major field and hence can not be treated as constituting a department .... The position of folklore in the curriculum of a liberal arts college presents a special problem, due to the fact that there is, except among specialists, the vaguest ideas only as to the relation of folklore to the traditional and well established subjects of a college curriculum, and, second, that in most colleges where folklore is offered as an undergraduate subject, it is directly correlated with and, so to speak, under the patronage of the department with which the specialist offering the course is connected and through which therefore the approach is made to the subject. That is, it is affiliated with one of the literature and

linguistic courses such as English, German, French, or the Classics, or with a course in social science such as Sociology, Anthropology, History, Geography, or Religion. One who attempts therefore to offer any sequential course of study in connection with folk-lore is at once confronted with an arbitrary division into subjects coordinated under special aspects but which have no necessary sequential bearing upon a subject like folklore. The aim of the course is to relate the imaginative life of the folk to their social culture. It studies the concrete forms which popular expression takes as influenced by custom and belief and by contacts with the outside world, the influence of such forms upon literature on the one hand, upon social culture on the other. It aims to bring the student in touch with modern theory in the field of folklore in the light of older methods of interpretation and to give practical help in recognizing folk forms of the past and in collecting and preserving disappearing forms alive today in oral art and in the practice of the folk group.

As to the applicability of folklore studies for Vassar graduates, Beckwith wrote the Committee on Vocational Guidance of several opportunities. "There are some teaching posts in this subject for women and the number of such posts will doubtless increase." She added "art" and the "opportunity for women in museum work," although ever the scholar wary of the romanticization of folklore, she cautioned that "its emotional value must always depend upon the intelligence with which the material is handled." Finally, she emphasized that "folklore is of especial value for those who intend to take up social work of any kind, especially among primitive peoples and in foreign countries. It gives a key to the folk mind."[18]

Beckwith utilized the loyal network of Vassar alumnae for the work of the Folk-Lore Foundation. She published a brochure on the foundation that was circulated to graduates; the brochure asked for details of field work or folklore collections that alumnae may undertake. She also solicited donations of books and funds for the publication of monographs reporting folklore fieldwork. Finally, she urged alumnae to join the American Folklore Society and "to contribute to the support of its Journal, which is edited by the leading Folk-lorists of this country and is the means of communicating results in Folk-lore. A strong Alumnae representation and interest in this Association will add to the influence of the college as a center for research."[19] The alumnae responded with generous support of the monograph series, called the Publications of the Folk-Lore Foundation of Vassar College. Particularly generous were Jennie Gouldy, Vassar class of 1875, who supported publications on Hawaiian folklore, and Elisabeth Howe (a friend of American Folklore Society founder William Wells Newell), Vassar class of 1882, who underwrote many Folk-Lore Foundation publications and contributed field collections on Polish immigrants to Buffalo.

Before the Vassar publication series in folklore ended, it featured fourteen monographs mostly on Jamaican, Native-American, and Hawaiian folklore.[20] In addition, Beckwith arranged to have leading folklorists lecture at Vassar, and the American Folklore Society met there in 1929 to further reinforce the influence of the college as a center for folklore scholarship.[21] Revising the brochure on the

Folk-Lore Foundation in 1931, she was able to write that "Between 1920 and 1930 interest in folklore has greatly increased in America. Scholars are much more will-ing to recognize the relation of folklore to art and literature and to the history of culture. In giving a place on its curriculum to this subject therefore the college is working in the same direction as modern educational theory."

After five years of supporting the folklore chair, Alexander agreed to renew her contribution on a year-to-year basis. After three years on this arrangement, Alexander made a commitment to support the chair until Beckwith's retirement. The terms of the chair allowed Beckwith generous amounts of research and writ-ing time in addition to granting regular sabbaticals and leaves. Looking for com-parative data to examine folklore, she divided her research during the 1920s and 1930s mainly among three different racial groups: Jamaican blacks, native Hawaiians (of Polynesian descent), and Native Americans in the Dakotas. Concentrating on the influence of culture and history over racial or mental char-acteristics among these groups, Beckwith furthered the scholarly and political agenda of cultural relativity championed by Franz Boas.[22] Refuting the racial theo-ries of "psychological unity" by nineteenth-century evolutionists, Beckwith in each case study focused on culture contact, geographical and social context, and histor-ical uniqueness rather than genetics or mental development as forces shaping the group's society and its artistic expressions. Although her fieldwork took her far from Poughkeepsie, she did not neglect folk groups close to home. She worked with Mid-Hudson descendants of Dutch settlers, from whom she collected folk songs, and modern Vassar College women, from whom she collected courtship and divination beliefs (Ring et al. 1953; Beckwith 1923).

With the Vassar collection, Beckwith had several goals. She wanted to show that "literate American homes," as she wrote, had an abundance of living folklore that functioned in everyday life. She desired to examine contemporary women's values as a special field of inquiry in addition to the beliefs of ethnic-regional groups that dominated the pages of the *Journal of American Folklore* and other journals of cul-ture. Instead of dictating the types of folklore she sought, she hoped to get a pic-ture of tradition from the tradition bearers themselves, much as she conceived the idea in her Hawaiian research. She recorded the beliefs that women used most commonly, thus suggesting gender as a significant social category for the produc-tion of folklore in America. She asserted women did not have to be "primitive" or ethnic to have a shared folklore. She emphasized that "certain classes of signs" repeatedly reported in folklore journals through collections of body signs, weath-er, and dreams were "negligible." At Vassar she found an overwhelming majority of material referred to, first, matters of luck and, second, love and marriage. She did not see the good-luck signs as survivals of superstitions, but instead as reflections of the everyday life of the women. She noted in the collection references that "relate to the interest of the group" such as obtaining wealth in careers, riding cars, writing letters, and finding company. She thought the generalized form of the good-luck signs was a tip-off that they lacked supernatural content but were significant nonetheless for framing identity at the intersection of femininity and college life. She categorized them as "a species of play" that "extends to mature folk in social life." She underscored the creativity in tradition by pointing to folkloric uses of "modern innovations" replacing horseshoes and flower petals and invention of new beliefs that served the purposes of the group. She argued that folklore was a renewable resource that could be sought among "modern" groups, exemplified by college women. Arguing for the constant adaptation of tradition as part of modernity, she wrote, "Even when the faith is lost, the form remains, and a fresh stock of similar forms are fashioned like them, but differing in content and direction according to the particular tastes and interests of the group by which they are cultivated" (Beckwith 1923, 2). It was a dramatic case at the time for the situational uses of folklore among small, often temporary groups as part of the diverse American cultural scene (see Beckwith 1931b, 4–7).

Beckwith traversed the globe to locate traditions that crossed national boundaries and to make a case for a discipline of folklore based on that search. She told Vassar's president that "during the summer of 1923 I was the guest of a friend to places of archaeological interest in England, France, and Spain; and during my sabbatical year, 1926–'27, I visited for the first time Italy, Greece, Palestine, Syria, India and familiarized myself as far as possible with their present folk life and the literature of their traditional past."[23] Beckwith's international experience played a major role in her guide to the method, and discipline, of folklore studies, which she published as *Folklore in America* in 1931. Her global concern for tracing cultural migrations and settlements is evident in her choice of "folklore in America" as opposed to the "American folklore" preferred by Constance Rourke, and later, Richard Dorson. Instead of taking a perspective emphasizing the exceptionalism of the United States, Beckwith wanted to show the many spirited ethnic "strains" that contributed to cultural formation across the American social landscape. She called for more consideration of cultural process of adaptation within the American scene. By way of example, she wrote, "Certainly the negro art which is coloring our American culture today is not African but Afro-American, as anyone can distinguish who is familiar with the clearly separate pattern of any other even English-speaking colony like the Jamaican. We need the emotional response to other national strains in the process of creating an American cultural life" (Beckwith 1931b, 64).

Folklore in America was also distinctive because it singled out a scholarly audience for the establishment of a folkloristic discipline. Anthropologist Melville Herskovits at Northwestern University wrote Beckwith promising to assign it in his folklore class (December 19, 1931). "I think it is a much-needed job and I am sure the students in my Folk Lore class will find it useful when I put it into their hands," he wrote. From the literary side of the fence, Benjamin Botkin at the University of Oklahoma also planned to use it in a new course on folklore he instituted, and asked Beckwith for suggestions on its content in a letter dated January 12, 1932. "It is a work that needed to be done and you have done it well," the future author of numerous "treasuries" of American folklore wrote. As late as 1959, Daniel G. Hoffman wrote in the *Journal of American Folklore* that "I have found no theoretical discussion which supersedes Martha Beckwith's suggestions, made almost thirty years ago, about the nature of those groups in America among whom folklore is found" (Hoffman 1959, 226).

Beckwith made several theoretical principles evident in *Folklore in America*. First she recognized the adaptive nature of tradition: "Folklore—that is, poetic fantasy based on tradition, custom, belief, or on some fresh form brought in from outside—is to be recognized in every form of folk expression, European or primitive. Every new folk grouping is a fresh problem in acculturation, which means the adaptation of experience, either traditional or acquired from a new environment or from fresh contacts, to those special forms of fantasy which arouse popular emotion within the group" (Beckwith 1931b, 10). "Folklore as a subject of intellectual discipline," she wrote, takes from literature the appreciation of "individual composition" and from anthropology the "expression of the development of human culture." Yet her goal was to define folklore broadly and distinctively to include a type of approach to material and social aspects of culture as well as the oral material (Beckwith 1931b, 6–8). By conceptualizing the scope of folklore in this way, Beckwith put forward folklore studies as more than a field combining anthropology and literature. It is an intellectual discipline that becomes, in her words, "a means of interpretation of the phenomena of culture studied under the more generally accepted disciplines of Religion, Art, Literature, Social Anthropology, Technology, and Archaeology" (Beckwith 1931b, 10).

Favoring a German-American concept of folklore over English, Scandinavian, and French models, Beckwith offered that folklore could be "more precisely" thought of as "folk art" (from the idea of *Volkskunde*) combining the collective culture and individual artist. "Every folk fantasy," she explained, "begins originally from an individual source, but it takes on, through infinite repetition and variation, the character of a group composition" (Beckwith 1931b, 3). Viewing folk expression from this dynamic perspective, she offered diverse examples of changing folk arts in family and age groups, from the ballads of isolated Newfoundlanders to the songs and rituals of college students. "Every social group," she generalized, "preserves bonds of fixed group observance whose preservation does not depend upon their practical but upon their traditional and aesthetic value" (Beckwith 1931b, 5). "Folklore," she summarized, "represents a living force taking shape in our midst today as in the past, building up tradition and governing the shaping of fantasy" (Beckwith 1931c, 66). Beckwith consciously tried to fashion a "modern" view of folklore as (1) tradition found in various types of artistic expression—literary, oral, social, and material; (2) emergent in everyday life as an interplay between individuals and their various group connections; and (3) adapting to new conditions to take on new forms and significant functions.

"According to the modern conception of folklore," as she put it, Beckwith offered guidelines for methods that followed her theoretical principles. "The folklorist is first of all a collector of verified data. He selects a carefully limited field for investigation and comparison in order that his results may be fairly inclusive within that field and he reports his data in the exact language of the folk with enough repetitions from the same and from other informants to check lapses of memory or individual variations in the relation." Taking the missionaries she knew so well to task for being "the most prejudiced recorders of customs whose standards differ from their own," she underscored the folkloristic "dictum" of "interpretations ... from the standpoint of the people themselves" (1931b, 50; 1928a, 278–79). Beckwith added to this call a special attention to the historical, cultural, and geographical context of the data:

> The folklorist wants to know what actually happened in the past to bring about the particular folk form he is studying. He cannot rely upon any generalization to establish these facts but must put them to historic proof. He must treat each case as a particular problem within its own limited field and be sure that he is comparing similar data in drawing conclusions from the variants within that field. He must observe folk data in relation to their setting. He must know, that is, what habits of life and custom and what particular style in art have determined their form. He must study each form in relation to the culture pattern of the group in which it is found. Thus folk data should never be isolated from their historic, geographic and cultural surroundings. (Beckwith 1931b, 65–66)

Refuting the sweeping evolutionary assumptions about racial unity in Frazer's *Golden Bough* (1890), Beckwith argued that "the same color woven into one pattern may be a quite different thing in another in which it appears under quite different conditions" (Beckwith 1928a, 279).

Beckwith had a special concern for American cultural conditions. She recognized that in their zeal to record "primitive" groups, anthropologists had neglected groups other than the "Indian and negro" and avoided discussion, she felt, about popular and European cultural influences. Beckwith had a vision for the eventual integration of American folklore collections considering such influences into a "regional characterization of folk groups" in America. Pointing to ethnographic models in France and Germany, she thought that the collections of individual folklorists could culminate in a folk atlas of American traditional practices in particular localities. She managed to acquire the endorsement of folklorists from anthropology and literature including professors Stith Thompson, Franz Boas, Alfred Kroeber, George Lyman Kittredge, Roland Dixon, and W. W. Lawrence for the project, but the Depression hurt her fundraising efforts.[24] As she explained to the American Council of Learned Societies, the project would cover "early settlers of this country from Europe and later immigrants who have settled in groups in one locality either in our large cities or in country districts and have contributed a particular character to the folk culture of that locality, as well as those who have been brought together by a common occupation. It will not attempt any collection of specific folk data, leaving such to the individual initiative of collectors in special areas, but it will attempt to map out these special areas and determine accurately their character and provenience."[25]

Although the grand atlasing project never got off the ground, Beckwith anticipated a movement within folklore studies to consider the regional and ethnic patterns operating in American folklife (see Glassie 1968; Yoder 1990). Her major contributions toward this end were in Hawaii, Jamaica, and in the Dakotas. Beckwith began working her collections from Hawaii made between 1914 and 1920 after she arrived at Vassar. Hawaii provided a prime example of a changing culture and history that can be viewed through traditional expressions. An island culture with influences from various Polynesian migrations and European contacts, Hawaii included a distinctive native language, religion, and folk literature. Beckwith published an extensive report on Hawaiian riddling in *American Anthropologist* during 1922. In the article, Beckwith drew attention to riddling as a process and ritual used in specific cultural contexts, rather than treating riddles as isolated literary texts. Archer Taylor, the premier scholar of proverbs and riddles of the day, wrote Beckwith, "I am glad to have it, because it is well done—and because it is so hard to get information about riddling among foreign peoples. The literature gives chiefly, nay exclusively, references to European, Indogermanic riddles."[26]

Corresponding with Laura Green who resided in Hawaii, Beckwith also developed several articles regarding beliefs and customs, especially those relating to birth and death. In these analyses, Beckwith hoped to show generally the functional cultural significance of folklore at times of life crisis, and specifically Hawaiian attitudes expressed in responses to passages through these periods (Beckwith and Green 1924, 1926, 1928). After 1928, the Bishop Museum awarded her the title of honorary research associate in Hawaiian folklore and she took several leaves between 1928 and 1938 to pursue folklore research on the islands. In 1931, she wrote President MacCracken to explain her situation there: "The museum offered every facility in the shape of an office, materials, library, typewriter and assistance during the entire period of my stay, and free access to the accumulation of manuscript texts from the royal collections and others. In return I filed and classified the papers bearing on ethnography, a task which gave me insight into the whole field of Hawaiian folk thought as it survives in text today. This view was supplemented by two months in the field in remotest parts of the islands."[27]

Beckwith's research into Hawaiian folklore culminated in the publication of *Hawaiian Mythology* in 1940. Luomala frankly considered the title "overly limited and modest." "The title does not reflect her comprehensive consideration of the oral art of the Hawaiians and other Polynesians in relation to their total culture," Luomala wrote in the introduction to the reprint in 1970. Luomala quoted a letter that Beckwith wrote her to explain the hope for the book: "My special interest in writing the mythology was to produce a book which covered what I conceive to be the province of a true mythology—not merely a series of tales, but, with the tales as major illustration or formal expression, to point out the ideas of the relation of man to the world he lives in, geographic, historic, social and political, which result in such expression, and to connect the particular forms of expression developed in Hawaii to those common with his throughout the known Polynesian area" (Luomala 1970, vii–viii; letter dated May 1955). Beckwith covered riddling contests, trickster stories, and romance legends, for example, in addition to documenting stories of Hawaiian gods and their offspring. While making a contribution by recognizing the individual creativity and social tradition that marks storytelling or "narrative art" in Hawaiian everyday life, she also faced criticism for her inattention to migration theory, particularly among the various Polynesian groups influencing Hawaii (Luomala 1970, vii). Coming to Beckwith's defense, Dorothy Lee promoted the significance of *Hawaiian Mythology* for its presentation of storytelling on native terms. She contended, "She draws no distinctions where the Hawaiian does not draw them. She has steeped herself so thoroughly in her material, that she accepts what most of us would have tried, at best, to justify. In this way, she can transfer directly to the reader, Hawaiian concepts unacceptable to the reasoning of the Euro-American mind" (Lee 1941).

Another island culture, this one in Jamaica in the Caribbean Sea, commanded much of Beckwith's attention during the 1920s. Her location of fields associated with, or symbolic of, the process of America but not on its mainland, indicated her transnational views of culture in the Americas. The islands she chose appeared isolated, but showed considerable influences from far-off shores. They were colonized and featured hierarchical social divisions that ranged from an educated aristocracy to a racialized folk. Beckwith first went to Jamaica for a vacation in 1919. Intrigued by the native folklife of the island's blacks as part of a colonized society, she returned for eight weeks during the winter of 1920–1921 and again in 1922–1923; then in 1924, she spent the entire spring semester exploring the island. She was accompanied by Helen H. Roberts, who recorded and transcribed music. During these visits, by Beckwith's own account, she "spent long hours in peasant homes listening to songs and stories; made several expeditions to the free Maroon settlements of Accompong and Moore Town; attended Sunday School picnics where ring-games were in progress, John Canoe performances at Christmas time, a revival meeting and a wake at Lacovia, a morning service at Mammy Forbes's balm-yard; and sought an interview with the healer, Bedward, during the excited period of the Christmas holidays preceding his predicted ascent into heaven and the ending of white rule in Jamaica" (Beckwith 1929, vii).

Beckwith saw the island's situation as a special problem of American acculturation that captured her interest in Hawaii and elsewhere. "Not African or Indian, east or west; not Spanish or British, it is a blend of all these into a fresh product reflecting the material background of the sunny fertile island itself and the mixed culture of those alien races who have come to call it home" (Beckwith 1929, xi). Her early collections were transcriptions of folklore genres that natives, many of them children at the roadside to whom she would offer pennies, felt little conflict in giving to the white stranger. She raised questions of culture contact with studies of African "Anansi" stories and English ballads among Jamaican blacks (Beckwith 1924a). She published several small studies on folk games, Christmas mummings, proverbs, and ethnobotany during the 1920s in her Folk-Lore Foundation series and then reprinted them together under the heading of *Jamaica Folk-Lore* in the American Folklore Society Memoirs Series in 1928. "Later, when the confidence of the people had been won and my own knowledge widened," Beckwith wrote, she probed deeper into the villages and into the protected traditions of custom, belief, and material and social life (Beckwith 1929, vii). While the *Folk-Lore* volume presented studies of traditional forms, her ambition for the professional folklorist was to uncover the inner life, the total life, of a culture, which she underscored as *Folk Life*.

The result of Beckwith's exploration was *Black Roadways: A Study of Jamaican Folk Life,* published in 1929. It was a pivotal study for presenting black culture as a rational system, and as a book held the distinction of being the first folklife study of blacks in the New World. Her special problem in the work was to assess the influence of colonial rule, and poverty, on the functional integration of culture. Jamaica's blacks retained their cultural separateness, she found, largely because of poverty imposed by British rule. Yet she maintained that black traditions "penetrate the life and thought of white and colored alike of the literate classes, and leave an impress upon their speech, attitude, emotion" (Beckwith 1929, x). In her conclusion she wrestled with tough questions of social reform. She wondered whether British rule could help blacks rise out of poverty and retain their traditions. She called for action "to bring the great mass of the folk out of their present social isolation into a more robust and wholesome way of thinking and living" (Beckwith 1929, 223). Modernization in the form of centralized education was not necessarily the answer, she thought. She argued that while education opened "the way for a few able," it "left the great masses bookless with no means of satisfying any possibly awakened curiosity" (Beckwith 1929, 224). She saw a healthy interaction of American tourists with the black folk to encourage consumption of traditional products, but bemoaned "the practice of the ruling classes to keep down folk prices to the folk level instead of stimulating excellence by paying commensurate prices" (Beckwith 1929, 223). Ultimately she believed in the value of colonialism and thought that blacks respected it. Her controversial closing answer was to call for "enthusiastic and tireless and wise leadership ... in the hands of trained social workers under government employ. The native respect for the government and for the white ruling class is a healthy sign in this little island group of African immigrants which augurs well for its ultimate solidifying upon a higher plane of genuine folk culture" (Beckwith 1929, 225–26).

Beckwith viewed in Jamaican folklife the integration of British and African traditions that formed a distinctive New World culture. She admired the "practical philosophy," "native wit," and "harmonious social life" of black Jamaican culture, while deriding its fostering of "shiftlessness." While one might expect the chapters on the settlements and religious centers, her section on the family appeared unusual for its attention to women's roles and life cycle. Her culminating chapter, entitled "Folk Art," covered the way that "the Jamaican Negro gives emotional expression to his inner life through the medium of voice and motion" (Beckwith 1929, 198). The book's scope and its confrontation of social issues extended well beyond the usual contents of folklore studies in the period. With the rhetorical shift to "folk life," Beckwith emphasized living tradition as a continuous process integrated into modern-day communities. She offered photographs, drawings, and maps to illuminate the everyday life of the island's black communities. In the text, she sifted through the many influences on black folk expression from adaptation to the environment and contact with European and American Indian populations.

Melville Herskovits, who used Beckwith's contribution in the preparation of his landmark work, *The Myth of the Negro Past* (1941), thought she needed more attention to variations of individuals, but he praised her for providing "the first ethnographic study of the life of any New World Negro which, to my knowledge, has been attempted. She tries to see the culture of the Jamaicans as a whole, and she describes it as a unit as she would describe the culture of any distinct people" (Herskovits 1930; Beckwith 1931a). Herskovits recognized the folklife approach in Beckwith's work that set it apart from folklore studies as a "portion of anthropology." It is less of a textual comparative study that marked other previous folkloristic works, including her own, than an exploration of tradition and all its complex social influences. To be sure, folklorists today bristle at Beckwith's use of stereotype-raising phrases such as "backward race" and "shiftlessness," and her colonial assumptions of deference of natives to the ruling population, but one has to admire, in the words of famed belief collector Newbell Niles Puckett, her "ethnographical zeal" and "folklorist enthusiasm" (Puckett 1929).

Black Roadways can be read not just as her suggestion of a folklife approach, but also an interpretation of New World nations that contain multiple cultures formed from the hybridization of traditions. This view explains her rejoinder to Herskovits that as an anthropologist he overstated the exclusive transplantation of relic African traditions. As a folklorist, she thought she understood the modern reality of interplay between tradition and modernity, transatlantic cultural sources and ethnic hybridization. "When we attempt to differentiate the purely African traits among these colonial Africans," she cautioned Herskovits, "it is necessary to take into account not only contacts with European superstitions in the New World but also with Portuguese, Dutch and British traders on the coast of Africa itself" (Beckwith 1931b, 223). Again, she invoked the separate identity of the folklorist for the special problems of folk cultures in modern societies as issues of tradition. "In all these matters," she chided Herskovits, "it seems safer for *the folklorist* to describe accurately the data in his own field than to hazard a guess as to original national sources" (Beckwith 1931b, 223; emphasis added). Folkloristic interest, she implied, lay in the contemporary formation and function, rather than origin, of culture.

On the islands of Hawaii and Jamaica, Beckwith had familiarity with the languages used by natives, but on the mainland she needed the aid of interpreters for major field experiences on American Indian reservations. On the recommendation of Franz Boas, and with government permission, Beckwith set out during the summer of 1926 to the Pine Ridge Reservation along the South Dakota-Nebraska border to record the "story forms" of the Oglala Dakota Sioux. She had three interpreters assisting her from the reservation. Other collectors had preceded her, but she hoped to make two distinct contributions to set her collection apart.[28] She wanted first to define the stories and storytelling art from the Oglala perspective, and second, she wanted to identify the narrative forms used by the Oglala so as to assess the style and meaning of their oral art. She revealed that although ethnologists had divided Dakota stories into European-American genres of myth, legends, tales, and so on, natives themselves divided stories into two classes: "myths" and "stories which tell about a tribe." She found that to the Dakota, myth is considered an "invention" rather than a story of an earlier age. With each of the classes of stories, she documented styles and structures used that characterized the performance of the tales, and she identified individual storytellers and their backgrounds. She published her collection with comparative notes and an introduction to the role of storytelling in the tribal culture as a special issue of the *Journal of American Folklore* (1930).

Beckwith turned her attention to other branches of the Sioux on three summer trips to the Fort Berthold Reservation in North Dakota between 1929 and 1932. There she collected "fast disappearing" traditional stories and accounts of ceremonies from aged members of the Mandan and Hidatsa. Again she documented storytelling forms from native points of view and discussed the stories as reflections of cultural life and formations of worldview. Yet in her focus on story forms, she stopped short of elaborating on the backgrounds and performances of individual artists that would mark later narrative research. Two "excellent story tellers," as Beckwith described them, related most of the stories in the collection. She faithfully transcribed and translated their tales with the help of interpreters, particularly one provided by music collector Frances Densmore (Densmore 1923).[29] Beckwith originally published her collections in the Folk-Lore Foundation series and reprinted the work in the American Folklore Society Memoirs Series under the title of *Mandan-Hidatsa Myths and Ceremonies* (1937).

When the American Folklore Society reprint came out, Beckwith was already sixty-six years old and had shown a remarkable record of activity including prolific publishing and rigorous fieldwork since taking off on her new career path at an advanced age. During the 1930s, the size of her folklore classes grew and she noticed a growing interest in folklore studies generally. She answered Mt. Holyoke College's query about her activities during the early 1930s by writing, "True to type, surrounded by books, bespectacled, an incurable scribbler, and finding life more interesting every day."[30] As the decade neared its close, Beckwith planned her retirement from teaching at Vassar and a move to a locale closer to Hawaii. It had appeared that Anne Alexander might permanently endow the chair in folklore at Vassar, but as Beckwith explained, "The gift would probably have been secured had not the depression year and the many other interests in scientific and educational fields for whose financing the donor had made herself responsible, put an end to that hope, a result rendered still more conclusive by the increased demands of the government, both state and national, since that time upon higher incomes."[31]

Beckwith appealed to Vassar to continue the line in folklore as a growing "modern field." She made the case to the college's president in 1932 that

> Vassar now holds a considerable reputation in this modern field and is gaining representation in national societies. In making new appointments in some allied field either of literature or of social science would it not be possible to look out for some candidate fitted to carry on the folklore as part of his program? Such a candidate should have ideally both literary-historical and ethnological training in order to give introductory work in folklore as affiliated here in America. Some of our ablest American folklorists such as Archer Taylor of Chicago, Louise Pound of Nebraska, Stith Thompson of Missouri, have the literary training alone. I should be ambitious for Vassar to include the two lines of interest and training.[32]

Such a person came on board the faculty when Dorothy D. Lee, one of Beckwith's former folklore students, joined the newly formed anthropology department. Yet the Folk-Lore Foundation and the introductory folklore course disappeared after 1939.

Beckwith left Vassar in 1938 with the title of research professor emeritus of folklore and established residence in Berkeley, California. When the end of World War II eased travel, she returned to Hawaii regularly to continue work on Hawaiian folklore. "I have found Berkeley," she wrote, "a half-way home between Hawaii and the East"; her home "became a center for literary folk, and for all who loved Hawaii and its people."[33] Berkeley also became a symbol of her approach to American culture as a matrix made from influences East and West. It was able to maintain various ethnic "strains," particularly from Asia, and develop new traditions. In her work at Berkeley, she constantly reminded American colleagues of influences into American culture from Asia to balance the transatlantic emphasis on European borrowing on the Eastern Seaboard.

Through the 1940s and 1950s, Beckwith reexamined Pacific traditions. Set against the background of social changes brought by war and modernization, she interpreted the changing functions of Pacific folklore. She especially looked more deeply into the mix of traditions around Hawaii and Polynesia. Beckwith's last major work, published when she was eighty years old, was *The Kumulipo, A*

Martha Beckwith in Honolulu, probably after 1945. (Archives, Mt. Holyoke College Library)

Hawaiian Creation Chant (1951), which she had translated from Hawaiian and to which she added extensive commentary. Reviewing the book in the *Journal of American Folklore*, Katharine Luomala commended it as "a milestone in Polynesian research, and for folklorists and anthropologists who wish to learn of Polynesian chants and their function in culture, this book on the most famous chant of all, is a fascinating introduction to the subject" (1951, 429–32). Besides this contribution, Beckwith worked on ethnobotany and folk medicine of her child-hood home in Maui, projects that brought her back to her earliest scientific and cultural explorations.[34] She also conceived of expanding or revising *Hawaiian Mythology* to include other Polynesian cultures, and wrote incisive articles on Polynesian mythology and story composition in preparation for a fuller treatment (Beckwith 1940, 1944). She even applied in 1949 for funding of new fieldwork in New Zealand to collect Polynesian narratives; she withdrew at the eleventh hour because, as she lamented, "I am having some trouble with my eyes and although they are still good, may not be able to work in future so intensively as I am accus-tomed to work and as I should wish to under government subsidy." The work in New Zealand would have brought her to the farthest reaches from which her Hawaiian, and American, homeland received ethnic Polynesian "strains." Ever determined and independent despite her elderly years and physical problems, she added, "I still hope to get to New Zealand for work on Polynesian mythology, but have other projects in mind for immediate attention, and should prefer to be on my own on such an expedition."[35]

Beckwith's vision worsened in 1950 and she suffered a stroke that curtailed her publishing after 1951. Her by-line still appeared in the *Journal of American Folklore* in 1953, however, when professional folklorists Tristram Coffin and Samuel Bayard edited a collection of songs made by her students in upstate New York in 1929 and 1930 (Ring et al. 1953). She must have smiled to see her efforts being expanded by authorities on tradition identifying themselves as professional folklorists. In her introduction written in 1937, she spoke of relying on a music specialist and Dutch scholar. Sixteen years later, the folklorists analyzed "Anglo-American texts and tunes," "fresh Dutch-American matter," and ultimately "local" ballads that showed a creative living tradition on the diverse American landscape.

Beckwith died on January 28, 1959, at her Berkeley home shortly after her eighty-eighth birthday. According to her wishes, her ashes were sent to the family burial plot on her beloved Maui. Back at Vassar, students and faculty offered a memorial tribute. Calling her "an inspiring teacher," with "single-minded devotion to scholarship" and "courage in the many difficulties of research in her chosen field," the tributaries praised her as "a charming and beautiful woman, the best type of Victorian lady and scholar."[36]

The Victorian label for Beckwith is meant lovingly to add dignity to her memo-ry, but it is misleading. Certainly informed by Victorian ideas of scientism, Beckwith nonetheless helped usher in twentieth-century, modern ideas of cultural relativism and diversity in her scholarship and public work. Indeed, she helped move folklore and folklife studies out of Victorian anthropology and into a new interdisciplinary combination for post-World War II folklorists. Most memorable in her scholarship are her Hawaiian and Jamaican studies. Her work came to the fore for a new generation of folklorists with the republication of *Hawaiian Mythology* in 1970. Beyond her work in Hawaii, Jamaica, and the Dakotas, Beckwith's ideas and collections merit attention for their contributions to the study of ethnic and regional lore, narrative and custom, race and gender, method and theory. She affected many associates with "the delights of the quest" for folk art, as she called it. She was instrumental in drawing women to the special problems of that quest. Her clarion call to women at Mt. Holyoke College sums her remarkable journey and her hope for fellow travelers:

> Squatting on the rug of an Indian tent on the Oglala Sioux reservation or watching the Fourth of July festival dance in the great camp circle; listening to African stories at night in a mountain village of Jamaica or sitting day by day with the old blind ex-sheriff who was born with a cowl and can see ghosts, or walking miles through the bush to visit an obeah sorcerer. Chatting with Dutch-American housewives in some farm-house in the valley; or going farther afield to a native coast village of Hawaii; to a Druse princess in the Lebanon mountains and a silk-worm cultivator in the village below; learning women's games at a girls' school in Delhi; touring country villages in the Punjab from the Grand Trunk road up into the Salt Range. If all these things will bring you too delight, then may you also bite the fatal apple and follow the toilsome ways of folk-lore. (Beckwith 1928a, 281–82)

Perhaps even more than inspiring followers of folklore's ways, Beckwith publicized the label of folklorist as an academic scholar of tradition. She developed a vantage for the folklorist from the university, where that figure could wield authority over public discourse about uses of American traditions. Applying the label of folklorist in her teaching and public presentations, she conceived a new intellectual hybrid formed from anthropological and literary concerns. It held a special place in America with its openness to innovation, she declared, and she surveyed the American field in a way that would lend the folklorist distinctiveness. She emphasized methods that would recognize the living traditions of America's groups, and the adaptive, artistic character of their lore. She took her stand for the folkloristic search for the authentic quality of tradition, and thereby laid a foundation for later debates about the diverse nature of American culture. She might have been better known if she could have established a department as well as filling a chair. Nonetheless, she served a pivotal role for the ensuing generation, who established academic programs by charging the folklorist with the main responsibility of explaining traditions in America. She also left issues on the table to enliven debate about ways that traditions should be presented, and indeed administered.

6

Alfred Shoemaker and the Discovery of American Folklife

WITH THE RISE OF FOLKLIFE IN THE TWENTIETH CENTURY AS A TERM FOR THE SOCIAL basis of tradition, America took on the look of a nation of composite groups. Folklife averred America's pluralism, its ethnic-regional diversity, and Pennsylvania became its model. Folklife was a rarely used term in America before Pennsylvania's Alfred Shoemaker raised it most forcefully as an alternative to folklore after World War II. By 1972, Richard Dorson observed that folklife "has vied with and even threatened to dominate folklore" (Dorson 1972d, 2). By the time America's bicentennial celebration rolled around in 1976, the United States had an American Folklife Center in the Library of Congress, an Office of Folklife Programs in the Smithsonian Institution, and a department of Folklore and Folklife at the University of Pennsylvania. Several American journals had folklife in their masthead, of which *Pennsylvania Folklife* was the oldest and largest.

Amid glorified monuments to great unifying figures of American history, folklife bursts on the Mall in the nation's capital every summer as a showcase of American pluralism (Adams 1990; Kurin 1990). Sponsored by the Smithsonian Institution, the Festival of American Folklife sounds keywords of diversity in its presentations. As the secretary of the Smithsonian offered in the introduction to a festival publication, "In the United States today there is increasing awareness and debate about questions of culture. The terms 'multicultural' and 'diversity,' 'equity,' 'conservation,' 'survival,' and 'pluralism' are becoming part of public discourse as national and local institutions evaluate their missions, audiences and constituencies" (Adams 1990, 5). Folklife, even more than folklore, provided a way to get at the vitality, the totality, of separate ethnic communities. Explaining folklife in "contemporary multicultural society" to festival-goers, Richard Kurin wrote, "Expressive, grass-roots culture, or folklife, is lived by all of us as members of ethnic, religious, tribal, familial, or occupational groups. It is the way we represent our values in stories, songs, rituals, crafts and cooking. Whether the legacy of past generations or a recent innovation, folklife is traditionalized by its practitioners; it becomes a marker of community or group identity. Folklife is a way that people say, 'This is who and how we are'" (Kurin 1990, 8).

While the rhetoric of folklife used in the festival encouraged "community or group identity" as the basis of plural America, the presentation at the festival favored groups "in need of empowerment," as one former staff member observed (Sommers 1996, 230). The director of the office sponsoring the festival phrased it in a less politically charged way: "The Festival gives voice to people and cultures not otherwise likely to be heard in a national setting" (Kurin 1989, 15). The history of the festival shows a procession from the safety of regional groups to communities claiming disenfranchisement or even victimization. Beginning with Regional America in 1967, the festival added a Native American Program (1968), Working Americans and Old Ways in a New World (1973), African Diaspora (1974), Community (1978), Folklore and Aging (1984), and Cultural Conservation (1985). A festival presenter reflected that at the festival, "'Folk' in fact means working class, marginalized, and grassroots; the traditions of the elite and powerful seldom are celebrated at FAF" (Sommers 1996, 230). She brought up the controversy over the American Trial Lawyers Program in 1986 as an example of this bias in the construction of folklife on the Mall. The folklorists did not question claims for the verbal artistry of trial lawyers as authentic tradition, but they disputed whether the festival "was an appropriate vehicle for the presentation of such a moneyed and powerful group, even with the intent of 'demystifying the powerful'" (Sommers 1996, 230). She pointed out, moreover, that during the Michigan Program the following year, "it was not the traditions of the engineers or designers we sought, although clearly theirs is valid occupational lore, but rather the lore of the worker on the assembly line, of the Union, of the ethnic workers who sought jobs in the industry" (Sommers 1996, 230; see also Cantwell 1991).

The rhetorical turn toward folklife before the Festival of American Folklife began affirmed recognition of unempowered groups as part of a view of a socially representative cultural democracy in the United States. Folklife study established the persistence of ethnic-religious communities bound by tradition that can be overlooked in a kind of cultural competition for public notice. The notice is important because of the presumption that mass culture overtakes folk cultures and fosters a consensus on the necessity for technological progress. Folklife study reminded Americans of the possibility of continuing tradition, and the benefits of self-esteem and belonging it brought. The special groups covered by folklife—the Amish and Cajuns, for example—were imperative for providing models of community in America. Folklife studies thus worked to chart ethnic-regional cultures that created a national map of difference.

Folklife showed difference in its very origin. Its roots lay not in the familiar English coining of a "good Saxon compound" of folklore, but in the foreign German term *Volksleben* and the Swedish *folkliv* (Yoder 1963; Erixon 1967; Fenton 1973; Bronner 1996c). The use of folklife argued for the interrelation of tradition in its cultural totality with reference to patterns created by oral, social, and especially material expressions (see Fenton 1967). The totality was rarely national, though. In its use of folk, it translated to a subcultural, and often marginalized, existence within a mainstream society. "Lore" implied unusual, surviving expressions that drew attention to themselves. "Life" appeared more functional; it invoked every-day, public activity as continuing tradition. It underscored the social bonds, the group identity, that lay at the foundation of a local culture. Its orientation was social-historical, to find precedent for a separate society, and ethnographic, to observe traditional practices and their living functions. Its inspiration was in German and Scandinavian scholarship, and its manifestation was in the plural eth-nic-regional communities of Pennsylvania. It flew in the face of comparative liter-ary methods of the prevalent historic-geographic school that seemed preoccupied with folktale texts. It went beyond an American anthropology of the exotic primi-tive in American Indians to an ethnography of familiar groups, often engaged by participants in the culture. It sought to bring issues of ethnic-regional identity and community to the fore as a new nationalism swept America.

The story of how Alfred Shoemaker made folklife prominent has its fair share of intrigue. It is a saga of a crusader up against formidable odds and a series of events that brought him rapid fame and a sudden fall. Alfred Shoemaker was used to going against the tide. A pacifist in time of war, a Pennsylvania-German speaker in an English-speaking world, a homosexual in a heterosexual society, Shoemaker exemplified difference and innovation. He established the first department of folk-lore or folklife in the United States, the country's first folklife society, and its first folklife publication. He created precedents for public folklife festivals, folklife archives, and cultural programming in popular media. Indeed, he brought mean-ing to the use of folklife as a rhetorical strategy for legitimizing cultural diversity and empowerment of marginalized groups. He put into circulation a new lexicon of tradition, including folk culture, material culture, and cultural source area. His model for the nation was in the state of Pennsylvania, in which he observed a com-monwealth of distinctive communities often put in precarious political roles. The Pennsylvania-German group to which he belonged had withstood state efforts to undermine the culture by suppressing the subcultural language and education.

In the story of Alfred Shoemaker is found the struggle to find reconciliation in the American discourse of culture between ethnic and national orientations to folklore. As a flamboyant public figure and academic scholar, Shoemaker simulta-neously appealed to a Pennsylvania-German audience and an international schol-arly "folk culture" fraternity. Removed from the ivory tower and anthropological assumptions about being an outsider to gain objectivity, Shoemaker saw benefits from his role as an insider to Pennsylvania-German culture to study its traditions. While his name may not be attached to present-day attempts to reconcile ethnic, national, and international folklife, his work significantly set the pattern for later attempts to intellectualize the public realm. In this discussion, I first examine reasons for the rise of folklife studies in the fertile soil of Pennsylvania and the development of the Pennsylvania-German tradition as a model for an unmeltable community in a multicultural society. I move then to Shoemaker's campaign to expand Pennsylvania-German historiography into a national scholarship encompassing all of America's groups.

Instead of isolating oral tradition into literary types as many folklore studies had done, Shoemaker's folklife studies gave special notice to observable crafts and arts as signs of functional traditions that contribute to the life of a community. Arts and crafts were integral to the function of a community, and they resulted in products including houses and town plans that remained visibly fixed on the landscape with ethnic imprints long after their makers had passed away. Folklife seen in a community's material products thus emphasized a total environment emphasizing the persistence of tradition. Folklife countered folklore's tendency to marginalize stories as surviving products of bygone ages. Folklife had a connotation of a living tradition, seen visibly in its arts and crafts used for the necessities of community life.

The legacy of rural art and craft studies in Pennsylvania reaching well back into the nineteenth century helped to convey an image of Pennsylvania as a place where hand-wrought tradition is momentous. It is an image filled with bank barns, fraktur, painted furniture, paper cutting, decorated stoves, baskets, quilts, and pottery. It is an image combining the hardy practicality associated with Pennsylvania settlers and the beauty they carved into their lives. This image undergirds much of today's folklife scholarship in general—emphasis on handwork, rural life, and domestic goods—and reflects several patterns that call particularly on the Pennsylvania experience.

That experience was a plural one. As opposed to the master narrative of ethnic homogeneity in early southern and New England settlement, Pennsylvania's saga featured an assortment of religious-cultural settlements from groups outside the English mold. Seeking refuge in Pennsylvania, groups such as Mennonites, Brethren, and Quakers formed distinctive ethnic and religious communities, often isolated from one another, that helped preserve Old World customs and language. In Pennsylvania, the character of communitarian group life in America became defined. Historian Michael Zuckerman emphasized the priority of Pennsylvania as America's first plural society. He explained: "The very diversity of the area demands the requisite attention to variation. Tribalism may have emerged among the Quakers of New Garden, but a far different familialism appeared close by among the Friends of the Welsh Tract. Sects may have solidified in revolutionary Philadelphia, but privatism prevailed in the revolutionary countryside a few miles up the Schuylkill" (1982, 23–24). Unlike New England, where studies of communities leaped to national generalization, in Pennsylvania study by geographic and cultural necessity was essentially local, primarily ethnic and religious. Since activities in the central Pennsylvania heartland often appeared outside of nation-making events in New England or the South, students of the region found value in locating the ordinariness of rural everyday life as a sign of communal importance.

The contrast of Pennsylvania to the nation is less a matter of landscape than ethnicity, amply demonstrated by the coverage of German heritage among Pennsylvania's many groups. Even in this nod to the dominance of German folklife in Pennsylvania's history, there is a plural, fragmented story. Historians often divide between "plain" sects, such as the Amish and Dunkards, and "church people" of Lutheran and Reformed faiths. Residents additionally distinguish between Old German, or the "Dutch" of colonial Pennsylvania, and New German brought over in the wave of late-nineteenth-century immigration. Pennsylvania's multiple identities, its communitarian sense of plural ethnicities, are bound in its varied history and settlement.

The Ethnic Connection

Pennsylvania began its settlement late, when compared to the other colonies on the Eastern Seaboard. The commonwealth also differed from its neighbors in the kind of settlers who came. Consistently, Pennsylvania attracted disenfranchised religious and ethnic groups from Europe. English Quakers during the late seventeenth century were joined by Dutch and Welsh brethren. Almost immediately the principle of a plural society emerged with this mixing of European ethnic-religious identities in a "holy experiment" of religious freedom. Attracted by promises of ethnic tolerance and a landscape reminiscent of their homeland, persecuted religious sects from German-speaking countries came next to give a contrasting image to the English roots of most Eastern Seaboard settlements. Mennonites, Amish, and Dunkers from Switzerland and the German Rhineland spread well inland into Pennsylvania and they established close-knit farming communities. The mountainous inland landscape influenced the separation of communities according to valleys. Still today, one hears reference to the subregional separation of the Oley Valley, Lehigh Valley, Hegins Valley, Mahatango Valley, and on it goes.

In many valleys bounded by imposing mountains in the Appalachian chain, an isolation and hardy self-sufficiency arose. In many Pennsylvania valley communities German language, art, and custom of the Old Country persisted well into the twentieth century. To be sure, the Germans, who mostly spoke a Plattdeutsch dialect, had contact with English speakers, and gave rise to an American German dialect they identified as the basis of a cultural group, called *Pennsylfannisch Deitsch*, or Pennsylvania Dutch. Within the range of settlement, subdialects formed, often arranged by valleys such as the Shenandoah, Lehigh, and Susquehanna (see

Buffington 1949). Many of the pioneers of Pennsylvania ethnic and folklife studies used linguistic training to tie the social boundaries of dialect to an ethnic culture (see Buffington et al. 1980). Alfred Shoemaker's dissertation, for instance, connected language use to cultural boundaries of an Amish community in Illinois (1940). The Pennsylvania linguistic scholars went beyond analysis of the dialectal nature of a community's language to make a case for the cultural integrity of ethnic characteristics of art, architecture, and belief associated with a language group.

Near the inland Pennsylvania-German settlements were many lowland Scots who had lived in northern Ireland, including many Presbyterians who had come during the eighteenth century to southeastern Pennsylvania for religious and economic opportunities. The result of this early settlement was an association of Pennsylvania's inland landscape with strong ethnic areas—particularly German and Scots-Irish communities. The distinctiveness of the arts and customs of these peoples, when compared to the predominant English background of the other colonies, helped create an image of ethnic islands within the new American nation. The family farm economy and supposedly stubborn hold onto Old World ways created an associated image of these areas as "folk" or "traditional" societies in contrast to the progressive nation.

An industrial connection to Pennsylvania ethnicity also became strong in a state that was host to the iron, coal, steel, lumber, and oil booms of the nineteenth century. When waves of southern and eastern European immigrants came to work in Pennsylvania industries during the late nineteenth century, they found encouragement from German and Scots-Irish precedents for maintenance of ethnic customs. Nonetheless, the life preserved by the colonial Germans was not matched by later immigrants who tended to maintain aspects of their culture such as food, domestic arts, dance, and music in a more ethnically mixed environment. By then spreading out across the state from Philadelphia to Scranton, Johnstown, and Pittsburgh, the new waves of Italian, Ukrainian, Serbian, Croatian, Polish, and Hungarian immigrants—to name a few of the nationalities—settled into a more urban experience than their German predecessors. Yet in Pennsylvania they were known for forming ethnic neighborhoods and establishing a vast assortment of ethnic clubs and churches that led to early urban anthropological and folkloristic interest (see Miner 1994; Gibbons 1882, 268–303; Culin 1887; Korson [1938] 1964). Apropos, the first local chapter of the American Folklore Society in Philadelphia, formed in 1889 to study the forms of folklore in America, diverged from the national society headquartered in New England by organizing its work around ethnic "fields" rather than folklore genres. It identified these fields as "Anglo-American," "Africo-American," and other "Local Foreign," such as "The Chinese Quarter," "The Italian Quarter," "The German Quarter," and "Gipsies" (*Philadelphia Branch* [1893] 1987, 71–72).

Other indications of this ethnic bias can be seen in nineteenth-century studies and societies. The Pennsylvania-German Society was formed in 1891 and featured many folklife topics in its publications, and other periodicals such as *Pennsylvania-German, Penn Germania,* and *German American Annals* began at the turn of the century. Thirty years earlier, *Atlantic Monthly* featured Phebe Earle Gibbons's essays on Pennsylvania traditions. Her organization revolved around ethnic topics: under "Pennsylvania Dutch," she covered Quiltings, Festivals, and Manners and Customs, and she discussed similar traditions for Swiss Exiles, Dunkers, Moravians, and Schwenkfelders. She collected her essays under the title of *"Pennsylvania Dutch," and Other Essays* and consumer demand encouraged three revised editions between 1872 and 1882. Another widely known statement of Pennsylvania's diversity before the turn of the century was Sydney George Fisher's *The Making of Pennsylvania* (1896). Fisher characterized the state and its folkways by its "mixture of languages, nationalities, and religions," and the way "these divisions led a more or less *distinct life* of their own in colonial times" (Fisher 1896, iii; emphasis added). Pennsylvania was no melting pot, according to writers in this part of America, and the studies of immigrant crafts verified this fact by showing the "extremely varied" character of Pennsylvania, as Fisher called it.

The divisions of religion that Fisher noticed led to the realization that some groups did not participate in America's polity. They desired a total way of life "separate from the world" and could accomplish that within Pennsylvania. The image of ethnicity and folklife in Pennsylvania often joined nonconformist sectarian life. Among the first popular descriptions of the Pennsylvania Germans, Phebe Gibbons's classic work viewed religion as the basis of groups that did not seek intercourse with other communities. While she could accept the idea of groups maintaining their Old World ties, the separation of the communities and lack of interest in negotiating politically surprised her. She repeatedly used the loaded term "sect" to underscore the difference, and communal separation, of the Pennsylvania groups. Although the groups she described did not use the term sect, it gave to her readers the impression of a small devoted community breaking away from the mainstream and living totally, maybe fanatically, within their faith.

Gibbons gave special attention to Amish and Mennonites and related their lives to the pursuit of plainness. She saw its manifestation in everything they did and the traditions they kept, including dress, transportation, and architecture. She also recognized the religious worlds within a world often retrievable only with reference to an insider's view. Here is the anecdote she gave to demonstrate this: "It is said that a person once asked an Amish man the difference between themselves and another Mennist sect. 'Vy, dey vears puttons, and ve vearsh hooks oont eyes;' and this is, in fact, a prime difference" (Gibbons 1882, 15). Don Yoder later used this connection of dress and sect to draw attention to "sectarian costume" research in the United States (1969). When he revised it for the textbook *Folklore and Folklife* (1972), edited by Richard Dorson, the material, a survey of dress used by sectarian groups mostly in Pennsylvania, became "folk costume."

Other early surveys of Pennsylvania featured religious sectarianism as a feature of Pennsylvania ethnicity. Oscar Kuhns in 1901 devoted a chapter of his *The German and Swiss Settlements of Colonial Pennsylvania* (1901) to Pennsylvania religions and offered the impression that Pennsylvania's Germans lived essentially in sectarian and church communities. Jesse Rosenberger's *The Pennsylvania Germans* (1923) gave a more even-handed account, but nonetheless spread the message that most of the Pennsylvania Germans "were possessed of strong religious convictions which dominated their lives, while the general character of all may be said to have been religious" (69). He devoted a separate chapter to the Mennonites as providing "a somewhat interesting additional distinctiveness in their religious history and characteristics" (Rosenberger 1923, 86). In a supplement to the popular volume in 1929, Rosenberger further conveyed an image of sectarian proliferation: "the number of sects first represented has since been considerably increased by schisms and by the formation of new sects, for the creation of which the Pennsylvania Germans have at all times shown somewhat of a propensity" (Rosenberger 1929, 27). If Pennsylvania became known in regional literature for its German stamp and general plurality of nationality groups, it also became specially associated with a growing number of ethnic sectarian communities tied to the land. This image defied the expectation of diminishing ethnic separation on the American landscape with the advent of industrialization.

THE CELEBRATION OF DECORATIVE AND PREINDUSTRIAL ARTS

The paradox of Pennsylvania's reputation for the heights of American industrialization and rural life owes to the lateness of settlement to the region relative to migration to the South and New England. The latecomers looking for land moved into Pennsylvania highlands because of the impression that other, more desirable lands had been taken. The highland settlement allowed for the isolation of homogeneous agricultural communities. With the spread of the population inland, demands for transportation and consumption increased. The lateness of settlement also encouraged the rapid introduction of industrialism that began sweeping Europe in the eighteenth century into the port of Philadelphia. Fisher believed that Pennsylvania's reputation for tolerance also contributed to the acceptance of innovation in the region (Fisher 1896). The same immigrants that brought masterful craft skills to the United States found themselves highly sought after by the growing numbers of manufacturers in Philadelphia and its outskirts. By the 1790s, more than one-third of all exports of the United States came from Philadelphia. In 1795, Oliver Evans introduced his automated gristmill in the Philadelphia area; to the amazement of the public, the mill received raw material and delivered a finished product on a large scale with little human intervention. Similar transformations were occurring in the printing, cloth, leather, and iron industries. The American factory system took shape in these technological advancements.

Artisans and small farm operations, a mainstay of the Philadelphia economy for more than a century, felt squeezed out by more mills and iron furnaces. By 1800 at least 167 furnaces and forges had been established in Philadelphia. By the early nineteenth century Philadelphia led the nation in manufacturing and population.

Pennsylvania's populations, especially its German settlers, were known for their hardy practicality bred by the challenge of agricultural life often under rough conditions. Out of this tradition, Pennsylvanians offered the nation the Conestoga Wagon and the Pennsylvania Rifle, known for their durability, efficiency, and economy. The German bank barns, fixtures on the Pennsylvania landscape, had an Old World look, but were admired for their efficiency. Larger than English barns, the bank barns used the hillsides for extra support and created extended space on the second level with an overhanging forebay. The forebay additionally served to protect livestock and equipment underneath (Glass 1986; Ensminger 1992). As practical as they were, the Pennsylvania Germans also conspicuously displayed signs of decoration and belief, and defied expectations that the poor folk lacked a developed, indeed boisterous, sense of art. Builders formed ventilation holes in the second level in geometric and natural shapes; elaborate weather vanes graced the tops of the barns; "hex" signs colorfully marked the front of the barn. The elaborate, colorful decoration featured motifs of ethnically distinctive tulips, birds, swirls, and hearts which added symbolic meanings of good fortune to the equipment of agriculture and farm living. They also seemed to certify the ethnic masterwork of practicality by covering in distinctive designs that drew attention to the value of the utilitarian object. To be sure, decoration often indicated a maker's cultural insignia and background, but it also marked the object as one made to last and to be cared for. This approach to the built environment carried over into the household, where rugs, quilts, towels, coverlets, documents, stoves, and furniture carried decorative flourishes. Even after the landscape appeared more industrial, the domestic interior perpetuated traditional arts, and the hearth and bed became dominant symbols of traditional ethnic life in Pennsylvania.

Awareness of a "folklife" in Pennsylvania emerged in recognition of the force of industrial change in the region, and in celebration of the domestic domains of rural stability. One can look to some of the nation's first folklife collections to see these influences on the attention to preindustrial and decorative arts. John Fanning Watson created a stir in the early nineteenth century, for example, by publishing his *Annals of Philadelphia and Pennsylvania in the Olden Time* (1830), in which he romantically recorded accounts of proud artisans. He claimed that during his lifetime great changes had occurred in the lives of the artisans. "In less than twenty years," wrote Watson, "our exports have grown from twenty to eighty millions.... Our inventions and improvements in the arts, which began but yesterday, make us, even now, 'a wonder unto many'" (Watson 1857, 2). Thus he sought to document the handskills of the aged before their proud traditions associated with the bonds of community and spirit passed. He recorded the reminiscences of wheelwrights, blacksmiths, and furniture makers. Many of these preindustrial arts did not disappear, as Watson feared, but the belief that their extinction was imminent, coupled with the assumption that Pennsylvania's conservative rural German settlers preserved the old ways, guided the hunt for traditional arts for many years to come. Indeed, the use of the term "folk art" and the decorative arts it described during the late nineteenth century were particularly associated with Pennsylvania researchers before the term became generally popular in American studies during the 1930s (Robacker 1959; de Jonge 1972; see also Bronner 1984a).

A pivotal figure in the late nineteenth-century boom of interest in preindustrial and decorative arts was Henry Mercer of Doylestown, Pennsylvania. Repeating some of Watson's rhetoric, Mercer claimed that "mechanical improvements in human handicraft at the beginning of the nineteenth century have suddenly transformed the American farmer from a pioneer relying for equipment upon his own skill and industry to a husbandman abundantly supplied with labor-saving devices." For Mercer, the value of preserving the old crafts was that "they gave us a fresh grasp upon the vitality of the American beginning" (Mercer [1897] 1987, 281). Himself an industrialist, Mercer nonetheless appreciated the integrity of handwork and its closeness to nature. In 1897, he installed a splashy exhibition of Pennsylvania folk crafts and arts entitled *Tools of the Nation Maker*, and followed with essays on fraktur, log houses, and decorated stove plates. Inspired by the establishment of Skansen, an outdoor folk museum in Sweden, Mercer then began building his dream of a folklife museum to house the collection and re-create the setting of preindustrial life, now known as the Mercer Museum. His collection was not alone, as indicated by the publication of F. J. F. Schantz's *The Domestic Life and Characteristics of the Pennsylvania-German Pioneer* (1900) and, later, the famed collection of the Landis brothers which led to the establishment of the Pennsylvania Farm Museum near Lancaster, Pennsylvania (Landis 1939, 1945; Cary 1989).

In answer to the historical tendency to neglect ethnic communities altogether or their culture to local history, Mercer had this argument: "in the largest sense the store of Eastern Pennsylvania and of its Bucks county is that of the whole Nation" (Mercer 1987, 282). He pointed out that Pennsylvania stood for the beginning of the country because it acted as middleman between the Old World and New. As a busy, mixed thoroughfare to the West, he opined, Pennsylvania laid claim to the cultural hearth of the largest part of the country. Tradition is especially prevalent here, he thought, because the "American pioneer" here more than elsewhere, "thrown for a time upon his own resources, turns back to conditions more primitive than those left behind in the Old World" (Mercer 1987, 282). He viewed this factor, together with the geographic and ethnic isolation of the region, contributing to the persistence of a folk culture on American soil. He gave special emphasis to the communal formations of the Germans in Pennsylvania: "the collection has been made in an old settled region, half Germanized one hundred years ago, and including to the northward a district where fixed conditions, having escaped the encroachments of railways, die slowly. Here in Bucks county, rather than in Dutch New York, Puritan New England, or the more decidedly English or French regions of the South, we might expect to trace readily the leaven of various trans-Atlantic ingredients of nationality which by degrees should be detected amongst a group of objects fashioned by English, Irish, Welsh, Dutch or German hands" (Mercer 1987, 282).

THE COMMUNITY EMPHASIS

In Pennsylvania, the idea of community is a material, not abstract, concept. When Pennsylvanians talk about community, they are talking about their towns and ethnic settlements (Zelinsky 1977; Hopple 1971–1972). Just travel the old pike in Central Pennsylvania from Harrisburg to Carlisle, a distance under twenty miles, and you can go through a dozen towns. There is no thought here of incorporating into a larger unit, as cities in the Midwest have done. And residents maintain fierce loyalties to their small towns, manifested in Old Home Days, local historical societies, and town festivals. Another indication is that residents still identify where they live by the small town name rather than the larger urban center around which it may revolve. Investigating the historical roots of this town identity, geographer Wilbur Zelinsky determined that the process of town founding advanced more vigorously in eighteenth-century southeastern and central Pennsylvania than over any other extended tract in British North America.

The Pennsylvania town has several distinctive characteristics. One peculiarity, when compared to other American regions, is the tightness of the settlements. Residences are built close together and close to the street, and as Zelinsky found, this tendency "appears in those attenuated one- or two-street villages that straggle far into the countryside" (1977, 127). Unlike town plans elsewhere, Pennsylvania towns often mix dwellings, shops, and offices in a single area and relegate churches, cemeteries, and schools to peripheral locations. Other common features in the Pennsylvania town are the diamond or square, often where a public market once stood, and a network of attractive alleys running through the town. Similar to many settlements in Germany, the compactness of the towns provides a contrast to sprawling outlying areas of farmland or woods that are kept fairly pristine. The effect is to attain an "urbane intimacy and lively visual variety" in town while maintaining a pastoral landscape on its outskirts. This pattern reflects the varied settlement characteristic of the plural sectarian society that originally came into Pennsylvania and fosters the bonds of traditions working in tightly knit communities. Part of the reason that folklife is associated with these communities is the location of crafts and services in each town. The compact town commonly featured blacksmiths, wheelwrights, tinsmiths, and other craftsworkers along the main street in addition to the farmers who brought crafts to sell at market. The profusion of towns throughout the landscape encouraged the establishment of many craft services and apprentice traditions through Pennsylvania. Documentation of crafts in

Pennsylvania was often a way to recall town life and the quality of goods found within one's town. It also spoke to the speculation that along with industrial change, urbanization threatened Pennsylvania's customary folklife revolving around the almost-communal towns. Traditional arts particularly showed local variation, and projected an "intimacy and lively visual variety" reminiscent of the towns.

Hence, local study of folklife and history has been strong in Pennsylvania. Watson's *Annals*, reprinted in many editions to the end of the nineteenth century, was an influence on the efforts to record folk traditions as part of town histories in Pennsylvania. The guide for study published in 1893 by the Philadelphia chapter of the American Folklore Society made the emphasis of community explicit. It urged the study of "usages of a community which are peculiar to itself, and which, taken together, constitute its individuality when compared with other communities." Henry Mercer's fame as a precursor of American folklife studies was indeed based on the study of his beloved Doylestown and surrounding towns in Bucks County for the Bucks County Historical Society. In this light, with the community holding the key to tradition and creative expression, one might better understand his particularly Pennsylvanian boast in 1897 that when considering folk crafts, "we need not look so far ahead to imagine the time when if we do anything like our duty, the student of these things, whoever he may be, will not go to Washington, Boston, New York, Chicago, or anywhere else in the country to study American history from this fresh point of view, but will be compelled to come to Doylestown" (Mercer 1987, 289).

The communities of Pennsylvania relate well to one another partly because of ethnic connections and the paths of transportation that tied the state into a region. Unlike the pattern in other states, migration from the eastern port of entry, namely Philadelphia, tended to stay within state lines. A reason, then, for the attention to arts particularly framed by Pennsylvania is that the state demarcates cultural as well as political lines. The Pennsylvania-German influence dips down below the Mason-Dixon line into north-central Maryland and northwestern Virginia, and north-central Pennsylvania bears a New England stamp, but generally the state uniquely represents a cultural region tucked between the older regions of New England and the South (Glassie 1968; Zelinsky 1973; Gastil 1975).

Affecting the construction of folklife in America as the description of a total way of life was the presence of distinctive religious communities described as sects and experimental societies. They were characterized as isolable subcultures with linked features of language, dress, occupation, custom, foodways, architecture, and craft. In addition to the "plain" sects such as the Amish, Dunkers, and River Brethren were enclosed societies such as Ephrata in eastern Pennsylvania and Harmony in western Pennsylvania. These settlements became American models for the "folk society" of the "little community" described by Robert Redfield in Mexico as a rural subculture within the modern state. Redfield offered its characteristics as "distinctiveness, smallness, homogeneity, and all-providing self-sufficiency" (Redfield 1950, 4; see also Loomis and Beegle 1951). John Hostetler

used this view of an "intimate, face-to-face" community tied to the land to organize his often-reprinted *Amish Society* (1963). Alfred Shoemaker isolated the
Amish and Mennonites as folk communities among the Pennsylvania Germans,
and placed them within the settlement landscape of the region: "The Amish and
'Team' Mennonite farms cluster around Garden Spot villages with such arresting
names as Bird-in-Hand, Intercourse, and Blue Ball. The Amish, who own some of
the richest farmland in America, and the less prosperous 'Team' Mennonites, who
for the most part inhabit the hill land, believe to a man that God has but one plan
for them: to till His acres and be non-conformers in the world which *man* has created" (Shoemaker 1959c; see also Smith 1961). The "little community" of the
Amish, the subject of Shoemaker's dissertation work, seemed appropriate to application of European folklife methods used for peasant communities.

THE EMERGENCE OF FOLKLIFE

The close integration of language, art, and custom in the ethnic and sectarian
enclaves of Pennsylvania suggested to many nineteenth-century chroniclers an
approach that examined traditional arts within the life of Pennsylvania's distinctive communities and regions. They saw the arts as part of the daily round of life
and an expression of the cultural inheritance maintained in the New World experience. Contributing to the appropriateness of this approach to Pennsylvania was
the influence of German ethnological methods which were widely read in German
intellectual circles in Pennsylvania academies (Yoder 1963). Early in the nineteenth
century, Christian Heinrich Niemann of Kiel in his journal *Schleswig-Holsteinische
Volkskunde* published a forty page questionnaire to show his method of assem-
bling a systematic description of a community or region (Jacobeit 1991, 70–71).
Wolfgang Jacobeit reflected that it was "one of the first attempts at interdisciplinary cooperation for a comprehensive investigation of an area and its people," and
it was appropriate to German-speaking areas known for their distinct regionalism
in language, arts, and architecture. Later questionnaires expanded the concern to a
connection of a people made separate by their work as well as by their land. The
essential components of an alternative to the Grimms' linguistic study of oral tradition as a type of literature had formed in this approach. It would emphasize the
observable behavior in daily life of a group or community, integration of its customs and crafts, and social function of its traditions. It fundamentally understood
traditions as ways of life that contribute to formation of separate identities, and it
asked how those traditions are maintained and adapted by the group. Its political
importance was that it supported the integrity of small communities against larger forces—national, industrial, and cultural—that would engulf them.

The appeal of folklife as a rhetoric of social difference became noticeable in the
literary work of Pennsylvania resident Ludwig August Wollenweber (1807–1888),
who published *Gemälde aus dem Pennsylvanischen Volksleben* (Pictures of

Pennsylvania Folklife) in Philadelphia and Leipzig in 1869. Wollenweber was a political refugee from the Rhenish Palatinate during the 1830s and settled in Philadelphia, and later further inland in central Pennsylvania. He founded and edited the *Philadelphische Demokrat* in 1839 and became an advocate for Pennsylvania-German welfare. In his opening line of *Gemälde* he emphasized "das Land und die Leut," the connection of people to a place and the separate identity and tradition they, that is Pennsylvania Germans, gain from it. He arranged beliefs by the season in which they were appropriate, and thus showed that they functioned within a round of daily life related to agricultural communities in the inland Pennsylvania-German region. In vignettes such as *Farmleben* or "farmlife" he submitted that the Pennsylvania Germans had established a separate tradition within the United States, but not without struggle (see Robacker 1943, 1034). Some of this tribulation is especially evident in his saga of *Die Berg Maria* (Mountain Mary, 1880), in which he wrote the opinion that the Pennsylvania Dutch fought in the Revolutionary War to throw off British tyranny so as to live their ethnic life freely.

There is a direct line from Wollenweber to later folklife scholars, for John Joseph Stoudt translated and introduced the Mountain Mary legend in 1974 as "the classical study of Pennsylvania Dutch life during the Revolutionary period" (Wollenweber 1974, 15). Phebe Gibbons included an English translation of Wollenweber's stories in her third edition of *"Pennsylvania Dutch," and Other Essays* in 1882. They provided reinforcement for her view of the distinctiveness of the Pennsylvania-German settlement. She emphasized the objectivity of the "life" she observed in her first paragraph: "I shall try to give from my own observation and familiar acquaintance, some account of the life of a people who are little known outside of the rural neighborhoods of their own State, who have much that is peculiar in their language, customs, and belief … " (Gibbons 1882, 11).

The theme of local separateness seen in folklife comes through an early, if not the first, American use of the term folklife. William Wells published "Folk-Life in German By-Ways" in the popular magazine *Scribner's Monthly* in 1873. Examining the very region of Hesse that the Brothers Grimm had made their case for a united voice of a national folk, Wells found more variation, and more persistence, among communities than the brothers.

> The German peasants form the most conservative communities in the world. Within a stone's throw of all the habits and customs of modern civilization, they will persistently maintain their speech, their costume, and their notions, both at work and at play. These differ also greatly in different regions, so that one can stand on a mountain summit, and look into valleys right and left, whose inhabitants wear different garbs, speak different dialects, and who, quite likely, may be of opposite faiths. These peculiarities are so marked that one well versed in folk-lore can divine among a score of men of different origin, the valley or the mountain range to which each one belongs. (Wells 1873, 590)

Wells advocated the localized study of folklife as opposed to the international study of folklore. "The study of German folk-life is therefore well-nigh exhaustless," he wrote, "and one who would do justice to it must choose some particular region, that its manners and customs may be considered apart" (Wells 1873, 590).

One German immigrant from Hesse who came to Pennsylvania and took up the study of folklife sounded a conciliation between ethnic community and national culture. Karl Knortz (1841–1918) was an educator and writer who believed that a national culture was inevitable in the United States but sought to involve plural, and especially German, influences on its formation (Assion 1988; Schamschula 1996). He appropriately published the first, even if slim, study of national folklife as *Zur amerikanischen Volkskunde* (On American Folklife, 1905). While making sweeping comments on American national character such as "Americans like to talk and they patiently listen to others, even when they talk about the most ridiculous things" and "The American wants to earn money in every situation," he also pointed out the persistence of sectarian German communities in Pennsylvania and Iowa (Knortz [1905] 1988, 42). He also paid attention to other ethnic "quarters" for Italians, Irish, and blacks that formed a distinctive community folklife. He contributed a methodological guide to folklife study as *Was ist Volkskunde und wie studiert man dieselbe?* (What is Folklife and How Does One Study That? 1900) in which he included questionnaires and suggested problems of interethnic relationships and acculturation as particular to the American scene (see also Knortz 1882; Schamschula 1996). Folklore was part of a larger study of *Volksleben*, or folklife, he urged, toward the understanding of social *Volkscharakters*, by which he meant the formation of collective identities (Knortz 1906, 3–5). If Knortz was not read widely in English, he had a measurable influence in German education circles that had a marked impact on American universities during the Gilded Age.

The University of Pennsylvania's German department became especially important in the connection of Pennsylvania-German language to folklife. Marion Dexter Learned (1857–1917), the chair of the department from 1895 to 1917, issued calls for systematic collection of folk cultural materials, and he mentored two mainstays of Pennsylvania-German folklife research—Preston Barba and Edwin Fogel. Fogel completed his dissertation on beliefs and superstitions of the Pennsylvania Germans under Learned, and offered it as a "serious attempt at putting into permanent form a phase of folk-life which will soon disappear into the background and thus be irretrievably lost" (Fogel 1915, iii). He credited Learned, "an inspiring leader," with allowing the study of folklife as a "chapter in the larger field of German American relations" and for encouraging an insider to study his own background. Learned became nationally known in scholarly circles for his views in his capacity as president of the Modern Language Association in 1909 and editor of *German-American Annals* from 1897 until 1917. As editor of a series of books called "Americana Germanica," Learned published Fogel's work alongside studies of the Harmony Society, Germans in Texas, and German Creoles in Louisiana.

Of special significance in spreading academic awareness of Pennsylvania's ethnic communities, Learned planned and published the first American ethnographic survey in the United States dealing with European rather than American Indian cultures (Learned 1907, 1911). Called the American Ethnographical Survey, it surveyed the Conestoga Valley, mostly in Lancaster County, for a range of folk cultural material, including language, architecture, and craft. It was notable, too, for its attention to localized group identity and its manifestation in thriving cultural forms (Learned 1903). The "culture census," as Learned sometimes referred to his survey, connected folklife with the method of ethnography, and according to Don Yoder, earned Learned the reputation of "one of the pioneers of the folklife studies movement in the United States" (Yoder 1971, 73; see also Old Penn 1911).

I could discuss other figures such as William Julius Mann, John Baer Stoudt, E. L. Grumbine, and Walter James Hoffman, all who contributed to a consciousness of Pennsylvania folk around the turn of the nineteenth century (Robacker 1943, 144–69; Mann 1880; Stoudt 1915; Grumbine 1905; Hoffman 1888). The upshot is that inspired by German ethnological methods and a political concern for the integrity of German communal life in America, Pennsylvania-German writers and students of language and culture developed a special approach toward folklife in Pennsylvania. Most of the writers had a connection to the Pennsylvania-German Society formed in 1891 with the intention of interpreting the group's folklife together with its history and literature. The folklife approach in Pennsylvania differed from the British-inspired approach prevalent in the American Folklore Society, formed in 1888. The folklore approach considered oral traditions separately from material traditions, and compared cross-culturally, rather than in the context of a single community or culture, to compile an evolution of the tradition's development.

The distinctiveness of the Pennsylvania, and especially Pennsylvania-German, scholar's approach helps explain the relative independence of Pennsylvania folklife studies from the main movements of American folklore study until the late twentieth century. Study of tradition in Pennsylvania stressed crafts and customs as part of folk tradition, and related them to social and oral parts of a community or regional culture. A sign of this emphasis to American folklorists came in 1888 with the first volume of the American Folklore Society's *Journal of American Folklore*. In it, Walter James Hoffman published "Folklore of the Pennsylvania Germans," in which he described flax raising, barn design, marriage custom, foodways, and quilting parties all related to the cultural history of Pennsylvanians around his native Reading. Work on German communities in America suffered with the rise of anti-German feeling in the United States during World Wars I and II. The *Journal of American Folklore* contained twenty articles on German Americans before World War I, and did not publish another one until 1931. The Pennsylvania-German Folklore Society formed in 1936 and published several volumes on folk crafts and arts, but it received scant attention from the American

Folklore Society, probably because the academics of the American society perceived it to be of regional or parochial rather than national interest. Indeed, the self-concerned tone of the introduction to the Pennsylvania-German Folklore Society may have sounded exclusive and hardly objective: "the sphere of this Society is, of course, ethnological seeking to record permanently the folk-mind *of our own people*. History, as such, is therefore to be subordinated, the main emphasis falling upon the cultural aspects of Pennsylvania German life" (emphasis added; Yoder 1971, 81–82).

Up until World War II, leading lights of Pennsylvania-German cultural studies such as Preston Barba, Thomas Brendle, John Joseph Stoudt, and Edwin Fogel barely received notice in folkloristic circles, although they published extensively on folk art, belief, and speech. To be sure, they were self-conscious about their scholarly contribution, but their main publishing outlets were within Pennsylvania-German societies, and few of them held major academic positions (Yoder 1971; see also Beam 1995). When tourist interest moved John Joseph Stoudt's cultural history of Pennsylvania Germans into wide circulation, he editorialized in his preface: "Pennsylvania Germans have been orphans in American studies.... The main barrier to better understanding has been language. Pennsylvania Dutch culture has been viewed as 'strange' and 'foreign' by authorities in American studies. The field has no academic home, for it belongs neither to German nor to history departments. Some rubricate it with folklore" (Stoudt 1973, 9). Aware of the academic trends mentioned by Stoudt and still loyal to Pennsylvania-German folklife, the young and brash Alfred Shoemaker took it upon himself to change the intellectual landscape of tradition in America.

THE CREATION OF THE FIRST DEPARTMENT OF FOLKLORE

The University of North Carolina at Chapel Hill is usually credited with the establishment of the first academic "curriculum" of folklore in 1939. Led by Ralph Steele Boggs, the curriculum contained nine courses taught by six professors from five different departments, making it possible for a folklore major toward the M.A. or a minor toward the Ph.D. (Boggs 1940, 95–96). In 1948 Stith Thompson established an interdepartmental program at Indiana University at Bloomington, which awarded its first Ph.D. to Warren Roberts in 1953. It was not until 1963 that Richard Dorson inaugurated the folklore department at Indiana. By using the term "department" Dorson argued that folklore joined the higher ranks of other disciplines. Folklore then took its rightful place as a distinctive study, not just an amalgamation of many studies. Pragmatically, it served as a budgeted power base to promote folklore studies at the undergraduate as well as graduate levels, spread course requirements on cultural studies, and fund graduate students.

Dorson's original appointment at Indiana University in 1957 was to chair what was then called "the committee on folklore." According to Dorson, when he came

… some half-dozen graduate students were seeking higher degrees in folklore. The courses they took originated almost entirely with established departments. That is, the course on the English and Scottish popular ballad belonged to the English department and would be cross-listed under Folklore. In effect, the folklore program simply drew upon the existing faculty and curricular resources of the university. I myself was budgeted full-time in the history department, and all the members of the folklore committee were budgeted in their respective departments of anthropology, English, Spanish, and so on. By such means the university cautiously launched new programs with a minimum of outlay. The programs might grow into departments, remain indefinitely in a limbo status, or wither away. They had to prove their vitality. (Dorson 1976c, 113–14)

"Vitality" at North Carolina and Indiana had an academic definition taking in numbers of students, faculty, and courses. Public outreach (in the way of festivals, museums, or centers) was not part of this strategy. Courses at North Carolina and Indiana stressed literary *forms* of folklore (ballad, epic, narrative) and their offerings crossed ethnic and national lines. When they covered the American scene, they emphasized the British inheritance. According to Boggs's survey, most folklore courses appeared in English departments, and the most common subject was English and American ballad (1940, 97).[1]

The approach at Franklin and Marshall, set in the heart of the "Pennsylvania Dutch" country, was different. Its emphasis on the integrated traditions of diverse ethnic-regional *groups* that formed local cultures within America had a relation to the ethnic-regional roots of the college. A small liberal arts college with ties to the German Reformed Church and Pennsylvania-German scholarship, it had for decades promoted teaching and research in local culture. One notable figure at the college was the Reverend Joseph Henry Dubbs (1838–1910, F&M class of 1856), Audenried professor of history and archaeology, who served as president of the Pennsylvania-German Society and wrote on folklore of the Pennsylvania Germans ("Dr." 1910; Yoder 1949, 5). When Dubbs died, none other than the college president, also a past president of the Pennsylvania-German Society, wrote a tear-jerking appreciation in *The Pennsylvania-German*. Franklin and Marshall's president spotlighted Dubbs's concern for local traditions which complemented the college's mission: "His knowledge of the founding of Pennsylvania, the early settlements of the German and the Scotch Irish, the planting of the first churches, and the development of the different religious denominations in this state was accurate, minute, and thorough, and there are few who will vie with him in this respect, and few, alas! who are qualified to receive his mantle" (Stahr 1910, 421).

H. M. J. Klein later filled Dubbs's chair and wrote on the folk customs of the Amish (1946). Dubbs's granddaughter, Elizabeth Clarke Kieffer, was on staff as reference librarian during the 1940s and 1950s and worked closely with the Pennsylvania-German collection. Edwin M. Hartman, headmaster of the Franklin and Marshall Academy connected to the college, chaired the organizing meeting of the Pennsylvania-German Folklore Society in 1936 (see Ziegler 1943, 182–83). The strong connection to the Pennsylvania-German culture made sense. Most of the students came from the region and many spoke Pennsylvania German as well as appreciating its folkways. When Theodore Distler (of German, if not Pennsylvania-German ancestry) came from Lafayette College to become president of Franklin and Marshall in 1941, he continued the legacy by supporting a strong German department, and in 1944, appointing J. William Frey its chair.

Frey, a Pennsylvania German, received his Ph.D. at the University of Illinois, where he completed a dissertation on the Pennsylvania-German dialect in eastern York County of Pennsylvania. He had studied comparative philology in Germany, and besides mastering dialects of German, he developed capabilities in at least fifteen other languages (see Beam 1981, xiii). Codirector of the Pennsylvania-German Folklore Society, Frey had a special love for folklore and folk song, and frequently entertained publicly using his native Pennsylvania-German folk song repertoire. When he returned to the United States he relied on his folklore collecting experience among the Pennsylvania Germans for dialect columns in York County newspapers, commercial recordings, and radio shows. Beginning in 1943, he edited and published *Der Pennsylvaanisch Deitsch Eileschpiggel*, taking its name from a folktale trickster figure in Pennsylvania-German lore. Begun at Lehigh University and later continued at Franklin and Marshall, the periodical was a miscellany of Pennsylvania-German folklore, fiction, poetry, history, bibliography, news, and commentary. Frey also contributed to scholarship with a chapter of *Pennsylvania Songs and Legends* on Amish folk music (1949) and a book-length grammar of Pennsylvania German (1942).

Frey and Distler, with the help of library director Herbert B. Anstaett, had an unusual opportunity to develop Pennsylvania-German folklore scholarship at Franklin and Marshall when Harvey Bassler donated a massive collection, forty-five tons in all, of rare books, pamphlets, fraktur, and prints, much of it obtained from indefatigable Pennsylvania-German collector Charles Unger of Pottsville, Pennsylvania (Yoder 1983, 11; Faill 1987, 5). On October 21, 1946, Distler wrote to the Reverend William Rupp of the Pennsylvania-German Society assuring him that the college would house the collection on the third floor of the Fackenthal Library, named after a former president of the Pennsylvania-German Society and a trustee of the college. Thinking of appropriate scholars to work with the collection, Distler in 1948 tapped Alfred Shoemaker. Frey had known Shoemaker at Illinois and Distler had previously hired him for the German department at Lafayette College. Another figure working with the collection, Don Yoder, joined the religion department as instructor in 1949. A Franklin and Marshall alumnus (class of 1942), Yoder had received his Ph.D. in 1947 from the University of Chicago. Both Shoemaker and Yoder had been involved with the Pennsylvania-German Folklore Society. The acquisition of the collection and faculty interest in folklore set the stage for the creation of the department of American folklore.

Other developments in Pennsylvania during the late 1940s supported academic and public interest in folklore. The Pennsylvania Historical and Museum Commission began a folklore division in 1948 and named Henry Shoemaker the nation's first state folklorist. Philadelphia was home to the American Folklore Society, and in 1944, the city hosted the society's annual meeting. In addition to claiming the Pennsylvania-German Folklore Society, the state also boasted a Pennsylvania Folklore Society, headed by Henry Shoemaker, and even a Harrisburg Folklore Society (H. Shoemaker 1943, 180–81). Folk festivals abounded in Pennsylvania. Bucknell University's George Korson produced successful festivals through the 1930s, Philadelphia provided the backdrop for the National Folk Festival for a number of years, and the Harrisburg Folklore Society hosted an annual summer festival (see Gillespie 1980; H. Shoemaker 1943, 181). Henry Landis meanwhile promoted the folk museum movement, based on European folklife models, with his open-air collection of Pennsylvania-German buildings, tools, and crafts near Lancaster (later to become the Pennsylvania Farm Museum and Landis Valley Museum).

Pennsylvania-German scholarship blossomed during the 1940s. Influential dissertations and studies on language and lore appeared by Albert Buffington, Alfred Shoemaker, J. William Frey, and Lester W. J. Seifert (Beam 1981, xvi; Weiser 1991, 22–23). Scholarly interest in Pennsylvania-German language and lore was connected to a longstanding academic tie between German studies and folklore. German language studies, with its legacy of folk narrative and linguistic research stretching back to the Brothers Grimm and others, used folklore extensively. In the United States, Archer Taylor and Wayland Hand, two leaders of the American folklore movement, for example, were Germanicists. Boggs's survey revealed that after English, folklore courses in the United States were most likely to be offered in anthropology and German studies.

Pennsylvania-German scholars often argued that the dialect had not received its due. They recognized that many German departments with elite views frowned upon the mongrel, even doggerel sounding Pennsylvania German. In response, many Pennsylvania-German scholars came to the academic study of folklore and culture, because they pointed out that the dialect's meaning and richness comes out in its cultural context, its use in folk expression such as proverbs and tales, and its adaptation to a new land with terms for buildings and implements. Folklore in the Dutch country, they pronounced, represented a great, often overlooked, artistic outpouring from a distinct regional culture (see Shoemaker 1954; Yoder 1990). This culture spread south, north, and west, and contributed to American culture generally (see Glassie 1968). American studies combining history and literature, however, usually emphasized the elite works that unified the country (see McDowell 1948a), although Richard Dorson loudly called for the integration of folklore studies within American civilization courses (Dorson 1950b, 346; see also Dorson 1971a, 78–93).

American studies developing among Pennsylvania scholars tended to accent the ethnic, regional, and religious mosaic of America (see Bronner 1989b; Yoder 1990). More than combining the literary and historical, Pennsylvania-German scholars working in American studies stressed cultural inheritance, especially within research on communities and groups, and the symbolic expressions of culture in material, social, and oral traditions. Colleges in Pennsylvania were among the pioneers of the American studies movement gaining speed during the 1940s. Indeed, years before, Penn State's Frederick Lewis Pattee, who counted folklore among his interests, became the first professor of American literature. Would it not make sense, then, to recognize American folklore with a professor bearing that title in the heart of a folk culture?

Enter Alfred L. Shoemaker. Franklin and Marshall hired Alfred L. Shoemaker as assistant professor of American folklore in 1948.[2] He also became head of the new "Department of American Folklore," which is first listed in the college catalogue for 1949–1950. Shoemaker's approach was to stress an ethnological approach to "folk culture." Shoemaker was well aware, indeed proud, that he was breaking new ground on the American scene. As he explained,

> In America most everybody interprets folklore to mean folktales, folksongs, rhymes, riddles—and little else.... However, those of us, like myself who have received our training in the folklore archives in Sweden and Ireland—the finest—do not share this narrow view. As far as we are concerned, folklore is the study of the material and intellectual culture of tradition-bound elements in our present-day societies. In addition to popular literature and popular beliefs and practices, folklore for us includes a study of our folk customs, games and pastimes, folk medicine, 'alda weverglawva' [Pennsylvania German term for folk beliefs], folk art, crafts, cookery, farms and farming and traditions—both mythological and historical. (Shoemaker 1949a, 1)

Shoemaker's approach and background coming into the discipline of folklore provides a contrast to other young leaders such as Dorson, Herbert Halpert, and Wayland Hand who emerged during this period. While they all founded academic homes for folkloristic study, Shoemaker charted his path toward the ethnographic study of folklife. More so than the other doyens of the field, Shoemaker put into practice an agenda for public presentations of folk culture. And perhaps because of that, and the appearance he gave of being on a crusade for his people, Shoemaker became more of an ethnic culture-hero.

Shoemaker was born in 1913 in Saegersville, Lehigh County, part of the Pennsylvania Dutch Country not far from Allentown. He grew up speaking Pennsylvania German and in high school joined a dramatic club that presented plays in Dutch and English using Pennsylvania folklife themes.[3] He attended Muhlenberg College in Pennsylvania (the common choice for Lutheran boys in the Dutch country), where he came under the influence of folklore professors and Pennsylvania-German specialists Preston Barba and Harry Reichard. According to a story circulating about Shoemaker's college days, an adviser casually suggested that Shoemaker educate himself beyond his coursework by reading. Shoemaker surprised the adviser later by reporting that he had read every book in the Muhlenberg College Library, and he wanted to know where he should go from there! Shoemaker was aware of the stigma that sometimes attached to a "Dutch accent," and he worked on his oration by reading aloud. He emerged from college with a flair for speech. As a later associate recalled, "his expression was magnificent, his manner impressive."[4] Dropping plans to become a Lutheran minister, he dedicated himself to the study of language and folk culture and championed the significance of Pennsylvania-German tradition.

After receiving his A.B. in 1934, Shoemaker studied in Europe, spending time at Munich, Heidelberg, Uppsala, and Lund, where he was exposed to folk-cultural research along ethnological lines. He returned to the United States to do graduate work at Cornell University and ended up majoring in German at the University of Illinois, known for its cultural as well as linguistic studies. The "Seminar in Deutsche Volkskunde" taught by Charles Williams was available in the German department, and folklore was a common subject of interest among Illinois graduate students (Boggs 1940, 101). Shoemaker received his Ph.D. from Illinois in 1940, completing a dissertation on the language and folklore of the Amish in Arthur, Illinois. Shoemaker's attention to social and cultural context of language distinguished the work. Applying his command of German dialects, Shoemaker served his country during World War II working for U.S. Army Intelligence in Europe. It was a traumatic experience, he later told friends, to see the wholesale destruction of precious cultures and intense violent hatred of peoples for one another, and it turned him toward pacifism (forced to carry a weapon, he carried it unloaded).[5]

Shoemaker poignantly referred to his wartime experience in an unusual place—a monograph on traditional rhymes and jingles of the Pennsylvania Dutch—intended for the general public.

> It was an evening during the war. My Counter Intelligence Corps team—three lawyers, a fellow college professor and myself—were stationed in Hayingen, a small industrial town in Lorraine. A mile or two away, across on the other side of the Moselle, the Germans lay entrenched. It was the long lull—those weary months of waiting—before the final offensive that carried our troops across the Rhine and brought an end to hostilities in Europe.
>
> From Hayingen, where we lay, and from the country 30 or 50 miles to the east, there had come, over 200 years before, the forebears of the Pennsylvania Dutch. They had left, weary of war and strife, to find peace and happiness in Penn's woods. And I, two centuries later, realized for the first time how strong must have been their longing to leave those parts for a better world—for the hills of the Lehigh, the Schuylkill and the Susquehanna.
>
> There was artillery fire overhead. I longed feverishly for a book—a book which would translate me into another world, one free of hatred and slaughter. And it was

then, that moment, that I came, quite by chance, upon a 38-page booklet, "77 Nursery Rhymes for Our Little Ones." It was in German, of course. I turned the pages nervously. There were the identical rhymes I had learned as a child from my own Pennsylvania Dutch grandmother. Deep emotions welled up within me.... (Shoemaker 1951, 3)

Shoemaker related himself in war to the experience that propelled a social movement to Pennsylvania, a Pax Americana in his mind. He used folklore (some may even say lost himself in it) to express the continuity of culture and something of the essence of his group's experience. Although the rhymes inspired questions for him of origin and diffusion, the "most important" he wrote, was "to what degree are these traditional rhymes a reflection of man's inner self?" (Shoemaker 1951, 16). This questioning of folklore's relation to self and society owed, he sometimes said, to his strange position in the army as an American with a subcultural identity of Pennsylvania-German background fighting Germans. In this regard, Shoemaker recounted on occasion his profound, yet disturbing, experience as a prisoner of war. While imprisoned he had friendly relations with a German commander who had been an ethnologist before the war. Their discussions of culture and folklife, the similarities and differences of their traditions, seemed to him to lift them away from the war. Shoemaker reported going into a deep depression when the commander was killed.[6]

Shoemaker spent summers after the war studying at the Irish Folklore Commission in Dublin and the Folklore Institute in Basel, Switzerland. These institutions offered him models for the systematic coverage of folk cultures, models he would later apply in Pennsylvania. A wealth of formal education and folk experience behind him, an insatiable thirst for books and field projects, an energy and charisma that suggested innovative leadership, Shoemaker attracted admirers among scholars and ordinary folk alike. Loud and boisterous, even crude outside the university, studious in the library, he was a man to be noticed as an outlandish personality. Some of this reputation came from his often bombastic speaking style, and his unashamed demonstrations of his Pennsylvania-German folksiness, which rubbed against stereotypes of the university scholar at the time. Stories of his prodigious efforts at reading, working, and organizing added to his legendary standing. His friends remember him variously as "a man of the people" and "a scholar's scholar."

To drive home the point of Shoemaker's duality as ordinary folk and academic folklorist, the story is told about the ivory-tower scholar who came to check out the remarkable Alfred Shoemaker. Climbing the stairs to the solitary third floor of the library, he was directed to an isolated desk impressively piled high with books and papers so that the occupant looked literally buried in his work. The visitor glowed with the idea of approaching a monastic scholar of the highest order. The visitor suffered a shock, however, when he spied Shoemaker, sporting a goatee on a folksy face, beaming behind the piles. As the visiting scholar told a colleague later,

"I expected a scholar, and I found a billy goat." "That's all right," Shoemaker supposedly remarked on hearing of the comment, "at least he'll remember me."[7] Beyond this suggestion of complexity to Shoemaker's personality, other traits found expression in adjectives used by former associates to describe Shoemaker: dynamic ("he was going to make things happen, you could tell"), tireless ("doing, he was always doing"), modest ("that was his Pennsylvania Dutch side coming in"), trusting ("too much so"), zealous, brilliant, visionary, idealistic, altruistic, outspoken, impatient, sensitive, and devoted.

Before coming to Franklin and Marshall, Shoemaker taught German at Lafayette and Muhlenberg colleges, and in 1947 became curator of the Berks County Historical Society in Reading. The *Journal of American Folklore* carried the news of his curatorial position with the commentary: "Dr. Shoemaker, a folklorist as well as an historical scholar, like Dr. Louis C. Jones of the New York [State] Historical Association, is keenly interested in the role which historical societies may play in the recovery and study of traditional culture" ("Historical" 1947, 425). In addition to his other duties, Shoemaker hosted a radio show in the Pennsylvania German dialect where he related folk narratives and wrote a column on regional culture for the Lancaster daily.

Shoemaker's first courses at Franklin and Marshall, according to a newspaper clipping in the college archives, were on the folklore of Southeast Pennsylvania and Pennsylvania Dutch folklore (September 29, 1948). Appealing to the public, Shoemaker taught the courses during the evening. Other courses taught by Shoemaker—Introduction to Folklore, General American and European Folklore—along with a mention of the department were announced in the *Journal of American Folklore* ("Folklore" 1949, 66).

The Franklin and Marshall catalogue gave the department its own listing under the heading "Folklore," with the following description:

> The aim of the Department of American Folklore is to give the student an understanding and an appreciation of the material and intellectual culture of tradition-bound elements within our American society. The courses in folklore will treat the following subject matter: popular oral literature, popular beliefs and customs, folk art and crafts, folk medicine, sports and pastimes, settlement and dwelling, folk speech, mythological and historical traditions, livelihood and household support, communication and trade, and the festivals of the year.

The courses covered folklore research in Europe and America, required fieldwork, and featured material and social traditions in a regional, ethnic, and community context. An unusual offering within the list for a folklore curriculum was a course on folk art.[8]

> 11. Introduction to Folklore. A survey of the beginnings in folklore research in Europe and America; the operation of folklore institutes and archives; theories and methods; the historical, geographical, sociological and psychological aspects of the subject.

12. General American and European Folklore. A survey course, comparative in nature, covering particularly the lore of groups in our American society, such as cowboys and lumberjacks. The American folksong will be studied in particular.

13. Folklore of Southeastern Pennsylvania. Particular emphasis on the folklore of the Pennsylvania Dutch. A course in folklore methods and techniques. A term report, based on field work, will be required of each student.

14. Pennsylvania Dutch Folklore. This course stresses popular oral literature (folktales, proverbs, riddles) and collecting techniques. A fair knowledge of the Pennsylvania Dutch dialect is a prerequisite.

15. Pennsylvania Dutch Folk Art. A study of fractur, primitives, barn signs, decorated household furnishings and ornamental objects.

16. Pennsylvania Folk Literature in Standard German. A study of popular ballads, folksongs, proverbs and riddles and of popular literature as disseminated by Pennsylvania-printed German broadsides, pamphlets, almanacs, books and newspapers. Prerequisite, a year's study of German.

With these courses, all under the heading of folklore, Shoemaker could boast the first department of folklore in the United States, and more undergraduate courses with the folklore prefix than any other institution. He could even claim listing as many courses under folklore as those offered in the largest graduate curricula at Indiana, North Carolina, and UCLA (see Boggs 1940; Dorson 1950b).

With his department Shoemaker hoped to signal the academic respectability of folklore in the United States. He had witnessed the success of folk culture studies in European academe and thought that folklore studies as a discipline could be similarly established in the United States. Although he recognized that Stith Thompson was moving toward the creation of an academic program, he considered his approach too limited to hold student interest or carry scholarly weight. He also resisted Thompson's literary assumption that historical reconstruction could derive from an aggregate of library texts or the anthropological premise that objectivity could be achieved from observation of a culture radically different from the observer. He sought an academic platform from which to launch studies that could be relevant to the communities from which they came. His case for the department at Franklin and Marshall was to argue the benefits for involvement of students in an understanding and promotion of their own tradition. He considered a public role for folklife as a way to involve groups in their own study and spread the ideas of folklife into a public philosophy. That philosophy involved the importance of local and ethnic heritage to a realization of a cultural identity and an American self.

He joined Dorson in railing against Benjamin Botkin's use, or misuse, of folklore in the public arena, because he felt that Botkin served to confuse the public about what folklore is by jumbling together examples from non-folk sources with hardly any cultural context or interpretation. Shoemaker disagreed with Dorson, however, about whether Botkin's pandering signaled that academic scholarship

Alfred Shoemaker as he appeared in *The Pennsylvania Dutchman* publicizing the 1951 Pennsylvania Dutch Folk Festival. (Pennsylvania Folklife Society, Ursinus College)

and popular public presentation could not mix. Before the days of state and federal funding for folk arts programming, Shoemaker put into action an agenda for using scholarly premises in public folklife presentations. His programming included festivals, radio shows, bus tours, outdoor museums, and popular pamphlets. To put these plans for a public presence into action, Shoemaker conceived of a center, the Pennsylvania Dutch Folklore Center, responsible for public activities associated with the department, raising money privately, and as was his tendency, he had grand designs.

Joining Shoemaker, the charismatic driving force behind the Pennsylvania Dutch Folklore Center, were able associates in J. William Frey and Don Yoder. Together, they had an applied scholarly purpose in promoting and preserving the folk culture of the Pennsylvania Dutch (or "German") culture in central Pennsylvania. They sought to foster Pennsylvania Dutch identity and community, threatened by post-World War II mass culture and lingering anti-German sentiment. Their choice of the vernacular term "Pennsylvania Dutch" over the more "bookish" (as Yoder called it) "Pennsylvania German" was a sign of the center's populist spirit and perhaps an indication of the separation of this culture from the fatherland and the experience of other immigrant groups. "Truly," Shoemaker underscored in a letter dated May 30, 1949, seeking support from Henry Francis du Pont, "this is the first time and place which the Pennsylvania Dutch have had to express themselves and preserve their cultural values." With the marvelous resources of the Unger-Bassler collection as a base, the center had an ambitious program of publishing a weekly newspaper covering folk culture in the region, collecting questionnaires and maintaining a folk archives, constructing an outdoor folk museum, sponsoring "folk tours" of European source areas of Pennsylvania culture, and producing a popular folk festival—the Pennsylvania Dutch Folk Festival (later the Kutztown Folk Festival)—which became America's largest regional folk festival (see Yoder 1983). "The publication of our paper," Shoemaker boisterously declared, "is only ONE phase of our important work. We want to imitate the Irish and Swedish folklore commissions by collecting and cataloguing literally millions of items pertaining to every bit of our traditional cultural life in southeastern Pennsylvania! We shall leave no stones unturned! We want thousands of photographs, thousands of wire and disc recordings, files and files of folktales, rhymes, recipes, games, pow-wow cures, etc., etc., and the ultimate building of the Pennsylvania Dutch Library right here on this campus! To this we have dedicated our lives and energies. We three editors are all in the thirties" (see also Shoemaker 1957).

No stone unturned indeed: Shoemaker's demanding routine was to start at his office and library early in the morning, spend afternoons and early evenings recording interviews and documenting folklife and material culture around the region (he made use of wire recorders and cameras), and into the night return to his office where he did not turn in until two or three in the morning. In this way he

PENNSYLVANIA DUTCH FOLK FESTIVAL

By ALFRED L. SHOEMAKER

Our folk-culture on parade — that's what we mean by a Pennsylvania Dutch Folk Festival. *N gross wayss I* unst you'd call it in dialect.

Yes, and there will be four full days — July 1, 2, 3, 4 — on the fair grounds at Kutztown. Our Folklore Center is going to make this an annual affair.

Let me give you a quick summary of what all there will be.

Saturday, July 1—that's the first day of the Folk Festival—you'll see fifteen or twenty old-timers mowing a four-acre wheat field, with cradles of course. Two women will follow each one of the *self-mayers*, one of them for *uff-u-recha* and the other for *uff-tru-inna*. (And in case you have never

forget the experience of listening to folk singers like Maggie Frey, Happy Hen Hollenbach and half a dozen others. And what is more, this is the first full-time program of Pennsylvania Dutch folksongs ever. The second part of this evening is an hour's entertainment by the Pennsylvania Dutch entertainers of the air: *Assabae and Sabina, Die Wunnernaas, Pumpernickel Bill,* the Sunbury *Nisnuts* and *Der Rote Gase-bauer Schumacher.*

A Fendue

Monday is a full day, too. "It gives" a Pennsylvania Dutch *fendue*, the first thing in the afternoon. There will be all the trappings, even down to a *mischt-haufa* with a traditional game of *eck balla.* Come and pick up some

MEET PRESTON BARBA— *Editor of the "Eck"*

By DON YODER

In 1935 a vocal infant—destined to be heard far beyond the Lehigh Valley—first saw the light of day in Allentown. The newborn babe was a newspaper column in the Allentown *Morning Call* entitled 'S Pennsilfawnisch Deitsch...

The Pennsylvania Dutchman, June 15, 1950, in its second volume, when circulation soared to 7,500. Alfred Shoemaker's article on the Pennsylvania Dutch Folk Festival is on the front page.

earned the reputation of scouring both the library and the field with an unusual systematic thoroughness (hence the story about his preparing and organizing "millions" of cards on local folk customs and reading every book in the Muhlenberg College Library!).

The grand scope of the center's efforts, academic and applied, and Shoemaker's leadership are evident in the center's weekly publication, the *Pennsylvania Dutchman.* The first issue carrying the subtitle "The Weekly Devoted to Pennsylvania Dutch Culture" (later it became "Devoted to the Folk Culture of the Pennsylvania Dutch") appeared on May 5, 1949. It carried news of the folklore department at Franklin and Marshall on the front page, and under the heading "The Folklore Center and You," Shoemaker explained the paper's exalted mission: "We, the Pennsylvania Dutch, were taught for generations to despise and disrespect our traditional culture. The task that we of THE PENNSYLVANIA DUTCHMAN have set ourselves is to teach NOT hate, NOT disrespect, but UNDERSTANDING, APPRECIATION, and, most important of all, a LOVE FOR OUR HERITAGE" (Shoemaker 1949b, 3). The weekly newspaper began with a remarkable circulation of 12,500, and continued successfully as a quarterly magazine. Besides editing the folklore section of the *Dutchman,* Shoemaker contributed almost two hundred essays to the publication between 1949 and 1961. Focusing

Tourist guide produced in 1955 by Alfred Shoemaker and Don Yoder, featuring the Amish as the centerpiece to the folk cultural attraction of central Pennsylvania. The guide carried the imprint of the Pennsylvania Dutch Folklore Center, Franklin and Marshall College, Lancaster.

particularly on folk custom, material culture, and language, Shoemaker's essays (and festivals) often implied that folk culture so close to the life of the Pennsylvania Dutch and other groups, once an embarrassment in front of elitist eyes, should be a source of social pride and honor, artistry and inspiration.

Although devoted to Pennsylvania-German ethnicity, Shoemaker by 1950 had a vision that the center's publications and activities could expand into a national institute, an American folklife center, that would extend the folk cultural approach to other communities and regions.[9] The Pennsylvania Dutch Folk Festival, for example, became the Kutztown Folk Festival under Shoemaker's leadership, and he included field-researched displays of Welsh, Ukrainian, Irish, and Slavic communities in Pennsylvania. The festival featured many tents for educational presentations to accompany performances of folk culture. Applying a pluralistic model of America, Shoemaker wanted the expanded festival under the guidance of the scholarly center to invite the participation of the folk communities themselves as well as a place for outsiders to understand and enjoy the communities' authentic expressions. The timing of the festival around American Independence Day had a symbolic value for Pennsylvania Germans able to celebrate their ethnic culture as part of an American celebration.

"The Center," Don Yoder remembered, "was based on European models and its purposes included the collecting, archiving and disseminating of scholarly information on every aspect of the Pennsylvania German culture. In 1956, under the influence of the European *Volkskunde* and folklife (regional ethnology) movements, we changed the title of our organization to the Pennsylvania Folklife Society and the name of the periodical published by our society from the *Pennsylvania Dutchman* to *Pennsylvania Folklife*. In this way we felt that we might do justice to all of Pennsylvania's ethnic groups" (Yoder 1982, 18). The archives and journal eventually moved to Ursinus College in Collegeville, Pennsylvania, and Yoder, longtime editor of *Pennsylvania Folklife*, left for the University of Pennsylvania in 1956. After a few years, in 1963, Yoder taught for the freshly formed Department of Folklore and Folklife.

The use of terms such as folk culture and folklife to designate an ethnological approach to the study of cultural traditions in America thus had its beginnings at Franklin and Marshall. Don Yoder reflected that "the term 'folklife,' now used widely in American scholarship (at the American Folklife Center at the Library of Congress and Department of Folklore and Folklife ... at the University of Pennsylvania), was first used in the scholarly context at F&M.... 'Folklife' got around the built-in limitations of the British 'folklore' by including material culture and other aspects of the totality of the culture, as well as the verbal 'lore' with which folklorists have traditionally busied themselves." Remarking on the contributions of Shoemaker's classes in folklife, Yoder recalled that "students did field work, reporting on interviews with 'powwow doctors' (native folk healers) and other typically Pennsylvania Dutch phenomena" (Yoder 1983, 8). Vincent Tortora,

First issue of *Pennsylvania Folklife*, winter 1957–1958. Alfred Shoemaker was listed as managing editor. The issue, produced as a slick popular magazine, included an article by Alfred Shoemaker on New Year's "fantasticals." The cover story on traditional architecture was unusual for an American folklore publication at the time.

Advertisements for books by Alfred Shoemaker published by the Pennsylvania Folklife Society in the "Special 1960 Festival Issue" of *Pennsylvania Folklife*.

a student in Shoemaker's classes, added that Shoemaker's interests went beyond Dutch folklife to the cultures of other ethnic, religious, and regional groups in America. Shoemaker made a special effort, Tortora emphasized, to have the class material in his American folklore class reflect the varied backgrounds of students and the cultural diversity of the United States.[10] Students saw their work for the class being put to use by the center. In Tortora's time, the eight to ten students in the class wrote for the *Pennsylvania Dutchman*, collected for the archives, and organized presentations for the festival.

The folk culture center, later reorganized as the Pennsylvania Folklife Society, offered another first when it replaced the *Pennsylvania Dutchman* with *Pennsylvania Folklife* in 1957 and thereby announced an expanded scope to a variety of folk cultures. The launching of *Pennsylvania Folklife* inaugurated folklife into the title of an American periodical. Until it ceased publication in 1997, *Pennsylvania Folklife* boasted the largest circulation for any American folklore journal, more than even the *Journal of American Folklore*. Yoder recognized that "the periodical was unique in America, for its purpose was to publish materials on one ethnic/regional culture and stimulate research from its readers" (Yoder 1990, 4). In addition, it set articles on folk beliefs, songs, and narratives alongside those for folk art and material culture. It published items in dialect and encouraged contributions from community members. Its contributors, from in and outside academe, the Pennsylvania-German editors insisted, wrote in an engaging narrative style.

Shoemaker's notoriety for his academic and public efforts earned him an invitation to the Midcentury International Folklore Conference at Indiana University in 1950. It was hosted by Stith Thompson, probably the preeminent folklorist in America at the time, who advocated an international study of folklore based on literary, rather than ethnological, principles. It gave Shoemaker an opportunity for international exposure for his campaign for application of folklife methods in the United States, although it appeared that he was a lonely voice. He drew support from Swedish scholar Sigurd Erixon who beseeched the audience to undertake "a comparative cultural research on a regional basis" in Europe and America that would expand the concept of folk tradition. He cited the urgency of the task: "In this period of great change there are still certain islands [of folklife], which we may call relic islands, and many traces of dying cultures within our reach. Our modern folk-life researchers must utilize the extraordinary possibilities which are thus placed at their disposal" (Thompson 1953, 252–53). Thompson understood the need to describe tradition broadly, but thought that folklife was an anthropological rather than folkloristic problem. For Shoemaker and Erixon, the issue was a way to study culture in terms of the groups in which humans live and work, and folklife presented a way to combine ethnology and folklore toward a view of social tradition in modern societies.

Shoemaker grappled Alan Lomax in a debate about the parochialism that folklife could produce. Shoemaker advocated establishment of archives such as the one at his center for each different ethnic-regional group, so that a total way of life within a socially based culture could be described. "Well, then we can't understand world folklore," Lomax interjected. He thought that comparisons needed to be made across genres within a "supernational archive" rather than for individual groups. Lomax added, "The material has to be brought together in order to make any sense of it, and I don't see why the Pennsylvania Dutch should have a priority on staying in its own backyard" (Thompson 1953, 98–99). Shoemaker fired back that every group had its own distinctive history and cultural character, and therefore the Dutch or another group needed to have its traditions understood in relation to one another. Comparison across genres, he thought, leveled out the differences among cultures, and fallaciously suggested equivalent functions.

Shoemaker rattled his fellow folklorists at the important midcentury conference in another dispute over the use of festivals. While Thompson and others were skeptical of the "bogus" folklore at festivals, others thought it was important to make folklore available to the public. In contrast to the idea of folk music or storytelling festivals emphasizing the aesthetic appeal of the texts and forms of folklore, Shoemaker hailed the distinctiveness of his festival as a folklife project to present the integration of a subculture. "I have felt all along here that the problems which I face are very much different from those of a good many of the folklorists present," Shoemaker told his colleagues. He explained a difference with reference to the social and material basis of the folklife festival:

> We had an enormous exhibition station and we put the arts and crafts of the community on display, both those of the past and those of the present. We had about four hundred feet of one of the buildings devoted to folk art exclusively. The thing that I was most interested in doing was presenting the culinary culture. What is more traditional in life than the cuisine? So I got four church groups in Cookstown to become interested. Each one of the four church groups made four or five distinctive dishes and so we actually had sixteen different traditional dishes of the Dutch country presented as part of the folk festival. Of course that was what the people were particularly interested in. As far as folk are concerned, I have never seen why we should limit ourselves exclusively to the oral tradition. To my mind that is only a very small segment of folklore and in the life of the people may not get as much attention as folk art, games, gambling, and so forth. That, by the way, has not been brought out here and it is an important aspect of culture. What are the traditional gambling games in a certain area? We put them on the stage, got people in the area to show how the gambling was carried on in the various taverns. In other words we tried to put the folk culture on parade. That is my definition of a folk festival. (Thompson 1953, 245–46)

Sensing resistance to folklife approaches from other conference participants, Shoemaker took his Swedish folklife allies Sigurd Erixon and Åke Campbell back to Pennsylvania to tour his center and appreciate its folklife projects (Thompson 1996, 267–68).

Dissatisfied with the reception to folklife at the midcentury conference, upon his return to Pennsylvania, Shoemaker cheekily organized his own conferences focusing on the folk cultural theme. On March 31, 1951, Shoemaker's center hosted the first "Pennsylvania Folk Life Conference" at Franklin and Marshall College. A significant statement that emerged from the conference was Don Yoder's address which appeared under the headline "Let's Take Our Blinders Off!" on the front page of the *Pennsylvania Dutchman* on May 1, 1951. In it, Yoder applied lessons of religious history to an American folklife effort. He worried that church histories could give the impression that continuities did not exist among a Protestant movement or a national setting. Underscoring the keyword of "discovery" to indicate a hidden social reality, Yoder asserted that "we have discovered that we have common American interests which cut across the artificial boundaries of denominationalism." He urged readers to beware of the danger of a kind of blind denominationalism in devotion to Pennsylvania-German folklife study, and called for a broad view of American "diversity." He argued that obstacles of "racialism" and "cultural separatism" needed to be overcome, so as to build an "objective study of Pennsylvania's folk culture" that would contribute to an understanding of the "cultural interplay" in the creation of an American "hybrid culture." Yoder implored followers of Pennsylvania-German culture to "focus our intellectual spotlights upon cultural interaction rather than stressing one group alone to the point of nationalistic stultification" (Yoder 1951, 6). Yoder set an agenda that would account for "all the present divergent cultures which still exist among us" and the cultural interaction of various groups in America that give rise to hybrid national traditions. He thus lay the groundwork for the transition of the Pennsylvania-German interests in *Pennsylvania Dutchman* to broader intercultural goals of *Pennsylvania Folklife*, and later, of *American Folklife*.

The center followed the folklife conference with sponsorship of annual summer seminars on Pennsylvania folk culture, beginning in 1952. "Academic folklorists have often been accused—and rightly so," a boastful blurb for the seminars announced, with a possible swipe at Stith Thompson's summer folklore institutes at Indiana University, "of talking and writing with great gusto about folklore but never actually rubbing elbows with the folk! Here, then, for the first time in the history of folk-culture studies in America is the opportunity to take advantage of the researches and contributions of the scholars and experts whilst at the same time becoming acquainted first-hand with the Pennsylvania Dutch folk in a concentrated but unexpurgated form" ("Pennsylvania" 1953). Laying claim to central Pennsylvania as "the richest and most diversified folk culture in America by far," the seminars offered that "serious students may at last study this folk culture on an academic plane."

The first set of folklife seminars featured a staff of twenty-six authorities, including professors (John Hostetler from Penn State in addition to Frey and Shoemaker), curators (Donald Shelley of the Henry Ford Museum and George O.

Bird of the Berks County Historical Society), community collectors (Thomas Brendle, Luther Schaeffer, Henry Kauffman, Earl Robacker, and William Troxell), and writers (Ann Hark, Arthur Graeff, and Frances Lichten, among others). "The student will be studying, observing and absorbing his subject in the heart of the very milieu upon which he is concentrating," the seminars stressed, and "registrants will have immediate avenues on all sides for exploring and testing the theories and conclusions of the classroom—in other words, they will *learn by doing*" ("Pennsylvania" 1952). The subjects ranged from definitions of "folk-culture" to folk song, tale, medicine, belief, art, and architecture. Bringing to light the applied purposes of the center, the seminars concluded with two panels, one on "how to put traditional folk-cultural materials to use" and another on "what has been the contribution of the folk-culture of the Pennsylvania Dutch Country to American life?"

The Department of American Folklore at Franklin and Marshall remained on the books through the academic year 1951–1952. Shoemaker's name then disappeared from the faculty listing after 1952–1953.[11] A number of factors did the department in. Shoemaker's efforts increasingly turned to the operation of the Pennsylvania Dutch Folklore Center. Of the three codirectors, Shoemaker was the most active, and had the grandest vision of its future. Vincent Tortora recalled that Shoemaker "didn't work well within a structure or pattern like teaching courses as a member of the faculty. He wanted to be free to pursue all his other activities of archiving, publishing, promoting, and interviewing and answer only to himself."[12] Florence Baver, who worked for Shoemaker at Kutztown and later founded the Pennsylvania Dutch Folk Culture Society, added that Shoemaker's first love was the people from whom he collected. He took to field research better than anyone she ever saw. He insisted on returning his work to "his people" by radio programs in the native dialect, newspaper columns, and festivals. He bragged of treating tradition bearers as intelligent people who appreciate hearing interpretations of their own culture, and he boasted of reaching more people with scholarship than uppity ivory-tower folklorists. He also separated himself from many festival promoters who tended to emphasize entertainment of artists instead of presentations of community life as Shoemaker wanted to spread. Scholars were expected to teach at that time, but Shoemaker left college teaching to devote himself to his center which allowed him to reach directly to the public and maintain his research and presentational activities. He nonetheless remained the teacher in his public seminars and many lectures across the region, and conceived of his center's purpose broadly as cultural documentation and education serving people at all levels.[13]

Given the restrictions of the college structure, it was unlikely that the department at Franklin and Marshall could expand beyond Shoemaker's faculty listing, and the center, besides having the greatest potential for growth, also allowed Shoemaker the greatest freedom to pursue multiple projects and roles. The summer festival brought great publicity and substantial income to the center, and issuing the newspaper and related publications became a major publishing venture. Meanwhile the archives ambitiously covered material, community, and social traditions beyond the oral genres usually indexed singularly in other American archives. Shoemaker cooperated with the growing tourist industry in the area, writing and editing many brochures and guides to the local culture (1953, 1954, 1955, 1956, 1959c). In addition, Shoemaker produced several scholarly monographs on folk custom and material culture in Pennsylvania (1959a, 1959b, 1960).

Franklin and Marshall's president had reason to be enthusiastic about the college's Pennsylvania-German connection when Harvey Bassler proposed funding a major library addition to house the folklore center. Bassler commissioned architectural plans for the project, but tragically in 1950 he died in an auto accident, ironically on the way to the center, before he could complete the funding arrangements (Yoder 1983, 11). Bassler's donations aside, Distler had been an avid supporter of Shoemaker's efforts, but the climate changed for the Pennsylvania-German connection at Franklin and Marshall when Distler retired in 1955. The new president sought to make Franklin and Marshall an elite national institution, and moved to reduce its faculty and student ties to the local culture. The speculative business ventures of the Pennsylvania Dutch Folklore Center led by the always independent and frequently cantankerous Alfred Shoemaker no longer sat well with the college president. The new president instituted sweeping changes in the curriculum, downplayed the German Reformed Church affiliation, and worked toward bringing students and faculty from outside of Pennsylvania into the college.

With the college's mission changed, the Unger-Bassler collection and center archives were transferred to Ursinus College, which maintained an interest in Pennsylvania-German studies and the nearby Kutztown Folk Festival. Only a folktale course in Franklin and Marshall's anthropology department gives any hint of the folkloristic legacy in the curriculum at Franklin and Marshall today. During the late 1980s, however, an exhibit at the college of Pennsylvania-German fraktur art recognized Shoemaker's contribution and Shoemaker supporters established a library fund in his honor (Faill 1987).[14] Before Shoemaker cut his ties to the college, he influenced a number of students and associates at Franklin and Marshall who remained active in culture studies. Among them were Vincent Tortora (who taught communications and languages at Hofstra and Adelphi colleges and produced several films on religious folk communities), Joel Hartman (professor of rural sociology at the University of Missouri), Florence Baver (director and curator of the Pennsylvania Dutch Folk Culture Society and Museum), and C. Richard Beam (director of the Center for Pennsylvania-German studies at Millersville University). Shoemaker's mark shows also every time the terms "folk cultural approach," "Continental plan" (for the layout of the Pennsylvania-German house), and "cultural source areas" (especially in searches for antecedents and "New World forms") are used in American scholarship (see Weaver 1986; Parsons 1980–1981).[15]

Shoemaker held colossal goals of promoting folklife to the public, and issued lofty promises of a better, more tolerant, more peaceful world as a result of folk cultural research. He operated at a kinetic pace, and had a capacity for brewing trouble by living on the edge. With all his grandiose plans, and his emotional state fragile, his friends worried that he set himself up for a crash. Renowned for his creative ideas, he was not highly regarded for his business acumen, although he scored a number of financial successes. He depended on associates to translate his groundbreaking, sometimes high-flown, ideas into practical terms. It is a credit to his foresight and understanding of folk culture's appeal that he had as many successes as he did. Often impatient, trusting to a fault, not one for tolerating formalities, Shoemaker's downfall might have been expected, but perhaps not so drastic or mysterious.

Exit Alfred Shoemaker. After enjoying tremendous success and renown for his folklife research and public promotions, Alfred Shoemaker felt the fabric of his life suddenly untangle in 1963. Wanting to capitalize on the success of the summer festival in Kutztown, Shoemaker proposed yet another gargantuan project, a fall harvest festival held on grounds the center had purchased east of Lancaster. Despite warnings from associates about overextending the resources of the Pennsylvania Folklife Society and the energies of the staff, Shoemaker brazenly charged ahead. He grandly envisioned a site comparable to the finest European museum and archives, operating year-round with historic buildings (a decorated brick-end bank barn was reconstructed on the site), research facilities, and festivals. He borrowed heavily for the project, and amassed great debts betting that his success streak would continue. When the time came for the "Pennsylvania Dutch Frolic" in the fall of 1963, heavy rains washed out the festival, and all that remained was a long line of creditors. Shoemaker faced ruin for himself and his beloved center.

The Pennsylvania Folklife Society recovered, Shoemaker did not.[16] He came out of it an emotional wreck and was committed to the State Hospital in Allentown. In 1964, he appeared homeless and destitute in New York City, and yet reportedly had the mental wherewithal for culling folklore. He frequently showed up tattered and bruised at Vincent Tortora's door talking excitedly about folktales he heard among Hispanic immigrants to the city and folk customs of street people among whom he dwelled. Stubbornly independent, Shoemaker often turned down offers of shelter and money. Rarely seeking aid for himself, he came to friends he knew to help others he considered less fortunate. By 1967, Shoemaker stopped coming around. He disappeared, and is presumed dead.[17]

Although Shoemaker's academic career, and his department at Franklin and Marshall, did not last long, both set important precedents for ethnological approaches to folklife, fieldwork, folk art and material culture, regional and ethnic folk culture, occupational folklife, and public folklife. The Cooperstown Graduate Program in American Folk Culture hatched by Louis C. Jones (with whom Shoemaker's name was linked in the *Journal of American Folklore*) sponsored jointly by the New York State Historical Association and the State University of New York at Oneonta from 1964 to 1979 bore a striking resemblance to the plan laid out by Shoemaker's department. Shoemaker's vision at Franklin and Marshall is hardly known in folklore historiography, although much of what he called for in the way of a folk cultural approach and public folklore is now being taken up in major academic programs and departments, as well as in public programs such as the American Folklife Center.[18] The influence of the Franklin and Marshall department was especially evident in Don Yoder's contribution to the Department of Folklore and Folklife at the University of Pennsylvania and the publication in 1976 of *American Folklife* (Yoder 1983). Further, many purposes of a public center devoted to Pennsylvania ethnic studies and connected with an academic department live on at the Center for Pennsylvania Culture Studies at Penn State Harrisburg, Center for Pennsylvania-German Studies at Millersville University, and the Pennsylvania German Cultural Heritage Center at Kutztown University. These institutions (and others applying folk culture studies) benefitted from Shoemaker's pathbreaking example, and maybe learned from his mistakes.

AFTER SHOEMAKER: THE PUBLIC FACE OF FOLKLIFE

Folklife as a term and concept was imported from Pennsylvania during the 1960s and flowered as a national term for a social vision of cultural diversity during the 1970s, anticipating the "multicultural" debate of the 1980s. In retrospect, countercultural movements of the 1960s may have helped create sympathy for the communal spirit of ethnic-regional folklife among young students. Civil rights struggles in the South, war on poverty in Appalachia, and ethnic politics in urban cities were also responsible for interest in folklife because they stimulated the search for models of community persistence rather than assimilation and modernization. Don Yoder's oft-cited essay "The Folklife Studies Movement" in *Pennsylvania Folklife* harped on this persistence in a national agenda for the "rediscovery of the total range of the folk-culture (folklife)" (Yoder 1963, 44). As a counter to modern society, folklife "is the opposite of the mass-produced, mechanized, popular culture of the 20th Century," Yoder wrote (43). He iterated the importance of tradition as oppositional to the dominance of modern mass culture by emphasizing folk culture as traditional culture, "bound by tradition and transmitted by tradition, and … basically (although not exclusively) rural and pre-industrial" (Yoder 1963, 43). He called for extending the folklife model of Pennsylvania-German concern, first to a statewide survey of Pennsylvania communities, and second to other regional folk cultures in the United States. He cheekily urged adoption of a folklife discipline for America as part of an international movement including Germany, Scandinavia, and Great Britain to view subcultures as integrated wholes.

Yoder's essay became a manifesto to expand folklife approaches to groups often neglected in American history or to present a culturally diverse view of American civilization. Austin Fife in Utah picked up the concept to emphasize the integrity of Mormons in the West as a functioning cultural tradition. With a broader purpose, he produced an exhibition at Utah State University entitled *Folklife and Folk Arts in the United States* in 1968 "to suggest a wide scope in geographic origin, chronological development, and distinctive ethnic groups" (Fife 1969, 9). Henry Glassie, who had come from the Cooperstown program to study under Don Yoder at Pennsylvania, produced *Pattern in the Material Folk Culture in the Eastern United States* (1968), which argued for the persistence of American regional-ethnic folk cultures from the colonial period to contemporary times. It contravened outlooks in American studies of a homogenizing nation with an emergent national character.

In addition to the formation of the Cooperstown program in New York State which featured required courses on "Folklife Research," Warren Roberts at Indiana University and Norbert Riedl at the University of Tennessee introduced folklife and material culture courses to cover community studies in their respective states (Roberts 1988, 2–8). Riedl appealed to American folklorists in the *Journal of American Folklore* (1966) to follow the lead of Don Yoder's manifesto for folklife. He suggested use of questionnaires and cultural mapping to create a comprehensive ethnographic survey and atlas of folk culture. To the opposition created between folklore and folklife, he suggested that rather than change the American Folklore Society into a folk culture or folklife society, he was calling for marshaling American folklorists to a new mission contributing to "any future material-oriented folk culture research in this country" (Riedl 1966, 562). The implication was that the materiality of tradition revealed a rootedness in place and a visibility of *cultural difference* that could be systematically studied and persuasively argued.

Folklife became further expanded during celebrations of America's bicentennial. While many events were supposed to invoke unity and independence relating to the founding of the new nation in 1776, the timing of the bicentennial after a period of social upheaval marked by movements for group rights for blacks, Hispanics, other minorities, and women urged a reflection on American social relations. The 1976 Festival of American Folklife for the bicentennial on the nation's symbolic center, on the National Mall in Washington, D.C., confronted the issue and made American folklife a synonym for a cultural accounting of America's diverse groups. As if to punctuate the significance of folklife at the time, the festival, begun modestly the decade before as an Independence weekend celebration, in 1976 lasted throughout the summer. The secretary of the Smithsonian Institution blared themes of diversity and localism for the festival: "What we have hoped—and have seen come to pass in many places—is that our Festival would illustrate the many roads to the better understanding of our *varied cultures*, that our visitors would return home to create their own celebrations out of their own cultural resources in their own local museums and schools" (emphasis added; Ripley 1976, 3).

American uneasiness about celebrating a violent revolution led the celebration to focus on lasting American principles such as freedom, tolerance, and pursuit of happiness that supported a present-day social balance (see Kammen 1978; Lomax 1976). It would be a festival "to cherish our differences," festival director Ralph Rinzler announced, and visitors witnessed sections devoted to Native Americans, European groups, African Americans, regional cultures, family and children's traditions, and working-class traditions (Rinzler 1976, 7). If festival-goers came to the festival to forget their troubles, Margaret Mead reminded them in the program: "We have seen a President resign. The tragedy of the Vietnam war continues to haunt us. We are in the midst of an economic recession. To give ourselves over to celebration and enjoyment, even on our 200th birthday, say the critics, is callous and heartless" (Mead 1976). By installing a festival of folklife that emphasizes the diversity of America's communities and the complexity of social traditions in everyday life, Mead suggested that "we shall be able to take heart in facing problems that are unsolved and otherwise may seem insoluble" (Mead 1976, 6). Difference of race, region, and ethnicity on the Mall, in other words, appeared to be a strength of American life, a sign of progress, rather than a condition to be lamented.

Although scaled down after the bicentennial, the Festival of American Folklife continued to have national visibility. In 1994, it was named the "Top Event in the U.S." by the American Bus Association as a result of a survey of regional tourist bureaus. That put it on a par with previous winners including the Olympics and the World Expo (Kurin 1996a). By 1995 the festival had featured tradition bearers from fifty-three nations, every region of the United States, scores of ethnic groups, more than a hundred American Indian groups, and some sixty occupational groups (Kurin 1996a, 253). Several ethnographies treated the festival itself as an invented tradition to be studied, and criticized (Cantwell 1991; Bauman, Swain, and Carpenter 1992; Price and Price 1995). Even though the Kutztown Folk Festival attracted more people, the American Folklife Festival attracted more scholarly attention because of its representation of traditions on the Mall, the nation's symbolic center. Although critics were frequently concerned about the exoticization of tradition bearers on festival stages, festival producers insisted on their sensitivity to community concerns. Director of the Office of Folklife Programs Richard Kurin defended the grass-roots intervention of the festival: "Research for the event and documentation of it have resulted in complex community-level collaborations, training, and a documentary archival collection held at the Smithsonian and disbursed back to various local institutions" (Kurin 1996a, 253).

Festival producers realized the implications of folklife's position on the Mall as a strategy of presenting, and creating, community. Politically, their translation of the folk on the Mall as neglected or disenfranchised groups in the polity such as Native Americans, African Americans, elderly Americans, and working-class Americans encouraged what they thought of as a more inclusive, decentralized cultural democracy. Kurin expounded:

The festival has had strong impacts on policies, scholarship, and on folks "back home." Many U.S. states and several nations have remounted festival programs and used them to generate laws, institutions, educational programs, documentary films, recordings, museum and traveling exhibits, monographs, and other cultural activities. In many documented cases, the festival has energized local and regional tradition bearers and their communities, and thus helped conserve and create cultural resources. It has provided models for the Black Family Reunion, the Los Angeles Festival, and other major civic cultural presentations, including America's Reunion on the Mall for the Clinton Inaugural. (Kurin 1996a, 253)

In festival and scholarship, folklife more than the concept of folklore became associated with efforts to maintain cultural diversity of marginalized groups through the conservation of community traditions. On the first working day of the bicentennial year of 1976, the American Folklife Preservation Act (Public Law 94-201) became law and resulted in the creation of the American Folklife Center in the Library of Congress to "preserve and present American folklife." The wording of the act emphasized keywords of "diversity" and "difference." I quote the declaration of findings and purpose of the act:

> The Congress hereby finds and declares—
> (1) that the diversity inherent in American folklife has contributed greatly to the cultural richness of the Nation and has fostered a sense of individuality and identity among the American people;
> (2) that the history of the United States effectively demonstrates that building a strong nation does not require the sacrifice of cultural differences;
> (3) that American folklife has a fundamental influence on the desires, beliefs, values, and character of the American people;
> (4) that it is appropriate and necessary for the Federal Government to support research and scholarship in American folklife in order to contribute to an understanding of the complex problems of the basic desires, beliefs, and values of the American people in both rural and urban areas;
> (5) that the encouragement and support of American folklife, while primarily a matter for private and local initiative, is also an appropriate matter of concern to the Federal Government; and
> (6) that it is in the interest of the general welfare of the Nation to preserve, support, revitalize, and disseminate American folklife traditions and arts.

In keeping with this "welfare" mission, the center coordinated fieldwork teams in Paradise Valley, Nevada; Lowell, Massachusetts; and South Georgia. It produced book-length catalogs on the American cowboy and Italian American folklife, published guides to national folklife resources, and sponsored conferences on belief and folk art (Jabbour 1996a, 1996b). The center incorporated the Archive of Folk Song in the Library of Congress and changed its name to the Archive of Folk Culture. It produced a splashy color booklet announcing American folklife as "a commonwealth of cultures" (Hufford 1991). It equated folklife to "community life and values," and related it to the reality of plural groups in America and the perception of change in the twentieth century. "We no longer view cultural difference as a problem to be solved," the booklet proclaimed. Instead, it made the case for difference as "a rich resource for all Americans, who constantly shape and transform their many cultures" (Hufford 1991).

The American Folklife Center has had legislative challenges since it was founded. The issue was not whether folklife was a valuable thing to preserve in America, but whether in a mad dash to balance the federal budget agencies charged with cultural research and programming should be publicly funded. The center was threatened with a loss of funding from a fiscally conservative House of Representatives in 1995, but the Senate restored it after a letter-writing campaign and support for the center's work in the popular press. To appeal to legislators, the center underscored its national scope in its budget battles by publicizing ways that its activity reached every state of the country. In 1996, Representative William Thomas (Republican-California) introduced a bill to repeal the American Folklife Preservation Act, thus removing an independent board of trustees and need for reauthorization, and incorporate the functions of the American Folklife Center within the Library of Congress. Thomas claimed that his proposal insured the survival of folklife collections, since it promoted folklife as a standing special collection of the library. At the same time that the Librarian of Congress James Billington offered that folklife would gain stature as part of the cultural references for American society, he also gave notice that the center's budget and activities would be curtailed. Alan Jabbour, the center's director, supported the move to remove the center as a vulnerable budget item open to legislative sniping. Things got really complicated when the House Appropriations Committee passed an amendment to transfer the center to the Smithsonian Institution, and the board of trustees of the center, going against the advice of Jabbour, led a public campaign for reauthorization.[19] The upper house ended up saving the day. Senator Mark Hatfield, chair of the Senate Appropriations Committee, praised the center's work for preserving the folklife of America's groups as being in the national interest. The Senate passed a bill with a measure for reauthorization of the center in the Library of Congress for 1997–1998, and the House went along. The president signed the bill, maintaining the center's folklife purpose, at least for a while.

A year after the center was established, the Office of Folklife Programs became an independent office of the Smithsonian Institution. Its director Richard Kurin explained that it "promotes the understanding and continuity of contemporary grass-roots cultures in the United States and abroad" (Kurin 1996b). A federal report entitled *Cultural Conservation: The Protection of Cultural Heritage in the United States* (1983) coordinated by Ormond Loomis argued for the growth of federal programs at the Smithsonian and the Library of Congress to protect "cultural heritage" in addition to historic properties covered by the National Historic Preservation Act of 1966. By calling this heritage cultural, rather than national or historic, the report assumed it would entail diverse ethnic, racial, and occupational groups. It offered that "productivity, freedom, and unity come from our cultural diversity" (Loomis 1983, iii). Citing the appeal of Alex Haley's *Roots* and Foxfire programs, the report maintained that, in fact, Americans needed, indeed demanded, a local or ethnic cultural identity, but found that mass cultural and national forces threatened to destroy traditions essential to perpetuating separate cultural identities. "Folklife," the report concluded, is especially useful in addressing the problem. Its shorthand definition of the term was "community life and values." Its longhand version taken from the American Folklife Preservation Act stressed the lack of a shared national culture: "the term 'American folklife' means the traditional expressive culture shared within the various groups in the United States: familial, ethnic, occupational, religious, regional."

This definition and its implication for a lack of national tradition or exclusiveness bothered several prominent folklorists, such as Richard Dorson. He advocated a model of national consensus of shared historic traditions in the mixture of American groups. He criticized folklife scholars for inadequate relation of folklore to the broad American historical experience. He especially assailed Don Yoder's *American Folklife* for not conveying a distinctive American cultural experience, and scattering traditions "found" in places as diverse as Canada, Mexico, and the Caribbean. In making an argument for a common national culture, Dorson feared that folklife gave the impression that none existed. He was especially irked that in separating a single group for cultural consideration, folklife approaches commonly overlooked ethnic interrelations and national connections (Dorson 1978c).

Yoder testily answered later that his model was "in a very real sense Pennsylvania's cultural pluralism, brought about by William Penn's invitation to English and Welsh Quakers, Scotch-Irishmen, Rhinelanders, Swiss, and anyone else who wanted to come, made Penn's Woods the basic prototype, the colonial model, for the pluralistic America that we have today" (Yoder 1990, 6). He reasserted that folklife studies are tied to the American experience as an experience of group life. Folklife study seen broadly beyond Pennsylvania, he wrote, views traditions pluralistically "in the context of that larger unifying society and culture of which all subgroups and traditions are functioning parts" (Yoder 1976b, 13). Yoder echoed Shoemaker's battle cry that American folklife in the twentieth century had to be "discovered," because it represented a social reality that went against an American myth of melting pot assumptions, or myths, propagated to give a false impression of assimilation and nationalism that was somehow natural and progressive.

Yet Yoder conceded that a temptation existed in folklife studies to provide ethnographies of particular groups and de-emphasize or criticize the role of the "unifying society and culture." If cultural comparison or historical contextualization are lacking, the result could easily be a fragmented picture of cultures within America, as I observed in a collection of ten folklife books published in 1989 covering groups such as Louisiana Cajuns, Lake Champlain fishermen, and Amana

Society members (Bronner 1990a). Built into the folklife effort was the assumption that data could become archived, comparative, even quantifiable. Europeans had a head start, pioneer American folklife scholars figured, but with the rapidly growing vigor of American folklife studies, they imagined that traditional cultures on the American continent could be charted and analyzed. Attempts to coordinate folklife research in the form of a cultural atlas for the United States have not been successful, and efforts to organize team research in communities have been all too infrequent. Invoking folklife could become a way to preserve the integrity of one's "people" as a community. It also is a way to present those people positively to the public as a living tradition. "The people at the center of folklife studies," Henry Glassie observed, "maintain their integrity and draw our admiration by holding to traditions that enable them simultaneously to express themselves and to meet their social responsibilities" (Glassie 1990, ix).

As folklife became nationalized from Shoemaker's rural regional-ethnic Pennsylvania-German model, new trends were apparent toward merging folklore and folklife into a conception of human agency in tradition. Urban and industrial crafts, modern children's arts, suburban yard arrangements, and memory arts of the aged were all presented as folklife during the 1990s. In some cases, the justification for calling such studies folklife was a matter of method or scope. It appeared that if a study employed ethnography—the systematic observation of communicated, symbolic behavior in cultural scenes—or if it included customary and material traditions, it could constitute folklife. Laurie Sommers reported that in the 1990s, folklorists in "public sector practice" used folklore and folklife interchangeably, and in academe at the same time Robert St. George beheld a "specious" distinction between the two terms (Sommers 1996; St. George 1995). Yet many folklife advocates justifiably worried that the significance of integrated communities like the Amish that received special attention for their social differentiation and totality of tradition would not be fully appreciated if folklife became subsumed under, or melded with, folklore (see Vlach 1985a; Bronner 1996c). To do away with some of the confusion, Jan Brunvand in his widely used textbook on American folklore proposed that "a safe generalization is that American folklorists have accepted the European concept of folklife as constituting their subject matter, and that they are borrowing from ethnography and ethnology for new field methods and theories" (Brunvand 1986b, 330). While conceptually defining folklife broadly as "the full traditional lore, behavior, and material culture of any folk group, with emphasis on the customary and material categories," Brunvand under the heading of "Folklife and Folklore," nevertheless called on "current usage" to form his narrower operational characterization of folklife "to mean only customary and material folk traditions, even though there is good reason to substitute the word immediately and permanently for the much-abused term 'folklore'" (Brunvand 1986b, 401).

To be sure, the bookshelf of American works with folklife in the title still paled in comparison to those using folklore. The UnCover database for the first six months of 1996, for example, listed 175 works with folklife as their keyword as opposed to 1,632 for folklore. The majority of folklife works covered a state, region, locality, or ethnic group. A few discussed occupational groups and urban neighborhoods. One could read into the titles that studying a group's folklife meant that it was threatened with disintegration or victimization. Showing the rationality of communal tradition, putting a human face on culture, argued for its integrity. Some studies, given the American penchant for individualism, suggested a person's choice of "folklife" for a symbolic kind of observable behavior made conspicuous in society. John Vlach cautioned that this favor for biographical studies, "cannot stop there with the universe inside the mind of a maker of objects; folklife studies are by the definition of the discipline also concerned with the maker's social universe" (Vlach 1985a, 70).

Folklife came to the fore in public and scholarly discourse primarily as a rhetorical reference to communal connection and group identity. The range of groups covered during the 1980s and 1990s went well beyond Shoemaker's concern for ethnic-regional cultures that were bounded by ancestry and rooted in place. It grew to include folklife for groups designated by gender, sexual preference, and disability, to name a few commonly used categories. Folklife as a way of following tradition appeared more common and everyday, and as a cultural formation of groups more extensively national. The political significance of widening designation of folklife groups is that as legitimized ways of life expressed through shared traditions, they vie for cultural protection as well as social equity with established ethnic groups. Hence Ward Goodenough in *American Folklife* referred to folklife as a way to record change of social attitudes to subcultures, and to promote maintenance of a diversity of groups within a "national community" (Goodenough 1976, 25). The rise of the folklife movement observed by Goodenough showed that in public discourse, determining the groups properly constituting American culture was open to debate—and intellectual construction. The heightened twentieth-century appeal of "life" in the discourse of culture was that as a subject, it offered a totality of experience to consider, and as an object, it represented the right of individuals to lead lives that did not conform to mass culture. In an era when the idea of community became increasingly elusive, folklife argued for communal persistence.

In the public discourse of American culture, the folklife approach that Alfred Shoemaker set in motion followed, and declared, groupness as the essence of tradition. That the rhetoric of "discovery" became attached to folklife is significant because it established two Americas. The reference to the common phrase for Columbus "discovering" America led to the nineteenth-century view of a new unified nation emerging from European and primarily homogeneous New England inheritance. The other comes from the twentieth-century "discovery" or "rediscovery" of American folklife. Its model lay in Pennsylvania's commonwealth of cultures. The suggestion of discovering America anew showed in a project to redraw the nation into communities of difference. In recognizing, even elevating, whole communities following tradition, the folklife movement involved evaluation, and judgment, of ways that Americans socialize. As a rhetorical quest, the twentieth-century discovery of American folklife forced reflection on the uncertainty of how they related to tradition, and to one another.

Henry W. Shoemaker and the Fable of Public Folklore

On October 2, 1947, the Pennsylvania Historical and Museum Commission made history by unanimously adopting the following resolution:

> RESOLVED, That the Historical and Museum Commission hereby authorizes the creation of the position of *State Folklorist*; and

> BE IT FURTHER RESOLVED, That *Henry W. Shoemaker*, Senior Archivist, be transferred from the Public Record Division (Archives) to the New Division of Folklore.

Receiving front-page attention from Pennsylvania newspapers, Henry Shoemaker (1880–1958) officially began his tenure as America's first state folklorist in March 1948 and served until February 1956. Despite leaving behind a documentary record of his accomplishment, his pathbreaking role for public folklore has gone mostly unrecognized. At least four chronicles of public folklore activities credited Henry Glassie with holding the first state folklorist position beginning in 1966, and formed a dominant narrative of public folklore's development disseminated in classrooms and professional forums (Baron and Spitzer 1992; Feintuch 1988; Loomis 1983; Hufford 1969). In fact, the official publication of the American Folklore Society describing the work of the folklorist singled out Glassie's position as a memorable first toward the "great expansion" of "state and local folk cultural programs" (Jackson, McCulloh, and Weigle 1984). The agreed-upon fable enthroned a young academic hero who ignited the charge demanded by a pluralist awakening of the 1960s and propelled numbers of unbroken folklore trajectories to the present day in the public sector. The historical illusion spread by this narrative raises two central questions I will address. First, if it was not the populist consciousness of the 1960s that prompted the creation of the state folklore position, what forces actually lay behind its formation in 1948? Second, why did

313

chronicles insist on a peculiar chronology commencing in the 1960s? Or put another way, why has Shoemaker's role been neglected? While the answers force an account of specific historical events, they also impel me to close the chapter with the revised historical narrative of public folklore work as state roles became diminished during the 1990s. From Progressivism to multiculturalism, the backgrounds of state folklore from Shoemaker's beginning to the end of the twentieth century raise issues of governmental responsibility for cultural programming, public attitudes toward folklore in cultural conservation, and scholarly conciliation of applied and "popular" folklore with academic scholarship.

The man who would become America's first state folklorist, Henry Wharton Shoemaker, was born in 1880 into one of America's wealthiest families in New York City. He was the first of three children born to Henry Francis and Blanche Quiggle Shoemaker. Neighbor to John D. Rockefeller and living in the vicinity of Vanderbilts, Havemeyers, and DePews, the Shoemakers were considered nouveau riche outsiders to the New York scene. Henry Wharton's parents had come a few years before his birth from Pennsylvania. His father had made his fortune in coal mining and railroading in the coal region around Schuylkill County and his mother came from a family of judges and diplomats in the forested Pennsylvania highlands near Lock Haven, west of the anthracite coal region. His father, a life-long member of the Pennsylvania Society of New York City, treated Pennsylvania nostalgically like the "old country." As Henry remembered, "As a boy [I] loved to listen to [my] father tell tales of old Orwigsburg, of Regina Hartman, the Indian captive." From these narratives, he recalled Pennsylvania as a marvelous land of "romance," somehow removed from "the maelstrom of higher historical criticism" he gained in school (Shoemaker 1923, 2).

Shoemaker acquired his early education from private tutors followed by attendance at the prestigious Dr. E. D. Lyons Classical School from 1889 to 1896. The work at school on the classics—especially English, Greek, and Roman—apparently stuck with young Henry Shoemaker. His sister later reminded her older brother of his youthful love of myths and epics in tracing the source of his sense of "romance." At Lyons, he came under the tutelage of William Edgar Plumley, originally from Lackawanna County in Pennsylvania, who instilled in his pupils a reverence for natural history. "Nature," one remembrance of Plumley pasted into one of Henry Shoemaker's scrapbooks stated, "possessed a most remarkable charm for him. It was his delight to wander among the fields and woods and to commune with nature when at her loveliest." A Presbyterian preacher, Plumley emphasized the spiritual experience of nature as manifestation of the divine. The Lyons School prided itself on developing students' skills in prose and poetry, music performance, and above all, immersion in the classics. Shoemaker's scrapbooks show that schoolteachers honored him for his command of Greek myths and French literature, and they also reveal by his notes that they neglected American history. While still at Lyons, Shoemaker edited and his brother managed the *Argyle News*, a monthly devoted to schoolboy athletics. Despite this stated purpose, Shoemaker strayed into a range of topics. To the announcements of club football, biking, and racing, Shoemaker added interviews with hunters, romantic poetry, and "mystery" stories. Shoemaker's editorializing in the magazine included an attack on control of New York politics by Tammany bosses and support for the Spanish-American War.

Shoemaker attended Columbia College in 1897 near his New York City residence. He intended to take up commercial art (owing to his admiration for Currier and Ives prints), but soon turned to literary interests, including classical studies, when he was not vigorously engaged in outdoor sports, including track, golf, and boating. He continued his interests in journalism by joining the staffs of the *Columbia Spectator* and *Columbia Jester*. At the tender age of eighteen Henry published a volume of poetry drawn from his work on *Argyle News* (1898), and two years later he published his first book of prose, calling it *From Lancaster to Clearfield, Or Scenes on the By-ways of Pennsylvania* (1900). Recalling the inspiration for the travel tale, Shoemaker stated, "I travelled over hilly, winding back roads where I enjoyed meeting interesting people and visiting strange, out-of-the-way places."[1] And while Shoemaker was doing all this, he volunteered his press services to the Republican County Committee in Manhattan. He was voted in by his classmates as class treasurer in 1900, and as his parting task, addressed the class dinner on "How to Become Famous."

Shoemaker credited a Columbia professor for turning his focus to folklore. As a junior, he took a composition course in which the rhetoric professor, George R. Carpenter, required a "daily theme" paper. "For want of subjects," Shoemaker recalled, he drew on the "old Pennsylvania stories" told by his family, and to his surprise, the professor raved about them. "'Go on with them,' he said; 'you have found an original field'" (Shoemaker 1917b, 6). Shortly after this incident, he published a character sketch of a folklore raconteur entitled "John Q. Dice, The Pennsylvania Mountaineer" in the *Columbia Jester*. Dice was a real-life figure from his mother's childhood home in Clinton County and the story, delivered in dialect, is a hunting tall tale about a wrestling match between buck and hunter after the ammunition is gone. Set against the backdrop of John Dice's rustic cabin, the tale-teller spun his yarn.

Shoemaker spent summers at his maternal home in the Pennsylvania mountains called "Restless Oaks" in McElhattan. A two-and-a-half-story country house near the West Branch of the Susquehanna River and the Bald Eagle Mountains, Restless Oaks stood beside extensive forestland. It was Shoemaker's favorite home and the all the more so because of the romantic history it offered. His ancestor Michael Quigley, "descendant of the Waldensian martyrs in the Piedmontese Alps of Europe," first settled there in 1768. His grandmother Cordelia, who died at age eighty-six in 1914, regaled the boy there with stories of the family and region stretching back into the eighteenth century. She also entertained him with folk songs accompanying herself on the piano, songs that her grandson well remembered many years later. She nurtured Shoemaker's interest in literature and the outdoors by reserving a room of the house for his use, and she arranged for him to inherit the estate. Recalling his summer days of boyhood at Restless Oaks, Shoemaker wrote that "those early impressions decided my whole life and I have been ever a loyal son of Pennsylvania."[2]

With the developed instincts of a Victorian naturalist "field collecting" specimens that revealed a hidden past, Shoemaker gathered in the details of what he saw and heard in the Pennsylvania highlands. Shoemaker reminisced,

> The collecting began when [I] was a small boy, on ostensible hunting and fishing trips, with certain old hunters in Clinton County, and it came to pass that [I] enjoyed their story-telling more than the game-slaying, and took more pleasure writing the stories than any other form of "compositions" in school and at college. Living mostly in a large city at the time, and born with an insistent longing for the woods and mountains, probably a heritage from some Indian ancestor, the quest for quaint stories of the long ago grew with the years, until it is now [my] favorite form of "hunting" (there is an open season twelve months in the year), with no "bag" limit, working in beautifully with [my] activities in forestry organization and the Pennsylvania Alpine Club. (Shoemaker 1924, 11)

While Shoemaker was at Columbia, his father made plans to shift his base of operations to Ohio as chairman of the board of the Cincinnati, Hamilton and Dayton Railroad. When the move came, the son came along as his father's private secretary. While in his father's employ he traveled through Ohio and Kentucky and was fascinated by the folk speech and legends he heard. "The desire came to write," he remembered, "and write [I] did, on the trains, in the evenings, at any spare time" (Shoemaker 1917b, 7). He reflected on the strong connections between the lore of this region and that of his favored Pennsylvania mountains. He read popular romantic writings steeped in Appalachian folklife by authors such as James Lane Allen (1849–1925) and John Fox, Jr. (1863–1919). Praising the "primitive strength and romantic chivalry" of the people from whom this folklore came, Shoemaker bemoaned the loss of "simplicity, sincerity and romance" as the "train of modernization," for which he worked, sliced through the mountains of Kentucky. "Big mining towns now flourish," he wrote, "in the most out-of-the-way valleys, railroads penetrate everywhere, old customs are being put to the test, will simplicity outlast the thirst for ease and prosperity?" (Shoemaker 1931, 9).

Increasingly disturbed by the environmental and cultural consequences of his father's railway business, the young Shoemaker rebelliously embraced the Progressive politics of conservation. To his father's dismay, he was a Progressive delegate to the Republican Party Convention in 1904 and became swept up by Roosevelt fever. Apparently referring to industrialists in his father's New York circle, young Shoemaker wrote that Roosevelt "possessed a remarkably clear understanding of the problem created by the abuse of wealth. Like David of old, he set out after the Goliath of ill-diverted wealth and privilege" (Shoemaker 1917a, 3). If Roosevelt was in his restraint of industrial development more moderate than Shoemaker would have liked, Shoemaker agreed wholeheartedly with Roosevelt's assertion that "the conservation of our natural resources and their proper use constitute the fundamental problem which underlies almost every other problem of our national life." Calling for practical management and invoking "forward-thinking" or "progressivism," Roosevelt explained that "the government has been endeavoring to get our people to look ahead and to substitute a planned and orderly development of our resources in place of a haphazard striving for immediate profit" (Roosevelt 1926a, 443). His goal was to increase the "usefulness," rather than exploitation, of the land to insure prosperity. He promised that with governmental regulation, he could promote industrial growth while protecting the precious American landscape.

Shoemaker joined in the broad Progressive impulse of the early twentieth century toward criticism and change. He chimed the theme of restoring economic individualism and political democracy associated with an earlier American tradition crushed by monopolized heavy industries and corrupt political machines. Shoemaker emphasized Progressivism as a nationalist American approach to industrial problems so as to separate it from supposedly "un-American" socialist and other radical "European" ideas. Conservation was important to this Progressive view because it protected the resources of the early American tradition and represented the control of industries for the public good. The rhetoric of conservation carried the implication of allowing for use of natural resources and also had the ring of a "conservative" rather than radical approach to reform.

The senior Shoemaker softened his suspicions of Roosevelt when the latter chose as his running mate Charles Fairbanks, formerly a senator from Indiana, who was the chief counsel to Shoemaker's industries and a family friend. Fairbanks acted to reconcile the Shoemaker father and son and courted their favor, not to mention their enormous wealth, for Roosevelt campaigns. The Shoemaker family frequently were guests at the Roosevelt White House and young Shoemaker's aspirations to be a diplomat, following a path in his mother's family line, became a topic of conversation. Fairbanks helped seal the deal that appointed young Shoemaker as secretary of American legations in Costa Rica and Portugal, followed by a post as third secretary of the American embassy in Berlin. But after five months in Berlin, Shoemaker wrote his mother to say that he had all he wanted, "namely the prestige and the experience," and he was tempted by an offer his brother made him for a brokerage partnership on Wall Street. Despite President Roosevelt's personal request that he stay on, Shoemaker returned to the United States in 1905.

The Wall Street enterprise was short-lived. Henry relied on the business acumen of his brother William to make the venture a success, and a year into the partnership William tragically died in an elevator accident. Henry kept the firm going for a few more years before dissolving it and concentrating on newspaper publishing. He envisioned using newspapers to advance his conservationist stands and apply his literary interests. He anticipated relocating out of the city to the forests of rural Pennsylvania, but his father pleaded with his son to tend to the family businesses after falling seriously ill in 1912. He wrote a friend in 1914 that "were it not for my business interests which I must have to keep things going, but which take so much of my time, I would have been able to have written more of Pennsylvania history and perhaps done something really worth while."[3] The family adviser sensed the son's frustration and bluntly counseled him, "It seems to me your gifts are pronounced as a writer along literary lines. Your tastes are not for figures and statements of account. You do not inherit the business traits of your father."[4]

After his father died in 1918, young Henry dove back into his cultural pursuits. Shoemaker had perhaps his most active period of writing stories on the Pennsylvania mountains in this period. He defended the coverage of folklore in his newspapers by claiming that "it is more than a pastime; it is a spiritual necessity. It is the inner life's history of the Pennsylvania frontier people. It is interesting to collect and valuable to preserve" (Shoemaker 1917b, 7). Echoing calls by Roosevelt, Shoemaker hoped that folklore would inspire an authentic American artistry based on the soul of the folk in the wilderness. Unlike Roosevelt, Shoemaker did not venture into the wild West to find America's soul; he came to the Pennsylvania highlands. Folklore there for Shoemaker identified a "source of a new spiritual renaissance in Pennsylvania," a reminder of an American tradition steeped in community and nature. As an officer of several historical and conservation groups, he encouraged recording local legends as the intersection of history, literature, and nature study. "In a humble way I want to be able to preserve the old traditions, which are fast passing away," he explained to the Reverend George P. Donehoo, a local historian in his own right. From this conservation, he professed, "will come a genuine literature."[5]

WRITING TRADITIONS

Henry Shoemaker had since the turn of the century been publishing collections of Pennsylvania legends he "bagged." He made his biggest splash by writing the legend of "Nita-nee" in 1902 connected with the tourist attraction of Penn's Cave in Centre Hall, Pennsylvania. The tragic romantic legend concerned the sad fate of a French Huguenot by the name of Malachi Boyer who fell in love with an Indian princess, Nita-nee of the Lenni-Lenapes, the chief's "Diana-like daughter." "But this was all clandestine love," Shoemaker wrote, "for friendly as Indian and white might be in social intercourse, never could a marriage be tolerated, until—there always is a turned point in romance—the black-haired wanderer and the beautiful Nita-nee resolved to spend their lives together, and one moonless night started for the more habitable East." Nita-nee's seven brothers caught up with Boyer and shoved him from the ledge above the mouth of Penn's Cave in Centre County to

Henry Shoemaker with the "Dauphin Sycamore" (near Linglestown, Pennsylvania, October 1920). Making a connection between nature and folklore, his inscription on the photograph reads: "It is said that this tree stands as a memorial to John Goodway, the last of the friendly Indians. Colonel Shoemaker is standing upon the spot where the Indian is believed to be buried." Photograph by Joseph Illick. (Pennsylvania State Archives, Department of Forestry Photo Collection)

Frontispiece to *Black Forest Souvenirs* (1914) by Henry Shoemaker. It creates icons of Shoemaker's favorite subjects from the extinct past. Above Shoemaker is a depiction of wild passenger pigeons, and below is rafting down the Susquehanna River. Clockwise from the top right are a mountain lion or panther, a frontier "Nimrod," an "Indian princess," a bison, an elk, an "Indian brave," a highland lumberman, and a wolf.

drown in the "greenish limestone water" below. "And after these years those who have heard this legend declare that on the still summer nights an unaccountable echo rings through the cave, which sounds like 'Nita-nee,' 'Nita-nee.'" From the time Shoemaker published this apparently romanticized account, controversy followed him. Critics were skeptical about his sources for a previously unreported legend (he claimed it was a "full-blooded" Seneca Indian he met in 1892) and questioned the intrusion of his imagination into his stories. Whether fabricated or real, it is Shoemaker's legend that has found its way onto innumerable postcards, travel brochures, and student papers explaining the origin of the Penn State Nittany Lion and the Nittany Mountains, and most recently even an advertisement for Wendy's Hamburgers.

Shoemaker the journalist sought narrative "scoops"—stories that had been usually uncollected and rooted in prominent natural sites or local events. He had an eye, he said, for the "picturesque" and "unusual." Owing to early criticism he received from a newspaper that he had not offered much that was unfamiliar, he vowed "to preserve legends that otherwise would be lost, not to rechronicle tales that had been told over and over again by newspaper paragraphers" (Shoemaker 1922). Thus his books contain few legends on familiar regional cycles such as Lewis the Robber, the Paxton Boys, or the Blue-Eyed Six, or ethnic tales such as those featuring the Pennsylvania-German trickster Eileschpigel. Shoemaker the writer sought stories that were "novel," mysterious, and surprising to his readers, rather than to present the most representative oral tradition, as folklorists might. Indeed, in some books it is unclear whether he qualifies stories as folklore because they are orally transmitted through time, a "folksy" mountaineer related the tale, or whether they had a deceivingly "folkish" feeling.

Yet there is in Shoemaker's many books the folklorist's sensitivity to the people for whom narrative was an everyday art. And if his descriptions of settings are to be believed, he equally demonstrated attention to the places, the contexts, in which storytelling thrived. Complaining that his collection of folklore began too late among central Pennsylvanians, Shoemaker offered that "people looked upon their individual lives as of little consequence, their deeds as simple duty" (Shoemaker 1912, xvii). Going on to discuss Native Americans from whom he recovered legends, he explained that "as to the Indians or their history, they were regarded with loathing or indifference. We have no one to-day who would collect the annals of English sparrows or Cooper's hawks. Fifty years ago, even, was not too late, as Indians were met with from time to time, and aroused no particular attention; they were tolerated as itinerant basket weavers or harvest-hands…. When the present writer came upon the scene 'all was over,' but there were gleams in the embers of romance and folk-lore that showed that they contained life. He was able to learn the legends from a few of the old people, who were boys when there were still borderers and Indians whose talk was interesting enough for them to listen to and remember." So Shoemaker concluded, "As there seemed to be no one else bent on chronicling and preserving them, the author, with a full realization of his limitations, has 'stuck at it'" (Shoemaker 1912, xvii–xviii, xvi).

The natural wilderness, Shoemaker argued, deserved preservation because every tree and rock potentially had history and folklore attached to it. And to him they seemed to have more "spirit" as a result than the products of his industrial age (later he bemoaned the advent of the nuclear age). Especially up in the mountains, befitting Christian mythology of wisdom derived from going to isolated mountaintops, one somehow had a clearer vista of life's meaning. In rivers, Shoemaker depicted the constant flow of the past and people who used them to explore the wilderness. And "it is in the forests that voices were first heard, linking us to the beyond" (Shoemaker 1913, xvi). In *Black Forest Souvenirs* (1914), Shoemaker recounted his trips "into the forest in 1908, 1909 and 1910." He romantically wrote: "These visits only accentuated the sense of sadness for the arboreal paradise that was no more, which on the wholesale plan, lumbering had swept away. The hand of man had changed the face of nature from green to brown. It was during these latter visits that [I] thought more of the ancient legends which were so easy to hear in 1898, but so difficult to obtain in 1910" (Shoemaker 1914, xvi). The titles of Shoemaker's books such as *Tales of the Bald Eagle Mountains, In the Seven Mountains, Juniata Memories, Black Forest Souvenirs, Allegheny Episodes,* and *Susquehanna Legends* thus refer repeatedly to endangered natural sites, particularly mountains, rivers, and forests.

For Shoemaker, folklore represented the realm between history and fiction, nature and culture, and it got everyday people talking about themselves, their past, and their preindustrial surroundings. To him folklore came from the spirited age of romance before "modern civilization" took over, and it reflected America's roots as the "glorious land of romance." Collecting and reading folklore "gives us greater pride of home and birth," Shoemaker reflected, "it enables us to love deeper our hills and valleys, by feeling that they were once the homes of brave and true men and women, white and red, whose lives were as highly colored as the heroes and heroines of classic antiquity, Theseus and Helen, Orpheus and Eurydice" (Shoemaker 1917b, 10). More than a field for scholars, appreciation for folklore was to Shoemaker a civic duty that should be spread by community organizations. As early as 1915, Shoemaker informed his audiences that "in some countries it [folklore] is collected under government patronage. England and Ireland have been devoting much time to it of late; Scotland has always made it a part of her national story. France, Germany, Russia, Japan and India would lose much of the picturesqueness of their literature did it not exist" (Allison 1915, 19–20). With his booster spirit and popular goals, Shoemaker found himself at odds with folklorists over what folklore was and how it should be presented. If he failed to woo scholars, he convinced his pals in government that promoting folklore perpetuated what Pennsylvania was all about—a modern-day Eldorado—and it became a centerpiece of the conservation and tourist program that eventually jumped ahead of other industries of steel, coal, oil, and lumbering.

The American "age of romance" that Shoemaker wanted to promote served to allay fears that America would be built over by a pernicious version of industrial capitalism. He worried that money and materialism were goals that overshadowed traditional values of civility and community. The cities and their new residents that commanded the artificial light of industrialization appeared to him a threat to America's colonial heritage. Like many other leaders who traced their roots to colonial settlement, Shoemaker was startled by the flood tide of eastern and southern European immigration raised by turn-of-the-century industrialization. In the mythology of Shoemaker's wilderness, not only Pennsylvania was being promoted, but old Protestant America itself. Pennsylvania held the wilderness, the "frontier," that epitomized the original American consciousness of the invitation extended by the New World's fertile Eden. Shoemaker was hardly alone in believing that in such a place, democratic principles and civil values thrived, and assimilation, or "Americanization," would be realized. In rhetoric that dripped old-time religion and evolutionary natural history, one could hear that from the mix of many pilgrim groups coming to the American Promised Land emerged a unique American type, a new Adam born of the Edenic wilderness. Shoemaker's distinction was his promoter's, some even said preacher's, zeal for spreading the good news in the marketing revolution brought by newspapers and periodicals around the turn of the century. Building a reverence for an imagined past that translated into Pennsylvania's special mystique, Shoemaker used his newspapers as his pulpit and his stories as testament for a modern era.

The kind of folklore he published had several persistent themes, most notably the intermixing of ethnic strains to produce a vigorous American type. His stories romanticized a harmonious golden age in the American wilderness before industrialization brought destruction to the land and its people. He was inspired by the work of fellow New Yorkers George Bird Grinnell, Ernest Thompson Seton, and Theodore Roosevelt who used stories of the wild to promote wildlife conservation. Although these leading conservationists centered their efforts on the romantic West, Shoemaker remained focused on Pennsylvania, which he considered America's first wilderness. From his position of cultural authority as the publisher of several city dailies, he became a leader of a Progressive campaign in the twentieth century to restore Pennsylvania's woods and preserve the state as a cherished home to wildlife as well as folklife. Touting rugged frontier figures of Daniel Boone and Davy Crockett as the new American pantheon born of the wilderness replacing Old World classical heroes, Shoemaker and his Progressive cronies in the Boone and Crockett Club in New York City (led by Theodore Roosevelt and George Bird Grinnell) set out to explore and save the wilderness. By saving a source of American distinction and wonder, they thought that they could recover a sense of American nationhood and spirituality at a time of rapid industrialization, immigration, and urbanization.

Shoemaker and his Progressive friends used their imaginations and their pens to promote a unified vision of America's genuine landscape and legend. It was a patriotic movement, Shoemaker often declared, to preserve the roots of America in the forested wilderness, and where better than in the only state with forests, or sylvan, in its name? Not born in the state, he nonetheless trumpeted Pennsylvania as "God's chosen wonderland," the "mystic region," "wooded paradise," and "glorious land of romance." His campaign is significant because while he was glorifying the abundance of the Pennsylvania wilderness, Shoemaker's adopted state was symbolizing the heights of industrial transformation. Railroad, coal, oil, iron, steel, and lumber industries laid their claim to the state's land and people in dramatic fashion after 1870. As Pennsylvania's image went—rustic or industrial—so it seemed the nation's would go.

PUBLICIZING TRADITIONS

In addition to writing the legends he heard for Pennsylvania newspapers, Shoemaker encouraged others to contribute similar material for newspapers he had bought in Altoona, Reading, Jersey Shore, and Bradford. His editorials expressed strong support for Progressive causes, particularly the conservation stands of Theodore Roosevelt and Gifford Pinchot. The Progressive stance Shoemaker took called for state management of natural and historical resources. Thus he vigorously supported the creation of state boards to create and manage wilderness areas, state parks, and public historical sites. In his newspaper editorials, in his books and many addresses, his many organizations and state commissions, he lobbied for restoring balance with nature, and the harmonious life and values it fostered.

If collecting and archiving folklore represented the preservation of folklore, encouraging its perpetuation by restoring its original settings and applying it to education, entertainment, and literature signified its conservation. Even before Shoemaker took the official state folklorist position with conservationist goals in 1948, he hosted "Raftsman Reunions" at Camp Shoemaker where he encouraged musical and narrative exchanges. The camp also served as a Boy Scout center, and Shoemaker held programs for storytelling around the campfire. His Alpine Club outings were also meant to explore and restore the original settings of the wilderness that he felt gave rise to folklore. He arranged for Pennsylvania Folklore Society meetings to be held in conjunction with the Pennsylvania Storytelling League or Poetry Society and he organized creative readings based on local folklore.

Besides meetings and books, festivals provided another opportunity for Shoemaker to popularize folklore among the general public. He served as chairman of the Pennsylvania Folk Festival and advised the Americans All Folk Festival (formerly the Festival of Nations). Bucknell University hosted the Pennsylvania Folk Festival through the 1930s and gave the festival's direction over to folklore collector George Korson. Korson wrote Shoemaker to state his aim to "popularize folklore by means of the folk festival and thus create interest in the subject and build up audiences who will enjoy such interesting works as yours."[6] Always one for pointing out the "usefulness" of public folklore activity, Shoemaker complimented Korson for enabling elderly and retired workers to have new life as performers. As chairman, he helped publicize the festival's goals and activities. The festival was remarkably successful, attracting as many as thirty thousand visitors.

Shoemaker had been involved in state efforts for conservation of natural resources as a member of the State Forestry Board and the State Geographic Board after 1918 and he used this experience to argue for historical and cultural conservation. Shoemaker served on the Forestry Board with Gifford Pinchot who went on to run for governor on a Progressive platform. Shoemaker wrote a biography of Pinchot for his successful campaign. Upon becoming governor in 1923, Pinchot appointed Shoemaker chairman of the Pennsylvania Historical Commission, an early example of a state-sponsored commission for public history. In this post, Shoemaker directed an extensive program for marking historical sites and undertaking archaeological excavations of Indian and frontier sites. Shoemaker claimed to have written over four thousand markers himself. He hoped that marked sites would increase appreciation among Pennsylvanians for local contributions to national history, instill a regional sense of pride, and help protect historic locations from industrial development. He expanded his public history role as officer of several county historical societies and president of the Pennsylvania Federation of Historical Societies.

Shoemaker founded and introduced the Pennsylvania Folklore Society to the federation in 1924. Shoemaker explained that the society would preserve "unwritten history" and encourage all Pennsylvanians to be involved in the collecting task. By the end of the 1920s, Shoemaker was Pennsylvania's best-known worker in the folklore and history fields. He published a daily column featuring folklore, conservation, and history topics for the *Tribune* that was carried throughout the state. A strong backer of Republican politics, Shoemaker was rewarded in 1930 by being named ambassador to Bulgaria.

Shoemaker credited his experience in Bulgaria between 1930 and 1933 with the idea of state-sponsored folklore organization. As early as 1936, Shoemaker told reporters "that the Bulgarian idea, that the government should subsidize the work of preserving folklore is worthy of emulation in the United States" ("Introducing" 1936). He touted government sponsorship of collecting trips and archives for folklore for its contribution to protection of the environment and its promotion of national spirit. Shoemaker admired the promotion of Bulgarian folk dances and costumes as a source of pride in national celebrations. He was particularly impressed by the work of the Bulgarian Ministry of Education. The ministry guided Bulgarian teachers in the collection and teaching of folklore, and published volumes to record "source materials of Bulgarian culture," such as folk songs, folktales, legends, and proverbs. Shoemaker contributed to the effort by offering a silver cup prize for the best book on Bulgarian folklore published each year. His interest in folklore research while he was minister resulted in his being awarded honorary membership in the folklore societies of Bulgaria, Romania, and Turkey. He also had a forest preserve in Bulgaria named in his honor. Apropos of Shoemaker's advocacy for wilderness areas, his preserve was the only one of twelve parks to be kept a primitive area where all forms of trees, plants, and wildlife were left undisturbed.

While in Bulgaria, Shoemaker's investments suffered greatly during the Depression. His banks failed, his newspaper went into the red, and his real estate values plummeted. He lost the family fortune but managed to hang onto his newspaper. His friend from the diplomatic corps, George Earle, had been elected governor of Pennsylvania in 1936 and gave Shoemaker a lift by appointing him to the paid position of state archivist, a post he held until 1948, except for two years as director of the State Museum. At the archives, Shoemaker began a folklore section, but complained that the post did not allow for "outdoors work collecting oral traditions." He may have startled an audience of historians by asserting that the State Archives,

> the most authoritative source of Pennsylvania history are entirely lacking in human interest. They consist of page after page of cabals of cunning politicians and self seeking soldiers. They contain nothing concerning the social, domestic, economic or cultural life of colonial and Revolutionary times. They give us no picture of the home life of the people, of that medley of races who made up colonial Pennsylvania. We soon become tired reading of the rancor, jealousy and hatred between various military and civilian factions and seek for a new fountain head of history. Therefore it is in the folklore and oral traditions of the people themselves that we must look for the adequate picture of the times.[7]

Such a call for an "adequate picture of the times" based on folk cultural research had more than the usual reception in Pennsylvania because of a growing number of folkloristic efforts related to public history after 1935. Arthur D. Graeff, who had been involved in the American Guide Series sponsored by the New Deal's Work Projects Administration, thought of the years after 1935 in Pennsylvania as a renaissance period of interest in lore that drew national attention. He thought that it was at least partly due to American response to Nazi folklore to make a claim for a superior Aryan folk spirit or character (Graeff 1955). Many writers during the 1930s touted American folklore as a rich trove of democratic society. It showed that unlike fascist regimes, a national society could be plural, including a special trinity of regional, "racial" or ethnic, and occupational cultures. Indeed, the Pennsylvania Folk Festival chaired by Henry Shoemaker used these categories to organize the sections of the festival. Benjamin Botkin offered his *Treasury of American Folklore* against Nazi efforts to speak "of folklore in terms of the 'racial heritage' or insists that a particular folk group or body of tradition is 'superior' or 'pure'" (Botkin 1944, xxvi). A familiar call went out for recovering authentic American lore before

it disappeared, especially in Pennsylvania where "traditions preserved orally flour-
ished as vigorously as in any North American region," according to Penn State professor Samuel Bayard (1945, 1). "To rescue it," Bayard advised during the 1940s,
quick action will be necessary, for to all appearances it will not survive delay. And
its disappearance through neglect will be a cultural loss to both the state and the
nation" (Bayard 1945, 14).

New Deal programs such as the American Guide Series recast the central issue
of cultural loss during the Great Depression. They marked a shift of attention
from the ways that previously poor "foreign elements" would assimilate to the dignity that native-born workers could muster in the face of Depression poverty.
Images of farmers forced off their land and migrants in search of work suggested
that the regional map of America was rapidly changing. Passage of immigration
restrictions had quieted the debate over the Americanization of ethnic cultures,
but reports of foreclosures and natural disasters increased awareness of breaks in
regional traditions. As industry suffered and migrations forced by the hunt for
economic opportunity spread, a new consciousness of workers and their attachment to place arose. Reminiscent of Shoemaker's Progressive campaign to "sell
Pennsylvania to Pennsylvanians" early in the century, the federally sponsored
American Guide Series—structured as state travel manuals featuring sites of historical and cultural interest—to "introduce America to Americans" as a "rich culture." Another indication of regionalism during the period was the American
Folkways series edited by novelist Erskine Caldwell. Over twenty regional
overviews connecting landscape, people, and culture came into popular circulation. With titles such as *Short Grass Country* (by Stanley Vestal) and *Blue Ridge
Country* (by Jean Thomas), writers extolled the virtues of "old-timers" and "unlettered farm workers," especially those in the South and West. Stories of cowboys in
the West, sharecroppers in the South, and lumberjacks in the upper Midwest gave
the impression of American ruggedness and persistence in the face of crisis.

In Pennsylvania, the voice of the folk in mines and mills, farms and forests,
came across in popular festivals and publications—many of them government
sponsored—to bolster the public spirit. The Pennsylvania installment of the WPA-
sponsored American Guide Series opened with a section on history followed by
chapters on ethnic folkways and traditions of mine, mill, and factory. S. K. Stevens
in his foreword underscored the connection of this documentation to economic
conditions and cultural re-creation. He wrote that the guide "should be a contribution to better citizenship through making Pennsylvanians conscious of their
traditions and backgrounds. In these troubled times such a work may well aid in
the preservation of those fundamental values so essential to the maintenance of
our democracy" (Writers Program 1940, vii).

Amidst this outburst of regional documentary activities stood Henry
Shoemaker, the genial elder statesman of Pennsylvania folklore, whose major
claim was not so much the professionalization, but the "popularization" of

Pennsylvania's traditions. As a devoted Progressive, he advocated the conservation of cultural and natural resources belonging to the "common citizen for the public good." If Shoemaker earned respect for his Progressive efforts especially during the 1920s, during the New Deal he lacked a flock of professional followers. New workers in the field stressed the realistic depiction of working-class industrial culture and the persistence of ethnic-regional communities. Through the 1940s the growing university system ascended as a source of cultural authority and young folklore professors in Pennsylvania's public eye such as Samuel Bayard, Alfred Shoemaker, and Don Yoder voiced skepticism about the appropriateness of government's involvement in the administration of regional heritage. Shoemaker pushed on, however, for a state program for building romantic regionalism around Pennsylvania's history and folklore. Later, Shoemaker quietly defended his stand in the conflicts over Pennsylvania's cultural re-creation: "I think if I can in any way uncover a portion of the magnificently rich lore of Pennsylvania, preserving it for posterity, I shall feel that the time and effort I put into the study has been greatly repaid me. Indeed there is no greater thing that a man can leave to posterity than the fruit of his life's work, knowing it will be preserved and widely used."[8]

In 1939, Shoemaker met with the national Federal Works Project editor Benjamin Botkin at the State Museum. Known for popularizing regional folklore, Botkin admired Shoemaker's work and he included two of his stories in the best-selling *A Treasury of American Folklore* (1944). If the New Deal project Botkin described at their meeting provided an inspiration for the state folklorist post, Shoemaker for his part did not admit it. Shoemaker was a vocal critic of the New Deal, although he agreed that government should be involved in conserving heritage in the name of the constitutional directive to care for the public's welfare.

Shoemaker received a chance to air his views when Governor Edward Martin, campaigning for the preservation of Pennsylvania historical sites as a way of instilling civic pride, took office in 1943. As an opponent of the New Deal, Martin was not usually one for adding governmental programs. He nonetheless advocated strong governmental promotion of state and local heritage to build "loyalty to those ideals and institutions that have fashioned the American way of life" (Pennsylvania Historical 1950, 24). He invoked the need for local patriotism during World War II and considered public history a way to foster American values. The governor proposed the creation of a powerful independent historical agency reporting directly to him. In 1945 he reached his goal when legislation merged the Historical Commission, the State Archives, and State Museum into a more active Pennsylvania Historical and Museum Commission that had a conservationist mission. Donald Cadzow, formerly state archaeologist, was named the first executive director and Sylvester Stevens became state historian. Both officials had interests in "conserving" the cultural heritage of the state. Stevens announced that "by arousing pride in what Pennsylvanians have done in the past for the state, for the

Nation, and for mankind, the Commission seeks to build up and encourage sound patriotism and true civic feeling" (Stevens and Kent 1947, 5).

The patriotic posturing that was occurring after World War II owed to the climate of political nationalism of the war years. The country's leaders urged Americans to stand together as a nation and define themselves by the democratic ideas and moral values for which the nation stood against evil fascism. The story the new commission planned to present included the patriotic events of the state and the popular story of its people. Key phrases recur in the commission's rhetoric of the period such as "the American way of life," "conserving heritage," and "love of country." The commission report for 1945–1950 declared, for example,

> We need in our Nation and in our Commonwealth, as never before, a new appreciation and understanding of our heritage. The danger of being deprived of the cherished institutions that constitute the American way of life is very real and imminent. Understanding must rest upon a greater diffusion of popular knowledge about our history and the historic roots of our development and progress. A deeper love of our country and appreciation of our heritage should rest upon the firm bedrock of love of state and community. This naturally translates itself into love of country and understanding of all our national ideals and aspirations as Americans. (Pennsylvania Historical 1950, 1)

In a statement that probably owed to Shoemaker's lobbying, the report emphasized that "conserving the raw materials of history is as necessary to the well-being of the Commonwealth as is the conserving of natural resources to its material strength" (Pennsylvania Historical 1950, 11).

The story the new commission planned to present included the patriotic events of the state and the popular story of the everyday people. For the latter, folklore and its image of people cooperating in communities entered the picture the commission wanted to prominently display. Indeed, several directors of state historical societies (especially in Progressive strongholds of New York, Minnesota, and Wisconsin), representing local and family legacies, took the lead in publishing and promoting public folklore as a means of publicizing the cultural connections of citizens to the state (see Jordan 1946; L. Jones 1950; Halpert 1985). Pennsylvania's state historian Sylvester Stevens argued that if the commission was to present the story of the state's people in various forms, it would need to actively retrieve oral as well as documentary materials for interpretation. He loudly announced: "I can testify in person to the serious lack of the folklore materials which are badly needed to enrich our understanding and enliven our appreciation of many aspects of our early Pennsylvania history" (Stevens 1965, xi). For the commission, the folklore coming out of "distinctive regional areas, from the occupational groups that comprise the laboring population, and from the numerous nationalities that have Pennsylvania their new home" was especially significant. Shoemaker's work had demonstrated to the commission that folklore was interesting to the public and that including it in conventional historical work could "invest the written record with an imagination and color that reflect the deep-seated, inner forces which lie close to human conduct" (Pennsylvania Historical 1950, 15).

CREATING A PUBLIC FOLKLORE FOR THE STATE

The State Archives had the primary responsibility for maintaining the written record, but the structure of the unit needed revision to accomplish the new goals of the commission. A committee reviewed the archives and recommended that a Folklore Division be created in the state historian's unit and a professional archivist be hired. Shoemaker was at first suspicious of the recommendation, because he thought that Cadzow and Stevens planned to remove him or minimize his influence. He accepted the post after receiving assurance that the Folklore Division would be separate from history and that a deputy could be hired. To underscore his independence, Shoemaker asked for the title of state folklorist, equivalent to Stevens's of state historian. He confided to a legislator, "Folk Lore has been a main interest of my life and the position seemed like official recognition of my life time's effort to collect and preserve Pennsylvania folk lore, and I would receive a salary in keeping with my long services and general training and experience."[9]

John Witthoft, formerly the State Museum's curator of anthropology, remembered that "many people in the state wanted folklore represented on the Commission. It was a popular subject after the 1940s, and Shoemaker seemed a logical person to do it. He had many friends across the state and he was closely associated with folklore."[10] Dolores Coffey, who served in the commission's executive director's office, added that "the position of chief or Director of the Folklore Division was a natural for Colonel Shoemaker. He was President of the Pennsylvania Folklore Society, a friend to many of the big folklore writers and collectors such as George Korson."[11]

On March 11, 1948, the commission announced Shoemaker's historic appointment and the next day, the Harrisburg *Patriot* featured on its front page the news that went out across the state's news wires: "Archivist Gets Folklore Post." "It is an interesting assignment," Shoemaker told the paper, for "Pennsylvania has the richest folklore heritage of any state in the union" ("Archivist" 1948, 1). Cadzow's explanation was that "the Commission decided that fuller use should be made of Colonel Shoemaker's abilities as a folklorist, and the new division was created to give full scope to his talents in this field" ("Archivist" 1948, 15). In his first day on the job, Shoemaker excitedly wrote a friend, "I am taking over a new department in the State Historical Commission, to collect and compile the Pennsylvania Folklore, and I think it is going to be interesting work with considerable time out-of-doors."[12] It was a position essentially created by and for Shoemaker, but Shoemaker hoped that such positions would be established in other states. He expansively planned, he informed Cadzow, to "correspond with all the American folklore societies."[13] Shoemaker's prime office space on Capitol Hill across from the governor's office seemed to confirm the importance of the position.

The *Journal of American Folklore* carried an announcement of the position in its fourth issue of 1948. Louis C. Jones, editor of *New York Folklore Quarterly*, also carried news of the groundbreaking role, and Shoemaker wrote him personally to thank him for acknowledging "the fact that our State of Pennsylvania was the first to have a State Folklorist." Fired up, Shoemaker went on to brag of other developments in the state: "It is not only the one to have the first State Folklorist, but it is also the first to have a chair in folklore in a university, at Franklin and Marshall College; also the Wyomissing Institute of Fine Arts, near Reading, has established a Division of Folklore."[14] Shoemaker testified to a sudden outpouring of folkloristic activities. "It looks as if Pennsylvania folklore," he gushed to Arthur D. Graeff, "after a long time in getting started, has taken on real life and there seems to be no end to it and its ramifications and details, which take in every aspect of our daily life."[15]

Shoemaker began a folklore archives in the office and wrote a weekly column on folklore that went to newspapers across the state. He took excursions into the countryside gathering material at least once a week and appeared at numerous state functions as representative of the commission. He used the office as headquarters of the Pennsylvania Folklore Society and issued its publications. Despite these groundbreaking activities, Shoemaker wrote many memos to Cadzow expressing his disappointment. After Don Yoder turned down the job of deputy, Shoemaker failed to get approval for another assistant. He did not get support for a publication series and his requests for new equipment went unfilled.

Well into his seventies as the Democratic administration of George Leader took office in 1956, Shoemaker hung onto the position in the hope that a successor could be named, but academic folklorists in the state such as Samuel Bayard and Alfred Shoemaker resisted the idea of a state folklorist position and discouraged others from being involved. Bayard and Alfred Shoemaker hurled criticism at Henry Shoemaker for distorting folklore study with political and romantic leanings. Alfred Shoemaker at first tried to take over the Pennsylvania Folklore Society and, when that bid proved unsuccessful, then formed the rival Pennsylvania Folklife Society. He publicly criticized literary distortions and political uses of folklore and named the state folklorist's work as a prime example.

The public row came to a head when Alfred and Henry vied for control of the huge and valuable Unger-Bassler collection of Pennsylvania-German manuscripts. Henry was sure he had snared the collection for the state for deposit in the public historical site of Conrad Weiser Park. Alfred Shoemaker meanwhile worked on Bassler to convince him that Henry had a Republican political interest in using the collection to present an assimilationist view of ethnic culture. Henry shot off a letter to Representative Daniel Hoch to complain: "As to the news concerning Dr. Bassler, his recent visit to me would indicate that he is one hundred per cent sold on Weiser Park, and he seemed very enthusiastic about the meeting and the

Henry Shoemaker as state folklorist giving an address at Tiadaghton Elm, July 4, 1951, legendary spot of the declaration of independence made by the "Fair Play Settlers" of Clinton County in 1776. Shoemaker referred to the incident as an example of folklore revealing "unrecorded history." (*Lock Haven Express*)

prospect of depositing the Unger collection in the old Marschall House. I cannot conceive of an organization less politically minded than the Weiser Park Board, as at the table the other night sat Democrats, Republicans and independents, and I know that I am one of the least politically minded persons in public life, and have served under Democratic presidents and governors as well as Republicans." Bassler ended up reneging on his pledge to Henry Shoemaker and donated the material to Franklin and Marshall College and Alfred Shoemaker's Pennsylvania Dutch Folklore Center. Dolores Coffey recalled that "it was a terrible blow to him [Shoemaker] when Alfred Shoemaker and Don Yoder began to criticize his work, and even more so when the criticism was published in the press.... I do know the Commission did not feel it could come to the Colonel's defense which might have been another blow."[16]

Alfred Shoemaker became especially annoyed at Henry's invitations to creative writers to elaborate on folklore, and resisted associations that the state folklorist made between the Folklore Society and storytelling leagues and poetry societies. The rift grew when Alfred, who promoted an ethnological approach, publicly ridiculed the superficiality of Henry Shoemaker's literary folklore collections. Alfred accordingly announced at one Pennsylvania Folklore Society meeting that to make the distinction between the shallowness of Henry's folklore and the depth of folklife research, "we will drop the term folk lore and substitute 'folk life' and 'folk culture.'"[17] Brandishing his expertise as an experienced publisher and journalist, Henry Shoemaker meanwhile made unflattering remarks about the appearance and content of Alfred's *Pennsylvania Dutchman*. "As to my personal comments on the 'Dutchman,'" Henry wrote Alfred, "I realized that the Pennsylvania Dutch, a far more valuable culture than New England, deserved a more fitting mouthpiece, on good paper, well illustrated, and ploughing out into new fields rather than repeating the old stories we have known all our lives."[18] In his statement, Henry Shoemaker revealed philosophical differences between his literary view of folklore and Alfred's ethnological perspective. Alfred systematically gathered objective data—mostly material and social such as barns, customs, foods, and crafts—that could be quantified and analyzed. For Alfred, the goal was to record the ordinary and characteristic lifeways of traditional communities, in their totality, and he demonstrated this goal in his special attention to the "Dutch Country" within America. In Alfred's view, America had a diverse social landscape underscoring the persistence of ethnic-religious cultures such as the Pennsylvania Germans. Henry, on the other side, wanted to record lore to inspire the public with imaginative local narratives that recovered America.

At the time, the feud between Alfred and Henry Shoemaker was reminiscent of a national one shaking the foundations of the American Folklore Society. Outspoken Richard Dorson (1916–1981), who taught folklore at Michigan State University and later chaired the Ph.D.-granting Folklore Institute at Indiana University, unleashed a firestorm by discouraging figures he called "popularizers" and "amateurs" from the leadership of the American Folklore Society. He located the center of this censurable activity in New York and Pennsylvania. In Dorson's view, the popularizers undermined the serious study of folklore, destroyed the integrity of authentic traditions, misrepresented folklore's meaning, and endangered the academic growth of a folkloristic discipline. He assailed literary tampering with a tradition bearer's texts as akin to desecrating a historian's manuscripts. While MacEdward Leach, secretary-treasurer of the American Folklore Society, thought that popularizers did a service by keeping folklore interests before the public hungry for colorful regional literature, Dorson damned their efforts as "fakelore" (Dorson 1971a, 26–27). Contrary to Shoemaker's conception of "state folklorist," Dorson thought that collection and analysis properly belonged in the authority-wielding academy, carried out by unsentimentalized students trained in a separate, objective discipline of folklore, and he argued against the expansion of public folklore positions like Shoemaker's (Dorson 1971a, 40–42).

As the first state folklorist, Shoemaker was given great latitude by the executive director of the commission to define his responsibilities. His planning for the position began with a two-year plan. In it he envisioned supervising three branches to the division: "collection, compilation, publicity." He planned for four "departments" engaging in fieldwork to insure that the division would have state-wide coverage:

> As there are four folk cultures in Pennsylvania, Western, Northern, Southern, and Eastern, four departments, with a collector assigned to each county, as the ultimate aim, equipped with typewriter, recording machine, to range these localities all the year round, gathering up ballads, legends, customs, proverbs, old words, but in the next two years if the Division could have four, or even two collectors in the field, one for each locality, all provided with a knowledge of Pennsylvania Dutch, in which form most of the Folklore exists, a beginning could be made. In the home office these collectors would [turn] in their findings monthly, either in shorthand notes or in typed form, where four office assistants would separate as to topics, and file in the most available manner for public use. There should be a secretary stenographer for each of these helpers, a secretary stenographer for the chief, a secretary stenographer for his assistant, and a messenger. The chief and his assistant would act as general program directors, interview callers, give out interviews, make addresses, write articles, and go out in the field as advisors. To the searchers, or on personal quests which seemed [expedient] for them to run down. Once a year the Division should publish an index by topics and localities of all materials collected, under the imprint of the Historical and Museum Commission. For the next two years in order to collect before it is too late, the ranks of old people, for example the old canal boatmen, raftmen, log drivers, charcoal furnace hands, wagoners are thinning, and we know hardly a civil war veteran survives. It would seem essential to have at least two workers in the field, their sustenance, returning to their homes Friday afternoons until Monday A.M., with automobiles, etc. provided, by State and (serviced, equipped with typing machines, recorders, etc.) Four compilers in the home office with Secretary stenographers, machines, etc. The chief

with Secretary stenographer, his assistant similarly equipped, and a messenger. This would mean a staff of fifteen including the chief and same [*space*] as was Division of Archives in 1912. When they were doing a good piece of work, but gradually cut down to four, including the Archives, when became only partly effective. It would seem that the Chief of Folklore should receive $5,000, as he gives the Division the experience of a life time, an energy and enthusiasm which only comes to one who began the work fifty years ago and knows every nook and corner of Pennsylvania, its people, history and folklore, to give him less discourages, especially after his years of research.

The four men in the field should receive $200 each monthly, and keep of selves, car [*space*] stationery. The office compilers $40 weekly, the six stationery stenographers, at the current rate of such employment, the messenger on the same basis. The assistant should be paid $3500, in which event would not have lost Prof. Don Yoder, and might still secure a great man like Prof. Sam Bayard. If it should be this level could not be reached, 1949–1951, I would feel that two field men the most important the compilers in the Harrisburg office cut to two, and four secretary stenographers instead of six and keep the messenger. The recapitulation of the reduced force would be, 2 field men, 2 cars, 2 recording machines, 2 office compilers, 4 secretary stenographers, 4 machines, 1 messenger, or 11 in staff. The work would lapse and lag on less. Why not get it off to a good start, or abandon it, single-handed your chief has done his best, but it is like putting him to count the grains of the sands of the ocean. Cutting down from four men in field to two, four office helpers to two, secretary-stenographers to two, I feel some progress could be made yet far out of line to my look ahead of March 13, 1948, yet the growth can only come by the size of staff in the field.[19]

After a year in the job, Henry Shoemaker reported feeling frustrated by the lack of staff. It forced him, he said, to follow a "conservative path." He outlined a "two fold purpose" for the position: "Not only does it preserve the history of a people according to law, geography and economics, but it preserves the manners, customs, the heart and soul of a people as well."[20]

Shoemaker prepared monthly reports to the executive director during his tenure as state folklorist, so he left a good record of what he accomplished. According to the reports, he went on an average of two to four collecting trips a month, mostly to areas he had not covered during his peak years of collecting before 1930. He wrote a weekly release on folklore for *Capitol News*, which was distributed to the state's newspapers. He delivered between two and four addresses per month, attended a similar number of organizational meetings, and appeared frequently on radio and television shows. He made appearances at ceremonies and other official functions, including dedications of historical markers, openings of exhibits, and events at inaugurations and Pennsylvania farm shows. He answered between 70 and 130 letters a month and received a similar number of visitors to his office. He prepared scrapbooks and card indexes on different topics with clippings, mostly Shoemaker's, on folklore. He distributed mimeographed folklore collections for distribution to members of the Pennsylvania Folklore Society and interested parties. He organized branches of the Pennsylvania Folklore Society, with the goal of placing one in every county of the state, "under competent chairmen, who will collect and send to the Folklore Division at Harrisburg, all material collected in their localities." By 1949, he claimed "a hundred enthusiastic volunteer workers in all the counties throughout the state" contributing material to the division.[21] To reach these far-flung workers, he proposed a number of regional meetings of the Pennsylvania Folklore Society to replace the annual meeting in Harrisburg, and he spoke frequently on "county" folklore, encouraging its collection by local historical and folklore societies. He hoped to compile these results into a massive state folklore archives and build a library of folkloristic books.

Shoemaker needed extra staff and funding to realize his ambitious plans. During one brief interval, he had paid fieldwork help from Victoria Smallzel, and on occasion he benefitted from extra secretarial or archival assistance, but for the most part he worked alone with a secretary. This is the way he described his day:

> I usually arrive at 8 a.m. and put out the things that I am planning to work with during the day. At 8:30 the mail begins to arrive, and by 9:00 I am ready to dictate answers to secretary-stenographer who arrives around 8:30. By 11 o'clock I am generally through the mail and have many of the letters answered. Around 11 my secretary goes for my light lunch and often gets her own. On other days, she goes out from 12 to 1 o'clock. Generally visitors do not come in until about 1, and they appear off and on for the rest of the day, some on appointments, others happen in. I have many phone calls, generally asking for information from nine until four thirty. In my spare moments I work on articles for Capitol News, and folk tales from my notes, being typed and filed. Or I work up my notes so as to make stories from them ready for typing. I endeavor to clear my days work by "going home time," and often succeed at this. The scope of folklore is the time put on it. I do about all that is possible with one helper.[22]

Early in television's development, Shoemaker, ever the communicator, saw great potential in using media to spread interest in folklore and gain research outlets. He wrote Cadzow, "I believe that television would be an ideal means for bringing the facts of Folklore to the public's attention and thereby getting more help from outsiders who know where some of the dying Folklore can be found. I have spoken on radio a number of times and on television two or three times and from the number of letters and phone calls I receive after these talks it seems to me that the public is interested and would be more so if they hear of it oftener." "Probably the best stroke," he added, "was connecting ourselves with *Capitol News* as these stories go to many newspapers every week and I get very interesting responses from people who know stories that I have not previously heard."[23]

In effect, Shoemaker had created a folklore wire service feeding information to the community outlets of local newspapers. Well experienced in column writing, Shoemaker made the most of the weekly news releases to publicize and popularize Pennsylvania folklore. While giving public notice to state folklore work, the releases also made many academic folklorists and historians cringe because of the sugared and watered-down versions of collections peddled to the public. Responding to the popularity of Paul Bunyan as a journalistically developed frontier folk hero, Shoemaker quickly offered a real-life Pennsylvania version in "Cherry Tree Joe McCreery," "his heroic deeds from Cherry Tree to Williamsport being sung in every lumber camp and mountain cabin."[24] Scrambling to come up with fresh material weekly, Shoemaker frequently paraphrased the collection of others, such as his elaboration of Arthur Graeff's research into the Pennsylvania-German legend of the recluse Mountain Mary. Shoemaker's releases especially gained notice when he issued timely columns on the origins and customs of holidays such as Halloween and Christmas. He additionally issued releases with flashy headlines commemorating anniversaries, particularly for the state's ethnic groups. He used the occasion of the three-hundredth anniversary of Jewish settlement in Pennsylvania, for example, to briefly trace other "lost colonies" in Pennsylvania of Acadians and Waldensians.[25]

PROFESSIONALISM AND AUTHENTICITY

Samuel Bayard wrote in *Pennsylvania Folklife* that the damage done in Pennsylvania from Shoemaker's public work was "enormous" and "probably irreparable." He protested the marriage Shoemaker had arranged between folklore and the Historical Commission and howled that the work of Shoemaker's office "had the long-run effects of misleading some of the public, alienating others, hampering normal collection and study of the material, and completely destroying the ethnological value of anything published." In the popularizer-professional debates of the 1950s, Bayard flatly dismissed Shoemaker "as arrant a faker and 'fakelorist' as ever existed."[26] Bayard wanted to legitimate the folklorist's work as a trained academic specialty. He expressed annoyance at Shoemaker's attribution of folklorist to every naturalist, local colorist, or historian he admired. Popularization in Bayard's opinion distorted, indeed dumbed down the complex reality of tradition and tampered with the authenticity of the folk's own literature. Bayard thought that Shoemaker had used folklore for political rather than scholarly ends and worried that any connection of heritage to a public agency corrupted the hard facts of tradition.

Exploding Shoemaker's public presentation of Pennsylvania folklore, Bayard struck at the state folklorist's most cherished assumptions. Of the idea that Pennsylvania folklore arose anew out of local conditions and events, Bayard argued for its being properly understood in reference to its diffusion from European sources. As to Shoemaker's claim that folklore is unrecorded history, Bayard asserted that "what the historian considers important is usually disregarded and forgotten by bearers of a folk tradition, while legends tend to cluster thickly around happenings that, historically speaking, are quite obscure." Bayard recognized Shoemaker's purpose of promoting the state's cultural uniqueness, but he pointed out that too much evidence denies this sentimental notion. Related to

"Purists" and "popularizers" at the American Folklore Society meeting, July 28, 1962, Indiana University. In the bottom row, far left, "popularizer" Benjamin Botkin sits next to his academic defender MacEdward Leach of the University of Pennsylvania. In the second row, far right, stands Richard M. Dorson of Indiana University, leader of the "purists." In the top row are Pennsylvania folklorists Samuel Bayard (second from left), a vocal critic of Shoemaker's "state folklorist" work, and George Korson (second from right), Shoemaker's successor as president of the Pennsylvania Folklore Society. The full roster is, from left to right, 1st row: Benjamin Botkin, MacEdward Leach, Erminie Wheeler Voegelin, Catherine Luomala, Thelma James, Wayland Hand, Francis Lee Utley; 2d row: Charles Seeger, Warren E. Roberts, Newbell Niles Puckett, Mody P. Boatright, Louis C. Jones, Stith Thompson, Archer Taylor, Arthur Palmer Hudson, Richard M. Dorson; 3d row: Morris E. Opler, Samuel P. Bayard, D. K. Wilgus, Edson Richmond, George Korson, Sol Tax.

this romanticism is Shoemaker's implication that folklore especially attaches to "picturesque" groups such as lumbermen, railroaders, and canallers. Yet it is among ordinary farmers in Pennsylvania, Bayard declared, "that the oldest, most enduring, and most enlightening popular lore normally persists." Then Bayard targeted Shoemaker by stating that "this piece of common knowledge to folklorists throughout the western world has never been emphasized by an 'official historian' publicizer of folklore in Pennsylvania" (Bayard 1959, 11).

Bayard's harshest cut may have ultimately been to Shoemaker's public service for Pennsylvania. He shattered Shoemaker's goal of finding the unique traditions of Pennsylvania. This obsession with uniqueness, Bayard grumbled, must be influenced by Shoemaker's position as state folklorist, which serves purposes of publicity and patriotism, not the mission of furthering cultural knowledge. "What a folklore investigator is concerned with in the traditions of a region," Bayard wrote, "is not the distinctive and unique ... but the characteristic and revealing" (Bayard 1959, 12). Bayard was not even willing to grant Shoemaker the usual credit for blazing new trails for others to follow, because "attempting a synthesis long before the folklore materials for it were available ... is none the less lamentable," especially since it may have the consequence of inhibiting solid fieldwork. Because Shoemaker gave the mistaken impression that folklore constituted a certain bygone romantic type of story, "the empty gesturing of the past," so Bayard called it, other genuine traditions that could have been collected have been neglected. Bayard advocated a scientific regionalism being developed by academic linguists, cultural geographers, and folklife scholars during the 1950s. It called for a comprehensive mapping of regions on the basis of objective data subject to variation across space and stability over time such as dialect words, houses, barns, foods, and town forms (Glassie 1968; Zelinsky 1973).

Scientific regionalism challenged cherished American myths of the country's ancestors in romantic highland "regions." In Pennsylvania, academic studies suggested that a "Pennsylvania Culture Region" differed markedly from Shoemaker's portrayal of a heartland in rugged northcentral Pennsylvania. The objective map showed a Philadelphia "cultural hearth" fostering a strong Pennsylvania-German imprint on the landscape in central and southeastern Pennsylvania and extending down into western Maryland and Virginia. Out of this farmland "core" a Middle-Atlantic region formed moving westward toward Pittsburgh (Glass 1986). So much for Henry Shoemaker's mystical priority of Pennsylvania's forested wilderness. This challenge extended to other romantic highland regions of the southern Appalachians, Ozarks, Rockies, and Adirondacks. The romantic regionalism that gave rise to the highland myths was subjective. It was based on the way that people narrated themselves, or rather, the way that the narrative was invented and popularized for some national or state need. Besides magnifying, indeed symbolizing the ruggedness of highland existence, as well as the equalizing and renewing effects of the woods, romantic regionalism offered a religious overtone to America's ideals by placing them on the holy mountaintop close to God and nature. Henry Shoemaker summarized that Pennsylvanians have their soul in the highlands and forests because they imagine their values in the legends of the fertile wilderness. He insisted that they use them to provide the "inner meaning," or self-perception of locality and national experience (see Bronner 1996d, 45–52).

Whether academic criticism or the aging Shoemaker's ill health and erratic behavior had an influence, the facts are that in 1956 Shoemaker was unceremoniously fired from the commission by Democratic governor Leader, then the youngest governor Pennsylvania had ever had. Shoemaker's line to friends was that he "was let out for 'age.'"[27] His health failing, Shoemaker also stepped aside as president of the Pennsylvania Folklore Society in 1956 and George Korson took over the helm. The society made its farewell with a reception honoring Shoemaker after the spring 1957 meeting and the publication of a special "Henry Shoemaker" issue of *Keystone Folklore Quarterly* edited by Frank Hoffmann. As if to rebuff Bayard's and Dorson's criticisms of the popularizers, Korson titled his piece "Henry W. Shoemaker, *Folklorist*" following a dedication by New York's popularizer Harold Thompson. During the summer of 1957, Shoemaker returned to his beloved home Restless Oaks, but in August he suffered a heart attack forcing him into the Lock Haven Hospital for seven weeks. After a second attack a year later he died at a Williamsport hospital on July 15, 1958. The *New York Times* carried a full column on his life accompanied by a photograph the next day. It highlighted his role as diplomat and historian, while Pennsylvania newspapers typically dwelled on his newspaper publishing, public service in Pennsylvania, and writings on folklore.

After Henry Shoemaker's departure from the Pennsylvania Historical and Museum Commission, another reorganization occurred when Governor Leader placed Frank Melvin as chair of the seventh Historical Commission. Sylvester Stevens replaced Cadzow as executive director and he consolidated the divisions, thus eliminating the Folklore Division. Despite attempts to bring folklorists to the commission within the History Division during the 1950s, Stevens failed to restore the state folklorist position until 1966, when MacEdward Leach of the University of Pennsylvania, who worked with Shoemaker, helped secure funding for an "Ethnic Culture Survey" within the commission by an act of the legislature. Stevens intended the job for the elderly Leach, but the revered ballad scholar took ill before the position could be filled. Henry Glassie, a graduate student still in his twenties in the Folklore and Folklife program at the University of Pennsylvania, took the job and Leach died shortly after.

Meanwhile during the 1960s, Richard Dorson, then director of Indiana University's Folklore Institute, kept up his campaign to evict "popularizers" and "amateurs" from folklore's disciplinary home (Dorson 1971a, 1976c). He claimed the scholarly goals of Indiana University's Ph.D. program should be the model for future development of the growing discipline rather than the applied and even popularizing tendencies of folklore studies at the University of Pennsylvania (Dorson 1971a, 11–13; Abrahams 1992a). Dorson strongly denounced two of Shoemaker's favorites in New York—Benjamin Botkin and Moritz Jagendorf. He belittled Shoemaker as a "regional collector" type who turns into a "parochial folklorist, ploughing the same field endlessly, collecting simply to collect" (Dorson 1971a, 23–24). He thought that Henry Glassie, who received his Ph.D. in 1969, might suffer the same fate as state folklorist, and plucked him away from his position at the Pennsylvania Historical and Museum Commission shortly after he assumed the post to come to Indiana University as an academic type.

In his first report as state folklorist for the commission, Glassie wrote of his activities, including setting up archives, holding conferences, and issuing publications, much as the previous state folklorist had done. He recognized the precedent of Henry Shoemaker but he sought to establish a professional reputation for the position and establish folklife principles. His successor was David Hufford, also a young Ph.D. candidate from the Folklore and Folklife program at the University of Pennsylvania. Although the Ethnic Culture Survey was only three years old in 1969, Hufford offered its history as the "first state program in the country devoted to the collection, study and preservation of America's traditional cultures." Hufford knew of Shoemaker's precedent but stressed the groundbreaking role of the Ethnic Culture Survey as a systematic ethnological instrument.[28] Glassie, who had not written on the program beyond his reports, and who had not been well received by fellow commission members, received treatment in Hufford's piece as a young pioneer hero combining material with verbal traditions. Hufford's history did not discuss the circumstances leading to the passage of the legislation in 1966 or the background of state folklore efforts in Pennsylvania and elsewhere. Beyond the one paragraph given to the formation of the survey, the rest of the article discussed current activities.

Yet it is Hufford's account from which other chronicles have borrowed. The impression was that from Henry Glassie, a progressive line of professional folklore could be traced. Glassie was young as was the idea of public folklore at the state level. The image could be conveyed of continuous professional growth from this propitious beginning. The source of public folklore could be placed in academe and the direction could be mapped away from the "amateurs" and public interested in folklore. It had a founding hero, a miraculous birth, and an unbridled, almost magical development. Professional folklorists, if they were to accept public folklore, needed this narrative to affirm, in the words of Roger Abrahams in 1992, that "the work of public folklorists, then, is not less objective or scientific than that of academic folklorists" (Abrahams 1992a, 25).

In addition to seeming objective, the work of folklorists for the state in the 1990s also could appear increasingly socially therapeutic. Folklorists advocated for underrepresented, culturally neglected groups in need of attachment to state services. Roger Abrahams's historical commentary in 1992 viewed state folklorists in relation to the cultural politics of the 1990s. What he called the "intercessory role" of public folklorists taking up the cause of the "disempowered" through government projects from the New Deal to the Great Society echoed through retrospectives beginning with *Cultural Conservation* by Ormond Loomis (1983) and *The Conservation of Culture* edited by Burt Feintuch (1988) to *Public Folklore* edited by Robert Baron and Nicholas Spitzer (1992) and *Conserving Culture* edited by Mary Hufford (1994). Abrahams's view was that "since the 1960s it has become the accepted position that all scholarship arises from the investigator's sociopolitical concerns," and he affirmed the liberal stance that "the primary despoilers of folk culture still are the power brokers who too often forget about life-quality considerations in working out their engineering plans, their business mergers, their multinational takeovers" (Abrahams 1992a, 26). Yet one piece left out of chronicles of public folklore is that a prime mover for a controlling governmental role in cultural conservation and folklore was Shoemaker, a power broker from the wealthy elite.

What, then, prompted the creation of the first state folklorist position? My reading is that it owed to the background of Progressivism in Pennsylvania, influence-peddling of a prominent public figure caught in a bureaucratic reorganization, Republican nationalism after World War II—and a good bit of happenstance. Its link to the Ethnic Culture Survey, usually touted as the first state folklore program, is the precedent it offered for an office within the statewide historical commission. To be sure, the goals of the survey were decidedly different, although many of its activities were dictated by the previous operation.

And why did a peculiar chronology arise and why was Shoemaker neglected? Some may claim that Hufford's published account of 1969 with its misleading historical claim provided a baseline picked up by future chroniclers. But then why did chroniclers not go beyond this document to examine other widely available folkloristic references such as the *Journal of American Folklore* or *New York Folklore Quarterly*, which carried news of Shoemaker's new position? It is conceivable that Shoemaker's amateur or romanticist image and conservative ideology did not fit with the prevailing views of professional folklore scholarship as it took shape in the 1960s and later became recast in the 1980s.

It is also true that beginning with Shoemaker would not have produced as neat or inspiring a narrative as starting with Glassie. The latter especially offers miraculous birth, virtuous father figure (MacEdward Leach) and revered roots (University of Pennsylvania), and a rapid, continuous growth from trained youth to professional maturity. Michael Owen Jones in *Putting Folklore to Use* (1994) quietly acknowledged Shoemaker's precedent as state folklorist but loudly hailed Glassie as the first to take the role "in the modern sense of 'folk-arts coordinator'" (16). After publication of the book, he wrote me to explain that he "liked the modern, professionalism of associating its [public folklore] start with Hank [Henry Glassie] and Dave [David Hufford]." Elsewhere in the letter he commented that "claiming public folklore began during the 60s with Penn academics fits well with a desire to claim professionalism … and it fits well with the spirit of young college folks at the time (anti-establishment, anti-war, etc.) and with the populism on which folklore study is rooted or at least attracts so many folklorists. To claim Shoemaker as a hero/founder/leader of public folklore just doesn't seem to have the same excitement, rightness, fit."[29]

Perhaps another reason that a mistaken chronology for public folklore arose is the peculiarity of the term "public folklore." Its dichotomy with "private" or academic folklore, which "public" suggests in practice, needed to be established in the 1960s, but seemed less convincing as roles crossed between scholars in academe and public agencies during the 1980s. College professors with administrative encouragement managed public festivals and ran outreach centers, and state folklorists offered courses and participated in academic programs. Moreover, whether "public" refers to the constituency or the source of support in the form of government can be irritatingly ambiguous (a problem shared in the parallel use of "public history") (Jones 1994; Kirshenblatt-Gimblett 1988). Michael Owen Jones tried to revise public folklore by demonstrating that folklorists in "public service" (i.e., employed in government agencies providing educational, arts, or cultural programming) represent one kind of applied folkloristics (Jones 1994). Barbara Kirshenblatt-Gimblett also supported use of "applied folklore," but worried that its rhetorical position opposite academe made it seem unscholarly, she sought an alternative base concept for its practitioners. She came up with "cultural objectification" as the common bond of public folklore with academic work (Kirshenblatt-Gimblett 1988).

The critiques by Jones and Kirshenblatt-Gimblett beheld a new era in which the university was no longer dominant in the production of scholarship. The search for, and canonization of, the first state folklorist undertaken by many writers symbolized the need for analyzing alternative organizational contexts in which folkloristic labor, or "cultural objectification," if one prefers, occurs. A problem arose in conceptualizing this practice because the labor was placed within broad cultural spheres rather than behavioral organizations. What has unfortunately transpired in several chronicles I have mentioned is that outlining historical events in the absence of organizational clarity helped to reify public folklore as a legitimate sphere and spreading social philosophy.

REVISION OF THE HISTORICAL NARRATIVE

In 1982, Governor Dick Thornburgh authorized a new state folklorist position for Pennsylvania after a lapse of a decade. Instead of being located at the Historical and Museum Commission, the position was put in an Office of State Folklife Programs in the Governor's Ethnic Affairs Commission (later the Pennsylvania Heritage Affairs Commission). Its rhetoric changed from that of a Folklore Division calling for state patriotism to a folklife program with a pluralistic agenda. Its overall purpose was "to advocate and encourage the presentation of folk artists and the interpretation of folk cultural traditions in the public forum." Although this sounded close to Shoemaker's precedent, and indeed it loudly sang out the cant of cultural conservation, the new office was assuredly focused more on ethnological objectives than the historical and naturalistic goals set by the original state folklorist position. Ignoring Henry Shoemaker's position in history, the Office of State Folklife Programs invoked the precedent of Henry Glassie's Ethnic Culture Survey, appropriately, as the first state folklorist project. It sounded concerns for the "diversity" rather than the former "unity" of Pennsylvania. Its structure included forty-nine "ethnic commissioners" representing separate communities such as Assyrian and Bangladeshi as well as African American and Native American. More than half of the commissioners came from the Philadelphia and Pittsburgh area. The Heritage Affairs Commission brandished keywords of "multicultural," "inter-ethnic," and "cultural heritage." It brought to the fore contemporary industrial and urban folk arts of recent immigrants and migrants much more than the poetic rural roots of Pennsylvania's frontiersmen. These folk arts happened to be in Pennsylvania rather than being Pennsylvanian. They belonged to artists rather than the romantic "soil" or regional "soul."

At the new Office of State Folklife Programs, the dynamic array of social movement and event in the modern city epitomized rather than antithesize the character of folkways. The public heard a lot more about Philadelphia and Pittsburgh from the Heritage Affairs Commission than it ever did in Shoemaker's state folklorist days, and it came in a way that verified, if not celebrated, the opportunities and excitements of the varied, fast-paced city. This pattern fit into a wider scholarly trend at the time emphasizing the essential role of folklore in media, industry, and urban life as many contemporary folklorists viewed their subject embracing modernity rather than opposing it. Giving validity to the mobility of community traditions in a diverse, teeming metropolis offered a strong political imagery for a changing society based on an unmeltable "cultural diversity."

That a new model—more social science than humanistic history, more industrial than natural—largely pushed aside the unified mythologizing of the American countryside did not mean that a romantic narrative did not still persist or contestation within agencies for producing the narrative did not occur. The new social sensitivity of the urban folk arts model offered a vision, described by Bess Lomax Hawes, former director of the National Endowment for the Arts Folk Arts Program: "It is a vision of a confident and open-hearted nation, where differences can be seen as exciting instead of fear-laden, where men of good will, across all manner of racial, linguistic, and historical barriers, can find common ground in understanding solid craftsmanship, virtuoso techniques, and deeply felt expressions" (Hawes 1992, 21). As the Progressives fashioned a response to rapid immigration and industrialization in a popular version of American tradition, so this new model offers an answer to new immigration (much of it from Latin America and Asia) and to mass incorporation. The wilderness is gone from the rhetoric but the need for a mystique that supports a sense of destiny and identity remains. Its mythology before the public may be less narrated and more "imaged" in art and performance, but it is no less imagined.

The dramatic shift of public folklore presentation between the Progressive era and the 1990s matches the chronology historian Michael Kammen has projected for the role of tradition in American culture (Kammen 1991). Since 1870, he has pointed out, the most significant role involved the deliberate Americanization of folk heritage through collected and presented narrative, speech, and song. Broadly speaking, what followed was an imperfect democratization in regions and occupations, and later pluralization in groupings of ethnicity, race, gender, age, sexuality, appearance, and class, to name some in the ever-growing list. Kammen also noted the influence of tourism on later uses of tradition, and Pennsylvania, with its whopping fifty-one separate tourist agencies, certainly attests to that trend in the state. Even more than attracting tourism, heritage-writing—indeed, a whole heritage industry—is being called on for purposes of "economic development," to promote community pride and image. Judging from the meteoric increase in museums, magazines, and films on heritage during the 1980s and 1990s, and the leveling off of American studies programs in universities, the production of heritage knowledge came increasingly from media and public agencies. If the 1980s reports on higher education are to be believed, the role for public agencies was heightened by the diminishing cultural authority of the academy. At the same time, American cultural education by many public agencies in the 1990s was a frequent target of conservative criticism in an effort to scale back or redevise governmental programs.

Pennsylvania's state folklorist position was a victim of that effort in 1995. Almost fifty years after Henry Shoemaker realized his Progressive vision of state government taking responsibility for cultural conservation for the sake of the "public good," a new administration dismantled a key agency created to carry out this state function. After Thomas Ridge became governor in 1995, his administration proposed eliminating the Department of Community Affairs, in which the Pennsylvania Heritage Affairs commission resided. The state administration relocated many agencies from Community Affairs into other departments, and it announced plans to abolish the commission and its Office of State Folklife Programs by June 30, 1996, and to seek repeal of the Heritage Affairs Act of 1992, which authorized the commission to offer cultural conservation activities. The Ridge administration called for "privatizing" such state services, but failed to create a mechanism for privatization. The director of the commission, Shalom Staub, resigned in October 1995, and indeed established a private, nonprofit organization called the Institute for Cultural Partnerships.

Shoemaker's Progressive guidelines of managing culture in a modernizing state, as well as promoting its tradition, took a dramatic turn in the reorganization and privatization of public heritage programs, and Pennsylvania—indeed, the nation—appeared to be controversially entering a new era of cultural and historical programming for the "public good." A change was also apparent from the pluralist mission of the period of state folklife and folk arts programs. Although the goals of cultural "diversity" and "conservation" were still apparent, the role of the state as the manager of cultural resources altered. New trajectories for organizations and communities charitably promoting tradition became manifest. The narrative of public folklore had to be changed accordingly to bring out the organizational or grass-roots precedent for folklore working on behalf of "the common citizen and the public good," to borrow Shoemaker's old phrase.

The proclamation of the new narrative became evident in a widely distributed report produced by the National Endowment for the Arts in 1996. Entitled, appropriately enough, *The Changing Faces of Tradition*, prepared by Elizabeth Peterson, it had the stamp of an official report on public folk arts activities across the United

States. Trained as a folklorist, Peterson had been director of a traditional arts program for a regional private, nonprofit arts organization. The news of her report was that the state did not carry the burden of cultural conservation, and what it did support was a seed from which communities could flower traditions. Responding to legislative pressure that cultural programming was a drain on fiscal resources, it gave a wealth of statistics to show that cultural conservation was a sound "investment" in the future of tradition, and a small one at that. The tone emphasized "folk arts" rather than "folklore" or "folklife" to underscore the creative, renewable sense of culture. Tradition constituted "rich artistic and community resources" to be shaped and renewed (Peterson 1996a, 90). It ushered "a vision for a future where communities are guided by local culture" (Alexander 1996).

The report broadcast the finding that most folk arts projects occurred *outside* institutional settings and they found much of their nurturance from private funding. It highlighted the work of private, nonprofit organizations devoted to folklore for the public good. The list ranged "from ethnic organizations, museums, libraries, schools, historical societies and local arts agencies to folk arts organizations" (Peterson 1996a, 9). Instead of grouching for the preservation of the endangered past, it beamed a creative future enriched by the organizational promotion of diverse traditions centered in family and home. It splashed the future-oriented headlines of public folklore for "Creating, Changing, Renewing" (Peterson 1996a, 32). It envisioned the imperative of "Organizing" for a changeful future restoring community within a mass culture (Peterson 1996a, 68). Avoiding reference to the intervention of state and government, the chair of the Endowment sung a populist keynote that "the folk arts are part of what make our homes and communities ours." She spread the message that they are therefore "our" responsibility. It is the collective "us," she carefully noted, that would "continue to support and sustain the traditional arts" (Alexander 1996). That responsibility seemed to translate to organizations outside of state authority (Peterson 1996a, 91).

While Henry Shoemaker's state folklorist position predictably was absent from the historical narrative of the NEA's reinterpretation of national cultural programming, so was Henry Glassie's Ethnic Culture Survey. The oldest organization providing impetus to the growing trajectory of the 1990s was the private, nonprofit National Council for the Traditional Arts (NCTA). "Founded in 1933," the summary read, the group is "the granddaddy of folk arts organizations." The same blurb used rhetoric of the 1990s to describe its work. "It is the nation's oldest *multicultural producing and presenting organization* dedicated solely to the presentation and documentation of folk and traditional arts in the United States" (emphasis added). It gave its flagship program as the production of the National Folk Festival, "the oldest multi-cultural folk festival in the country" (Peterson 1996a, 64). Other organizations linked to this precedent do not have to produce festivals, but they may engage in "multicultural producing and presenting" that includes museum exhibition, multimedia and publication projects, technical assistance and advocacy for artists and communities, and educational programs for schoolchildren and their teachers. Profiled in the report were City Lore (founded in 1986, New York City), Texas Folklife Resources (founded in 1985), and Vermont Folklife Center (founded in 1982).

If the NCTA is the granddaddy, then a daddy in this revised historical narrative is the National Endowment for the Arts pilot project of apprenticeship programs in 1983. Although involving the state, the programs bring out the decentered nature of state involvement. Their rhetoric minimizes the authority of the state and emphasizes individual artists in their communities. The report found that most "coordinators" (a less authoritarian term than "state folklorist" or "office director") called apprenticeships "the foundation of their folk arts program or among their three most important projects" (Auerbach 1996b, 24). The program spread from three projects in 1983 to thirty-eight in 1995. As if to emphasize the historical significance of apprenticeships, the NEA produced a separate report in the same year as *Changing Faces of Tradition* called *In Good Hands*, prepared by Susan Auerbach. Its subtitle gave the historical baseline of a new period of folk arts organization as the beginning of the apprenticeship programs in 1983. Auerbach explained that the ascendancy of the "model program" of apprenticeships owed to its decentered local emphasis. They "are responsive to local needs and conditions at hand," she wrote. "Policy makers appreciate the diversity built into the cost-effective programs," and "the concept of intergenerational teaching and learning has strong appeal to the public as well as artists and ethnic communities." The direction of program control, she predicted, would move to those communities. She offered precedents in Texas, New Hampshire, and Hawaii for private organizational administration and community management. Attention turns to the programs in this historical narrative because they are "Investing in the Future of Tradition," as the headline of her essay in *Changing Faces* blared.

The public folklorist from State Folklorist Henry Shoemaker to the folk arts coordinator at present has kept watch on tradition for the public good. Although working from different historical narratives, they equally hoped to shape the future in their attention to the past. Shoemaker's saga was one that took in conservation of nature, to preservation of the legacy of the nation's founding, to installment of a Progressive vision of state authority over resources—cultural, historical, and natural. In support of assimilation and "Americanization," it defined folk traditions for the purpose of nation-building and conceived a state role of promoting local patriotism. One might now forecast a period in which American folk tradition is geared toward emotional community-building in order to deal with the uncertain identities of individuals in a global mass culture, where electronic communication and constant mobility create a need for organizing belonging. The state and the folklorist equally seem to be giving up authority for tradition. They may urge, guide, and coordinate, but avoid giving the impression of running the show.

Judging from the aftermath of Pennsylvania's state folklorist position and folk arts reports of the 1990s, public folklorists may even be put in the troubling position of being cultural accountants worried about investments for the future of tradition. In this trend, the historical narratives for locating work for the public good have been decentered as much as the cultural conservation project has become increasingly privatized and diversified. At times, they compete for ordering the priority of work in the name of tradition, both public and private. To be sure, the expansion of traditions of concern in the public sector has opened a wide range of possibilities and provoked useful academic response from corners of history, anthropology, and sociology in addition to folklore. In the challenge to the ways that arts and humanities are public responsibilities, folklorists are noticeable among public agents for tradition as they assess the dizzying array of communities and organizations, identities and symbols representing the American memory of the past, its perception of the present, and its vision of the future.

8

Richard Dorson and the Great Debates

RICHARD DORSON (1916–1981) WAS ONCE DESCRIBED AS THE MAN WHO DID FOR folklore what Kinsey did for sex (Brunvand 1982, 347). It is an image of a man putting his subject forward before the public seriously, and controversially, and placing it on scholarly footing from the 1950s through the 1980s. The similarity between the two luminaries went beyond the fact that both Dorson and Kinsey were associated with institutes at Indiana University, and both had a cultural impact on attitudes of Americans about themselves. Dorson's subject was, like sexuality, often considered raw entertainment rather than the stuff of science. Because of this perception, Dorson expressed the uneasy relationship of folklore to mass media, and pointed to the absence of eroticism in popularized folklore texts to show that mass culture lies and folk culture speaks honestly. It was a keynote he chimed through many public presentations starting with criticisms of folklore treasuries and ending with barbs at Foxfire programming in elementary schools. As if to connect him to the challenge of Kinsey, Dorson referred in his last survey of folklore studies to the deposit of "Unprintable Ozark Folklore" by Vance Randolph at the Sex Research Institute (Dorson 1982b, 101; Randolph 1976). While both figures considered their books and views after World War II liberating, and above ideology, they also ended their careers besmirched for their biases (Morantz 1977).

Dorson touted a new academic, indeed a new class of scholars devoted to revealing the profundity of the ordinary. The academics thought in terms of movements, of democratizing the ivory tower, of wielding influence in the troubled public realm. A prime example for them was the interdisciplinary study of American culture and formation of an objective history of tradition. To be sure, surveys of the 1940s revealed the steady expansion of courses on folklore and American culture in American universities before Dorson came on the scene (Boggs 1940; Dorson 1950b; Wise 1979). But while folklore entered established language or anthropology departments with increasing frequency, or as an interdisciplinary enterprise,

349

Dorson worked forcefully for a separate disciplinary home in folklore that would promote connections to American studies and crusade for its place in the scholarly landscape (Dorson 1963c, 1972a). He launched his campaign for legitimacy in great debates waged in magazines, books, and meetings that drew wide public notice. The issue on the table was the proper representation, and interpretation, of historic American culture in light of the post-World War II rise of mass media and nationalism. First he took on popularizers regarding the authenticity of tradition, and then he scrapped with colleagues in the academy over the historical realization of a national tradition.

Dorson's distinctive position among folklorists of his era is that unlike most of his anthropological and literary colleagues, he championed an historical consciousness of folklore's role in what he envisioned as an American civilization arising from the unique conditions of the New World. He would speak often of a special American type with its own traditions, a distinctive "American folklore" rather than imported "folklore in America." Maybe "shout" or "argue" would be more apt terms for his presentation, since he had the effect of making the discourse on tradition in American culture more acrimonious by distinguishing between the positive values of the private academic and the commercial public. Beating back popularizers, ideologues, and creative artists who would use folklore in response to popular taste, he set an intellectual tone for the presentation of folklore in which academic authority would dictate what the public would believe about their tradition. He insisted that folklore was not fair game for writers and film producers. Instead, it was an academic specialty open to highly qualified experts. Accordingly, he touted American folklore studies as a discipline as well as a subject with its own special theories and methods. Above all, he often exclaimed, its students would have exclusive license to speak for American culture in public and academic circles.

Analyzing Dorson's influence is complicated by his often wavering intellectual position, between the public and academy, international and national realms. Academically, Dorson directed an astounding eighty-six dissertations and had a hand in many more, and he unashamedly boasted of imperially placing his students in college positions across the country. His messages of the need for establishing authenticity in folklore and the academic rigor of folklore studies iterated in his internationalist textbook *Folklore and Folklife: An Introduction* reached many thousands of students every year in large lecture halls. His *American Folklore* and, later, *Handbook of American Folklore* meanwhile pressed ahead with the exceptionalism of American culture. Although his books covering a national tradition reached a wide audience, his "doctoral children" in their publications did not necessarily adopt his historical view of American civilization. Michael Owen Jones's dedication to *Craftsman of the Cumberlands* (1989) epitomized many students' feelings toward their mentor: "Richard M. Dorson (1916–1981), historian and folklorist, who inspired many of us in his charge, whether or not we followed the path of folklore studies quite as he did." Inspiring he was, for the academic pursuit of cultural knowledge through folklore studies, for the veneration of the authentic artifact of tradition, for the use of history and the empirical experience of field-work (Georges 1989a; Abrahams 1989; Ben-Amos 1989). There is little denying his tremendous organizational influence and his pivotal role in setting the agenda for academic research and its role in popular culture and public discourse from the 1950s through the 1980s (Harrah-Conforth 1989). His legendary battles pitting "genuine" folklore against fakelore, and universalist emphasis on traditional behavior in America against an exceptional historical American tradition, helped to galvanize intellectual energy to the role of folklore study in characterizing as well as documenting a complex culture such as America's. The sometimes rancorous public discourse at meetings and in the press drew attention to the political significance of folklore as a tool of cultural production, even manipulation, in addition to its naive intellectual use for cultural stereotyping. Dorson the public intellectual, therefore, needs to be understood as critic of mass culture and promoter of academic authority in a discourse of American culture in the post-World War II decades.

Citation indexes list Dorson as America's most quoted folklorist for three decades, and indeed one of the most cited Americanists during that period. He preached the "gospel," as he put it, of American folklore, of a national tradition, through scholarship rather than popularized texts, but his *America in Legend* (1973a) published by the leading American publisher of Random House drew wide notice in the media and enjoyed huge sales as a Book of the Month Club selection in 1974. With major titles to his credit on American folklore and history, he is still remembered as the ultimate Americanist, but he spent considerable time abroad and published books on Japan, Africa, and Britain. He was Fulbright professor of American studies at the University of Tokyo for an academic year (1956–1957), and twice received Guggenheim fellowships to study the history of British folklore studies (1949–1950, 1964–1965). At times, he could sound antinationalist, or internationalist, or regionalist, but often his backtracking was in the form of warnings against the extremes of nationalism as fascism rather than an abandonment of his position on the integrity of an American tradition. He taught that a folklorist in a lifetime could barely collect a county with anything resembling comprehensiveness, no less represent a nation, and yet he may be best remembered for popular editions of *American Folklore* (1959, 1977) in Chicago's History of American Civilization Series, edited by fellow Harvard alumnus Daniel Boorstin.

Dorson praised Boorstin, the academic turned public historian, with best exemplifying American studies—"combining literary, social, cultural, and folk history, and following the contours of the civilization produced in the United States" (Dorson 1979). Reading further into their mutual admiration, one finds a significant reinterpretation of American self-awareness in their effort. By emphasizing the cultural components of American history—much of it based in cities, regions, occupations, industries, and immigrants—they relocated American tradition in a democratic social process that went well beyond the Turneresque reduction of a unified American character to frontier settlement or Charles Beard's interpretation of elites' economic self-interest. The America they described showed cultural democracy set into motion by experiences Boorstin and Dorson knew from their urban and ethnic observations. Underscoring Dorson's use of cultural traditions to optimistically account for an exceptional, dynamic America, Boorstin prefaced Dorson's book with the claim that "the folklore of a people is as distinctive as anything else about them. The new American places—the colonial fireside, the backwoods bearhunt, the city slum, or the college campus—make a difference. American literacy and the American standard of living change the channels of folklore" (Boorstin 1959, ix–x).

Boorstin and Dorson collaborated on what they saw as a common cause for a distinctive American culture recovered historically, and in so doing engaged an intellectual establishment in debate. "You're a man after my own heart," Boorstin wrote Dorson after reading *American Folklore*. Noting reviews critical of Boorstin's downplay of great historical events and figures in favor of charting everyday life, Dorson meanwhile urged Boorstin on by writing, "I prophesy you will dethrone Parrington and shave Beard to a whisker."[1] They worked on their sweeping national surveys at the same time, and in fact, they sent letters to each other competing for who would reach their deadlines first. Boorstin prepared *The Americans: The Colonial Experience* (1958) with advice from Dorson on folklore references, and Dorson relied on Boorstin for material in his chapter on colonial traditions (see also Boorstin 1965, 1973). They were both in Japan on Fulbright grants at the same time in 1957, and frequently listed each other for grant recommendations. Dorson backed Boorstin's battle against historians of the time about accepting cultural evidence, and in commenting on a negative review by John Higham, he opined: "Like too many historians he doesn't appreciate culture, in the anthropological sense, and has to keep dragging in liberal and conservative labels, to pigeonhole other historians. The new historiography in *The Americans*, to my view, is its treatment of colonial civilization in categories to cultural anthropology—religion, law, language, education—which each reflect what Herskovits calls the focus and drift of a culture."[2] After visiting with Dorson in Bloomington, Indiana, in 1959 Boorstin gratefully wrote, "I'm increasingly amazed by your grasp of American history and culture in the large, as well as your intimacy and mastery of folklore. For me, it's a wonderful thing to have the advantage of your guidance in this field which is so important to my work, and in which I'm such a novice."[3] Boorstin made his final tribute in Dorson's obituary which was carried nationally by United Press International: "He was a man of great stature who produced monumental works in the field of folklore" (September 14, 1981).

Dorson commands attention because he was the most vocal proponent in public discourse on an American national tradition evident through folklore

(Abrahams 1989; Wilson 1989). My concern is with the way Dorson tried to direct the conversation on American culture toward a realization of authentic local folk traditions that could represent a national consensus. I will begin my discussion of Dorson's outlook on tradition with his debate on "fakelore" and the popular representation of American folklore. This will take me into an account of several battles engaged by Dorson, including the protracted one with Benjamin Botkin over the purity of folkloric texts and its implication for establishing an authoritarian, "New Class" voice for interpreting American tradition. This will lead to a discussion of scholarly response to Dorson's "theory for American folklore" which attempted to develop a historical approach to American tradition, and the related dichotomy between "American folklore" and "folklore in America."

My observations depend on Dorson's lectures and his talks with me as much as my reading of his papers. I came to Indiana because my collegiate advisers told me he was America's preeminent folklorist. I served as his editorial assistant and I often questioned him about what he wrote. Because I had come to Indiana from New York where I had worked on *New York Folklore Quarterly* and taken courses from one of his nemeses, Louis C. Jones, he used to regale me with stories of his clashes with the New York popularizers and their journal (I heard the other side from Jones). Dorson was regularly a topic of conversation among his students and colleagues, and in my assessments I took into account his image in and out of academe. I was a student in his memorable American Civilization class and I had him on my dissertation committee. I heard every paper he gave at American Folklore Society meetings from 1975 until his death. I have vivid memories of traveling with him to Hoosier Folklore Society meetings and seeing him at social occasions in his home, at my home, and at the university. Wherever he appeared, he was a center of attention and every chat touched on folklore, either a recent "find" he had to relate, or a publication on the subject he had in press. One oral history of Dorson went even further to describe him as "the center of everything that happened." "He had energy and style," the account explained, "You didn't like it necessarily, or didn't believe it or want to believe it; but he had some kind of style, and great energy. And around energy, people congeal" (Harrah-Conforth 1989, 346). He had public and academic notoriety from the ample press covering his campaigns and controversies. He wielded authority as the director of the Folklore Institute through three decades, so I listened to what foundation officials, publishers, and readers had to say about him. He was a man on several missions, among them setting the public straight on folklore and building appreciation for American tradition from a historical perspective. He was, as his colleague Edson Richmond reflected, a man remarkably obsessed, and equally a man of extraordinary influence (Richmond 1981).

Dorson was born March 12, 1916, to affluent parents of German-Jewish background in New York City. Although he was aware of his ancestry, he denied having much of an ethnic identity during his childhood. He later referred to the cultural persistence of New York's many ethnic communities; however, at his Park Avenue address he considered himself assimilated.[4] He eventually affiliated with the Unitarian church which sounded his scholarly keynote of unity from variety. It held an appeal to him as a liberal theology stressing inquiry, progress, and diversity of individual ideas in the unity of spiritual thought (Faust 1909, 2:426). Leaving his multiethnic New York City base in his youth, Dorson followed the path of elite institutions in New England announcing arrival into the unity of American society. He attended Phillips Exeter Academy, a prestigious boys' preparatory school in New Hampshire, with historic roots in the young Republic (established 1781). He was unsure of a career goal when he devoted himself to raise his dismal grade in history at Exeter and snared a prize for the most-improved student in the subject. Showing scholarly promise, he advanced to Harvard, but by his own account, his undergraduate energy was largely devoted to squash and tennis competition, and he probably took greater pride at that time in becoming intercollegiate squash champion and earning a high ranking in tennis than in pursuing scholarship.

Despite his admission of slacking in the classroom, it was not because he held his professors in low esteem. At Harvard during the mid-1930s, Dorson majored in history and literature, and was attracted to eminent Americanists such as Perry Miller, F. O. Matthiessen, Ralph Barton Perry, Arthur Schlesinger, Sr., Kenneth Murdock, and Howard Mumford Jones in a new scholarly movement to promote the integrated study of American history, literature, and arts, especially from the colonial to national periods before the Civil War. Dorson reminisced that "the talk and the writing in those days was all of the American experience, now suddenly revealed as an independent, mature, intricate, and noble civilization" (Dorson 1971a, 79–80; see also Dorson 1976a; Hylton 1987). It was rebellious talk and writing about innocents in a wicked academic world and an anti-intellectual society (Berkhofer 1979, 341). It sought a consensus of American culture from the democratic experience of the agrarian American republic into the plural, even fragmented, appearance of industrial-ethnic America. As part of this movement, Dorson was perhaps closest at Harvard to Professor Howard Mumford Jones, who provided the following justification for the blossoming of scholarly interest in American culture, "In a period of intense economic and social strain ... *the country needs to cling to its traditions*; it needs, in Van Wyck Brooks' phrase, a 'usable past'" (emphasis added; Hylton 1987, 4). In the upper echelons of Harvard's administration, the new program in American civilization that Dorson joined could also be supported to meet the perceived threat at the time of "alien" ideologies such as communism and fascism (Hylton 1987, 6). From the viewpoint of many of the students and faculty in the program's first classes, an essential task was to clarify the Americanism of American ideas.

Concerned that the academic study of America would struggle in a fragmented disciplinary university structure built on English and German precedent, advocates for an American civilization program sought an interdisciplinary American academic enterprise reflecting American conditions. Americanist refugees from English escaped the reign of socially removed philology and a distant British canon, while a newly formed path from history led away from ancient European sites toward the modern cultural as well as political emergence of the United States. In the midst of a "machine age" in which immigrants, industrial workers, and regional migrants—the so-called "common man"—drew attention to a changing, diverse country, American studies located the nation's cultural roots in pastoral-religious allegories such as the "myth of the garden" and "myth of the innocent Adam" that proclaimed the uniqueness and holism of American experience (Smith 1950; Marx 1964; Mechling 1989d, 14–15). The Americanists shaped contexts for their work that suggested the possibilities of cultural as well political democracy—built on the consensus model of pluralism among common people—in a new troubled age corrupted by abuses of capitalism, racism, and technology (Marx 1979; Mechling 1989d). The new movement, in fact, allowed, and even encouraged, new participants in the academy—particularly ethnic Catholics and Jews—with cultural subjects to shake the dominance of white Anglo-Saxon Protestants and their elitist studies in the university (Hollinger 1975; Marx 1979).

The American studies movement rallied enthusiasm by denouncing obstacles and enemies to the cause of Americans appreciating an American heritage. It reminded its participants of the need for fight—within the elitist academy and the anti-intellectual public sector (Mechling 1989d, 24). Dorson seemed to have taken this message to heart when he pronounced the birth, indeed the spirit, of American studies in the "crusading fervor" of the Harvard Americanists and described himself as a "cliffhanger" and "fighter"—and his subject "misunderstood," "unknown," and "untaught," indeed an "orphan" (Dorson 1976c, 1–4; Dorson 1976b, 30; Dorson 1975b, 237). Declaring the urgency of American studies as a reform project in a troubled era and molding it after a consensus notion of the protean American experience, the movement pumped America as exceptional in the world, especially in its expansion and variety, its boldness on the frontier and fondness for new beginnings (Hacker 1947; Smith 1950; Mechling 1989d, 24; Kammen 1993).

Extending the idea of the emergence of a new American type, Dorson reflected on the creation through the Harvard program of a new academic type befitting a modernist generation breaking with European scholasticism and shaping a future from an American tradition. It was a type Dorson described as "having a certain flair that denotes a liberated spirit." "I think in terms of types," Dorson admitted, and the new academic type was willing to behold America broadly and positively. Dorson, the epitome of this type, was dissatisfied with the fragmentation of history and literature into minute specialties of period and area and was attracted to heated discussions among faculty and students about a new interdisciplinary conception combining history, literature, and culture that could grandly be called American civilization. "What they shared," Dorson marveled, "was a sense of exhilaration of America as a civilization, and at possibilities of the intellectual discovery of the meaning of America" (Dorson 1979, 369–70). To Dorson and others in the early days of the movement, America was "exhilarating" and "astonishing" (two favorite Dorson adjectives), for America held cultural riches of its own and this awareness could be revitalizing for America's sense of self. If American history had been tardily found and inadequately taught, American culture still awaited discovery, and it promised great, unique marvels along with a store of dilemmas.

After receiving his undergraduate degree in 1937, Dorson moved to Vermont, traveled, and thought about his future before he returned to Harvard to study with a highly charged devotion to American studies. He reflected that he came back energized by his reading of frontier humor and historic narratives of American heroism that had spread through the country (Dorson 1937). It was "cultural" or "folk" material that lay outside the purview of most academic history and literature studies of the time. Yet to Dorson it helped explain America, and he became anxious to study and teach it, and write about it. He joked that his freshly found enthusiasm for scholarship must have "confounded his professors" (Dorson 1941a, 509). He wrote Howard Mumford Jones on February 8, 1938, "Last year when taking a seminar with you in Southern literature, I chose for the subject of my paper, as you may remember, 'The Humor of the Southwestern Frontier.' At the time you said, 'What is the point of taking this when it has already been covered by Meine, Devoto, etc.?' I am now in a position to say that the field had by no means been covered and in fact one of the most fascinating sources has been almost untouched." That source was folklore.

The new doctoral program that attracted him, the world's first devoted to American studies, was called the History of American Civilization, and Dorson became the fifth student to receive the degree in 1943. He entered with the intention, he wrote in 1938, of "becoming a writer and critic of Americana."[5] His fellow students included others who would later carry the American studies banner such as Daniel Aaron and Henry Nash Smith. It was Smith, remembering Dorson's work on frontier humor, who suggested to him that he could study folklore with Celticist Kenneth H. Jackson at Harvard. Dorson arranged for a reading course with Jackson and chose folklore as one of his doctoral areas. From Jackson, Dorson became more aware of comparative international folklore study and its analysis of folktale types and motifs, and their diffusion. He followed this course with attendance at a summer folklore institute at Indiana University directed by Stith Thompson, at that time a leading proponent of the "Finnish" historic-geographic method of comparatively analyzing international folktales. He also encountered anthropological approaches, especially the idea of folklore as the mirror of a group's cultural history espoused by Africanist Melville Herskovits from Northwestern University, who was a student of Franz Boas and was active in the American Folklore Society (Dorson 1963b, 1971a, 18–21; Herskovits [1941] 1946, 1958).[6] From American history, then, Dorson took the nationalist vista of America as a civilization, and from folklore study he considered the internationalism of cultural diffusion and literary analysis.

As Dorson read more folklore scholarship, he attempted to reconcile the "paradox" that folklore studies should develop "most energetically" along national lines while by "its very nature" it "requires an international breadth of vision" (Dorson 1973c, 1; see also Montenyohl 1989). Following the work of Stith Thompson and Archer Taylor, he recognized that "the materials of folklore transcend all barriers of language and culture, traversing continents and spanning oceans in vast leaps and drifting across borders in easy stages. 'Cinderella' has circled the globe. The 'Shanghai gesture,' popular among American schoolboys as a thumb and finger wiggle of derision, roamed all over Europe in the past four centuries. One extended family of water goblins unites the Japanese *kappa* with the Scottish kelpie. In ballad and legend, romance and epos, the same protean hero performs the same sequence of marvelous exploits. Proverbs and riddles glide from one tongue to another to settle comfortably in a new idiom" (Dorson 1973c, 1; see also Taylor [1931] 1951, 1972, 1985; Thompson [1946] 1977). "But," he asserted, "the galvanic force behind concerted, subsidized, and firmly organized folklore studies is the force of nationalism.... The same impulses that have led to the self-study of national history and national literature have urged the pursuit of national folklore. Today the well-equipped political state possesses its accredited historical records, its approved literary masterpieces, and its classified folklore archives" (Dorson 1973c, 1).

In his dissertation "New England Popular Tales and Legends" (1943) Dorson brought an international and national perspective together to make a case for the transformation, indeed the exceptionalism, of American oral tradition from its Old World sources. Studying early New England storytelling culled from printed sources, Dorson separated the "comic anecdote and local legend, the tall story and trickster yarn" of New England from the myths, fairy tales, and sagas of Old World culture. He wrote: "Americans wove the fresh materials of their experiences and livelihoods into story stuff dyed with Old World supernaturalism and New World extravagance, and by the devious routes of folklore channels, stories passed into popular currency, and crusted into a traditional lore" (Dorson 1946b, 3). Thus a national cultural tradition was planted; it grew from the bottom up. Dorson published his dissertation as *Jonathan Draws the Longbow* in 1946 and dedicated the book to his American studies teachers at Harvard. Dorson made some scholarly impact with the book, for it was awarded the prestigious Chicago Folklore Prize. He began the book with a sentence that he would elaborate in a remarkable publication list comprising twenty-four books and over two hundred articles: "American culture, late to arise in the history of civilizations, exhibits a folklore with distinctive qualities" (Dorson 1946b, 3).

Dorson first stumbled onto folklore study, he said, "accidentally through an undergraduate paper on Mark Twain's debt to the oral tall-tale tradition of the frontier," and he became so involved in the topic that he published excerpts from Davy Crockett's almanacs in 1939 (Dorson 1937, 1939, 1971a, 4). That summer, he traveled around the country "on the trail of Paul Bunyan interest" and other American folk heroes, and met with the major folklorists and writers working in the field, including a core of scholars from New York State working to popularize American folklore: Benjamin Botkin, Louis C. Jones, and Harold Thompson (Dorson 1941a, 401). After publishing two articles based on his folk hero research in regional journals, Dorson received national attention from intellectuals in 1941 with an essay on "America's Comic Demigods" in the highly respected *American Scholar*. Standing back from the American center, he claimed to be able to see whole, and objectively, rather than in a fragmented and biased perspective of literary scholars. It is worth quoting his opening lines for indication of later Dorson hallmarks: a provocative writing style often bordering on the grandiloquent, a faith in American exceptionalism, and a sharp jab at those who did not see things his way.

> From a nation lean in folk annals and too short-lived to boast an heroic age there has suddenly sprung a knavish breed of blustering superheroes. Survey the American callings and the chances are you will find in each the same titanic character—whether hunter, trapper, flatboatman, cowboy, sailor, lumberjack, farmer, oil driller, iron puddler, wheat thresher or hobo. This native portrait at once buffoon and strong hero, braggart and superman, joker and work giant, stands as America's unique contribution to the world's store of folklore. It is a strange snub by American literary scholars that they have been inclined to read in the comic demigod only an overblown juvenile fable. (Dorson 1941a, 389)

The essay included Dorson's first debunking of the association of American folklore with Paul Bunyan. He thought that the popular fascination with Paul Bunyan was a sign of the growing dominance of mass media in twentieth-century communications as it took a booster role of forming an American superhero mythology. He exposed the "Paul Bunyan myth" as essentially "manufactured," and he suggested that authentic legends of "American tradition" properly existed in the conditions of the nineteenth century when figures such as Mike Fink and Davy Crockett ignited an orally circulating legacy of earthy legends and tall tales. He used the term "American tradition" repeatedly to describe ideas and traits at the foundation of an American national character (see Wilson 1989). Dorson was careful to differentiate between folk tradition made up of recordable historic forms such as legends and folktales and an exploitable tradition conceived as a present-day spirit for which new Bunyanesque forms could be written. Dorson expounded that if an authentic folklore of recordable historic forms could be identified in the United States, American culture could stand comparatively, and proudly, next to the grand traditions of European nations and ancient civilizations with heroic ages. His hope was to raise the level of the American tradition to the "dignity" of serious literature, to give recognition to an American heroic age. His evidence for this majestic epoch hinged on the recognition of legends about Davy Crockett during the nineteenth century as a national mythology (see Dorson 1942). Into the twentieth century, Dorson found cultural malaise as this mythology had been transmogrified by mass media and commerce. "For the present at any rate," he concluded, "the Bunyans and Finks and John Henrys occupy a burlesque level, if an unerasable place, in American tradition—perhaps doomed for further indignities in the folklore of the comic strips, perhaps destined for immortality in the unwritten American epic" (Dorson 1941a, 401).

Dorson's intellectual heroes in his campaign for studying the American tradition were crusading figures who forged new organizations or scholarly directions. They combined serious history and literary study into public notice of a "glorification of things American" (Dorson 1941b). In his early work, he often cited Moses Coit Tyler (1835–1900), founder of the American Historical Association and author of books on the literature of the new nation, who he religiously called "historian of the American Genesis." Another favorite was Constance Rourke (1885–1941), author of *American Humor* (1931) and *Davy Crockett* (1934), who he thought had "ingeniously" and "brilliantly" traced folk themes in a national popular literature and made humor—usually taken lightly as entertainment—a subject of serious cultural inquiry. He saw his labor on top of this Americanist foundation to be the expansion of studies of social history and folk tradition past the eighteenth century into immigration, labor, and regionalism of the nineteenth and twentieth centuries (Stern 1989). To offset the risk of provincialism in American studies, he repeatedly called for an awareness of the international currents of folklore, and different national traditions of folklore studies (Dorson 1973c). He saw great promise in the engagement of empirical fieldwork to record authentic living traditions from the grass roots (Dorson 1971a, 25). If popularizing media and elitist literary scholars could not be trusted with getting American tradition right, then a new scholarship of American studies and folklore studies resting on the promise of social history and cultural fieldwork would.

After a year of yeoman teaching at Harvard, Dorson moved up the professor ranks in the history department at Michigan State University. He stayed for thirteen years before coming to Indiana University's doctorate-granting Folklore Institute. With the presence of Stith Thompson and his student Warren Roberts, Indiana had been known as a center of philological analysis based in the library that involved searches for international origin and diffusion of folktales. Prior to coming to Indiana, Dorson had a conversion experience to fieldwork. Both history and literature which he had pursued at Harvard were based on the reading of printed texts mostly drawn from "the elite or intellectual culture" that "covers the small cerebral segment of the population" (Dorson 1971a, 91). He made his early employment of field collection of oral texts sound like a discovery of America, its real people, and its genuine cultural expression. "The folklorist," he reflected, "is

crossing the square, or scaling the walls, that divide the book-learned from the tradition-oriented sectors of society, and in my foray into the Upper Peninsula of
Michigan in 1946 I crossed the Straits of Mackinac by ferry to enter an uncharted
world of folk societies. As I now realize, I could have found the folk anywhere, but
at the time I needed a symbolic crossing in my voyage of discovery" (Dorson
1976b, vii).

With a fellowship from the Library of Congress for studies in the history of
American civilization, he stayed "exhilarated and astonished" in the Upper
Peninsula for five months in 1946. There he found living oral traditions that he had
earlier assumed to be historical relics. He gushed that "the bards and troubadours of
Homer's day and King Arthur's court were all there, reciting in a variety of
American accents their wondrous sagas" (Dorson 1976b, viii). In folklore fieldwork,
he thought he had struck the pure mother lode of popular, mass, and elite culture
(Dorson 1971a, 90–93). Instead of reconstructing an evolutionary model of folk culture "at the bottom of American civilization," and elite at the top, he relativistically
set popular, mass, and elite cultures alongside one another with folk culture feeding
them all (Dorson 1971a, 91).

In his classes at Michigan State, Dorson required his students to engage in fieldwork for living American traditions, as Jan Harold Brunvand recalled. He wrote of
his course with Dorson in 1954:

> Our term projects were huge grab bags of lore wrested from roommates, friends, and
> relatives; we tried to embellish them with as many comparative notes and Dorson-type
> field anecdotes as possible. Each project from the large class got a pointed witty com-
> mentary from the instructor and then went into the archives; that is to say, it was
> dumped into overflowing filing cabinets in the narrow hall leading to Dorson's over-
> stuffed office on the top floor of creaky old Morrill Hall. The major essay question for
> the final went something like "If your parents ask you what folklore is and why you were
> studying it, how would you answer them?" (Brunvand 1975, 15–16)

Brunvand recognized Dorson's captivation of an audience with his storytelling.
"The real guts of the course," he said, "was the storytelling: encounters with the legendary Suggs, adventures in the Upper Peninsula, first-person reports about the
exploits of Davy Crockett in the Heroic Age, duels fought with concocters and collectors of fakelore." When Brunvand came to Indiana University in 1957 to study
English, Dorson brazenly pressed him by asking, "what the hell are you doing as an
English major?" Brunvand remembered that "his most convincing logical argument
was that English majors were a dime a dozen, but that in a few years every university in the country would be clamoring for folklorists. But I think what really convinced me to switch was some wild stories he soon began telling about a meeting he
had recently attended in Chicago where he did battle again with the demons of
fakelore and cultists of the folksy" (Brunvand 1975, 15–16). Dorson viewed his students as missionaries for the cause and he annually reviewed his battles for a

national tradition based on a "genuine" folklore in a class for the folklore department he introduced, Folklore in American Civilization, which he cross-listed with history.

The Michigan experience "exhilarated and astonished" Dorson in other ways. He found a greater variety of ethnic, occupational, and native traditions than he had imagined in his literary work in New England. As a result, he altered his nationalistic vista of American culture to take into account a communitarian view of ethnic and regional diversity. His answer was to tie a native and ethnic presence as threads in a weave of American culture. In his foreword to *Bloodstoppers and Bearwalkers*, he observed that three great strands of "folk traditions of Indians, European ethnic groups and occupational workers" could be found in the formation of a national American culture. In any region of the United States, therefore, "fieldwork done in depth in a relatively limited area can illuminate the entire American scene" (Dorson 1976b, viii). Only in a limited area, he surmised, could a collector get an adequate representation of the traditions that represent culture. He urged a holistic approach that avoided the parochialism of concentrating on one group but saw the group as part of a historical process of "co-existing cultures" that came together within the American experience (Dorson 1961a). From this premise, he envisioned American folklorists' mission: to compile a record of an America based on collections of focused regional-ethnic-occupational traditions. Rather than being connected to separate communities, these "diversified folk cultures," he offered, were streams feeding into an American sea. In his words, they "contributed vigor and strength to American life" (Dorson 1976b, ix).

Dorson created a colorful picture of a collected America in 1964 with the publication of *Buying the Wind: Regional Folklore in the United States*. It contained "bona fide" stories and beliefs collected by individuals in their limited regional-ethnic-occupational fields, including Maine Down-Easters, Pennsylvania Dutchmen, southern mountaineers, Louisiana Cajuns, Illinois Egyptians, southwestern Mexicans, and Utah Mormons. He admitted that the work presented was an incomplete portrait and his introduction, "Collecting Oral Folklore in the United States," urged a professional mission to record American traditions. Toward the end of life, he was still sounding this call and organized a meeting of folklorists in 1980 to prepare an encyclopedia of American regional folklore, but the project collapsed after his death a year later. Even in his last fieldwork-based book, *Land of the Millrats* (1981), he described his experience in the urban-industrial city of Gary, Indiana, as a "foray into 'de region.'" Drawing parallels with *Bloodstoppers*, Dorson viewed the plural ethnic and occupational traditions of the "Calumet Region" of northwest Indiana, and reflected that "as a folklorist interested in regional theory and the common traditions shaping a region, I was intrigued by the notion of an urbanized region, seemingly a contradiction in terms, and one so self-aware that it pinned the label on itself. Had the Region generated a distinctive folklore within its boundaries and become a subject of talk and legends?"

(Dorson 1981, 2–3). It was a question he asked in equal frequency about the nation, for both region and nation represented to him the American social process of consensus from the mix of subcultures.

The idea of a powerful cultural center and unempowered periphery is significant to Dorson's treatment of both folklore as a subject and folklore studies as an object. He argued for recognition of folklore's move to the center of culture, where it objectively belonged as the root of cultural development, from the margins where elitist literary scholars had put it. He tied the relation of elite English emphasis in American culture with the control of white Anglo-Saxon Protestant scholars. His presentations argued essentially for the move of the "other" groups— ethnic, occupational, and regional—from which folklore is generated to the center of culture. He followed his regional study of the Upper Peninsula of Michigan with two collections from African-American communities in Michigan and Arkansas (1956c, 1958). He argued there, in fact, that the American black narrative tradition was a new hybrid formed primarily from European and some African influences. Unlike other studies of tales that had been narrowly textual, Dorson gave special attention to the distinctive storytelling styles of black raconteurs. Accordingly, he also called for the disciplinary unity and distinctive style of the "mixed brew" of folklore studies from the margins to the center of scholarship. Even within folklore studies, he used this rhetorical strategy to show that while national and international studies could coexist, the former should be more central. The movement from the margin to the center is evident in his concern for entry into folklore studies. He wanted to know the path from which students came to his folklore center, and, in fact, his students produced a collection of anecdotes recalling their arrival from distant scholarly homes (Reuss 1975). Similarly, his "Theory for American Folklore" had as its prologue the search for a student from outside disciplines to an inside core of folklore studies (Dorson 1959b).

Dorson's approach to the presentation, and professionalization, of folklore to the public was largely in response to two popular trends in American book and magazine publishing he held in contempt. One was the journalistic (he would say "juvenile") rendering of regional and occupational folk heroes such as that done by writers James Stevens in *Paul Bunyan* (1925) and Frank Shay in *Here's Audacity!* (1930). The other was the anthologizing of American folklore from literary sources into national celebrations of its native creativity such as *A Treasury of American Folklore* (1944) by B. A. Botkin and *The American Imagination at Work* (1947) by Benjamin Clough. Dorson often prefaced his criticism by claiming that he was not, *per se*, opposed to popularization, but he thought it could be done by academics eradicating, rather than stooping to, public ignorance.

Dorson implied he had a moral obligation to "call down" authors if they "are manipulating folklore simply to make a quick buck, and in so doing sacrifice their personal integrity" (Dorson 1959b, 238). Intellectually, Dorson objected to their often chauvinistic boosterism of an American character, misrepresentation of the genuine American tradition in the reliance on "spurious and synthetic" literary editing, and cleansing simplification for children and general audiences.

Dorson detested the writers and editors of folklore for a popular market because they obscured the authenticity of folklore as social product of real-life common folk. He righteously declared that by rewriting materials they ruined the sanctity of the original document, thus detracting from the analytical use of the scholar and the dignity, indeed the social meaning, of the American epic. In a critique of the artistic quality of modern mass culture, he derided the work of popularizing writers and editors as commercialized "fakelore."

THE FAKELORE DEBATE

Dorson made a name of himself in 1950 with his introduction of "fakelore" in *American Mercury* (with a circulation of over eighty thousand). If not the largest magazine in America, it was one of the nation's most quoted and discussed (Spivak and Angoff 1944, 3). The publication had a lively reputation because of the previous editorship of H. L. Mencken and the contributions of renowned American writers including Sinclair Lewis, William Faulkner, Theodore Dreiser, and F. Scott Fitzgerald. Among the authors of the 1920s publishing in *American Mercury* were artist-critics such as Benjamin Botkin developing a regional literature out of folk materials (Botkin 1926, 1935). During the 1940s the magazine regained prominence by publishing snappy literature by promising young authors, incisive cultural assessments of national arts, and anti-Communist essays that celebrated the American enterprise. Critic Marsha Siefert reflected that "the revival of the Mencken focus, with a new emphasis on the virtues and substance of America (rather than only its foibles), made it a natural home not only for pieces on American folklore of the kind that Dorson had already published, but also for contributions by young authors who had the kind of writing talent that Dorson did" (Siefert 1989, 64).

Dorson sought to infuse "daring" and "flair" in his historical writing, and he drew upon what he called the "artistic" models of his Harvard Americanist teachers, who he thought "not only explored, but contributed to, American mythmaking" (Dorson 1977d). Dorson believed that his colorful "Menckenisms" such as ringtailed roarers and whopper-mouthed woodsmen were more than enlivening prose for a general readership. Talking to me once about how intellectuals gain fame in a public, mostly anti-intellectual, culture, he remarked "notoriety goes to the coiners of terms." He elaborated elsewhere on his change of heart that led him to "abandon efforts at polite and decorous criticism and resort to forceful language": "American mass culture was highly commercial, blatant, loud, aggressive, and the book industry partook of these traits; in another age, say Victorian England, subtle thrusts might be appreciated, but in twentieth-century United States one needed to shout at the top of his voice" (Dorson 1976c, 7). The lack of response to his understated reviews of Botkin's *Treasury of New England Folklore* led him to think in terms of combining the loudness of contemporary mass culture with the flourish of British Victorian oratory and American grandiose talk. Despite his academic position, he was deliberately unacademically combative to give notice to the malaise of commercial culture and the scholarly seriousness of folklore. He imagined an American version of the controversies taken up by the "Great Team" of Victorian English folklorists, as he dubbed them. He referred to their unrelenting debates and the ways that their arguments over theory and the meaning of folk tradition in an industrializing, civilizing world drew them respect as intellectual authorities (Dorson 1968). He admired the British folklorists for their oratorical flourish, their authoritarian air, and their societal importance. He would announce: "I yearned for a caustic critic—an Andrew Lang tilting at Max Müller or a Joseph Jacobs in turn jabbing at Lang, men who held the British public spellbound for four decades with the virtuosity of their debating skills" (Dorson 1971a, 51).

Dorson sought disputes to enliven scholarly discourse. As review editor of the *Journal of American Folklore*, Dorson invited Botkin to harshly review his *Bloodstoppers and Bearwalkers*. He prodded Botkin on October 6, 1952: "This is not a peace offering; say what you please without pulling any punches. I am quite ready and anxious to have other points of view than my own represented in the review section, as long as they have some thinking behind them." Thus Dorson promoted debate for its scholarly service in sharpening intellectual positions and standards, and he equally relished the public spotlight it could bring. As sport, raising controversy invited a match of rhetorical skills, and Dorson had great confidence in his abilities to triumph in defense of the unpopular position, especially since he thought of that position typically being the intellectual one.

Although Dorson often expressed admiration for the intellectual fervor expressed in the debates of the British folklorists, his polemics had an American reference. Discussing his choice of fiery words aimed at the popularizers, I recall him quipping, "This isn't discourse, it's combat," and many of his terms describing the intellectual quarrels of the Great Team or his own debates were military references of "battles," "barrages," and "clashes" (see Dorson 1968, 1976c, 1–30). One can understand his adoption of military rhetoric from the journalism of World War II, and in his debates with the popularizers he raised the specter of attacking a totalitarian threat from mass culture. As orator and critic, he took the role of defender of democracy in folk culture against corrupting, expanding forces. In his rhetoric he implied analogies of the manipulation and dishonesty of a homogenizing mass culture with the totalitarianism of fascism. In the drama he staged with his early debates, the progressive voice of cultural democracy needed to triumph to save society.

Dorson's first skirmish was over the authenticity of Paul Bunyan. By the 1940s, Bunyan's spread in mass media as a folk hero had become a national phenomenon.

Frontispiece from *Paul Bunyan*, by James Stevens, published by Alfred Knopf, New York (1925). The woodcut is by Allen Lewis.

Bunyan's woodsman virtues of being kindly and down-to-earth, remarkably strong, fantastically large, and fiercely independent were often touted in the popular press and children's books as the substance of American character, especially in times of hardship such as the Great Depression and the World War (Shephard 1924; Stevens 1925, 1932, 1947; Wadsworth 1926; Bowman 1927; Rounds 1936; McCormick 1939; Turney 1941; Miller 1942; Untermeyer 1946). In the fashion of creating an American epic hero, poets including Robert Frost, Carl Sandburg, and W. H. Auden (who wrote a libretto) latched onto the Bunyan figure (Hoffman 1952, 128–64; see also Morrissette 1932). They thought of Bunyan as a home-bred American folk figure inspiring the American spirit much as countries in Europe had their ancient national heroes. In Dorson's fieldwork with Michigan lumberjacks, however, he did not collect anything similar to the tall tale cycle concocted by Stevens, although he admitted that there may have once been a small kernel of oral tradition on Bunyan (Dorson 1941a, 393; Dorson 1951c, 233–35).[7] "Lumberjacks did not tell Paul Bunyan stories," Dorson asserted, "but they did relish anecdotes about sly and eccentric bosses" (Dorson 1976b, viii). And for Dorson the field-recorded item was the test of cultural reality. It represented the purity of the folk teller that rendered the authenticity of the relic past, he asserted, and in an academic manner could be analyzed, much as the historian's cherished documents, for the objectively determined pattern of American culture. Dorson was alarmed that popularizers had the power to create a tradition for the commercial present and obscure the truthfulness of the rough-hewn past. He resented the public association of what he considered a "sickly sweet" fabrication over the gritty social substance of folklore.

H. L. Mencken at *American Mercury* had originally published Stevens's stories of Bunyan in 1924, and in 1925, the commercial house of Alfred Knopf turned Stevens's *Paul Bunyan* into a hot seller and the most successful of the Bunyan books. Stevens claimed to have heard Bunyan stories in the lumber camps and to have embellished them to supply a quintessential American folk hero. His introduction offered the unsubstantiated origin of Bunyan in "a mighty-muscled, bellicose, bearded giant named Paul Bunyon" who participated in the French Canadian Papineau Rebellion against English rule in 1837. In Stevens's narratives, however, Bunyan's rebellion against colonial domination was replaced with support of American industry and capitalism. "History, industry, invention, and oratory were, to his mind, the four grand elements of human life," Stevens wrote of the Americanized Bunyan (Stevens 1925, 225).

Stevens the writer had replaced the legendary quality of a localized Bunyan story told in a camp with national mythmaking. To witness this, judge Stevens's mythological narrative introducing the book: "This forest warrior, with a mattock in one hand, a great fork in the other, powerful as Hercules, indomitable as Spartacus, bellowing like a furious Titan, raged among the Queen's troops like Samson among the Philistines" (Stevens 1925, 1). Stevens gave the impression that the stories in his book were taken from the lips of hearty lumberjack tellers. "This folk lore," he wrote, "survives as shining memorials to sturdier and nobler days. And the legend of Paul Bunyan is certainly the greatest of these creations; for it embodies the souls of the millions of American camp men who have always done the hard and perilous pioneer labor of this country. It is true American legend now, for Paul Bunyan, as he stands to-day, is absolutely American from head to foot" (Stevens 1925, 7).

During the 1940s *American Mercury* continued appealing to public interest in the courageous Americanness of colorful folk heroes with a Dorson essay on Sam Patch, among others (Dorson 1947). Unlike Stevens the creative artist, Dorson played the role of the historical detective finding a paper trail recounting mill hand Patch's dramatic jumps over Niagara Falls and other waterfalls, and uncovering legends that arose about Patch's life and fatal leap over the Genesee Falls in 1829. Charles Angoff, who had succeeded Mencken as editor of *American Mercury*, wanted, in Dorson's words to "keep some of the old fires stoked." By this he meant exposing "the fraudulent and perfidious" in a grudge match between accuser and accused (Dorson 1976c, 5; Siefert 1989, 68). It was also an issue that *American Mercury* and its readers took to heart because of the political importance of rendering a distinctively and authentically virtuous American tradition as the Cold War began. Dorson mentioned to me that Angoff's offer of a printed debate appealed to his competitive instinct honed on the squash and tennis court. Indeed, he drew attention to a head-to-head contest in a later essay by changing the "and" in the title between "folklore" and "fakelore" to the agonistic term "versus" (Dorson 1974a).[8] He hoped to be the Harvard champion again, and send a stinging message that folklore, whether on the pages of a popular magazine or in the halls of academe, needed to be researched, not "written." Dorson further insisted that it needed to be analyzed "properly" by the university professionals acting as cultural interpreters for the public.

Angoff shared with many other editors the opinion that folklore had become by 1941 a national topic of conversation. Bunyan was a household word that cropped up in cartoons, advertisements, and magazine stories (Felton 1947; Hoffman 1952; Dorson 1956a). Many artists and writers used what they identified as folk themes to create a national epic. Stephen Vincent Benet gained fame, for example, for "writing" folktales such as *The Devil and Daniel Webster* (1937, adapted before the end of the decade into an opera, drama, and movie) and the renowned literary figure Carl Sandburg mined American folk idioms for a number of poems in *The People, Yes* (1936). Sandburg had also worked to popularize American folk songs and published arrangements in *American Songbag* (1927). Marking the bridge between artist and popularized scholarship, Sandburg wrote the foreword to Botkin's *Treasury of American Folklore* (1944) for the commercial house of Crown Publishers. In music, folk festivals such as the National, White Top, and Pennsylvania folk festivals drew massive crowds during the 1930s and "folk" singers such as Bradley Kincaid, Leadbelly, and Woody Guthrie gained notoriety (Lawless 1960). In art, Thomas Hart Benton, one of the celebrated "regionalist painters," captured folksy characters from American tradition in several well-publicized murals, including one for Indiana at the 1933 World's Fair and another in 1937 at the state capitol of Missouri (Kammen 1991, 434–35; Benton 1983, 247–76).

Film producer Walt Disney created perhaps the biggest splash of folklore in mass media with the release of *Snow White and the Seven Dwarfs* in 1937, his first animated feature. Based on an internationally disseminated folktale (Aarne-Thompson Tale Type 709) identified in Germany by the Brothers Grimm (no. 53), the Disney film turned the story into a highly stylized and hugely successful musical comedy. Disney followed this success during the 1940s and 1950s with several animated features based on Grimms' collection and tall tales of American folk heroes including Johnny Appleseed, John Henry, and Pecos Bill. The popular press in New York sought out some academicians to comment on the phenomenon, and nearby folklorists active in the public spotlight such as Louis C. Jones and Harold Thompson were often quoted as folklore authorities (Kammen 1991, 432–34; Thomsen 1993). Angoff referred to this public interest in a preamble to the debate between Dorson and Stevens: "During the past two decades, the subject of American folklore has not only won the attention of more and more academicians, but has also won widespread interest among the general reading public. It therefore merits critical examination." Angoff implied a struggle for cultural authority between the "professor" represented by Dorson and the "artist" defended by Stevens (see Davidson 1940; Brown 1946; Thompson 1951; Utley 1952).

In "Folklore and Fake Lore" in *American Mercury*, Dorson lumped together Stevens the journalist writer and Botkin the Ph.D. editor as despicable "commercializers" and "money-writers." Bemoaning public ignorance of its own tradition on the one hand and berating its wretched exploiters on the other, he arrived clearly picking a fight:

> In recent years folklore has boomed mightily, and reached a wide audience through best-selling books, concert and cabaret folksingers, even Walt Disney cartoons. But far from fulfilling its high promise, the study has been falsified, abused and exploited, and the public deluded with Paul Bunyan nonsense and claptrap collections. Without stirring from the library, money-writers have successfully peddled synthetic hero-books and saccharine folk tales as the stories of the people Americans may be insufficiently posted on their history and culture, as the famous *New York Times* survey indicated, but their knowledge of these subjects is erudition, compared with what they know about their own folklore. The saddest aspect of this fraud is that the spurious article is so dull and thin, and the genuine material so salty and rich. (Dorson 1950b, 336)

Especially explosive was Dorson's charge of ideological manipulation. "These comic demigods are not products of a native mythology," he acerbically wrote, "but rather of a chauvinist and fascist conception of folklore. They must be 100 per cent native American supermen, all-conquering, all-powerful, braggart and whimsically destructive. By such distorted folk symbols the Nazis supported their thesis of a Nordic super-race, and touted Hitler as their greatest folklorist" (Dorson 1950b, 336). Considering that the military and ideological campaign against Nazi Germany was still fresh in the public's memory, Dorson's melding of fakelore with fascism must really have hurt. Rather than the praise heaped on the rewritten Bunyan from literati and public alike, Dorson pummeled the popularized Bunyan as the worst of commercial and ideological exploitation. Bunyan provided Dorson a tie between Stevens and Botkin, since Stevens wrote "folklore" using Bunyan, Botkin anthologized literary stories of Bunyan as folklore, and Botkin's *Treasury* was advertised as a "Paul Bunyan of a book."

Dorson did not explicitly define "fakelore" in the essay, but he was dead sure about folklore's meaning: "Folklore by any definition requires the proof of oral vitality" (Dorson 1950b, 336). With the value-laden term "fakelore" Dorson intended to cast aspersions on contemporary writers who tampered or misrepresented folklore in their entertaining stories. "My promulgation of the term 'fakelore' was intended as a shorthand attention-getter to make people aware of a difference between bona fide and phony folklore," Dorson later recalled (Dorson 1974a, 59). He contrasted the negative intentionality of "fake" with the "folk," or analytical use of print sources "in which folk traditions have found lodging more or less accidentally and casually" (Dorson 1972g, 465). After all, he had mined printed nineteenth-century newspapers for his *Jonathan Draws the Longbow*, but he argued for this work as a form of naturalistic fieldwork "to provide historical antecedents for contemporary specimens of oral and material culture" (Dorson 1972g, 466). He could allow that classic American writers such as Hawthorne and Irving had adapted "folk themes," but their writing should not be confused with the performance of folklore (Dorson 1971a, 186–203). Dorson viewed their literature as a historical artifact of cultural process, as opposed to contemporary anthologizers and journalists who misrepresented literary works as the stuff of folklore—and the basis of American culture. Using the tone of a moral play, Dorson set folklore as the true cultural expression of sincere, hardworking folk and fakelore as the commodity of devious and greedy exploiters. Dorson made the judgment that fakelore, if not exposed, would take a reprehensible life of its own and eventually obliterate all attempts at saving the pure strains of genuine American tradition. He lambasted authors and artists as charlatans who would steal for cheap profit and misrepresent for hurtful propaganda the cultural property of humble, unsuspecting tellers.

After use of "fakelore" caught on, Dorson clarified his meaning of the term as the presentation of "spurious and synthetic writings under the claim that they are genuine folklore." He allowed "fakelore" to become a single term, although originally he had meant it to be intentionally separated into "fake" and "lore" as opposed to the united, historical "folklore." Dorson did not deny Stevens's right to create stories in the style of folktales, but he insisted on distinguishing between the historically "real" oral accounts of folklore and the fictional lie that his literature was in itself folklore. He resented retellings of folklore as distracting the appreciation of everyday tradition bearers and undermining the "serious" investigation of folklore as a cultural mirror. His argument for authenticity hinged on the ironic categorization of mass culture as *anti*-cultural. In Dorson's sense, culture had an organic meaning in that cultures grow from the expressions of groups tied to place and community. Dorson detested that folk tradition had been made into entertainment in contemporary society instead of a part of the everyday life of ordinary people which he associated with "culture." Dorson implied that academics had to be culture's intellectual defenders against "popular taste" engendered by the dulling force of mass media and its commercializing agents in contemporary life. Assessing the situation as another American exception, Dorson thought that "there appears to be no close parallel in other nations to the fakelore issue in the United States, where popularization, commercialization, and the mass media *engulf* the culture" (Dorson 1976c, 14, emphasis added).

Dorson turned the charge of fakelore into a cultural critique of the anti-intellectual and pro-ideological effect of American mass media. He warned that the temptations of commercialism and mass media diluted the "salty and rich" core of American folklore and detracted from the essential message of its glorious earthiness. Concerned for preserving the American historical spirit of "democracy," reflected in the varied and vernacular social spirit of American folklore, Dorson resented that Paul Bunyan had been turned by media into a triumph of American industrialism rather than a reference to a living tradition of lumberjack legends criticizing camp bosses and their corporate management. He further pointed out a fondness for erotic themes in folklore in the living tradition as opposed to the bowdlerized family entertainment of folktales produced for the mass media. The connection of these charges for Dorson was that the democracy of folklore meant that culture would be seen as it was found, in all its vernacular reality, and it signified a middle ground, objectively above ideology, or at least between right and left. Dorson, the realist academic, claimed to speak for the integrity of folklore and its powerless tradition bearers, since they were chauvinistically and commercially manipulated in the media, and it was this exploitative "manipulation" that Dorson hammered time and again.

Dorson burned another Bunyan editor, Harold Felton, with rhetoric even more acidic than that hurled at Stevens. Reviewing *Legends of Paul Bunyan* (1947), Dorson stabbed the book and the mass culture of which it was a part in one stroke:

> This anthology of the literature that has grown around Paul Bunyan exalts still further the nation's leading fake-hero. It testifies to the gullibility of the public, the irresponsibility of publishers and editors, the timidity of folklore scholars, and the dismal insipidity of some American writers. Here is no excusable Ossianic lie, with a witty fraud and a poetic talent to palliate the act. Here is chiefly ignorance, commercialism, and the shoddiest of

creative power. The surest proof that most of these "legends" are not folklore lies in the puerility; no self-respect folk would pass them on. (Dorson 1951c, 233)

Dorson implied that scholarship did not serve a degrading master, but as merchandise fakelore was subject to popular taste, akin to the rule of the vulgar mob. The mob could be forgiven for its ignorance, he intimated, but what he could not allow was that it was manipulated or controlled by conniving media and commercial elites who sought to change thinking and obscure the grit of vernacular tradition. Thus Dorson harped on the "fabrication" and "manufacture" of Bunyan, and he explained that the Bunyan fad signified a "cultural adolescence in the American nation, which has grown up on Greek and Roman and Norse gods, and now feels a childish glee in discovering its own homemade, all-conquering deity." Preferring the social reality of vernacular texts, Dorson trashed the Paul Bunyan phenomenon as "safe, harmless and patriotic stuff. Nothing in the legends can offend, save their banality, for all the juice has been extracted" (Dorson 1951c, 234). Dorson's command for a proper handling of the Bunyan phenomenon was to first folkloristically uncover the early oral tradition or historically show the rise of Paul Bunyan in American popular entertainment (see Hoffman 1952). Instead, he complained, readers got an "omnibus" in which "all types of Bunyan writing are piled together, whether the plain, anecdotal yarns of Charles E. Brown or the overblown whimsy of Mr. Stevens, so long as they deal with the mammoth kitchen or upside down mountains" (Dorson 1951c, 235).

Dorson contemptuously called Stevens "a badly mixed up man" and accused him and his ilk of passing off their vapid creations as the voices of the folk. He implied that Stevens lied about his sources and misrepresented his background in the storied environment of the lumber camps. In Dorson's biting words,

> In an expanded introduction to a new edition of his book, he [Stevens] squeals at the Ph.D.s and professors who ask him for documentation. Then he admits spending three years looking for some, in vain. He now mentions six story-tellers by name, and a "hundred" others anonymously, but gives no texts. He says that his Paul Bunyan is the real McCoy, but that he invented most of it. He accuses other authors of stealing his legend—which he has assigned to all America—even if they heard it from jacks, for the jacks read it in his book. I would like to meet the lumberjack who would recite such stuff—or any novel—aloud. He calls himself a "timber beast and sawdust savage," and writes fluff. (Dorson 1950b, 337).

The barbs must have cut Stevens, and aroused readers of *American Mercury,* as a classic battle between critic and artist turned into a debate about the future of American culture and the value of spreading mass media. But while Dorson and Stevens were sharply divided on the value of creatively presenting folklore in contemporary popular culture, both agreed that Bunyan should not be used for "chauvinist" or commercial exploitation to boost a blind patriotism or culturally false tourism. Dorson admonished that Stevens's "invention" should not be called folk-lore because folklore had a scholarly, and therefore authoritative definition. To Dorson, Stevens did not collect, or write, folklore; he concocted insipid "fluff" not worthy of the public attention it received. Stevens testily answered that as an artist he could alter what he wanted to produce a creative work for the public, and Dorson could study his unaltered texts as he wanted for a different, specialized audience. For Stevens the spread of Bunyan in mass media invigorated modern culture with art, built an appreciation for forestry, and raised the vernacular voice of forest "poesy" into respectable poetry. Stevens defended his genuine experience with the oral tradition of lumbermen by recounting his life in the woods. Stevens wrote:

> I swing on Dr. Dorson's charge, "Stevens is a badly mixed up man [on Paul Bunyan]," and bat it right back at him. His confusion is between the tasks of the anthropologist and those of the artist with folklore…. The scientist of long technical training and experience will use folklore to reflect vital phases of human tribes in times past. The artist adopts folklore for the work of his imagination. He sees Paul Bunyan as substance for art, in the tradition of Twain with King Arthur's court, of Byron with Don Juan, of Marlowe with Faustus, of Homer with Odysseus. On that great way I make my trifling tracks. (Stevens 1950, 343–44)

If the argument sounds petty, remember that as a struggle for authority over public consciousness, the stakes in the debate were substantial for the period. Modern scholar and artist scrapped for oversight over American tradition.

Stevens's categorization of historian Dorson as the anthropologist may appear surprising, but Dorson's argument for the social group basis of culture sounds anthropological and, considering his background, at times startlingly antinational-ist. It is also true that at the time the antifascist, sociocultural line had been strong-ly voiced by anthropologists such as Franz Boas and many of his students who used folklore to show the cultural relativity of tribal and minority groups (Barkan 1992, 66–95; Herskovits 1953, 86–101). Boas, had, according to George Stocking, trans-formed the conception of culture away from race and nationality to "the burden of tradition, and to the processes of human reason" (Stocking 1968, 233; see Boas [1928] 1986, 1940). So when Dorson made pronouncements in "Folklore and Fake Lore" such as "There is no such thing as the lore of the nation, or of regions, but only the lore of groups," he may have indeed sounded to Stevens like a Boasian anthropologist (Dorson 1950a, 342). This view merits some explanation, since Dorson never considered himself anthropological or antinationalist. What appears to be a contradiction is a result of Dorson's brew of history and folklore in forming his view of national tradition. History, organized nationally, taught Dorson the influence of the developing political nation-state in the life of its residents (Stern 1989). He would indeed argue that the environment and experience of New World settlement especially transformed American life into a unique culture rather than consisting mainly of altered transplants of Old World traditions.

Folklore, Dorson understood, crossed national lines and connected narrators with groups. He edited the Folktales of the World book series and the anthology *Folktales Told around the World* (1975) with this view in mind. When arguing solely for folklore, then, he could sound internationalist or diffusionist. On his folklore fieldwork in the Upper Peninsula, for example, he could comment, "Folk traditions follow their own courses much like parallel railroad tracks which never meet," implying that each example of folklore has its own life history and varied group associations (Dorson 1976b, 7). But when added to the background of history, which tended in his mind to be traced to national movements, then the picture appeared more nationalistic. In writing up his fieldwork for *Bloodstoppers and Bearwalkers*, Dorson overlaid national history upon the anthropological idea of folklore in culture to come up with a communitarian reconciliation by combining the cultural "minuscule" with the historic "region" and "nation." He declared, for example: "the Peninsula contains in minuscule the nation's varied folk culture. A dramatic century of land and water conquest, of mining and lumber booms, has generated a rich historical and local lore" (Dorson 1976b, 2).

One may also evaluate Dorson's apparent backtracking on the nationalist line by considering the folklore genres with which he was preoccupied. At the time Dorson studied folklore, a great concern spread among "comparativists" such as Stith Thompson and Archer Taylor for charting from literary analysis the diffusion of folktale motifs and types from source areas around the globe. Boasian and Malinowskian anthropologists meanwhile recorded myths from so-called primitive groups to determine their reflection of a society's particular cultural history and the social and psychological function of those myths within the society. Dorson's interest since his undergraduate days had been largely in legend because of its narrative based on historical events and figures of community, region, and nation. Besides criticizing the historic-geographic literary scholars and cultural anthropologists for their indifference to legendary material, he bemoaned a lack of attention to living traditions such as jokes and anecdotes among modern occupational groups such as college students and steel workers (Dorson 1949, 1981). When he referred to folktale or myth in his work, as he did in "Folklore and Fake Lore," he tended to take more of an internationalist or comparativist tack. When he brought up legend, occupational narrative, or humor, it tended to be in a historical and frequently nationalistic light (see Dorson 1973a, 1976b). And it was the study of legend, occupational narrative, and humor against the background of American history that Dorson especially relished as revealing social life. As if to show the possibility of using folktales for nationalist interpretation, he interpreted national characteristics of Japanese folktales in a book on folklore and nationalism (Oinas 1978). "Anyone speaking of national characteristics depicted in folktales treads shaky ground," Dorson recognized, but he thought, "Japan offers as strong a case as may be found anywhere" (Dorson 1975d, 241). Significantly, Dorson in Japan and America stuck to an emphasis on the text and its types, rather than the particularistic social group, to be able to show the ways that texts can become both varied and shared within a regional, urban, and national whole.

Dorson never reprinted "Folklore and Fake Lore," although he published two books of essays in which fakelore was a central theme. He indicated to me that the charge of Nazi fascism was overheated and the nationalistic theme understated for his later sensibilities. He reprinted "Fakelore," a reflective review of the issue first published in Germany in 1969, in *American Folklore and the Historian* (1971). He closed the essay with a much stronger call for a historical search for national tradition than he made in "Folklore and Fake Lore":

> *Fakelore* was intended as a rallying cry against the distortion of a serious subject. It seems almost incredible that such elementary principles as the necessity for fieldwork and the faithful rendering of texts had to be debated. It all goes back to the curious lack of specialization in American folklore, which fell into a no-man's-land between comparative folklorists and scholars in American studies. To overcome this lack of any body of theory fitting the needs of the United States, I presented two lengthy papers to the Society, "A Theory for American Folklore" (1957) and "A Theory for American Folklore Reviewed" (1968). In essence, this theory holds that the folk traditions of countries colonized in modern times—in North and South America and Australia—must be correlated with their major historical developments from colonization to industrialization. (Dorson 1971a, 14)

Dorson even declined to reprint the original essay in a book entitled *Folklore and Fakelore* (1976). Instead, he introduced the book with a new essay, "Folklore, Academe, and the Marketplace," another review of the issue with an update of new battles since 1969. The thrust of his later argument hinged more on the position of an intellectual class toward the commercial or mass culture. In his summary of "Folklore and Fake Lore," he ignored the questions of chauvinism and nationalism raised in the original essay, and recapitulated the tone of the piece as an attack on the temptations of the popular marketplace to distort genuine folklore. The significance of the original essay, Dorson told readers, was that "this exchange presented for the first time the clash of viewpoints between the academic (the Victorians would have said scientific) folklorist and the [commercial] writer using folklore themes" (Dorson 1976c, 5).

Dorson disdained extremist uses to which folklore could be put from the left as well as from the right. During the 1970s, he responded to leftist critics who skewered his *America in Legend* for omitting ethnic folk heroes and heroines and for exalting the bloodthirsty Indian-killer Mike Fink as a legendary hero. "Fink and Crockett were indeed violent and even racist personalities," Dorson replied. "Still, to invent substitutes for them merely produces a new fakelore" (Dorson 1976c, 27). During the Cold War of the 1960s he raised this concern for ideological control of folklore in his public objection to Soviet governmental reins on folklore scholarship (Dorson 1976c, 71–72).

Dorson appeared much more forgiving of uses of folklore for "cultural" rather than "ideological" nationalism, especially when they resulted in political independence of a minority group or the unification of culturally connected people. Thus he set the work of the Brothers Grimm as the "reconstruction of a proud Germanic past," and the ways that folklorists in Ireland "all fought for the revival of the Gaelic tongue and heritage against the stifling cloak of English culture" (Dorson 1976c, 67–70). In the United States, he considered the pressures of "official" ideology and government less pervasive than the temptation of popular taste, which as he said, "contains its own latent ideology" (Dorson 1976c, 72). He implied that this ideology of popular taste in commercial culture is anti-intellectual or professional, capitalistic, and hegemonic. To the criticism that Dorson's championing of "professionalism" was elitist and conservative, Dorson responded that he preferred to call it "the search for truth and standards of excellence" (Dorson 1975b, 237–38). From his perspective, American folklore scholarship should serve neither the right nor the left, and in setting the middle course, he imagined an objective, essentially positivist handling of folklore so that intellectuals could rationally interpret culture and guide the public's cultural knowledge (Dorson 1951c, 234; Dorson 1957).

Jay Mechling commented further that Dorson's choice of the "middle way" lay in "the consensus school's claim [of] 'givenness' of American experience, in contrast with Europe's reliance on ideologies." The claim to givens of American experience, it can be argued, follows American philosophical emphases on pragmatism, flexibility, and realism, and Mechling cites Dorson's intellectual comrade Daniel Boorstin as a main proponent of this view (Mechling 1989d, 22). In fact, Dorson avoided using ideological or theoretical "isms" (and he vowed to never, never use the charged term "paradigm" that had come into vogue among radical historians) in his rhetoric. He surveyed folklore studies as a whole many times with reference to various "theories," but pragmatically preferred to describe "techniques," "directions," and "concepts" that in the name of disciplinary consensus would bring together diverse viewpoints (Dorson 1951b, 1951a, 1959c, 1963a, 1969, 1972b, 1982b).

Dorson thought that Botkin's nonmethodological treasuries were antithetical to the rational scholar's agenda. "Patchwork catch-alls," "haphazard scrapbooks," and "scissors and paste jobs" Dorson called them. He cursed folklorists who would defend the treasuries as somehow constituting a model of research, and he dismissed writers who gave positive reviews to the anthologies as obviously having little or no background in American studies (Dorson 1971a, 27). The treasuries further represented to Dorson a dangerous combination of chauvinist nationalism and pandering commercialism. Introduced by Botkin as a book "as big as this country of ours—as American as Davy Crockett and as universal as Brer Rabbit," the *Treasury of American Folklore* sold over a half-million copies in 1944 and was chosen as a Book-of-the-Month Club selection. It went into numerous editions and led to a whole bookshelf of other "Treasury" volumes. Stevens also had a negative opinion of Botkin's treasuries, but for a different reason. Speaking as an artist, he thought that Botkin's literary choices should have been better. He wrote: "Most of the pages of his *Treasury* represent little more than the whimsies swapped by drugstore cowboys and the printed maunderings of the boozy hacks who infested the Frontier, from Cumberland Gap to the Golden Gate.... His book reminds me of the squirming mass of worms to be dug from the right spot behind any rotting, abandoned barn" (Stevens 1950, 349).

Dorson decried Botkin's confusion of folklore in literature with folklore in the field and Botkin's resulting misrepresentation of national tradition as overly Anglo-Saxon and refined. Dorson ridiculed Botkin the editor-folklorist as "the dude fisherman who buys his catch at the market" (Dorson 1950a, 338). Because Botkin did not record his fieldwork, Dorson claimed, "he gives us not close-ups of story-telling action or folk societies. Because we cannot trust them, we never are sure how much is real tradition, or what has been left out. I can testify that his bulky collections graze the country's folklore wealth" (Dorson 1950a, 338–39). Essentially, Botkin had included material that Dorson considered folksy rather than folklore. Dorson accused Botkin on the one hand of loosely using the omnibus "American" label to succeed at the "box office," and on the other hand, of creating a false and overly glorified picture of America that smacks of "exclusive nativism."

To Dorson's way of thinking, the anthologizers stretched the "term folklore out of all meaning, and shrink the definition of American to old stock Anglo-Saxons" (Dorson 1950a, 338). Promoting an image of America with diverse communities acting together in a cultural process of consensus, Dorson asked why immigrant and Indian traditions were left out of Botkin's treasury and why historical social differences among classes and regions of America were not represented in folklore collection. To answer these crucial questions, Dorson sounded a call for a library of in-depth field collections of communities similar to his *Bloodstoppers and Bearwalkers* "gathered and interpreted with insight, integrity, and some sense of social meanings" (Dorson 1950a, 343).

Readings of Botkin's essays without taking into consideration their different social vantages during the 1950s might suggest that he and Dorson really were not that far apart on the need for fieldwork, or the issue of representing the pluralism of American traditions in ethnic, occupational, and regional communities, or even the matter of a historical national tradition (Botkin 1946a, 1949a, 1962; J. Hirsch 1987). A veritable gulf existed between them, however, concerning the public presentation of folklore and the uses or "applications" to which folklore is put. Botkin poetically sounded the call of a humanist for "folkness," the use of traditional ideas which could invigorate mass culture through creative artists, while Dorson insisted on folklore's treatment as a precious historic artifact whose form needed to be kept intact to keep its original cultural integrity and scientific value (Botkin 1931, 1932; Dorson 1957). As an oral artifact, folklore for Dorson gained definition; it took on reality as a cultural form. Its sincerity and authenticity could be set in contrast to its other, commercial mass culture.

It bothered Dorson that Botkin was vague, even evasive, about folklore's objective place in culture. Botkin felt uncomfortable with folklore's "esoteric associations" and ambiguous connection with a distant past (Botkin 1932). While Dorson was sure about the definition and need for "folk" and "folklore" as keywords necessary for discourse about community and expression, Botkin seemed ambivalent about them, since as scholarly inventions, he argued that they seem "to have become the possession of the few who study it rather than of the many who make or use it" (Botkin 1944, xxi; see also Botkin 1932). If Dorson found Botkin's populist presentation of literary retellings in the treasuries culturally and historically abhorrent, Botkin viewed Dorson's presentation in *Bloodstoppers* as boringly inventorying trivial "survivals," rather than showing the creative power of folklore as "humane learning" (Botkin 1952b, 1955b). The principle that Botkin stuck to since the days of editing *Folk-Say* remained: "There is a point where collection and classification, with all their superstructure of definition and analysis, break down and creative (including re-creative) interpretation must begin. Not what is the folk and what is folklore but what can they do for our culture and literature is the question that should concern our writers and critics" (Botkin 1930, 17).

Dorson's swipe at Botkin was a bold professional move. Fifteen years Dorson's senior, Botkin had been president of the American Folklore Society (1944), had founded and edited the annual *Folk-Say*, had a best seller to his credit in the *Treasury of American Folklore* (1944), and had respected posts teaching at the University of Oklahoma, and directing the Federal Writers Project folklore programs and the Library of Congress's Archive of Folk Song. Botkin championed work in the American folklore field and was chosen to write the definitive survey of "American Folklore" for the *Standard Dictionary of Folklore, Mythology, and Legend* in 1949. Dorson had first met Botkin in 1939 and kept up a friendly correspondence. Botkin praised Dorson's volume on Crockett, and Dorson in turn worked with Botkin on a proposal for a book on tall tales of American folk heroes for a series Dorson planned on American Folk Literature. On July 6, 1939, Botkin wrote Dorson to encourage him: "The function of such a series, I agree with you, is to introduce to a wider public the native literature of the folk order, which has value for the scholar as well as interest for the general reader."[9] Dorson advised Botkin to organize the industrial, occupational, and urban lore collected in Chicago and New York by the WPA project for the book, but plans for the book stalled when Botkin could not get permission to publish the material. Dorson expressed his disappointment about the project's demise when he wrote Botkin on January 21, 1940, but offered that "personally, I do not consider the negotiations a loss, since they gave me the opportunity of becoming acquainted with you."[10]

Dorson and Botkin were both Harvard alumni (Botkin earned his B.A. in 1920, but rarely referred to it; Dorson often did) and Jewish ancestry (Dorson rarely

Benjamin Botkin working at the Archive of Folksong (now the Archive of Folk Culture), Library of Congress, c. 1945. (Special Collections, University of Nebraska)

referred to it; Botkin often did). Botkin had come from working class roots in Boston while Dorson grew up in bourgeois comfort in New York City. Botkin was known for his shy and quiet ways, while Dorson was outgoing and outspoken. They also differed in their curricular focus and extracurricular activity. Dorson the intense sports competitor embraced history and American civilization. Besides studying for the M.A. in English from Columbia, which he received in 1921, Botkin wrote poetry, "communed with nature," and found employment in New York City settlement houses and English and Americanization classes for new immigrants (Botkin 1935; Jackson 1966, 2–3). After his social work experience in New York City, Botkin returned to academic studies at Nebraska, where he studied folklore with Louise Pound and produced a dissertation on the American play-party song, for which he received the Ph.D. in English and anthropology in 1931 (Botkin 1937).

Following the success of the first *Treasury* volume in 1944, Botkin resigned from the Archive of Folk Song to write and edit full time in New York, helped by prestigious fellowships from the Guggenheim Foundation in 1951, and later the Louis M. Rabinowitz Foundation (1965) and National Endowment for the Humanities (1967). He was a major star in the firmament of folklore studies. Indeed, reverence had been paid to Botkin's treasuries in most reviews by folklorists until Dorson expressed mild criticism at the end of a review of *Treasury of New England Folklore* in the magazine *Saturday Review of Literature* (1948): "The chief complaint I am making is that Mr. Botkin is trying to present a full body of regional folklore without benefit of field work" (Dorson 1948a, 9).[11] According to Dorson, within the folklorist fraternity the review was considered "devastating," not only because Botkin was a respected authority, but also because folklorists were expected to support their own in public outlets to attract adherents to the subject (Dorson 1971a, 6). Dorson thought the subject could be better served through imposition of scholarly authority, and he faulted folklorists generally for inadequately defining their field, surveying its terrain, indicating its problems, and explaining its discipline (Dorson 1948b, 76).

When it came time to scorch Stevens's Bunyan for *American Mercury*, Dorson turned up the heat on Botkin, who had anthologized six literary renderings of Bunyan in *Treasury of American Folklore* and written on Bunyan as the epitome of an American folk hero (Botkin 1946b). Once again Dorson faulted Botkin for not doing fieldwork and reporting, essentially, the wrong stuff as folklore. Dorson caustically wrote: "His Anglo-Saxon sources provide an endless suffocation of tall tales and gags, but not a single instance of the blood-stopping charm, or the dialect yarn, or the personal saga—since these are unreported forms, though widespread, known only to the folk" (Dorson 1950a, 339). These were also forms collected together by Dorson in *Bloodstoppers and Bearwalkers*, and they suggested the uncensored reality of grassroots folklore. Dorson fretted that Botkin's selections showed "the tough folk mind a thing of gossamer and ribbons" (Dorson 1948b, 76). Botkin returned that Dorson was guilty of "harping on the more lurid and violent aspects" of life and overblowing "discoveries" of unartistic, trivial survivals (Botkin 1952b).

Dorson's strident accusation against Botkin of chauvinistic English-American nativism must have especially stunned Botkin, since he was known for liberal views on American pluralism, and in his Federal Writers' Project he had promoted special fieldwork attention to living traditions of ethnic and occupational groups (Botkin 1946a, 1946b). Dorson went after the Federal Writers' Project manuscripts Botkin used in *A Treasury of New England Folklore* as "for the most part disappointing and amateurish, devoid of milieu and commonplace in content" (Dorson 1948b, 76–77). Dorson's most crushing blow against Botkin in the essay was that Botkin could not distinguish genuine folklore or else had sold out his values for the devil's money. "Mr. Botkin defines folklore, fairly enough, as 'the stuff that travels and the stuff that sticks,' but this is not the same as the stuff that is shoveled together to fill a bargain volume," Dorson snorted (Dorson 1950a, 339).

If Dorson was retaliating for Botkin's criticism of Dorson's *Jonathan Draws the Longbow* in 1947, he did not say. Botkin had dished out the same complaint that Dorson later leveled at Botkin: he had not done fieldwork. Botkin wrote that Dorson unfortunately "by-passed (to use his own term) 'direct oral sources,' except for a few introductory generalizations on oral story-telling habits and an occasional reference to oral parallels or variants." As a result, he does little "to illuminate the actual influence of print on the folk tale but rather confines his attention to the mutations of tale types and motifs on the single level of print" (Botkin 1947a, 79). In fact, Botkin also accused Dorson of neglecting the cultural background and "living tradition" of the region, yet another charge that Dorson later shot back at Botkin. It must have irked Dorson that Botkin also considered Dorson a fellow "treasure-digger," who had helped to break down "the resistance of purists in the fields of both literature and folklore who refuse to regard folklore as worthy of literary scholarship or literary folk tales as worthy of folklore scholarship" (Botkin 1947a, 79). Dorson made sure that no one would confuse his work with Botkin's.

Dorson was especially savage in his review of Botkin's *Treasury of Southern Folklore* (1949). "Mr. Botkin's gift, it would seem, is for the vapid and inane generalization," Dorson screeched (Dorson 1950c, 481). Damning the book as a "rehash of rehashes," he warned that the stories edited by Botkin "are excessively flat and dull and badly written, besides having nothing to do with folklore." Dorson charged that Botkin had stooped degradingly low to "meet the taste of the modern reading audience":

> [Robert] Chambers and [William] Hone [Victorian British antiquarians] made mental demands on their readers; Botkin makes none, and caters to his audience much as do newspapers, digests and omnibuses, with short, breezy selections, good for a laugh or a human-interest angle, that also appeal to superficial regional patriotism with familiar names and places: anecdotes of Lee, Andy and Stonewall Jackson, Huey Long, hillbilly stories, Confederate sagas, Negro dialect jokes, flotsam about the old plantation, cotton, moonshiners, the Mississippi, New Orleans cookery—something for everybody, and what drugstore bookbuyer will cavil at disparity of sources or the many removes from oral tradition? (Dorson 1950c, 482)

Botkin's treasuries drew Dorson's ire because their popularity implied a successful standard of scholarship. He did not want them to be the works from which judgments of folklore scholarship or American tradition would be made. Dorson railed that they "lessened the prestige of the study in the eyes of scholars in other disciplines." They showed little fieldwork, elementary library research, and were "unmindful of folklore's relation to culture in time and place" (Dorson 1950c, 482). The *Treasury* became symbolic in Dorson's mind for the incoherence of the discipline and the trouble with mass culture. In an example of his using the subject of folklore to represent the object of folklore studies and American civilization, Dorson bitterly commented that "Burgoo" would be a more apt term than treasury for Botkin's anthologies: "Burgoo" is a dish "neither liquid nor solid, neither soup, hash, nor goulash, but partook of the nature of all of them" (Dorson 1950a, 354). He chided other folklorists for attaching folkloristic merit to this kind of work or approving of the popular attention to folklore the volumes brought.

Looking back over the first *Treasury*, one can find the phrases that made Dorson bristle early on in the introduction. Botkin wrote:

> When I began to think of a book of American folklore, I thought of all the good songs and stories and all the good talk that would go into it, and of what a richly human and entertaining book it would be. A book of American folklore, I thought, should be as big as this country of ours—as American as Davy Crockett and as universal as Brer Rabbit. For when one thinks of American folklore one thinks not only of the folklore of American life—the traditions that have sprung up on American soil—but also of the literature of folklore—the migratory traditions that have found a home here. (Botkin 1944, xxi)

In the volume, Botkin stressed the aesthetic and entertainment value of folklore rather than its cultural roles. Although he recognized "migratory traditions," he chose to stress "the English idiom in the United States," not for nativistic purposes, so Botkin wrote, but for "practical purposes." He felt that a book of "folklore in America" would be too unwieldy and he preferred the "unity" that resulted from concentrating on "American folklore" "as an expression of the land, the people, and their experience" (Botkin 1944, xxiv).

To be sure, Botkin began his treasury with American bravado. His first sections are mostly literary retellings of legends regarding "Heroes and Boasters," such as Crockett and Mike Fink followed by anecdotes of "Boosters and Knockers." Parts three and four concern "Jesters" and "Liars" and contain entertaining jokes and tall tales, including comical "yarns" about Paul Bunyan. Parts five and six have migratory folktales, songs, and rhymes, including African-American animal tales, British-American ballads, and children's lore. Overall, the contents of the volume give the impression of defining through literature an American tradition of legendary hyperbolic characters and events, although as Dorson pointed out the historical, social, or cultural connection of these characters and events is not clear. However disappointing to Dorson the objective historian who recorded events and texts as they were, Botkin's purpose was ultimately aesthetic. Botkin made selections that he considered artistic examples of indigenous traditions that could inspire creative work in contemporary culture. Botkin wanted "to show both the discrete and the discursive folk imagination at work" (Botkin 1944, xxv; see also Clough 1947). The key to the volume's significance, and ultimately the real bone of contention for Dorson, then, was its popular service "as an inspiration and a source-book for writers, teachers, and all others who are concerned with the materials of an American culture" (Botkin 1944, xxvi).

Rather than defend the treasuries, Botkin answered a year after Dorson's review in *New York Folklore Quarterly* with a plea for ending the mudslinging so as to improve folklore's public image. Invoking the cultural center in calling for "a little Christian civility," Botkin announced that "it is high time that folklorists realized that their internal squabbling and bickering, accompanied by much backbiting and sniping and open display of ill temper and bad manners, are doing their cause more harm than good, as far as the general public is concerned" (Botkin 1951a, 78). Thereafter Botkin refrained from engaging Dorson in public or reviewing his books. Well after Botkin had published his last treasury, Dorson was still unrelenting in blasting away at the anthologies in many surveys of the discipline through the 1970s.[12] The fakelore debate spread beyond Botkin and continued long after the early round of essays during the 1950s, and in folkloristic discourse generally, Botkin's treasuries became the ultimate symbols of besmirched "popularized" tradition (see Dorson 1974a, 1976c, 1–30; Bluestein 1994).

Dorson thought that the assault on fakelore and popularizers was necessary for raising the integrity of folklore as well as folklore studies in the public eye. The issue became a theme running through several presidential addresses and major sessions at the American Folklore Society (Utley 1952; Halpert 1957; Dorson 1968). Francis Lee Utley in his presidential address of 1951 commented that "nothing has disturbed your president more in this year of his ritual passage than the disintegrative quarrels which make our Society function at only a small fraction of its potential" (Utley 1952, 111). Utley wanted the American Folklore Society to be inclusive and make it a home for popularizer and scholar alike. Dorson wanted to coldly drive popularizers out of the organization since membership implied credentials as a cultural authority. Dorson insisted that the fight needed to continue to set the public straight on the genuine article of folklore and the standards set by scholars for its study (Dorson 1957).

THE APPLIED FOLKLORE DEBATE

It may appear that the "war of the folklorists" or the "battle of the books," as Botkin referred to it, was a personal tiff, but the fact that so many figures claiming cultural authority got into the act and the arguments continued for so long shows a broader significance. It related folkloristic discourse to the rise of mass culture alarmingly witnessed during the post-World War II decades (Botkin 1952a). Dorson's answer to a sense of contemporary cultural malaise was to find long-standing "authentic" folklore from the grass roots. It served as alternatives to mass culture in subcultural persistence and the independence of traditional forms from the past into the present. He suggested intellectuals as custodians for this tradition and universities as repositories for its study. In contrast, Botkin's message resonated with the promise of an engulfing mass culture enhanced by a sense of tradition in new guises.

Botkin's ideal "culture" and definition of democracy were at odds with Dorson's. It is from this difference that the larger meaning of their debate for their times can be drawn. Whereas Botkin spoke of culture as activity in contemporary society, as an ongoing process of popularization, Dorson tended to refer to culture by its historical forms shared locally and communally. Botkin wanted to invigorate "modern life" and its popular expressions of literature and broadcast media with the imaginative appeal of folklore. His goal was thus to create an "applied" folklore for use in society which he contrasted with that of the purist who serviced his or her discipline.

Writing on the "Folkness of the Folk," Botkin referred to folklore as an answer to modern cultural malaise:

> The ultimate aim of applied folklore is the restoration to American life of the sense of community—a sense of thinking, feeling, and acting along similar, though not the same lines—that is in danger of being lost today. Thus applied folklore goes beyond cultural history to cultural strategy, to the end of creating a favorable environment for the liberation of creative energies and the flourishing of the folk arts among other social, cooperative activities. In a time of increasing standardization it becomes an increasingly important function of the applied folklorist to discover and keep alive folk expressions that might otherwise be lost. And in a country of great regional diversity such as ours, the balanced utilization of regional as well as ethnic resources is vital to the enrichment and fulfillment of American life and expression. In this way the folklorist may outgrow the older "survival" theory of the "partial uselessness" of folklore and renew the continuity and survival values of folklore as the "germ-plasm of society." (Botkin 1962, 54–55)

In answer to Dorson's call for academic authority, Botkin argued that "whereas a pure folklorist might tend to think of folklore as an independent discipline, the applied folklorist prefers to think of it as ancillary to the study of culture, of history or literature—of people" (Botkin 1962, 50). For "restoring the sense of community and continuity to modern life," and "in securing and making available socially and artistically satisfying examples and versions of folk expression," therefore, "the folklorist should take the initiative," which meant participating in and creating new forms of popular culture (Botkin 1962, 55). Folkloristic initiative, Botkin contended, included reading folklore to children in elementary schools, writing new literature based on folklore, and promotion of folk festivals,

all in the name of creating "understanding and enjoyment"—a favorite Botkin
phrase (Botkin 1953). The folk festival, for example, he called "an important form
of utilization and application, for understanding as well as enjoyment, through
participation and the celebration of our 'commonness'—the 'each' in all of us and
the 'all' in each of us. For what we participate in here is not only a performance
and a revival but cultural—intercultural—democracy" (Botkin 1962, 51). Botkin's
Treasury was applied folklore, because it showed the ways that hidden treasures of
folklore for stirring imagination had been used by writers in the past, and the
ways they could be applied to a new "machine age." Botkin liked to explain his use
of folklore as subject and object by the double meaning of "folklore in the making" to refer to his treasuries. By this he referred to the cultural process of folklore,
its shifting back and forth between oral tradition and print, or broadcast media,
and its renewal by creative artists in popular, repeated traditions (Botkin 1938;
1944, xxv; J. Hirsch 1987, 26).

What was positively "folklore in the making" for Botkin was negatively
"fakelore" for Dorson. Botkin emphasized in the *Treasury of American Folklore*: "If
this book is intended to bring the reader back to anything, it is not to the 'good old
days' but to an enjoyment and understanding of living American folklore for what
it is and what it is worth" (Botkin 1944, xxii). This intention for reinvigoration of
popular culture through creative applications of folklore and folkness became
repeated in the many popular *Treasuries* by Botkin and others that followed, often
loosely organized around regions and localities (see Botkin 1947b, 1949b, 1951b,
1954, 1955c, 1956; Botkin and Harlow 1953; Ausubel 1948; Tidwell 1956; Life 1961).[13]

For Dorson, "living traditions" meant a continuity of form from the past. Like
Botkin, he recognized folk traditions in urban centers, in industries, even in mass
media. Like Botkin, Dorson emphasized the pluralism of groups—ethnic, occupational, and regional—of which folklore played a major role. Dorson was stricter
than Botkin, however, in his view of the oral vitality and social connection of folklore, and he had more of a methodical historical approach to tracing a group's traditions (Dorson 1946a, 1961b; Botkin 1940, 1955a). Assessing "Folklore in the
Modern World," for example, Dorson differentiated between authentic and spurious "updating" of traditions:

> The Davy Crockett who was a living legend in the 1830s and 1840s resurfaced a cen-
> tury later as a Walt Disney boy scout with no folk roots. In our time the cowboy has
> become a subject for popular films and recordings rather than a dispenser of anecdote
> and folksong. Meanwhile the youth culture has generated a lively druglore and rock fes-
> tival scene attuned to the vibrations of the 1960s and 1970s. Many of the themes in this
> new druglore can be recognized as *time-honored in tradition*—for instance, the battle of
> wits between the stupid ogre and the underdog trickster, here represented by the narcs
> (narcotics agents) and heads (consumers of marijuana and LSD). As Hartland said, tra-
> dition is ever being created anew. (Dorson 1976c, 47; see also Dorson 1973a, 257–303;
> 1978d, emphasis added)

Dorson's folklore came from a genuine social folk, who he first defined as community groups and later as "anonymous masses of tradition-oriented people" (Dorson 1976c, 46). He made a further distinction between the official culture of corporations, universities, media, and arts that dictate rules and the unofficial culture in which tradition-oriented people find their own modes of expression (Dorson 1976c, 45). Traditions to Dorson were living in the sense that they were continuous in form or function for the cultural process of a social folk.

For Botkin traditions were living in that they could be adapted by the official culture for aesthetic and educational uses. While Botkin also believed that folklore arose from the cultural process of groups, he embraced an idea of "folk-say" which extended folklore in print and other mass media to revitalize popular culture (Botkin 1931; J. Hirsch 1996). It included "literature about the folk as well as the literature of the folk" (Botkin 1962, 52). As his friend Bruce Jackson reflected, Botkin "refused to distinguish between what people wrote, what happened in a movie, and what was said on a streetcorner. For him, the stuff and process of folklore were truly protean. Not in the academic's limited sense of an item's being able to move from place to place and redaction to redaction, but in a profounder sense: from words in air to words on a page and back out again, from one kind of meaning here to a vastly different kind of use there, from one kind of use here to a radically different kind of use there" (Jackson 1986, 29). Living traditions, then, were creative adaptations to the present applied for future use. Botkin presented the axiom that "for every form of folk fantasy that dies, a new one is being created, as culture in decay is balanced by folklore in the making" (Botkin 1962, 50). He explained that revivals (unorganized and organized in local and national folk festivals) and local renascences (working from above downward) were all part of "folklore in the making." Botkin therefore made less of a distinction than Dorson between folk and popular culture and showed less concern for the historical development or international spread of folk themes.

Botkin argued that the goal of folklore study was its "utilization" to aesthetically and emotionally stimulate the human spirit or to remedy social problems. This was in contrast to Dorson's intellectual goal of building scholarship. Dorson was to Botkin the "purist" oblivious to society's social progress. In Botkin's words:

> Utilization adds one more string to the folklorist's bow. And since the word *folklore* already means both the material studied and the study itself, it is time we had a term like *applied folklore* to designate the use of folklore to some end beyond itself. To some end beyond itself, because any one who does anything with folklore, from the original folk singer or story-teller to the scholar, is *using it*. But as long as the folklorist stays *inside* folklore and regards it "from the point of view of folklore itself," he remains a "pure" folklorist. It is only when he gets *outside* of folklore into social or literary history, education, recreation, or the arts, that he becomes an "applied folklorist." (Botkin 1962, 50)

Following his use of folklore to combat fascism, Botkin turned the attention of applied folklore during the 1950s with the polarization of the world into

American and Soviet blocs. Botkin's alarm about the tension of the Cold War came through in his call for applied folklore to further intercultural understanding (Botkin 1953, 1962). He disconcertedly wrote: "At this moment in history, when the creation of understanding in the world community is essential to survival, students and users of folklore and the folk arts must become 'members of the whole world'.... It seems clear that as 'members of the whole world' folklorists have a stake in culture and in the world community, and it is up to them to make themselves heard in the councils of cultural strategy, or else—. But there must not be an 'or else'" (Botkin 1962, 55).

Dorson's answer to Botkin and other "activists" on applied folklore for a long time was firm: "I contend that it is no business of the folklorist to engage in social reform, that he is unequipped to reshape institutions, and that he will become the poorer scholar and folklorist if he turns activist" (Dorson 1971b, 40). I do not believe that Dorson meant to sound heartless; his tone spun off from his signal protection of the integrity of the academic enterprise. Writing on "Applied Folklore," he posed the question, "How can the scholar, and especially the folklorist, remain aloof and uninvolved in the face of the world's tragedies and crises, and inequities near-at-hand that he directly perceives?" He answered:

> Well, in my view he is very much involved, simply as a folklorist. Look what an impact upon the landscape of learning the folklorist has already achieved—not nearly as considerable as he would wish, but still a sizable dent. This is where I see the folklorist playing his activist role: within the university arena, where he must bring all his energy, persuasive powers, and political acumen to bear if he is to defend, explain, and advance his subject. Folklore studies in the nineteenth and twentieth centuries have done more than any other field of learning to bring attention to the culture of the overlooked sectors of the population. No subject is more humanistic, more people-oriented than folklore. Today the folk narrator and bard have won recognition in books, sometimes as their author, in recordings, and even on the documentary screen. This is the achievement of the folklorist, in which he can take pride. By teaching, studying, collecting, and writing about folklore, the scholarly folklorist is making a noble contribution to man's knowledge of man. And these activities will absorb all his skills and strength. If he wants to divert them into a reformist role for which he is not equipped, he will succeed neither as a scholar nor as a philanthropist. (Dorson 1971b, 40–41)

For Dorson, "fighting the battle of fakelore" was his involvement as an educator in the world's problems rather than his application as a folklorist (Dorson 1971b, 42). The organization of folk festivals and the study of the folk, he argued, are worlds apart, and the former properly belongs to the shady entrepreneur, the latter to the enlightened scholar (Dorson 1971b, 41).

Dorson's last published survey was kinder to applied folklore, if it was conceived as "public folklore" (Dorson 1982b). He recognized the spread of "public folklore" as a respectable term and a job description for academically trained folklorists in a bicentennial afterglow he characterized as a "folklore boom" (Dorson

1978b). "Public folklore" at least reinforced separation from the private realm of authentic cultural production and equally private orbit of academic study. He noted the establishment of the American Folklife Center, Smithsonian Institution's Festival of American Folklife, and state folklorist programs as prominent examples of the quickly growing public folklore movement involving professional folk-lorists. He helped perpetuate the fable that Henry Glassie, then a renowned university professor, had been the first state folklorist. Accordingly, he thought "public folklore" could be an adequately neutral term that allowed for a conception of a scholarly role in the public sector. He had, in fact, accepted a National Endowment for the Humanities grant for a public folklore project called the "Indiana Communities Project," involving technical assistance by folklorists for community heritage programming. Dorson approved of the way that communities initiated the projects, however, rather than folklorists dictating the application of their study. He reiterated his concern for "fidelity to tradition," including ensuring "the authenticity of the performances and craft demonstrations" at festivals and fairs.

Dorson reflected that public folklore "can lead into a new form of fakelore, or it can substantially enlarge the audience for the genuine values of folklore" (Dorson 1982b, 103). The elder Dorson uttered his warning as a vibrant generation of academically trained folklorists had gained employment in the public folklore movement, and sought to serve the causes, among others, of cultural conservation, social reform, and community enhancement. If they mostly followed Dorson in rejecting Botkin's treasuries as the route to go for public folklore, it is also true that Botkin's views on applied folklore reemerged positively in many public forums (Widner 1986; J. Hirsch 1988; Jones 1994).

Dorson's battle with Botkin and Stevens was one of many through his career where he entered the public realm to take on the commercial popularizers and collaborating scholars. He became engaged in a debate in the pages of *Atlantic Monthly* with Maine writer John Gould defending his professorial representation of Down Easters' folklore. He hurled criticism at Eliot Wigginton's journalistic Foxfire program of involving schoolchildren in oral history and folklore collecting in their communities (Dorson 1973d, 1974c; Wigginton 1974; see also Clements 1996). He envisioned problems in maintaining scholarly standards and recording the saltiness of genuine folklore in an elementary education project with journalistic rather than folkloristic goals. He took Foxfire to task for spreading "the old romantic stereotype of folklore as associated with primeval mountain people tucked in the hollers and secluded from the modern world" (Dorson 1973d, 157). Foxfire exalted the folksy, rather than the folk, Dorson implied. He also criticized the Ford Foundation for not consulting folklorists before deciding on the merits of the projects for funding. If it had, it would have acknowledged a need for a "science of folklore," "where the guilds are powerful and the public defers to their expertise" (Dorson 1974c, 158). Dorson reiterated that the folklorist needed to be "concerned with truth and knowledge as opposed to falsification and error, with the distinction between folklore and fakelore" (Dorson 1974c, 159).

Wigginton defended Foxfire's collections as "absolutely accurate—the result of careful fieldwork and the verbatim testimony (via tape recordings) of hundreds of informants in the field" (Wigginton 1974, 37). He insisted that depictions of Appalachia such as that of Aunt Arie, who did not have television or running water, in Foxfire were part of the social reality, rather than romanticism, of the region. Then he shot back that Foxfire projects did not have to conform to folkloristic standards to accomplish its educational goals of involving schoolchildren in their own culture. He pounded Dorson for not involving his Ph.D.'s in the social relevance of high schools and public projects. He wound up his defense with the offensive stance that

> if, in the end, the project still does not measure up to the academic criteria laid down by the gods of folklore, that's just too damn bad. My primary concern is, has always been, and will remain *not* with whether or not some Beta Club students will go on to college knowing exactly how the professional discipline of folklore works, but whether or not my high school kids will make it through high school *at all*, and what stance they will eventually take toward the dying, exploited communities they live in. And I would challenge some of those Ph.D. folklorists to get out here in the mud and get their diplomas dirty and pitch in where they can really do some good instead of sniping at little folks from the safety of their certificate-lined walls. (Wigginton 1974, 39)

Dorson retorted that he had every right as an academic folklorist to "snipe" since Foxfire purported in its grant to the Ford Foundation to collect and publish "folklore." Dorson insinuated that Foxfire had shamefully profited from false pretensions of conducting serious folklore research. He pointedly wrote: "Mr. Wigginton may not have intended to get into folklore, but he is in it up to his ears and his *Foxfire* books are influencing many Americans. It is he who is playing god as the oracle of the folk" (Dorson 1974c, 39). Dorson accepted Wigginton's invitation to come to Rabun Gap, Georgia, to observe the Foxfire project and Wigginton came to Bloomington to engage in what Dorson termed another "Great Debate" (Dorson and Carpenter 1978, 7; Wigginton 1978). Dorson softened a bit after crediting the values that Foxfire sought to "implant and develop were indeed ... the humane and traditional values that our study of folklore would reveal" (Dorson and Carpenter 1978, 7). He suggested several ways that folklorists could indeed cooperate with educators to produce honest and useful Foxfire-type projects. Wigginton followed by inviting Dorson to write on the standards of folklore scholarship in one of the popular Foxfire books (see Dorson 1977e). Dorson nonetheless complained afterward to students that the noninterpretative thrust and romantic impulse of the Foxfire books had not changed. "Popularization finds its gullible publics," he sighed.

Ideological uses of folklore occupied Dorson even more than popularization during the politically charged 1970s. He took on the New Left in 1970 at the

American Historical Association, and reviewed the proceedings in the *Journal of the Folklore Institute* (Williams 1975; Dorson 1975b). Resenting the American academic neglect of class struggle and cultural hegemony, the young rebels criticized the consensus model of a national cultural democracy as perpetuating Cold War delusions and social prejudices, and they assaulted Dorson's preoccupation with professionalism as creating an hierarchical, elitist superstructure. Dorson's self-image as a liberal fighter against the university establishment and popular commercialism collided with the New Left assertion that Dorson's cant of professionalism promoted "conformism at home and imperialism abroad" (Williams 1975, 228).

Dorson responded to his New Left critics with "shock" at being categorized with "establishment figures." He saw in folklore studies progressive forces for participation of women and minorities within society and appreciation for the cultural integrity of communities and their "common man, the people, the folk." Restaging arguments for American studies during the 1930s, Dorson iterated that "folklorists have had to fight, and still fight, for every inch of recognition…. My own sense of the battleground is that the cause of folklore studies must be fought primarily within the universities. The rigid departmental structure of the American university is the bastion that must be scaled" (Dorson 1975b, 237, 239).

Dorson stood firm in defending the nonpartisan search for truth by proclaiming that "folklorists, on the whole, did not commence field investigations with a-priori assumptions of the folk, whether liberal, conservative, radical, populist, or whatever" (Dorson 1976c, 23). In fact, he emerged from the debate with the observation that much common ground existed between him and the New Left historians in the folkloristic attention to the cultural and historical dimensions of ordinary folk (Dorson 1976c, 23–24). But some of Dorson's activities in the name of professionalism irked proponents of the New Left. He used his presidential address to the American Folklore Society in 1968 to answer Soviet communist criticisms of his "pragmatic historicism" or "bourgeois" nationalist views on folklore as "reactionary" (Zemljanova 1964; Dorson 1971a, 62–64; see also Klymasz 1976).

Dorson engaged in Cold War rhetoric to encourage Congress to counteract Soviet uses of folklore by continuing funding of educational projects in folklore as part of the National Defense Education Act (Dorson 1962; see also Fife 1961). He appealed to Congress: "Trained folklorists can expose the Communist use of folklore behind the Iron Curtain and within the labor unions in the democracies" (Dorson 1962, 163). Embittered by the trivialization of funded folklore projects in the *Wall Street Journal*, Dorson rose to say, "The kind of stereotyped and uninformed thinking that links folklore with church music can cripple the efforts of the free world to combat the communist states, who know well how to reach the hidden millions with the shrewd manipulation of folklore, legend, and myth" (Dorson 1962, 164).[14] His words drew the notice in 1969 of Indiana University student radicals who singled him out in an editorial as an academic "prostitute" for

seeking funds from the federal government fighting a barbarous war in Vietnam
(Dorson 1976c, 340). Yet Dorson testified against the formation of a federally funded American Folklife Center within the Library of Congress because he feared it
would "propagate" official versions of folk culture under a governmental impri-
matur (Dorson 1971b, 41; see also Coe 1977; Cantwell 1991).

While the source of many of Dorson's new detractors came from the Left during the 1970s, especially as youthful rage built up at home during the Vietnam War,
Dorson saved one of his fiercest charges during the 1970s for the right-wing politics of Duncan Emrich. Emrich had a career of national service, frequently connected to the nation's capital. After receiving his Ph.D. from Harvard in 1937,
where he studied under George Lyman Kittredge, he went into the military and
took several diplomatic posts. He worked in Army Intelligence, and served as a
member of General Dwight D. Eisenhower's staff (McNeil 1996b). He went to the
United States Information Agency, and from 1953 to 1955 he became a celebrity
with weekly radio broadcasts about folklore for NBC. Like Ben Botkin, Emrich
had been chief of the Archives of American Folk Song at the Library of Congress
(1945–1955) and had published several popularized anthologies of cultural texts
with whimsical titles such as *The Nonsense Book* (1970), *The Hodgepodge Book*
(1972), and *The Whim-Wham Book* (1975). Although many of Emrich's volumes
were general works on American tradition, Emrich's specialty was on the romance
of the American cowboy and the American West in folk song and poetry. When he
was a professor at American University, he produced a celebratory anthology,
Folklore on the American Land (1972), aimed at the general public with the goal of
increasing "awareness of our greatness and goodness as a people." Against the
background of social protest during the Vietnam War, Emrich closed his preface
by declaring, "I love my country and its traditions, and I happily and without apology wear my heart upon my sleeve for them" (Emrich 1972, xi).

Emrich supported Dorson's opposition to the American Folklife Preservation
Act which proposed creating a federal office for folklife programming. But
Emrich's tone dismayed Dorson. Emrich saw a communist conspiracy infiltrating
government. He wrote Dorson on May 22, 1970:

> I am most fearful of the possibility that the Lomax/Seeger/Joan Baez et al. ilk will
> move in on a superb institution like the Smithsonian. Just as they are at the moment
> hoodwinking the Hill. I think that we are in very perilous times, and that these charac-
> ters are chief contributors, working slowly from a point at least twenty years ago. You
> will recall that Pete Seeger took the 5th amendment at least twice; that Alan Lomax
> stayed out of the country for three years during the existence of the McCarran Act; that
> *Sing Out* follows the communist party line, and leavens it with the real folksongs in
> order to "excuse" themselves. I am close to it here, and it literally frightens me.

The same letter applauded Dorson's use of fakelore and added that singers like
Seeger and Baez were "phony folk," "riff-raff running up and down the land and

appearing at 'folk festivals' as 'folksingers' or on college campuses as 'folksingers'.… And we have vicious phonies like PS [Pete Seeger], JB [Joan Baez], and others who use the 'folksinger' bit to promulgate leftist (communist) propaganda quite true. As you know. And we might circulate whatever you may wish to write simply to test those who have or do not have the guts to stand up for our great traditions."[15] Despite their common concern, Dorson distanced himself from Emrich by publicly pinning the fakelore stigma on him.

Writing in *Western Folklore*, Dorson blasted Emrich's appeal to the "romantic, chauvinistic, anti-intellectual consumers of fake folklore." Dorson excoriated Emrich for omitting any traditions that did not glorify America. He sarcastically wrote: "The examples are wonderfully jumbled together, across the centuries and across the country, as if American folklore were one big homogenized stew" (Dorson 1973e, 141–43). Sounding pluralist calls for social reality, Dorson wanted to know where "ethnic folklore, obscene folklore, black folklore" were in Emrich's "big package." Emrich had, in fact, deliberately downplayed the impact of immigrant traditions, insisting that American folklore "should be a leveler, a freer, a common denominator, and not a divider or separator" (Emrich 1972, x). Commenting on the separation of black folklore in other collections, Emrich blithely offered: "I was brought up in New England, to me all these things were American" (Emrich 1972, x).

Dorson had no patience for Emrich's "patriotic fervor," his "sentimentalities about the American heritage" and "Eisenhower syndrome." He assailed Emrich's "sleazy formula" and "attempt to capture the all-American market (folklore properly collected and analyzed is regional and local)" (Dorson 1973e, 151). To Dorson, Emrich's volumes were worse "gimcrackery" than Botkin's treasuries because they seemed even more of a hodgepodge with "no underlying philosophy or theory, not even any folk." Dorson summed up: "This is not the fakelore of tampered texts but of ideological selectivity. In place of the class protest fanned by fakelore on the left, we have here a sugary unity promoted by fakelore on the right" (Dorson 1973e, 142).

Dorson used his scathing review of Emrich to show at least one New Left critic his defense of the truth against manipulation from both the right and left (Dorson 1975b). In declaring that folklore should not be tainted by commercial culture and ideology, he stuck to his guns throughout his life, and he understood the implication that "scholars often respond to the psychic pressures of their time as supinely as do the popularizers, and will manipulate folklore, and history, to support their biases" (Dorson 1976c, 27). He somehow believed that his own work was above ideology or the new nationalism into which he came of age.

Jay Mechling recognized Dorson's ideology as a member of the New Class which arose dramatically after World War II in America (Mechling 1989d, 24–25; Berger 1979). By this analysis, as the American economy moved from industrial production to consumerism, a New Class based on control of information wedged into the power held by the old middle class based in business and industry. Many children of ethnic and working class parents were attracted to informational professions in academe, government, law, and media because, besides being seen as open fields demanded in a growing, diversifying society, they carried an association with achievement of intellectual merit rather than connections of family and money. Even so-called bourgeois children learned this lesson, since money could make them economically comfortable but not necessarily socially acceptable in a power establishment (Hertzberg 1989, 330–31). To this class, the available, righteous path to having credentialed status in America lay in education and communication, for they provide forums for an objective demonstration of ability and competition of ideas rather than the patronage of privilege. Dorson's rhetorical coupling of "integrity" with "scholarship," and "exploitation" with "commercial [culture]" and "chauvinistic [ideologies]" bear out such New Class values.

New Class values also came out in Dorson's veneration, especially in his American Civilization class, of Vernon Parrington's *Main Currents in American Thought* (1927–30), for the way it characterized American intellectual history as a struggle of rational intellectual values of progress and democracy against commercial interests of acquisition and domination. In Parrington's narrative, the struggle culminated in the contemporary critique of industrialism and the old middle class (Parrington 1930; see also Dorson 1946a, 95; 1971a, 55).[16] Indeed, the New Class in its celebration of the intelligentsia often countered the commercial values of the old class and its claim to power with liberal, centrist attitudes toward building an inclusive, humanitarian society (Hertzberg 1989, 264–75; Hollinger 1975). If the rhetorical move of having an "ignorant" public or "commercial" sector granting authority to universities as a merit-based organization of expertise suggested a hierarchy of power, then balance might be claimed by insisting on the egalitarianism and rationality *within* information organizations as a model for society.

The New Class revised the narrow republican image of America to allow for varied experience in a broadening of cultural possibilities (Hollinger 1975). Cultural pluralism and social democracy were appealing, if incomplete concepts, then, for they understood the need of new and marginalized groups to have legitimacy in a national consensus. The trade off for many of the ethnic intelligentsia was that they accept assimilation in the drive toward professionalism (Hollinger 1975). A secular cosmopolitanism arose in which intellectuals often wrote as "general Americans" or embraced social scientific pursuits such as psychoanalysis and cultural history built on ethnic concerns (Hertzberg 1989, 264–75). Or, as in the case of Alfred Kinsey, "his own liberalism was grounded in the conviction that nothing human should be alien to the realm of science" (Morantz 1977, 564). Mechling observed in Dorson's case a similar position for rational objectivity as a "defense of the new center of the culture—namely, the New Class—and his view of pluralism-in-microcosm … [serving] the class's ideology" (Mechling 1989d, 25). In the New Class exchange of information for status, claims to scientific and technical expertise, the objectivity of standards and achievement, and the rhetoric of professionalism became paramount in imagining a nonideological, rational society (Mechling 1989d, 25). Traditions still mattered, but were viewed as belonging to the old ethnic and occupational communities from which the New Class came.

The old communities received sympathy from New Class scholars as representing the spirit of cultural democracy. That spirit reinforced the right of New Class to rise into prominence over the privilege from above of old money and family title. Sympathetic to the folk because it had been overlooked and underestimated, New Class rhetoric expressed admiration for the folk's integrity, honesty, and social reality. The New Class showed its ability to rise socially and achieve power by education and control of information. The combination of sympathy for social reality and drive for middle-class mobility became translated into a liberal "cosmopolitanism." David Hollinger explains the cosmopolitanism of the New Class as one in which "particular cultures and subcultures are viewed as repositories for insights and experiences that can be drawn upon in the interest of a more comprehensive outlook on the world" (Hollinger 1975, 135).

THE NATIONALISM DEBATE

One of the "comprehensive outlooks" noticeable in the post-World War II years is the emergence of a revised nationalism. Propagandists drew American nationalism during World War II as a patriotic devotion to moral democracy over immoral fascism. The factions of America indeed needed to be united to fight as a nation. The popular press hailed the uniqueness of the American character reflected in folk types of bold, adventurous heroes on the frontier and in current battles. These heroes were thought to be "democratic" because they symbolized the shared trait of American commonness—whether urban, rural, ethnic, or religious. Other phrases of the period expressed this commonness: "American dream," "American creed," and "American way of life."

If America, then, was not based on one national ancestry or main occupation, it could stand for certain ideas and values, the most important of which seemed to be democracy. Philip Gleason added that "democracy was thus more than a political system or an institutional arrangement: it was a way of life" (Gleason 1984, 353). If America was to build a moral difference with the scourge of Europe, both from the right and the left, then another component had to be the uniqueness of an emergent, democratic American culture, defined by a loose conception of a consensual whole drawing on social commonness and variety. In the new nationalism, devotion to the democratic nation-state is dedication to its ideas, for unlike totalitarianism or communism, democracy allows for participation of different views and ways of life. The nation-state affords its citizens freedom to live as they pleased (ironically, this praxis of freedom expressed as "this is a free country" often constitutes the

"American way of life"), but when the nation-state calls on its citizens to help beat back a threat to democracy, its citizens are obliged to follow and unequivocally support its effort. So the wartime message went.

American studies during the 1950s contributed to conceptions of the American character in the "myths, symbols, and images" that Americans owed to their historical and cultural experience. Under the guise of replacing ideology with an intellectual search for patterns in the American historical and cultural experience, Dorson's colleague at Harvard, Henry Nash Smith, especially touted the prevalence of the "Myth of the Garden," of America as an abundant new land that gave rise to new traditions and possibilities (Smith 1950). Smith thus explained that America could indeed be socially diverse and owe to European settlement, but have intellectual coherence. Central to the revised intellectual concept of nationalism was "culture" or "civilization." Both terms suggested something large and complex, expressive and ideational. Boasian anthropology informed the popularity of culture, although in American studies "culture" became broadened to expressions of shared ideas that went beyond small, bounded communities tied to place and ethnic tradition. If America had a separate history from its colonial settlement to the founding of the republic and the emergence as a powerful nation, then it followed that it should have a distinctive cultural history in the spirit of Boas's particularism (Sklar 1971).

Dorson's use of "civilization" to describe America suggested that the cultural history of America is one of progress and expansion. Its cultural features had intellectual and artistic value and could be compared internationally, especially to ancient societies that left cultural imprints as they expanded. "Civilization" had a wartime reference in its assumption that if Europe destroys itself as a formerly vital civilization, then America would be the last bastion of a Western or humanistic civilization (Gleason 1984, 352). In fact, "civilization" later gave way to "culture" as the preferred term for describing a holistic American studies project (Mechling, Merideth, and Wilson 1973; Spiller 1973; Wise 1979). The culture concept had built into it vagueness because it covered both ideas and the expression of those ideas. And those expressions in a work such as Henry Nash Smith's could vary from canonical literature to folk legends. Following the suggestion of Constance Rourke in 1942, some American studies scholars such as Walter Blair and Franklin Meine saw a nationalist mission to find in folklore the "roots" of American culture. Dorson began with her premise in *Jonathan Draws the Long Bow*, but after the conversion experience of fieldwork, and informed by New Class values, he revised and publicized the use of folklore in the culture concept of American nationalism.

The pivotal moment Dorson chose to announce his nationalistic "Theory for American Folklore" was significant for an organizational reason. It strengthened in his mind the consensus of folklore, history, and literature in American studies and anthropology. It was the first time that the American Folklore Society met with the American Studies Association in addition to the American Anthropological

Association. He viewed an organizational mix, and older generation, interested variously in the literary and historical development of an American civilization, the pluralist basis of culture in geographically bound groups, the origin and diffusion of folktale motifs and types internationally, and the creative use of folklore. His opening paragraph used humor to pose a serious challenge of a new American generation for a nationalist direction formed out of the old mix. He wrote: "I can point to the success of such union already pragmatically demonstrated in the nuptials between the secretary-treasurer of the American Folklore Society, MacEdward Leach, and his charming spouse, a holder of the doctor's degree in American Civilization from the University of Pennsylvania. The argument of this paper will be that the child of such union is the properly reared American folklorist of the next generation" (Dorson 1971a, 15). Hoping to stage another great galvanizing debate, he arranged for elder leaders of the organizations to comment on his presentation.

He structured his presentation of his theory according to the organization of the midcentury American studies model. Out of troubled old approaches, new and improved ones emerge that would be appropriate to the needs of the unique American scene. Dorson identified seven existing views of folklore, each flawed for the study of folk traditions in the United States: comparativism (internationalist historic-geographic), cultural anthropology, folk song and folk music specialization, special pleading (myth-ritual, sexual symbolism, class struggle), regionalism, literary history, popularization. He softened his blow by claiming that each approach admirably served its own ends, but was faulty for not being comprehensive in its outlook on the special American case. His new type, he promised in an appeal to pluralist consensus, would show the "common ground" of the "science of folklore" and the "history of American civilization," and he hoped for a "cooperative inquiry into the behavior of folklore within the American environment" (Dorson 1971a, 47).

Dorson presented his case pragmatically rather than philosophically. His intent was to locate the distinctive purpose, and therefore scholarly respectability, of American folklore studies. He imagined a young student interested in folklore seeking "professional order." Once "acculturated," he opined, the student would become accustomed to thinking of analyzing literary or cultural types but would not be part of an intellectual type that could vie for disciplinary power. Echoing New Class rhetoric, Dorson yearned for "one standard vocabulary, the common frame of reference, and the accepted critical or empirical approach within which controversy arises" instead of "a kaleidoscope of activities" and "multiplicity of accents" that may marginalize the new entrants, who he described as "transients or refugees" from "a host." So he pragmatically outlined an approach that would turn the subject of folklore into an object, combine and transform previously held approaches into a comprehensive outlook.

With reference to folklore's role in the scholarly landscape, much of Dorson's paper concerned "problems and inquiries the American folklorist will be equipped to undertake" (Dorson 1971a, 29). Dorson's bias toward analyzing the connection of American traditions to the nation's distinctive historical periods and movements was bound to disturb many of his internationalist colleagues. The conclusion followed from the method that folklore must be correlated with, and studied as an outgrowth of, major and dramatic historical events *unique* to the American nation. Within the sequence of great debates in which Dorson engaged, his polemic brought to the fore the revised nationalist role of folklore and importance of historical authenticity within the American discourse on culture into the Cold War years.

Essential to the idea of a new nationalism is the view that America's uniqueness, and unity, comes from social variety brought together by democratic consensus. In countries such as England, Germany, and Japan, Dorson found "tidy" cultural histories of relative social homogeneity. Although Dorson recognized the echoes in his argument of European romantic nationalism, and similar historical arguments for national cultural uniqueness, he viewed a social landscape in America more complex than for England, Germany, and Japan where folklore became interpreted as ancient poetic stirrings of a national soul (W. Wilson 1982c, 1989; see also MacGregor-Villarreal 1989). Dorson insisted that national folklore emerged in the United States in a distinctive sequence to bring together diverse groups under the prevalent "type" in a certain historical period: religious for the colonial period, political or democratic in the era of the new republic, economic from the close of the Civil War to the 1960s, and finally the humane in the "modern" period. In countries such as Australia and Canada whose diverse social histories he called "analogous" to the United States, Dorson beheld "a far simpler situation" of ethnic transplantation or fusion between European and Indian inheritance. Dorson contended that the United States had folk types of the Yankee and immigrant, American black and Indian, whose elusive common ground needed explanation. Further separating America as a special case to Dorson was that it "looks back to no ancient racial stock, no medieval heritage, no lineage of traditions shrouded in a dim and remote past" (Dorson 1971a, 28).

What America did have, he claimed, were "great dramatic movements" that naturally influence the formation of folklore, even that which is socially diverse. The movements he saw as especially distinctive were exploration and colonization, revolution and the establishment of a democratic republic, the westward surge, the tides of immigration, the slavery debate that erupted in civil war, and the triumph of technology and industrialization. They further conjured special American themes such as regionalism, patriotism and democracy, and mass culture. With such a survey, it became obvious to Dorson that the explanatory power of historical context had been neglected in the folkloristic enterprise, and his theoretical contribution was to suggest that the distinctive historical framework of traditions and institutions had shaped an American character. Dorson thus argued that although America had changed dramatically, especially in the twentieth century, it

Richard Dorson (standing) introducing Stith Thompson (seated, far right) to his class in the theory and techniques of folklore at the Folklore Institute, Indiana University, fall 1962. (IU Photographic Services, Indiana University)

had some traditions, or ideas, that persisted through its history. Indeed, by this argument America could not be explained without reference to its folklore which revealed a coherent American history influencing authentic cultural experience. And without American folklore appearing emergent and indigenous, in contradistinction to a transplanted folklore in America, the claim for a separate culture or civilization could not be made (McDowell 1948b).

This nationalist argument was hardly a question before the 1930s, for folklore was often attached to peasant, ancient, or aboriginal societies, and outside of American Indians and African Americans, the United States as a field of study was ironically underrepresented in the anthropological pages of the *Journal of American Folklore*. Whether analyzed by Thompson's international comparativism or Boas's cultural particularism, folklore appeared variable over space, but stable over time, and therefore not prone to modern historical national movements. Alexander Haggerty Krappe, author of *The Science of Folklore* (1930), signaled a prevalent purist attitude when he wrote: "there exists no such thing as American folklore, but only European (or African, or Far Eastern) folklore on the American continent, for the excellent reason that there is no American 'folk'" (Krappe 1930, 291). Thirty years later, a British reviewer of Dorson's *American Folklore* (1959) could observe, "The United States is still surprisingly adolescent in some respects but no nation surely has been more persistent in examining its folklore" (Peate 1960, 61). Several Americanists made a claim for a distinctive American folklore within the historical context of a rising American civilization after the 1930s. Constance Rourke was especially influential in her observation of a dominant "folk strain" in the formation of an American character played out in popular culture and Martha Warren Beckwith in her legitimation of America as a field for research of living traditions (Rourke [1931] 1959; Beckwith 1931b). Reacting to Krappe's comment, Ben Botkin used both Rourke's and Beckwith's ideas to buttress his argument for some "indigenous" American folklore that comes from its special history, landscape, and society (Botkin 1940; 1944, xxiv; 1949a). In reply to the view of an absent American folk, Botkin before Dorson had answered that there is "not one folk but many folk groups—as many as there are regional cultures or racial or occupational groups within a region" (Botkin 1929, 12; 1944, 44).

Dorson in his 1941 essay on American comic demigods had sought to make finer distinctions between authentic traditions belonging to these groups and popular reinterpretations used by Botkin and Rourke for expressing folklore, although he understood the need to broaden the definition of folklore beyond ancient myths and fairy tales. Dorson's essay inspired Wilson Clough in 1943 to ask, "Has American Folklore a Special Quality?" He agreed that to make the case alongside other nations, American folklore would need to show new examples that bear the stamp of "true" folklore—indigenous, of obscure origin, and of unknown authors. Authenticity, he agreed with Dorson, translated to intensity of subcultural experience. It is distinctive because of the historic "divorce from the European inheritance and its more static environment." Therefore, a distinctive, if adolescent, American history influences a native folklore that is "more democratic, the more human, the more valuable, for the absence of the naively supernatural" (Clough 1944, 119). In short, it contains as part of the national character, a more pronounced realism and pragmatism.

The closest precedent to Dorson's "theory" is University of Minnesota professor Philip Jordan's pronouncement in 1946 of a "New Folklore." He had in preparation a book on the National Road that made a case for an emergent folklore about a road, indeed a middle ground between south and north, that represented the growth of a national self-identity as Americans moved westward (Jordan 1948). Dorson credited Jordan with uncovering incipient forms of American backwoods humor that became traditional in the new nation (Dorson 1946a, 91; 1971a, 116; Jordan 1938). Jordan had done more than Dorson was willing to admit, however, to locate the authenticity of folklore within a historic process, and in fact Jordan had beaten Dorson to the punch with his criticism of popularized Bunyan tales. Four years before Dorson's famous "Folklore and Fake Lore" essay, Jordan had condemned narratives about Bunyan that had been "commercialized in vulgar fashion" and peddled to a "credulous public ... duped daily by market-place sharpsters" (Jordan 1946, 278–79). Jordan's main case was that if the definition of folklore was to be other than ancient survivals or literary fabrications, it needed tests of authenticity, and it needed trained, professional folklorists (Jordan 1946, 279–80). "Folklore, in its broader definition, includes larger areas of human experience when it surveys traditional modes of political, economic, and social activity," Jordan wrote in his 1946 manifesto (275). Jordan's special historic "areas quite unique to folklore" brought in America's westward movement, immigration, industrialism, and urbanization. Jordan presaged Dorson's stated interest in contemporary "folkstuff" of the white-collar world and the "unofficial culture" of the city. He lamented that "little attempt has been made to comprehend the folk mind" and Dorson equally ended his presentation with the hope that American folklore will "illuminate the American mind" (Jordan 1946, 277; Dorson 1971a, 48). Although Dorson did not cite Jordan in his presentation of a "Theory for American Folklore," he drew support from his Harvard associates. He pointed to Henry Nash Smith's interpretation of the cultural specialness of the American frontier and Daniel Boorstin's view that because American civilization differed so widely from that of Europe, it needed to be studied through new categories (Dorson 1971a, 33, 48).

Although Dorson's Americanist approach cut against the grain of most folkloristic work during the 1950s, the discussion from the floor did not turn into the grand theoretical debate or galvanizing experience that Dorson wished for. Several speakers picked up the old fakelore issue, since Dorson saved his harshest words for the popularizers among the existing views of folklore. Others also returned a charge that Dorson had once shot at Botkin—the chauvinism of a nationalistic perspective. Melville Herskovits, the Boasian anthropologist, probably took greatest exception to Dorson's nationalistic view, challenging Dorson's definition of an American culture. He commented: "so far as any specific folkloristic quality, no matter how defined, is concerned, there is no single American culture. There are the enclaves, the pockets, the localities, where peoples of different origin or occupation have developed particular ways, whether because of internal circumstance or historical derivation" (Herskovits 1959, 217). Herskovits balked at the use of "American character" and pointed out the danger of obscuring subcultural persistence and difference outside of an imagined American consensus: "The use of a concept as vague and overinclusive as this, it seems to me, should everywhere be avoided, even where it is used in passing, as is the case here. Certainly in view of the varying ethnic derivations and, in particular, the different historical backgrounds of the segments in the total population of this country, it loses any precision. It thus tends to block, rather than to further the ends of analysis" (Herskovits 1959, 217). He feared that Dorson's approach could lead to political chauvinism and scholarly balkanization.

William Hugh Jansen especially raised the warning flag of Nazi Germany as a harsh lesson for nationalistic folklorists in America (Jansen 1959a, 236). The honored elder Stith Thompson meanwhile joined Jansen in worrying about the methodological isolationism that could result from a lack of comparison with other countries and cultures. Daniel Hoffman admired Dorson's search for a national tradition, but sighed that "our quest for the unity of a defining principle is once again baffled by the protean multiplicity of American folklore" (Hoffman 1959, 227). He also had great difficulty with Dorson's facile linking of post- and preindustrial cultural processes. Hoffman complained that Dorson was not purist enough: "I cannot accept the assertion that 'mass culture breeds its own special varieties of folklore.' What is culturally viable as folklore in American life seems to me to pertain by definition to the pre-industrial and transitional phases of our history" (Hoffman 1959, 230). Louis Jones hit Dorson from the popularizer side by rejecting the recasting of folklore into a specialized study that would have a mission without reference to the interests of the public good.

Dorson's rejoinder accepted the concerns of his discussants. He sounded the tone of consensus, but stuck to the assertion of America as a special case: "I certainly never meant to give the impression of wanting our students to become single-minded, and narrow-minded, American folklorists. But it seems to me that the person who is concerned with folk tradition within the United States needs to be aware that there are special problems of the historical background of our country, and I was considering simply those problems which are approached by students of American literature who have had no formal training in folklore at all" (Dorson 1959b, 238). To the worry of chauvinism, he assured his listeners that students needed to be familiar with the folklore of at least one other country, and that awareness should prevent exalting one national tradition over all others. As for scholarly isolationism, he came out pragmatically: "And if a person is studying American folklore, there is no reason why he cannot be a comparative folklorist, or musicologist, or anything else. He is simply one type of folklorist, not necessarily to the exclusion of other types" (Dorson 1959b, 238).

In hindsight, it appears to me that Dorson emphasized a clarion call for an American professionalism based on the presence of an American historical field more than a signal of new direction. Dorson in his review of the "theory" a decade later questioned the impact of the presentation since "American folklore studies continued along their merry separate ways, and the seven sinful schools kept on sinning with increased vigor" (Dorson 1971a, 51). He found detractors to duel, of course, but his strategy for nudging an historical approach to American tradition into folklore studies turned to claiming young students in the "folknik" generation of the 1960s. He counted the work of Alan Dundes on the futuristic orientation in American worldview, Roger Abrahams on urban black folklore, Jerome Mintz on Hasidic culture, and Charles Keil on black blues music as fitting into his conception of interpreting traditions—old and new—against the background of special historical conditions of the United States. If this choice of the "Theory" was not self-conscious on the part of the authors (although two of them had been Dorson's students), then Dorson offered that "the 'Theory' will claim them as true American folklorists who perceive the intimate bonds between the culture of the folk and the history of the American experience" (Dorson 1971a, 77). As Dorson had hoped, the young folklorists of the 1960s had more of a disciplinary self-identity drawn from university study, and Dorson was their dean. He made it a point to venture beyond Indiana University and teach during the 1970s at folklore study centers at the University of Pennsylvania and University of California at Berkeley, and keep up a grueling lecture schedule.

Through the new university-trained folklorists of the 1960s and 1970s, Dorson spread his watchwords into American culture of fakelore, fieldwork, and folk history. In 1972, he issued a basic textbook with his introduction devoted to concepts of folklore and folklife studies. He again surveyed existing "theoretical points of view," beginning with the old Finnish historical-geographical method and ending with later approaches including his own, which he now called "the hemispheric theory." He had separated the Old World from the New, and expanded his idea for national tradition from the United States to other countries in South and North America. He seemed more equivocal about the presence of a unique American tradition when he wrote, "Clearly one cannot speak about an Old World national tradition with its relative stability, rootedness, and long ancestry, in the same fashion as the New World blends. (Australia, also a colonized continent with separate aboriginal and settlers' traditions, belongs with the Americas in this formulation)" (Dorson 1972b, 43–44). More so than before, Dorson recognized the subcultural forces of ethnicity and race, even if he took less stock of class conflict (relegating it to the misrepresentations of the "ideological" concept). Dorson summarized: "According to the hemispheric theory, the folklore of each New World country needs to be analyzed in terms of its ethnic-racial and historical ingredients. In one country the African element may be high, in another the Indian, in another the colonial German. The task for the New World folklorist is to examine closely the processes of syncretism, adaptation, acculturation, retention, accommodation, revitalization, recession, and disappearance that determine the ultimate product" (Dorson 1972b, 44).

Dorson ended his survey with the latest concept—"contextual"—that many new students of folklore were embracing. Calling them "young Turks," he included some of the same names he had listed in his review of the "Theory": Alan Dundes and Roger Abrahams. Later these figures would point out that a contextual "school," *per se*, did not exist, but various interpretations of "performance," "dynamics," and "artistic communication" did. In structuring some of the work of the new generation into an umbrella concept, Dorson showed the continued growth of folklore studies as a discipline and the liberated spirit of its students. By placing it after his theory, he also implied that they took their cue from his call for new directions appropriate to the American scene. Reflecting on Dorson's use of "young Turks," Dan Ben-Amos wrote, "Anyone who reads into this epithet the resentment a senior figure in the field might feel toward a young, rebelling horde is

In a posed 1962 photograph taken in the Folklore Archives at Indiana University, Richard Dorson shows his Israeli student Dan Ben-Amos the cover of *Folktales of Israel* (edited by Dov Noy), a new addition to his Folktales of the World series for the University of Chicago Press. The cover of *Folktales of Japan* (edited by Keigo Seki) is on the table. Ten years later, Dorson identified Ben-Amos (then teaching at the University of Pennsylvania), in *Folklore and Folklife: An Introduction,* as one of the "young Turks" espousing "contextual" approaches to "folklore traditions" and heralding "a new departure in the writing of folklore books of the future." (IU Photographic Services, Indiana University)

not sensitive to the personal affinity Dorson felt for the group. More likely, he anticipated with relish a spirited debate that could ensue from a contextualist manifesto" (Ben-Amos 1989, 52).

Dorson's last debate echoed his first. In a published challenge in 1978, he urged a final fight between "folklore in America vs. American folklore" (Dorson 1978c). The distinction between the two had been voiced during the 1940s by Ben Botkin in response to Alexander Krappe's assertion that there was no such thing as an indigenous American folklore (Botkin 1949a; see also Dorson 1983b, 328). And ironically, Dorson had been critical of Botkin for overplaying the nationalist card. The difference in Dorson's rhetoric in 1978 was that he linked the "folklore in America" approach to the contextualism of the young Turks, as well as comparative, psychological, and structural approaches. He viewed these approaches together as getting away from the historical, communitarian view of his revised nationalism. He regarded "*folklore in America* as part of a universal model," and as in other debates, he found it important "to distinguish between universal and national models" (Dorson 1983c, 323). He tried to shatter the universal model by scoffing at its "fantasy of predicting human behavior" wherever it may be found in spontaneous social situations. Dorson's position was not as extreme as his polemic implied, since he had in his scholarship claimed attention to context—historical and social—and had early on criticized Botkin for not considering the processes of storytelling performance (Dorson 1950a; see also Dorson 1972e). He wanted to direct the consideration of context, however, through history toward national themes and problems. What was mainly lacking in "folklore in America," he most strongly declared, was the special relation of cultural expressions of Americans to the national democratic experience. The ultimate issue for Dorson revolved around the use of the past to explain an American tradition.

Together with a young faculty member at the Folklore Institute, I offered Dorson explanations for the apparent neglect of American historical experience in the work of contemporary folklorists (Bronner and Stern 1980). Dorson implied that considerations of folklore in America defied comparison and therefore meaningful analysis, but we pointed out the appeal of ethnographic perspectives recording the frames of the variable present in a contemporary era of communication. Carrying the empiricism of fieldwork further than Dorson's text collecting, such perspectives allowed for observation of folklore as it is enacted. With such attention to individual behaviors, the influence of historical experience seemed distant, much as we were intellectually drawn to its holism. We challenged Dorson's contention that folklore in America and American folklore represented opposing methods, the second an indefensible one. Dorson had presented his methodology as the *only* historical approach, but we knew of or conceived others less ethnocentric and rigid. We thought that Dorson's approach led to a tautology, which was based on the assumption of a unique national history giving rise to a unique folklore whose existence testified to the validity of viewing American history in terms of dramatic, exceptional events. We saw explanatory possibilities in a behavioral and cultural history tied to social ethnography (Joyner 1975; Abrahams 1976; Bronner 1982, 1986b, M. Jones 1982).

Using Dorson's own criticism of Botkin, was it possible that the inadequacy of Dorson's sources compelled him "to use a topical or thematic arrangement, a far less satisfying method than a survey by folk groups, which would enable us to know just who possesses the lore" (Dorson 1948b, 77)? Dorson's placement of folklore in America in opposition to American folklore, we contended, set up false dichotomies in scholarship, particularly since there was no consensus regarding a folklore-in-America approach. It was a "type" of his own making. Finally, we argued that Dorson's explanation of folklorists not availing themselves of historical methodology—lack of familiarity with historiography—appeared wrong or at least presumptuous (see de Caro 1976). Indeed, the "performance-centered" editors of the notable volume *Theorizing Folklore* (1993) observed that history played a central role in the essays. One "axis of historical concern," they noted, was a diachronic analysis of cultural forms. Although as Elizabeth Fine noted, this historical rediscovery "promises to reveal additional insights about the relationship of performance to social life and other modes of communication," it appeared less about Dorson's goal of identifying national tradition than in locating precedents for behavior (Fine 1996). The second axis for the editors of *Theorizing Folklore* that would have bristled the objectivist Dorson was a critical, often political, scrutiny of folklore as context, and folklore studies as an issue of cultural construction and recontextualization (Briggs and Shuman 1993, 115–21). This move suggested to the editors a departure from what they considered Eurocentric nationalism and the arrival of a performance-centered model of the folk exploring "the diversity of intra-group difference" as well as "artistic communication in small groups" (Briggs and Shuman 1993, 121–24).

Dorson's assumption of an overriding national tradition created difficulties for folklorists because it smacked of ethnocentrism or the folk cultural basis in the local and subcultural. Simply knowing another country's history, as Dorson once suggested, was not enough to get around the problem, since it can merely compound nationalistic modeling, as it might have in Dorson's selected comparisons to Japan and England. Following several arguments in *Theorizing Folklore*, in fact, one can read in folklore a counter-national force, since it dramatized instances of individual control and could express human values that were subversive to a state civilization. Dorson drew much of his case for a national tradition, maybe too much of his case, from selected narrative examples. He thus appeared to overemphasize an overarching tradition extrapolated from supposedly complete, static forms in "untampered" stories and customs. His arguments for representativeness from isolated authentic examples seemed to us as much of a stretch as Botkin's. His acceptance of an encompassing national character blocked recognition of a growing concern among young students of tradition for uncovering specific behavior and cognition ascribed to individuals, *one* of whose identities might be "American." It was for these reasons that we felt historical methodology, namely the one advocated by Dorson, had not been incorporated into folklore studies.

We were not arguing that certain dramatic events and movements were not particular to the American experience, nor that historical periodicity was not a significant context. Rather, we were pointing out that many folklorists felt uneasy with the extent to which Dorson identified overgeneralized American themes as traditions which can be expressed culturally. A problem arose in Dorson's reference to themes as "traits," implying an ontological status comparable to the cultural reality of folklore. To many folklorists they were arbitrary categories with little relation to the cultural context of situated folklore performance. One example is his declaration that the theme of boosterism—attributes of "salesmanship" and "promotionalism"—was "an essential trait of the American character" because one can find antecedents "in the frontier boast of the backwoodsman and glib talk of the Yankee peddler" (Dorson 1978a, 181–82). But is it really unique, and can it be directly linked in a causal chain to these historic examples? After all, the practice of promoting one's wares, it could be argued, is fundamental broadly to competitive market economies and not exclusive to the United States. Moreover, Dorson did not show the agency that might have led to certain kinds of expressions of boost-erism in the United States. What about the guild systems of nineteenth-century England and Scandinavia that attempted to lure clientele by parading elaborate insignias? What is to be made of European towns raising their prestige at the same time by organizing local festivals to draw in trade, of London street criers who huckstered their products and were portrayed in engravings as early as the eigh-teenth century? Although Americans arguably may have elevated advertising to fine art, such boosterism at best was a matter of degree, not of uniqueness. And we questioned the causal relation without some presumptive agency that Dorson implied between a categorical "theme" and cultural behavior.

Although Dorson recognized dangers in overstressing the Americanness of American conditions, he nevertheless appeared guilty of pushing the "uniqueness argument" to an extreme in his later years (Dorson 1982b, 1983b). In various essays after 1975, he pushed for recognition of the exceptionalism of American folklore, of American folklore studies, of American history, and periods within American history, and of a historical theory for American folklore. In the *Handbook of American Folklore* (1983), he positioned his essay on "A Historical Theory for American Folklore" first, followed by a supportive chapter by Lawrence Levine on "How to Interpret American Folklore Historically." He allowed two others to trail, one by Roger Abrahams lumping together ethnographic and sociological approaches, and the other by Archie Green on the positive uses of American liber-al thought (of popular sovereignty and democratic equity, of enlightenment rights and communal needs). In discussing the debate between D. K. Wilgus and Stanley Edgar Hyman over the latter's claim that Child ballads in America deteriorated from supernatural to realistic elements, Dorson consented to Wilgus's criticism that this process of "modernization" occurred in England as well (Dorson 1978c, 105–6). Still, Dorson felt obliged to insist that modernization has been keenly developed by American enterprise. The recognition of intensification was hardly sufficient to brand the resulting folklore as "American" while its European coun-terpart was stamped "un-American."

Another example of forced assignment of the American theme by Dorson occurred in his claim for the historical interpretation of his students' work. In his editorial comments on Janet Langlois's "Belle Gunness, the Lady Bluebeard: Community Legend as Metaphor" (1978), Dorson saw as her point the manifesta-tion of boosterism through the widespread popularity of a local legend. A close reading of her essay, however, reveals no references to any such booster spirit. In addition, Langlois failed to follow Dorson's own criterion for designating research "American folklore" which was that "the writer present the relation of folklore to American cultural, social, political, and economic history in chronological frame."

Indeed, the main point of her article was that historical time is of little consequence in explaining these narratives, for underlying them are symbolic references to a static system of social relationships. In her analysis of the "story of the cows" in which Belle Gunness insisted that her neighbor release Belle's property, Langlois stated, "Whose cows initiated the action, which was antecedent and which was consequent act is not as important as the relationship between the neighbors." In sum, we worried that rather than explain events, Dorson was using history to show national identity beyond the awareness of participants in the culture.

Dorson was eager to debate, for he felt we had espoused, rather than explained, undesirable trends in folklore studies. In fact, we had both been immersed in American studies and more than most appreciated the benefits of history. Capping his rebuttal, he insisted that our "failure to appreciate that attitudes, beliefs, practices, possess their own histories ... is symptomatic of a general malaise among folklorists in America, who lock themselves into a parochial present and blind themselves to the buried treasure of America's past" (Dorson 1980c, 89). He was not any less friendly to me after the debate appeared in print. In fact, he was happy to "stir up the troops," he told me, and he supported his plaint of folklorists' presentism by mentioning that he found it indicative that the festschrift prepared in his honor by students and colleagues was entitled *Folklore Today* (1976). He appreciated the professional honor, to be sure, but mentioned that "there wasn't much history or American civilization in there." In the debate with us, he hoped to again survey the terrain, show what was missing, and direct the discipline.

Shortly after publishing his rejoinder, Dorson edited a special issue of the *Journal of the Folklore Institute* concerning the historical theme in American folklore (Dorson 1980a). Significantly, his editorial remarks seemed to retreat from some bold assertions made earlier. Although he iterated his concern for the prevalence among folklorists of folklore in America over American folklore, Dorson actually shifted ground when proclaiming: "The training and energies of folklorists in the United States are insufficiently directed toward the traditions arising out of the American historical experience. We must also utter the caution that folklore studies are comparative, cross-cultural, and international, but the matter here is one of balance, and paradoxically American folklorists are neglecting their own turf" (Dorson 1980a, 91). He indicated that his historical view was another relative "type" rather than the synthesis he had hoped for. By drawing attention to American folklorists' "own turf," rather than their specific approaches, Dorson moved the focus of the American theme from method to scope. The American folklore perspective was reduced from a claim of theory to a listing of Dorson's favorite topics. His themes of colonization, westward expansion, and so forth lost their determinative force and became historical headings. Indeed, William Clements's psychological study of Pentecostal narrators and Gary Alan Fine's sociological analysis of legends about fast food in modern society included in the historical theme issue ran directly counter to Dorson's own thematic methodology (Clements 1980; Fine 1980b).

From one position Dorson never budged. He believed America's history was being neglected by American folklorists and its folklore was overlooked by historians. What he perhaps did not fully realize is what new students of American folklore sought for folk cultural data in America's past. Dorson had been drawn to texts from which he could extrapolate national or regional character or the temper of the times, while many students applied an interest in explaining enacted behavior in social situations to find actor and action statements within historically described events (Isaac 1982; Bauman 1983b; Abrahams and Szwed 1983; Abrahams 1992b; Bronner 1982, 1986b). Although Dorson had proposed that when the folklorist does historical research he or she "should rest content with establishing the vigor and continuity of traditional behavior," many folklorists were not willing to rest there. They looked for interpretation that could go beyond to finding "reflection" of a historical period, region, or country, and get at the workings of mind (Glassie 1975; Dundes 1980a). It had become evident that Dorson's use of "behavior" was misleading. He still adhered to a notion of static outputs of behavior—his "typed" narrative—rather than detailing the actions and thoughts, the motivations and aspirations, the actual conduct and communication of the human actors and settings involved in behavior that were being studied by young students of what he called folklore in America. Ironically, the so-called "contextualists" called him guilty of a charge he leveled at Botkin: lacking in "portraits of the master storytellers, the drama of collecting, and the folk setting" (Dorson 1948b).

Although Dorson had been very much involved in studies of the behavior of folklore performance and individual performers, and although he appreciated more than most folklorists the international and subcultural dimensions of folklore creation and diffusion, young folklorists associated him increasingly with the nationalist line that they considered methodologically restrictive and ethnocentrically conservative. Dissatisfaction stemming from acceptance of unsubstantiated causal explanations for American behavioral phenomena led American folklorists during the 1970s to seek alternative perspectives. Whether influenced by anthropology, sociology, or psychology, many of these folklorists strove to explain occurrences by detailed investigations of all situational factors that produced events and affected individuals. The locus of observation, or ethnography, had become even smaller than Dorson's "collecting" in a county or region. In the synchronic and ethnographic approach that Dorson on occasion found too behavioral and overly localized, and therefore too marginalized, researchers examined the ways that "American" is used by individuals in their everyday activities. Dorson looked at "American" as a historical rather than cognitive category. Dorson typically sought thematic generalization and national unity from his data. More of his students examined cultural specificity and cultural conflict from theirs.

The distance between students and Dorson was especially evident in the growing tide of ethnic studies. Dorson felt he was a banner bearer for this interest, since he early took on the melting pot popularizers of "100 percent Americanism" with admonitions about the persistence of ethnic traditions in the American experience. While he held up his collections of black folklore as objective analyses, they unmistakably appealed for an ongoing process of cultural democracy in America. Showing the integration of European influences on black folklore confirmed an integrative process in America that was likely to continue. This is how he explained the persistence of ethnic folklore within a national tradition. Ethnicity and race were not melted away, but rather integrated into a national experience. Dorson's view was influential on the likes of Nathan Glazer, who reflected that "those of us who were students of ethnicity and race in the 1960s and held the perspective that assimilation—or, if one prefers the milder term, integration—was what happened to ethnic and racial groups in America, could look unconcernedly on many of the signs of continuing black separation and difference" (Glazer 1997, 149–50). Among those signs were the explosion of urban race riots as the 1960s ended, conflicts over community control of schools, and growing black nationalism. Against this background, more students of the 1970s suggested that collection of folklore offered a view of intentionally alienated groups prevented from cultural citizenship by racism, poverty, and victimization. Dorson recoiled at the suggestion that a cultural democratic process could fail America.

Before a view of an emerging racial separatism in American life had been widely dubbed "multiculturalism," Dorson had to confront its issues, especially as his students formed interpretations that varied from his in the team project to collect folklore in the largely black, troubled city of Gary, Indiana, in the late 1970s (Carpenter 1978). To be sure, Dorson rethought his previous progressive assertions in light of his experience in Gary. Calling it alternately "the armpit of the nation" and "land of the millrats," he did not see the decay of Gary nearly as "America in minuscule," as he had the rurally benign Upper Peninsula of Michigan (Dorson 1981). But he still held to his integrationist view of, or hope for, America. One way that Dorson dealt with the growing challenge was to invoke scholarly authority to avoid politics by faulting the concern for growing separatism as a misguided result of method, especially ethnography.

Increasingly citing ethnography rather than history, many of Dorson's students tended to construct "American" as a context rather than an identity. It appeared increasingly in their dissertations as a complex of personal, familial, regional, ethnic, religious, economic, and political factors, among others, to which individuals refer differently depending upon their particular circumstances. In this construction, the force, the continuity, of tradition appeared less essential to folklore's mission. Students contemplated that in the ethnography of contemporary cultural events, functions of activities, and their integration into small groups, that respond to immediate conditions are more evident. Dorson recognized some of this trend in his embrace of "personal narratives" expressed by individuals, including some of his own making, but he treated the subject anecdotally and underestimated the analysis that was being brought to the multivalence of individual performance (Dorson 1977f; see also Stahl 1989; Kirshenblatt-Gimblett 1989a; Georges 1989a; Braid 1996). Those young scholars who focused on personal narratives that defied historical analyses of form, indeed of tradition as inheritance from the past, discussed the sense by which persons considered themselves to be manifesting particularly American and ethnic behavior without the causation of supposedly "well-known" historical themes and events (Georges 1984; Stern and Cicala 1991; Mechling 1993; Oring 1994; Dolby 1996). A different kind of process came into view with personal narratives. The personal narratives raised issues of the ways that individuals create traditions for themselves, and often, the ways that the new expressions reflected frustrations of marginalization.

Ethnographic attention to identity and process, often coupled with universalist concern for explaining human behavior, affected the perception by many baby-boom folklorists of Dorson's concept of fakelore in addition to his claim for the uniqueness of American cultural experience. While still distinguishing between authentic and created experience, folklorists of the 1980s and 1990s referred increasingly to examples of festivals, tourist presentations, and literary retellings as "folklorism" (Voigt 1980; Bendix 1989; Sweterlitsch 1996). There was not the assumption of commercial exploitation, but rather, exploration of needs for community-building and identity formation. As a form of cultural production, folklorism was considered an extension of a process of tradition that needed to be analyzed for its structure, development, and function. It could be described ethnographically, therefore, as much as folklore (Bauman, Sawin, and Carpenter 1992). Many analyses blasted the strict dichotomy between the private world of folklore and the public realm of mass culture that Dorson had promoted to boost professionalism in the private intellectual sector of academe (Kirshenblatt-Gimblett 1988; Abrahams 1992a; Mechling 1993; Hanson 1993; Dégh 1994; Bluestein 1994). Folklorists had found a way to intellectualize, rather than alienate, the public realm.

The American civilization model had been revised to take into account ethnography of the multiple situational frames of everyday experience. Focused less on cultural consensus and more on separation, new perspectives looked to incorporate fresh "isms" that Dorson avoided: feminism, multiculturalism, racism, sexism, classism. The implication of this shift was that it spotlighted groups other than the American trinity of region, occupation, and ethnicity. Both reducing the scale of social units and expanding the scope of traditional associations, the ethnographies covered identities and associations that were frequently analyzed as transnational or even counternational. In some cases, ethnographic studies focused tightly on behavioral "dyads"—the bond, and tradition, formed between two persons, and in one study even between a person and animal (Oring 1984b; Bendix 1987; Mechling 1989d). They often considered identities of gender, age, class, sexuality, family, indeed of individuality. Thus the national construction of American identity in contrast to Europe, or fascism, or communism, appeared less real, especially as the

Cold War ended. Ethnography returned identity to individual circumstances and reconnected Americans to universal concerns of gender and race, for example.

Preferring to see "expression" and "narrative" in specific cultural performances, ethnography also challenged the reality of a folk literature. Questioning fixed literary genres of traditional tales and legends, it blurred genres with contextual attention to ways that tradition emerges through the "dynamics," "strategies," and "interactions" of everyday conversation, behavioral gesture, and body image. Writing on "American Folklore and American Studies" during America's bicentennial, Richard Bauman and Roger Abrahams commented that studies emphasizing the "minuscule" rather than the whole—biography, repertoire, and performance style of folk performers and their sociocultural context—"have enriched the study of American folklore." "This approach," they concluded, "will note not only the specifics of performance, but the cultural equipment and expectations as well, and thus encompass both the unity and diversity of American expressive culture as enacted in social life" (Bauman and Abrahams 1976, 377).

Dorson fervently held to the idea of a liberal, enlightening spirit of folklore to reveal the relation of cultural groups to one another from the pluralist margins to the national center. Dorson's view of himself as an "other" in the study of "others" is significant to his work (and the work of many folklorists inspired by him) interpreting culture for the public. He had, in fact, planned, but never completed, a pluralist volume on the "Other America in Legend" to complement his more nationalistic *America in Legend* (1973). Returning to the distinction between folklore as objective reality and public image, he hoped to separate popular stereotypes from ethnic, racial, regional, industrial, and urban inheritance, and "consciousness" of grouped otherness (Dorson 1982b, 86–97). His thinking had been shaped, no doubt, by his late-in-life battles with the New Left and Old Right, his students' increasingly vocal concern for ethnicity and multiculturalism, and his ethnographic team "foray" into the "multiethnic" city (Dorson 1981).

Discipline from Discourse

It can be argued that in significantly setting a tone of cultural discourse during the post-World War II years, Dorson revealed much of his own experience in his concern for a move of marginalized others to the center. Going in his life history from the ethnic city to the pastoral imagery of New England, he was aware of his relatively new arrival in American society. He struggled for his identity as an authoritarian "professional" in the university, and he referred to the fragility of his identity in folklore and American civilization studies from roots in "established" history and literature. In his many reminiscences, he boasted of his Algeresque pluck, intimating that his experience of scrapping from a subcultural background to a national center was the real American one. Dorson made much of his early emergence from the city and academy to find America in the rural, isolated landscape of the multiethnic Upper Peninsula, and when he returned to write he made his argument that this was the real America in minuscule. His last fieldwork returned him to the familiar ground of the city, which he had marginalized as strange because of its density of industry and self-identity of difference.

Going north to urban, multiethnic Indiana, he made his case that "all three great folk traditions in the United States—the regional, the ethnic, and the occupational—can be observed and recorded in cities" (Dorson 1981, 232). In his rhetoric, Northwest Indiana and the Upper Peninsula were both "realities" that had been obscured or denied by commercial and scholarly fantasies. Even the recordable historic forms he presented as the real stuff of folklore expressed his concern with marginality and change. He began with the reality of American historic legends which he had claimed had been overlooked in the rush for international literary folktales. It is significant that he was especially drawn to hero cycles and their implication of beginning with lowly status and rising to popular support. Through his career, he pointed to immigrant dialect tales, a genre he claimed to discover. They represented to him the move of a second generation from ethnic marginality to centrality while recognizing its subcultural cultural roots. Indeed, the narratives were collected from sources most like himself—students and scholarly colleagues of the New Class. With the "personal narrative" that he analyzed from his own experience as well as those of his students, he found his ultimate issue—the entry of tradition toward the center of individuality in modern existence.

Leaving behind folklore vs. fakelore and folklore in America vs. American folklore, the discipline that Dorson ushered in confronted a fresh scholarly posturing and reconciliation: between central artistic text and social context at the periphery (Dorson 1972b, 45–47; Dorson 1982b, 71–72; Jones 1979; Ben-Amos 1979; Georges 1980; Ben-Amos 1993). In Dorson's mind, the new controversy was really about integrating the social sciences and humanities in folklore, and in that tension confronted anew the relation of scholarship to the public. He related well to the fray because he had made reference to such an integration with his "theory." Priding himself on his "open-mindedness" as long as professional standards were maintained, Dorson appeared to welcome the sophistication of the younger "contextualist" generation and looked for a "Hegelian synthesis" of text and context (Dorson 1982b, 72). He predicted: "The emergence of this sophisticated circle of youthful academic folklorists heralds a new departure in the writing of folklore books of the future. Texts and annotations will be subordinated to close analyses of group dynamics and psycho-cultural relationships. Fieldwork will become a more elaborate enterprise than the securing of verbatim texts" (Dorson 1972b, 47). His worry was that the "close analyses" suggested by the contextualists disengaged the public from the scholarly discourse of culture. He lambasted students and colleagues for using theoretical jargon that was inaccessible to the public. He wanted to educate the public with scholarship, rather than remove them from the discussion.

In light of the emergence of the challenge from within his discipline, Dorson revived his "theory" to create another consensus: the ways that history configured with "group dynamics" recognized peoplehood, and further, how folklore represented shared values and an ongoing cultural process he considered, or publicized, as American. Through all his debates, Dorson insisted on the American common ground that folklorists should have "the ideals of truth itself, fair play, equality, democracy, freedom, and the work ethic" (Dorson 1983c, 325).

Dorson had indeed followed and applied what he perceived as American tradition. With the integrity of professionalism, he hoped to have its ideals reinstilled in the American public, in contemporary mass culture, which he thought of as troubled and in need of reform. He believed Americans "needed" the folk, and fought for its honor. Upon reflection, he also required the folk and its American connection to satisfy his own sense of self and those sharing New Class values (Dorson 1974b, 1978e). In the discourse he spread through students' work and popular publications, folk stood for authenticity and honesty in a corruptible, shallow modern culture. He called on the folk's protectors to be incorruptible fighters and honest professionals. The folk, and America, he finally informed professional and layman alike, represents "a common humanity, out there somewhere" (Dorson 1978e, 269).

9

Displaying American Tradition
in Folk Arts

THE TWENTIETH CENTURY WAS THE ERA OF THE GREAT FOLK ART EXHIBITION AND festival in America. Blockbuster folk art shows such as *American Folk Art: The Art of the Common Man* at the Museum of Modern Art in 1932 and *The Flowering of American Folk Art* at the Whitney Museum of American Art in 1974 inspired countless collections, books, and commentaries harping on the essential national spirit of America found in its folk art. They also had their detractors who wanted to use the eye-catching forms of folk art to different social and aesthetic purposes. *The Arts and Crafts of the Homelands Exhibition* of 1919 publicized a contrary definition of America as a pluralist society composed of immigrant groups, and it must have held appeal for its attendance topped the magic one million mark. Staged outdoor events from the 1960s to the 1990s organized on the pluralist theme, such as the Festival of American Folklife, National Folk Festival, Newport Folk Festival, and Kutztown Folk Festival, became mass entertainment.

Exhibition and festival share the designation of displaying, indeed elevating, folk tradition as *art*. In so doing, they formed arguments for the proper roles of Americans as viewers, producers, and consumers of tradition. By installing artifacts or presenting performances to attract popular notice, they mounted varying social visions of traditional creativity within modernized existence. This chapter explores these social visions with special reference to folk art exhibitions alternately advocating national unity and cultural pluralism and to the uses of folk arts in festival and other display events to realize a behavioral perspective of performed tradition.

Although to this point in the book my emphasis in analyzing folk tradition in the discourse of American culture has been on the written and spoken word, the debates that folk art exhibitions have inspired in America lead me to consider how

413

social concepts became presented in tangible ways and became supported by cultural rhetoric. As an invented term for a class of objects, folk art brought together potentially opposed ideas. While problematic, the term also significantly drew attention to itself for marking the changing role of tradition in modernizing society. Its formation begged the question of the groups that properly held an authentic claim for producing a distinctly American culture. Yoking folk to art especially brought into question conceptions of social class in the American experience. Art had European associations with aristocratic taste as well as embodying beauty and skill unattainable to the lowly masses. In literary usage, it conveyed originality and genius. It meant change. It announced the future. Folk meanwhile represented the stable past steeped in the tradition of groups and classes without power.

With the insertion of folk" between "American" and "art" to describe objects in galleries, curators invited reflection on the cultural characterization of American society. Showing beauty and originality among artists drawn from ordinary circumstances implied a national tradition united by the spirit of individual expression that left behind the hold of European culture and led to the future. It was a future prefiguring the strength of American nationalism and its catapult into modernity. Problems of defining this invented category of objects did not deter enthusiasm for its use in collecting and exhibiting, especially in the American art world center of New York City. From this center, folk art became a publicly recognizable term for crude work of the people admired for its boldness of color, line, and expression.

Natives and Immigrants in Folkloristic Presentation

A rival use of art outside the gallery world emerged that emphasized the functional uses of decoration in everyday lives of diverse communal groups. Otis Mason, curator of ethnological collections at the new United States National Museum in the Smithsonian Institution, first referred to a "folk fine art" in his presidential address to the American Folklore Society in 1891 (Mason 1891, 103). Eskimos, Indians, and Polynesians had their traditional designs heralded as art in extravagant expositions in London in 1891, Chicago in 1893, and Atlanta in 1895. In these exhibitions of arts that seemed exotic to Victorian viewers, folklorists and anthropologists collected objects that were divided between those that illustrated tradition and those that were traditional because of their use. They classified the latter as useful or decorative art. Often the prefix "folk" was not necessary since the assumption was that the objects came from traditional or "savage" societies. In such societies, there would not be distinction between folk and fine arts; everything was traditional. Alfred Haddon's influential *Evolution in Art* (1895), explained that "the term 'art' now has a tendency to be confined to designate the Fine Arts as opposed to the Useful Arts; not only so, but instead of including personal decoration, ornamentation, painting, sculpture, dancing, poetry, music, and the drama, the term is very often limited to ornamentation, painting, and sculpture." Art in a social sense meant broadly "a creative operation of the intelligence, the making of something either with a view to utility or pleasure" (Haddon 1895, 1). For the word folk at the time, the first editor of the *Journal of American Folklore* made the claim that it "was primarily invented to describe the unwritten popular traditions of civilized countries" (Newell 1888b, 163). Folklorists, especially European and American folklorists, applied anthropological concepts to complex, literate societies and "folk art" came into use to differentiate between the dominant "fine arts" of the elite and other arts of "lower classes" such as peasants.

Outdoor folk museums in Sweden, Norway, and Denmark established during the late nineteenth century symbolized the richly embroidered folk art of peasants as signs of continued nationalism in an age of industrial empire in Europe. Saving and celebrating the relics of the past as artistic, Danish folklorist Peter Michelsen observed, "served the cause of progress," by allowing a transition to the "radical changes in the entire material culture of the peasantry.... This cultural upheaval caused the relics of the earlier way of life to be ruthlessly swept aside, and gave the folk museums and open-air museums formed at this time a mission to fulfill" (Michelsen 1966, 227–28).

Books simultaneously appeared describing peasants' art as genuine folk art and associating it with the character-building daily round of a passing traditional life. Germans coined the word *Volkskunst* while the French referred to *l'art populaire*. German Alois Riegl brought out *Volkskunst, Hausfleiss und Hausindustrie* in 1894, F. Zell published *Volkskunst in Allgau* in 1902, and Scandinavian N. Nicolayson published *Kunst og haandverk ha Norges fortid* from 1881 to 1899. The rage for peasant art entered fashionable designs of the period and reached across Europe from England to Russia. For English-speaking audiences, *The Studio* published a series of books on the folk art of Sweden and Iceland (1910), Austria and England (1911), Russia (1912), Italy (1913), the Netherlands (1913), and Switzerland (1914). The International Folk-Lore Congress of 1900 held in Paris had as one of its main themes *art populaire*. The proceedings took up the relationship of folk art to fine arts, especially those established by earlier civilizations like the Greeks and Romans, and its implication for aesthetic systems existing within Western societies.

Several prominent American folklorists at the close of the nineteenth century noticed this artistic trend and its relation to culture. Daniel Brinton (at the University of Pennsylvania), Otis Mason (at the Smithsonian Institution), Frederick Ward Putnam (at the Peabody Museum), Washington Matthews (at the Bureau of American Ethnology), and Stewart Culin (at the Brooklyn Institute Museum) pushed for wider American appreciation of traditional art and material culture. At the 1893 Folk-Lore Congress in Chicago, organizer Fletcher Bassett made a special point of calling for the collection of objects, and listed "artistic and emblematic folklore" as a major heading of folk studies. Stewart Culin contributed by exhibiting Native American and American immigrant folk objects at Madrid in

1892, Chicago in 1893, Philadelphia in 1894, and Atlanta in 1895. Frederick Starr collected Mexican decorative masks and ceremonial objects which he displayed in London and about which he published a catalog under the imprint of the Folk Lore Society in 1899.

With the turn of the century, Stewart Culin made calls that presaged the twentieth-century move toward examining modern folk arts. He made comparisons of primitive art to modern-day aesthetics in essays such as "Primitive American Art" (1900) and "The Origin of Ornament" (1900). "When we examine the products of man's handicraft," he wrote, "as represented both by his prehistoric remains, as well as by the rudest effort of the existing savage, we everywhere find evidence of an aesthetic sense, of an effort, not only at mere utility, but at decoration and ornament, analogous to that which is universal among cultivated people at the present day" (Culin 1900a, 235). This examination was crucial, Culin and his crowd asserted, because of the changes that industrialization had brought to American traditional arts during the late nineteenth century.

Pennsylvania collectors such as Henry Mercer and Edwin Barber had gained notoriety for bringing out a legacy of regional folk art in America comparable to esteemed European peasant work. They published essays filled with the rhetoric of discovery on Pennsylvania-German fraktur, pottery, and ironwork. At the American sesquicentennial celebration in 1926 held in Philadelphia, an exhibition of Pennsylvania folk art installed by Hattie Brunner included decorated craft items such as illuminated manuscripts, papercuts, ironwork, pottery, and textiles. Brunner highlighted the significance of this ethnic folk art for its inherited techniques of handwork, cultural context of the object in an ethnic-regional tradition, and functions in daily community life. In a region touted as America's first plural society, where German dialects still thrived, and where coal regions brought in a flood of immigrants from eastern and southern Europe, an explosion of color and design burst forth. Brunner and other dealers showed brightly illuminated manuscripts and painted furniture from an immigrant culture of the colonial past maintaining its ethnic distinctiveness. When the furniture from the Mahantango Valley of Pennsylvania came into view at the sesquicentennial exhibition, the English-American unpainted version seemed weak indeed. This Pennsylvania painted furniture, one New York collector exclaimed, was the real "epitome of folk art" (Earnest 1984; see Reed 1987).

Pennsylvania art and culture did not fit well into a unified vision of America, and Pennsylvania writers promoted folklife approaches to the diverse communities within the region. The *Annual of the Pennsylvania German Folklore Society* ridiculed the rage for folk art coming out of New York galleries as "antiquarian" and "unscientific." The folkloristic interest in Pennsylvania was inclined less toward the visual, leisurely, decorative products, and more toward those of labor in communal societies, as existed in the Pennsylvania-German settlements. In this view of labor in community life, pottery, textiles, ironwork, and manuscript illumination were rooted in traditionally learned crafts in which an aesthetic function was integrated with utility. They were the stuff of folk art related to folk life. Promoting this view, John Baer Stoudt published *The Shenandoah Pottery* in 1929, and his son John Joseph carried on with general studies of illuminated manuscripts (or fraktur) and iconography in *Consider the Lilies* (1937) and *Pennsylvania Folk Art: An Interpretation* (1948). Preston Barba wrote in the *Annual* that folk art should be tied to a social world of folklore, not to the "individual achievement" of the art world. He argued that folk art is a "result," not a "product." "It's a living link in the long chain of a people's social existence," he emphasized (Barba 1954, 4).

Edwin Barber and the Pennsylvania folklorists influenced some collectors in New York and New England, including Albert Pitkin, who used "folk" as an adjective for art with his *Early American Folk Pottery* (1918). His folk, he stated, was an "American Folk, as exemplified in the work of our English and European ancestors who were among the early settlers in this country. The Pottery made by aborigines will have no consideration, because it was unglazed ware, and because it belongs essentially to Ethnological study" (Pitkin 1918, 83). A similar rhetoric separating traditional crafts of early American settlers as folk art from the "ethnological" culture of aborigines was evident in Fanny Bergen's groundbreaking study of quilts as "The Tapestry of the New World" (1894). She concluded that "the interest which attaches to these old quilts is not only due to the light that they throw on the degree of artistic advancement (or lack of it) that characterized the household industries of our grandmothers, but the needlework itself is often extraordinarily beautiful, fine, and intricate, approaching in these respects the finest of the old tapestries" (Bergen 1892, 69).

Pitkin boasted of getting out of the gallery and into the field: he interviewed the "old potters, in their homes," who were threatened, he said, with extinction. With such research, a shift could be discerned from objects illustrating folklore of primitives or used in folk custom, to decorative objects of regional and immigrant groups in America. Their collected objects were not savage or primitive in the sense that Haddon had noted, but were still outside of "fine arts." As American society entered the twentieth century, a fear arose of mass society, a society governed by formal rules and tastemakers. Some ethnic and regional museums such as Henry Mercer's Bucks County Historical Society and the Norwegian-American Museum in Decorah, Iowa, collected and displayed the arts of traditional communities to fulfill an educational purpose similar to that of the European folk museums. Industrialist Henry Mercer declared that industrialization was indeed progress, and therefore inevitable, but he called for saving the remnants of preindustrial life to appreciate the efforts of settlers in the building of the nation. He called his first major exhibition of his collection drawn primarily from Pennsylvania-German sources, *Tools of the Nation Maker* (1897) (see Mercer 1987).

The background of the *Nation Maker* exhibitions showing that America had a quickly disappearing "material culture" lay in social dilemmas tugging at the nation around the turn of the century. Beside the promotion of industrialism as the great leap into the future of the twentieth century stood reminders of the upheaval that change had brought. Disruptive labor strikes, economic panics, and radical protests commanded headlines alongside news of the industrial splendor of the 1893 World's Columbian Exposition in Chicago and growth of American big business (see Trachtenberg 1982). Poverty spread while "conspicuous consumption" and affluence rose. There were reports on the plight, or curse, depending on the writer's political persuasion, of immigrants and minorities. There was condemnation, or praise, of isolated rural regions in relation to the progress of the nation. The admiration for industrial modernism stood alongside an antimodern revival of older values, from religious fundamentalism to the aestheticism of the Arts and Crafts movement (see Lears 1981). Studies of old rural crafts and art abounded amidst a celebration of modern urban invention. Not that these dilemmas were new, but rather public attention to them was heightened by journalists, reformers, and photographers. Folklorists, whose studies gained public notoriety in the antimodern (and isolationist) trend, increasingly turned to "neglected" or "disappearing" subjects at home—regional and immigrant oral tradition. The research of American folklorists turned toward the nation's heart, rather than, as it had before, outward to international studies of the primitive's mind.

Reflecting this trend were Allen Eaton's exhibitions of *Arts and Crafts of the Homelands*, first put up in Buffalo in 1919, and the *America's Making Exposition*, opening in New York City in 1921. Eaton was trained as a sociologist at the University of Oregon and influenced by folklorists in New York City such as Stewart Culin. Eaton was born in 1878 in Union, Oregon, and became an art professor and state legislator before being asked to assemble an arts and crafts exhibition for the Oregon Building at the 1915 Panama-Pacific International Exposition in San Francisco. It was the only state building at the exposition that displayed crafts as part of the arts. Losing his bid for reelection and dismissed from the University of Oregon for anti-war activities, Eaton came to New York City in 1918 and found work with the Emergency Fleet Corporation, a division of the United States Shipping Board. In this work, he came to know hundreds of newly arrived immigrants. In 1920 he became associate director of the Department of Surveys and Exhibitions of the Russell Sage Foundation, established to improve social conditions in America. He earned the promotion by receiving tremendous notice for the *Arts and Crafts of the Homelands* exhibition, opening in 1919. He turned his attention to another social transformation in America when he began surveys of rural regions increasingly marginalized by industrialization and urbanization. His efforts culminated in 1937 with a major exhibition of rural arts for the United States government. His displays of tradition were more like festivals than galleries, and he invited groups to select the objects and performances used to represent their culture. As David B. Van Dommelen recalled, "Not only did Eaton accept for display all objects brought to him by working immigrants, but he decided that, in order to illustrate a total integration of these gifts, dances, costumes, songs and foods from around the world would also be included" (Van Dommelen 1985, 36).

An example of the commentary that Eaton's lively and sympathetic representation of America's diverse folk cultures in the *Arts and Crafts of the Homelands* exhibition drew comes from the *Portland Spectator:*

> These exhibitions of things made by unschooled but sensitive people who know not the rules of composition and color, but who felt strongly the impulse to create beautiful objects and responded to the impulse, will not only help us to appreciate more fully the folk culture of the many homelands from which America is made up, but they will give us a vision of what we may reasonably hope to see in a renaissance of all the arts in our country. Perhaps the greatest thing, however, this will do is to help us understand that art in its true sense, whether it be folk or fine, is the expression of joy in work. (Van Dommelen 1985, 36)

Eaton's intention of showing the joy of the work came through in his display of woodcarving, embroidery, and egg decorating accompanied with performances by immigrant groups to bring life to the arts as a social creation. The *Homelands* exhibition and *America's Making Exposition* confirmed the value of immigration to American life. Both shows traveled widely, and together they attracted well over a million viewers, resulting in a book by Eaton, *Immigrant Gifts to American Life* (1932).

Other exhibitions of immigrant folk art as a connection of the European peasant to the hyphenated American sprang up in Omaha, Minneapolis, Cleveland, and New York City during the 1920s. Curators following this folk art held the belief that immigrant groups would quickly become assimilated, so their folk arts arising out of their utilitarian craft traditions should be preserved and appreciated for contributing to the richness of American life. Some of these exhibitions and festivals had strong support from social service agencies including settlement houses and the Young Women's Christian Association (YWCA). The YWCA sponsored International Institutes that produced almost 200 folk festivals and handicraft exhibitions during the 1920s (Eaton 1932, 93). The International Institute of St. Paul, Minnesota, beginning in 1919, presented ethnic arts in various displays and later produced the Festival of Nations, which led to the formation of the Folk Arts Foundation of America (Kaplan 1980). The International Folk Arts Society formed in Omaha in 1926, according to its bylaws, "(1) To encourage and foster friendly relations among the various nationalities of Omaha, and (2) To promote and enrich American art by exhibiting and cultivating that brought to us from other lands" (Eaton 1932, 96).

Eaton's exhibitions presented American experience as a narrative of continuous immigration and cultural enrichment. They told the story of the great wave of immigration that came to America around the turn of the century as a dramatic but not unusual chapter in the story of America. Eaton insisted that immigrants

Three generations of women posing alongside a "family of wooden dolls from Russia" at the Russian section of the *Arts and Crafts of the Homelands* exhibition installed at the Albright-Knox Art Gallery, Buffalo, New York, in 1919. The participants demonstrated the "living" tradition of the textiles and the uses of folk art in the home. Typical of publicity photographs from the exhibition, this inclusion of young and old representatives of the ethnic group implied tradition passed down from one generation to the next. (Albright-Knox Art Gallery Archives, Buffalo, New York)

presented opportunities rather than threats to American identity. The *Arts and Crafts of the Homelands* exhibitions, he vowed, promoted the "conservation of the choice customs, traditions, and folkways of these various [foreign-born] peoples" toward a better America. The mix of visitors to the exhibitions provided testimony of a socially diverse America, for the exhibitions brought out members of ethnic communities and overall attendance for an art exhibition was astounding for the period. Eaton boasted that "undoubtedly one of the measures of the influence of an exhibition is the interest indicated by attendance. In Buffalo it was the opinion of many that it would not be possible to get large numbers of people to come to the Albright Art Gallery.... In the two weeks during which the exhibition lasted, the attendance amounted to 42,961 persons, the largest number on record for any two consecutive weeks since the gallery had been dedicated nine years before"

(Eaton 1932, 63–64). Such numbers would set records even today in most galleries. Although counts were not kept at the Rochester and Albany sites, newspaper reports noted that the halls were filled to capacity. Encouraged by clamor for the displays and performances, promoters took the exhibition to additional sites in Syracuse, Utica, and New York City.

Eaton was not about to let the objects on display speak for themselves. He introduced extensive social education programs that became hailed as an innovation to art exhibitions. As Eaton reported, "Thousands of school children visited the exhibition and were instructed in the folk and industrial arts of foreign countries by the staff of the gallery or those in charge of booths" (Eaton 1932, 63–64). The repeated object lesson was the benefit, aesthetic and social, of an American ethnic pluralism. The picture of a door used as a frontispiece to *Immigrant Gifts to American Life* (1932) gave a compelling image of entry into a society enriched by its ethnic variety. Emblazoned on the page was the new ornate entrance to Saint Mark's Church in Philadelphia. The caption informed readers that the magnificent church doorway had "iron work by Samuel Yellin from Poland; wood-carving by Edward Maene from Belgium; stained glass by Nicola D'Ascenzo from Italy."

Eaton organized his exhibitions in large halls, such as the great rotunda of the New York State Educational Building in Albany and the Rochester Exposition Grounds, to suggest outdoor culture-scapes: the feelings of field and sea, community and participation. He created settings for work and performances including Greek fishing boats and dances featuring hundreds of Russian, Italian, and Ukrainian children in folk costume, thereby underscoring the link of environment to living custom. Encouraging demonstrators and performers ranging in age from young to old, Eaton broadcast the impression that one generation to the next pridefully transmitted arts within ethnic families and communities and they could be appreciated by a wider public. In the world Eaton exhibited, arts, like the cultures they expressed, were alive, persistent, buoyant. Across from a striking photograph showing a "Czech father teaching little son to dance at the Buffalo exhibition," Eaton cheered that visitors can observe "artists and craftsmen in native costume working at the wheel, the loom, the bench, the easel, and the frame, actually creating objects of art associated with the life of the countries from which millions of our citizens have come." Impressing upon his public a continuum of tangible and non-tangible traditions as integrated "folk arts," Eaton made sure to draw visitors to displays as "programs" involving "native music, songs, and folk dances." For the immigrants already here, the exhibition "may develop opportunities for the gifted to live by their gifts." It was an invitation to continue their culture. For non-immigrants, the exhibition promoted tolerance and the possibility of a peaceful simultaneity between multiple communities and the nation.[1] Visitors were urged "to hear with their own ears, and to feel with their hearts this wealth that is ours for the caring…. But most of all we hope that it will bring about a better understanding between all the people;

Norwegian, Danish, and Swedish section of the *Arts and Crafts of the Homelands* exhibition installed at the Albright-Knox Art Gallery, Buffalo, 1919. The exhibition was divided into sections representing immigrants' countries of origin. In addition to representing such "homelands," the sections had the look of rooms in an immigrant home. Costumed participants demonstrated "living" traditions of textiles and the uses of folk art in the home. (Albright-Knox Art Gallery Archives, Buffalo, New York)

and no matter how successful this undertaking may be we hope that it may be looked upon not as the end, but as the beginning of a greater co-operation among all citizens in appreciating and conserving the finest and best of our community and national life" (Eaton 1932, 34–35).

Set behind the background of progressive changes to American life that immigrants during the great wave brought, Eaton proposed a revision of the ways that America's heritage was conceived. Eaton claimed that "our people are coming into a greater appreciation of their folk arts as they inquire into the many ingredients and influences that have gone into the making of America." Making reference to the art world's obsession with the emergence of the New Republic, Eaton offered a longer cultural view in an essay entitled "American Folk Arts": "This quest goes back beyond the founding of a new nation on this continent, to the original American, the Indian, whose folk arts form the first part, chronologically, and a distinguished part, of American's cultural heritage…. We are a nation of people

The Jugoslav String Orchestra and Singers at the *Arts and Crafts of the Homelands* exhibition installed at the Albright-Knox Art Gallery, Buffalo, 1919. Performances of dance and music were regularly featured during the exhibition and culminated in a gala "All-American Night" on the last night. Twenty-two nations (mostly from eastern and southern Europe) were represented. In the finale, according to a press release, the "new Americans in the costumes of their homelands assembled in a striking pageant as loyal and patriotic upholders of Columbia, who will typify the spirit of the new land." (Albright-Knox Art Gallery Archives, Buffalo, New York)

gathered here from every continent on the earth, and from a hundred homelands." Offering a pluralist summary borrowing Martha Warren Beckwith's rhetoric of spirited ethnic "strains," Eaton concluded, "There is considerable evidence that we are beginning to prize the folk arts of the many human strains that make up our population" (Eaton 1944, 201; see Beckwith 1931b, 64).

MODERNISM AND NATIONALISM IN THE ART WORLD

Eaton tended to use "folk arts" rather than "folk art" as an indication of the variety of everyday expression used by diverse "human strains" in American society. Eaton's exhibitions stressed a plurality of "arts" integrated into various cultures. Dance, song, dress, and even foodways became arts defined as activities functioning within the culture rather than objects evaluated for fitness outside culture. To

Allen Eaton and Lucinda Crile at display in the *Rural Arts Exhibition,* which they directed, 1937. (Theodor Horydczak Collection, Library of Congress)

Eaton such folk arts, as expressions of persistent subcultures, were gifts of communities to the nation. In contrast, Holger Cahill, espousing the view of the New York art world, argued that folk art was a treasure of the self, mirroring the spirit of the republic. Cahill's conception of folk art, which informs contemporary institutions such as the Abby Aldrich Rockefeller Folk Art Center, the Museum of American Folk Art, the Shelburne Museum, and the New York State Historical Association, celebrates the power of image. The type of folk art they collected is used to form a romantic narrative in images, of a pastoral America built on unity and harmony. Beginning with its usage by the art world during the 1920s, "folk art" separated image from process and community.

The impetus for this separation came from the rise of interest among art world patrons and artists promoting folk art. Displays of American art during the 1920s relied on a new breed of affluent art patron who broke with the status of purchasing European fine art by collecting the plain portraits and rough-hewn sculptures from the American countryside. Patrons equally of new vogues of modern art and folk art such as Electra Havemeyer Webb and Abby Aldrich Rockefeller bought much of their folk art material from New York and New England dealers who

Holger Cahill. (Archives of American Art)

scoured the large antique auction houses of central Pennsylvania. Working with museum curator Holger Cahill and art patron Abby Aldrich Rockefeller, New York's enterprising dealer Edith Gregor Halpert came regularly to Pennsylvania for purchases of folk art and in her downtown New York gallery offered the works for a new decorative purpose tailored to her clients' needs (Metcalf and Weatherford 1988). The folk art gracing the walls of Rockefeller's New York apartment retained the decorative and spirit-giving purpose of antiques. In fact, when Cahill installed folk art exhibitions in Newark and New York, he tried to preserve the positioning of Rockefeller's prized possessions, such as *Peaceable Kingdom* by Edward Hicks and *Baby in Red Chair* by an unknown artist, in her home in a decorative, almost living-room, setting (Rumford and Weekley 1989, 8–11). The objects were of a bygone era but moved to walls and pedestals that flattered patrons and gallery-goers even more than the often anonymous artists. With their collections of home-grown antiques meant to decorate their estates, these upper-class women announced their independence from a previous European-centered generation and elevated the American antique into art. Not surprisingly, the decorative forms they collected were typically larger and more select than the average craftswork of ethnic communities.

Abby Aldrich Rockefeller (1874–1948) canonized her folk art and its connection to both modernism and nationalism by donating her extensive collection of paintings and sculptures in 1939 to Colonial Williamsburg and the Museum of Modern Art. She reflected at the time to writer Mary Ellen Chase on the driving themes of her collecting. She told Chase that the folk art she was attracted to recorded "those years in American history when, after the baffling problems of a new world had been solved by the colonists and after the War of the Revolution had finally shattered an earlier dependence upon the culture and learning of England, a new American people began for the first time to stand alone, to work out its own destiny as a nation" (Chase 1950, 148). She identified in this passage the unified lineage from Protestant England to a new American type. Then she elaborated on this era of the New Republic as a golden age of prosperity and harmony: "an era of relative prosperity, which followed the disturbance of war, and a more leisurely existence than had been possible in years of settlement were conducive to the development of art" (Chase 1950, 148). Described as a forceful woman with a combative personality who used art as ammunition for a "good fight" in defense of her nationalist cause, she wanted to create a stir in the art world as a way to reach America (Chase 1950, 131). While her management of the Museum of Modern Art mainly brought in art aficionados, she hoped that her folk art collection with her aesthetic and nationalist message would more widely reach common people. Thus she gave the bulk of her folk art collection to Williamsburg, which had a founding principle to recall the spirit as well as surroundings of the new nation (Freeze 1989).

Rockefeller had a home in Williamsburg as well as residences in Pocantico Hills, New York; Seal Harbor, Maine; and New York City, where she did much of her folk art collecting. She had an appreciation for New England history and art from her youth in Providence, Rhode Island, where she received a classical education at a school for girls. She also respected the theme of a prospering nation grown from humble roots because of narratives from her father. He had risen from a lowly position of bookkeeper in a grocery firm to become a powerful United States Senator. He had encouraged her to travel to Europe as a youth, and she was attracted to art museums on her travels. It gave her an aesthetic education and a certain jealousy of the cultural capital and nationalism that European nations acquired through the encouragement and display of native art. The American art she surrounded herself with and later displayed to the public boosted the image of a rising nation as a narrative of her family's historic saga from modest middle-class New England roots to international prominence. Intersecting with her art and Protestant church associations, she joined the Mayflower Descendants, National Society of Colonial Dames, the Women's National Republican Club, the Colony Club, and the Cosmopolitan Club. She married John D. Rockefeller, Jr., son of the founder of the Standard Oil Company and, with a fortune behind her, indulged in philanthropy and support of American modern and folk art. Rockefeller had faith in the therapeutic value of art as well as its redemptive power for the nation. Together with another folk art patron, Stephen C. Clark (who supported the collection of the New York State Historical Association at Cooperstown), she organized the War Veterans' Art Center in 1944, which offered art classes to disabled veterans until 1948. She also created a model workers' home for employees of Standard Oil in New Jersey, whereby she tried to demonstrate the uplifting power of an aesthetic environment.[2]

Rockefeller enlisted support from credentialed curators for her aesthetic cause. With her power of the purse, she encouraged more scholarly attention to building a sense of American tradition in art to rival Europe's. She turned increasingly to Newark Museum curator Holger Cahill, who had experience with collections of Scandinavian peasant as well as European fine arts (Vlach 1985b). Holger Cahill acted as her expert agent in choosing prize items for her collection, and he was instrumental in adding southern colonial items to complement her New England material (Chase 1950, 149). He helped her realize her philosophy of celebrating rising individuality in the New Republic as the basis of an individually expressive modernism in America. She had aesthetic inclinations toward bold colors and unusual abstractions, and as Chase emphasized, she gave her staunchest support to their value as American art (Chase 1950, 139). As chair of the committee that organized the Museum of Modern Art and as folk art patron, she called for works expressing an American imagination and "freedom of expression" (Chase 1950, 136). She delighted equally in promoting "little known" American modernist artists or folk artists into something much larger, much more symbolic. Of folk art, Rockefeller believed that "although the paintings merely as paintings are sometimes amateurish and even crude, they emanate an honesty and integrity not soon forgotten." In a conclusion that trumpeted a brassy keynote resounding through major national events from Cahill's *Art of the Common Man* in 1932 to Jean Lipman and Alice Winchester's *Flowering of American Folk Art* (1974), Rockefeller expressed the sentiment that folk artists conveyed "not only the character and quality of their imaginations, but as well the *spirit of a country*" (Chase 1950, 150; emphasis added).

The objects associated with Rockefeller and Cahill's art of the "common man" characterized a dominant white Protestant American stock and nationalized history. The usage came out of a potent combination of a modernist artistic movement and a post-war craze for American antiques collecting. Antiques collecting was partly in response to the lack of "European" art goods during the war and an interest by a new generation in locating power in America. The stress on antiques of the American colonial period carried over from the centennial of 1876 and Columbian Exposition of 1893 and the entrance of America into colonial rule and world prominence. Critic Virgil Barker commented on an exhibition of colonial paintings at the Whitney Studio Club in 1924: "The discovery of our artistic past which is now progressing with increasing rapidity satisfies more than the collecting instinct, for such paintings and miscellaneous objects as were brought together in this exhibition have the tang of reality" (Barker 1924, 161). Not being schooled but being old and domestic, the art objects—mostly portraits and occupational carvings—were considered antiques in the early twentieth century. They were the products of the colonial forebears, representative of a national history.

The celebration of colonial antiques as consumables for the home during the early twentieth century gave the domestic environment a feel of being a nurturing haven of rural tradition while rapid changes occurred in the factory and city. Broaching "The Superstition of the Antique," the Newark Museum pronounced, "There comes a moment in the history of every civilization when it turns back to look at the ground it has covered, before crossing the pass and plunging down to new discoveries on the other side. On the threshold of a new age it experiences an overwhelming desire to build an artificial paradise out of the ruins of the past" (Hinks 1928, 10). Walter Dyer writing in *The Lure of the Antique* (1910) wrote of antique collectors, "we are a home-loving people, and the things of the homes, and our reverence for the past around the hearthstone of our forebears. Also we are for the most part descended from Europeans, and there is born within us a respect for antiquity. We have no Rhenish castles here; no Roman roads undulate over our hilltops. The oldest we have is just coming of age, but we are glad of that, and do our homage" (Dyer 1910, 4).

Much of the antiques craze after World War I reflected an attempt to rescue America's country past as industrialization and urbanization appeared to cover over the landscape. The fondness in the antiques market for colonial New England material also suggested a nativist taste in opposition to new immigrant cultures coming into the country, mostly from eastern and southern Europe. Colonial antiques promoted during the period primarily comprised domestic furnishings, china, implements, and decorative items. The antique spoke of a domestic American past, rugged in its texture, conveying harmony and New England purity and restraint (Stillinger 1980; Davidson 1970). The antique gave the modern interior an image of the domestic and domesticated past, a unified middle-class Americanized past. The prestigious Metropolitan Museum of Art supported this view with the opening in 1924 of the American Wing, an exhibition of decorative arts. From the exhibition came the book *The Homes of Our Ancestors,* which bemoaned the disturbance by southern and eastern European immigrants of an American sense of self growing out of the cradle of New England homes. Repeatedly calling the refined style of domestic tranquility in America's colonial settlement a gloried "tradition," indeed America's true heritage, the curators announced that the museum's display of colonial New England furnishing was meant to offset intrusions of immigrant taste. They proclaimed, "Much of the America of to-day has lost sight of its traditions. Their stage settings have largely passed away, along with the actors. Many of our people are not cognizant of our traditions and the principles for which our fathers struggled and died. The tremendous changes in the character of our nation, and the influx of foreign ideas utterly at variance with those held by the men who gave us the Republic, threaten and, unless checked, may shake its foundations. Any study of the American Wing cannot fail to revive those memories, for here for the first time is a comprehensive, realistic setting for the traditions so dear to us and so invaluable in the Americanization of many of our people, to whom much of history is little known" (Halsey and Tower 1924, xxii).

As the curators of the American Wing acknowledged, it seemed to be a stretch to label furnishings once part of the antiques market as art. While exuding noble qualities of self-control, stability, and refinement, English colonial domestic furnishings appeared embarrassingly dull, devoid of color and design, especially in contrast to boisterous new immigrant traditions. To compensate for the "dullness" of New England antiques, their patrons claimed that furnishings and decorations collected as antiques were paintings, sculpture, and decorative arts. They were deserving of praise for their American authenticity, if not their vibrancy (see Wolfe 1997).

Antiquity and modernity came together in art at the *International Exhibition of Modern Art,* better known today as "The Armory Show" of 1913. The show was international in scope but critics especially heralded the arrival of American modernism. Works by artists such as Bernard Karfiol, John Sloan, and Stuart Davis were on display with Picasso and Kandinsky. The art was modern and yet it was primitive. Critic W. D. MacColl commented that the modern painters "achieve the first place by the force of a pure native power that is in them." He observed that in showing the "progress of art" out of primitive power, the modernists had triumphed over "machinery" and continued a "classic tradition" (MacColl [1913]

1970, 179, 181). Other critics were less generous. Art critic Royal Cortissoz writing in the New York *Tribune* and *Century* equated modern art with the invidious influences of immigration, which introduced alien elements shaking the foundation of the nation (Cortissoz [1913] 1970).

Some American modernists replied that their designs had roots in the American soil. They were inspired by American primitives such as the "naive" painting and sculpture of the eighteenth century that showed abstraction of line, disregard for perspective, and boldness in color. "Modernism" called attention to the blandness of machine-built modernity. It sought roots and inspiration in the reality of the authentic primitive. Charles Messer Stow, writing in the *Antiquarian* in 1927 on "Primitive Art in America," reported, "Indeed, certain of the ultra-modern painters, whose work now and then comes to the attention of bewildered lookers, confide that they are endeavoring to return to the primitive in their art" (Stow 1927). An exhibition at the Whitney Studio Club in 1924 arranged by painter Henry Schnackenberg showed some of the primitives and their relation to modernism. There were many paintings and watercolors, pieces of pewter, woodcarvings, a brass bootjack, and a plaster cat. Stow wrote of the show, "In the midst of a sophisticated existence it is refreshing to turn to something that totally lacks sophistication. And these early paintings give that refreshment. Seeing them is like getting all at once a new outlook, a new viewpoint, a new approach to the world. By contrast their realism seems most attractive to us, even though it be crude" (Stow 1927). Wealthy New Yorkers, he observed, were impressed, and they drew connections of their present condition to that of the paintings. "They may truly be said to have retained their 'primitive' feeling. Many of them are products of that time of stress of the early nineteenth century, that time when the people of the new nation were forced, whether they like it or not, to take one of the forward steps in civilization" (Stow 1927).

Modern artists such as Robert Laurent and Bernard Karfiol amassed substantial collections of nineteenth century paintings and sculpture of anonymous itinerants and amateur artists from antiques shops. The connection among the objects they selected was the aesthetic of primitive line and color. This connection brought together a dominant native aesthetic overriding foreign or subcultural influence. As galleries took notice of the commodification of the "naive" aesthetic in the Museum of Modern Art and Newark Museum, they displayed objects formerly assigned to the antiques market as saleable art. Folk became a commercial term to separate a commodity from the fine arts above and antiques below. It was an art that challenged the assumptions of art schools and epicurean control of taste, yet it supported the system by using the fine arts as the standard of judgment. Because the collection of these objects grew out of a fine arts view, painting and sculpture were emphasized rather than the craft and ornament of the anthropological concern for use and the subculture from which the object came. Assembled together, the objects became "Americana," standing intuitively for a lost bucolic American vintage, the art collectors claimed. The objects played up the commonality of America's predominantly small-town, white Anglo-Saxon Protestant past, and while patronizing ethnic and racial contributions, underscored the bourgeois New England or Tidewater roots of the newly dubbed folk imagery. The modernists, according to historian Jackson Lears, with their premodern *objets d'art* created "a surrogate religion of taste well suited to a secular culture of consumption" (Lears 1981, 192).

Modernist artists during the 1920s supported the categorization of folk art in the terms of highly valued, and consumable, fine arts. By using "folk," modernists added an emotional quality to the work. Seeking tradition for a break with the past, modernist sculptors such as Elie Nadelman constructed an art of the abstract based on so-called American folk art. Painters as well as sculptors admired the boldness of design, the removal of boundaries and restrictions, that characterized cultures able to express their inner feelings. American weathervanes and decoys used as wall decorations provided studies of American "primitives" in abstract form. Artists placed the objects on a wall or pedestal and noted that their lines and colors could be compared to the new abstract art.

It was important for the modernists to draw out the *creation* rather than the *creativity* of folk art. In this way, art could still be based on value and judgment rather than culture. The art world affirmed that art was an act of creation; it came into being where there was nothing before. It expressed the excitement, the genius, of Biblical creation (Mason 1988). During the 1920s, however, a new word mirroring "relativity," came into use. "Creativity," philosopher Alfred North Whitehead argued, emerges from tension in a plurality of forces, not from unity; creativity arises from everyday struggle with the past and present, with self and other (Kristeller 1983; Bronner 1992b). Thus anthropologist Franz Boas, a German immigrant to the United States and honorary chairman of the National Committee on Folk Arts as part of the International Commission on Folk Arts, drew notice by hailing primitive art not as creation, but as creativity fundamental to human existence. All humans, he argued, share a basic human impulse to perfect form coming from the life of people as part of their everyday traditions (Boas [1927] 1955).[3] In contrast to this idea of tradition incorporating relativity and creativity, tradition in a nativist mode needed to be defined according to America's founding by New England Protestants and away from new immigrant groups. Those things worthy of consumption became tied to the nationalistic display of domestic production from the colonial period.

The boom of colonial Americana drew front-page attention from the *Saturday Review* in July 1926. The article led with the announcement, "The American Past has become a national industry." It continued, "There are almost as many 'antique' signs in Connecticut as gas stations, and it is impossible to guess at the millions which have been spent in refurnishing ornate Louis XIV houses and apartments with plain but far more costly American pine and maple." The cause, the *Review*'s editor Henry Seidel Canby declared, "is a change in the country itself." He failed to give specifics of the change but summarized the feeling by saying, "An era ended in the decade that included the war, so that 1910 seems more archaic to our children than did 1870 to us." The celebration of Americana projected into the complex twentieth century the desired stable image of nineteenth-century "Americanization," Canby opined. Thus "vanity and an acuter sense of our history as a great common people are partly responsible for the vogue of Americana" (Canby 1926, 913, 916). To underscore the theme, the front page was balanced with an article on "American Folk-Lore" by Ernest Sutherland Bates. "One of the few indubitably good results of our recent patriotic movement," he observed, has been the increased interest in days "'when America was young'—twenty, fifty, or one hundred years ago, according to locality. We have begun to realize ... that we are just emerging from a most romantic and picturesque phase, rich in many of the raw materials of art" (Bates 1926, 913-14).

Although the gallery meaning of folk grew out of nativist and modernist forces of the period, it was given sanction by an attachment, as is so often the case with taste movements, to an intellectual figurehead—Holger Cahill. On staff at the Newark Museum, Holger Cahill had been exposed to the presentation of European peasant arts and showed an interest in what he thought might be an analogous nationalistic collection for America put together by the modernists (Vlach 1985b). Cahill was born in Iceland in 1887 and grew up in North Dakota and Manitoba, Canada. He came to New York City in 1905 and worked as a journalist and studied art history at Columbia University. Shortly before assuming curatorial duties at the Newark Museum in 1922, Cahill visited Sweden and was inspired by the outdoor folk museum Skansen, with its peasant arts, in Stockholm. He toured other folk museums in central Europe and reported his admiration for the Norwegian national museum Nordiska Museet. Upon his return to the United States he saw a connection between the Scandinavian exhibition of peasant folk arts and American antiques when he visited an artists' retreat in Ogunquit, Maine, founded by artist Hamilton Easter Field. Field had decorated the fishing shacks turned into studios with local curios, including decoys and weather vanes. The objects were often used as inspiration for the artists' paintings and sculptures. According to John Vlach, the artists "were fascinated when they discovered that there was 'primitive' art to be found in their own backyards. Furthermore, they were delighted that their modern abstractions could relate them not to exotic art from Africa or Mexico but to art from their native or adopted soil" (Vlach 1985b, 151).

In the early 1930s Cahill produced the exhibitions that set the fine art rhetoric for generations to come. He first produced a show in 1930 on *American Primitives*, which he subtitled *An Exhibit of the Painting of Nineteenth-Century Folk Artists*, followed a year later by one on *American Folk Sculpture*. The most significant exhibition came in 1932 at the Museum of Modern Art, entitled *American Folk Art: The Art of the Common Man in America, 1750–1900*. Cahill had visited the collection of

Art of the Common Man exhibition, 1932, directed by Holger Cahill and featuring objects from the collection of Abby Aldrich Rockefeller, as installed at the Rhode Island School of Design. (Abby Aldrich Rockefeller Folk Art Center)

modernist Robert Laurent with gallery owner Edith Halpert, and, with contributions of sculptor Elie Nadelman and collectors Abby Aldrich Rockefeller and Isabel Wilde, he created a gallery view of objects as art. For the folk sculpture show he included cigar store Indians, decoys, weathervanes, ship figureheads, and stove plates. He wrote in his introduction to the catalogue: "In grouping together these carven images which have previously been little known or studied other than for their interest as pleasant mementos of the past, the exhibit offers testimony that there has always existed in this country a robust native talent for sculpture, which has been capable of expressing itself spontaneously and with characteristics of its own" (Cahill 1931b).

Cahill legitimized folk art with his exhibition at the Museum of Modern Art in New York City. He resolutely announced,

> This exhibition represents the unconventional side of the American tradition in the fine arts. The pictures and sculptures in it are the work of craftsmen and amateurs of the eighteenth and nineteenth centuries who supplied a popular demand for art.... It is a varied art, influenced from diverse sources, often frankly derivative, often fresh and original, and at its best an honest and straightforward expression of the spirit of a people.

> This work gives a living quality to the story of American beginnings in the arts, and is a chapter, intimate and quaint, in the social history of the country. (Cahill 1932, 3)

Although Cahill hedged some in the catalogue about what to call the material—considering provincial, primitive, and popular—he settled on folk art because he favored continuity with European national traditions. But in its American version, since peasants were absent, Cahill emphasized the abstract and "quaint" appearance of small-town artisans and unschooled artists. The qualities that marked gallery collecting for years are evident in his introduction and choice of objects. They constitute paintings and sculpture showing artistic abstraction—a boldness or crudity of line and color—produced by town artisans and homemakers and used by merchants of a rising middle class. In Cahill's words, "The quality of American folk art which first strikes the observer is quaintness" (Cahill 1932, 17). Further, it offered authenticity to the claim for a national American tradition, as Cahill indicated when he concluded his introduction to the Museum of Modern Art exhibition, "Their art mirrors the sense and the sentiment of a community, and is an authentic expression of American experience" (Cahill 1932, 28).

Invoking European Romantic Nationalism reminiscent of the Brothers Grimm, Cahill suggested that American folk art, as he recast it, "compares favorably with the folk arts of Europe. It is as rich as any, as fresh, as original, and as full of the naive and honest expression of the spirit of the people." But rather than based on folk as an adjective for learned tradition, this art was based on folk as a noun referring to the common "folks," especially those in an "increasingly affluent and status-conscious middle class" (Cahill 1931a, 39). The folk art he found to represent this class often derived from the early nineteenth-century and reflected the heritage of English Northeast colonial settlement.

Although Cahill referred to the middle-class connection to his selection of folk art, "common man" sounded more democratic, more in keeping with the myth of America as a classless society, and was a phrase frequently used in New Deal rhetoric of the 1930s. Folk art, Cahill wrote, was the "expression of the common people, made by them and intended for their use and enjoyment. It is not the expression of professional artists made for a small cultured class, and it has little to do with the fashionable art of its period." "Common people" compensated for the absence of a recognizable peasant class in America that could be romanticized. Necessarily vague as a social category, "commonness" appeared to be defined by what it was not—a patron elite or professional artist class known in New York's art world. Realizing the vagueness of folk art in terms of commonness, Cahill turned the defining process around and used the exhibition to establish a definition. He explained folk art "as it is defined by the objects in this exhibition, is the work of people with little book learning in art techniques, and no academic training" (Cahill 1932, 6). The objects are part of a dichotomy, between academic and nonacademic, educated and non-educated, and by extension, between upper and lower classes. In effect, Cahill suggested that upper-class collectors use a definition based on their taste to select appropriate objects and then allow the objects to establish a folk art canon. Despite his circular reasoning, Cahill's definition, as Beatrix Rumford, former director of the Abby Aldrich Rockefeller Folk Art Collection at Williamsburg, noted in 1980, "is still being quoted, and curators and collectors continue to regard the 1932 catalogue as an indispensable reference" (Rumford 1980).

With fine arts categories of painting, sculpture, and decorative arts as references in his exhibitions, Cahill emphasized appreciation of folk art away from its cultural context. The placement of the large objects allowed visitors to view them at a distance to observe their overall form. Cahill presented paintings, sculpture, and decorative arts as surfaces, celebrated for their freshness and originality. He encouraged quiet viewing of individual images apart from one another in the subdued exhibition interiors. His galleries offered a vision of the "creation" of America that challenged the "creativity" promoted by Eaton, whose exhibitions featured the intricacy of craftswork and thus encouraged viewers to examine the artifacts at close range while surrounded by references to the makers' communities.

A pattern among exhibitions in the United States emerged pitting Eaton's culturally diverse view of America against Cahill's unified aesthetic depiction. Eaton offered an image of a changing, adapting social mix in a country gaining strength from immigrant traditions and contributions of many cultural groups. Eaton's culturally diverse view drew metaphors from the new physics of relativity and the ethnology of culture in speaking of the dynamics of American plural cultures. Cahill's rhetoric came from art history tied to national history. It offered a view of a unified national tradition emerging from the background of early European settlement. It was a tradition of a common culture of middle-class vernacular characterized by free individual expression and nationalistic loyalty.

"Circles" and "Treasures" of Folk Art

A striking juxtaposition of the two rival social visions revealed in folk art was the staging of exhibitions in Minneapolis in 1989. While the two exhibitions simultaneously used the term "folk art" to present American traditions, they shared little else in common. Walking through the two galleries, one would hardly have known that they contained depictions of the same subject. Yet they shared a concern for the home-grown symbols that genuinely characterize America. In a heartland city more than a half-century after Cahill's and Eaton's exhibitions, the conflicts over defining America's tradition and its future became vividly apparent.

Treasures of American Folk Art from the Abby Aldrich Rockefeller Folk Art Center, installed at the Minneapolis Institute of Arts, presented portraiture, sculpture, and decoration drawn mostly from America's preindustrial heritage. The curators selected the works of artists "neither especially poor nor extremely rich but simply the average citizens of America—'the common man.'" The result, the curators claimed, was "a fresh insight into the American past," exposing "both particular and general social and cultural preferences" (Rumford and Weekley 1989, 18). The Americans portrayed in this exhibition had much in common, as producers and consumers, participating in a unified national tradition.

Unlike the historical unity of the *Treasures* show, *Circles of Tradition: Folk Arts in Minnesota*, installed at the University of Minnesota Art Museum (renamed the Frederick R. Weisman Art Museum at the University of Minnesota in 1993), offered works, mostly emerging from craft traditions, representing a variety of communities and traditional arts active in a single state. "Minnesota has the reputation of being a homogeneous enclave of Scandinavian Americans," the museum's director wrote, and "we hoped that a survey would reveal much more diversity.... And, after realizing the diversity of the traditional arts in Minnesota, we believed that the state *could* serve as a microcosm for developing new ways of looking at the traditional arts that were valid generally" (King 1989, viii). The Americans in this exhibition were a varied ethnic lot and the settings in which they work were diverse.

In their objectification of American tradition, these displays, distinguished from presentations of fine art, proclaimed the roots, the character, of the nation in its everyday customs and beliefs. Agreement on the nature of this tradition has been lacking, however, particularly in this century. For more than seventy years the conflict of American traditions that arose after a giant wave of immigration brought into question America's historical unity has been especially evident in folk art exhibitions. Although the duality of exhibitions I focus on exists in many other cities, Minneapolis is especially appropriate because of its simultaneous reach to mixed audiences including academic and public organizations, art and folklife societies, and ethnic and civic groups. Earlier in this century, Minneapolis was home to Holger Cahill, inspiration for the "common man" approach in the *Treasures* show, and also headquarters for the Folk Arts Foundation of America, devoted to preserving and presenting the "diverse elements in our national life." Recognizing the contrasting approaches to American folk art, the University of Minnesota Gallery and the Center for the Study of Minnesota Folklife in 1980 sponsored a "Midwestern Conference on Folk Arts and Museums" in St. Paul to bring squabbling sides together for discussion. As with other such attempts at conciliation, little headway toward agreement was made at this conference (*Abstracts* 1981).

My interest in this analysis of the two exhibitions in Minneapolis is in the underlying strategies and structures American folk art exhibitions use for their representations of traditions and what they imply ideologically when they do. I am asking about the significance of the argument over the objects properly constituting folk art not as a definitional problem but a rhetorical one related to social views. The argument rages, I believe, because implicitly it refers to one's very conceptions of America's past and of present social conditions. With a lack of agreement on national tradition, folk art has persistently been a tool of persuasion to win over the public to a view of America as either culturally diverse or historically unified. The popularity of folk art exhibitions in this country, then, attests to the struggle to visibly define an American tradition with consolidating symbols.

Why is there this inextricable tie between folk art and national tradition? According to European Romantic philosophers of the eighteenth and nineteenth centuries, in folk art lay the spirit and soul, the genius—indeed the unity of a people. These philosophers observed that in contrast to the division of countries under monarchies and aristocracies, a division of nations by culture should emerge. Folk arts expressing the life of the mass of ordinary people, especially peasants, reflected the claims of a group's cultural integrity and, hence, nationhood. The political use of folk arts in Europe became enough of an issue after World War I that the League of Nations set up the International Commission on Folk Arts. Its preamble declared: "Throughout the civilized world it is now being recognized that in the folk arts lies a regenerative and stabilizing influence for contemporary life and art; that each country has in its folk arts an asset of incalculable value; and that the time has come to assemble and record these folk arts before they perish at their source and to make them available for study and use" (*A Folk Arts Service*; see also Olrik 1934).[4]

In the United States the link of folk art with national identity has been dramatically put on display in countless exhibitions, particularly since America's bicentennial (see Teske 1988; Dewhurst and MacDowell 1984). The special conditions of the United States, however, lent confusion to the application of folk arts according to European Romanticism. Unlike the clear connection to peasant work and communally shared traditions in Europe, folk arts in American exhibitions variously expressed the grass-roots strength of the nation or the distinctiveness of groups within it. Folk arts also variously reflected American tradition as self-taught or communally shared.

Circles of Tradition was the result of a field survey by folklorist Willard Moore, who covered over fifteen thousand miles of Minnesota to document living artists engaging in traditional activities. The use of "folk arts" in the subtitle, the touring of the exhibition to towns throughout the state, and the attention in the book accompanying the exhibition to music, dress, storytelling, holiday customs, and foodways emphasized that these activities are part of community life. Moore organized his material, his artifactual "texts," similar to narrative folklore texts, into the cultural contexts of first, "work, play, and survival in a northern land," second, "spiritual community," third, "adjustment to change," and fourth, "continuity and variation." Much as narrators express their culture through folktale texts and adjust their tales in response to immediate community and environmental influences or "contexts," so folk artists construct artifacts that capture an intimate social relationship.

Visitors to the *Circles* show encountered the contexts as groupings of objects, photographs, and narratives within several rooms. The objects represented

Norwegian-style Cedar Fan, made by Walter Torfin, 1985, Duluth, Minnesota, from the exhibition *Circles of Tradition: Folk Arts in Minnesota.* In the exhibition, this carving using a traditional form was labeled a "perceived tradition." It might have been "integrated" in another context, but the craft was not totally integrated into Torfin's community setting. (Frederick R. Weisman Art Museum at the University of Minnesota)

different kinds of traditions or "circles of traditions." The first rooms the visitor entered constituted "integrated" traditions, followed by "perceived" and "celebrated" traditions. In an accompanying exhibition brochure, Moore presented a conceptual model of the contexts transecting "tradition" as divided into three concentric circles. His choice of the circle is rhetorically significant, since it is a traditional symbol of magic and community. The inner and most traditional circle is "integrated": "within it lie the art forms, techniques, materials, and symbolic meanings that are most fully interwoven with the rest of community life." Here one found jars of canned vegetables, Ukrainian Easter baskets, and Laotian-American ceremonial dress. Here people share their arts with one another in community; they pass on tradition by face-to-face interaction and learning. The middle circle represents "perceived traditions." These are traditions often thought of as authentic, when in fact they have changed over time. Twentieth-century

Rosemaled Bowl, made by Judith Nelson, 1988, Minneapolis, Minnesota, from the exhibition *Circles of Tradition: Folk Arts in Minnesota.* Although this bowl was included under "perceived traditions" in the exhibition because its maker had a connection to Norwegian tradition, other examples of a rosemaling revival were placed under "celebrated traditions" because their makers were not connected to ethnic learning traditions or community contexts. (Frederick R. Weisman Art Museum at the University of Minnesota)

Polish-American *wycinanki* (colorful designs from papercuts), for example, bear a diminished resemblance in form, technique, or function to the original European practice. The outermost circle contains "celebrated traditions," which include the work of artists who for personal and aesthetic reasons choose to create objects not necessarily related to their own heritage or social roles. Here one found yard constructions and rosemaled bowls.

Of the three "circles of tradition" in the exhibition, the integrated tradition arguably has a preeminent status. It celebrates people making connections to the land and to one another. The strength of community over the individual and nation predominates in the integrated tradition. Yet taken together, the products of all the circles form a brightly colored quilt of the people of Minnesota. Even the poster for the exhibition illustrated variety in traditional arts: it juxtaposed objects such as painted fish decoys, Scandinavian carved fans, and Ukrainian Easter eggs on a textured family quilt. All the traditions vividly displayed regional and ethnic

Section on "Work, Play, and Survival in a Northern Land" within the "integrated traditions" circle at the exhibition *Circles of Tradition: Folk Arts in Minnesota* installed at the University of Minnesota Art Museum (now the Frederick R. Weisman Art Museum). Hand-crafted objects such as the Finnish kick sled (*Potkukelkka*), Norwegian skis, and Latvian mittens are surrounded by photographs emphasizing the environmental and cultural contexts that encourage the adaptation of these functional folk traditions to northern Minnesota everyday life. (Frederick R. Weisman Art Museum at the University of Minnesota)

expression persisting and adapting to everyday contexts of work, play, and custom. Wall panels showed photographs of objects being made and explained customs surrounding the objects. The objects, such as Laotian rice cakes in banana leaves, Latvian mittens, and Jewish marriage contracts lacked great visual impact by themselves, but with accompanying photographs of makers and their environments, the objects gained stature as community expression. They portrayed a sense of sharing, a balance of people and place. A dynamic plurality of customs and peoples appears to be the natural—and moral—order of life.

Treasures of American Folk Art displayed the "best" objects from the collections of the Abby Aldrich Rockefeller Folk Art Center in Williamsburg. As the preface of the accompanying book stated, the *Treasures* show celebrated Rockefeller's tasteful eye and generous pocketbook for American folk art. The title *Treasures* conveyed a sense of value attached to individual objects, and the installation stressed fine art, rather than cultural categories. Its abundant use of pedestals and rectangular lines emphasized artifice and technological control. Most of the objects were forms of painting and sculpture with scanty labels—a tactic that directed viewers' attention to form rather than context. Communities were not shown as much as outstanding individuals who created works notable for their form and color. In contrast to Moore's living traditions drawn from sometimes struggling classes, the *Treasures* show, as the narrative of Beatrix Rumford and Carolyn Weekley emphasized, featured "our middle-class American ancestors." Progress in the form of "burgeoning industrialization, improved road and canal systems, westward expansion and development," they announced, comprised "factors that contributed to the common man's prosperity" and "resulted in a new sense of individual and national identity," factors evident in folk art (Rumford and Weekley 1989, 8, 18).

The difference between the two exhibitions *Circles* and *Treasures* became magnified in the books published to accompany them. *Treasures* was an oversize book with an appearance suggesting a framable work of art. It was image-laden and short on text. In the book's very design, one appreciated the emphasis on decorative purpose and communication through images established in Cahill's exhibitions. *Circles* was of standard paper size and emphasized text. Several chapters explained the objects' contexts and featured ethnographic photographs. *Circles* encouraged reading, questioning, and even exploration, while *Treasures* invited aesthetic appreciation, and maybe consumption.

The cover of *Treasures* showed a painting of an innocent looking, well-dressed blond boy holding a finch in a flowery interior (entitled *Boy with Finch*, attributed to John Brewster, Jr., New England or New York State, ca. 1800). The book's first section contained similar paintings. These portraits, including the famous *Baby in Red Chair*, celebrated as an "endearing image," are among the "favorites" of visitors to the Folk Art Center, according to Rumford and Weekley. The connection of the approach in the *Treasures* show to Cahill's exhibitions can be seen in the emphasis made on portraits. Portraits were the first and the largest group of images put forward by Cahill as folk art. (They were conspicuously absent in Eaton's exhibition.) According to Cahill, portraits by a less-than-accomplished hand were folk because they were "quaint"; they commonly lacked a known artist and seemed refreshing in their depiction of plain features.

Landscapes and townscapes were also portrayed plainly. In the *Treasures* show, *Peaceable Kingdom* by Edward Hicks was a central image conveying harmony and pastoralism in the imagined unity of a new nation. Hicks's romanticization of William Penn's treaty with the Indians on the Philadelphia riverside under a majestic elm is another frequently exhibited expression of American harmony. The Hicks rendition of the legendary seventeenth-century event is actually an adaptation of a Benjamin West painting of 1771, which is typically included in the fine arts canon. Hicks probably admired Penn's Quaker principles of trust and friendship with the Indians amidst God's gifts of a sublime American landscape, and the image has been used subsequently and most frequently in advertising and politics to connote fair dealing and social unity (Showalter 1996; Kashatus 1996). Rumford and Weekley called Hicks "the most celebrated of America's folk painters of religious

Unidentified artist, *Baby in Red Chair,* possibly Pennsylvania, c.
1810–1830, oil on canvas, from the exhibition *Treasures of American Folk
Art from the Abby Aldrich Rockefeller Folk Art Center.* This "endearing
image," according to the curators, "is among the favorites" of visitors to
AARFAC. Indeed, it is the opening image to the preface of the catalog
accompanying the exhibition and thus conveys the characteristics of
"quaintness," "wholesomeness," and "innocence" associated with American
folk art generally. The authors' interpretation of the painting emphasizes
aesthetic form: "The baby's legs are convincingly foreshortened, but the
chair is not, providing an interesting pattern of softly colored forms moving in and out of space." (Abby Aldrich Rockefeller Folk Art Center)

Edward Hicks, *Peaceable Kingdom*, Bucks County, Pennsylvania, 1832–1834, oil on canvas, from the exhibition *Treasures of American Folk Art from the Abby Aldrich Rockefeller Folk Art Center.* Iconic images by Edward Hicks connect this exhibition to Holger Cahill's of the 1930s. Cahill considered Hicks an American Rousseau and called his landscapes forerunners of the Hudson River School. The authors of the *Treasures* catalog praise Hicks as "one of the most familiar and beloved folk artists." (Abby Aldrich Rockefeller Folk Art Center)

pictures," and "by the early twentieth century, one of the most familiar and beloved folk artists" (Rumford and Weekley 1989, 90–93).

Hicks's work is another link between Cahill's show in 1932 and the *Treasures* exhibition. Cahill hailed Hicks as "an American Rousseau," forerunner to painters of the Hudson River School (Cahill 1932, 15–16). Created in Philadelphia, the same city highlighted as diverse by Allen Eaton in the frontispiece to *Immigrant Gifts*, Hicks's expression of Quaker and regional associations alongside Statue of Liberty weather vanes and Victorian mourning pictures become American melting pot perspective (see Vlach 1988, 121–42). Williamsburg's recontextualization of Hicks as an American image of peaceful unity is paralleled in other frequently exhibited collections such as those of Meyer and Vivian Potamkin. During the Vietnam War, the Potamkins collected and exhibited the Hicks images to convey a contemporary "message of peace" during the divisive conflict on the home front.[5] Vivian Potamkin explained to reporters, and in the catalogue of the show, that she was especially drawn to the feature of William Penn settling a treaty with the Lenape, which Hicks often put in the background of his *Peaceable Kingdom* versions (Cullen 1996). She considered the scene of two cultures existing in harmony as a symbol of peace, although the curator of the Potamkin exhibition worried about possible criticism of the destruction of Native American culture some visitors may view in the pictures (Cullen 1996, E8). The opening panel of the exhibition nonetheless declared, "Within everyone lies a desire for peace. Art collectors Meyer and Vivian Potamkin found an expression of that quest for harmony amid the brushstrokes of a folk art painting." A whole room behind the panel was devoted to a wall mural of a Vietnam battle scene with Hicks's *Penn's Treaty* enshrined under glass below. Despite the contextualization of Hicks's painting for its peaceful image, the artist completed at least six versions of Washington crossing the Delaware in celebration of the Revolutionary War, but these works rarely make it into folk art shows (see Kammen 1978, 82).

The landscapes and portraits central in Cahill's folk art imagery support the Peaceable Kingdom theme. Paintings such as Charles Hoffmann's depiction of a Pennsylvania-German community become not regional or ethnic expressions but constructions of harmonious American landscapes. It is no wonder that Edward Hicks is so celebrated in folk art: his farm scenes conjure the notions of natural creation, proprietorship, and the unique character of the American scene. The curators of *Treasures* hung Pennsylvania-German fraktur and *Scherenschnitte* (scissors-cutting) as aesthetic creations rather than as expressions of cultural creativity or tradition. Pennsylvania-German fraktur, such as the birth and baptismal certificate by Friedrich Bandel, lost its cultural connection but gained a relation of form when placed next to the Anglo-American birth record from New England for Mary E. Wheelock. Fraktur emphasizing religious texts in dialect among the Pennsylvania Germans, documenting cultural rites of passage and ordinarily kept hidden in dower chests, were framed and displayed like decorative pictures.

In a revealing photograph in Rumford and Weekley's book, two painted boxes from New England were set on top of a painted Pennsylvania-German dower chest. Viewed together, they appeared to be similar shapes, given character by color and line, rather than by region or group. Their lines remained constant as if put into the world by creation. The religious and the secular blended; cultural meanings became obscured by form.

The handling of sculpture in the *Treasures* show resembled the presentation of painting in Cahill's exhibitions. Sculpture's surface quality attracted the viewer. Sculpture, like painting, reinforces an American vernacular apart from group tradition; it conveys an American nationalism with sculpted heroes and sovereign eagles. Ship carvings and weather vanes appeared as self-contained creations, apart from their original context. Although many of the sculptures in their original contexts were once intended to signify labor, they now invited aesthetic appreciation in the *Treasures* exhibition. The sculpted human figures formed an American pantheon.

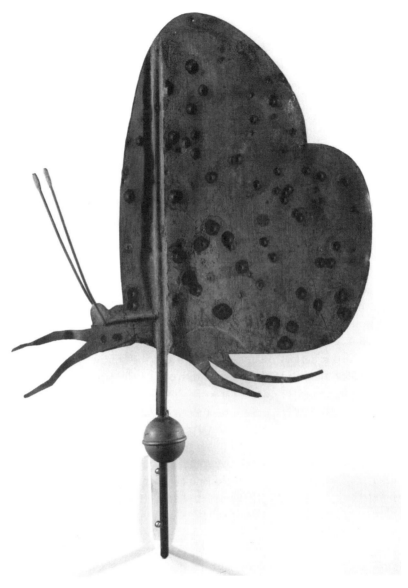

Unidentified maker, *Butterfly*, c. 1850–1875, painted sheet copper, from the exhibition *Treasures of American Folk Art from the Abby Aldrich Rockefeller Folk Art Center*. This weather vane is treated as sculpture when taken off the barn and placed on a pedestal. The dents on the butterfly's wings that seem to give the work an abstract design were caused by people shooting at the vanes to make them spin, a common pastime. (Abby Aldrich Rockefeller Folk Art Center)

Both the *Circles* and *Treasures* shows exhibited quilts as the epitome of folk art, but the character of the selections in each differed sharply. In the *Circles* show, quilts with comparable designs related to intergenerational families or ethnic and community traditions (Old Order Mennonite and African American, for example) received primary attention. Many quilts remained on the beds for which they were intended. In the *Treasures* show, only quilts with unique forms or designs merited display. What qualified quilts as art was not their social connection or cultural creativity, but their text of individualism: the self-referential use of color, line, and arrangement. Quilts as a feminine commodity in shows such as *Treasures* stand above hooked and woven rugs, which are often given secondary importance because of their utilitarian associations. Quilts are bolder in their use of color and design and have persisted as an art world image of the rural American past. Along with painting and sculpture, they also defy regionalization and ethnic association more so than other "arts" such as gravestones and architecture given special attention in folklife scholarship (see Glassie 1968, 1972; Bronner 1989b; Vlach and Bronner 1992).

While shows such as *Treasures* sometimes spawn exhibitions on different regions of America, thematic or celebratory shows of important collections are more common.[6] The images in such events support one another and give the impression of a whole based on artistic creation, but their selectivity is conspicuous. In contrast, shows such as *Circles* emphasize inclusiveness. The former apparently flows from the patron and the latter from the culture. *Treasures* called for a good "eye" for form and color representative of modernism while *Circles* required a more tactile feeling for creators at work.

For more than seventy years the patterns in the two models have seemed irreconcilable, although some recent convergence is evident. *Circles* mounted objects that expressed individual taste even if it relegated them to the outermost circle of tradition. *Treasures* contained twentieth-century material and acknowledged southern African-American collections to augment its earlier collections. It should be pointed out, however, that the move to add black folk art to the art world canon fits more into what Nathan Glazer calls the "southern model" of ethnicity, in which society divides by race, rather than the multiethnic "northern model" apparent in *Circles* (see Glazer 1983, 314–36).[7] In the art world's use of the southern model, nationalism produced by a dominant stock is still appreciable. Yet taking into consideration the challenge of Pennsylvania-German folklife to the national model, the Museum of American Folk Art installed an exhibition of traditional Pennsylvania-German barn decorations, and folklorists have produced more studies of individual and even idiosyncratic artists (Yoder and Graves 1989; Jones 1989; Ferris 1982; Marshall 1983). Although common ground has opened in the consideration of creativity and tradition together in human practice, divisions remain strong.

Images of folk art express the changes and conflicts of both the past and present "American Kingdom"—peaceable or turbulent. After the ethnic transformation of

American society during the late nineteenth century, classical patriotic symbols appeared convincing (see Kammen 1991; Bodnar 1992; Glassberg 1990). When countries of Europe reinforced their nationhood by celebrating unified folk traditions, America—often called a "nation of nations"—could barely boast a sense of its own self. Questions arose whether it possessed an "American" folk tradition at all (see Dorson 1971a, 94–107; Kammen 1991, 407–43), and partly in response an American studies movement arose to examine the national unity of American art, literature, and history (see Dorson 1976a, 1971a, 78–93; Wise 1979, 293–337, esp. 331–35).

In America the dispute over folk art persists as a representation of tension between national and folk cultures and their respective backgrounds in class and ethnicity. The nationalistic *Treasures* exhibition has commanded more publicity and prestige than the folkloristic *Circles* show. Since America's sesquicentennial the organization, wealth, and power in the art world behind *Treasures* resulted in the "triumph," as one prominent folk art museum director called it, of new images for the twentieth century based on those of stability in early nineteenth-century life (L. Jones 1982, 147–66). *Peaceable Kingdom* and *Baby in Red Chair* are more than "favorites" of the Abby Aldrich Rockefeller Folk Art Center; they have become popular images offering a stabilizing middle-class consensus as national tradition. This appeal has been challenged during the 1980s and 1990s by multicultural images that highlight the creative labor of diverse ethnic groups (see Teske 1994; Siporin 1992; Glassie 1989; Noyes 1989; McClain 1988).

Whether triggered by national anniversaries, new immigrant waves, demands for collective rights, major communication transformations, or anticipation of entering a new century, folk art during the twentieth century repeatedly became a primary reference in a contested discourse over how life was—and will be—lived. Especially since America's bicentennial of independence, communal folk art images have been more apparent, although they typically have emerged from organizations outside of institutional power (such as cultural agencies, learned societies, and community groups). From such organizations during the 1990s, traditional textiles, baskets, and ceramics representing labor and community have challenged the prevailing imagery of painting and sculpture (see Vlach 1988, 1991b; Glassie 1992). In 1991, for example, the *Journal of American Folklore* adopted a new cover format featuring an African-American basket, an English-American quilt design, and a southern face jug.

Exhibitions such as *Treasures* with their ideology of historical unity appear aesthetically impressive, although not as intellectually convincing as ethnographic shows such as *Circles*. One conclusion, then, is that the approach of *Circles* bears merit because it is more intellectually defensible than *Treasures*, but this judgment sidesteps the issue of social demands for the different approaches. Despite years of criticism for contrivance of a national spirit, aesthetically impressive presentations such as *Treasures* remain emotionally persuasive for many viewers. Although both approaches are exaggerated social visions, Americans are not moving quickly toward resolving this conflict—even when confronted with simultaneous, polarized exhibitions such as these two in Minneapolis. Nor are they likely to do so. American curators and scholars have invested the term "folk art" with power as a keyword for society, or as one art world editor offered, a "juicy term" not likely to be given up (Jules Laffal, editor of *Folk Art Finder*, quoted in Benedetti 1987, 6). From it is squeezed an undeniable authenticity, the "right stuff" of America. Socially, it points to the impossibility and simultaneously the necessity to characterize the American "people," or their commonality. In its American version, the rhetoric of folk art grew with a strong emotional core exhorting the very spirit of the nation's contested traditions.

ART AND THE ELEVATION OF TRADITION

There is a significant sense in which folk art and folklore are joined by tradition in a discourse of culture. Influenced by the use of *folk art* to elevate tradition into a spiritual power, extensions of art beyond physical things to verbal expressions became apparent in scholarly discourse, especially after World War II. But when they did, it led to behavioral conceptions of American identity that challenged the existing debate in folk art between diversity and unity. Folk art clasped folklore to form a view of tradition operating universally among individuals to imbue modern life with meaning. Folk art as commentary on the virtue of culture became a strategy to explain the persistence of folklore in widening, transnational mass culture. In devising a behavioral model of folk art, proponents inspired a move from the gallery to the festival to display the celebration of tradition in action.

Festival as a strategy of displaying folk art encouraged performances and designations of participants as "folk artists." It brought dance, music, and drama under the tent of folk arts that enriched the presumed drabness of modern life. Having a festival was celebratory, and bringing different types of performances together under the heading of festival fostered a positive response to the range of tradition. As the folk art exhibitions of the 1930s variously established the boundaries of material as part of American tradition, so the burgeoning festivals at the same time defined varied songs, dances, and crafts as cut from the same cloth of tradition. The organized events designed to present traditions became repeatable, "annual" traditions unto themselves. Traditional festivals such as Mardi Gras or Fiesta de Santa Fe did not appear to Americans to be as numerous in their land as in Europe, and the twentieth-century construction of festivals of folk arts appealed to a sense of locality and ethnicity suggested by the older sense of the folk festival. With roots in the Appalachian handicrafts revival and immigrant arts expositions of the early twentieth century that so inspired Allen Eaton, the festivals mushroomed during the 1930s as music and dance concerts in celebration of the "common man." A lull in their development occurred during World War II because of travel restrictions and war conditions. After the war, the folklife festival that demonstrated arts and crafts of regional-ethnic groups burst on the American scene. The National Endowment for the Arts encouraged the growth of festivals after the 1960s and, with the support of state "folk arts coordinators," fostered promotion of festivals as grand displays of folk artists and their plural communities. They were usually booster events combining entertainment and education and meant to invigorate communities as well as build support for folk arts.

The move from folklore to folk arts to represent the elevation of tradition in modern life owes much to Martha Warren Beckwith's campaign to connect the professional folklorist to issues of art during the 1920s. Unlike the anthropologist who sought out primitive groups of remote cultures or the literary scholar who dealt with verbal texts of civilization, the folklorist was a new hybrid who interpreted artful expressions of traditions within industrialized societies, she insisted (Beckwith 1931b, 5-8). The task at hand, she underscored in her manual for the field, was to recognize how folklore "develops as a living and social art" (Beckwith 1931b, 66). In 1929, her book *Black Roadways* made the point by culminating in a last chapter entitled "Folk Art." The art of the people she observed was not so much materially crafted as expressed in the stories and rituals they enacted. To show their tie to everyday life, she subtitled her book *A Study of Jamaican Folk Life.*

While the treatment of folklore as art could be demonstrated in scholarship, Beckwith also considered ways it could be shown with integrity to the public. In her manual of folklore, she lauded "the establishment of folk theatres in which the people themselves take an active and creative part," and thought that they had a special role for preserving "in our immigrants a sense of the dignity and beauty of their old national traditions" (Beckwith 1931b, 64). During the 1930s she served on the National Committee on Folk Arts formed in New York City by folk dance promoter Elizabeth Burchenal to bring together rising authorities on material as well as performing arts and consider their proper presentation to the public as a widening range of "folk arts." Beckwith gave her nod to festival as an active display format in two groundbreaking reviews for the *Journal of American Folklore* in 1938. It was startling to have such reviews in a bookish journal, but she insisted that the burgeoning festivals of the day were as important as books for the statements they publicly made on tradition. She touted the value of the National Folk Festival in Washington, D.C., and the Mountain Folk Festival in Berea, Kentucky, in presenting traditions as creative works enriching American life. She underscored the work of the performers in these settings as that of "folk artists" and worried whether the gritty force of tradition properly came through in the unnatural setting of the stage (Beckwith 1938).

The National Folk Festival, founded in 1934, was unusual at the movement's beginning because it was multiethnic. Other festivals such as the Mountain Folk Festival in Berea, Kentucky, or the Mountain Dance and Folk Festival in Asheville, North Carolina, tended to be regionally focused and implied a monocultural environment. The monocultural festivals sought performers who reached fellow residents to boost the esteem and unity of regions and groups marginalized by mass culture. The National presented the diverse range of America with musical performances by American Indians, blacks, French, and Mexicans to reach a country-wide public. Building on its pluralist vision of America, the National also tried to show an occupational range by featuring cowboys, lumberjacks, and sailors (Gillespie 1996). First produced in St. Louis, Missouri, it moved to various sites during the 1930s. It was organized by Sarah Gertrude Knott, who had a background in dramatic performing arts rather than folklore. Despite her independence from scholarship, her energy and vision drew the interest of professional folklorists such as Martha Beckwith. One point of disagreement, however, was Knott's rejection of the term "folklife" as condescending to the artistic merit of the musical performers, while Beckwith insisted on it to signify the integration of art as part of the daily life of multiple groups. Another point of contention was Knott's use of "revival" artists who adapted folk material and whom she contrasted with presumably authentic "survival" performers who had preserved practices through the generations.

Beckwith and most folklorists favored the representation of authentic American tradition with the survival performers. The National attracted others making a connection between folklore study and display such as George Korson, who produced his own popular multiethnic festivals in Pennsylvania during the 1930s in addition to collecting mining lore of various ethnic groups (Gillespie 1980). The shift to the polestar of arts became evident at the National when its sponsoring organization, the National Folk Festival Association, became the National Council for the Traditional Arts (NCTA) in 1976 under the leadership of Joseph Wilson. The Mountain Festival at Berea that Beckwith reviewed also shifted its emphasis from staged music and dance to the wide range of arts, and in 1988 the Commonwealth of Kentucky designated Berea as the "folk arts and crafts capital of Kentucky" (Ramsay 1996). The full-fledged folklife festival that emphasized the integration of folk arts in the life of a community meanwhile took off especially from professional folklorist Alfred Shoemaker's Pennsylvania-Dutch events after World War II.

That art became thrust into displays of tradition in exhibitions and festivals during the 1930s suggests a connection of this trend with changing views of art as experience at that time. In the industrial letdown of the 1930s, social critics stressed human capriciousness over mechanical efficiency. With doubts about the satisfactions of material existence, many critics proposed the compassionate realm of experience as humanity's essence, and saving grace. Art, creativity, and tradition came to the fore to express social objects of experience that sustained people through the worst of times. Social activist Joseph Freeman, for example, declared in 1935, "Art, then, is not the same as action; it is not identical with science; it is distinct from party program. It has its own special function, the grasp and transmission of experience. The catch lies in the word 'experience'" (Freeman 1935, 10). Pragmatist philosopher John Dewey helped spread the keyword of experience by publishing

Experience and Nature (1925) and *Art as Experience* (1934); A. Irving Hallowell, president of the American Folklore Society in 1940, expanded the theme to culture studies in *Culture and Experience* (1955). Hallowell stated the problem well:

> it should be possible to formulate more explicitly the necessary and sufficient conditions that make a human existence possible and which account for the distinctive quality of human experience. A human level of existence implies much more than an existence conceived in purely organic terms…. The unique qualitative aspects of a human existence that arise of conditions of human experience which are not simple functions of man's organic status alone, and that have variable as well as constant features, must be thoroughly explored in all their ramifications and given more explicit formulation. (Hallowell 1967, vii–viii)

Hallowell signaled for folklorists a philosophical turn from approaching folklore as fixed forms to be biologically preserved and classified to dynamically observed experiences that enlivened existence.

The development of performance analysis of folk arts from changing views during the 1930s of art as dramatic experience that served social ends has a common source in the formation of American pragmatist philosophy and its debt to the "dynamics" and "interactions" in physics. In 1985, in fact, several folklorists reflected in *Western Folklore* on the relation of the pragmatist philosophy of William James, especially in relation to perception of truth and explanation of belief, to folkloristic interpretation (Mechling 1985; see also Bronner 1990c). Jay Mechling observed that in relation to pragmatism, "Folklorists join others in seeing human cultures as collective exercises in creative meaning-making, in 'practical reason,' wherein meaning is an interactive, emergent, and contextual accomplishment. Moreover, the folklorist brings to the interpretive approach the additional insight that practical reason is 'artlike,' that we are studying not 'mere' discourse but stylized communication that is as often as expressive as it is instrumental" (Mechling 1985, 303–4).

As far as pragmatists were concerned with perceptions of meaning in events, folklorists applied ideas of expressions that reflected thinking serving the individual's needs and interests. The importance of an event's context came out in John Dewey's claims that the practical bearings ideas have on experience can be observed in the circumstances of their use, especially of a public nature. Moreover, the idea of emergent tradition from the interaction of people in a situation can be seen in pragmatist George Herbert Mead's proposal for the importance of process and the application of rigor to the interpretation of social situations. Mead favored a physical sciences metaphor over the evolutionary biological framework for describing society. In the physical sciences metaphor of actions and reactions, one found a relativism where judgments of superiority could not be made. Different situations operated under separate systems and gave rise to varied expressive, even artistic, results.

Pragmatist influences on the application of art to the process of folklore can be significantly found in William Bascom's oft-cited writings on "verbal art." Introducing the modification of art in the *Standard Dictionary of Folklore* (1949–50) as a definition for folklore, Bascom expounded on this use of "art" at the American Folklore Society's annual meeting in the "art capital of the world," New York City. Even before the paper was published, Bascom's view, in recognition of its portent perhaps, received a rebuff by literary scholar Samuel Bayard in the pages of the American Folklore Society's journal. Arguing for an emphasis on form as the distinction between folklore and other expressions, Bayard concluded that he saw no precedent or justification for the relation of art and folklore (Bayard 1953). His line of textual preservations and readings of folklore stretched from his teacher at Harvard George Lyman Kittredge back to the Brothers Grimm. He recognized the possibility that a shift to "verbal art" would move the predominant debate from the texts and sources of tradition to the processes in some kinds of universal experience.

The paper that Bascom read appeared as "Verbal Art" in the *Journal of American Folklore* in 1955. To the anthropologist Bascom, verbal art described the core of folklore study, spoken forms, to distinguish it from the customs and beliefs that anthropology claimed. Bascom asserted that the term placed folktales, myths, proverbs, and related forms "squarely alongside the graphic and plastic arts, music and the dance, and literature, as forms of aesthetic expression, while at the same time emphasizing that they differ from the other arts in that their medium of expression is the spoken word. From this point one can go on to examine the relation of verbal art to the other art forms, drawing helpful parallels and determining what special features it has which grow out of this medium" (Bascom 1955, 246). Bascom differentiated between folklore that was primarily social—such as customs—and folklore that was primarily expressive, textural, and artistic—such as tales and myths. His emphasis was on recognizing the aesthetic forms of folklore; the term "verbal art" combined attention to expressive form and to its medium.

As a museum director and a collector of African primitive art, Bascom had culled his rhetoric from the growing consideration of crafts and primitive material culture as "folk arts" in the postwar period. Previous anthropological use of folklore suggested to him a tight weave in the fabric of group life under study—Indian tribes, Sea Island blacks, Mexican peasants. But he felt that folklore in the postwar era became less attached to isolable cultural groups. He observed folklore being collected from distinctive individuals who had a knowledge of traditional expressions and who might be connected to an abstracted community. As folklore appeared to carry less utility and as it seemed more marginal in an era of electronic communication, it moved to the realm of special creativity, of art. He mustered support from a trend toward democratization of the arts heralded by Allen Eaton and continuing into the post World War II period. The democratization of the fine arts to embrace "primitive" art and photography had spread in the 1930s with the celebration of the common man in the Index of American Design and various Work Progress Administration (WPA) projects. The point reached a height of sorts with the exhibition in the Metropolitan Museum of Art in 1944 by Grandma Moses, a self-taught painter of past everyday life, who subsequently enjoyed extraordinary fame.

As the meaning of *art* in the postwar period opened to broader interpretation, it came to signify expressive, creative social values in contrast to modern or commercial workaday values of conformity and banality. It could exist among others besides fine artists. Landscapes, foods, furniture, and crafts created for a social life considered romantic or nostalgic could be touted as art to draw attention to their handmade fragility in a mass culture. Sociologist Howard S. Becker recognized, for instance, that "quilts are not art because no one treated them like art. They were the physical embodiment of families and communities, but that was not reason to preserve them; if they were not preserved they could not be admired and eventually seem to have the artistic qualities they might or might not have…. That has changed, as it has for many other products of family and community industry, as museums have either devoted themselves to preserving native crafts or recognized artistic merit in such work" (Becker 1982, 257–58). As folk art the objects connected to a loose sense of community, and somehow imparted vernacular honesty. It aestheticized ordinary experience for an intimate audience.

While new uses of art elevated tradition and stressed its creative components, a potential problem for folklorists was that art often carried with it elitist connotations of judgment and value. It was commonly evaluated from outside a localized culture. It consisted of a body of images and articles that was accepted by tastemakers—a body whose value was decorative and mercantile rather than utilitarian. And because art, or the lack of it, was used to measure the social value of cultural groups, scholars concerned with the integrity of cultural groups often applied it to describe, and defend, their collected materials. The formation of the Folk Arts Division of the National Endowment for the Arts represents such elevation of traditions by often marginalized groups into art. Its major projects have featured artists outside the art worlds—in presumably endangered communities usually defined as ethnic, racial, or regional (Peterson 1996a). Its rhetoric echoed through the work of local and state "folk arts coordinators" who formerly had preferred the label "state folklorist." The major coordinating task became to identify and display endangered, marginalized works of creative tradition in festivals, schools, and exhibitions. Whereas installing exhibitions had been their primary function during the 1970s and 1980s, in the 1990s they reported spending more of their time planning programs involving performances and demonstrations (Peterson 1996a). The urgency of their task was created by the image that a diversity of American tradition would be lost if its folk arts were not presented before a wide public. During the 1990s, the urgency also included a plaint that more than diversity, the very evidence of performance would be lost. Art raised the social status of artist and group before a public judge, but it could also signal cultural weakening.

One answer to the implication of marginalization of a group's folk arts was to situate art as spontaneously generated in various performances. Art therefore appeared everywhere—in conversation, gesture, and craft. Groups could be variable and temporary; people could simultaneously hold connections to many groups. In "Toward a Definition of Folklore in Context," the most widely cited article on folklore through the 1970s and 1980s, Dan Ben-Amos contributed to the rhetorical development of *art* by defining folklore as "artistic communication in small groups." Ben-Amos went beyond the combination of form and medium that Bascom had suggested in the term "verbal art" by emphasizing the transmission—the behavioral and textural qualities—of lore. Examples of the behavioral or textural qualities of art, Ben-Amos observed, can be "rhythmical speech, musical sounds, melodic accompaniment, or patterned design." He admitted that his attention to such behavior is "a reverse argument for the arts. Accordingly, a message is not considered artistic because it possesses these qualities, but it is these textural features that serve as markers to distinguish it as artistic." In this view the texture of art is set apart from everyday ways of acting and folklore, too, is isolated. Ben-Amos stressed that "folklore, like any other art, is a symbolic kind of action. Its forms have symbolic significance reaching far beyond the explicit content of the particular text, melody, or artifact … the time and locality in which the action happens may have symbolic implications for which the text cannot account" (Ben-Amos 1972, 11). The importance of artistic action to the conception of folklore came even more to the fore when Richard Bauman published *Verbal Art as Performance* (1977) and, following Bascom and Ben-Amos, characterized folklore as "artistic action in social life" (vii).

Bauman's references to artistic action followed social studies that examined the ways that Americans, freed from the deep roots of community, could speak or dress differently to take on various roles, which had the effect of impressing a select audience. Commonly this kind of action model was arranged into the communications metaphor of frames. Political scientist Harold Lasswell in 1948, for example, described diplomacy in terms of "attention frames." He defined them as "the rate at which comparable content is brought to the notice of individuals and groups." In contrast to the frame of folk cultures, he said, the frame of modern urban life is "variable, refined, and interactive" (Lasswell 1949, 102–15). Of especially lasting influence was sociologist Erving Goffman's "frame analysis" in *The Presentation of Self in Everyday Life* (1956) and *Behavior in Public Places* (1963). Using the theatrical metaphor of performances, Goffman described framed events that serve the symbolic function of "impression management," demanded by the postwar economy (Goffman 1956, 1963; Abrahams 1977, 102–8; Bauman 1972, 33–34).

The emphasis on action and the individual conveys an image of the ungrounded variability of modern living. Indeed, Bauman praised the efforts of performance analysis "to really comprehend what modernity means and to see what genuine expressive and esthetic responses emerge to deal with it" (Bauman 1983a, 155). In this image of modern living, an electronically mediated modern world, speaking needs to become performance to be heard; speaking gains meaning as the medium of staged sincerity. In a modern era marked by what Bauman calls "differentiation," or individualization, life seems more complex and demands more scripts. Individuals become actors adjusting their roles to immediate conditions. In the postwar shift, too, from a manufacturing economy to one based on service and information, "performing" services and speaking in routines become more part of daily life (Abrahams 1978). It is not surprising, then, that folklore with its intimate connection of speaker and listener and its connotation of sincerity should have drawn the attention of scholarship seeking meaning from communication in society.

Interpreting the theatrical nature of modern life restored some of the humanistic orientation to the study of culture. The metaphor of "performance" was still steeped in behavioral analysis, but it replaced the laboratory metaphor with an artistic one. In emphasizing display and performance, in the assumption of expressive actions as strategies used in specific situations, the nature of an actor was separated from the act, and the physical stage was isolated from its social surrounding. Less aware of a specific audience and left alone to become more ritualized, people used performance to manage a public life in a world of strangers. This seemed to replace the familiar community who shared a knowledge of common texts. The assumption was that with the breakdown of community, an audience consisted of strangers who needed performed symbols to denote status, knowledge, and feeling.

In an action model of behavior, the stability and three-dimensionality of material arts described less the activity of folklore than the variability and fluidity of performing arts. In Ben-Amos's and Bauman's rhetoric, art's position was significantly adjectival; art described a quality of action rather than an entity or article. While emphasizing the position of groups in the generation of folklore, Ben-Amos and Bauman devalued the importance of the collective whole in the conception of folklore or raised the significance of individual creativity. Bauman defended the move by pointing out that "tradition, the collective, the communal, the conventional, are not forsaken here; rather, the individual and the creative are brought up to parity with tradition in a dialectic that is played out within the context of situated action, viewed as a kind of practice" (Bauman 1992, 33). References to "small groups" and "social life" underscored the adaptability of folklore to varying situations and changing identities. No longer a thing of the past, folklore became continually re-created and appeared integral in modern life. Indeed, the use of folklore appeared more *active*, since it appeared to be a human tool, not simply a reflection of culture or a repetition of tradition. Dramatic in its display whether as a craft or a story, folklore appeared elevated as folk arts in competition for public appreciation of cultural virtue.

When folklore was viewed as dramatic performance, however, the objective reality of an American tradition frequently appeared in doubt. Life could appear as

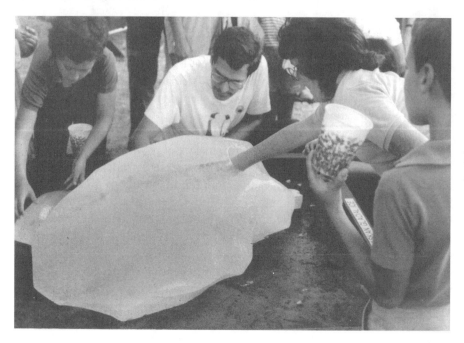

Visitors to the Festival of American Folklife touch a piece of glacial ice brought to the National Mall, Washington, D.C., to represent traditions of Alaska, July 1984. Photograph by Simon Bronner.

variable events not bound by the isolation of place or the continuity of time. Unlike the museum display where tradition appeared fixed, public performance resisted borders of time and location. It was an event that was situated rather than an artifact that was preserved. Bauman referred to the "immediacy" of events, for example, and offered performances as "enactments," framed into "public displays" (Bauman 1983a, 157). To represent this view to the public, many performance-oriented folklorists conceived of displays to the public that would be active and experimented with festival formats to show performed traditions as situated arts (Gillespie 1996). Indeed, one handbook labeled the production of festivals as *Presenting Performances* (Wolf 1979). In celebrations of folk arts within festivals, tradition appeared enlivened and significant. But the need to construct a festival also implied a need to boost tradition, a sign of cultural weakening. Especially since the United States is not known for its folk festivals the way, say, Japan is, festivals were understood as contrived events meant for promoting fragmented or minimized arts. I have seen a marked change in festivals from the 1960s, when they were meant to present neglected folk artists, to celebrations of diversity as a living tradition and, since the 1990s, to participatory events stressing the ubiquity of performed tradition.

Alaskan fisherman explaining tools of his trade to a family visiting the Festival of American Folklife, July 1984. Photograph by Simon Bronner.

East Lansing High School students working on a homecoming float at the Festival of Michigan Folklife, East Lansing, Michigan, August 1996. Photograph by Simon Bronner. (Michigan State University Museum)

In an example of encouraging participation in tradition at a festival, visitors learn to dance the Macarena at the Children's Area Stage, Festival of Michigan Folklife. Photograph by Mary Whalen. (Michigan State University Museum)

Conceived in 1967 to represent the cultural pluralism of America, the Festival of American Folklife in Washington, D.C., attracted notice during the 1980s and 1990s for trying to program performances of tradition away from the boundaries of stages. It offered apparently spontaneous rituals and children's play on its grounds. These events were often not isolated as American traditions, but rather explained as vital human responses to various needs. Festival planners added that "the festival encourages visitors to participate—to learn to sing, dance, eat the foods, and converse with people represented in the program" (Kurin 1996a, 253). In 1983, festival planners built a replica of the Atlantic City boardwalk to show the kinds of interactions that occurred in a traditional slice of New Jersey (Gillespie 1996). Usually unromanticized workers, including taxi drivers, meat cutters, and construction workers, engaged visitors in conversations that brought out their performed traditions. In 1995, a site to show Cape Verdian traditions had no stage, but at certain times, program participants led visitors in a ritualized dance through the grounds. Despite these efforts, the festival could also be criticized by the performance-oriented folklorists for its labeling of traditions into fixed groups and the separation of "folk artists" from everyday life as unusual entertainers (Bauman, Sawin, and Carpenter 1992, Price and Price 1995; Sommers 1996).

The Festival of Michigan Folklife sponsored by the folk arts division of the Michigan State University Museum worked performance into its programming by revolving its displays around life themes. In 1997, summer visitors wandered around tents presenting many ways that the automobile spurred traditions. It could be a place—a situation—for enacting play, and it could also be a product that inspired artistic traditions by assembly-line workers and car decorators alike. In 1996, the organizers asked me to be a "presenter" at a tent meant to invite participation in tradition. The theme that year was the life cycle, and while some tents had bakers artfully showing their decoration of wedding cakes or weavers preparing special costumes for life's events, the one I staffed stood out because the demonstrators did not seem to qualify as "artists." It had teenagers from a local high school folding colorful paper into wire fencing to make a homecoming float. It was a slow, tedious process although it formed a creative act. As is usual in the tradition, the youth tried to coax volunteers to help in the labor-intensive task. My job was to give the big picture of the whole event and invite visitors to participate or return to see the work develop. I could tell that visitors that bothered to check out the site were startled by the scene. They did not expect casually dressed teenagers milling about to be engaging in "folk arts." No one sang or danced. They did not have special skills. Visitors saw no stage, detected no relics, and discerned no ethnic-religious connection. The site was artificial, to be sure; usually the event occurred in the fall at students' homes and the planning had a certain amount of secretiveness and competitiveness to it (Dewhurst 1996). Still, some visitors at the summer festival found themselves altering their thinking of folk arts. Those who had worked on such a structure in the past or present were invited to share their accounts with the students to show continuities in the annual reenactment of tradition. The idea was that visitors became the tradition bearers instead of viewers of an exoticized other. With the process winding along slowly, those participants that stayed usually ended up socializing and narrating, thereby showing the integration of "folk arts." Although they usually did not have an awareness of being "performers" or "artists," they were nonetheless participating in a contemporary situation where traditionalized creative events occurred.

Many folklorists implied that in their ordinary performances, people revealed themselves and even found themselves. Roger Abrahams commented, for example, that "reality itself … appears to be layered, made up of different levels of intensity and focus of interaction and participation. A very precious commodity is being negotiated, after all, one which is remarkably vital and which, in fact, we might call our socio-cultural vitality. For it is in these states of ritual or performance, festive or play enactments that in many ways we are most fully ourselves, both as individuals and as members of our communities" (Abrahams 1977, 117).

Even work could be divided into artistic events for people to find their vitality. Michael Owen Jones gave a behavioral orientation on this in his oft-cited essay, "A Feeling for Form, as Illustrated by People at Work" (1980a). Taking art to mean this "feeling for form," even in apparently mundane tasks such as cleaning tuna, Jones concluded that "it is precisely this perspective emphasizing the art of work that is needed both to understand the nature of *homo faber* and to improve the very conditions as well as goods and services whose quality is so often deplored. At present, most people whose labor is simplified, specialized, and standardized must content themselves with subtle (some might be tempted to say 'pathetic') attempts to develop and elaborate tasks into forms having esthetic value crucial to their sense of self worth and being" (Jones 1980a, 268). For Jones, the process of action carried not just displays of routine, but also suggested inner feelings of worth, of being. Folklore thus could be constructed to make a commentary on the fragmentation of the present moment. Its historical role, its former use as "roots" to culture, had been transformed into an ethnography of the emerging message made possible by aestheticized events. Performance analysis looked at individuals as actors in a modern drama that was spontaneous and disjointed. It proposed to give social significance to modernity's minimal units—its situations. Tradition could become an art of the moment.

Performance owed some of its appeal in the display of tradition to the commonly held perception in post-1960s society that showmanship and "impression management" were more necessary for the self to be recognized in the run of modern life. As Americans left home for far-off climes and felt their ties to family, church, and community slacken during this period, more scholarship contemplated how individuals reestablish identity and connect to tradition in unfamiliar surroundings. One answer was by enacting symbolic performances that heightened special forms of experience. To Bauman, for example, "performance thus calls forth special attention to the heightened awareness of the act of expression, and gives license to the audience to regard the act of expression and the performer with special intensity" (Bauman 1977, 11). The artistic expressions that were associated with the processes of folklore were signs of identity-forming intensity, of sincerity, of really being alive. Really being alive was an issue because of fears that television, governmental regulation, and service work, among other mass cultural phenomena, had made Americans less active, less creative, less feeling. At the same time, the tendency of modernization to alienate individuals from social ties to tradition meant that belonging to community appeared more elusive. A performance orientation imagined Americans as citizens of humanity who had to ask who they really were and how forms of cultural identity carried meaning beneath the surface allure of modern life. Performance invited formation of, and participation in, symbolic experience.

Praxis and the Representation of Action

The everyday experience of labor, of daily routines, rarely translates well into the display of art or performance, but it fits well with the idea that creatively following tradition is a human condition. From behavioral perspectives comes a view of the display of tradition that avoids the rhetoric of art as an aestheticized thing or of performance and embraces routine activity as widely representative of a cultural mode of thinking. Such displays can be seen in community events not meant to present performances as much as represent actions considered significant to local lives and symbolic of tradition. It may not fit neatly into the installation of folk art in a gallery, staging of folk arts at a festival, or recording of verbal art as performance. It may be called *praxis* by scholars outside the displays, but within them, participants may say that "it's what we *do*," or "it's our tradition," and thereby express its quintessential character.

   The circulation of praxis in public discourse of the 1980s to describe the meaningfulness of routine activities attracted the notice of popular columnist William Safire in 1989. Known for commenting on the vogue of words and their social backgrounds, he spread the headline "Praxis Makes Perfect" in the *New York Times* to mark a shift from neutral "practice" to socially charged "praxis" (Safire 1989). He thought that the demonstrations for democracy by students in Beijing's Tiananmen Square had much to do with the spread of the term from scholarship to the press. The translation of the term by the students implied that they would change by organizing "doing" rather than protest. They would encourage the standardization of behaviors in China's daily life that would represent a democratic spirit. The dissidents claimed to install an alternative "praxis" that provided the meaning of democracy even though they understood that they were still under communist dominion. Safire took notice after the demonstrations that two political senses of praxis came through in press reports: an old view of "'practicality,' such as is put forward by 'capitalist roaders' and free-marketers, and 'action,' such as that undertaken by hunger-striking, freedom-seeking students" (Safire 1989). Safire noted that praxis in public discourse carried the meaning of "action based on will," and Safire quoted American philosopher Sidney Hook on the "selective behavior" beyond practicability which is praxis, the realization that knowledge made apparent in symbolic action across a range of events could express meaning and emotion.

Closer to home, the hotly disputed Hegins Pigeon Shoot in central Pennsylvania from 1989 to 1994 conspicuously forced nationwide speculation about praxis. There may seem hardly a comparison between demonstrations for democracy in a world-class city and a display of destroying pigeons in a spot absent on most maps. But the media reports explaining the fuss made over pigeons dramatically broadcast ways that displayed behavior came to symbolize different worldviews that extended well beyond Hegins. They picked up on the protestors' theme that more than the event was in dispute; questioning tradition generally implied a challenge to the authority of a past in need of change. The protestors objected to the social "praxis" perpetuated through time of abusing animals and violating the dignity of life. The traditionalized shooting, protestors implied, represented a root cause of society's ills of social violence, environmental decline, and moral crisis. They intimated that pulling out this root was a natural extension of civil rights movements breaking with institutionalized traditions to create a more tolerant, egalitarian, and compassionate humanity.

The shooting for supporters showed a grounding in tradition, community, and land that had been seriously eroded with the domination of modern urban living over American worldview. Hegins was the kind of small place that went its own way, complaining of an America that seemed to pass it by. Its older residents recalled when the labors of hunting, fishing, and farming that characterized Hegins life were national pursuits. They saw the decadent city "over there" and on television, and media events built around social protests were even more distant. When buses emblazoned with city sources rolled into Hegins challenging what it was about, Hegins could blithely go about its own business no more. Different ways of doing and living came hostilely face to face for cameras to vividly see.

The shoot was a form of display organized by residents and meant primarily for residents of the rural valley. It was not a tradition that any of the state's folklorists chose to have performed in a folk festival or celebrate in an exhibition. At least one folklorist wanted to make a film on the ubiquitous hunting culture of Pennsylvania, but his grant proposal was turned down by an arts agency because the panel did not think the activity constituted folk *arts*. None of the coveted National Heritage Awards given by the National Endowment for the Arts Folk Arts Division has ever gone to a hunter. The arts agencies did not recognize or favor the aestheticized customs of traditional hunting and shooting contests. When I prepared a presentation with Jay Mechling at an American Studies Association meeting about the Hegins Pigeon Shoot, we heard that the "tradition"

Shooter prepares for release of pigeons from one of the boxes at the Hegins Pigeon Shoot, Labor Day, 1993. Photograph by Simon Bronner.

One of many confrontations between animal rights protestors (left) and pigeon shoot supporters at Hegins, Pennsylvania, Labor Day, 1992. Photograph by Simon Bronner.

was an affront to many students of culture used to receiving scholarship advocating respect for marginalized groups. Although we did not come down on one side or the other, we heard several responses accusing us of supporting the event by rationalizing the irrational behavior of Hegins Shoot participants. Several audience members argued with us that this was not a tradition to encourage. It deserved the category of repulsive ritual rather than folk arts. Inclined toward the rhetoric of civil rights and away from the destructive aspects of hunting, their relativism apparently had its limits.

In most states today, the Pigeon Shoot would be illegal, although forms of the shoot were once widespread in early America. It carried on legally in Pennsylvania and was a regular feature of many private hunting and fishing clubs. It was part of hunting-related practices including turkey shoots and snake hunts that were widespread in Pennsylvania. The place of rural Pennsylvania as a haven for hunting traditions is indicated by the fact that Pennsylvania usually led the nation in the number of hunting and fishing licenses issued. And it should be noted that Pennsylvania has the country's largest rural population. The beginning of hunting season is a major event, and the opening of deer season is usually a school holiday. Hunting and shooting contests for many participants, usually men, are rich in tradition, so they said, and draw much of their appeal from it. Hunters extolled their commune with nature, rituals initiating novices and recognizing seasoned veterans, engaging in long rounds of storytelling at the primitive lodges, and donning earthy dress and body appearance that separate the activity from modern life. They commonly brought out arts of taxidermy and woodcarving to display their trophies of adventures in the wild. In their talk, they often connected to the days of yore in the primitive wilderness and imagined themselves as part of a classic American story of triumphing in the woods.

Hegins is in the middle of an isolated rural area known for its vistas of field and stream and legacies of hunting and farming. Yet the cities of Harrisburg, Scranton, and Philadelphia loom close by since a superhighway cut through the woods and mountains. The mountains that once set this valley apart suddenly do not seem so much a barrier to urban encroachment. Harrisburg, the state capital, is only an hour or so away by car. It is surely a different place, residents constantly reminded me as I made the trip to Hegins from the capital. Pennsylvania German could still be heard in the valley's public places, and even the children who did not speak it often had a "Dutchy" accent. As a lush valley circled by imposing mountains, it sometimes could feel like a world away. The juxtaposition of city and country, their stark contrast in this part of the country, is one reason that Hegins became a text of praxis.

What made Hegins so noticeable was that it was the largest public contest of pigeon shooting in the country. The community festival at Hegins galvanized public opinion when national media picked up the story of protestors descending on the tiny town. It was a scene reminiscent of northern buses of freedom riders

Animal rights protestor with a sign criticizing the defense of the Hegins Pigeon Shoot as a tradition, Labor Day, 1992. Photograph by Simon Bronner.

Pigeon Shoot supporter sporting one of many T-shirts invoking the importance of tradition to justify the Labor Day event, 1993. Photograph by Simon Bronner.

coming down South in the Civil Rights movement of the 1960s. In the 1990s, the media smelled a skirmish in the culture wars: animal rights protestors against traditional values. The protestors consisted mostly of women from urban areas such as New York, Baltimore, and Philadelphia; they devoted their Labor Day holiday beginning in 1989 to block the operation of Hegins's annual community festival. Having had successes in urban settings, and being savvy in using protests to attract national media and publicize their cause, leaders of animal rights organizations proposed assaulting the bastions of American culture in its old heartland. They viewed the isolation of Hegins as a sign of its backwardness and wanted to draw media to the shame of the town in progressive America. They derided the event as a "blood sport" and referred to shooters as barbarians.

Participants at Hegins thought that the contest was part of coming home. There were some who predicted that the shoot might have dwindled in its impact on the valley in favor of family picnicking if the protestors had not come, but the coverage of the event raised the stakes for hanging on. What happens at the contest is that shooters, mostly men, stand seventy-five feet away from a set of boxes lined in front of them. The boxes, called "traps," hold live pigeons and are connected by strings to a booth where a man can open the lids by pulling on strings. The shooter does not know in advance which box will open, since it is chosen randomly by a man "pulling the strings." The challenge, then, is to aim and shoot quickly as the birds take off. The birds tend to ascend slowly, however, and most shooters hit their mark close to the ground. In an event meant to eliminate the birds, the majority of birds are picked off. The birds fall without much evidence of blood, although feathers typically fly. Thus attendees sported T-shirts declaring patriotically, "Let Freedom Ring and Feathers Fly." Townspeople generally considered the shoot a wholesome pursuit, as another T-shirt announced with the phrase aimed at urban decadence, "Shoot Pigeons, Not Drugs."

The event is a fund-raiser for the community park and is a capstone to the Labor Day homecoming. It announces the end of summer and the foregrounding of fall recreational hunting season that structures the lives of many families in the valley. The Hegins park called the event a tradition because it had been active for almost fifty years and invoked occupational hunting activities that were once part of the seasonal cycle dating back to the beginning of settlement of the central Pennsylvania valleys in the eighteenth century. The Hegins valley retains its Pennsylvania-German cultural cast and agrarian landscape, but it has suffered economically and socially as declines in coal mining and agriculture have forced younger generations to migrate away since the end of World War II. During the summer and especially on Labor Day weekend it is common for family reunions to take place in the valley, drawing back kin to the rustic roots of the "old-time" valley.

The shoot, unnecessary to the needs of modern daily life, nonetheless was a retained, reorganized activity that expressed rural values recognized in the region.

When protestors came, supporters viewed the demonstration less as an objection to the event and more as an attack on their *way of life*. Their views of labor in an agricultural valley centered on dominance over land and beast and many could cite Biblical passages to underscore the idea of human dominion over nature. They also understood the shoot as elimination of a detested pest in their farm existence. They thought the pigeons as disgusting as the droppings they scattered over barns and sheds. They referred to the pigeons as diseased rats rather than as animals with lives to be respected. While families watched adults take aim and shoot, young boys gathered the downed birds in sacks and unceremoniously disposed them. If the shot birds were not dead when they were picked up, the boys finished the job. Protestors saw this division of roles as initiating the boys into the acceptability of violence. The boys understood it as taking an appropriate task of cleaning up before they could be in charge. They willingly took responsibility in the social structure of the community.

The townspeople of Hegins refused to give up their public display of killing birds. They loudly retaliated against the protestors because they felt that an urban authority and moral system had eroded the foundation of their rural society. Between protestors, police, media, and supporters of the shoot, attendance sky-rocketed into the thousands. The crowds strained the capacity of the park and turned most of their attention to the confrontation. State Police carted away pro-testors who stormed the site and tried to release birds from the traps. A breakaway group of protestors engaged in civil disobedience reminiscent of the Civil Rights movement and lay down in the shooters' lines of sight. As protestors and towns-people pressed toward each other, bloody scuffles broke out, and hundreds were arrested. It became a media event sending out a narrative pitting a relic of small town America against a modern urban moral order. In maintaining the festival (even though a minority of the attendees actually shoot), supporters made a claim for community authority.

Some protestors set up a first-aid tent for injured birds that got away. The pro-testors made it a studio to focus the media on the brutalized animals and thus show the barbarism of the deed. Meanwhile, the calmest of the supporters beheld the landscape and down-home sights of which the symbolic activity was a part. Not being organized about exploiting the media, many rough-edged supporters to their discredit were recorded swilling beer and hurling abuse, and sometimes dead animals. One photographed supporter drew national front-page attention by smilingly demonstrating how the bag boys finished off the birds by wringing their necks until they died. Others ridiculed the calls of the protestors for extend-ing the cause to exploitation of animals. They ate hamburgers in front of the veg-etarian protestors and boasted T-shirts illustrating the delicacy of pigeon pies. They yelled for the protestors to fix the cities rather than attacking the country. Some supporters tagged the urban protestors as abortion rights advocates, but appeared confused when they heard pro-life stands from the protestors.

The shouts and signs during the confrontation at Hegins divided between the protestors' rhetoric of "rights" for the animals and moral grounding of the shoot, and supporters' messages of respect for tradition and community. Many signs from the protestors called for breaking tradition to join a universal, progressive order of humanity. "Is 7000 Deaths Worth a Tradition?" a protestor's sign proclaimed in reference to the average number of birds killed at the shoot. "Shame on America," "Join the Human Race," and "Hunters are Killers" were others. Some of the women brought sexual politics into it by accusing the shooters of brandishing their phallic guns in a sad, transparent show of their manly prowess. Shooting for Hegins residents, even for those who did not engage in the practice, became not so much a performance to be questioned as much as a symbolic action that connected to a series of other activities involving dominion over the land. As the protests built up during the early 1990s, many supporters came to the festival in military camouflage wear to show their embattled state. As the State Police exerted more control over the event, they moved the protestors further away from the site, and their effectiveness for the media was reduced. The protestors failed to close the shoot down, and in 1995 they shifted their protest away from the display event to the state capitol in Harrisburg. One organizer of the protest who talked to me about the move thought that the organization could be more effective in the new setting because legislators shared their understanding of activities of political organizing and rights talk.

If performance's metaphor is dramaturgical, praxis's is epistemological. It follows from the classical distinction between *theoria* and *praxis*; theoria is concerned with knowing for its own sake, while praxis realizes knowledge expressed through activities in social life (Dolgin et al. 1977; Markovic 1979). It suggests evaluation of basic actions that express meaning to individuals within a society. It points, in the words of Richard Bernstein, to an "understanding of the ways in which men *are* what they *do*, of how their social *praxis* shapes and is shaped by the complex web of historical institutions and practices within which they function and work" (Bernstein 1971, 306). "The Japanese Tradition of 'Smaller is Better,'" one exemplary text of praxis asserts, comes from the way of knowing in folding common in Japanese society. Things that are folded pervade society and help explain its "compact culture." Folding takes large ideas and renders them small, thereby making them graspable and comprehensible (Lee 1984). The folded fan devised in Japan takes scenes and reduces them in the hand. The traditional folded fan is used by men and women alike and represented in advertising and arts as an icon of Japaneseness. Children learn folding early as a fundamental way of creating beauty in the reductive behavior of the *origami*, and use it above all to miniaturize the national symbol of the crane. In their religious practice, the Japanese signal their wishes by folding them on paper. Sentences and poems follow the pattern of going from the largest idea to the small. Superlative terms are those expressing tiny detail and being packed in. Places of honor are designated by folded backgrounds.

Bowing, so basic to acknowledging social relationships, is itself a form of folding the body. The praxis of folding, of reducing, can bridge the past and present from the miniaturization of trees and rock gardens, where space is scaled down to the MiniDisc and folded earphone. The Japanese have taken the table-top television screen and put it in the fold of the hand. The Japanese contrast their packing in of knowledge within a hand's grasp and American ideas of expansiveness gained from sweeping vistas and yawning sprawl. They question the ways that Americans express their ways of knowing by enlargement. Panoramas, wider and wider screens, and spacious cars are the mark of American technology. Importance is bestowed by upward aspiring monuments, giant heroes, and gaping spreads.

How praxis is differentiated from performance in the American rhetoric of display is conspicuously evident in Roger Abrahams's widely read essay on contemporary uses of Romantic Nationalism. Dissatisfied with the limits of an approach that declares the uniqueness of single performances, he reflectively wrote on developing an event orientation that builds a comparative view of "praxis" (Abrahams 1993, 25). Although the trend of performance analysis had been to fragment experience to individuals, he asked whether activities that produce folklore could indeed still be related to national patterns. Or considering the ubiquitous influence of "cultural diversity" during the 1980s and 1990s, and looking for an understanding of "the role of folklore in society," Stephen Stern found promise in a "concept of praxis" that "may assist us to wed performance to the larger philosophical issues that imbue folklore events with significance ... " (Stern 1991, 26). Shortly after Stern made his observation, Paul Hanson reflected on the aging influence of performance orientations in *Toward New Perspectives in Folklore* (1972) and pronounced that "folklorists are now in a position to expand their understanding of performance as speaking praxis beyond isolated folklore events" (Hanson 1993, 332). If Abrahams and Hanson drew attention to the reality of the nation-state and the ways that social structures manage cultural communication, the significance to Stern is presumably political as well as cultural, at least in the ways that power relations in a view of cultural diversity and unity can be approached between folklore events and various social ideologies and organizations affecting them. Concerned about "hazards" of reducing the social units in performance-centered folkloristics during the 1980s, the editors of *Theorizing Folklore* (1993) reported that growing interest in nationalism and the organizational construction of tradition "led to growing questioning of the adequacy of analyses that do not make reference to these sorts of '*macro*' processes" (Briggs and Shuman 1993, 121; emphasis added).

The idea of organization commonly comes up in discussion of praxis, because the use of praxis springs from an altered view of modern life, one that is structured less by variable situations and more by organizations. During the 1980s, the public became more accustomed to hearing about the worlds of power, organized worlds that were creating cultures of their own. The public heard about the corporate world and, later, corporate cultures, about the fashion world and, later, about the culture of consumption. In a modern society that was noted for its increasing indi-vidualism, organizational settings define more identities: the office, the military, the city, the media, the school, the profession, the government. Thus the individual and the organization often have a syncretic relationship: organizations help guide individuals' choice and action, and they instill a feeling of belonging and cultural association (Cohen 1974; Handy 1976; Jones et al. 1988; Jones 1996). Organizing becomes a common praxis in modern life, a way of traditionalizing from the widening, and often dizzying, array of choices available to individuals forming social identities in a mass culture. Although conceived as an offshoot of occupa-tional folklore study, concern for organizational tradition to Michael Owen Jones, a folkloristic mover and shaker of organizational theory, casts a wide net to take in "many folklore forms and examples as instances of *organizing*. Festivals, parades, religious ceremonies, family reunions, and annual clambakes require organized effort if they are to occur and be judged satisfying" (Jones 1996, 533; emphasis added). Expanding the range of tradition to organized privatized events and their organization in terms of fundamental praxis, Jones presented a strong case that "most family outings, sandlot baseball games, impromptu picnics, and birthday parties are spontaneous organizations. They exemplify organizing in its funda-ment; people cooperating, channeling resources, and distributing roles and activi-ties for a designated purpose" (Jones 1996, 533).

The term *praxis* comes into play because it refers to a type of action separable from conceptions of art and performance. Praxis implies "practice," essential in an idea of tradition as the ritualized tasks of daily life rather than its division into spe-cial performances, but it has more social and intellectual connotation than the neu-tral "practice." In praxis is the idea that individuals as participants in continuities of time and place follow and adjust customary modes of behavior and thought. In praxis, more so than in performance, the view of social structure and historical condition become more paramount. The verbs that describe cultural forms of praxis discussed so far—folding, shooting, organizing, reducing, enlarging—are the kinds of productive activity where the final product is not the sole end, but where the doing and the experiences and symbols involved are equally important.

The source of a concern for praxis comes from a society where process appears increasingly removed from the product. Modern Americans fit descriptions of consumers, spectators, attendants. The prefabricated suburban home can become a public gallery of artistic activity by individual manipulation and decoration of the yard from the mailbox to the garden. Yard art can be looked at for its tradi-tionalizing process of arranging consumed goods into a personally meaningful landscape that carries social significance. Many studies have documented yard arrangements with wonder because the results seemed artistically bizarre. The process of production, however, is explainable in terms of a praxis. Makers share the action of taking available materials from the consumer society and converting them, in the style of craftsworker, into a symbol of identity and feeling. They use the consumer praxis of arranging rather than the productive activity of crafting to express creativity. Many practices draw attention to themselves because they display skill in activity, from storytelling to pigeon shooting. For many, the process takes on a symbolic significance for its exercise of personal control and its relation to the consuming, conforming standards of organizational life. Many studies of the "arts of work" (a reversal of the gallery emphasis on "works of art") examine the process of control as a basis of traditionalizing. In creating routines shared among auto workers on the assembly line, in aestheticizing the tedious cleaning of tuna, in decorating the faceless corporate office, modern folk engage in forms of praxis that achieve the emotional creativity of tradition, so folklorists have informed humanities scholarship in the discourse of American culture (see Dewhurst 1984; Jones 1990).

The display of tradition in representative activities in fact may not be public but may be for the self in a play of emotions. The display is perceived, made cognitive, rather than performed for an audience. In my book *Chain Carvers* (1985), for instance, I argued that in the private trick of "cutting in" the wood to produce the chains, elderly carvers found a reassurance that they could be cut into society (see also Bronner 1996a). To George Blume, born and raised in the country and in a mode of craft production stressing self-reliance and communal values, the factory and its corporate structure lured him because the old economy in which he existed was breaking down. Still, he maintained the old values in symbolic material forms. He made long expansive chains, usually from the very wood the factory used for furniture, to show his prowess despite the advance of age. Earnest Bennett carved tiny replicas of tools from the farm that no longer were prevalent and thereby announced their specialness. Another factory worker, Linus Herbig, made miniature chairs and put them in bottles to show their fragility and attract closer attention. In these apparently whimsical and decorative forms, the objects held no social threat to the corporate structure. Yet the activities of miniaturization, bottling, caging, and chaining expressed labor that had been marginalized. The craftsworkers signaled a way of doing things that had been rendered small and that they wanted to elaborate. What they meant could be perceived differently in various settings. When I showed them in Japan, their reduction of experience was perceived as a sign of empowerment; in the United States their encasement was typically seen as trivialization.

The various perceptions of culture bundled in orientations toward art, performance, and praxis mark struggles to determine the role of identity-forming tradition in modern life. Semantic changes in the keyword *culture* represent changes in intellectual perception of identity. In the late eighteenth century, culture was the tending of natural growth, the kind that human training close to what the rooted homeplace provided. In the nineteenth century, culture became a thing, "a general habit of the mind having close relations with the idea of human perfection." Culture was something that could be cultivated in society and raised the status of creative pursuit. Identity was broadly conceived in civilization and often into hierarchies of taste. It was associated with intellectual development or the general body of the arts (Williams 1983, 87–93). In the twentieth century, culture has been increasingly perceived as variable, relativized communication, and the most particularized communication could become an act of culture (Hall 1959; Leach 1976). In this view, the constant redisplay of tradition is understood as part of a modern need to pin the jelly of communicated culture to the wall. If culture became realized through a composite of fleeting events, then it needed to be defined at dramatic moments, and thereby was habitually reified through displays of tradition to various publics. If American culture was a problem to describe because of its ethnic and geographic diversity before the twentieth century, it became even more of a problem in behavioral perspectives on communication that fragmented experience. It was easier to imagine a region or nation when culture was a thing bound to the land.

As the stability of an American culture has become more elusive, there is a renewed search to locate traditions that center people's actions in a consuming modern life. In the effort to clarify culture when people consume more than they produce, the traditions that draw attention are the kind that are repeatable, variable, and observable. If people do not offer recognizable stories and things as were once imagined, they can reconceive traditions that express and narrate action. Tradition, then, clarifies guides to what people do, and why they do it. Moving toward the twenty-first century, public formats for the display of tradition show culture as creativity, a process of fabricating social meaning from activity. Questions arise in the discourse about how much control humans have over their expressiveness and how much they are able to adjust their identities in life's various frames of experience. If orientations toward art, performance, and praxis differ as to the extent to which tradition is followed, they nonetheless share the view that its interpretation is relative to the dislocating experience that modern living provides.

Williamsburg's "treasured" displays of tradition as paintings and sculptures of national unity, Minnesota's "circles of traditions" as labor of ethnic and regional groups, Michigan's demonstration of performances in folk arts, and Hegins's sticking to their guns have a common strategy of organization. They offer to reunite public actors with their art. In the twentieth century, they have been powerful instruments of persuasion to view the creativity of tradition within modernity. Once primarily a contest of themes that commanded the folk art exhibition showing Americans as a collective whole or members of plural groups, the search for definition of life in America has expanded to the art of the moment presented in festival, performance, and activity. Forms of displaying tradition in America have been notable for their alternative visions of the relation of self to society for a future America. Although the pluralist theme in folk arts arguably has been ascendant in popular discourse since the 1990s, it still must contend with the force of displays conjuring American tradition as an unfinished project. There is still time for recasting the present and past into fragmented performances, representative actions, and national symbols, they remind us. The spread of display strategies argues for finding ways to follow and guide tradition, for ways that as Americans or individuals, people realize their roles in the flow of time. Presumably, it is a search forced by a modern existence that strains the ties of individuals to culture, and impels them to organize belonging.

Epilogue

The Future of Tradition

NOTHING FOCUSED MY ATTENTION ON AMERICAN TRADITIONS LIKE BEING AWAY from them. This book began as I contemplated the youth of America's national relics against the ancient ruins of England and I heard countless times how the United States and England were two nations divided by a common language. It ended in Japan where I heard fewer hints of commonality with the United States. Pundits on both sides of the Pacific presented Japan to be essentially different from America. While England and the United States were both part of what has been called Western tradition, Japan and America split apart into East and West. Set against the background of this sharp division, several prominent figures discussed in this book went to Japan to reflect on the meaning of American culture. Lafcadio Hearn pondered materialism, Richard Dorson contemplated nationalism, and Alice Bacon mused on feminism. Judging by the keynotes sounded by an expanding chorus of authors taking up comparisons, Japan is America's reverse mirror. It especially shows in conceptions of tradition.

The Japanese I met talked assuredly about the cultural unity of their country. They understood the basis of their traditions in a common racial stock, an ancient lineage, a group orientation, and a shared narrative of their distinctiveness. Much as I heard rebellious scholars give abundant evidence of the illusion of Japan's homogeneity and uniqueness, that did not check the flow of references to the Japanese as a separate race isolated on its islands and thereby able to form a distinctive culture (see H.W. Smith 1995; Weiner 1997). When the entrance examination for the national university I attended asked for an essay in English on the center of Japan's tradition, the American graders were amazed at the high level of agreement in the returned answers. Ninety percent of the students placed the heart of the nation's tradition in the same spot—the ancient temples of Kyoto. The examiners could not imagine that kind of consensus for a similar question put to Americans.

475

Well after the examination, I saw a qualification for the placement of Kyoto as the center of Japanese tradition in a headline that declared, "Kyoto Plays Tradition Card to Lure Students Back." Going to Kyoto is a kind of pilgrimage for most schools in Japan, but the traditionalists have become concerned by competition from, of all places, Tokyo Disney Land (Iida 1997). That clinched for them the connection of America with novelty and consumerism and Japan with antiquity and spiritualism. To whisk the students into the American past, I provided "Electronic Field Trips" to historic America produced on Laserdisc (ABC News 1997). After getting used to the futuristic idea of transporting them electronically to absorb America's shrines, I ruminated on the disc's representation of American memory. Eighteen sites were featured with a careful eye to multicultural inclusiveness of American social experience. No capitols, no monuments to presidents, certainly no plantations. A student appeared puzzled and asked, "But where is the *kokoro*?" She meant the heart and soul, the ancient spiritual center of American tradition, as the Japanese conceived it. I paused and explained America's decentering.

I realized the ubiquity of festivals as one source of the Japanese view of tradition. The country has thousands of local festivals whose histories have stretched back centuries. Each one re-enacts the importance for the Japanese of continuity with the past and bonds with community and nation. Instead of proclaiming adaptation to the changing times, they preserve original customs intact. They all seem to draw from the dramatic start of the New Year celebration, which encourages participation in familiarly known rituals for family, neighborhood, and nation. "Starting the Year with Tradition," one headline of a national newspaper at the time blared appropriately across its pages (Sakane 1997). As obviously industrialized, indeed modernized by Western standards, as the Japanese have self-consciously become, there are constant reminders that they believe that tradition as an inheritance of their ancient racial past persists into the present. "The Old in the New," one typical essay explains of Japan's resilient tradition. Read the narrative of continuity as the author offers to attend to "craftsmen who, while preserving Japan's tradition of consummate craftsmanship, are striving to create new types of craftwork suitable to modern living. In the process, we explore the root—the spirit of craftsmanship—of Japan's technological prowess" (Muda 1997).

Having heard so often about the sturdiness of tradition in the edifice of Japanese unity, I witnessed cracks in the facade when I took students to a Japanese folklife museum and they were taken aback by what they did not know of their own traditions. Given to express values of filial piety, they seemed embarrassed by their neglect of practices familiar to their parents and many generations before. The fragility of some traditions in a place where residents supposedly follow traditions unswervingly is evident in a national program since 1950 to protect "folk cultural properties" and "intangible cultural properties" (Saitsu 1996). The national public television station promotes tradition with regular broadcasts of folk performing arts and festivals, and features a weekly program called "Hometown

Traditions" usually focused on crafts, foods, and occupations. The national newspapers (and there are many in contrast to the few in the United States) almost daily carry a photograph of Japanese citizens engaged in an old folk art or custom. At the same time, they regularly report surveys revealing anxieties about the transforming effects of modernization and "internationalization" on the continuity of Japanese traditions such as language, food, and family.

Upholders of Japanese tradition express special worry about the rebelliousness of Japan's uniformed high school girls, dubbed "The Boom Brigade," against the ways of the past. The national press gives ample coverage to their voracious appetites for novelty, supposedly influenced by American consumerism. Although appearing to be a statement of individual difference, in Japan it is probably more of a sign of conformity to the age group, which helps spread fads of virtual-reality pets, loosely worn high sweat socks, and miniature digital photographs. Presuming America as the unquestioned home of novelty, one American news reporter noted in alarm that Japan may have outdone the United States in industry, and now in fadism (Watanabe 1997). As much as the girls shock their elders by dyeing their hair and wearing outrageous platform shoes, they are expected to conform to tradition by the time they work for companies and marry. Another consolation for Japanese elders is that they imagine that new fashions incorporated into their culture since the end of World War II have been transformed so as not to interrupt Japanese tradition. They proudly recognize American imports from baseball to burgers but with a decided Japanese cast (see Whiting 1989; Sakaiya 1993).

So sure are the Japanese of their national culture that they judge their uniqueness by contrasts with the United States, while measuring their progress by their similarities. It is in this constant exercise that separate identities, or some may say stereotypes, for both Japan and the United States become reified within their joint embrace of modernity (see McClean 1992). The columns the attributes form extend far down the page: America is individualistic, Japan is group-oriented. America is dangerous, Japan is safe. Americans go for the large and expansive, the Japanese like things compact and detailed. The Japanese are polite, closed, formal, while the Americans tend to be brutally direct, open, informal. America is spacious and has many natural resources, Japan is cramped and has few caches of raw materials. America is diverse, Japan is homogeneous. America is new, Japan is old. Since many cultural features from America are admired, it rarely occurred to the people I talked to in Japan that the United States could have a sense of tradition comparable to theirs. They perceived America as a place where the past gave way constantly to the future, where radical individualism prevented bonds to groups fostering tradition, and racial and ethnic diversity made it difficult if not impossible to reach consensus or represent a common tradition.

I know Americans who feel the same way about their nation, but I maintain that public discourse in the United States, especially in the twentieth century, has instilled a distinctive American sense of tradition. It has consistently provided extra depth to America's shallow roots. A major dispute has been about where those roots lay and how they affect the country's development. There has been an ongoing project to identify the social and intellectual attributes of national tradition, and innumerable arguments about how far one can generalize shared modes of thought from cultural evidence through time. Instead of claiming homogeneity as a basis for national tradition, there has been a tendency to offer America's varied "strains" as its distinguishing cultural feature. Yet a bone of contention has been the processes of integration or, less delicately stated, assimilation, working on America's varieties. Do they gravitate toward a model of Americanness, or are they unsuspectingly shoved toward it? Whose model is it, anyway? The question of whether the varieties of America naturally come together forming an American type, keep their difference, or have it kept for them fans the fire of debate. For all the declarations of how Americans stand together, one can easily find pronouncements of how they live apart. Weighing the balance between unity and diversity has been a defining characteristic of American scholarship as well as the national experience.

If this falling out set the old debates over American tradition, redirected conversations are apparent from placing the United States in a global stream rather than an isolated spot. They also arise from observation of border-crossing complexities in the many situational choices, many identities available, within an individualistic, future-oriented society. If that sounds blind to the past, it should be remembered that as never before "folk histories," narratives of the past and cultural surroundings of ordinary people, especially members of often neglected ethnic groups, are more in evidence as backgrounds to many of the new discussions. One can increasingly hear questions of how individuals and organizations negotiate social unities, cross racial and sexual borders, and organize usable pasts at the local subcultural as well as international mass cultural levels (see Cross 1991; Roberts 1993; Hannerz 1996; Sollors 1997; Gubar 1997). The inquiry takes on significance as ways of categorizing Americans, and thereby explaining their traditions, shift, multiply, and blur in a swirl of cultural interactions associated with modernizing America. At Harvard symposia I attended in 1997 on new American agendas, the talk was all of *cross*racial, *multi*ethnic, and *trans*national intersections causing fissures in conventional boxes of ethnicity, religion, race, and gender. I heard arguments about the character of *emergent* traditions for interracial, interfaith, and international families. The border crossing in American cultural studies, sometimes invoked as the "California model," came out in the discussion of cultural cross-fertilization between Asia and the United States as air travel and media regularly bring Pacific cultures into view as never before. The gut issue in the revised debate is about the choices that individuals make about their expressions and identities, and those imposed upon them. It brings into relief the meaning, indeed the worth, of a variety of American cultural projects to uphold or change traditions in daily local practice set against the limits of national polities.

A significant contribution has been made to all this by American folklorists and, I hasten to add, notables not identifying themselves as "folklorists" but who use the stuff of tradition to rationalize American history and culture. They have consequentially given form and expression to tradition. Laboring over the authenticity of examples given in folklore's name, they have given recognition to the "right stuff" of tradition. They have encouraged cultural literacy in the texts of folklore and opened debate to proper representation in a canon of American tradition. They have shaped a discourse about the meaning of culture, modernity, and community that has become a major force in the intellectual construction of America. Their collections of specimens from the "field"—somewhere out there— have inventoried the cultural environment close to home. In their many portrayals of groups showing cultural vitality, they have framed a multilayered picture of social diversity and often spotlighted its relation to nation and state. Once devoted to what was spoken and sung, they moved to expand and democratize American arts by extending the creativity of tradition in material and performing expressions. They have monitored the cultural impact of novel forms of communication such as photocopiers and computers and thereby established tradition as a fundamental process of being human, indeed of being modern.

As independent as folklorists have sometimes been in scholarship, they have ceaselessly made interdisciplinary connections, joining their evidence to history, literature, sociology, anthropology, linguistics, and art. Folklore has been a hardy stream irrigating many fields in American learning. Like members of other learned professions pointing to society and culture, folklorists and their fellow travelers have perpetually fretted about their inadequate numbers, intellectual authority, and popular force. Yet in a cascade of book, gallery, film, and festival before various publics, they have conveyed folklife as American life, renewed folklore into the present, and elevated tradition to art. All told, they have impressively spread a consciousness of tradition as a vital cultural feature of America. This has come with some organizational cost to the great scholarly crusade of Beckwith, Shoemaker, and Dorson up until the late twentieth century to chart American folklore studies on its own course. Some of folklorists' success has meant a loss for the independence of folklore as a prophetic disciplinary lens on tradition, since the opening of the subject to an orientation toward local and native expressions within modernizing society has offered imperial academic realms like history and literature broadening opportunities to gain work from the social bottom up, and to see relatively from the inside out.

The American idea of tradition folklorists assembled before the end of the twentieth century differs from that of the Japanese and English, who have primarily taken their sense from an ancient past and common racial stock. By emphasizing that tradition emerges from social connection, many American folklorists located tradition without a long time line or a rooted place. That activities draw attention to themselves as repeatable, variable signs of some shared identity increasingly qualified them as cultural expressions. The social connections defined loosely as communities could be overlapping and temporary. That made it possible to simultaneously conceive of community traditions being maintained intact for private purposes and also being changed in the swirling midst of different communities for various publics to experience. American tradition could therefore be enacted, kept flexible, as symbolic action, rather than set in distant time, entrenched in place, or fixed in form. It involved everyone in the process of folklore even as it identified the special groups that thrived on it. If the United States was not group oriented, as the Japanese insisted, the nation nonetheless grew to believe that it cherished myriad communities and tendencies toward organizing belonging around them.

American individualism showed in folkloristic ideas that people could choose traditions, even create them, to express themselves. While the image of time, or more appropriately continuity, still could frame tradition, it usually did not have to be ancient or geographically rooted to be culturally significant. By viewing tradition as a function of human needs for deriving meaning from life, instead of a result of remote existence, then Americans could more fully contemplate their identity within globalized mass culture, their diversity within a nation-state, and their creativity in industrialized, consumer society. While this allowed more expressions of the situated self in the sense of tradition appropriate to a mobile, modernized society like the United States, it also permitted tradition to be future-oriented. It promised that traditions would continue to emerge to establish identity even when people pull up roots. To be sure, tradition as a heritage from the past may still be called inspiring relics, but in progressive America, it often draws its meaning from being popularly directed to the future by alteration and adaptation. In rhetoric taken from a physics of speeding, transforming atoms, many references to "dynamics" and "interactions," which threaten to overshadow a biology of cultural soil, underscore the future orientation of tradition. And like atoms of the nuclear age, traditions can be redirected, recombined, and reformed, and the immense results of human intervention contemplated.

Tradition and the folklore that gave it form became significant to the contestation of American social visions because variously defined they provided the historical precedent and cultural basis for charting uncertain roads ahead. Maybe that is why everyone is talking about culture. As culture has appeared more indefinite, it has become more manipulable and apparently more necessary to actualize. To bring it into reality has frequently meant to bring it into display so as to publicize it, emotionalize it, politicize it. As institutions of family, church, and state that had their holds upon socialized behavior, or praxis, diminished with the rise of modernity, culture became a hot commodity in a public marketplace where diversifying organizations vied for production of meaningful symbols and values (see Eagleton 1997, 2B3). Reference to tradition helped rationalize the many claims for culture through the twentieth century. Often these claims became the basis for social and political movements, brandishing notions of rights and entitlements as outcomes of cultural consciousness in the public arena. I have in front of me headlines of the 1990s from the American press that bear this politicization out: "An Affront to Tradition (Administration's Policy on Immigration)," "A 20-Year Tradition: Female Cadets," "Affirmative Action: An American Tradition," and "If the Boy Scouts Can't Live by Their Traditional Values, Who Can?" Another indication, and maybe a portent of the future of staged tradition, is the way that American folklife events deliver their social messages globally on the Internet. In 1997, the Northwest Folklife Festival in Seattle broadcast performances live over the World Wide Web. What are the themes producing meaningful symbols and values? "Women's Work," "An African Aesthetic in Two Worlds," and "Labor History and Arts."

Folklore frequently served to narrate images of "following tradition" at the heart of culture, to signal the values parents inculcated in children, the legacies that the nation defends, the environments humanity and nature require, and the differences that communities protect. It could be made apparent in popularized rhetoric spread in schools and media, in various forms of display from galleries to festivals, in the tourist productions of preindustrial tradition from the Amish to Zuni. Because folklore gave tradition its form and expression, it permitted *reproduction* in the public marketplace. Traditions could be peddled to legitimate forms of social praxis represented in campaigns ranging widely from "traditional values" to "gay rights." The payoff was institutionalization of ways of doing things, of thinking about values for the future inherent in tradition. The situation is not America's alone, but it became especially noticeable there because of highly vocal, widely publicized flaps over qualifying, multiplying identities of race, ethnicity, sexuality, and gender, among others.

Everyone is talking about culture because it has an expressive, symbolic value in directing attention, and organizing roles, in a public marketplace where competing social visions and often clashing political orders are hawked. People believe that it reduces to a core the dizzying array of contentious modern issues to resolve. In addition to symbolizing culture in discourse, their talk invites judgment of it. Arguments over its character, indeed its fate, seem to inevitably lead to cries for its rehabilitation. Objectifying tradition and thereby leaving it open to critical analysis is risky but can help advance the evaluation of possible social unities in American society. In a decentered America, a contest is discernible for the authority that will lead the discussion of culture and guide the decisions that really matter. They involve nothing less than the nation's recentering.

As political investment in the enterprise of culture increases, speculation turns to the ways that tradition writ large has been, and will be, followed. Catapulted into the public eye, tradition attracts interests from scattered quarters, academic and otherwise. The turf of tradition, once the recognized domain of folklorists, has become common ground. Challenging academic authority, public agencies and private organizations retread tradition as the way to rationalize culture and legitimize social vision. The public marketplace has become crowded with bidders for the role of explaining American culture, and in the process clashes are apparent over the groupings that constitute, indeed exemplify national culture. Folklore has been a subject used to record and realize culture with the object of presenting it, and ultimately controlling it. Questioning tradition's purpose and power for social grounding, the discourse of American culture in the modernizing twentieth century has summoned the past and present in tradition to confront, sometimes direct, the future of experience.

Bibliographic Essay

FROM THE BEGINNINGS OF THE AMERICAN STUDIES MOVEMENT, FOLKLORE AND FOLKLIFE research has lent authenticity to a claim for an American tradition. In *American Humor* (1931), often cited as a pathbreaker in opening American culture to interdisciplinary scrutiny, Constance Rourke explained the rise of a national consciousness in the development of folklore born of the American experience. "No other people has created its folklore and tried to assimilate it and turn it to the purposes of the creative imagination and of self-understanding, all within a brief span," Constance Rourke later declared in *The Roots of American Culture* (1942, 243). Rourke believed that a distinctive American folklore formed out of the special circumstances of the new nation: "The wonder is that a people whose elements have been far from homogeneous should have steadily created a distinctive lore from its earliest days, and that the hold among us upon these materials should have been so stubborn against all the forces of modern civilization which tends to scatter them to the four winds" (Rourke [1931] 1959, 244).

For Rourke's faculty colleague Martha Beckwith, American society was too diverse and derived too greatly from foreign sources to be described as a single tradition. She outlined many living ethnic and religious "strains in the process of creating an American cultural life" in *Folklore in America* (1931), published the same year as *American Humor* (see Beckwith 1931b, 64). In the phrasing of her title, Beckwith set her social vision as a contrast to "American folklore." In her pluralist view, folklore as the possession of small social groups crossed national lines, and she drew comparisons with the material found in America to examples dispersed around the globe. We can only imagine the lively debates she and Rourke had in the English faculty lounge at Vassar, and their different keynotes reverberated in many public discussions of American identity through the twentieth century as momentous immigration, industrialization, and urbanization forced reevaluation of the relation of the future to the nation's roots.

This tension between using folklore as evidence of a distinctive new national tradition or a diverse configuration of old imported traditions was especially noticeable in publications on American life from the 1960s into the 1980s. Richard M. Dorson, who championed the connection of folklore research to American studies since he emerged in the 1940s among the first holders of the Ph.D. in American civilization, was especially vocal in expressing an intellectual priority for locating an "American Folklore" over "Folklore in America." He devoted several books, especially *American Folklore* (1959), *American Folklore and the Historian* (1971), *America in Legend* (1973), *Man and Beast in American Comic Legend* (1982), and two special issues of the *Journal of the Folklore Institute* (1978, 1980) to the theme. In reviews, he railed against collections neglecting his Americanist theme such as *Folklore in America* (1966) edited by Tristram P. Coffin and Hennig Cohen, and *Folklore on the American Land* (1972) by Duncan Emrich.[1]

To be sure, Dorson observed differences among Americans—regional, ethnic, and occupational—evident in folklore across the varied American landscape. His books *Bloodstoppers and Bearwalkers: Folk Traditions of the Upper Peninsula* (1952), *Buying the Wind: Regional Folklore in the United States* (1964), and *Land of the Millrats* (1981) attest to that. Yet he saw these differences converging into a unifying American self under the weight of historical forces. At the first joint meeting of the American Studies Association and the American Folklore Society in 1957, he called attention to a distinctive set of historical patterns—exploration and colonization, revolution and the establishment of a democratic republic, westward movement, immigration, slavery and civil war, and industrialization and technology—that "shaped and created new folklore, or new adaptations of old folklore themes" peculiar to American society. This address, entitled "A Theory for American Folklore," became the centerpiece of his influential book *American Folklore and the Historian* (Dorson 1971, 15–48).[2]

Laying out his "American Folklore Bibliography" for *American Studies International* in 1977, Dorson continued his advocacy for American folklore studies highlighting historical themes and conditions unique to the United States. He further emphasized that this kind of American folklore research "is an indispensable component of any American studies program, for it deals directly with the lives and ideas of the average man and woman, of work groups, of minority cultures, ultimately of all segments of American society" (1971a, 23). In keeping with his approach, his bibliography gave first priority to studies of national folklore, especially historical events and heroes. Secondarily he covered studies of regional, urban, Afro-American, immigrant-ethnic, and Amerindian societies in America, but even then, he selected those studies that showed change from an older tradition into a new American form.

Primarily concerned with oral genres such as tales and songs, Dorson nonetheless recognized the expansion of the American study of folk traditions to material expressions such as art and architecture, but he devoted only one paragraph to "folklife and material culture." Worried about the ethnographic challenge of folklife and material culture to his model, he voiced suspicion of the communitarian orientation of folklife research, and its uncovering of cultural persistence and diversity. He saved some of his highest praise for Constance Rourke's historical literary work, and considered his own efforts as building on her ideas. Claiming that the realization of historical inquiry into folklore was only just emerging in American studies, Dorson's forward-looking message in 1971 for the international American studies community was that "the best books on American folklore are yet to be written" (1971a, 23).

As the historically oriented Constance Rourke had her anthropological detractor in Martha Beckwith, so too did Dorson have dissenting folklorists who sought behavioral connections to American studies. Writing in the 1976 bibliography issue of *American Quarterly*, Richard Bauman and Roger Abrahams with Susan Kalčik reiterated the split between American folklore and folklore in America and surveyed the familiar categories of region, ethnicity, race, occupation, and genre. They closed with attention to "a social inter-actional perspective, centering around the notion of performance" that they felt was modi-fying the traditional organizing principles of American folklorists. In this perspective researchers observed varying individual "performances" of traditional behavior influenced by the immediate sociocultural context. This idea led to more consideration of the lives of individual American folk performers and artists from a wide range of backgrounds and the processes for learning and expressing folklore under various American conditions. Thus Bauman, Abrahams, and Kalčik pointed to studies of biography, repertoire, and perfor-mance style of folk performers leading to increased interest in "community, locale, and per-sonal experience as formative influences" in diverse American contexts (1976, 377).

Although addressing changes in folklore studies, Bauman, Abrahams, and Kalčik equal-ly implied a shift in the mission of American studies from one of uncovering, in Rourke's words, the "common storage of experience and character," usually centered on literary arts, to one seeking to describe American lives and identities in everyday cultural practice. This shift suggests questioning that leaves behind the issue of whether American traditions were created or imported (seen as a process, they are obviously both), and moves to the complex use of traditions by and for individuals in various settings that are part of American life.[3] Additionally, inquiry can follow the ways that Americans carry multiple identities through their lives and the patterns of forming, expressing, and manipulating those identities. This kind of inquiry opens American studies to global applications, since these identities are in question when Americans or American expressions enter into surroundings outside the United States. This new questioning characterizes many new studies since the surveys of the 1970s on folklore and folklife in relation to American studies.

If there has been a trend since the 1970s, it has been that writing on folklore in American studies appears more "ethnographic."[4] The basis of fieldwork using interview and observa-tion to describe the communication of symbols among people in contemporary cultural scenes and artifacts is conspicuous in many studies. And during the 1990s, a rejuvenation of the historical component of tradition is evident, thus forming a new folkloristic synthesis of art, literature, culture, and history. Rather than trying to describe America as a whole, more attention has been made to describe the complexity of American scenes and peoples that influence, and have influenced, the sense of the whole and its parts. Thus studies of Louisiana Cajuns, Pennsylvania Germans, city firefighters, and corporate humorists are all American studies that connect to cultural studies abroad. Implying the importance of social identities, these studies are complemented by a movement in folklore and folklife research to consider the importance of settings and practices they suggest (the schools, workplaces, and leisure spots) within the common scenes of American life.

Particularly in its emphasis on the processes of "tradition," folklore and folklife research notably contributes to American studies by identifying longstanding values and beliefs inherent in socially shared expressions that connect to individual lives as part of the American experience. One indication of the scholarly appeal of folklore in American stud-ies has been the rise of folklore and folklife courses in American studies programs and departments from a handful in 1971 to thirteen percent of all folklore courses offered in the United States in 1986. The previous domination of ballad and song gave way to American folklore and folklife as the dominant folkloristic subject taught in American colleges (twenty-six percent), just behind the introductory course (Baker 1971, 1986a). The numbers are probably even higher today. One can understand the folkloristic connection by recalling that the basis of American studies methodology in "myth, symbol, and image" prevalent during the 1950s and 1960s borrowed heavily, even if problematically, from folkloristic ideas of mythology's connection to a shared cultural consciousness or worldview (see Dundes 1972; Toelken 1979; Smith 1950; Tate 1973). Further, terms representing attention to behavioral manifestations of social perceptions of the past and present such as "folkways," "tradition," and "memory," concepts again emanating from folklore and folklife research, have since the 1980s taken prominent places as keywords of new major American studies titles (Fischer 1989; Glassberg 1990; Kammen 1991; Levine 1992).[5]

In this essay I will update the surveys of the 1970s with particular attention to new interdisciplinary arguments on the nature of American identities and lives using folklore as evidence. I therefore depart from the social organization of the older surveys to present a categorization emphasizing research problems of folkloric "processes" in relation to American studies. I begin with studies focusing on types of American folk expression and their performers. More studies now refer to "expression" rather than genres to draw attention to native perspectives on what is being said, sung, or made as an expression of self and society. I discuss aspects of ethnicity, region, and occupation in the next section on American "Identities and Communities." In this category, I also add a description of the growing bookshelf for identities of age, gender, sexual preference, and physical ability not described in earlier surveys. I then move on to consider studies of "Settings and Contexts" for these identities and communities. Under this heading, I especially cover studies of work, school, and recreational contexts as well as landscape and material culture. I will close with a brief guide to the study of American folklore, including Internet sources for historiography and bibliography.

EXPRESSIONS AND PERFORMERS

Surveys of folklore before World War II often pointed to folk songs as a primary example of America's rich folk heritage. Abundant collections attested to the preservation of old English and Scottish ballads while some such as G. Malcolm Laws in *Native American Balladry* (1950) indexed songs that are unique to the American scene. Most folk song surveys still available categorize both native and imported sources (See Cazden et al., 1982; Randolph 1982; McNeil 1987–1988, 1993; List 1991). Since the 1970s more folk song studies have examined the functions of musical traditions especially as they have adapted to popular culture associated around the world with American tastes. *Folk Music and Modern Sound* (1982), a collection of essays edited by William Ferris and Mary L. Hart, sets the tone for many books that explore folk music and folklore's relation to country music, blues, jazz, Cajun, zydeco, polka, and a variety of other ethnic expressions in America. Perhaps the most sweeping study relating folk tradition to commercial culture is Bill C. Malone's *Country Music, U.S.A.*, which first appeared in 1968 and was revised in 1985. He strongly argued for the influence of southern traditions on American musical culture and he expanded this argument in *Southern Music, American Music* (1979). Some challenge to his thesis along with a survey of a neglected northern country music tradition can be found in my *Old-Time Music Makers of New York State* (Bronner 1987). During the 1990s, country music has been a common ground for American studies scholars and folklorists, judging from a spate of interpretative books such as Curtis Ellison's *Country Music Culture* (1995), George Lewis's *All That Glitters* (1993), and Cecilia Tichi's *High Lonesome* (1994). While folkloristic works focus on the communitarian character of country music in regional and ethnic traditions, American studies scholars have been attracted to country music's claim as America's traditional music.

Some folk musical studies examine less of the regional associations in country music and blues traditions and explore more of the themes inherent in American texts and performances. Archie Green studied recorded coal-mining songs, for example, in *Only a Miner* (1972), while Norm Cohen used commercial recordings to examine the theme of railroads in American folk song in *Long Steel Rail* (1981), and Paul Oliver surveyed the cultural meanings of blues themes in *Songsters and Saints* (1984). Beyond country music and blues, ethnic music in America is finally receiving its due with books such as *Tenement Songs* (1982) by Mark Slobin, *Italian Wind Bands* (1990) by Emma Rocco, *A Passion for Polka* (1992) by Victor Greene, *Barrio Rhythm* (1992) by Steven Loza, and *The Makers of Cajun Music* (1984) by Barry Jean Ancelet. The title of Ancelet's book underscores the attention to individual performers or "makers" that was influenced by *Folksongs and Their Makers* (1971) by Henry Glassie, Edward D. Ives, and John F. Szwed. Other studies of individual performers can be found in *Joe Scott, the Woodsman-Songmaker* (1978) by Edward Ives, *Adirondack Voices* (1981) by Robert D. Bethke, and *Virginia Piedmont Blues* (1990) by Barry Lee Pearson. Studies that question the performance styles and creative traditions of performers are *Early Downhome Blues* (1977) by Jeff Todd Titon, *Big Road Blues* (1982) by David Evans, *Singing in the Spirit* (1992) by Ray Allen, and *African Banjo Echoes in Appalachia* (1995) by Cecilia Conway. The issues of authenticity and cultural transformation that bring American studies, popular culture, and folklore research together are taken up in *Transforming Tradition: Folk Music Revivals Examined* (1993) edited by Neil V. Rosenberg.

Besides what is sung, what is traditionally said holds a special interest for students of folklore. The proverb is a basic form of folk speech that is often used to express a shared cultural wisdom, and, appropriately, Wolfgang Mieder has surveyed the cultural unity and diversity of American proverbs in *American Proverbs* (1989), *A Dictionary of American Proverbs* (1991), and *Proverbs Are Never Out of Season* (1993). In keeping with the theme of this book of the importance of the rhetoric of tradition in public, often politicized, discourse, his contribution of *The Politics of Proverbs* (1997) should be singled out for attention. International in his scope, Mieder covers rhetorical strategies of proverb use by history-changing figures such as Adolph Hitler and Winston Churchill in addition to American leaders. Elsewhere, he has provocatively suggested the cross-cultural possibilities for comparing American proverbs to other national collections (see Mieder 1992). A suggestive ethnic study of proverbs examining cross-cultural encounters is Roger Mitchell's "Tradition, Change, and Hmong Refugees" (1992), which analyzes the use of folk proverbs by Southeast Asian refugees to adjust to the startlingly different American scene.

Another traditional expression with international connections is the "modern" legend. Many of the legends deal with American icons such as cars, fast-food chains, corporations, fads, and celebrities. *American Folk Legend* (1971), edited by Wayland Hand, contained important general essays by Linda Dégh and Alan Dundes on the modern legend along with chapters on American historical legendry promoted by Richard Dorson (see Dorson 1971c, 1973a, 1982b). The overlap of legendary belief and documentary history in American naming of places is evident in Ronald Baker's *From Needmore to Prosperity* (1995). Historical folk legendry (not to mention American naming traditions) deserves more attention than it has received, while studies of modern legendry, particularly in American settings, have thrived. In *The Vanishing Hitchhiker* (1981) Jan Harold Brunvand offers a general introduction to American modern legendry and follows the work with several updated collections (1984, 1986, 1989, 1993). Gary Alan Fine focuses on themes of sexuality and commercial culture in American modern legendry in *Manufacturing Tales* (1992). Ronald L. Baker provides an exemplary collection of historical and modern legendry for a single state in *Hoosier Folk Legends* (1982); another strong regional collection is *Storytellers: Folktales and Legends from the South* (1989) by John Burrison. Several new studies promise more explorations of African-American and Amerindian narrative traditions (see Roberts 1989; P. Turner 1992, 1993; Brady 1984; Lankford 1987; Cunningham 1992). An intersection of ethnic and narrative theories from folklore and the concerns for national and popular culture from American studies has been in the role of tradition in the mass media as demonstrated by Linda Dégh in *American Folklore and the Mass Media* (1994), Harold Schechter in *The Bosom Serpent* (1988), and Jackson Lears in *Fables of Abundance* (1994) (see also Lears 1988).

American folk humor, since Rourke's day a strong link between folklore and American studies, has enjoyed renewed attention by folklorists. Recent studies and collections explore the diversity of American humor, modern forms of folk humor, and the symbolic meanings of joke cycles. Three praiseworthy regional collections, for example, are *Jokelore* (1986) by Ronald Baker, *Ozark Mountain Humor* (1989) by W. K. McNeil, and *Midwestern Folk Humor* (1991) by James Leary. Essays on modern joke cycles taken from different perspectives are featured in *Jokes and Their Relations* (1992) by Elliott Oring, and *Cracking Jokes* (1987) by Alan Dundes. Dundes, collaborating with Carl Pagter, has also been instrumental with books such as *Work Hard and You Shall Be Rewarded* in opening photocopied folk humor often found in corporate America to scholarly scrutiny (1978, 1987, 1991). As with explorations of other narrative expression, a number of recent studies consider more closely the perspective of individuals and their often varying audiences. *Humor and the Individual* (1984a) edited by Elliott Oring brings together several such studies to raise questions about the role of the joke teller in American society (see also Dégh 1995, 285–305, 325–40).

Often combining legendary and humorous elements is the "personal narrative" or "personal experience story." This recounting, according to traditional models of events in one's life, is gaining notice for what it reveals about narrative process and contextual influences. Sandra Dolby Stahl contributed *Literary Folkloristics and the Personal Narrative* (1989) toward this study, and a spate of titles on the subject should be forthcoming judging from scholarship in journals (see Dorson 1977f; Titon 1980; Wilson 1991; Kirshenblatt-Gimblett 1989a; Dégh 1995, 70–78). If these essays are useful to American studies for exploring the ways that Americans frame their experiences in narrative, another suggestive study, "Tales of America" by Knut Djupedal (1990), opens for inquiry the stories told about America by returning emigrants. More work could also be done on the culturally relative formation of narrative experience in childhood, as Brian Sutton-Smith has explored in *The Folkstories of Children* (1981) (see also Sullivan 1992; Bronner 1992d; Friel 1995).

Studies of customs including American holidays, folk medicine, games, and rites of passage lag behind those on song and story, although some excellent contributions have been made since the 1970s. Folk medicine is represented by *American Folk Medicine* (1976) edited by Wayland Hand, *Magical Medicine* (1980) by Wayland Hand, *Healing, Magic, and Religion* (1985) edited by Jack Santino, *Black Folk Medicine* (1984) edited by Wilbur H. Watson, and *Herbal and Magical Medicine* (1992) edited by James Kirkland, Holly Mathews, C. W. Sullivan III, and Karen Baldwin. The medical profession has become more aware of folk medical scholarship, often subsumed under the category of "unorthodox" or "alternative" medicine in studies such as *Other Healers* (1988), edited by Norman Gevitz, and *Hand Trembling, Frenzy Witchcraft, and Moth Madness* (1987) by Jerrold E. Levy, Raymond Heutra, and Dennis Parker.

Ritual, festival, and play are related topics that combine interests in tradition and culture from a number of disciplines. Combining psychology, anthropology, and folklore, Brian Sutton-Smith has contributed now classic studies in play, such as *The Folkgames of Children* (1972) and *The Masks of Play* (1984, edited with Donna Kelly-Byrne). Two folkloristic books showing the diversity of games in America are *Texas Toys and Games* (1989) edited by Francis Edward Abernethy and *Step It Down* (1987) by Bessie Jones and Bess Lomax Hawes. These books are more collections than studies, but may be useful as guides to the range of activities engaged in by Americans, as will a collection such as *The Folklore of American Holidays* (1991), edited by Hennig Cohen and Tristram Potter Coffin. More in the way of studies that tend to emphasize the creative and pluralistic celebration of holidays are Jack Santino's *All Around the Year* (1994) and *Halloween and Other Festivals of Death and Life* (1994). A regional study of customs is *Ozark Baptizings, Hangings, and Other Diversions* (1984) by Robert K. Gilmore, and a focused study available for a holiday tradition is *O Freedom! Afro-American Emancipation Celebrations* (1987) by William H. Wiggins, Jr. An overview of traditions related to the life cycle is provided in *Rites of Passage in America* (1992) edited by Pamela B. Nelson, and a focused study of a modern rite of passage is *Birth as an American Rite of Passage* (1992) by Robbie E. Davis-Floyd.

Especially gaining strength, if publication output is an indication, is the study of folk art, architecture, and foodways. *Common Places* (1986) edited by Dell Upton and John Michael Vlach is a flagship anthology in folk architectural research. Its sections indicate the directions of this research: definitions and demonstrations, construction, function, history, design, and intention. For demonstrations of imported traditions and their adaptation in America, for example, one can consult *America's Architectural Roots* (1986) edited by Dell Upton (see also Noble 1992), *The Pennsylvania Barn* (1992) by Robert Ensminger, and *Building Traditions among Swedish Settlers in Rural Minnesota* (1983) by Lena Andersson-Palmqvist. Warren E. Roberts's *Log Buildings of Southern Indiana* (1984), John Morgan's *The Log House in East Tennessee* (1990) (see also Jordan 1985), Gabrielle M. Lanier and Bernard L. Herman's *Everyday Architecture of the Mid-Atlantic* (1997), and Peter Nabokov and Robert Easton's *Native American Architecture* (1989) are especially good for questions of form and construction. Studies of history and function, especially in regional and ethnic contexts are offered in *Folk Architecture in Little Dixie* (1981) and *Paradise Valley, Nevada* (1995) by Howard Wight Marshall, *Hollybush* (1984) by Charles E. Martin, *Architecture and Rural Life in Central Delaware, 1700–1900* (1987) by Bernard L. Herman, *Homeplace* (1991) by Michael Ann Williams, *Big House, Little House, Back House, Barn* (1984) by Thomas Hubka, *The Dutch-American Farm* (1992) by David Steven Cohen, *Back of the Big House* (1993) by John Michael Vlach, and *Ozark Vernacular Houses* (1994) by Jean Sizemore. The outstanding work for design and intention is Henry Glassie's *Folk Housing in Middle Virginia* (1975). A forum bringing together these concerns from American studies, folklife research, archaeology, and history has been *Perspectives in Vernacular Architecture* (see Carter and Herman 1989, 1991; Cromley and Hudgins 1995). A global reference that includes an extensive North American section and discussion of folkloristic approaches to architecture is *Encyclopedia of Vernacular Architecture of the World* (1997), edited by Paul Oliver.

The bookshelf of folk art studies mostly divides between studies of regions and groups and individual artists. The leading collections of essays are *Folk Art and Art Worlds* (1992) edited by John Michael Vlach and Simon J. Bronner and *Perspectives on American Folk Art* (1980) edited by Ian M. G. Quimby and Scott T. Swank. Exemplary state and regional surveys include *Local Color* (1982) by William Ferris, *Passing Time and Traditions* (1984) edited by Steven Ohrn, *Circles of Tradition* (1989) edited by Willard B. Moore, *Craft and Community* (1988) edited by Shalom Staub, *Southern Arizona Folk Arts* (1988) by James S. Griffith, and *Folk Arts of Washington State* (1989) edited by Jens Lund. Some praiseworthy studies of ethnic groups include *The Afro-American Tradition in Decorative Arts* (1978) by John Michael Vlach, *Afro-American Folk Art and Crafts* (1983) edited by William Ferris, *Arts of the Pennsylvania Germans* (1983) by Scott Swank, *Decorated Furniture of the Mahantango Valley* (1987) by Henry M. Reed (see also Bronner 1992e), and *Material Culture and People's Art among the Norwegians in America* (1994) and *Norwegian Folk Art* (1995), both edited by Marion Nelson. A suggestive survey of folk art by American women is *Artists in Aprons* (1979) by C. Kurt Dewhurst, Betty MacDowell, and Marsha MacDowell. Among studies of specific crafts, quilt studies are prominent; see *Kentucky Quilts and Their Makers* (1976) by Mary Washington Clarke, *Michigan Quilts* (1987) edited by Marsha MacDowell and Ruth D. Fitzgerald, *Stitched from the Soul* (1990) by Gladys-Marie Fry, *African American Quiltmaking in Michigan* (1997) by Marsha MacDowell, and *To Honor and Comfort: Native Quilting Traditions* (1997) by C. Kurt Dewhurst and Marsha MacDowell. Other excellent folkloristic studies exist for pottery, rug weaving, and wood carving; see John Burrison's *Brothers in Clay* (1983), Charles G. Zug's *Turners and Burners* (1986), Geraldine Niva Johnson's *Weaving Rag Rugs* (1985), and my own *Chain Carvers* (1985), revised as *The Carver's Art* (1996). *American Folk Masters* (1992) by Steve Siporin celebrates in sweeping style the achievements of individual folk artists that have been recognized nationally. Focused biographical and contextual studies of folk artists include *Charleston Blacksmith* (1992) by John Michael Vlach, *The Wood Carvers of Córdova, New Mexico* (1980) by Charles L. Briggs, *Dulcimer Maker* (1984) by R. Gerald Alvey, *A Bearer of Tradition* (1989) by Rosemary Joyce, and *Craftsman of the Cumberlands* (1989) by Michael Owen Jones. Jones expands on his influential behavioral ideas in *Exploring Folk Art* (1987), and in a series of compact studies he edits for the University Press of Mississippi (see Kitchener 1994; Sherman 1995). Several suggestive studies explore modern assemblages of objects as "folk environments" in *Personal Places* (1984) edited by Daniel Franklin Ward (see also Sheehy 1991; Kitchener 1994). Examples of such assemblages that particularly address American studies concerns are the essays by Jack Santino on folk displays of yellow ribbons and flags that show American responses to national crisis and seasonal displays at Halloween that reveal American attitudes toward nature (Santino 1992a, 1992b).

More studies could be done on the themes in verbal and visual art. Some texts that propose this approach are *The Pueblo Storyteller* (1986) by Barbara A. Babcock and Guy and

Doris Monthan, *Religious Folk Art in America* (1983) by C. Kurt Dewhurst, Betty MacDowell, and Marsha MacDowell, *Hex Signs* (1989) by Don Yoder and Thomas Graves, and *American Wildlife in Symbol and Story* (1987) edited by Angus K. Gillespie and Jay Mechling. The first work examines the popularity of depicting a female storyteller among Pueblo potters. The third book interprets the use of geometric designs among Pennsylvania Germans, and the fourth publication considers the representation of the rattlesnake, alligator, and bear, among others, in American folklore and popular culture. In regard to the analysis of symbols and themes across a number of expressive forms, one should consult Alan Dundes's essays on shared American tendencies. *Interpreting Folklore* (1980), for example, contains essays on American future and visual orientation, fondness for patterning in "threes," and male preoccupation with football.

Foodways represent studies of foods as well as traditions associated with them such as preparation, preservation, and dining. Because of the social character of dining, foodways studies often stress social and behavioral aspects of everyday and festive life. Charles Camp's *American Foodways* (1989) serves as a folkloristic survey of American traditional eating habits. Anthologies on the subject include *Foodways and Eating Habits* (1983) edited by Michael Owen Jones, Bruce Giuliano, and Roberta Krell, *Ethnic and Regional Foodways in the United States* (1984) edited by Linda Keller Brown and Kay Mussell, and *"We Gather Together"* (1992) edited by Theodore C. Humphrey and Lin T. Humphrey. The outstanding survey of a state's diverse ethnic foodways is *The Minnesota Ethnic Food Book* (1986) by Anne R. Kaplan, Marjorie A. Hoover, and Willard B. Moore. A focused study of a foodways tradition is *Clambake* (1992) by Kathy Neustadt, and a thought-provoking consideration of the Anglo-American structure of "three solid meals a day" is "The Logic of Anglo-American Meals" (1982) by Michael P. Carroll.

The interconnection among folk art, architecture, and foodways in a society forms what scholars call "material culture." The material culture bookshelf includes the general anthology *American Material Culture and Folklife* (1992), which I edited, and *Living in a Material World* (1991), edited by Gerald Pocius, which is a result of a conference on Canadian and American approaches to material culture. With American studies in mind, I offered a book-length interpretation of the relation of American material folk culture to mass society in *Grasping Things* (1986). The realm of "folklife," which includes material culture and social customs based in community, has benefited from the works of Don Yoder, notably *American Folklife* (1976) and *Discovering American Folklife* (1990). Jan Harold Brunvand surveys the genres of American folklife and folklore in *The Study of American Folklore* (1986), accompanied by *Readings in American Folklore* (1979). Richard Dorson takes up the task in *Folklore and Folklife* (1972), although the book covers more than the American experience. He concentrates more on American forms and performers in the *Handbook of American Folklore* (1983). *Folk Groups and Folklore Genres* (1986) edited by Elliott Oring offers introductory essays on narrative, objects, religion, ballads and folk songs, riddles and proverbs, and balances them with attention to the social context of ethnicity, religion, occupation, and childhood. Taking a processual approach to folklore and folklife, Barre Toelken writes on *The Dynamics of Folklore* (revised edition, 1996) while Robert Georges and Michael Owen Jones present several views of folklore as "historical artifact," "describable and transmissible entity," "culture," and "behavior" in *Folkloristics* (1995).

IDENTITIES AND COMMUNITIES

In *Folklore Matters* (1989), Alan Dundes understands the importance of folklore as "one of the principal means by which an individual and a group discovers or establishes his or its identity" (35). The advantage of folklore as evidence is that it, in Dundes's words, "gives a view of a people from the inside-out rather than from the outside-in" (35). It allows scholars of American studies to grasp the complex ways Americans view their identities, often simultaneously held, of ethnicity, religion, region, community, gender, and family, as well as nationhood. Susan D. Rutherford, for example, offers folklore communicated through sign language as evidence of a distinctive cultural identity held among others in the "American deaf community" (Rutherford 1983). Because folklore is often shared privately among a group of people, it often reveals, as Rutherford discovered, the connections within a community as well as its deep-seated values and beliefs. Folklore is often gathered to give an intimate cultural view of communities and subcultural identities, although Dorson made a claim for an overarching American tradition based on a shared narrative knowledge in *America in Legend* (1973).

Cases for American regional identity typically use traditional speech, music, food, and architecture bound to a landscape for evidence. Dorson's early survey of regional traditions in *Buying the Wind* (1964) emphasized isolated oral traditions, but later works tended to highlight regional "performances" and more symbolic evidence from festivals and material arts. While Dorson tended to assume that regional lore remains constant, the later studies explored the ways people in a region dynamically express distinctive traditions variously influenced by historic and ethnic conditions. Examples of this approach can be found in *Sense of Place* (1990) edited by Barbara Allen and Thomas Schlereth. In this view oriented more toward cultural lives functioning in communities than literary comparison across broad expanses, the cultural sense of place tends to be smaller and more adaptive than the larger sections of the South and West, for example, mapped earlier. Book-length studies and anthologies showing the "cultural lives" perspective are *The Ramapo Mountain People* (1974) and *Folk Legacies Revisited* (1995) by David Steven Cohen, *Pinelands Folklife* (1987) edited by Rita Zorn Moonsammy, David Steven Cohen, and Lorraine E. Williams, *Don't Go Up Kettle Creek* (1983) by William Lynwood Montell, and *The Last Yankees* (1990) by Scott E. Hastings, Jr. The South has been especially well covered in regional studies, such as those in a series edited by Lynwood Montell for the University Press of Mississippi (see Ancelet, Edwards, and Pitre 1991; Bucuvalas, Bulger, and Kennedy 1994; McNeil 1995a; Williams 1995). In addition to the identities fueled by the cultural lives in a region, a few anthologies and studies such as W. K. McNeil's *Appalachian Images in Folk and Popular Culture* (1995) and George H. Lewis's "The Maine Lobster as Regional Icon: Competing Images over Time and Social Class" (1989) have explored the images of regional traditions held by those outside the region.

Surveys of folklore within state and county boundaries typically underscore the diversity of ethnic-regional-community identities. The outstanding study of a state's traditions is *The Lore of New Mexico* (1988) by Marta Weigle and Peter White. Other notable works on states, many sponsored or influenced by "public" folklore programs with state agencies, include *"And Other Neighborly Names"* (1981) edited by Richard Bauman and Roger D. Abrahams, *Michigan Folklife Reader* (1987) edited by C. Kurt Dewhurst and Yvonne R. Lockwood, *Idaho Folklife* (1985) edited by Louie W. Attebery, *Arts in Earnest* (1990) edited by Daniel W. Patterson and Charles G. Zug III, *The Folklore and Folklife of New Jersey* (1983) by David Steven Cohen, *An Arkansas Folklore Sourcebook* (1992) edited by W. K. McNeil and William M. Clements, *Folklife in the Florida Parishes* (1989) by the Louisiana Folklife Program, and *South Florida Folklife* (1994) by Tina Bucuvalas, Peggy A. Bulger, and Stetson Kennedy. Especially suggestive for American cultural studies is the kind of work exploring cultural exchange and formation at the borders of the United States. Examples are *Folklore and Culture on the Texas-Mexican Border* (1993) by Américo Paredes and *A Shared Space: Folklife in the Arizona-Sonora Borderlands* (1995) by James S. Griffith.

Urban identity in folklore and folklife research has been well recognized since the publication of the essays in *The Urban Experience and Folk Tradition* (1971) edited by Américo Paredes and Ellen J. Stekert. Focused studies on urban folklore and folklife include Richard M. Dorson's *Land of the Millrats* (1981), Eleanor Wachs's *Crime-Victim Stories* (1988), and Amanda Dargan and Steven Zeitlin's *City Play* (1990). Margy McClain discusses "cultural identity" in Chicago in *A Feeling for Life* (1988), and Sally Harrison-Pepper examines street performing in New York City in *Drawing a Circle in the Square* (1991). Phillips Stevens contributes a collection of essays on folklore in Buffalo for a special issue of *New York Folklore* (1984). Impressive presentations of ethnic communities within an urban environment are Dorothy Noyes's *Uses of Tradition: Arts of Italian Americans in Philadelphia* (1989) and Jerome Mintz's *Hasidic People* (1992). *Alley Life in Washington: Community, Religion, and Folklife in the City, 1850–1970* (1980) by James Borchert particularly uncovers African-American cultural patterns in the nation's capital. A suggestive study interpreting the interaction of ethnic folk traditions and American urban and popular culture is Jenna Weissman Joselit's *The Wonders of America: Reinventing Jewish Culture, 1880–1950* (1994).

Sweeping ethnic folklore studies are now available for Italian Americans (Malpezzi and Clements 1992), German Americans (Barrick 1987), Mexican Americans (West 1988), Romanian Americans (Thigpen 1980), and Jewish Americans (Sherman 1992). More regionally focused studies cover Louisiana Cajuns (Ancelet, Edwards, and Pitre 1991), Pennsylvania Germans (Burke and Hill 1991; see also Beam 1995), San Francisco Chinese (Hom 1992), Italian Americans in the West (Taylor and Williams 1992), and Laotian Hmong in Michigan (Dewhurst and MacDowell 1984). A collection of essays examining the adaptation of ethnic folklore in modern life is *Creative Ethnicity* (1991) edited by Stephen Stern and John Allan Cicala. Examples of studies focusing on specific traditions related to ethnic identity are Yvonne Lockwood's "The Sauna: An Expression of Finnish-American Identity" (1977) and Larry Danielson's "St. Lucia in Lindsborg, Kansas" (1991).

African-American folklore and folklife scholarship claims a rapidly growing bookshelf. The "folklore in America" question of imported traditions continues in publications such as *Africanisms in American Culture* (1990) edited by Joseph E. Holloway. Coverage of African-American folklore and folklife has been greatly expanded by the publication of *Afro-American Folktales* (1985) edited by Roger D. Abrahams (standing in contrast to Dorson's *American Negro Folktales* [1967] which argued for primary influence on the narratives from European and American sources), *Afro-American Folk Art and Crafts* (1986) edited by William Ferris, and *By the Work of Their Hands* (1991) by John Michael Vlach. The classic study of Afro-American folk preaching has meanwhile been revised as *Can These Bones Live?* (1988) by Bruce Rosenberg complemented by a study by Gerald L. Davis, *I Got the Word in Me and I Can Sing It, You Know* (1985). For contrast in the contemporary African-American experience, one can compare the isolated Sea Islands community in

When Roots Die (1987) by Patricia Jones-Jackson and the middle-class urban black life in *The World from Brown's Lounge* (1983) by Michael J. Bell. Most noticeable in new scholarship interpreting African-American traditions is the integration of folkloristic and historical approaches. Exemplary titles are *Black Culture and Black Consciousness: Afro-American Folk Thought from Slavery to Freedom* (1977) by Lawrence W. Levine, *Down by the Riverside: A South Carolina Slave Community* (1984) by Charles Joyner, *From Trickster to Badman: The Black Folk Hero in Slavery and Freedom* (1989) by John W. Roberts, *Long Gone: The Mecklenburg Six and the Theme of Escape in Black Folklore* (1987) by Daryl Cumber Dance, *I Heard It through the Grapevine: Rumor in African-American Culture* (1993) by Patricia Turner, *New Raiments of Self: African American Clothing in the Antebellum South* (1997) by Helen Bradley Foster, and *Singing the Master: The Emergence of African-American Culture in the Plantation South* (1992) by Roger Abrahams.

Closely related to issues of race and ethnicity is the role of religion as an expressive identity for Americans. Yet studies of American folk religion have lagged behind those for ethnicity. Among the select studies in folk religion, there are praiseworthy folkloristic studies of Baptist and Pentecostal sects: *Powerhouse for God* (1988) by Jeff Todd Titon and *Handmaidens of the Lord* (1988) by Elaine Lawless. Other studies that examine religious preachers and believers are Donald E. Byrne's *No Foot of Land* (1975) about Methodist itinerants and William A. Wilson's *Folklore of Mormon Missionaries* (1982). A special issue of the *Jewish Folklore and Ethnology Review* (1991) edited by Guy Haskell surveys "Jews in the Heartland." "Growing Up Catholic and American: The Oral Tradition of Catholic School Students" (1986) by Louise Krasniewicz is a suggestive essay on the perceived "clash of values" between Catholic and American experience in Catholic schools. While Krasniewicz uses personal narrative as her primary evidence, Daniel Patterson offers a hefty study of the Shaker spiritual (1979) and a volume on southern folk religion he co-edited with James L. Peacock and Ruel Tyson (1988). Studies of specific religious rituals and customs include *Votive Offerings among Greek-Philadelphians* (1980) by Robert Teske and *Old Ship of Zion: The Afro-Baptist Ritual in the African Diaspora* (1992) by Walter F. Pitts. Active sectarian societies such as the Amish and Hasidim are covered in Donald Kraybill's *The Riddle of Amish Culture* (1989) and Jerome Mintz's *Hasidic People* (1992).

A growing trend in American studies is consideration of occupational identity expressed in folklore and folklife (see Green 1993). The intellectual grounding of such an approach is offered in *Working Americans: Contemporary Approaches to Occupational Folklife* (1978) edited by Robert H. Byington; it implies that the social organization of "community" and "class" is imbedded in the formation of occupational traditions. Several studies examine the lore and life of fishermen; see *The World of the Oregon Fishboat* (1986) by Janet Gilmore, *I Heard the Old Fisherman Say* (1988) by Patrick Mullen, and *Lake Erie Fishermen* (1990) by Timothy C. Lloyd and Patrick Mullen. On dry land, some exemplary studies are Robert McCarl's *The District of Columbia Fire Fighters' Project* (1985) and Maggie Holtzberg-Call's *The Lost World of the Craft Printer* (1992). A special issue of *New York Folklore* (1987) edited by Mary Arnold Twining on migrant workers opens an important field for further investigation. Farming and mining probably deserve more cultural attention in American studies as "occupational" (and in the case of hunting and fishing "recreational" cultures) than they have received; some suggestive studies are *Threshing in the Midwest* (1988) by J. Sanford Rikoon, *Backwoodsmen* (1995) by Thad Sitton, *Buck Fever*

(1990) by Mike Sajna, and *Tinged With Gold: Hop Culture in the United States* (1992) by Michael A. Tomlan. Especially contributing to American studies, Allen Tullos demonstrates in *Habits of Industry* (1989) the ways that a regional folk culture became transformed by the textile industry in the Carolina Piedmont. While the emphasis in studies of occupational folklore has been on craft labor and industrial work, corporate life receives attention in *Inside Organizations* (1988) edited by Michael Owen Jones, Michael Dane Moore, and Richard Christopher Snyder. Often taking a behavioral approach, this kind of study is less on the formation of "class" and more on the processes and symbols that mediate between needs of the individual and the organization and those that sustain cultural continuity among organization members.

An organization of immediate concern for Americans is the family, and the ways that Americans traditionally express their familial identity is the subject of *A Celebration of American Family Folklore* (1982) by Steven J. Zeitlin, Amy J. Kotkin, and Holly Cutting Baker. A focused study of a family's folk traditions is *Last Chivaree: The Hicks Family of Beech Mountain* (1996) by Robert Isbell. American children's expressions within family contexts have received renewed attention in books such as *One Potato, Two Potato* (1976) by Mary and Herbert Knapp, *American Children's Folklore* (1988) by Simon Bronner, *He-Said-She-Said* (1990) by Marjorie Harness Goodwin, and *Children's Folklore: A Source Book* (1995), edited by Brian Sutton-Smith, Jay Mechling, Thomas W. Johnson, and Felicia R. McMahon. At the other end of the life course, the defining role of life-review for the identities of the elderly is explored in *The Grand Generation* (1987) by Mary Hufford, Marjorie Hunt, and Steven Zeitlin, *Remembered Lives* (1992) by Barbara Myerhoff, and *Listening to Old Voices* (1992) by Patrick B. Mullen (see also Titon 1980; Pearson 1984; Kirshenblatt-Gimblett 1989a). Somewhere in between childhood and old age, the modern American preoccupation with "mid-life crisis" is interpreted by Stanley Brandes in *Forty: The Age and the Symbol* (1985).

Many American folklorists are reexamining the ways that traditions collected from women express an identity of gender. The anthology *Women's Folklore, Women's Culture* (1985) edited by Rosan A. Jordan and Susan J. Kalčik is not exclusively about American women or concerned with American studies, but most of the essays explore American settings. Espousing a "feminist" approach to "gendered" traditions, a variety of scholars contributed to *Feminist Messages: Coding in Women's Folk Culture* (1993) edited by Joan Newton Radner and *Feminist Theory and the Study of Folklore* (1994) edited by Susan Tower Hollis, Linda Pershing, and M. Jane Young. Similarly, a special issue on "Folklore and Feminism" in the *Journal of American Folklore* (1987) edited by Bruce Jackson contains several feminist perspectives on "traditional gender roles" in America, including articles on American Mormon and Pentecostal women, Amerindian mythology, and the American ritual of birth (see also Stoeltje 1988). Consideration of manliness as a developed tradition in America can be found in *The Men from the Boys* (1988) by Ray Raphael. Joseph Goodwin takes up the special identity of gay men expressed through folklore in *More Man Than You'll Ever Be* (1989).

SETTINGS AND CONTEXTS

The studies in this section typically have concerns that overlap with those in previous sections, but because they often present as their focus the contextual influence of American settings, it is worth considering them as a distinctive area of exploration in the relation of

American studies and folklore research.[6] One indication of this shift of focus is a special section of the journal *New York Folklore* on "Folklore in the Industrial Workplace" (1988) edited by Mia Boynton. The rhetoric of the workplace as a setting is important to interpret the ways that participants symbolically respond to one another as well as to the setting as part of the complex "American scene." For example, essays examine the function of humor in a lumberyard and the expressive responses of a woman in a typically male setting of a steel plant. *Inside Organizations* (1988) edited by Michael Owen Jones, Michael Dane Moore, and Richard Christopher Snyder is especially suggestive for American studies. It contains studies of typical American settings such as Girl Scout camps, booster festivals, military hospitals, and service agencies, as well as restaurants, aircraft factories, health care agencies, and corporate offices. Michael Owen Jones includes several studies of his own on restaurant, academic, and corporate settings in *Exploring Folk Art* (1987). He particularly scrutinizes the symbol-making power of organizations and the metaphoric value of their verbal and material culture.

Richard Dorson realized the contextual trend when he devoted the largest section of his last major work, the *Handbook of American Folklore* (1983) to "American Settings." Under this heading, he included brief overviews of "Office Folklore," "Factory Folklore," "The Folk Church," "Urban Folklore," "Suburban Folklore," and "Hanging Out: Recreational Folklore in Everyday Life," among others. Although not constituting a large bookshelf, work in organizational and contextual studies steadily grows. Michael Bell's *The World from Brown's Lounge* (1983) examines a bar setting for black middle-class play. Also using a bar setting, *The Cocktail Waitress* (1975) by James Spradley and Brenda Mann is an exemplary ethnography of "woman's work in a man's world" and includes discussions of narrative and customary traditions in response to the bar's social and material environment. I devoted the book *Piled Higher and Deeper* (1995) to the expressive culture of students on college campuses and over the Internet (see also Baker 1983; Toelken 1986; Mechling 1989c). An exceptional study of an ethnic setting is Barbara Myerhoff's portrait of life in a Jewish senior center in *Number Our Days* (1978) (see also Heilman 1976). A suggestive study exploring the folk rituals and customs of modern hospitals is "Customary Observances in Modern Medicine" (1989) by David Hufford.

The contextual influence of an American organization is especially evident in Gary Alan Fine's study of Little League baseball, *With the Boys* (1987). Jay Mechling explores the organizational settings of Boy Scouts in several essays (1980, 1981), and Bill Ellis compares legend telling in different summer camps in "'Ralph and Rudy': The Audience's Role in Recreating a Camp Legend" (1982). Children in institutions receive additional attention in Roberta Krell's poignant study, "At a Children's Hospital: A Folklore Survey" (1980). American soldiers in Vietnam attract a similar cultural investigation in a special issue of *Journal of American Folklore* (1989) edited by Bruce Jackson.

Many of the recent book-length folkloristic studies of American settings examine outdoor contexts of hunting and recreation. Mary Hufford offers *Chaseworld* (1992) about fox hunting in New Jersey's Pine Barrens region. John Miller's *Deer Camp* (1992) is an ethnographic portrait of the male preserve of deer hunting camp, while Edward Ives's *George Magoon and the Down East Game War* (1988) is more of an historical study of a conflict in Maine over hunting rights. In *You Hear the Ice Talking* (1986), I. Sheldon Posen examines the contextual influence of ice on Lake Champlain in the American Northeast. *City Play*

(1990) by Amanda Dargan and Steven Zeitlin applies a similar analysis to New Yorkers' adaptation to the urban setting of sidewalks and stoops.

What could be a more basic setting than the home? Yet many studies have neglected the varying ways that Americans have viewed and used this setting for material and verbal performance. I have contributed to the inquiry in *Grasping Things* (1986), and other publications include *Homeplace* (1991) by Michael Ann Williams, *Getting Comfortable in New York* (1990) edited by Susan L. Braunstein and Jenna Weissman Joselit, *Home Sweet Home* (1983) edited by Charles W. Moore, Kathryn Smith, and Peter Becker, and "Living Room Furnishings, Ethnic Identity, and Acculturation among Greek-Philadelphians" (1979) by Robert Thomas Teske. Studies of how setting alters verbal performance can be found in "Inside Millie's Kitchen" (1990) by Felicia McMahon and "A Traditional Storyteller in Changing Contexts" (1981) by Patrick B. Mullen.

Guides, Histories, Bibliographies, and Internet Sources

American Folklore: An Encyclopedia (1996) edited by Jan Harold Brunvand is the latest reference guide for students of American studies to the topics and approaches within American folklore and folklife research. Brunvand published a third edition of his widely adopted textbook *The Study of American Folklore* in 1986 and revised it further in 1998. He asks, "Does America Have a Folklore?" and spends the next 555 pages demonstrating that indeed it does, with examples of items and genres "found in" America and those "originated" there (Brunvand 1986, 38). Richard Dorson's *Handbook of American Folklore* (1983) emphasizes even more than Brunvand the American studies connections to folklore in contributors' brief essays under large sections on "American Experiences," "American Cultural Myths," "American Settings," "American Entertainments," and "American Forms and Performers." One regional model for an encyclopedic survey using folklore and folklife is the *Encyclopedia of Southern Culture* (1989) edited by Charles Reagan Wilson and William Ferris. It contains a separate section on "folklife" that includes genres, types, collectors, and performers in southern tradition (451–527).

Placing folklore and folklife research in American intellectual history was the intent of my *American Folklore Studies* (1986; see also Kammen 1991; Zumwalt 1988). Essays in *Folk Roots, New Roots* (1988) edited by Jane S. Becker and Barbara Franco address similar issues, particularly from a New England vantage. I offer a collection of essays by folklorists from Victorian America in *Folklife Studies from the Gilded Age* (1987) and, similarly, W. K. McNeil presents historic essays on the much romanticized Appalachian region in *Appalachian Images in Folk and Popular Culture* (1995). The history of public involvement in Appalachian folk culture is the subject of David E. Whisnant's *All That Is Native & Fine* (1983).

Making a great contribution to the recognition of folklore research and American studies has been the spate of biographies of individual folklorists. Richard Dorson's career as folklorist and Americanist has yet to be fully chronicled, but an assessment of his contributions is discussed in "Richard M. Dorson's Views and Works: An Assessment" (1989) and "Special Section: Richard Dorson" (1989), both edited by Robert Georges (see also Brunvand 1982). Other biographies of figures in American folklore research are *Good Friends and Bad Enemies: Robert Winslow Gordon and the Study of American Folksong* (1986) by Debora Kodish, *Folklorist of the Coal Fields: George Korson's Life and Work* (1980) by

Angus Gillespie, *Vance Randolph: An Ozark Life* (1985) by Robert Cochran, *Wealth and Rebellion: Elsie Clews Parsons, Anthropologist and Folklorist* (1992) by Rosemary Lévy Zumwalt, *Paper Medicine Man: John Gregory Bourke and His American West* (1986) by Joseph C. Porter, *The Indian Man: A Biography of James Mooney* (1984) by L. G. Moses, and *Daniel Garrison Brinton: The 'Fearless Critic' of Philadelphia* (1988) by Regna Darnell. A *Folklorist's Progress* (1996) by Stith Thompson is an autobiography with commentaries on his life of scholarship by Marguerite Thompson Hays (his daughter), Warren E. Roberts, and Herman B. Wells.

While these previous studies typically focus on academic figures who contributed to American folkloristic scholarship, the history and practice of "public" folklore in government, arts agencies, and historical and cultural organizations have received attention in several edited volumes, including *The Conservation of Culture* (1988) edited by Burt Feintuch, *Public Folklore* (1992) edited by Robert Baron and Nicholas R. Spitzer (1992), and *Conserving Culture* (1994) edited by Mary Hufford. The bookshelf of historical works in public folklore has not been adequately developed, but two foundational studies are a study of the first state folklorist in my *Popularizing Pennsylvania: Henry W. Shoemaker and the Progressive Uses of Folklore and History* (1996) and a survey of a public-oriented folklore organization in *The Texas Folklore Society* (1992) by Francis Edward Abernethy. Several critical essays on public folklore have taken up the symbolic uses of folk festivals, especially the Smithsonian's prominent Festival of American Folklife (see Bauman, Swain, and Carpenter 1992; Cantwell 1993; Price and Price 1995). This cultural criticism bears comparison to historical studies of "uses of tradition" in public fairs, parades, and pageants, such as David Glassberg's *American Historical Pageantry* (1990), John Bodnar's *Remaking America* (1992), Robert Rydell's *All the World's a Fair* (1984), and Susan Davis's *Parades and Power* (1986) (see also Kammen 1991). Expanding the consideration of folkloristic practice is *Putting Folklore to Use* (1994) edited by Michael Owen Jones, which sets "public" folklore (usually conceptualized as cultural programming for governmental and arts agencies) as "applied" folklore alongside museum agency, medical practice, social work, occupational and psychological therapy, urban and regional planning, economic and organizational development, cultural tourism, and education. A statistics-filled report containing essays on the impact of "applied" public programs in America devoted to traditional arts is *The Changing Faces of Tradition* (1996), edited by Elizabeth Peterson (see also Auerbach 1996a).

A number of bibliographies exist to help you make your way through the wide and varied terrain of folklore's fields. *American Folklore* (1977) by Cathleen C. Flanagan and John T. Flanagan is limited to the years 1950 to 1974, and is organized by genres, but lacks annotation. Organized by ethnic groups, *American and Canadian Immigrant and Ethnic Folklore* (1982) by Robert A. Georges and Stephen Stern is well annotated and indexed. Bibliographies of specific ethnic and regional groups are *An Annotated Bibliography of Chicano Folklore from the Southwestern United States* (1977) by Michael Heisley (for on-line sources, see *Hispanic American Periodicals Index* and *Chicano Database*), *Native American Folklore, 1879–1979* (1984) by William M. Clements and Frances M. Malpezzi, *Tennessee Folk Culture: An Annotated Bibliography* (1982) by Eleanor E. Goehring, *Folklife in New Jersey: An Annotated Bibliography* (1983) by David Steven Cohen, and *Ozark Folklore: An Annotated Bibliography* (1987) by Vance Randolph. A survey of titles on gender that includes many American titles is *Women and Folklore: A Bibliographic Survey* (1983) by Francis A. de Caro.

David Shuldiner has done a great bibliographic service for folk traditions of the elderly in *Folklore, Culture, and Aging: A Research Guide* (1997).

The bibliographic bookshelf that surveys specific genres and fields has *Folklore and Literature in the United States* (1984) by Steven Swann Jones, *American Folk Art: A Guide to Sources* (1984) edited by Simon Bronner, *American Folk Architecture* (1981) by Howard Wight Marshall, *Traditional Crafts and Craftsmanship in America: A Selected Bibliography* (1983) by Susan Sink, *Folk Music in America: A Reference Guide* (1986) by Terry E. Miller, *The Blues: A Bibliographic Guide* (1989) by Mary L. Hart, Brenda M. Eagles, and Lisa N. Howorth, and *Contemporary Legend: An Annotated Bibliography* (1992) by Gillian Bennett and Paul Smith.

As the last bibliography shows, folklore is material that often invites cross-cultural comparison. Susan Steinfirst's general guide to the international reference shelf of folklore and folklife research (1992) may be helpful for placing American work in global perspective. In addition, the Modern Language Association annually updates its bibliographic volume on folklore and makes it available in print as well as electronic form. On-line resources for American folklore are archived in Gopher and World Wide Web pages for the American Folklife Center at the Library of Congress. Print references with strong folkloristic contents are *America: History and Life* (also available in CD-ROM form), *American Studies: An Annotated Bibliography* (Salzman 1986), and *Arts and Humanities Index*. On-line sources such as *Anthropological Literature*, *UnCover*, *Current Contents*, *Table of Contents*, *Religion Index*, and *Sociofile* cover a number of folklore and folklife journals. Many serials featuring American material such as the *Journal of the Folklore Institute*, *Pennsylvania Folklife*, and *Kentucky Folklore Record* have separate volumes devoted to indexes. Especially important are the *Centennial Index* and supplement to the *Journal of American Folklore* (Jackson, Taft, and Axlerod 1988; Taft 1994). A special volume indexing folklore theses and dissertations, in need of updating, has been prepared by Alan Dundes (1976), and in addition to having a catalogue of more recent folklore dissertations, University Microfilms Incorporated in Ann Arbor has a service for searching for specific titles and subjects of dissertations.

Folklore and folklife research abounds in films, videotapes, and sound recordings as well as in print, and the Center for Southern Folklore has produced two volumes entitled *American Folklore Films and Videotapes* (1982) to guide users. Recordings also provide important research materials; since 1984 the American Folklife Center has annually published a list of outstanding recordings in *American Folk Music and Folklore Recordings* coordinated by Jennifer Cutting. The American Folklife Center additionally issues helpful "sourcebooks" such as *Folklife Sourcebook* (1994) compiled by Peter T. Bartis and Hillary Glatt and *Maritime Folklife Resources* (1980) compiled by Peter T. Bartis. The sourcebooks cover organizations, journals, and recording companies, to name some of the contents. Significant discographies of American folk material include *Traditional Anglo-American Folk Music* (1993) by Norm Cohen and *Ethnic Music on Records* (1990) by Richard K. Spottswood. A few guides to field recordings in archives are also available, such as the Native-American materials in *A Guide to Early Field Recordings (1900–1949) at the Lowie Museum of Anthropology* (1991) by Richard Keeling and regional records in *The Northeast Archives of Folklore and Oral History: A Catalog of the First 1800 Accessions* (1986) by Rita Breton, Joan Brooks, Catherine Fox, Florence Ireland, and Edward Ives.

Resources for "getting into traditions" seem to multiply daily on the Internet. Folklore discussion groups often post reviews and announcements in addition to featuring conversational "threads" on folklore topics. Lively nonspecialist newsgroups exist for general topics of folklore (folklore), urban legends (alt.folklore.urban), and college folklore (alt.folklore.college). "Moderated" lists encourage professional participation on legends (alt.folklore.suburban) and folkloristic issues (afs-l and newfolk). If that does not satisfy the net surfer, lists can be found for folk music, ballads, storytelling, folk dance, medicine, foodways, humor, military folklore, ghost stories, mythology, material culture, and a multitude of ethnic and international traditions. Sites on the World Wide Web offering graphic capabilities have quickly grown in number and degree of usefulness. The American Folklife Center at the Library of Congress offers handy bibliographies and guides, and connections to its tremendous Archive of Folk Culture (http://lcweb.loc.gov/folklife). The center runs a regularly updated service on-line called "Folkline" which lists jobs, fellowships, internships, grants, and conferences involving folklore. The homepage of the Smithsonian Institution's Center for Folklife Programs and Cultural Studies has significant resources such as materials for educators, an index to the Smithsonian Folkways catalogue of recordings, and detailed information on the annual Festival of American Folklife (http://www.si.edu/folklife/start.htm). The American Folklore Society website contains information on its publications and activities (http://afs-net.org). A valuable feature is a set of links to its many "sections" covering special interests such as history, education, folk belief and religion. For the broad heading of American studies, with ample representation of matters of tradition, one can consult the "Crossroads" site at http://www.georgetown.edu/crossroads.

More than a dozen American university folklore programs run homepages that have links to folklore resources in addition to describing educational approaches to the study of traditions. They also often provide useful information on research projects, special events, publications, syllabi, and student and faculty access. The one I go to most is Harvard's because of its extensive set of links and clear organization (http://www.fas.harvard.edu/~folkmyth). Among the connections to be found are folklore archives, centers, societies, electronic journals, publishers, syllabi, information guides, and special projects. One can click on announcements for the American Folklore Society annual meetings and newsletters through the site. Another impressive homepage is at UCLA, which in addition to making guides available to its immense set of archives, offers a glimpse of future developments with special text and graphic collections on-line in brilliant color for folk art and Los Angeles folk culture (http://www.humnet.ucla.edu/ humnet/folklore/archives). It also offers an innovative public service with the interactional site called "Ask the Folklore Expert!" Some sophisticated homepages for folkloristic figures and topics are popping up as publishing on the Internet becomes more popular, and they increasingly offer valuable illustrations and photographs in addition to texts. For this book, for instance, I made use of websites for Joel Chandler Harris (http://xroads.virginia.edu/~ug97/remus/ remus.html), Lafcadio Hearn (http://www2.gol.com/users/steve), Abby Aldrich Rockefeller (http://www.rockefeller.edu/archive.ctr/aar.html), George Washington Cable (http://etext.virginia.edu/railton/huckfinn/hftourhp.htm), Vance Randolph (http://lcweb.loc.gov/spcoll/193.html), and John and Alan Lomax (http://www.surfin.com/users/alperry/Alan_Lomax.html). Others with bibliographic guides can be found for topics as wide-ranging as urban legends (http://www.snopes.com, http://www.urbanlegends.com, and

http://www.nardis.com/~twchan/afuref.html), folklore from Vietnam veterans (http://
129.162.150.173/folk.htm), life histories collected by the WPA folklore project from 1936 to
1940 (http://rs6.loc.gov/wpaintro/ wpahome.html), cross-cultural data on trickster narratives (http://members.aol.com/ pmichaels/glorantha/tricksref.html), and folk arts in basic
education (http://www.carts.org). Some sites take the form of electronic journals such as
American Folk for folk artists (http://www.americanfolk.com) and *Newfolk for New
Directions in Folklore* (http://www.thunder.ocis.temple.edu/~cbaconsm/newfolk .html).

The most global set of links to folklore topics I have found is at a site called "Mythology,
Folklore, and a Little Bit of Religion Compiled by Sarah Craig" and can be accessed through
Harvard's folklore homepage. It is alphabetically arranged by areas from Afghan to
Zoroastrian, but users should be forewarned that the links range widely in quality. It has a
section devoted to American folklore connecting to sites for Mexican-American tales of La
Llorona and, inescapably, Paul Bunyan. There are even links to "Cowboy Hat Terms" or
"Folklore of the Color Green" if you happen to be searching for that information. Other
sections at the site relating to American tradition include Afro-Caribbean, Canadian,
Caribbean, Cherokee, Christian, Guam, Hawaiian, Hopi, Iroquois, Latino, Lenni-Lenape,
Native American, Navajo, Nez Perce, Potawatomi, and Sioux.

All these traditions that can be explored electronically also suggest more studies in the
future on traditions of the Internet, and there is a volume announcing the arrival of
Internet Culture (1997) edited by David Porter. Barbara Kirshenblatt-Gimblett specifically
questions the ramifications of computer communication for the study of folklore in her
essay, "From the Paperwork Empire to the Paperless Office: Testing the Limits of the
'Science of Tradition'" (1996). I consider the impact of folklore over the Internet for college
students in the Afterword of my *Piled Higher and Deeper* (1995). Other exploratory essays
on the folklore of computer communication have been written by Karla Jennings (1990),
John Dorst (1990), and Michael Preston (1996a, 1996b).

Premise and Promise

Since 1977 when Richard M. Dorson anticipated that the best books on American folklore
had yet to be written, an impressive library of works has appeared proclaiming the social
diversity and cultural complexity of American lives. Besides expanding the range of folklore to folklife concerns of material culture and community formation, researchers increasingly seek out the multiple cultures that interact in an American commonwealth (see
Hufford 1991). There is probably more consideration now than in Dorson's day of America,
and individuals affected by America, in an increasingly transnational world. Researchers
can be heard asking more questions about the influences of tradition on the behaviors and
attitudes that Americans take on in many settings, organizational and physical, in the
United States and abroad. The guiding problem for the relation of folklore and folklife
research to American studies no longer revolves exclusively around the simplistic opposition of imported and emergent traditions, an opposition that in its formation portrays
American culture as a completed project, and an exclusive one at that. The tendency in the
growing library of settings and performers, expressions and identities, has been to view
America in process. The main problem statement therefore concerns the rhetorical uses of
traditions from various perspectives—the individual, the community, the region, the

nation—and the way those uses help construct cultural meaning. The task of interpreting intellectual construction and cultural production undergirds many new American studies of tradition waiting for the light of print and screen. The promise of these studies is their inquiry into the adaptive nature of everyday lives, and the ways that those lives can reveal the varied nature of cultural experience.

Notes

Chapter 1. The Problem of Tradition

1.   The definition and uses are taken from *The American Heritage Dictionary of the English Language* (1976). The Latin root of tradition is *tradere*, to hand over or deliver. There is also a legalistic definition listed of the transfer of property to another.

2.   The *International Dictionary of Regional European Ethnology and Folklore* (Hultkrantz 1960) lists "Folk Tradition Research" as a title occasionally used in Scandinavian countries (144). "Tradition sciences" and "tradition research" as cognates of social sciences and social research were used as a theme for the 22nd Nordic Congress of Ethnology and Folkloristics at Liperi, Finland, on June 9–11, 1981, and published as *Trends in Nordic Tradition Research*, ed. Lauri Honko and Pekka Laaksonen (1983). Although tradition science or research is not a label for a university department in the Nordic countries either, the organizers used it as a key concept to bind existing disciplines of ethnology and folkloristics, primarily, and secondarily of anthropology and comparative religion (see Honko 1983). In England, prominent Victorian folklorist Edwin Sidney Hartland defined folklore as "the science of tradition," but academic titles did not pick up the reference to tradition science (Hartland [1899] 1968; see also Sanderson and Evans 1970; Fenton 1993).

3.   The MLA database in 1994 showed that "folkloristics" appeared 113 times in titles. This figure compares with 5,051 hits of "folklore" and 275 for "folklife," but these appearances include uses of folklore and folklife as the materials of tradition as well as their study. "Folklore studies" or "folklore research" appeared 1,830 times, while "folklife studies" or "folklife research" came up 33 times. "Folk studies" showed up 164 times. "Folklore science" or "science of folklore" shows up primarily to describe early approaches, especially evolutionary ones, such as Alexander Haggerty Krappe's 1930 classic *The Science of Folklore* (see Burson 1982).

4.   Three volumes covered evening concerts (VRS-9184, 9185, 9186), two volumes, entitled "Traditional Music at Newport, 1964" covered the workshops (WRS-9182, 9183), and two were devoted to blues (VRS-9180, 9181).

5.   Previous to the publication of the first Foxfire volume by Doubleday, Wigginton organized distribution of six hundred copies of an offset magazine called *Foxfire* in 1967 (see Wigginton 1989).

6.   This message was carried on a large poster in Spanish and English encouraging participation in the census. Other posters specifically appealed to African and Asian Americans. For the social implications of the ways that the census is taken, see Anderson 1988.

7.   The Traditional Values Coalition has a website with the heading "Standing Firm ... Taking Action" (*Standing Firm* is also the title of Dan Quayle's book of 1994). The issues of concern listed in the mission statement of the Coalition as of May 1997 are: "Religious Liberties" ("freedom of worship and expression in church, outside clinics, at work, school and on the public airwaves"), "The Family" ("teen pregnancy, the re-definition of the family and domestic partnerships"), "Sanctity of Human Life" ("abortion ... assisted suicide, baby harvesting, RU-486, euthanasia"), "Homosexuality" ("politicization of the gay lifestyle and demands for special recognition ... preserving the heterosexual ethic"), and "Pornography" ("taxpayer funded 'art,' pornography addiction and the sexual victimization of women and children"). Its newsletter for spring 1997 voiced outrage that the lead character of the popular television show *Ellen* came out as a lesbian. The group called for combating what it called "homosexual advocacy" in public schools and urged readers to fight pornography in print and on television. A search with the Yahoo! index for sites using "traditional values" produced thirty-one hits, mostly for American organizations identifying themselves as religious or conservative. Examples are "Citizens for Excellence in Education" ("helps Christians and conservatives restore academic excellence and traditional moral values to the public schools"), "The Citizen's News" ("reflecting traditional American values and conservative viewpoints"), "Federalist Society of Mississippi" ("reordering priorities within the legal system to place a premium on individual liberty, traditional values and the rule of law"), "American Family Association" ("devoted to the preservation of traditional family values"), "Pathlight Productions" ("producing entertainment focused on traditional family values, strong Christian morals, and God-given direction"), and "Piaonline" ("dedicated to the simple fact that traditional American values are values to be proud of").

8.   "The Religious Left" is described in a website for Truland Web Journal, established in March 1995 in New York. It lists constituent groups of the Interfaith Alliance, Interfaith Working Group, Religious Coalition for Reproductive Choice, Unitarian Universalism, Christian Socialist Movement, Religious Society of Friends, and Office for Social Justice. The Interfaith Working Group is more vocal than the others on its stands for policies of supporting "gay rights, reproductive freedom, and the separation of church and state." There is also a link at the site to the webpage for Religious Socialism prepared by the Democratic Socialists of America. While the religious left appears less united, publicized, or powerful than the religious right, it represents part of the wide-ranging "progressive" and "activist" coalition.

Chapter 2. Folklore and Ideology during the Gilded Age

1.   Letter from Stewart Culin to William Henry Holmes, November 30, 1906 (Smithsonian Institution Archives).

2.   Stewart Culin, "Boxes and Containers." Typescript (Stewart Culin Papers, Brooklyn Museum).

3.   Stewart Culin, "The Perfect Collector," n. d. Typescript (Stewart Culin Papers, Brooklyn Museum).

4.   Review from the *Indianapolis Journal* and letter come from "Twins of Genius" website documenting the Mark Twain-George Washington Cable tour of 1884–1885 (checked May 1997). The site is part of electronic text sources made available by the University of Virginia.

5.   Texts from Harris's works and reviews of his books are taken from the Joel Chandler Harris website called "Project Navigation," edited by Melissa Murray and Dominic Perella (checked May 1997), made available by the University of Virginia.

6.   Stewart Culin, "The International Jew." Typescript (Stewart Culin Papers, Brooklyn Museum).

7.   Letter from Adolph Bandalier to Stewart Culin, April 13, 1912 (Stewart Culin Papers, Brooklyn Museum).

8.   Letter from Adolph Bandalier to Stewart Culin, January 16, 1912 (Stewart Culin Papers, Brooklyn Museum).

9.   Letter from George Dorsey to Stewart Culin, October 17, 1918; Letter from George Dorsey to Stewart Culin, March 16, 1910 (Stewart Culin Papers, Brooklyn Museum).

CHAPTER 3. THE ENGLISH CONNECTION, FROM CULTURAL SURVIVALS TO CULTURAL STUDIES

1.   Suggesting the alliance of English and American intellectual history, W. K. McNeil's history of American folklore scholarship before 1908 (1980) followed Dorson's outline in *The British Folklorists* (1968). Essays on the English inheritance were included in the first volume of the *Journal of American Folklore*; see, for example, William Wells Newell, "English Folk-Tales in America" (1888c). See also Clemens Klöpper, *Folklore in England and America* (1899).

2.   The multicultural heritage in games tended to be studied much later. For the influence of African-American heritage, for example, see Jones and Hawes 1987. For Asian-American games, see Scherbatskoy 1976, and for regional games, see Abernethy 1989; Page and Smith 1993.

3.   The Opies in the *Oxford Dictionary of Nursery Rhymes* (1952) trace the first line of "This Little Pig" to an English song composed in 1728, and find a reference to the rest of the text in 1760, but cannot account for its popular origin or spread (348–50). The first line of "This Little Pig" did not necessarily evolve into the rest of the text. Halliwell-Phillipps (1849), for example, recorded "This pig went to market/Squeak, mouse, mouse, mousey/Shoe, shoe, shoe the wild colt/And here's my own doll dowsy" as a rhyme told to children who would not try on shoes (102). The Opies additionally do not consider the implications of the text's rhythm, performance, or repetition. Other textual references are found in Brewster et al., 1958, 185; Welsch 1966, 187; and Ford 1968, 11.

4.   The Opies (1959) offer the "Dark, Dark" material as a narrative under the heading of "Spookies," but Tucker (1977) found that Girl Scouts from Ellettsville, Indiana, referred to the material as a "poem" (see 209–10). Well aware of textual variation, they used the structure as a guiding principle to organize the words. Shelley, for example, says, "Okay, it's sorta like those two but it's a little different" (497), and Beth offers, "Well, you know how you did, 'There's a dark dark road,' except I said it's black black" (502). A literary rendition of the narrative is Leach 1959, 51.

5.   The narrative of the origins of cultural studies usually is drawn to English scholarship in communication and culture such as Hoggart 1957 and Thompson 1955. For surveys of cultural studies, see Grossberg, Nelson, Treichler 1992; Inglis 1993; During 1993; Davies 1995.

CHAPTER 4. THE AMERICANIZATION OF THE BROTHERS GRIMM

1.   The manuscript was found in the 1920s, edited and published by Franz Schultz (1924). For a discussion of editions of the manuscript and scholarship related to it, see McGlathery 1993, 41–44. Dating to 1810, the collection is often referred to as the Ölenberg manuscript because it was found among Brentano's posthumous papers in the library of the Trappist monastery in Ölenberg.

2.   For varying defenses of the genuineness of the Grimms' representation of Viehmann's German tales, see Ward 1988 and Rölleke 1988. A similar controversy surrounds the identity of the storyteller "Old Marie," who may indeed have been young and of "French origin" (see McGlathery 1993, 40–41).

3.   *Cinderella* was followed by an even more expensive and elaborate animated feature, *Sleeping Beauty,* in 1959 designed for a wide-screen process. The Disney studios continued producing animated adaptations of fairy tales even after Disney's death. Recent productions include *Beauty and the Beast* (1991) and *Aladdin* (1992). The *Detroit News* estimated that in the six times that *Cinderella* has been released to theaters, 75 million people have seen it, and it grossed 315 million dollars (October 6, 1997). When the film was first issued on video in 1988, it sold eight million copies before April 1989, when it was withdrawn. It was rereleased in 1997 as the second most requested title in the Disney library, behind only *The Little Mermaid* (see *Detroit News* site: http://detnews.com/menu/stories/1908.htm). Disney produced a made-for-television movie of *Cinderella* with a multiracial cast for airing on November 2, 1997. It featured Brady (African American) as Cinderella, Paolo Montalban (Asian American) as the prince, Whitney Houston (African American) as the fairy godmother, and Whoopie Goldberg (African American) as the queen (see publicity for the show at the creative Hollywood site: http://www.creativehollywood.com/newton/Cinderella.html). For reviews of Disney's special attraction to fairy tales, see Zipes 1994; Schickel 1968; Stone 1988.

4.   The series included "Cinderella" which appeared in 1985 with Jennifer Beals, Matthew Broderick, Jean Stapleton, Eve Arden, and Edie Mclurg in leading roles. "Sleeping Beauty" was shown in 1983 with Bernadette Peters, Christopher Reeve, and Sally Kellerman. "Rapunzel" in 1982 featured Jeff Bridges and Gena Rowlands along with Shelly Duvall.

5.   The conference was Dauphin County Library System's 28th Annual Conference held at the Pennsylvania State University at Harrisburg on May 23, 1996. The buy-or-burn metaphor juxtaposes American consumerism with the specter of book burnings of objectionable material in Nazi Germany with favor given for the American trend. Indeed, the deck was stacked in favor of multicultural literature. Faith Ringgold spoke on African-American storytelling, Gary Soto on stories from Spanish-speaking American neighborhoods, and Jewel Grutman and Gay Matthaei on Native-American tales.

6.   This idea is associated with Herder in the German context but is not uniquely his. That societies follow a pattern of natural development, and possess a "poetical," then "heroic," age early in their history, owes much to Giambattista Vico (1688–1744). That human history moves in cycles was an old and widely discussed idea in Vico's day. The distinctive reference given by the Romanticists was to an "ideal, eternal history traversed in time by every nation in its rise, growth, decline and fall" (Berlin 1976, 64). History takes precedence over other kinds of knowledge because it represents the development of human nature itself. Human nature appears to be an activity, and necessarily a social one. For a discussion of these ideas of history, and the relation of Vico and Herder, see Berlin 1976.

7.   To be sure, there was American folkloristic concern for *Märchen,* but it was often presented as a literary or European problem, and many of the folklorists working with the genre were from Europe. Once the major source of folkloristic interest, *Märchen* during the 1980s were viewed as an understudied genre in America, according to folklorists such as Linda Dégh, W. F. H. Nicolaisen, Wolfgang Mieder, Steven Swann Jones, and Kay Stone. Dégh blamed the lack of attention on "context-centrism" of American folklorists that ignored "accumulated disciplinary knowledge" gained from Europe (Dégh 1995, 28–29). She presented her *Narratives in Society: A Performer-Centered Study of Narration* (1995) as an attempt to show the continuity of European narrative scholarship with present ethnographic trends, and she demonstrated the oral vitality of *Märchen* by writing on living storytellers in their

European communities. As editor of a book series entitled *Folklore Studies in Translation,* Dan Ben-Amos introduced, during the 1980s, two classics of European *Märchen* scholarship by Max Lüthi to American audiences (1982, 1984). Yet he noted that the genre attracted studies that ran counter to "the ethnographic research of narrative performance in particular cultures and specific situations." His hope was that the work "has provided us with an analytical base that can be extended to other genres and other cultures" (Ben-Amos 1982, xii). Alan Dundes during the 1980s drew attention to interpretative consideration of individual tales in the Grimm canon; he edited "casebooks" on *Cinderella* (1988) and *Little Red Riding Hood* (1989) that included reprints of interpretations from folklore studies and other fields.

CHAPTER 5. MARTHA WARREN BECKWITH AND THE RISE OF ACADEMIC AUTHORITY

1.   Martha Warren Beckwith served on the National Committee of the National Folk Festival in 1938 and was a consultant to the United States Section, International Commission on Folk Arts, in 1935 (see Beckwith 1933, 416; 1938, 442–44). Among her proudest moments were in the folk arts in education field, she wrote, "when the Hawaiian Board in Honolulu decided to use our publications as a text-book in Hawaiian" (see Beckwith 1928a, 281).

2.   Of the group, Dorothy Demetracopoulou Lee (Vassar class of 1927), who taught at Vassar and Harvard, and Katharine Luomala, who served as editor of the *Journal of American Folklore* from 1952 to 1953, are probably best known. Lee's books include *Valuing the Self* (1976) and *Freedom and Culture* (1959). Among her folklore contributions are *Wintu Myths* with Cora Du Bois (1931); "A Study of Wintu Mythology" (1932); "The Loon Woman Myth" (1933); "Greek Accounts of the Vrykolakas" (1942); "Greek Tales of Nastradi Hodjas" (1946); "Greek Tales of Priest and Priestwife" (1947); and "Greek Personal Anecdotes of the Supernatural" (1951). Although not one of Beckwith's students, Katharine Luomala was by her own account deeply influenced by Beckwith's guidance (see Luomala 1962, 1970). Some representative works by other associates and students of Beckwith include Greenleaf 1933; Green 1923, 1926, 1929; Lewis 1946; Ring 1953; Treadwell 1930; Pukui 1933; and Roberts 1925, 1928.

3.   Mary Elspeth Fleming, "I Remember," newspaper clipping, c. 1959 (Mount Holyoke College Archives).

4.   See Lawrence 1911, 1928. Beckwith took some of Lawrence's approach in "A Note on Punjab Legend in Relation to Arthurian Romance" (1927) and "Pushkin's Relation to Folklore" (1937) and quoted him extensively in *Folklore in America* (1931b, 63–64).

5.   Boas's *The Mind of Primitive Man* (1911), *Tsimshian Mythology* (1916), and *Primitive Art* ([1927] 1955) were frequently used by Beckwith in courses and articles. Annotating the first and third titles for her folklore course, she wrote, "The first is the classic of the modern American school of social anthropology. The second applies his theories to an objective field. It is 'an attempt to give an analytical description of the fundamental traits of primitive art' as based on two principles: 'the fundamental sameness of mental processes in all cultural forms of the present day' and 'consideration of every cultural phenomenon as the result of historical happenings.'" (Letter and reading lists from H. N. MacCracken to Martha Beckwith, December 30, 1929, Special Collections, Vassar College Library).

6.   "Vassar Trustees Make Changes in College Faculty, Associate Professor M. W. Beckwith Becomes Professor on New Folk Lore Foundation." *Poughkeepsie Eagle News,* February 17, 1920; Letter from Martha Beckwith to President MacCracken, February 14, 1938 (Special Collections, Vassar College Library).

7.   Letter from Martha Beckwith to President Henry N. MacCracken, December 29, 1919, and to President MacCracken, February 14, 1938 (Special Collections, Vassar College Library). According to a letter specifying the terms of the donation from Alexander & Baldwin, Ltd., to President MacCracken, January 6, 1920, the amount of the gift was twenty-five hundred dollars annually (Special Collections, Vassar College Library).

8.   Letter from C. B. Bourland to President H. MacCracken, November 26, 1919 (Special Collections, Vassar College Library).

9.   Letter from Elizabeth Deering Hanscom to President MacCracken, November 26, 1919 (Special Collections, Vassar College Library).

10. Letter from Gertrude Schoepperle Loomis to Martha Beckwith, May 11, 1920 (Special Collections, Vassar College Library). Gertrude Schoepperle Loomis (1882–1921), who like Beckwith had written a dissertation on the folkloric sources of the romance, died prematurely at the age of thirty-nine, a year after Beckwith arrived at Vassar. Her unexpected passing probably dashed Beckwith's hopes for a folklore department at Vassar (see Schoepperle 1960, 1920; Loomis 1927).

11.   Letter from Franz Boas to H. N. MacCracken, December 2, 1919 (Special Collections, Vassar College Library).

12.   Letter from William W. Lawrence to Henry Noble MacCracken, December 19, 1919 (Special Collections, Vassar College Library).

13.   Letter from A. Thorndike to Henry Noble MacCracken, December 4, 1919 (Special Collections, Vassar College Library).

14.   Letter from Alexander & Baldwin, Ltd., to President MacCracken, January 6, 1920 (Special Collections, Vassar College Library).

15.   "Vassar Trustees," *Poughkeepsie Eagle News*, February 17, 1920.

16.   Letter from Charles Peabody to Martha Beckwith, February 21, 1920 (Special Collections, Vassar College Library).

17.   "Folk-lore: The Art of Oral Tradition." Typescript (Special Collections, Vassar College Library).

18.   Undated letter from Martha Beckwith to Miss Conrow (Special Collections, Vassar College Library).

19.   Alumnae were also involved in collecting in Dutchess County (see Ring et al. 1953). In addition, a collecting expedition by Elisabeth Greenleaf and Grace Yarrow was sponsored by the Folk-Lore Foundation and the results published as *Ballads and Sea Songs of Newfoundland* (Greenleaf 1933).

20.   Titles in the Publications of the Folk-Lore Foundation of Vassar College are: 1. *Folk Games of Jamaica,* collected by Martha Beckwith, with music recorded in the field by Helen Roberts, 1922; 2. *Christmas Mummings in Jamaica* by Martha Beckwith, with music recorded in the field or from phonographic records by Helen Roberts, 1923; 3. *Hawaiian Stories and Wise Sayings*, translated by Laura Green, 1923; 4. *The Hussay Festival in Jamaica* by Martha Beckwith, with music recorded by E. Harold Geer, 1924; 5. *Hawaiian String Games* by Joseph Emerson, 1924; 6. *Jamaica Proverbs*, collected by Martha Beckwith, 1925; 7. *Folk Tales from Hawaii* by Laura Green, 1926; 8. *Notes on Jamaican Ethnobotany* by Martha Beckwith, 1927; 9. *The Legend of Kawelo*, translated by Laura Green, 1929; 10. *Myths and Hunting Stories of the Mandan and Hidatsa Indians,* collected by Martha Beckwith, 1930; 11. *Folklore in America: Its Scope and Method* by Martha Beckwith, 1931; 12. *Myths and Ceremonies of the Mandan and Hidatsa*, collected by Martha Beckwith, 1932; 13. *Hawaiian Folk Tales*, 3d series, text and translation by Mary Pukui, 1933; 14. *Mandan and Hidatsa Tales*, 3d series, collected by Martha Beckwith, 1934. Some numbers of the series were republished in the Memoir Series of the American Folklore Society: *Jamaica Folk-Lore,*

1928 (including nos. 1, 2, 6, 8); see also *Mandan-Hidatsa Myths and Ceremonies,* 1937 (nos. 10, 12, 14).

21.   According to records at Vassar College, the speakers included Franz Boas, W. W. Lawrence, Ella Young (who held the James Phelan lectureship in Celtic mythology at the University of California), Mary A. Jordan, and Ruth Benedict.

22.   See Boas 1911, 1940, especially "The Aims of Anthropological Research" (243–59) in the latter volume; Stocking 1974, especially Part X "Anthropology and Society"; Stocking 1982, "Franz Boas and the Culture Concept in Historical Perspective" (195–233). For discussion of some inconsistencies in Boas's treatment of the relativity of ethnic groups, see Glick 1982.

23.   Letter from Martha Beckwith to President MacCracken, February 14, 1938 (Special Collections, Vassar College Library).

24.   Letter from Martha Beckwith to Rockefeller Foundation, March 28, 1931 (Special Collections, Vassar College Library). For calls for and progress reports of the folk atlasing movement, see Nicolaisen 1973, 1975; Taylor 1965; Erixon 1955; Wildhaber 1972.

25.   Letter from Martha Beckwith to American Council of Learned Societies, December 13, 1930 (Special Collections, Vassar College Library).

26.   Beckwith 1922. Letter from Archer Taylor to Martha Beckwith, November 7, 1924 (Special Collections, Vassar College Library).

27.   Letter from Martha Beckwith to President H. N. MacCracken, May 5, 1931 (Special Collections, Vassar College Library).

28.   At the time Beckwith went to study the Oglala Dakota Sioux, the tribe's traditions had already garnered scholarly attention. See Walker 1905, 1917; Boas 1925b; Meeker 1901; Bushotter 1888; Densmore 1918; Dorsey 1891, 1889; Wissler 1907. For Boas's ideas that informed Beckwith's collection of Native-American narrative, see Boas, "Mythology and Folk-Tales of the North American Indians" (1914), and "Stylistic Aspects of Primitive Literature" (1925).

29.   For other collections of the Mandan-Hidatsa used by Beckwith, see Matthews 1877; Lowie 1913; and Will 1912. Although Beckwith's collections among Native Americans are not usually cited as praiseworthy among her works, in a review of Native American collections, William N. Fenton in 1947 offered Beckwith as among the few "notable exceptions" who had applied a rigorous method of analysis and taken stories directly from the native language. He noted that "Beckwith makes a pretty good case of taking materials in Indian English, allowing for lapses of Indian memory and not retouching the material to enhance its attractiveness." See his "Iroquois Indian Folklore" (1947), particularly 388–94.

30.   Alumni Activity Form, February 1932 (Archives, Mt. Holyoke College Library).

31.   Letter from Martha Beckwith to President MacCracken, February 14, 1938 (Special Collections, Vassar College Library).

32.   Letter from Martha Beckwith to President MacCracken, May 21, 1932 (Special Collections, Vassar College Library).

33.   Letter to Theresa (no surname given), March 30, 1950; Mary Elspeth Fleming, "I Remember" (Archives, Mt. Holyoke College Library).

34.   "Field Notes on Herb Medicines," unpublished papers (Library of the Bernice P. Bishop Museum; see also Luomala 1970, xii–xiii).

35.   Letter from Martha Beckwith to Dr. MacCracken, December 29, 1949 (Special Collections, Vassar College Library).

36.   John Peirce, Winifred Smith, and Richard Brooks, "A Memorial Minute to Martha Warren Beckwith," March 9, 1959, typescript (Special Collections, Vassar College Library).

Chapter 6. Alfred Shoemaker and the Discovery of American Folklife

1.   The emphasis on British American folklore and balladry during the 1940s is evident in a guide to American folklore scholarship written by Levette Davidson (1951). In a chapter entitled "American Folklore Specialists, 1950" Davidson puts a heading "Other Non-English Folklore" last and lists Alfred Shoemaker, Wayland Hand, Roman Jakobson, Jonas Balys, R. D. Jameson, Charles Speroni, and Ruth Rubin (see Davidson 1951, 125).

2.   The first chair of folklore in the United States was Martha Warren Beckwith, who held the post of research professor on the Folk-Lore Foundation at Vassar College beginning in 1920. She also had a Pennsylvania-German connection as an honorary vice president of the Pennsylvania-German Folklore Society. (See the chapter on Beckwith elsewhere in this volume and Luomala 1962; Bronner 1992e; Glazier 1996.) Stith Thompson claimed to be the first American professor of English and folklore in 1939 (Thompson 1996, 160). Shoemaker's title of assistant professor of American folklore was the first post to use "American folklore," as far as searches have revealed thus far.

3.   Interview with Martha Best, July 8, 1991.

4.   Interview with Joel Hartman, July 15, 1991.

5.   Interview with Joel Hartman, July 16, 1991.

6.   Interview with Henry Glassie, October 20, 1991.

7.   Interview with Joel Hartman, July 16, 1991.

8.   The "Seminars on American Culture" run by the New York State Historical Association at Cooperstown, New York, beginning in 1948 offered intensive summer seminars for two weeks that qualified for credit through two State Teachers' Colleges (later State University of New York) and Colgate University. Under the direction of Louis C. Jones, the courses included American Folklore, American Folk Art, and Folklore Collecting (see Dorson 1950a, 346; Davidson 1951, 111). Shoemaker's course, however, appears to be the first regular college offering in American folk art (cf. Boggs 1940; Dorson 1950b).

9.   Interviews with Martha Best, July 8, 1991; Florence Baver, July 9, 1991; Joel Hartman, July 15, 1991.

10.   Interview, June 20, 1991.

11.   According to a letter dated June 22, 1970, from the dean's office at Franklin and Marshall to Ronald Baker, Shoemaker "retired" from the department, although he stayed on with the college's Pennsylvania Dutch Folklore Center. With Shoemaker's retirement, the department was discontinued and a folklore teaching line was not transferred elsewhere.

12.   Interview, June 20, 1991.

13.   Interview with Florence Baver, July 9, 1991.

14.   Interview with Martha Best, July 8, 1991.

15.   William Woys Weaver in "The Pennsylvania German House: European Antecedents and New World Forms" (1986) credits Shoemaker with introducing the "Continental type house" as a folk form (see Shoemaker 1954, 12). Shoemaker promoted the form as evidence of the profound German influence on American culture through Pennsylvania-German adaptation; for later statements on the form, see Bucher 1962 and Glassie 1968.

Shoemaker is still invoked when searches for folk cultural antecedents occur. Commenting, for example, on the Winter 1980–1981 issue of *Pennsylvania Folklife*, editor William Parsons wrote: "The articles by Ensminger, Jordan and Stevens, which constitute the bulk of this WINTER issue of PENNSYLVANIA FOLKLIFE, stand, in the opinion of the

Editor, in the best of the tradition established by Professor Alfred L. Shoemaker. His specialty articles on Pennsylvania Barns, both the Forebay Barn types and Bottom Barns, elicited further items by an entire group of authoritative contributors" (94).

16.   As part of the society's recovery, Shoemaker's detractors permanently severed his ties with the society. While the Pennsylvania Folklife Society was reorganized and prospered under new direction, many workers for Shoemaker at Kutztown remained loyal to him. Many quit working for the new festival, complaining of increased pandering of Pennsylvania Dutch stereotypes (which Shoemaker abhorred) and the festival's commercial departure from Shoemaker's scholarly premises. One result of the split was the founding in 1965 of the Pennsylvania Dutch Folk Culture Society in Lenhartsville, Pennsylvania. Smaller than the Pennsylvania Folklife Society, it continues to maintain archives, library, outdoor museum, public activities, and publications under the direction of Florence Baver, a Shoemaker associate. One bridge between Shoemaker's heyday and the period that followed was Don Yoder's work for the Pennsylvania Folklife Society. Yoder helped the Folk Culture Society in its early years as well as editing *Pennsylvania Folklife* for the reorganized Pennsylvania Folklife Society.

17.   According to Martha Best, a friend of Shoemaker since they attended high school together, attempts at locating him through the Red Cross, Salvation Army, and Social Security Administration have all been futile. Family members could not help. Shoemaker was unmarried and his sisters lost touch with him. The last time Best saw Shoemaker was in 1967 when he came to Pennsylvania from New York to attend her mother's funeral. According to Best, he was in good spirits and talked, probably quixotically, of planning another folklife project or center out of New York (interview with Martha Best, July 8, 1991). He checked on the progress of the Pennsylvania Dutch Folk Culture Society in Lenhartsville during the late 1960s, but never returned to any posts after 1963 (interview with Florence Baver, July 9, 1991). According to recollections I gathered, Shoemaker was last heard from during the late 1970s. Herbert Miller, who worked for Shoemaker at Kutztown, remembers Shoemaker visiting at Miller's home near Lenhartsville (interview, July 9, 1991).

The mystery of Shoemaker's whereabouts, the saga of his dramatic rise and fall, the reputation of an enigmatic man with ideas well ahead of his time, inspired legend, as narrative accounts of "sightings" and anecdotes mentioned in my essay indicate.

18.   Statistical evidence for the changes in folklore offerings within academe is provided by Ronald Baker's surveys published in 1971, 1978, and 1986. Whereas Baker's early survey showed that Anglo-American ballad and folk song (thirty-three percent) still dominated folklore offerings, it also showed the rise of the introductory folklore course (fifty-five percent) since the 1940 and 1950 survey by Boggs and Dorson, respectively. By 1986, ballad and folk song dramatically dropped to seven percent, while American folklore with twenty-six percent moved behind introductory folklore courses. In keeping with Shoemaker's interests, it is noteworthy that after American folklore the categories of highest frequency are "regional American folklore" and "ethnic American folklore." By 1986 a new category championed by Shoemaker among folklore offerings appeared of "material culture," accounting for seven percent of all offerings (equal to percentages for balladry and mythology courses).

As Shoemaker anticipated, folklore courses between 1971 and 1986 increasingly took up ethnological methods. In 1971, seventy percent of folklore courses were taught in English with only nine percent in anthropology and eight percent in a combination of English and anthropology. By 1986, the percentage for English dropped to fifty-eight and rose for anthropology to thirty-two. Most dramatic was the rise in American studies from almost nothing to thirteen percent in 1986. Shoemaker moved from foreign language study to folklore and American studies; overall, folklore courses in foreign languages dropped from five to 1.5 percent. Meanwhile, courses carrying folklore prefixes rose from two to six percent of all offerings.

Shoemaker differed from these trends at least in the kind of institution for which he worked. Baker's surveys show that folklore courses increasingly were offered by public universities (forty-six percent of the publics offer folklore as opposed to thirty-three percent of the privates; F&M is a small private college) and at large institutions (eighty percent of institutions with over twenty thousand students have folklore courses; thirty-five percent of schools with one to five thousand students have folklore courses). For example, today in central Pennsylvania around Franklin and Marshall, Penn State University campuses at University Park and Harrisburg carry the lion's share of folklore courses in the region.

By 1986 the B.A. with a major, minor, or concentration in folklore was available from about sixty colleges, up from less than ten in 1971, and graduate curricula also rose in number. Shoemaker argued for folklore as a basic collegiate offering, one that explored cultural values basic to students' understanding of their lives and those around them. Appropriately, the total amount of folklore courses has risen from 60 around the time that Shoemaker taught (about ten percent of the total was taught by Shoemaker alone!) at Franklin and Marshall (see Dorson 1950b) to 170 in 1971 (Baker 1971) to 509 in 1986 (Baker 1986a).

19.   Much of this discourse was carried on over the Internet. The text of the bill appeared on the Folklore discussion list and other traditional culture lists on May 21, 1996, and the Committee on House Oversight approved the bill on May 23. Alan Jabbour circulated a statement of support for H.R. 3491 on May 24 and the Librarian of Congress's statement appeared on May 28. Numerous criticisms of the measure and the center's response appeared through June, including strong statements from Joe Wilson of the National Council for the Traditional Arts and Steve Goldfield of the University of California at Berkeley. On June 20, 1996, a statement from the president of the American Folklife Center, the chair of the American Folklife Center board of trustees, and director of the National Council for the Traditional Arts addressed to "Folk Arts Advocates" urged a letter-writing campaign in opposition to the repeal to senators and representatives. On June 26, Representative David Obey (Democrat-Wisconsin) introduced his amendment to transfer the American Folklife Center to the Smithsonian, and it was reported over the Internet to many lists through the National Coordinating Committee for the Promotion of History (NCC) Washington Update (vol. 2, no. 21 June 27, 1996). The final outcome of the president signing a bill for reauthorization of the center in the Library Congress for 1997–1998 was reported in the *Folklife Center News* for 1996 (vol. 18, nos. 3–4).

Chapter 7. Henry W. Shoemaker and the Fable of Public Folklore

1.   "Extracts from Lancaster to Clearfield: H. W. Shoemaker's First Prose Volume" (Typescript, Pennsylvania State Archives).

2.   Letter from Henry W. Shoemaker to Stuart Kinser, September 11, 1914 (Private Collection).

3.   Ibid.

4.   Letter from J. Arbuckle to Henry W. Shoemaker, November 15, 1916 (Private Collection).

5.   Letter from Henry W. Shoemaker to the Reverend George P. Donehoo, September 29, 1913 (Historical Collections and Labor Archives, Pennsylvania State University).

6.   Letter from George Korson to Henry W. Shoemaker, November 23, 1935 (Private Collection).

7. "The Value of Folklore and Witchcraft Beliefs in Pennsylvania History" (Typescript, Lycoming County Historical Society).

8. Letter from Henry W. Shoemaker to Victoria Smallzell, March 22, 1955 (Pennsylvania State Archives).

9. Letter from Henry W. Shoemaker to Marion Patterson, November 24, 1947 (Private Collection).

10. Interview with John Witthoft, West Chester, Pennsylvania, December 9, 1992.

11. Letter from Dolores Coffey to Simon Bronner, December 17, 1992.

12. Letter from Henry W. Shoemaker to Forest Sweet, March 12, 1948 (Pennsylvania State Archives).

13. Memorandum from Henry W. Shoemaker to Donald Cadzow, November 20, 1947 (Pennsylvania State Archives).

14. Letter from Henry W. Shoemaker to Louis C. Jones, October 28, 1949 (Pennsylvania State Archives).

15. Letter from Henry W. Shoemaker to Arthur D. Graeff, May 21, 1948 (Pennsylvania State Archives).

16. Letter from Henry W. Shoemaker to Honorable Daniel K. Hoch, February 21, 1947 (Private Collection); letter from Dolores Coffey to Simon Bronner, January 21, 1993.

17. Minutes of Pennsylvania Folklore Society meeting, 1951 (Lycoming County Historical Society).

18. Letter from Henry W. Shoemaker to Alfred Shoemaker, May 5, 1950 (Pennsylvania State Archives).

19. Memorandum from Henry W. Shoemaker to Donald Cadzow, "A Two Years' Look Ahead by the Folklore Division," August 23, 1948 (Pennsylvania State Archives).

20. Minutes of Pennsylvania Folklore Society, May 15, 1948 (Pennsylvania State Archives).

21. Memorandum from Henry W. Shoemaker to Donald Cadzow, August 23, 1949 (Pennsylvania State Archives).

22. Report from Henry W. Shoemaker to Donald Cadzow, March 22, 1955 (Pennsylvania State Archives).

23. Memorandum from Henry W. Shoemaker to Donald Cadzow, January 25, 1955 (Pennsylvania State Archives).

24. Press Release, Folklore Division, Pennsylvania Historical and Museum Commission, January 12, 1950 (Pennsylvania State Archives).

25. Press Release, Folklore Division, Pennsylvania Historical and Museum Commission, December 17, 1957 (Pennsylvania State Archives).

26. Letter from Samuel Bayard to Simon Bronner, April 21, 1993.

27. Letter from Henry W. Shoemaker to Miriam Dickey, May 15, 1956 (Juniata College Archives).

28. Interview with David Hufford, Logan, Utah, June 10, 1994.

29. Letter from Michael Owen Jones to Simon Bronner, September 23, 1994.

CHAPTER 8. RICHARD DORSON AND THE GREAT DEBATES

1. Letter from Daniel Boorstin to Richard Dorson, February 4, 1959; Richard Dorson to Daniel Boorstin, August 15, 1958 (Dorson Mss., Lilly Library, Indiana University). Boorstin was two years older than Dorson, and graduated from Harvard in 1934. While Dorson was at Michigan State University and Indiana University, Boorstin was in the history department at the University of Chicago.

2.   Letter from Richard M. Dorson to Daniel Boorstin, April 10, 1959 (Dorson Mss., Lilly Library, Indiana University).

3.   Letter from Daniel Boorstin to Richard M. Dorson, June 2, 1959 (Dorson Mss., Lilly Library, Indiana University).

4.   Dorson was clearly uncomfortable with what little Jewish identity he experienced in his childhood. Proud of his participation in elite American institutions such as Exeter and Harvard, he nonetheless mentioned to me anti-Semitism he faced at Exeter. I thought about his comment when I noticed that in his reading of the Brothers Grimm he singled out derision of Jews and the middle class in their fairy-tale corpus as evidence of problems of creating a liberal, inclusive nationalism (Dorson 1966a, xviii–xix). Although Dorson occasionally attended a meeting of the Jewish section of the American Folklore Society, he never considered an extended study of Jewish culture apart from American culture. Dorson's scholarship on Jewish folklore consisted of two essays on Jewish-American dialect humor. His interpretation stressed the force of assimilation in the American scene and the penetration of Jewish lore ultimately into the American tradition: "These contemporary, urban, dialect folktales about Jewish acculturation form a fresh and lively addition to the varied strands of American humorous lore" (Dorson 1960a, 117; see also Dorson 1960b). He stressed similar patterns in the stories he collected to non-Jewish lore to point out their Americanness as a response of children of American immigrants and an example of living lore among modern, urban educated folk. He avoided any reference to his ethnicity in these essays, and in his many reminiscences late in his life, he hardly referred to any Jewish identity. He made one passing reference to himself as a *mensch*, a Yiddish word for a decent human being (Dorson 1971b, 41). In unpublished transcripts of fieldwork in multiethnic Gary, Indiana, an informant responding to questions about ethnicity asked Dorson about his. After a long pause, his answer was "I was originally Jewish," referring therefore to his ethnicity as a past identity (for his comments on the persistent ethnic identity of Gary, Indiana, see Dorson 1981, 109–64).

5.   Letter from Richard M. Dorson to Mr. Brooks, February 24, 1938 (Dorson Mss., Lilly Library, Indiana University).

6.   Influenced by Herskovits's *Myth of the Negro Past* ([1941] 1958), Dorson sought out Herskovits to advise his collection of folktales collected from blacks in Michigan but challenged Herskovits's thesis of African origins of black American folktales when he published *American Negro Folktales* (1967) (see also Dorson 1975a). Funded in 1952 by the American Council of Learned Societies Faculty Study Fellowship, Dorson spent a postdoctoral year at Northwestern studying with Herskovits. Dorson eulogized Herskovits in the *Journal of American Folklore* (1963b).

7.   For commentaries on the Bunyan issue during the 1940s and 1950s, see Haney 1942, Charters 1944, Gartenberg 1950, Loehr 1951, Hoffman 1952, Dorson 1956b. A recent summary of the rage for Bunyan is Walls 1996.

8.   Dorson announced tennis as a basic influence on his life alongside his attendance at Phillips Exeter and Harvard in his essay "History of the Elite and History of the Folk" published in *Folklore: Selected Essays* (1972, 249, 256–57). Another example of his referencing of tennis in scholarship was his challenge to Lauri Honko, prominent in Finnish folkloristics, to a tennis match when he visited Indiana University in 1978. Dorson was victorious and he announced to his students that the match pitted two great powers in folklore studies—the old represented by Finland and the new signified by the United States—with the upstart Americans ultimately triumphing. Alan Dundes recalled Dorson's fighting spirit in recounting that he made much of his appointment to distinguished professor, a notable achievement for an underdog folklorist Dorson thought, on the same day he scored

an upset to enter the finals of a local tennis tournament (Dundes 1982, xv). Brunvand recalls the connection of Dorson's sports drive to his academic work this way: "Considering Dick Dorson's lifestyle—lived with great enthusiasm—it was highly likely that it would end either during scholarly labors or on the tennis court. Fittingly, then, while playing tennis, on June 28, 1981, Richard M. Dorson collapsed and went into a coma from which he never recovered" (Brunvand 1982, 352).

9.   Letter from Ben Botkin to Richard Dorson, 6 July 1939 (Dorson Mss., Lilly Library, Indiana University).

10.   Letter from Richard Dorson to Ben Botkin, 21 January 1940 (Botkin Mss., Special Collections, University of Nebraska).

11.   Dorson later acknowledged that another folklorist, Stanley Edgar Hyman, had also criticized at length Botkin's treasuries around the same time (Dorson 1971a, 8; see Hyman 1948).

12.   Dorson's last review of Botkin's books was of *A Treasury of Mississippi River Folklore* in *Minnesota History* (1956). Dorson claimed that his "quarrel is less with Botkin than with folklorists who praise his patchworks as models of research" (Dorson 1971a, 27). Dorson contributed in 1966 to a volume of essays honoring Ben Botkin (see Dorson 1966b and Jackson 1966). If the two men seemed to have made a truce during the 1960s, supporters of Botkin nonetheless kept up criticism of Dorson's tactics and ideas. See Dorson 1971a, 12–13; Halpert 1957; Jones 1959; Jackson 1984a, 1986; and Stekert 1987.

13.   The treasury approach to presenting American folklore was still evident in commercial publishing through the 1980s and 1990s, although no single prominent figure carries the association with the style that Botkin had in the 1950s (see Battle 1989; Cohn 1993).

14.   Fifteen years later Dorson invoked the authority and prestige of the *Wall Street Journal* in boasting of the "folklore boom" during the bicentennial years. He credited the newspaper with recognizing folklore-folklife and tennis (another Dorson obsession) as "hot" growth industries (Dorson 1978d).

15.   Letter from Duncan Emrich to Richard Dorson, May 22, 1970 (Dorson Mss., Lilly Library, Indiana University).

16.   Parrington's biography carries much of the outline of New Class heroism: charting intellectual territory alone and gaining fame on the basis of the merit of his argument. A stranger from the hinterland to the exclusive world of Harvard, he was "exhilarated by the freer intellectual atmosphere of the East, yet naive and hence vulnerable there to its cosmopolitanism and its social elitism," so Gene Wise has pointed out. In fact, Wise in his survey of American studies claims that from 1927 to 1965, the American studies project was largely inspired by Parrington. He was "a single mind grappling with materials of American experience, and driven by concentrated fury to create order from them" (Wise 1979, 298–301). Dorson saw a line from Parrington to his comrade-in-arms Daniel Boorstin; he wrote Boorstin before publication of *The Americans*: "I prophesy you will dethrone Parrington, and shave Beard to a whisker" (August 18, 1958; Dorson Mss., Lilly Library, Indiana University).

Chapter 9. Displaying American Tradition in Folk Arts

1.   For the connection of simultaneity with a multicultural view of modernity born in a twentieth-century era of communication, see Lowe 1982; Bronner 1986a, 94–129.

2.   This information comes from the Abby Aldrich Rockefeller Personal Papers, Rockefeller University Archives. See "Biographical Sketch," at the website for the Papers (http://www.rockefeller.edu/archive.ctr/aar_biog.html).

3.   For elaboration on Boas's ideas of perfecting form in folk art, see Jones 1987, 119–31; Herskovits 1953, especially chap. four, "Man, The Creator"; Beckwith 1929, especially chapter XIII, "Folk Art"; Beckwith 1931a. Not insignificant to Boas's contributions to cultural relativity and related ideas of "creativity" are the ways that his views, influenced by his Jewish roots, countered German stereotypes of Jewish and immigrant folk creativity as a sign of disease (see Gilman 1991; Stocking 1982, 149–50).

4.   The United States Section of the International Commission under the leadership of Elizabeth Burchenal unsuccessfully tried during the 1930s to establish "a central authority for the whole field of folk arts of the United States." Among its "expert consultants" were representatives of conflicting views including Holger Cahill and Edith Halpert from the art world and Franz Boas and Martha Beckwith taking an ethnological perspective.

5.   The exhibition *An Image of Peace: The Penn Treaty Collection of Mr. and Mrs. Meyer P. Potamkin* was mounted at the State Museum of Pennsylvania from April 14 to October 20, 1996. See Cullen 1996 and Pennsylvania Historical and Museum Commission 1996.

6.   For tributes to collectors, see National Gallery of Art 1987; Hartigan 1990. For examples of thematic folk art books, heavily image-laden and short on text, see Barber 1993; Lipman, Warren, and Bishop 1986; Jones 1975; Bishop 1977.

7.   For a critique of the art world's handling of black folk art, see Metcalf 1983.

Bibliographic Essay

1.   For retrospective essays on Richard Dorson's roles as Americanist and folklorist, see Georges 1989a, and particularly the contributions of Jay Mechling (1989d), "Richard M. Dorson and the Emergence of the New Class in American Folk Studies" (11–26); Roger D. Abrahams (1989), "Representative Man: Richard Dorson, Americanist" (27–34); William A. Wilson (1989), "Richard M. Dorson as Romantic-Nationalist" (35–42); Stephen Stern (1989), "Dorson's Use and Adaptation of Prevailing Historical Models of American Folklore" (43–50). Historical background for the relationship of folklore to American studies can be found in Dorson's memoirs of his experience in the American civilization program at Harvard in *The Birth of American Studies* (Bloomington: Indiana University Publications, 1976). For Dorson's last survey of folklore studies before his death in 1981, see his essay "The State of Folkloristics from an American Perspective" (1982).

2.   The book also included essays that should be known by American studies professionals: "Folklore in Relation to American Studies" (78–93), "The Question of Folklore in a New Nation" (94–107), and "Folklore Research Opportunities in American Cultural History" (108–28). For precedents for Dorson's call in "A Theory for American Folklore," see Jordan 1946, 1953; McDowell 1948b; and L. Jones 1956.

3.   For criticisms of and alternatives to the American folklore versus folklore in America debate, see Bronner and Stern 1980; Bronner 1982; and L. Jones 1982.

4.   Some writings that discuss the rise of ethnographic approaches among folklorists from the 1970s to the 1990s are: Bauman and Sherzer 1974; Toelken 1979; Dorson 1982b; Abrahams 1983; Limon and Young 1986; Bronner 1988b; Bauman 1989; Schoemaker 1990.

5.   It could be argued that judging from the use of keywords to describe American life in American studies, during the 1970s the anthropological "culture" replaced the humanistic "civilization." The increasing use of folkloristic terms such as "tradition," "process," "memory," "narrative," and "folkways" in American studies suggests a more behavioral understanding of American experiences. See Jones 1982, Bronner 1982, 1986, 1988; Perin 1988; Bellah et al. 1985; and Varenne 1986. Indeed, the argument in folklore studies over Dorson's "Theory for American Folklore" during the 1950s and 1960s and the consequent

movement toward new questions of process and emergence anticipates the raging debate today in American studies over whether America is a unified or multicultural country. In this regard, Alice Kessler-Harris's presidential address to the American Studies Association of 1991, published in *American Quarterly*, on the multicultural debate called for a "processual notion of America" (Kessler-Harris 1992).

It is also worth pointing out that the relationship between the behavioral study of folklore and American studies has been institutionalized at schools such as Indiana University (Bloomington, Indiana), which allows for a joint Ph.D. degree in folklore and American studies. George Washington University offers a folklife program within the American studies Ph.D. Other American studies Ph.D.-granting institutions such as the University of Pennsylvania, University of New Mexico, Bowling Green State University, and Michigan State University have strong folkloristic components, and thus contribute to the influence of folkloristic keywords in American studies scholarship.

6. The use of contextualism in folklore and folklife research may indeed well inform American studies. Robert F. Berkhofer, Jr., states that "if the disparate interests that comprise American studies are united about anything, it is the necessity of contextual knowledge" (1989, 589). Two such examples of the possibilities of applying folkloristic ideas of context and tradition in American studies are Glassie 1978 and Mechling 1979; see also the seminal statements of Ben-Amos 1972, 1977, and 1984.

References

Aarne, Antti. 1907. *Vergleichende Märchenforschungen.* Helsingfors: Finnische Literaturgesellschaft.

———. 1910. *Verzeichnis der Märchentypen.* Folklore Fellows Communications, no. 3. Helsinki: Suomalaisen Tiedeakatemian Toimituksia.

Abbott, Ethelyn. 1913. *Folk Tales from Grimm: A Dramatic Reader for Third and Fourth Grades.* Chicago: A. Flanagan.

Abbott, Philip, and Michael B. Levy, eds. 1985. *The Liberal Future in America: Essays in Renewal.* Westport, Connecticut: Greenwood.

ABC News. 1997. *Historic America: Electronic Field Trips.* Laserdisc. New York: ABC, Inc.

Abernethy, Francis Edward, ed. 1989. *Texas Toys and Games.* Dallas: Southern Methodist University Press.

———. 1992. *The Texas Folklore Society, 1909–1943.* Vol. 1. Denton: University of North Texas Press.

Abrahams, Roger D. 1968. "Introductory Remarks to a Rhetorical Theory of Folklore." *Journal of American Folklore* 81:143–58.

———. 1976. "Folklore and History in the Study of Afro-America." In *Folklore Today: A Festschrift for Richard M. Dorson,* ed. Linda Dégh, Henry Glassie, and Felix Oinas, 1–9. Bloomington, Indiana: Research Center for Language and Semiotic Studies, Indiana University.

———. 1977. "Toward an Enactment-Centered Theory of Folklore." In *Frontiers of Folklore,* ed. William Bascom, 79–120. Boulder, Colorado: Westview Press for the American Association for the Advancement of Science.

———. 1978. "Towards a Sociological Theory of Folklore: Performing Services." *Western Folklore* 37:161–84.

———. 1979. "Folklore in Culture: Notes toward an Analytic Method." In *Readings in American Folklore,* ed. Jan Harold Brunvand, 390–403. New York: W. W. Norton.

———. 1981. "Shouting Match at the Border: The Folklore of Display Events." In *"And Other Neighborly Names": Social Process and Cultural Image in Texas Folklore,* ed. Richard Bauman and Roger D. Abrahams, 303–22. Austin: University of Texas Press.

———. 1983. "Interpreting Folklore Ethnographically and Sociologically." In *Handbook of American Folklore,* ed. Richard M. Dorson, 345–50. Bloomington: Indiana University Press.

———. 1985a. *Afro-American Folktales.* New York: Pantheon.

———. 1985b. "Pragmatism and a Folklore of Experience." *Western Folklore* 44:324–32.

———. 1986. "Ordinary and Extraordinary Experience." In *The Anthropology of Experience*, ed. Victor W. Turner and Edward M. Bruner, 45–72. Urbana: University of Illinois Press.

———. 1987. "'Roots and Wings': An Overview of the FAIE Program." In *Folk Arts in Education: A Resource Handbook*, ed. Marsha MacDowell, 77–80. East Lansing: Michigan State University Museum.

———. 1988. "Rough Sincerities: William Wells Newell and the Discovery of Folklore in Late-19th Century America." In *Folk Roots, New Roots: Folklore in American Life*, ed. Jane S. Becker and Barbara Franco, 61–76. Lexington, Massachusetts: Museum of Our National Heritage.

———. 1989. "Representative Man: Richard Dorson, Americanist." *Journal of Folklore Research* 26:27–34.

———. 1992a. "The Public, the Folklorist, and the Public Folklorist." In *Public Folklore*, ed. Robert Baron and Nicholas R. Spitzer, 17–28. Washington, D.C.: Smithsonian Institution Press.

———. 1992b. *Singing the Master: The Emergence of African-American Culture in the Plantation South*. New York: Penguin.

———. 1993. "Phantoms of Romantic Nationalism in Folkloristics." *Journal of American Folklore* 106:3–37.

Abrahams, Roger D., and Susan Kalčik. 1978. "Folklore and Cultural Pluralism." In *Folklore in the Modern World*, ed. Richard M. Dorson, 223–36. The Hague: Mouton.

Abrahams, Roger D., and John F. Szwed, eds. 1983. *After Africa*. New Haven: Yale University Press.

Abstracts of Papers Delivered at a Midwestern Conference on Folk Arts and Museums. 1981. St. Paul: University of Minnesota Gallery and the Center for the Study of Minnesota Folklife.

Ackerman, Robert. 1990. "J. G. Frazer." In *Classical Scholarship: A Biographical Encyclopedia*, ed. Ward W. Briggs and William M. Calder III, 77–83. New York: Garland.

Acton, H. B. 1953. "Tradition and Some Other Forms of Order." *Proceedings of the Aristotelian Society*, n.s., 53:1–28.

Adams, Robert McC. 1990. "Cultural Pluralism: A Smithsonian Commitment." In *1990 Festival of American Folklife*, ed. Peter Seitel, 5–6. Washington, D.C.: Smithsonian Institution.

Aeppel, Timothy. 1996. "More Amish Women Are Tending to Business." *Wall Street Journal* (February 8), B1.

Aleichem, Sholem. 1973. *Tevye's Daughters*. Ed. Teiji Nagawa. Tokyo: Kenyusha.

Alexander, Jane. 1996. "Foreword." In *The Changing Faces of Tradition: A Report on the Folk and Traditional Arts in the United States*, ed. Elizabeth Peterson, 5. Washington, D.C.: National Endowment for the Arts.

Allen, Barbara. 1996. "Regional Folklore." In *American Folklore: An Encyclopedia*, ed. Jan Harold Brunvand, 618–19. New York: Garland.

Allen, Barbara, and Thomas J. Schlereth, eds. 1990. *Sense of Place: American Regional Cultures*. Lexington: University Press of Kentucky.

Allen, Ray. 1992. *Singing in the Spirit: African-American Sacred Quartets in New York City*. Philadelphia: University of Pennsylvania.

Allies, Jabez. 1852. *On the Ancient British, Roman and Saxon Antiquities and Folk-Lore of Worcestershire*. London: J. H. Parker.

Allison, Christine. 1993. *Teach Your Children Well: A Parent's Guide to the Stories, Poems, Fables, and Tales that Instill Traditional Values*. New York: Delacorte Press.

Allison, William M., Jr. 1915. *Henry W. Shoemaker: An Appreciation.* Altoona: Times Tribune.

Almeida, Raymond A. 1995. "*Nos Ku Nos*: A Transnational Cape Verdean Community." In *1995 Festival of American Folklife*, ed. Carla M. Borden, 18–26. Washington, D.C.: Smithsonian Institution.

Alvey, R. Gerald. 1984. *Dulcimer Maker: The Craft of Homer Ledford.* Lexington: University Press of Kentucky.

Ames, Kenneth L. 1980. "Folk Art: The Challenge and the Promise." In *Perspectives on American Folk Art*, ed. Ian M. G. Quimby and Scott T. Swank, 293–324. New York: W. W. Norton.

Ammerman, Peggy. 1989. "The Simple Life." *Chicago Tribune* (May 7) 12:21.

Ancelet, Barry Jean. 1984. *The Makers of Cajun Music.* Austin: University of Texas Press.

Ancelet, Barry Jean, Jay Edwards, and Glen Pitre. 1991. *Cajun Country.* Jackson: University Press of Mississippi.

Anderson, Brian. 1985. *Grimm Tales in English.* London: British Library.

Anderson, Margo J. 1988. *The American Census: A Social History.* New Haven: Yale University Press.

Andersson-Palmqvist, Lena. 1983. *Building Traditions among Swedish Settlers in Rural Minnesota.* Stockholm: Nordiska Museet, The Emigrant Institute.

Andrews, E. Benjamin. 1896. *The History of the Last Quarter-Century in the United States, 1870–1895.* New York: Charles Scribner and Sons.

Andrews, Ruth, ed. 1977. *How to Know American Folk Art.* New York: E. P. Dutton.

Annan, Noel. 1966. "The Strands of Unbelief." In *Ideas and Beliefs of the Victorians: An Historic Revaluation of the Victorian Age*, ed. Harman Grisewood, 150–56. New York: E. P. Dutton.

Anttonen, Pertti J. 1993. "Folklore, Modernity, and Postmodernism: A Theoretical Overview." In *Nordic Frontiers: Recent Issues in the Study of Modern Traditional Culture in the Nordic Countries*, ed. Pertti J. Anttonen and Reimund Kvideland, 17–31. Turku: Nordic Institute of Folklore.

"Archivist Gets Folklore Post: Col. Henry Shoemaker Is Assigned to Collect Tales of State's Heritage." 1948. *Harrisburg Patriot* (March 12), 1, 15.

Argetsinger, Amy. 1997. "Amish Market Cultivates an Eager Clientele: High Quality, Low Prices. Quaint Merchants Lure Customers to Mall Near Annapolis." *Washington Post* (March 16), B1.

Asad, Talal, ed. 1975. *Anthropology and the Colonial Encounter.* London: Ithaca Press.

Ashton, John W. 1957. "Folklore in the Literature of Elizabethan England." *Journal of American Folklore* 70:10–15.

Assion, Peter. 1988. "Karl Knortz and His Works." *Folklore Historian* 5:2–12.

Attebery, Louie W., ed. 1985. *Idaho Folklife: Homesteads to Headstones.* Salt Lake City: University of Utah Press.

Auerbach, Susan. 1996a. *In Good Hands: A Portrait of State Apprenticeship Programs in the Folk & Traditional Arts, 1983–1995.* Washington, D.C.: National Endowment for the Arts.

———. 1996b. "Investing in the Future of Tradition: State Apprenticeship Programs." In *The Changing Faces of Tradition: A Report on the Folk and Traditional Arts in the United States*, ed. Elizabeth Peterson, 24–31. Washington, D.C.: National Endowment for the Arts.

Aughey, Arthur, Greta Jones, and W. T. M. Riches. 1992. *The Conservative Political Tradition in Britain and the United States.* Cranbury, New Jersey: Associated University Presses.

Ausubel, Nathan, comp. 1948. *A Treasury of Jewish Folklore.* New York: Crown.

Axelrod, Alan, ed. 1985. *The Colonial Revival in America.* New York: W. W. Norton.

Babcock, Barbara A. 1993. "'At Home, No Women Are Storytellers': Potteries, Stories, and Politics in Cochiti Pueblo." In *Feminist Messages: Coding in Women's Folk Culture*, ed. Joan Newlon Radner, 221–48. Urbana: University of Illinois Press.

Babcock, Barbara A., Guy Monthan, and Doris Monthan. 1986. *The Pueblo Storyteller: Development of a Figurative Ceramic Tradition*. Tucson: University of Arizona Press.

Bacchilega, Cristina. 1989. "Folk and Literary Narrative in a Postmodern Context: The Case of the Märchen." *Fabula* 29:302–16.

Bacon, Alice Mabel. 1893. "Proposal for Folk-Lore Research at Hampton, Va." *Journal of American Folklore* 6:305–9.

———. 1894. *A Japanese Interior*. Boston: Houghton Mifflin.

———. 1896. *The Negro and the Atlanta Exposition*. Baltimore: Trustees of the John F. Slater Fund.

———. 1898. "Work and Methods of the Hampton Folklore Society." *Journal of American Folklore* 11:17–21.

———. 1905. *In the Land of the Gods: Some Stories of Japan*. Boston: Houghton Mifflin.

Bacon, A. M., and E. C. Parsons. 1922. "Folk-Lore from Elizabeth City County, Virginia." *Journal of American Folklore* 35:250–327.

Baker, Ronald L. 1971. "Folklore Courses and Programs in American Colleges and Universities." *Journal of American Folklore* 84:221–29.

———. 1978. "The Study of Folklore in American Colleges and Universities." *Journal of American Folklore* 91:792–807.

———. 1982. *Hoosier Folk Legends*. Bloomington: Indiana University Press.

———. 1983. "Folklore of Students." In *Handbook of American Folklore*, ed. Richard M. Dorson, 106–14. Bloomington: Indiana University Press.

———. 1986a. "Folklore and Folklife Studies in American and Canadian Colleges and Universities." *Journal of American Folklore* 99:50–74.

———. 1986b. *Jokelore: Humorous Folktales from Indiana*. Bloomington: Indiana University Press.

———. 1995. *From Needmore to Prosperity: Hoosier Place Names in Folklore and History*. Bloomington: Indiana University Press.

Ballard, Linda M. 1994. "Out of the Abstract: The Development of the Study of Irish Folklife." *New York Folklore* 20:1–13.

Banfield, Beryle. 1979. *Black Focus on Multicultural Education: How to Develop an Anti-Racist, Anti-Sexist Curriculum*. New York: E. W. Blyden.

Barba, Preston A. 1954. *Pennsylvania German Tombstones: A Study in Folk Art*. Allentown: Schlecter's for the Pennsylvania German Folklore Society.

Barber, James G. 1993. *To the President: Folk Portraits by the People*. Washington, D.C.: National Portrait Gallery and Madison Books.

Barkan, Elazar. 1992. *The Retreat of Scientific Racism*. Cambridge: Cambridge University Press.

Barker, Virgil. 1924. "Notes on the Exhibition." *Arts* (March), 161.

Barnard, F. M. 1965. *Herder's Social and Political Thought: From Enlightenment to Nationalism*. Oxford: Clarendon Press.

———, trans. and ed. 1969. *J. G. Herder on Social and Political Culture*. Cambridge: Cambridge University Press.

Barns, Cass G. 1930. *The Sod House*. Lincoln: University of Nebraska Press.

Baron, Robert, and Nicholas R. Spitzer, eds. 1992. *Public Folklore*. Washington, D.C.: Smithsonian Institution Press.

Barone, Michael. 1994. "A History of Culture Wars." *U.S. News and World Report* (August 1), 40.

Barons, Richard I. 1982. *The Folk Tradition: Early Arts and Crafts of the Susquehanna Valley.* Binghamton, New York: Roberson Center.

Barrick, Mac E. 1968. "Finger Games and Rhymes." *Pennsylvania Folklife* 17(4):44–47.

———, ed. 1987. *German-American Folklore.* Little Rock: August House.

Barron, Elwyn A. 1892. "Shadowy Memories of Negro-Lore." *The Folk-Lorist* 1:46–53.

Bartis, Peter, comp. 1980. *Maritime Folklife Resources: A Directory and Index.* Washington, D.C.: American Folklife Center, Library of Congress.

Bartis, Peter, and Hillary Glatt, comps. 1994. *Folklife Sourcebook: A Directory of Folklife Resources in the United States and Canada.* 2d ed. Washington, D.C.: Library of Congress.

Bascom, William R. 1949–50. "Folklore." In *Standard Dictionary of Folklore,* ed. Maria Leach, 1:398. New York: Funk and Wagnalls.

———. 1955. "Verbal Art." *Journal of American Folklore* 68:246.

———. [1954] 1965. "Four Functions of Folklore." In *The Study of Folklore,* ed. Alan Dundes, 279–98. Englewood Cliffs, New Jersey: Prentice-Hall.

———. 1977. "Frontiers of Folklore: An Introduction." In *Frontiers of Folklore,* ed. William Bascom, 1–16. Boulder, Colorado: Westview Press for the American Association for the Advancement of Science.

———. 1983. "Malinowski's Contributions to the Study of Folklore." *Folklore* 94:163–72.

Basile, Giambattista. 1927. *Il Pentamerone, or, The Tale of Tales.* Trans. Sir Richard Burton. 1637; rpt., New York: Boni and Liveright.

———. 1976. *Il Penatamerone: lo cunto de li cunti.* Ed. Benedetto Croce. 1637; rpt., Rome: G. Laterza.

Bassett, Fletcher S. 1892. *The Folk-Lore Manual.* Chicago: Chicago Folk-Lore Society.

———. 1898. "The Folklore Congress." In *The International Folk-Lore Congress of the World's Columbian Exposition,* ed. Helen Wheeler Bassett and Frederick Starr, 17–23. Chicago: Charles H. Sergel.

Bates, Ernest Sutherland. 1926. "American Folk-Lore." *Saturday Review of Literature* 2 (July 10):913–14.

Battle, Kemp P., comp. 1989. *Great American Folklore: Legends, Tales, Ballads, and Superstitions from All Across America.* New York: Touchstone.

Bauer, Gary L. 1991. "If the Boy Scouts Can't Live by Their Traditional Values, Who Can?" *USA Today* (June 17), A8.

Baughman, Ernest W. 1966. *Type and Motif Index of the Folktales of England and North America.* The Hague: Mouton.

Bauman, Richard. 1972. "Differential Identity and the Social Base of Folklore." In *Toward New Perspectives in Folklore,* ed. Américo Paredes and Richard Bauman, 31–41. Austin: University of Texas Press.

———. 1977. *Verbal Art as Performance.* Rowley, Massachusetts: Newbury House.

———. 1983a. "Folklore and the Forces of Modernity." *Folklore Forum* 16:153–58.

———. 1983b. *Let Your Words Be Few: Symbolism of Speaking and Silence among Seventeenth-Century Quakers.* Cambridge: Cambridge University Press.

———. 1986. *Story, Performance, and Event: Contextual Studies of Oral Narrative.* Cambridge: Cambridge University Press.

———. 1989. "American Folklore Studies and Social Transformation: A Performance-Centered Perspective." *Text and Performance Quarterly* 9:175–84.

———. 1992. "Folklore." In *Folklore, Cultural Performances, and Popular Entertainments: A Communications-Centered Handbook,* ed. Richard Bauman, 29–40. New York: Oxford University Press.

———. 1996. "Folklore as Transdisciplinary Dialogue." *Journal of Folklore Research* 33:15–20.

Bauman, Richard, and Roger D. Abrahams, eds. 1981. *"And Other Neighborly Names": Social Process and Cultural Image in Texas Folklore.* Austin: University of Texas Press.

Bauman, Richard, Roger D. Abrahams, with Susan Kalčik. 1976. "American Folklore and American Studies." *American Quarterly* 28:360–77.

Bauman, Richard, and Américo Paredes, eds. 1972. *Toward New Perspectives in Folklore.* Austin: University of Texas Press.

Bauman, Richard, Patricia Sawin, and Inta Gale Carpenter. 1992. *Reflections on the Folklife Festival: An Ethnography of Participant Experience.* Bloomington: Special Publications of the Folklore Institute, Indiana University.

Bauman, Richard, and Joel Sherzer, eds. 1974. *Explorations in the Ethnography of Speaking.* Cambridge: Cambridge University Press.

Bayard, Samuel P. 1944. *Hill Country Tunes.* Philadelphia: American Folklore Society.

———. 1945. "Unrecorded Folk Traditions in Pennsylvania." *Pennsylvania History* 12:1–13.

———. 1953. "The Materials of Folklore." *Journal of American Folklore* 66:1–17.

———. 1959. "English-Language Folk Culture in Pennsylvania." *Pennsylvania Folklife* 10:11–13.

Beam, C. Richard. 1981. "Preface to the Second Edition." In *A Simple Grammar of Pennsylvania Dutch* by J. William Frey, iii–xxxiv. Lancaster, Pennsylvania: John Baers and Son.

———, ed. 1995. *The Thomas R. Brendle Collection of Pennsylvania German Folklore.* Vol. 1. Schaefferstown, Pennsylvania: Historic Schaefferstown.

Beard, George M. 1970. "Causes of American Nervousness" (1881). In *Democratic Vistas, 1860–1880,* ed. Alan Trachtenberg, 237–47. New York: George Braziller.

Bechstein, Ludwig. 1872. *As Pretty as Seven and Other Popular German Tales: A Companion to Grimms' German Popular Stories.* London: J. C. Hotten.

Becker, Howard. 1982. *Art Worlds.* Berkeley: University of California Press.

Becker, Jane S., and Barbara Franco, eds. 1988. *Folk Roots, New Roots: Folklore in American Life.* Lexington, Massachusetts: Museum of Our National Heritage.

Beckwith, Martha Warren. 1907. "Dance Forms of the Moqui and Kwakiutl Indians." In *Proceedings of the International Congress of Americanists, Fifteenth Session, Quebec, 1906,* 2:79–114. Quebec.

———. 1916. "The Hawaiian Hula-Dance." *Journal of American Folklore* 29:409–12.

———. 1918. "Review of *Tsimshian Mythology* by Franz Boas." *Journal of Germanic and English Philology* 17:460–70.

———. 1919. *The Hawaiian Romance of Laieikawai.* In Thirty-third Annual Report of U.S. Bureau of American Ethnology (1911–1912), 285–666. Washington, D.C.: Smithsonian Institution, Government Printing Office.

———. 1922. "Hawaiian Riddling." *American Anthropologist* 24:311–31.

———. 1923. "Signs and Superstitions from American College Girls." *Journal of American Folklore* 36:1–15.

———. 1924a. "The English Ballad in Jamaica: A Note upon the Origins of the Ballad Forms." *Publications of the Modern Language Association* 39:455–83.

———. 1924b. *Jamaica Anansi Stories.* New York: Memoirs of the American Folklore Society, no. 17.

———. 1927. "A Note on Punjab Legend in Relation to Arthurian Romance." In *Medieval Studies in Memory of Gertrude Schoepperle Loomis,* 49–74. New York: Columbia University Press.

———. 1928a. "In Praise of Folk Lore." *Mt. Holyoke Monthly* 35:277–82.

———. 1928b. *Jamaica Folk-Lore*, with music recorded in the field by Helen H. Roberts. New York: Memoirs of the American Folklore Society, vol. 21.

———. 1929. *Black Roadways: A Study of Jamaican Folk Life*. Chapel Hill: University of North Carolina Press.

———. 1930. "Mythology of the Oglala Dakota." *Journal of American Folklore* 43:338–442.

———. 1931a. "Black Roadways: A Rejoinder." *Journal of American Folklore* 44:22–23.

———. 1931b. *Folklore in America: Its Scope and Method*. Poughkeepsie, New York: Folklore Foundation.

———. 1931c. "Review of *American Humor* by Constance Rourke." *Journal of American Folklore* 44:311–13.

———. 1933. "The White Top Festival." *Journal of American Folklore* 46:416.

———. 1934. *Mandan-Hidatsa Myths and Ceremonies*. New York: Memoirs of the American Folklore Society, vol. 32.

———. 1937. "Pushkin's Relation to Folklore." In *Pushkin, the Man and the Artist*, 187–204. New York: Paisley Press.

———. 1938. "National Folk Festival, Washington. Mountain Folk Festival, Berea College." *Journal of American Folklore* 51:442–44.

———. 1940. "Polynesian Mythology." *Journal of the Polynesian Society* 49:19–35.

———. 1943. "Review of *Roots of American Culture* by Constance Rourke." *Journal of American Folklore* 56:222–23.

———. 1944. "Polynesian Story Composition." *Journal of the Polynesian Society* 53:177–203.

———. 1951. *The Kumulipo, A Hawaiian Creation Chant*. Chicago: University of Chicago Press.

———. 1970. *Hawaiian Mythology*. 1940; rpt., Honolulu: University of Hawaii Press.

Beckwith, Martha, and Laura C. Green. 1924. "Hawaiian Customs and Beliefs Relating to Birth and Infancy." *American Anthropologist* 26:230–46.

———. 1926. "Hawaiian Customs and Beliefs Relating to Sickness and Death." *American Anthropologist* 28:176–208.

———. 1928. "Hawaiian Household Customs." *American Anthropologist* 30:1–17.

Belanus, Betty, coordinator. 1985. *Folklore in the Classroom*. Indianapolis: Indiana Historical Bureau.

Bell, Michael J. 1983. *The World from Brown's Lounge: An Ethnography of Black Middle-Class Play*. Urbana: University of Illinois Press.

———. 1988. "No Borders to the Ballad Maker's Art: Francis James Child and the Politics of the People." *Western Folklore* 47:285–307.

Bellah, Robert N., Richard Madsen, William M. Sullivan, Ann Swidler, and Steven M. Tipton. 1985. *Habits of the Heart: Individualism and Commitment in American Life*. New York: Harper and Row.

Ben-Amos, Dan. 1972. "Toward a Definition of Folklore in Context." In *Toward New Perspectives in Folklore*, ed. Américo Paredes and Richard Bauman, 3–15. Austin: University of Texas Press.

———. 1977. "The Context of Folklore: Implications and Prospects." In *Frontiers of Folklore*, ed. William R. Bascom, 36–53. Boulder, Colorado: Westview Press.

———. 1979. "The Ceremony of Innocence." *Western Folklore* 38:47–52.

———. 1982. "Foreword." In *The European Folktale: Form and Nature*, by Max Lüthi, viii–xiv. Philadelphia: Institute for the Study of Human Issues.

———. 1984. "The Seven Strands of *Tradition*: Varieties in Its Meaning in American Folklore Studies." *Journal of Folklore Research* 21:97–132.

———. 1989. "The Historical Folklore of Richard M. Dorson." *Journal of Folklore Research* 26:51–60.

———. 1993. "'Context' in Context." *Western Folklore* 52:209–26.

Ben-Amos, Dan, and Kenneth S. Goldstein. 1975. "Introduction." In *Folklore: Performance and Communication*, ed. Dan Ben-Amos and Kenneth S. Goldstein, 1–7. The Hague: Mouton.

Bendix, Regina. 1987. "Marmot, Memet, and Marmoset: Further Research on the Folklore of Dyads." *Western Folklore* 46:171–91.

———. 1989. "Tourism and Cultural Displays: Inventing Traditions for Whom?" *Journal of American Folklore* 102:131–46.

Benedetti, Joan M. 1987. "Who Are the Folk in Folk Art? Inside and Outside the Cultural Context." *Art Documentation* 6:3–8.

Benet, Stephen Vincent. 1937. *The Devil and Daniel Webster.* Toronto: Farrar & Rinehart.

Bennett, Gillian. 1991. "English Folklore and the Land of Lost Content." *Folklore Historian* 8:26–37.

———. 1994. "Geologists and Folklorists: Cultural Evolution and 'The Science of Folklore.'" *Folklore* 105:25–37.

———. 1996. "The Thomsian Heritage in the Folklore Society (London)." *Journal of Folklore Research* 33:212–20.

Bennett, Gillian, and Paul Smith. 1992. *Contemporary Legend: An Annotated Bibliography.* New York: Garland.

Bennett, William J. 1993. *The Book of Virtues: A Treasury of Great Moral Stories.* New York: Simon and Schuster.

Benton, Thomas Hart. 1983. *An Artist in America.* 4th rev. ed. Columbia: University of Missouri Press.

Bercovitch, Sacvan, ed. 1995. *The Cambridge History of American Literature.* Vol. 2. Cambridge: Cambridge University Press.

Bergen, Fanny D. 1892. "Quilt Patterns." *Journal of American Folklore* 5:69.

———. 1894. "The Tapestry of the New World." *Scribner's Magazine* 16:360–70.

Berger, Peter L. 1979. "The Worldview of the New Class: Secularity and Its Discontents." In *The New Class?*, ed. Bruce Briggs, 49–56. New Brunswick, New Jersey: Transaction Books.

Berkhofer, Robert F., Jr. 1979. "The Americanness of American Studies." *American Quarterly* 31:340–45.

———. 1989. "A New Context for a New American Studies?" *American Quarterly* 41:588–613.

Berkow, Ira. 1987. "The Coloring of Bird." *New York Times* (June 2), D27.

Berlin, Isaiah. 1976. *Vico and Herder: Two Studies in the History of Ideas.* New York: Viking.

Bernstein, Richard J. 1971. *Praxis and Action.* Philadelphia: University of Pennsylvania Press.

Bethke, Robert D. 1981. *Adirondack Voices: Woodsmen and Woods Lore.* Urbana: University of Illinois Press.

Bettelheim, Bruno. 1977. *The Uses of Enchantment: The Meaning and Importance of Fairy Tales.* New York: Alfred A. Knopf.

———. 1989. "Little Red Cap and the Pubertal Girl." In *Little Red Riding Hood: A Casebook*, ed. Alan Dundes, 168–91. Madison: University of Wisconsin Press.

Beye, Charles Rowan. 1990. "Milman Parry." In *Classical Scholarship: A Biographical Encyclopedia*, ed. Ward W. Briggs and William M. Calder III, 361–66. New York: Garland.

Birdsall, Esther K. 1973. "Some Notes on the Role of George Lyman Kittredge in American Folklore Studies." *Journal of the Folklore Institute* 10:57–66.

Bishop, Robert. 1977. *The All-American Dog: Man's Best Friend in Folk Art.* New York: Museum of American Folk Art.

Black, Rick. 1992. "Shadow from Developers Dims Amish Paradise." *Chicago Tribune* (May 10) 1:21.

———. 1993. "Amish Country Being Overrun by 20th Century." *Los Angeles Times* (June 28), A5.

Blair, Betty A. 1991. "Iranian Immigrant Name Changes in Los Angeles." In *Creative Ethnicity: Symbols and Strategies of Contemporary Ethnic Life,* ed. Stephen Stern and John Allan Cicala, 122–36. Logan: Utah State University Press.

Bledstein, Burton J. 1976. *The Culture of Professionalism: The Middle-Class and the Development of Higher Education in America.* New York: W. W. Norton.

Bluestein, Gene. 1994. *Poplore: Folk and Pop in American Culture.* Amherst: University of Massachusetts Press.

Blumenreich, Beth, and Bari Lynn Polansky. 1975. "Re-evaluating the Concept of Group: ICEN as an Alternative." In *Conceptual Problems in Contemporary Folklore Study,* ed. Gerald Cashion. Folklore Forum Bibliographic and Special Series, no. 12.

Bly, Robert. 1991. *Iron John.* New York: Harper Collins.

Boas, Franz. 1896. "The Limitations of the Comparative Method of Anthropology." *Science* 4:901–8.

———. 1911. *The Mind of Primitive Man.* New York: Macmillan.

———. 1914. "Mythology and Folk-Tales of the North American Indians." *Journal of American Folklore* 27:374–410.

———. 1916. *Tsmishian Mythology.* Thirty-first Annual Report of U.S. Bureau of American Ethnology, 29–1037. Washington, D.C: Smithsonian Institution, Government Printing Office.

———. 1925a. "Stylistic Aspects of Primitive Literature." *Journal of American Folklore* 38:329–39.

———. 1925b. "Teton Sioux Music." *Journal of American Folklore* 38:319–24.

———. 1938a. "An Anthropologist's Credo." *The Nation* 147:201–4.

———. 1938b. "Mythology and Folklore." In *General Anthropology,* ed. Franz Boas, 609–26. Boston: D. C. Heath.

———. 1940. *Race, Language and Culture.* New York: Free Press.

———. 1945. *Race and Democratic Society.* New York: J. J. Augustin.

———. 1955. *Primitive Art.* 1927; rpt., New York: Dover.

———. 1986. *Anthropology and Modern Life.* 1928; rpt., New York: Dover.

Bødker, Laurits. 1965. *Folk Literature (Germanic).* Copenhagen: Rosenkilde and Bagger.

Bodnar, John. 1985. *The Transplanted: A History of Immigrants in Urban America.* Bloomington: Indiana University Press.

———. 1992. *Remaking America: Public Memory, Commemoration, and Patriotism in the Twentieth Century.* Princeton: Princeton University Press.

Boggs, Ralph Steele. 1940. "Folklore in University Curricula in the United States." *Southern Folklore Quarterly* 4:93–109.

Bolden, Thomas Jefferson. 1899. "Bre'r Rabbit's Box." *Southern Workman* 28:25–26.

Bolte, Johannes, and Lutz MacKensen, eds. 1930. *Handwörterbuch des deutschen Märchens,* 2 vols. Berlin: DeGruyter.

Bolte, Johannes, and Georg Polívka. 1963. *Anmerkungen zu den Kinder- und Hausmärchen der Brüder Grimm,* 5 vols. 1913–1932; rpt., Hildesheim: Georg Olms.

Bondi, Nicole. 1995. "Time's Up for Wimpy Cinderellas." *Detroit News and Free Press* (November 11), C1.

Boorstin, Daniel. 1958. *The Americans: The Colonial Experience.* New York: Vintage.

———. 1959. "Preface." In *American Folklore* by Richard M. Dorson, ix–xi. Chicago: University of Chicago Press.

———. 1965. *The Americans: The National Experience*. New York: Vintage.

———. 1973. *The Americans: The Democratic Experience*. New York: Random House.

Borchert, James. 1980. *Alley Life in Washington: Family, Community, Religion, and Folklife in the City, 1850–1970*. Urbana: University of Illinois Press.

Bosma, Bette. 1987. *Fairy Tales, Fables, Legends, and Myths: Using Folk Literature in Your Classroom*. New York: Teachers College Press.

Botkin, B. A. 1926. "Sanctuary." *American Mercury* 7:14.

———. 1929. "The Folk in Literature: An Introduction to the New Regionalism." In *Folk-Say*, ed. B. A. Botkin, 9–20. Norman: University of Oklahoma Press.

———. 1930. "Introduction." In *Folk-Say: A Regional Miscellany, 1930*, ed. B. A. Botkin, 15–18. Norman: University of Oklahoma Press.

———. 1931. "'Folk-Say' and Folklore." *American Speech* 6:404–6.

———. 1932. "The Folkness of the Folk." *English Journal* 26:461–69.

———. 1935. "*Folk-Say* and *Space*: Their Genesis and Exodus." *Southwest Review* 20:321–35.

———. 1937. *The American Play-Party Song, with a Collection of Oklahoma Texts and Tunes*. Lincoln: University of Nebraska.

———. 1938. "The Folk and the Individual: Their Creative Reciprocity." *English Journal* 27:121–35.

———. 1940. "Folklore as a Neglected Source of Social History." In *The Cultural Approach to History*, ed. Caroline F. Ware, 308–15. New York: Columbia University Press.

———, ed. 1944. *A Treasury of American Folklore*. New York: Crown.

———. 1946a. "Living Lore on the New York City Writers' Project." *New York Folklore Quarterly* 2:252–63.

———. 1946b. "Paul Bunyan Was OK in His Time." *New Masses* (April 23), 12–14.

———. 1947a. "Review of *Jonathan Draws the Longbow* by Richard Dorson." *New York Folklore Quarterly* 3:78–81.

———. 1947b. *A Treasury of New England Folklore*. New York: Crown.

———. 1949a. "American Folklore." In *Standard Dictionary of Folklore, Mythology, and Legend*, ed. Maria Leach, 43–48. New York: Funk and Wagnalls.

———. 1949b. *A Treasury of Southern Folklore*. New York: Crown.

———. 1951a. "A Little Christian Civility." *New York Folklore Quarterly* 7:78–79.

———. 1951b. *A Treasury of Western Folklore*. New York: Crown.

———. 1952a. "Battle of the Books." *New York Folklore Quarterly* 8:235.

———. 1952b. "Review of *Bloodstoppers and Bearwalkers* by Richard Dorson." *United States Quarterly Book Review* 8:412–13.

———. 1953. "Applied Folklore: Creating Understanding through Folklore." *Southern Folklore Quarterly* 17:199–206.

———. 1954. *Sidewalks of America: Folklore, Legends, Sagas, Traditions, Songs, Stories and Sayings of City Folk*. New York: Bobbs-Merrill.

———. 1955a. "Folklore and History." *Manuscripts* 7:256–60.

———. 1955b. "Love and Learning." *New York Folklore Quarterly* 11:74–75.

———. 1955c. *A Treasury of Mississippi River Folklore*. New York: Crown.

———. 1956. *New York City Folklore: Legends, Tall Tales, Anecdotes, Stories, Sagas, Heroes and Characters, Customs, Traditions, and Sayings*. New York: Random House.

———. 1962. "The Folkness of the Folk." In *Folklore in Action: Essays for Discussion in Honor of MacEdward Leach*, ed. Horace P. Beck, 44–57. Philadelphia: American Folklore Society.

Botkin, B. A., and Alvin F. Harlow, eds. 1953. *A Treasury of Railroad Folklore: The Stories, Tall Tales, Traditions, Ballads and Songs of the American Railroad Man.* New York: Crown.

Bottigheimer, Ruth B. 1986. "Silenced Women in the Grimms' Tales: The 'Fit' Between Fairy Tales and Society in Their Historical Context." In *Fairy Tales and Society: Illusion, Allusion, and Paradigm,* ed. Ruth Bottigheimer, 115–32. Philadelphia: University of Pennsylvania Press.

———. 1988. "From Gold to Guilt: The Forces Which Reshaped *Grimms' Tales.*" In *The Brothers Grimm and Folktale,* ed. James M. McGlathery, 192–204. Urbana: University of Illinois Press.

Bourke, John G. [1895] 1987. "Folk Foods of the Rio Grande Valley and of Northern Mexico." In *Folklife Studies from the Gilded Age: Object, Rite, and Custom in Victorian America,* ed. Simon J. Bronner, 183–216. Ann Arbor: UMI Research Press.

Bowman, James Cloyd. 1927. *The Adventures of Paul Bunyan.* New York: Century.

Boynton, Mia, ed. 1988. "Folklore in the Industrial Workplace." Special section of *New York Folklore* 14(1–2):1–106.

Brady, Margaret K. 1984. *"Some Kind of Power": Navajo Children's Skinwalker Narratives.* Salt Lake City: University of Utah Press.

Braid, Donald. 1996. "Personal Narrative and Experiential Meaning." *Journal of American Folklore* 109:5–30.

Brandes, Stanley. 1985. *Forty: The Age and the Symbol.* Knoxville: University of Tennessee Press.

Brandt, Mindy. 1993–94. "Tourism and the Old Order Amish." *Pennsylvania Folklife* 43 (winter):71–75.

Brauner, Cheryl Anne. 1983. "A Study of the Newport Folk Festival and the Newport Folk Foundation." M.A. thesis, Memorial University of Newfoundland.

Braunstein, Susan L., and Jenna Weissman Joselit, eds. 1990. *Getting Comfortable in New York: The American Jewish Home, 1880–1950.* New York: Jewish Museum.

Breton, Rita, Joan Brooks, Catherine Fox, Florence Ireland, and Edward D. Ives. 1986. *The Northeast Archives of Folklore and Oral History: A Catalog of the First 1800 Accessions.* Orono, Maine: Northeast Folklore Society.

Brewer, Teri, ed. 1994. *Perspectives on Folklore, Tourism and the Heritage Industry.* Middlesex, England: Hisarlik Press.

Brewster, Paul G. 1943. "Notes on Contributions of the Clergy to Folklore and Allied Fields." *Southern Folklore Quarterly* 7:173–86.

Brewster, Paul G., Archer Taylor, Bartlett Jere Whiting, George P. Wilson, and Stith Thompson, eds. 1952. *The Frank C. Brown Collection of North Carolina Folklore: Vol. One.* Durham, North Carolina: Duke University Press.

Briggs, Charles L. 1980. *The Wood Carvers of Córdova, New Mexico: Social Dimensions of an Artistic "Revival".* Knoxville: University of Tennessee Press.

———. 1988. *Competence in Performance: The Creativity of Tradition in Mexicano Verbal Art.* Philadelphia: University of Pennsylvania Press.

Briggs, Charles L., and Amy Shuman. 1993. "Introduction." In "Theorizing Folklore: Toward New Perspectives on the Politics of Culture," ed. Charles Briggs and Amy Shuman, 109–34. *Western Folklore* 52(2,3,4).

Briggs, K. M. 1967. *The Fairies in English Tradition and Literature.* Chicago: University of Chicago Press.

"British Fear 'Snow White' Will Cause Nightmares." 1938. *New York Times* (February 6), L37.

British Library. 1985. *Grimm Tales in English: Exhibition Notes.* London: British Library.

Brody, Ed. 1992. *Spinning Tales, Weaving Hope: Stories of Peace, Justice and the Environment.* Philadelphia: New Society.

Bronner, Simon J. 1981. "Investigating Identity and Expression in Folk Art." *Winterthur Portfolio* 16:65–83.

———. 1982. "Malaise or Revelation? Observations on the 'American Folklore' Polemic," *Western Folklore* 41:52–61.

———, ed. 1984a. *American Folk Art: A Guide to Sources.* New York: Garland.

———. 1984b. "Folklore and the Behavioral Sciences." *Anthropos* 79:251–55.

———. 1984c. "Folklore in the Bureaucracy." In *Tools for Management*, ed. Frederick Richmond, Barry Nazar, and Kathy Nazar, 45–57. Harrisburg, Pennsylvania: PEN Publications.

———. 1985. *Chain Carvers: Old Men Crafting Meaning.* Lexington: University Press of Kentucky.

———. 1986a. *American Folklore Studies: An Intellectual History.* Lawrence: University Press of Kansas.

———. 1986b. *Grasping Things: Folk Material Culture and Mass Society in America.* Lexington: University Press of Kentucky.

———, ed. 1987a. *Folklife Studies from the Gilded Age: Object, Rite, and Custom in Victorian America.* Ann Arbor: UMI Research Press.

———. 1987b. *Old Time Music Makers of New York State.* Syracuse: Syracuse University Press.

———. 1988a. *American Children's Folklore.* Little Rock: August House.

———. 1988b. "Art, Performance, and Praxis: The Rhetoric of Contemporary Folklore Studies." *Western Folklore* 47:75–102.

———. 1989a. "Anglo-American Aesthetic." In *Encyclopedia of Southern Culture*, ed. William Ferris and Charles Wilson, 458–60. Chapel Hill: University of North Carolina Press.

———. 1989b. "Folklife Starts Here: The Background of Material Culture Scholarship in Pennsylvania." In *The Old Traditional Way of Life*, ed. Robert E. Walls and George H. Schoemaker with Jennifer Livesay, 230–43. Bloomington, Indiana: Trickster Press.

———. 1990a. "The Fragmentation of American Folklife Studies." *Journal of American Folklore* 103:209–14.

———. 1990b. "'Left to Their Own Devices': Interpreting American Children's Folklore as an Adaptation to Aging." *Southern Folklore* 47:101–15.

———. 1990c. "'Toward a Common Center': Pragmatism and Folklore Studies." *Folklore Historian* 7:23–30.

———, ed. 1992a. *American Material Culture and Folklife.* 1985; rpt., Logan: Utah State University Press.

———, ed. 1992b. *Creativity and Tradition in Folklore: New Directions.* Logan: Utah State University Press.

———. 1992c. "Elaborating Tradition: A Pennsylvania-German Folk Artist Ministers to His Community." In *Creativity and Tradition: New Directions*, ed. Simon J. Bronner, 277–325. Logan: Utah State University Press.

———. 1992d. "Expressing and Creating Ourselves in Childhood: A Commentary." *Children's Folklore Review* 15:47–59.

———. 1992e. "Martha Warren Beckwith, America's First Chair of Folklore." *Folklore Historian* 9:5–53.

———. 1995. *Piled Higher and Deeper: The Folklore of Student Life.* Rev. ed. Little Rock: August House.

———. 1996a. *The Carver's Art: Crafting Meaning from Wood.* Lexington: University Press of Kentucky.

———. 1996b. *Ethnic Ancestry in Pennsylvania.* Harrisburg: Pennsylvania State Data Center.

———. 1996c. "Folklife Movement." In *American Folklore: An Encyclopedia,* ed. Jan Harold Brunvand, 282–85. New York: Garland.

———. 1996d. *Popularizing Pennsylvania: Henry Shoemaker and the Progressive Uses of Folklore and History.* University Park: Penn State Press.

Bronner, Simon J., and Stephen Stern. 1980. "American Folklore vs. Folklore in America: A Fixed Fight?" *Journal of the Folklore Institute* 17:76–84.

Brooks, Van Wyck. 1958. *America's Coming-of-Age.* Garden City, New York: Doubleday Anchor.

Brown, Carolyn. 1987. *The Tall Tale in American Folklore and Literature.* Knoxville: University of Tennessee Press.

Brown, Linda Keller, and Kay Mussell, eds. 1984. *Ethnic and Regional Foodways in the United States: The Performance of Group Identity.* Knoxville: University of Tennessee Press.

Brown, Roger. 1973. *A First Language: The Early Stages.* Cambridge: Harvard University Press.

Brown, Sterling. 1946. "The Approach of the Creative Artist." *Journal of American Folklore* 59:506–7.

Bruns, Gerald L. 1991. "What is Tradition?" *New Literary History* 22:1–22.

Brunvand, Jan Harold. 1975. "Dorson Draws the Longbow." In *Roads Into Folklore,* ed. Richard Reuss, 15–16. Bloomington, Indiana: Folklore Forum Bibliographic and Special Series, no. 14.

———. ed. 1979. *Readings in American Folklore.* New York: W. W. Norton.

———. 1981. *The Vanishing Hitchhiker: American Urban Legends and Their Meanings.* New York: W. W. Norton.

———. 1982. "Richard M. Dorson (1916–1981)." *Journal of American Folklore* 95:347–53.

———. 1984. *The Choking Doberman and Other "New" Urban Legends.* New York: W. W. Norton.

———. 1986a. *The Mexican Pet: More "New" Urban Legends and Some Old Favorites.* New York: W. W. Norton.

———. 1986b. *The Study of American Folklore: An Introduction.* 3d ed. New York: W. W. Norton.

———. 1989. *Curses! Broiled Again! The Hottest Urban Legends Going.* New York: W. W. Norton.

———. 1993. *The Baby Train and Other Lusty Urban Legends.* New York: W. W. Norton.

———, ed. 1996. *American Folklore: An Encyclopedia.* New York: Garland.

———. 1998. *The Study of American Folklore: An Introduction.* 4th ed. New York: W. W. Norton.

Bucher, Robert. 1962. "The Continental Log House." *Pennsylvania Folklife* 12(4):14–19.

Buck, Roy C. 1978. "Boundary Maintenance Revisited: Tourist Experience in an Old Order Amish Community." *Rural Sociology* 43:221–34.

Bucuvalas, Tina, Peggy A. Bulger, and Stetson Kennedy. 1994. *South Florida Folklife.* Jackson: University Press of Mississippi.

Buffington, Albert F. 1949. "Linguistic Variants in the Pennsylvania German Dialect." *Publications of the Pennsylvania German Society* 13:217–52.

Buffington, Albert F., Don Yoder, Walter Klinefelter, Larry M. Neff, Mary Hammond Sullivan, and Frederick Weiser. 1980. *Ebbes fer Alle-Ebber Ebbes fer dich; Something Fore Everyone—Something for You. Essays In Memoriam Albert Franklin Buffington.* Breinigsville, Pennsylvania: Pennsylvania German Society.

Bulger, Peggy A. 1992. "Can't We Pass on Fairy Tales without Being Accused of Satanism?" *Atlanta Journal* (November 6), A11.

Burke, Susan M., and Matthew H. Hill, eds. 1991. *From Pennsylvania to Waterloo: Pennsylvania-German Folk Culture in Transition.* Kitchener, Ontario: Joseph Schneider Haus.

Burne, Charlotte Sophia. 1913. *The Handbook of Folklore.* London: Sidgwick & Jackson.

Burnett, John. 1978. *A Social History of Housing, 1815–1970.* Newton Abbot, England: David and Charles.

Burrison, John A. 1983. *Brothers in Clay: The Story of Georgia Folk Pottery.* Athens: University of Georgia Press.

———. 1989. *Storytellers: Folktales and Legends from the South.* Athens: University of Georgia Press.

Burson, Anne. 1982. "Alexander Haggerty Krappe and His Science of Comparative Folklore." *Journal of the Folklore Institute* 19:167–95.

Bushotter, George. 1888. "A Teton Dakota Ghost Story." *Journal of American Folklore* 1:68–72.

Butcher, Philip. 1948. "George W. Cable and Booker T. Washington." *Journal of Negro Education* 17:462–68.

———. 1962. *George W. Cable.* New York: Twayne.

Byington, Robert H., ed. 1978. *Working Americans: Contemporary Approaches to Occupational Folklife.* Los Angeles: California Folklore Society.

Bynum, David. 1974. *Four Generations of Oral Literary Studies at Harvard University.* Cambridge, Massachusetts: Center for the Study of Oral Literature.

Byrne, Donald E. 1975. *No Foot of Land: Folklore of American Methodist Itinerants.* Metuchen, New Jersey: Scarecrow Press.

Cable, George Washington. 1885. *The Silent South: Together with the Freedmen's Case in Equity and the Convict Lease System.* New York: C. Scribner's.

———. 1886. "Creole Slave Songs." *Century* 31:807–28.

———. 1888. *The Negro Question.* New York: American Missionary Association.

———. 1892. "A Negro Folk-Song." *The Folk-Lorist* 1:54.

Cahill, Holger. 1931a. "American Folk Art." *American Mercury* 24:39.

———. 1931b. *American Folk Sculpture: The Work of Eighteenth- and Nineteenth-Century Craftsmen.* Newark: Newark Museum.

———. 1932. *American Folk Art: The Art of the Common Man in America, 1750–1900.* New York: Museum of Modern Art.

Callahan, Tom. 1987. "The Complexities of Complexions: Struggles in Living Color on All the Playgrounds." *Time* (June 22), 80.

Camp, Charles. 1989. *American Foodways: What, When, Why and How We Eat in America.* Little Rock: August House.

Campbell, Marie. 1958. *Tales from the Cloud Walking Country.* Bloomington: Indiana University Press.

Canada, Craig. 1992. "What's behind 'Traditional Values'?" *San Francisco Chronicle* (July 4), A18.

Canby, Henry Seidel. 1926. "Americana." *Saturday Review of Literature* 2 (July 10), 913, 916.

Cansler, Loman D. 1968. "Midwestern and British Children's Lore Compared." *Western Folklore* 27:1–19.

Cantwell, Robert. 1988. "When We Were Good: The Folk Revival." In *Folk Roots, New Roots: Folklore in American Life,* ed. Jane S. Becker and Barbara Franco, 167–94. Lexington, Massachusetts: Museum of Our National Heritage.

———. 1991. "Conjuring Culture: Ideology and Magic in the Festival of American Folklife." *Journal of American Folklore* 104:148–63.

———. 1993. *Ethnomimesis: Folklife and the Representation of Culture.* Chapel Hill: University of North Carolina Press.

Carpenter, Inta Gale, ed. 1978. *Folklorists in the City: The Urban Field Experience.* Special issue of *Folklore Forum*, 11(3).

Carpenter, Inta Gale, and Ricardas Vidutis, eds. 1984. *Culture, Tradition, and Identity.* Special issue of *Journal of Folklore Research* 21(2/3).

Carroll, Michael P. 1982. "The Logic of Anglo-American Meals," *Journal of American Culture* 5:36–45.

Carter, Thomas, and Bernard L. Herman, eds. 1989. *Perspectives in Vernacular Architecture, III.* Columbia: University of Missouri Press.

———, eds. 1991. *Perspectives in Vernacular Architecture, IV.* Columbia: University of Missouri Press.

Cary, Ruth Anna. 1989. "The Mercer Museum and the Landis Valley Farm Museum: Exhibitions of Typology and Ethnicity in Pennsylvania." *Folklore Historian* 6:38–75.

Cashman, Sean Dennis. 1988. *America in the Gilded Age from the Death of Lincoln to the Rise of Theodore Roosevelt.* 2d ed. New York: Columbia University Press.

Cather, Katherine Dunlap. 1918. *Educating by Story-Telling, Showing the Value of Story-Telling as an Educational Tool for the Use of All Workers with Children.* Yonkers-on-Hudson, New York:World Book.

Cazden, Norma, Herbert Haufrecht, and Norman Studer. 1982. *Folk Songs of the Catskills.* Albany: State University of New York Press.

Center for Southern Folklore. 1982. *American Folklore Films and Videotapes: A Catalog.* Vol. II. New York: R. R. Bowker.

Chamberlain, Alexander F. 1896. *The Child and Childhood in Folk-Thought.* New York: Macmillan.

———. 1904. "Mythology and Folklore of Invention." *Journal of American Folklore* 17:14–22.

Charters, W. W. 1944. "Paul Bunyan in 1910." *Journal of American Folklore* 57:188–89.

Chase, Mary Ellen. 1950. *Abby Aldrich Rockefeller.* New York: Macmillan.

Chase, Richard. 1943. *The Jack Tales.* Boston: Houghton Mifflin.

Chen, David W. 1996. "Amish Going Modern, Sort of, about Skating." *New York Times* (August 11) 1:20.

Cheney, Lynne. 1987. *American Memory: A Report on the Humanities in the Nation's Public Schools.* Washington, D.C.: National Endowment for the Humanities.

———. 1990. *Tyrannical Machines: A Report on Education Practices Gone Wrong and Our Best Hopes for Setting Them Right.* Washington, D.C.: National Endowment for the Humanities.

———. 1995. *Telling the Truth: Why Our Culture and Our Country Have Stopped Making Sense—And What We Can Do about It.* New York: Simon and Schuster.

"Chicago Folk-Lore Society." 1892. *The Folk-Lorist* 1:5–12.

Child, Francis James. 1965. *The English and Scottish Popular Ballads.* 5 vols. 1884–1898; rpt., New York: Dover.

Chinen, Allan B. 1992. *Once upon a Midlife: Classic Stories and Mythic Tales to Illuminate the Middle Years.* New York: Jeremy P. Tarcher/Perigee.

"Clapping Rhyme." 1985. *Australian Children's Folklore Newsletter* 9:12.

Clarke, Mary Washington. 1976. *Kentucky Quilts and Their Makers.* Lexington: University Press of Kentucky.

Clements, William M. 1980. "The Pentecostal Sagaman." *Journal of the Folklore Institute* 17:169–95.

———. 1996. "Foxfire." In *American Folklore: An Encyclopedia*, ed. Jan Harold Brunvand, 303–5. New York: Garland.

Clements, William M., and Frances M. Malpezzi. 1984. *Native American Folklore, 1879–1979: An Annotated Bibliography.* Athens, Ohio: Swallow Press.

Clodd, Edward. 1885. *Myths and Dreams.* London: Chatto and Windus.

Clough, Benjamin, ed. 1947. *The American Imagination at Work: Tall Tales and Folk Tales.* New York: Alfred Knopf.

Clough, Wilson O. 1944. "Has American Folklore a Special Quality?" *Southern Folklore Quarterly* 8:115–21.

Cocchiara, Giuseppe. 1981. *The History of Folklore in Europe.* Trans. John N. McDaniel. Philadelphia: Institute for the Study of Human Issues.

Cochran, Robert. 1985. *Vance Randolph: An Ozark Life.* Urbana: University of Illinois Press.

Coe, Linda C. 1977. *Folklife and the Federal Government.* Washington, D.C.: Library of Congress, American Folklife Center.

Coffin, Tristram, ed. 1968. *Our Living Traditions: An Introduction to American Folklore.* New York: Basic Books.

Coffin, Tristram, and Hennig Cohen, eds. 1966. *Folklore in America.* Garden City, New York: Doubleday.

Cohen, Abner. 1974. *Two-Dimensional Man: An Essay on the Anthropology of Power and Symbolism in Complex Society.* Berkeley: University of California Press.

Cohen, David Steven. 1974. *The Ramapo Mountain People.* New Brunswick, New Jersey: Rutgers University Press.

———. 1982. *Folklife in New Jersey: An Annotated Bibliography.* Trenton: New Jersey Historical Commission.

———. 1983. *The Folklore and Folklife of New Jersey.* New Brunswick, New Jersey: Rutgers University Press.

———. 1992. *The Dutch-American Farm.* New York: New York University Press.

———. 1995. *Folk Legacies Revisited.* New Brunswick, New Jersey: Rutgers University Press.

Cohen, Hennig, and Tristram Potter Coffin, eds. 1991. *The Folklore of American Holidays.* 2d ed. Detroit: Gale Research.

Cohen, Norm. 1981. *Long Steel Rail: The Railroad in American Folksong.* Urbana: University of Illinois Press.

———. 1993. *Traditional Anglo-American Folk Music: An Annotated Discography of Published Sound Recordings.* New York: Garland.

Cohen, Ronald D., ed. 1995. *"Wasn't That a Time!": First Hand Accounts of the Folk Music Revival.* Metuchen, New Jersey: Scarecrow Press.

Cohn, Amy L., ed. 1993. *From Sea to Shining Sea: A Treasury of American Folklore and Folk Songs.* New York: Scholastic.

Collins, Carvel. 1957. "Folklore and Literary Criticism." *Journal of American Folklore* 70:9–10.

Commager, Henry Steele. 1950. *The American Mind.* New Haven: Yale University Press.

Conroy, Patricia L. 1979. "Creativity in Oral Transmission: An Example from Faroese Ballad Tradition." *Arv: Scandinavian Yearbook of Folklore* 3:25–48.

Conway, Cecilia. 1995. *African Banjo Echoes in Appalachia: A Study of Folk Traditions.* Knoxville: University of Tennessee Press.

Coontz, Stephanie. 1992. *The Way We Never Were: American Families and the Nostalgia Trap.* New York: Basic Books.

Cooper, Anna Julia. 1969. *A Voice from the South by a Black Woman of the South*. 1892; rpt., New York: Negro Universities Press.

Cortissoz, Royal. [1913] 1970. "The Post-Impressionist Illusion." In *The Call of the Wild (1900–1916)*, ed. Roderick Nash, 175–79. New York: George Braziller.

Cothran, Kay L. [1973] 1979. "Participation in Tradition." In *Readings in American Folklore*, ed. Jan Harold Brunvand, 444–48. New York: W. W. Norton.

Cott, Jonathan. 1992. *Wandering Ghost: The Odyssey of Lafcadio Hearn*. Tokyo: Kodansha.

Courlander, Harold. 1967. *The African*. New York: Crown.

———. 1986. "Kunta Kinte's Struggle to Be African." *Phylon* 47:294–302.

Cowan, Ruth Schwartz. 1983. *More Work for Mother: The Ironies of Household Technology from the Open Hearth to the Microwave*. New York: Basic Books.

Cox, Cynthia Anne. 1994. "'Postmodern Fairy Tales' in Contemporary Children's Literature." *Children's Folklore Review* 16:13–19.

Cox, Marian Roalfe. 1895. *An Introduction to Folk-Lore*. London: David Nutt.

Craig, Gordon A. 1982. *The Germans*. New York: G. P. Putnam's Sons.

Creeden, Sharon. 1994. *Fair Is Fair: World Folktales of Justice*. Little Rock: August House.

Cromley, Elizabeth Collins, and Carter L. Hudgins, eds. 1995. *Gender, Class, and Shelter: Perspectives in Vernacular Architecture, V*. Knoxville: University of Tennessee Press.

Cross, William E., Jr. 1991. *Shades of Black: Diversity in African-American Identity*. Philadelphia: Temple University Press.

Crowley, Daniel J. 1966. *I Could Talk Old-Story Good: Creativity in Bahamian Folklore*. Berkeley: University of California Press.

Culin, Stewart. 1887. *China in America: A Study in the Social Life of the Chinese in the Eastern Cities of the United States*. Philadelphia: privately printed.

———. 1890. "Folk-Lore Museums." *Journal of American Folklore* 3:312–13.

———. 1894. "Retrospect of the Folk-Lore of the Columbian Exposition." *Journal of American Folklore* 7:51–59.

———. 1900a. "The Origin of Ornament." *Free Museum of Science and Art Bulletin* 2:235–42.

———. 1900b. "Primitive American Art." *University Bulletin* 4:191–96.

———. 1901. "A Summer Trip among the Western Indians." *Free Museum of Science and Art Bulletin* 3:1–175.

———. 1924. "Creation in Art." *Brooklyn Museum Quarterly* 11:91–100.

———. 1927. "The Road to Beauty." *Brooklyn Museum Quarterly* 14:41–50.

———. 1975. *Games of the North American Indians*. 1907; rpt., New York: Dover.

Cullen, Sandy. 1996. "Works of 'Penn's Treaty' Link Cultural Issues." *Harrisburg Patriot-News* (April 14), E1:8.

Cunningham, Keith. 1992. *American Indians' Kitchen-Table Stories*. Little Rock: August House.

Cushing, Frank Hamilton. 1897. "Primitive Motherhood." *The Work and Words of the National Congress of Mothers*, 3–47. New York: D. Appleton.

Cutting, Jennifer, coordinator. 1984–. *American Folk Music and Folklore Recordings: A Selected List*. Washington, D. C.: American Folklife Center, Library of Congress.

Cutting, Robert F. 1992. "In Amish Country, the Scenery and Food are Good and Plenty." *Boston Globe* (December 13), B1.

Dance, Daryl Cumber. 1987. *Long Gone: The Mecklenburg Six and the Theme of Escape in Black Folklore*. Knoxville: University of Tennessee Press.

Daniels, Roger. 1990. *Coming to America: A History of Immigration and Ethnicity in American Life*. New York: Harper Collins.

Danielson, Larry. 1991. "St. Lucia in Lindsborg, Kansas." In *Creative Ethnicity: Symbols and Strategies of Contemporary Ethnic Life*, ed. Stephen Stern and John Allan Cicala, 187–203. Logan: Utah State University Press.

Dargan, Amanda, and Steven Zeitlin. 1990. *City Play*. New Brunswick, New Jersey: Rutgers University Press.

Darnell, Regna. 1988. *Daniel Garrison Brinton: The "Fearless Critic" of Philadelphia*. University of Pennsylvania Publications in Anthropology, no. 3, Philadelphia: University of Pennsylvania Department of Anthropology.

Darwin, Charles. 1874. *The Descent of Man*. 2d ed. New York: A. L. Burt.

Davidson, Donald. 1940. "Current Attitudes toward Folklore." *Tennessee Folklore Society Bulletin* 6:44–51.

Davidson, Hilda Ellis. 1987. "Changes in the Folklore Society, 1949–1986." *Folklore* 98:123–30.

Davidson, Levette J. 1951. *A Guide to American Folklore*. Denver: University of Denver Press.

Davidson, Marshall B. 1970. "Those American Things." *Metropolitan Museum Journal* 3:219–33.

Davies, Ioan. 1995. *Cultural Studies and Beyond: Fragments of Empire*. London: Routledge.

Davis, Gerald L. 1985. *I Got the Word in Me and I Can Sing It, You Know: A Study of the Performed African-American Sermon*. Philadelphia: University of Pennsylvania Press.

———. 1996. "'Somewhere over the Rainbow … ': Judy Garland in Neverland." *Journal of American Folklore* 109:115–28.

Davis, Susan G. 1986. *Parades and Power: Street Theater in Nineteenth-Century Philadelphia*. Philadelphia: Temple University Press.

Davis-Floyd, Robbie E. 1992. *Birth as an American Rite of Passage*. Berkeley: University of California Press.

de Caro, Francis A. 1976. "Concepts of the Past in Folkloristics." *Western Folklore* 35:3–22.

———. 1983. *Women and Folklore: A Bibliographic Survey*. Westport, Connecticut: Greenwood Press.

Deetz, James, and Edwin S. Dethlefsen. 1982. "Death's Head, Cherub, Urn and Willow." In *Material Culture Studies in America*, ed. Thomas Schlereth, 295–305. Nashville: American Association for State and Local History.

Dégh, Linda. 1971. "The 'Belief Legend' in Modern Society: Form, Function, and Relationship to Other Genres." In *American Folk Legend: A Symposium*, ed. Wayland D. Hand, 55–68. Berkeley: University of California Press.

———. 1981. "Grimm's *Household Tales* and Its Place in the Household: The Social Relevance of a Controversial Classic." In *Fairy Tales as Ways of Knowing: Essays on Märchen in Psychology, Society and Literature*, ed. Michael M. Metzger and Katharina Mommsen, 21–53. Bern, Germany: Peter Lang.

———. 1986. "Introduction [to special issue on the comparative method in folklore]." *Journal of Folklore Research* 23:77–86.

———. 1994. *American Folklore and the Mass Media*. Bloomington: Indiana University Press.

———. 1995. *Narratives in Society: A Performer-Centered Study of Narration*. Helsinki: Academia Scientiarum Fennica.

Dégh, Linda, Henry Glassie, and Felix Oinas, eds. 1976. *Folklore Today: A Festschrift for Richard M. Dorson*. Bloomington, Indiana: Research Center for Language and Semiotic Studies, Indiana University.

de Jonge, Eric. 1972. "The Thing about Folk Art." *National Antiques Review* 4 (February):10–13.

Denhardt, Robert B. 1981. *In the Shadow of Organization*. Lawrence: University Press of Kansas.

Densmore, Frances. 1918. *Teton Sioux Music.* Washington, D.C.: Bureau of American Ethnology Bulletin.

———. 1923. *Mandan and Hidatsa Music.* Washington, D.C.: Bureau of American Ethnology Bulletin, no. 80.

DeSpain, Pleasant. 1994. *Multicultural Tales to Tell.* Little Rock: August House.

Dewey, John. 1925. *Experience and Nature.* Chicago: Open Court.

———. 1934. *Art as Experience.* New York: Minton, Balch.

Dewhurst, C. Kurt. 1984. "The Arts of Working: Manipulating the Urban Work Environment." *Western Folklore* 63:192–211.

Dewhurst, C. Kurt, and Yvonne Lockwood, eds. 1987. *Michigan Folklife Reader.* East Lansing: Michigan State University Press.

Dewhurst, C. Kurt, Betty MacDowell, and Marsha MacDowell. 1979. *Artists in Aprons: Folk Art by American Women.* New York: E. P. Dutton.

———. 1983. *Religious Folk Art in America: Reflections of Faith.* New York: E. P. Dutton.

Dewhurst, C. Kurt, and Marsha MacDowell. 1983. *Michigan Hmong Arts: Textiles in Transition.* East Lansing: Michigan State University Museum.

———. 1984. "Region and Locality." In *American Folk Art: A Guide to Sources,* ed. Simon J. Bronner, 117–38. New York: Garland.

———. 1997. *To Honor and Comfort: Native Quilting Traditions.* Santa Fe: Museum of New Mexico Press.

Dewhurst, Marit. 1996. "Beyond the Field: The Traditions of a High School Homecoming." In *Michigan Folklife Annual,* ed. Ruth Fitzgerald and Yvonne Lockwood, 51–55. East Lansing: Michigan State University Museum.

Dickey, Miriam E. 1955. "Henry W. Shoemaker: Pennsylvania Folklorist." M.A. thesis, Western Reserve University.

DiMaggio, Paul, John Evans, and Bethany Bryson. 1996. "Have Americans' Social Attitudes Become More Polarized?" *American Journal of Sociology* 102:690–755.

Djupedal, Knut. 1990. "Tales of America." *Western Folklore* 49:177–89.

Dobruskin, Mauro. 1990. "Folklore y posmodernidad." *Revista de Investigaciones Folkloricas* 5:46–52.

Dolby, Sandra K. 1996. "Essential Contributions of a Folkloric Perspective to American Studies." *Journal of Folklore Research* 33:58–64.

Dolgin, Janet L., David S. Kemnitzer, and David M. Schneider. 1977. "As People Express Their Lives, So They Are . . . ." In *Symbolic Anthropology: A Reader in the Study of Symbols and Meanings,* ed. Janet L. Dolgin, David S. Kemnitzer, and David M. Schneider, 3–44. New York: Columbia University Press.

Dorsey, J. Owen. 1889. "Teton Folk-Lore." *American Anthropologist,* o.s., 2:143–58.

———. 1891. "Games of Teton Dakota Children." *American Anthropologist,* o. s., 4:329–45.

Dorson, Richard M. 1937. "Frontier Humor." A.B. thesis, Harvard University.

———, ed. 1939. *Davy Crockett: American Comic Legend.* New York: Rockland Editions.

———. 1940. "The Yankee on Stage—A Folk Hero of American Drama." *New England Quarterly* 13:467–93.

———. 1941a. "America's Comic Demigods." *American Scholar* 10:389–401.

———. 1941b. "Moses Coit Tyler, Historian of the American Genesis." *Southwest Review* 26:416–27.

———. 1942. "Davy Crockett and the Heroic Age." *Southern Folklore Quarterly* 1:133–51.

———. 1943. "New England Popular Tales and Legends." Ph.D. diss., Harvard University.

———. 1946a. "Historical Method and American Folklore." *Indiana History Bulletin* 23:84–99.

———. 1946b. *Jonathan Draws the Long Bow*. Cambridge: Harvard University Press.

———. 1947. "The Story of Sam Patch." *American Mercury* 64:741–47.

———. 1948a. "Review of *A Treasury of New England Folklore* by B. A. Botkin." *Saturday Review of Literature* 31(January 17):9–10.

———. 1948b. "Review of *A Treasury of New England Folklore* by B. A. Botkin." *American Literature* 20:76–77.

———. 1949. "The Folklore of Colleges." *American Mercury* 68:671–77.

———. 1950a. "Folklore and Fake Lore." *American Mercury* 70:335–43.

———. 1950b. "The Growth of Folklore Courses." *Journal of American Folklore* 63:345–59.

———. 1950c. "Review of *A Treasury of Southern Folklore*, edited by B. A. Botkin." *Journal of American Folklore* 63:480–82.

———. 1951a. "Five Directions in American Folklore." *Midwest Folklore* 1:149–65.

———. 1951b. "Folklore Studies in the United States Today." *Folklore* 62:353–66.

———. 1951c. "Review of *Legends of Paul Bunyan* compiled by Harold Felton." *Journal of American Folklore* 64:233–35.

———. 1952. *Bloodstoppers and Bearwalkers: Folk Traditions of the Upper Peninsula*. Cambridge: Harvard University Press.

———. 1956a. *Negro Folktales in Michigan*. Cambridge: Harvard University Press.

———. 1956b. "Paul Bunyan in the News, 1939–1941." *Western Folklore* 25:26–39, 179–93, 247–61. Revised as "Paul Bunyan in the News" in Dorson 1976, *Folklore and Fakelore*, 291–336.

———. 1956c. "Review of *A Treasury of Mississippi River Folklore*." *Minnesota History* 35:39–41.

———. 1957. "Standards for Collecting and Publishing American Folktales." *Journal of American Folklore* 70:53–57.

———. 1958. *Negro Tales from Pine Bluff, Arkansas, and Calvin, Michigan*. Bloomington: Indiana University Folklore Series, no. 12.

———. 1959a. *American Folklore*. Chicago: University of Chicago Press.

———. 1959b. "Discussion." *Journal of American Folklore* 72:237–39.

———. 1959c. "A Theory for American Folklore." *Journal of American Folklore* 72:197–212. Reprinted in Dorson 1971.

———. 1960a. "Jewish-American Dialect Stories on Tape." In *Studies in Biblical and Jewish Folklore*, ed. Raphael Patai, Francis Lee Utley, and Dov Noy, 111–76. Bloomington: Indiana University Press.

———. 1960b. "More Jewish Dialect Tales." *Midwest Folklore* 10:133–46.

———. 1961a. "Ethnohistory and Ethnic Folklore." *Ethnohistory* 8:12–30.

———. 1961b. "Folklore and Cultural History." In *Research Opportunities in American Cultural History*, ed. John F. McDermott, 102–23. Lexington: University of Kentucky Press.

———. 1962. "Folklore and the National Defense Education Act." *Journal of American Folklore* 75:160–64.

———. 1963a. "Current Folklore Theories." *Current Anthropology* 4:93–112.

———. 1963b. "Melville J. Herskovits, 1895–1963." *Journal of American Folklore* 76:249–50.

———. 1963c. "Should There Be a Ph.D. in Folklore?" *American Council of Learned Societies Newsletter* 14(4):1–8.

———. 1964a. *Buying the Wind: Regional Folklore in the United States*. Chicago: University of Chicago Press.

———. 1964b. "Oral Tradition and Written History: The Case for the United States." *Journal of the Folklore Institute* 1:220–34.

———. 1966a. "Foreword." In *Folktales of Germany*, ed. Kurt Ranke, v–xxv. Chicago: University of Chicago Press.

———. 1966b. "The Question of Folklore in a New Nation." In *Folklore and Society: Essays in Honor of Benj. A. Botkin*, ed. Bruce Jackson, 21–34. Hatboro, Pennsylvania: Folklore Associates.

———. 1967. *American Negro Folktales*. Greenwich, Connecticut: Fawcett.

———. 1968a. *The British Folklorists: A History*. Chicago: University of Chicago Press.

———, ed. 1968b. *Peasant Customs and Savage Myths: Selections from the British Folklorists*. Chicago: University of Chicago Press.

———. 1969. "A Theory for American Folklore Reviewed." *Journal of American Folklore* 82:226–44. Reprinted in Dorson 1971, 49–77.

———. 1970. "Introduction: The Anglo-American Folklore Conference." *Journal of the Folklore Institute* 7:91–92.

———. 1971a. *American Folklore and the Historian*. Chicago: University of Chicago Press.

———. 1971b. "Applied Folklore." In *Papers on Applied Folklore*, ed. Dick Sweterlitsch, 40–42. Bloomington, Indiana: Bibliographic and Special Series, no. 8, *Folklore Forum*.

———. 1971c. "How Shall We Rewrite Charles M. Skinner Today?" In *American Folk Legend: A Symposium*, ed. Wayland D. Hand, 69–96. Berkeley: University of California Press.

———. 1972a. "The Academic Future of Folklore." In *Folklore: Selected Essays*, 295–304. Bloomington: Indiana University Press.

———. 1972b. "Concepts of Folklore and Folklife Studies." In *Folklore and Folklife: An Introduction*, ed. Richard M. Dorson, 1–50. Chicago: University of Chicago Press.

———. 1972c. "Esthetic Form in British and American Folk Narrative." In *Folklore: Selected Essays*, 80–98. Bloomington: Indiana University Press.

———, ed. 1972d. *Folklore and Folklife: An Introduction*. Chicago: University of Chicago Press.

———. 1972e. "Oral Styles in American Folk Narrators." In *Folklore: Selected Essays*, 99–146. Bloomington: Indiana University Press.

———. 1972f. "Techniques of the Folklorist." In *Folklore: Selected Essays*, 11–31. Bloomington: Indiana University Press.

———. 1972g. "The Use of Printed Sources." In *Folklore and Folklife: An Introduction*, ed. Richard M. Dorson, 465–77.

———. 1973a. *America in Legend: Folklore from the Colonial Period to the Present*. New York: Pantheon.

———. 1973b. "Folklore Studies in England." In *Folklore Research around the World: A North American Point of View*, ed. Richard M. Dorson, 16–26. Port Washington, New York: Kennikat Press.

———. 1973c. "Introduction by the Editor." In *Folklore Research around the World*, ed. Richard M. Dorson, 1–4. Port Washington, New York: Kennikat Press.

———. 1973d. "The Lesson of Foxfire." *North Carolina Folklore Journal* 21:157–59.

———. 1973e. "Review of *Folklore on the American Land* by Duncan Emrich." *Western Folklore* 32:141–43.

———. 1974a. "Folklore vs. Fakelore—Again and Again." *Folklore Forum* 7:57–63.

———. 1974b. "Heart Disease and Folklore." *Folklore Preprint Series*, 1(10). Bloomington, Indiana: Folklore Publications Group.

———. 1974c. "Professor Dorson's Response [to Eliot Wigginton]." *North Carolina Folklore Journal* 22:39–40.

———. 1975a. "African and Afro-American Folklore: A Reply to Bascom and Other Misguided Critics." *Journal of American Folklore* 88:151–64.

————. 1975b. "Comment on Williams." *Journal of the Folklore Institute* 11:235–39.

————, ed. 1975c. *Folktales Told around the World.* Chicago: University of Chicago Press.

————. 1975d. "National Characteristics of Japanese Folktales." *Journal of the Folklore Institute* 12:241–56.

————. 1976a. *The Birth of American Studies.* Bloomington: Indiana University.

————. 1976b. *Bloodstoppers and Bearwalkers: Folk Traditions of the Upper Peninsula.* 1952; rpt., Cambridge: Harvard University Press.

————. 1976c. *Folklore and Fakelore: Essays toward a Discipline of Folk Studies.* Cambridge: Harvard University Press.

————. 1977a. "Afterword." In *Foxfire 4*, ed. Eliot Wigginton, 482–85. Garden City, New York: Anchor.

————. 1977b. *American Folklore.* 1959; rpt., Chicago: University of Chicago Press.

————. 1977c. "American Folklore Bibliography." *American Studies International* 16:23–37.

————. 1977d. "The Legend of the Missing Pajamas and Other Sad Sagas." *Journal of the Folklore Institute* 14:115–24.

————. 1977e. "The Scholar as Artist." *Chronicle of Higher Education* (November 7), 40.

————, ed. 1977f. "Special Double Issue: Stories of Personal Experience." *Journal of the Folklore Institute* 14(1–2).

————. 1978a. "Boosterism in American Folklore." *Journal of the Folklore Institute* 15:181–82.

————. 1978b. "The Folklore Boom 1977." *Journal of the Folklore Institute* 15:81–90.

————. 1978c. "Folklore in America vs. American Folklore." *Journal of the Folklore Institute* 15:97–112.

————, ed. 1978d. *Folklore in the Modern World.* The Hague: Mouton.

————. 1978e. "We All Need the Folk." *Journal of the Folklore Institute* 15:267–69.

————. 1979. "The American Studies Type." *American Quarterly* 31:368–71.

————. 1980a. "The America Theme in American Folklore." *Journal of the Folklore Institute* 17:91–93.

————. 1980b. "The Reception of the British Folklorists, or, Have You Read the Great Team?" In *Folklore Studies in Honour of Herbert Halpert*, ed. Kenneth S. Goldstein and Neil V. Rosenberg, 145–56. St. John's, Newfoundland: Memorial University.

————. 1980c. "Rejoinder to 'American Folklore vs. Folklore in America: A Fixed Fight?'" *Journal of the Folklore Institute* 17:85–89.

————. 1981. *Land of the Millrats.* Cambridge: Harvard University Press.

————. 1982a. *Man and Beast in American Comic Legend.* Bloomington: Indiana University Press.

————. 1982b. "The State of Folkloristics from an American Perspective." *Journal of the Folklore Institute* 19:71–105.

————, ed. 1983a. *Handbook of American Folklore.* Bloomington: Indiana University Press.

————. 1983b. "A Historical Theory for American Folklore." In *Handbook of American Folklore*, ed. Richard M. Dorson, 326–37. Bloomington: Indiana University Press.

————. 1983c. "Interpretation of Research." In *Handbook of American Folklore*, ed. Richard M. Dorson, 323–25. Bloomington: Indiana University Press.

Dorson, Richard M., and Inta Gale Carpenter. 1978. "Can Folklorists and Educators Work Together?" *North Carolina Folklore Journal* 26:3–13.

Dorst, John D. 1988. "Postmodernism vs. Postmodernity: Implications for Folklore Studies." *Folklore Forum* 21:216–24.

————. 1990. "Tags and Burners, Cycles and Networks: Folklore in the Telectronic Age." *Journal of the Folklore Institute* 27:179–90.

Dow, James, La Vern Rippley, and Steven M. Benjamin. 1980. "Amana Folk Art: Tradition and Creativity among the True Inspirationists of Iowa." In *Papers from the St. Olaf Symposium on German-Americana*, 19–30. Occasional Papers of Society for German American Studies No. 10. Morgantown: Department of Foreign Languages, West Virginia University.

"Dr. Joseph Henry Dubbs Died This Afternoon." 1910. *Daily New Era* (Lancaster, Pennsylvania) (April 1).

Dresser, Norine. 1996. "The 'M' Word: The 1994 Archer Taylor Memorial Lecture." *Western Folklore* 55:95–111.

DuBois, W. E. B. 1986. *Writings*. New York: Library of America.

———. 1989. *The Souls of Black Folk*. 1903; rpt., New York: Penguin.

———. 1996. *The Philadelphia Negro: A Social Study*. 1899; rpt., University of Pennsylvania Press.

Du Brow, Rick. 1992. "Murphy Brown to Dan Quayle: Read Our Ratings." *Los Angeles Times* (September 23), F1.

Dundes, Alan. 1964a. "On Game Morphology: A Study of the Structure of Non-Verbal Folklore." *New York Folklore Quarterly* 20:276–88.

———. 1964b. "Texture, Text, and Context." *Southern Folklore Quarterly* 28:251–65.

———. 1965. "What Is Folklore?" In *The Study of Folklore*, ed. Alan Dundes, 1–3. Englewood Cliffs, New Jersey: Prentice-Hall.

———. 1966. "The American Concept of Folklore." *Journal of the Folklore Institute* 3:226–49.

———. 1969a. "The Devolutionary Premise in Folklore Theory." *Journal of the Folklore Institute* 6:5–19.

———. 1969b. "Thinking Ahead: A Folkloristic Reflection of the Future Orientation in American Worldview." *Anthropological Quarterly* 42:53–71.

———. 1971. "On the Psychology of Legend." In *American Folk Legend: A Symposium*, ed. Wayland D. Hand, 21–36. Berkeley: University of California Press.

———. 1972. "Folk Ideas as Units of World View." In *Toward New Perspectives in Folklore*, ed. Américo Paredes and Richard Bauman, 93–103. Austin: University of Texas Press.

———, comp. 1976. *Folklore Theses and Dissertations in the United States*. Austin: University of Texas Press.

———. 1980a. *Interpreting Folklore*. Bloomington: Indiana University Press.

———. 1980b. "The Number Three in American Culture." In *Interpreting Folklore*, 134–59. Bloomington: Indiana University Press.

———. 1980c. "Texture, Text, and Context." In *Interpreting Folklore*, 20–32. Bloomington: Indiana University Press.

———. 1980d. "Who Are the Folk?" In *Interpreting Folklore*, 1–19. Bloomington: Indiana University Press.

———. 1982. "Introduction." In *Man and Beast in American Comic Legend*, by Richard M. Dorson, ix–xix. Bloomington: Indiana University Press.

———. 1985. "Nationalistic Inferiority Complexes and the Fabrication of Folklore: A Reconsideration of Ossian, the *Kinder- und Hausmärchen*, the *Kalevala*, and Paul Bunyan." *Journal of Folklore Research* 22:5–18.

———. 1986. "Fairy Tales from a Folkloristic Perspective." In *Fairy Tales and Society: Illusion, Allusion, and Paradigm*, ed. Ruth B. Bottigheimer, 259–70. Urbana: University of Illinois Press.

———. 1987. *Cracking Jokes: Studies of Sick Humor Cycles and Stereotypes*. Berkeley: Ten Speed Press.

————, ed. 1988. *Cinderella: A Casebook*. 1982; rpt., Madison: University of Wisconsin Press.

————. 1989a. *Folklore Matters*. Knoxville: University of Tennessee Press.

————. 1989b. "Interpreting 'Little Red Riding Hood' Psychoanalytically." In *Little Red Riding Hood: A Casebook*, ed. Alan Dundes, 192–238. Madison: University of Wisconsin Press.

————, ed. 1989c. *Little Red Riding Hood: A Casebook*. Madison: University of Wisconsin Press.

————. 1991. "Bruno Bettelheim's Uses of Enchantment and Abuses of Scholarship." *Journal of American Folklore* 104:74–83.

Dundes, Alan, and Carl Pagter. 1978. *Work Hard and You Shall Be Rewarded: Urban Folklore from the Paperwork Empire*. Bloomington: Indiana University Press.

————. 1987. *When You're Up to Your Ass in Alligators: More Urban Folklore from the Paperwork Empire*. Detroit: Wayne State University Press.

————. 1991. *Never Try to Teach a Pig to Sing: Still More Urban Folklore from the Paperwork Empire*. Detroit: Wayne State University Press.

Dunn, Charles W., and J. David Woodard. 1996. *The Conservative Tradition in America*. Lanham, Maryland: Rowman and Littlefield.

During, Simon. 1993. *The Cultural Studies Reader*. London: Routledge.

Dyer, Walter A. 1910. *The Lure of the Antique*. New York: Century.

Eagleton, Terry. 1997. "The Contradictions of Postmodernism." *New Literary History* 28:1–6.

Earnest, Adele. 1984. *Folk Art in America: A Personal View*. Exton, Pennsylvania: Schiffer.

Eaton, Allen H. 1932. *Immigrant Gifts to American Life*. New York: Russell Sage Foundation.

————. 1937a. *An Exhibition of the Rural Arts*. Washington, D.C.: U.S. Department of Agriculture.

————. 1937b. *Handicrafts of the Southern Highlands*. New York: Russell Sage Foundation.

————. 1944. "American Folk Arts." *Studio* 27:201–3.

————. 1949. *Handicrafts of New England*. New York: Harper and Row.

————. 1952. *Beauty behind Barbed Wire: The Arts of the Japanese in Our War Relocation Camps*. New York: Harper and Brothers.

Eaton, Allen, and Lucinda Crile. 1946. *Rural Handicrafts in the United States*. Washington, D.C.: U.S. Department of Agriculture with Russell Sage Foundation.

Edmonson, Munro S. 1971. *Lore: An Introduction to the Science of Folklore and Literature*. New York: Holt, Rinehart and Winston.

Educational Policies Commission. 1937. *The Unique Function of Education in American Democracy*. Washington, D.C.: National Education Association of the United States and the Department of Superintendence.

Efron, John M. 1995. *Defenders of the Race: Jewish Doctors and Race Science in Fin-de-Siècle Europe*. New Haven: Yale University Press.

Eisenstadt, S. N. 1969. "Some Observations on the Dynamics of Traditions." *Comparative Studies in Society and History* 11:451–75.

————. 1972. "Intellectuals and Tradition." *Daedalus* 101:1–19.

Eliot, Marc. 1993. *Walt Disney: Hollywood's Dark Prince*. New York: Birch Lane Press.

Eliot, T. S. [1919] 1960. "Tradition and the Individual Talent." In *Selected Essays*, 3–11. New York: Harcourt, Brace, and World.

Ellis, Bill. 1982. "'Ralph and Rudy': The Audience's Role in Recreating a Camp Legend." *Western Folklore* 41:169–91.

Ellis, John. 1983. *One Fairy Story Too Many: The Brothers Grimm and Their Tales*. Chicago: University of Chicago Press.

Ellison, Curtis W. 1995. *Country Music Culture: From Hard Times to Heaven.* Jackson: University Press of Mississippi.

Emrich, Duncan. 1972. *Folklore on the American Land.* Boston: Little, Brown.

Ensminger, Robert F. 1992. *The Pennsylvania Barn: Its Origin, Evolution, and Distribution in North America.* Baltimore: Johns Hopkins University Press.

Ergang, Robert Reinhold. 1931. *Herder and the Foundations of German Nationalism.* New York: Columbia University Press.

Erixon, Sigurd. 1955. "International Maps of Folk Culture." *Laos* 3:48–87.

———. 1967. "European Ethnology in Our Time." *Ethnologia Europaea* 1:3–11.

Etzioni, Amitai. 1996. *The New Golden Rule: Community and Morality in a Democratic Society.* New York: Basic Books.

Evans, David. 1982. *Big Road Blues: Tradition and Creativity in the Folk Blues.* Berkeley: University of California Press.

Evans, Melanie. 1997. "Teacher Retells Tales of Tolerance." *Minnesota Daily* (March 3), 1, 8.

Evans-Pritchard, Deirdre. 1987. "The Portal Case: Authenticity, Tourism, Traditions, and the Law." *Journal of American Folklore* 100:287–96.

Evans-Pritchard, Edward. 1981. *A History of Anthropological Thought.* New York: Basic Books.

Everhardt, Gary. 1976. "Of Our National Heritage . . . ." In *1976 Festival of American Folklife,* ed. Bess Lomax Hawes and Susanne Roschwalb, 3. Washington, D.C.: Smithsonian Institution.

Faill, Carol E. 1987. "Fraktur." In *Fraktur: A Selective Guide to the Franklin and Marshall Fraktur Collection,* 5–8. Lancaster: Franklin and Marshall College.

"Faith, Traditional Values Gaining Hold on Americans, Polls Show." 1989. *Washington Times* (June 23), B5.

Farrer, Claire. 1976. "Play and Inter-Ethnic Communication." In *The Anthropological Study of Play: Problems and Prospects,* ed. David F. Lancy and B. Allan Tindall, 86–92. Corwall, New York: Leisure Press.

Faust, Albert Bernhardt. 1909. *The German Element in the United States.* 2 vols. Boston: Houghton Mifflin.

Feintuch, Burt. 1976. "A Contextual and Cognitive Approach to Folk Art and Craft." *New York Folklore* 2:69–77.

———. 1981. "Dancing to the Music: Domestic Square Dances and Community in Southcentral Kentucky (1880–1940)." *Journal of the Folklore Institute* 18:49–68.

———, ed. 1988. *Conservation of Culture: Folklorists and the Public Sector.* Lexington: University Press of Kentucky.

———. 1992. "From the Editor." *Journal of American Folklore* 105:131.

Felton, Harold W., comp. and ed. 1947. *Legends of Paul Bunyan.* New York: Alfred Knopf.

"Feminist Mutant Fairy Tales, Snow White to Nancy Drew." 1993. *Washington Times* (April 24), C2.

Fenner, Thomas Putnam, Frederic G. Rathbun, and Miss Bessie Cleaveland. 1901. *Cabin and Plantation Songs as Sung by the Hampton Students.* 3d ed. New York: G. P. Putnam's Sons.

Fenton, Alexander. 1967. "An Approach to Folklife Studies." *Keystone Folklore Quarterly* 12:5–21.

———. 1973. "The Scope of Regional Ethnology." *Folk Life* 11:5–14.

———. 1993. "Folklore and Ethnology: Past, Present and Future in British Universities." *Folklore* 104:4–12.

Fenton, William N. 1947. "Iroquois Indian Folklore." *Journal of American Folklore* 60:383–97.

Ferris, William. 1982. *Local Color: A Sense of Place in Folk Art*. New York: McGraw-Hill.

———, ed. 1986. *Afro-American Folk Art and Crafts*. 1983; rpt., Jackson: University Press of Mississippi.

Ferris, William, and Mary L. Hart, eds. 1982. *Folk Music and Modern Sound*. Jackson: University Press of Mississippi.

Fiedler, Leslie. 1979. *The Inadvertent Epic: From Uncle Tom's Cabin to Roots*. New York: Simon and Schuster.

Fife, Austin E. 1961. "Research in Folklore under the National Defense Education Act." *Journal of American Folklore* 74:146.

———. 1969. "Folklife and Folk Arts in the United States Exhibit." In *Forms upon the Frontier: Folklife and Folk Arts in the United States*, ed. Austin and Alta Fife and Henry H. Glassie, 9–22. Logan: Utah State University Press.

Fine, Elizabeth C. 1996. "Performance Approach." In *American Folklore: An Encyclopedia*, ed. Jan Harold Brunvand, 554–56. New York: Garland.

Fine, Gary Alan. 1979. "Folklore Diffusion through Interactive Social Networks: Conduits in a Preadolescent Community." *New York Folklore* 5:87–126.

———. 1980a. "Children and Their Culture: Exploring Newell's Paradox." *Western Folklore* 39:170–83.

———. 1980b. "The Kentucky Fried Rat: Legends and Modern Society." *Journal of the Folklore Institute* 17:222–43.

———. 1987a. "Joseph Jacobs: A Sociological Folklorist." *Folklore* 98:183–93.

———. 1987b. *With the Boys: Little League Baseball and Preadolescent Culture*. Chicago: University of Chicago Press.

———. 1992. *Manufacturing Tales: Sex and Money in Contemporary Legends*. Knoxville: University of Tennessee Press.

Finnegan, Ruth. 1977. *Oral Poetry: Its Nature, Significance and Social Context*. Cambridge: Cambridge University Press.

———. 1991. "Tradition, But What Tradition and for Whom?" *Oral Tradition* 6:104–24.

Fischer, David Hackett. 1989. *Albion's Seed: Four British Folkways in America*. New York: Oxford University Press.

Fischer, J. L. 1960. "Sequence and Structure in Folktales." In *Men and Cultures*, ed. Anthony F. C. Wallace, 442–46. Philadelphia: University of Pennsylvania Press.

Fisher, Sydney George. 1896. *The Making of Pennsylvania*. Philadelphia: J. B. Lippincott.

Fishkin, Shelley Fisher. 1993. *Was Huck Black? Mark Twain and African-American Voices*. New York: Oxford University Press.

Fiske, John. 1900. *Myths and Myth-Makers: Old Tales and Superstitions Interpreted by Comparative Mythology*. Boston: Houghton Mifflin.

Flanagan, Cathleen C., and John T. Flanagan. 1977. *American Folklore: A Bibliography, 1950–1974*. Metuchen, New Jersey: Scarecrow Press.

Fogel, Edwin Miller. 1915. *Beliefs and Superstitions of the Pennsylvania Germans*. Philadelphia: American Germanica Press.

Foley, John Miles, ed. 1987. *Comparative Research on Oral Traditions: A Memorial for Milman Parry*. Columbus, Ohio: Slavica.

———. 1988. *The Theory of Oral Composition: History and Methodology*. Bloomington: Indiana University Press.

A Folk Arts Service for the United States. N.d. New York: International Commission on Folk Arts, League of Nations.

"The Folk Film." 1938. *New York Times* (June 26), E8.

"Folklore Courses." 1949. *Journal of American Folklore* 62:66.

Ford, Robert. 1968. *Children's Rhymes, Children's Games, Children's Songs, Children's Stories.* 1904; rpt., Detroit: Singing Tree Press.

Fortier, Alcee. 1895. *Louisiana Folk-Tales.* Boston: G. E. Stechert for the American Folklore Society.

Foster, Helen Bradley. 1997. *New Raiments of Self: African American Clothing in the Antebellum South.* New York: Berg.

Fowler, Roger. 1991. *Language in the News: Discourse and Ideology in the Press.* London: Routledge.

Frazer, Sir James G. 1890. *The Golden Bough: A Study in Comparative Religion.* London: Macmillan.

———. 1900. *The Golden Bough: A Study in Magic and Religion,* 3 vols. London: Macmillan.

———. 1961. "Preface." In *Argonauts of the Western Pacific: An Account of Native Enterprise and Adventure in the Archipelagoes of Melanesian New Guinea,* by Bronislaw Malinowski, vii–xiv. 1922; rpt., New York: E. P. Dutton.

Freeman, Joseph. 1935. "Introduction." In *Proletarian Literature in the United States,* ed. Granville Hicks, Joseph North, Michael Gold, Paul Peters, Isidor Schneider, Alan Calmer, 1–28. New York: International Publishers.

Freeze, Gary. 1989. "Colonial Williamsburg." In *Encyclopedia of Southern Culture,* ed. Charles Reagan Wilson and William Ferris, 1253. Chapel Hill: University of North Carolina Press.

Frey, J. William. 1942. *A Simple Grammar of Pennsylvania Dutch.* Clinton, South Carolina: The Jacobs Press for J. William Frey.

———. 1949. "Amish Hymns as Folk Music." In *Pennsylvania Songs and Legends,* ed. George Korson, 129–62. Philadelphia: University of Pennsylvania Press.

Friel, Tara. 1995. "'Once upon a Time' to 'Happily Ever After': The Development of Children's Narrative Skill." *Children's Folklore Review* 18:3–52.

Frost, William Goodell. [1899] 1989. "Our Contemporary Ancestors in the Southern Mountains." In *Appalachian Images in Folk and Popular Culture,* ed. W. K. McNeil, 91–106. Ann Arbor: UMI Research Press.

Fry, Gladys-Marie. 1975. *Night Riders in Black Folk History.* Knoxville: University of Tennessee Press.

———. 1990. *Stitched from the Soul: Slave Quilts from the Ante-Bellum South.* New York: E. P. Dutton.

Fuchs, Lawrence H. 1994. "Immigration, Multiculturalism, and American History." *National Forum: Phi Kappa Phi Journal* 75:42–45.

Fumento, Michael. 1995. "HBO Anti-white Washes with Its 'Fairy Tales.'" *Detroit News* (June 2), A11.

Gág, Wanda. 1938. *Snow White and the Seven Dwarfs.* New York: Coward-McCann.

Gailey, Alan. 1989. "The Nature of Tradition." *Folklore* 100:143–61.

Gardner, Emelyn. 1920. "Some Play-Party Games in Michigan." *Journal of American Folklore* 33:91–133.

Garner, James Finn. 1994. *Politically Correct Bedtime Stories: Modern Tales for Our Life and Times.* New York: Macmillan.

Garry, Patrick M. 1992. *Liberalism and American Identity.* Kent, Ohio: Kent State University Press.

Gartenberg, Max. 1950. "W. B. Laughead's Great Advertisement." *Journal of American Folklore* 63:444–49.

Gaster, Moses. 1887. "The Modern Origin of Fairy-Tales." *Folklore* 5:339–51.

Gastil, Raymond D. 1975. *Cultural Regions of the United States.* Seattle: University of Washington Press.

Georges, Robert A. 1969. "Toward an Understanding of Storytelling Events." *Journal of American Folklore* 82:313–28.

———. 1976. "From Folktale Research to the Study of Narrating." *Studia Fennica* 20:159–68.

———. 1980. "Toward a Resolution of the Text/Context Controversy." *Western Folklore* 39:34–40.

———. 1984. "The Many Ways of Being Greek." *Journal of Folklore Research* 21:211–20.

———. 1986. "The Folklorist as Comparatist." *Western Folklore* 45:1–20.

———. 1987. "Timeliness and Appropriateness in Personal Experience Narrating." *Western Folklore* 46:115–20.

———. 1989a. "Introduction: Richard M. Dorson's Conceptual and Methodological Concerns." *Journal of Folklore Research* 26:1–10.

———, special editor. 1989b. "Richard M. Dorson's Views and Works: An Assessment." *Journal of Folklore Research* 26(3):1–80.

———, guest editor. 1989c. "Special Section: Richard Dorson." *Western Folklore* 48(4):325–74.

Georges, Robert, and Michael Owen Jones. 1995. *Folkloristics: An Introduction.* Bloomington: Indiana University Press.

Georges, Robert, and Stephen Stern, comps. 1982. *American and Canadian Immigrant and Ethnic Folklore: An Annotated Bibliography.* New York: Garland.

Gerber, David. 1977. "Haley's *Roots* and Our Own: An Inquiry into the Nature of a Popular Phenomenon." *Journal of Ethnic Studies* 5:87–111.

Gevitz, Norman, ed. 1988. *Other Healers: Unorthodox Medicine in America.* Baltimore: Johns Hopkins University Press.

Gibbons, Phebe Earle. 1882. *"Pennsylvania Dutch," and Other Essays.* 3d ed. Philadelphia: J. B. Lippincott.

Giles, Paul. 1994. "Reconstructing American Studies: Transnational Paradoxes, Comparative Perspectives." *Journal of American Studies* 28:335–59.`

Gillespie, Angus K. 1980. *Folklorist of the Coal Fields: George Korson's Life and Work.* University Park: Pennsylvania State University Press.

———. 1996. "Festival." In *American Folklore: An Encyclopedia*, ed. Jan Harold Brunvand, 249–52. New York: Garland.

Gillespie, Angus K, and Jay Mechling, eds. 1987. *American Wildlife in Symbol and Story.* Knoxville: University of Tennessee Press.

Gilman, Sander. 1991. *The Jew's Body.* New York: Routledge.

———. 1996. *Smart Jews: The Construction of the Image of Jewish Superior Intelligence.* Lincoln: University of Nebraska Press.

Gilmore, Janet C. 1986. *The World of the Oregon Fishboat: A Study in Maritime Folklife.* Ann Arbor: UMI Research Press.

Gilmore, Robert K. 1984. *Ozark Baptizings, Hangings, and Other Diversions: Theatrical Folkways of Rural Missouri, 1885–1910.* Norman: University of Oklahoma Press.

Glass, Joseph W. 1986. *The Pennsylvania Culture Region: A View from the Barn.* Ann Arbor: UMI Research Press.

Glassberg, David. 1990. *American Historical Pageantry: The Uses of Tradition in the Early Twentieth Century.* Chapel Hill: University of North Carolina Press.

Glassie, Henry. 1968. *Pattern in the Material Folk Culture of the Eastern United States.* Philadelphia: University of Pennsylvania Press.

———. 1972. "Folk Art." In *Folklore and Folklife: An Introduction,* ed. Richard M. Dorson, 253–80. Chicago: University of Chicago Press.

———. 1973. "Structure and Function, Folklore and the Artifact." *Semiotica* 7:313–51.

———. 1974. *Barn Building in Otsego County, New York.* Cooperstown: New York State Historical Association.

———. 1975. *Folk Housing in Middle Virginia.* Knoxville: University of Tennessee Press.

———. 1978. "Meaningful Things and Appropriate Myths: The Artifact's Place in American Studies." In *Prospects 3,* ed. Jack Salzman, 1–49. New York: Burt Franklin.

———. 1989. *The Spirit of Folk Art: The Girard Collection at the Museum of International Folk Art.* New York: Harry N. Abrams.

———. 1990. "Foreword." In *Discovering American Folklife,* by Don Yoder, ix–xi. Ann Arbor: UMI Research Press.

———. 1992. "The Idea of Folk Art." In *Folk Art and Art Worlds,* ed. John Michael Vlach and Simon J. Bronner, 269–74. 1986; rpt., Logan: Utah State University Press.

———. 1995. "Tradition." *Journal of American Folklore* 108:395–412.

Glassie, Henry, Edward D. Ives, and John F. Szwed. 1971. *Folksongs and Their Makers.* Bowling Green, Ohio: Bowling Green University Popular Press.

Glazer, Nathan. 1983. *Ethnic Dilemmas, 1964–1982.* Cambridge: Harvard University Press.

———. 1997. *We Are All Multiculturalists Now.* Cambridge: Harvard University Press.

Glazier, Stephen D. 1996. "Beckwith, Martha Warren (1871–1959)." In *American Folklore: An Encyclopedia,* ed. Jan Harold Brunvand, 78–79. New York: Garland.

Gleason, Philip. 1984. "World War II and the Development of American Studies." *American Quarterly* 36:343–58.

Glick, Leonard B. 1982. "Types Distinct from Our Own: Franz Boas on Jewish Identity and Assimilation." *American Anthropologist* 84:545–65.

Goehring, Eleanor E. 1982. *Tennessee Folk Culture: An Annotated Bibliography.* Knoxville: University of Tennessee Press.

Goffman, Erving. 1956. *The Presentation of Self in Everyday Life.* Edinburgh: Social Sciences Research Centre, University of Edinburgh.

———. 1959. *The Presentation of Self in Everyday Life.* Garden City, New York: Doubleday.

———. 1963. *Behavior in Public Places: Notes on the Social Organization of Gatherings.* New York: Free Press.

Goforth, Frances S., and Carolyn V. Spillman. 1994. *Using Folk Literature in the Classroom: Encouraging Children to Read and Write.* Phoenix: Oryx Press.

Goldberg, Christine. 1996. "Comparative Approach." In *American Folklore: An Encyclopedia,* ed. Jan Harold Brunvand, 151–54. New York: Garland.

Gomme, Alice Bertha. 1964. *The Traditional Games of England, Scotland, and Ireland.* 2 vols. 1894, 1898; rpt., New York: Dover.

Gomme, George Laurence. 1884. "Folk-Lore Terminology." *Folk-Lore Journal* 2:347–48.

———. 1892. *Ethnology in Folklore.* London: K. Paul, Trench, Trubner.

———. 1908. *Folklore as an Historical Science.* London: Methuen.

Goodenough, Ward H. 1976. "Folklife Study and Social Change." In *American Folklife,* ed. Don Yoder, 19–26. Austin: University of Texas Press.

Goodwin, Joseph P. 1989. *More Man Than You'll Ever Be: Gay Folklore and Acculturation in Middle America.* Bloomington: Indiana University Press.

Goodwin, Marjorie Harness. 1990. *He-Said-She-Said: Talk as Social Organization among Black Children.* Bloomington: Indiana University Press.

Gordon, Michael, ed. 1972. *The Nuclear Family in Crisis: The Search for an Alternative.* New York: Harper and Row.

Grady, Henry Woodfin. 1885. "In Plain Black and White: A Reply to Mr. Cable." *Century* 29:909–17.

Graeff, Arthur D. 1955. "Renascence of History." *Pennsylvania Folklife* 6(5):36–38.

Grant, Campbell, and Jane Werner. 1952. *Walt Disney's Snow White and the Seven Dwarfs.* New York: Simon and Schuster.

Grant, Carl, ed. 1995. *Educating for Diversity: An Anthology of Multicultural Voices.* Boston: Allyn and Bacon.

Green, Archie. 1972. *Only a Miner: Studies in Recorded Coal-Mining Songs.* Urbana: University of Illinois Press.

———. 1983. "Interpreting Folklore Ideologically." In *Handbook of American Folklore*, ed. Richard M. Dorson, 351–58. Bloomington: Indiana University Press.

———. 1984. "Folklore and America's Future." *Kentucky Folklore Record* 30:65–78.

———. 1993. *Wobblies, Pile Butts, and Other Heroes: Laborlore Explorations.* Urbana: University of Illinois Press.

Green, Laura C. S. 1923. *Hawaiian Stories and Wise Sayings.* Poughkeepsie: Folklore Foundation.

———. 1926. *Folktales from Hawaii.* Poughkeepsie: Folklore Foundation.

———. 1929. *The Legend of Kawelo.* Poughkeepsie: Folklore Foundation.

Greene, Jack P. 1993. *The Intellectual Construction of America: Exceptionalism and Identity from 1492 to 1800.* Chapel Hill: University of North Carolina Press.

Greene, Victor. 1992. *A Passion for Polka: Old-Time Ethnic Music in America.* Berkeley: University of California Press.

Greenfield, Meg. 1977. "Uncle Tom's Roots." *Newsweek* (February 14), 100.

———. 1992. "Quayle and 'Family Values.'" *Newsweek* (June 22), 76.

Greenleaf, Elisabeth. 1933. *Ballads and Sea Songs of Newfoundland.* Cambridge: Harvard University Press.

Grider, Sylvia. 1976. "The Supernatural Narratives of Children." Ph.D. diss., Indiana University.

Griffis, Rev. Wm. Elliot. 1893. "The Original of Uncle Remus' Tar Baby in Japan." *The Folk-Lorist* 1:146–49.

Griffith, James S. 1988. *Southern Arizona Folk Arts.* Tucson: University of Arizona Press.

———. 1995. *A Shared Space: Folklife in the Arizona-Sonora Borderlands.* Logan: Utah State University Press.

Grimm, Jacob, and Wilhelm Grimm. 1812. *Kinder- und Hausmärchen.* Berlin: Reimer.

———. 1823. *German Popular Stories Translated from the Kinder und Haus Marchen Collected by M. M. Grimm, from Oral Tradition.* Trans. Edgar Taylor. London: C. Baldwyn.

———. 1826. *German Popular Stories.* Trans. Edgar Taylor. Boston: Cummings, Hilliard.

———. 1839. *Gammer Grethel, or, German Fairy Tales and Popular Stories, from the Collection of M. M. Grimm and Other Sources.* London: J. Green.

———. 1840. *Gammer Grethel; or German Fairy Tales and Popular Stories, from the Collection M. M. Grimm and Other Sources.* Boston: James Munroe.

———. 1846a. *The Fairy Ring: A New Collection of Popular Tales, Translated from the German of Jacob and Wilhelm Grimm.* Trans. John Edward Taylor. London: John Murray.

———. 1846b. *German Fairy Tales and Popular Stories as Told by Gammer Grethel.* Trans. Edgar Taylor. London: Joseph Cundall.

———. 1854a. *The King of the Swans, and Other Tales: A Story Book for Holiday Hours.* Philadelphia: Whilt and Yost.

———. 1854b. *Stray Leaves from Fairy Land, for Boys and Girls: New Translations from the German of Jacob and Wilhelm Grimm.* Trans. J. Edward Taylor. Philadelphia: G. Collins.

————. 1867. *Grimm's Goblins, Selected from the Household Stories of the Brothers Grimm.* Boston: Ticknor and Fields.

————. 1878. *The Golden Bird and Other Tales. Collected by the Brothers Grimm.* London: George Routledge.

————. 1960. *The Grimms' German Folk Tales.* Trans. Francis P. Magoun, Jr., and Alexander H. Krappe. Carbondale: Southern Illinois University Press.

————. 1966. *Teutonic Mythology.* 4 vols. Trans. James Steven Stallybrass. 1844; rpt., New York: Dover.

Grossberg, Lawrence, Cary Nelson, and Paula Treichler, eds. 1992. *Cultural Studies.* New York: Routledge.

Grossman, Cathy Lynn. 1992. "Lancaster County, PA: Family Is First for Devout 'Plain People.'" *USA Today* (August 13), D8.

Grumbine, E. L. 1905. *Folk-Lore and Superstitious Beliefs of Lebanon County.* Lebanon, Pennsylvania: Lebanon County Historical Society.

Guarendi, Ray. 1990. *Back to the Family: How to Encourage Traditional Values in Complicated Times.* New York: Villard Books.

Gubar, Susan. 1997. *Racechanges: White Skin, Black Face in American Culture.* New York: Oxford University Press.

Guerber, H. A., ed. 1896. *Märchen und Erzählungen für Unfänger.* Boston: D. C. Heath.

Gummere, Francis B. 1959. *The Popular Ballad.* 1907; rpt,. New York: Dover.

————. 1973. *The Beginnings of Poetry.* 1901; rpt., Philadelphia: Richard West.

Guroian, Vigen. 1996. "Awakening the Moral Imagination: Teaching Virtues through Fairy Tales." *Intercollegiate Review* 32:3–13.

Gustavsson, Sven, ed. 1989. *Tradition and Modern Society.* Stockholm: Almqvist and Wiksell.

Guttmann, Allen. 1967. *The Conservative Tradition in America.* New York: Oxford University Press.

Hacker, Louis M. 1947. *The Shaping of the American Tradition.* New York: Columbia University Press.

Haddon, Alfred. 1895. *Evolution in Art: As Illustrated by the Life-Histories of Designs.* New York: Charles Scribner's Sons.

"Hail the Conquering Hero." 1964. *Newsweek* (October 19), 94–98.

Haley, Alex. 1976. *Roots.* Garden City, New York: Doubleday.

————. 1982. "Alex Haley's Commencement Address." *Xavier Review* 2:69–75.

Hall, E. T. 1959. *The Silent Language.* Garden City, New York: Doubleday.

Halliwell-Phillips, James Orchard. 1849. *Popular Rhymes and Nursery Tales: A Sequel to the Nursery Rhymes of England.* London: John Russell Smith.

Hallowell, A. Irving. 1967. *Culture and Experience.* 1955; rpt., New York: Schocken.

Halpert, Herbert. 1957. "Some Undeveloped Areas in American Folklore." *Journal of American Folklore* 70:299–305.

————. 1985. "A Note on Charles E. Brown and Wisconsin Folklore." *Midwestern Journal of Language and Folklore* 11:54–59.

Halsey, R. T. H., and Elizabeth Tower. 1924. *The Homes of Our Ancestors: As Shown in the American Wing of the Metropolitan Museum of Art of New York.* Garden City, New York: Doubleday, Doran.

Hammer, Dean C. 1992. "Meaning and Tradition." *Polity* 24:551–67.

Hand, Wayland D., ed. 1961. *The Frank C. Brown Collection of North Carolina Folklore: Popular Beliefs and Superstitions from North Carolina.* Vols. 6–7. Durham, North Carolina: Duke University Press.

———. 1963. "Die Märchen die Brüder Grimm in den Vereinigten Staaten." *Hessische Blätter* 54:525–44.

———, ed. 1971. *American Folk Legend: A Symposium.* Berkeley: University of California Press.

———. 1976. *American Folk Medicine.* Berkeley: University of California Press.

———. 1980. *Magical Medicine: The Folkloric Component of Medicine in the Folk Belief, Custom, and Ritual of the Peoples of Europe and America.* Berkeley: University of California Press.

———. 1981. "Introduction." In *Popular Beliefs and Superstitions: A Compendium of American Folklore from the Ohio Collection of Newbell Niles Puckett,* ed. Wayland D. Hand, Anna Casetta, and Sondra B. Thiederman, xxv–lviii. Boston: G. K. Hall.

Handler, Richard. 1992. "Anthropology Is Dead! Long Live Anthropology!" *American Anthropologist* 95:991–99.

Handler, Richard, and Jocelyn Linnekin. 1984. "Tradition: Genuine or Spurious." *Journal of American Folklore* 97:273–90.

Handlin, Oscar. 1951. *The Uprooted.* New York: Grosset and Dunlap.

Handy, Charles B. 1976. *Understanding Organizations.* New York: Penguin.

Haney, Gladys J. 1942. "Paul Bunyan Twenty-Five Years After." *Journal of American Folklore* 55:155–68.

Hannerz, Ulf. 1996. *Transnational Connections: Culture, People, Places.* New York: Routledge.

Hansen, Gregory. 1996. "The Relevance of 'Authentic Tradition' in Studying an Oldtime Florida Fiddler." *Southern Folklore* 53:67–89.

Hanson, Paul W. 1993. "Reconceiving the Shape of Culture: Folklore and Public Culture." *Western Folklore* 52:327–44.

Hanson, Russell L. 1995. "Tradition." In *A Companion to American Thought,* ed. Richard Wightman Fox and James T. Koppenberg, 681–83. Oxford: Basil Blackwell.

Harker, Dave. 1985. *Fakesong: The Manufacture of British "Folksong," 1700 to the Present Day.* Milton Keynes, England: Open University Press.

Harrah-Conforth, Jeanne. 1989. "Dorson and the Indiana University Folklore Program: Oral Histories." *Western Folklore* 48:339–48.

Harris, Joel Chandler. 1881. *Uncle Remus, His Songs and Sayings: The Folklore of the Old Plantation.* New York: D. Appleton.

———. 1892. *Uncle Remus and His Friends: Old Plantation Stories, Songs, and Ballads, with Sketches of Negro Character.* Boston: Houghton Mifflin.

Harris, Joseph. 1996. "Kittredge, George Lyman (1860–1941)." In *American Folklore: An Encyclopedia,* ed. Jan Harold Brunvand, 421–22. New York: Garland.

Harrison-Pepper, Sally. 1991. *Drawing a Circle in the Square: Street Performing in New York's Washington Square Park.* Jackson: University Press of Mississippi.

Hart, Mary L., Brenda M. Eagles, and Lisa N. Howorth. 1989. *The Blues: A Bibliographic Guide.* New York: Garland.

Hartigan, Lynda Roscoe. 1990. *Made with Passion: The Hemphill Folk Art Collection in the National Museum of Art.* Washington, D.C.: National Museum of Art.

Hartland, Edwin Sidney. 1894–96. *The Legend of Perseus: A Study of Tradition in Story, Custom, and Belief.* London: D. Nutt.

———. 1908. *The Science of Fairy Tales: An Inquiry into Fairy Mythology.* 1891; rpt., London: W. Scott.

———. [1899] 1968. "Folklore: What Is It and What Is the Good of It?" In *Peasant Customs and Savage Myths: Selections from the British Folklorists,* ed. Richard M. Dorson, vol. 1, 230–51. Chicago: University of Chicago Press.

Harwood, John. 1992a. "Campaign '92: Dan Quayle, for Better or Worse, Has Assumed the Tone-Setting Role for the GOP's Campaign." *Wall Street Journal* (June 8), A12.

———. 1992b. "Clinton and Bush Stress Initiatives to Foster Traditional Family Values." *Wall Street Journal* (May 22), A12.

Haskell, Guy H., ed. 1991. "Jews of the Heartland," special issue of *Jewish Folklore and Ethnology Review* 13(2).

Hastings, Scott E., Jr. 1990. *The Last Yankees: Folkways in Eastern Vermont and the Border Country*. Hanover, New Hampshire: University Press of New England.

Hauser, Arnold. 1958. "Popular Art and Folk Art." *Dissent* 5:229–37.

Haut, Judith. 1992. "'I Know a Story about That': One Young Child's Use and Understanding of Narrating." *Children's Folklore Review* 15:33–46.

———. 1994. "How Can Acting Like a Fieldworker Enrich Pluralistic Education?" In *Putting Folklore to Use*, ed. Michael Owen Jones, 45–61. Lexington: University Press of Kentucky.

Hawes, Bess Lomax. 1992. "Introduction." In *American Folk Masters: The National Heritage Fellows*, by Steve Siporin, 14–21. New York: Harry N. Abrams.

Hearn, Lafcadio. 1885a. *"Ghombo Zhebes." Little Dictionary of Creole Proverbs, Selected from Six Creole Dialects*. New York: W. H. Coleman.

———. 1885b. *La Cuisine Creole: A Collection of Culinary Recipes from Leading Chefs and Noted Creole Housewives, Who Have Made New Orleans Famous for Its Cuisine*. New York: W. H. Coleman.

———. 1890a. *Two Years in the French West Indies*. New York: Harper and Bros.

———. 1890b. *Youma: The Story of a West Indian Slave*. New York: Harper and Bros.

———. 1924. *Creole Sketches*. Ed. Charles Woodward Hutson. Boston: Houghton Mifflin.

———. 1926. *Editorials*. Ed. Charles Woodward Hutson. Boston: Houghton Mifflin.

———. 1957. *Children of the Levee*. Ed. O. W. Frost. Lexington: University of Kentucky Press.

———. 1964. *Sketches of New Orleans*. Franklin, New Hampshire: Hillside Press.

———. 1984. *Writings from Japan: An Anthology*. Ed. Francis King. New York: Penguin.

Hearne, Betsy. 1988. "Booking the Brothers Grimm: Art, Adaptations, and Economics." In *The Brothers Grimm and Folktale*, ed. James M. McGlathery, 220–23. Urbana: University of Illinois Press.

Heffley, Lynne. 1995. "HBO's 'Fairy Tales' a Kick of Diversity." *Los Angeles Times* (March 25), F18.

Heilman, Samuel C. 1976. *Synagogue Life: A Study in Symbolic Interaction*. Chicago: University of Chicago Press.

Heisig, James W. 1977. "Bruno Bettelheim and the Fairy Tales." *Children's Literature* 6:93–114.

Heisley, Michael. 1977. *An Annotated Bibliography of Chicano Folklore from the Southwestern United States*. Los Angeles: Center for the Study of Comparative Folklore and Mythology.

Hennig, John. 1946. "The Brothers Grimm and T. C. Croker." *Modern Language Review* 41:44–54.

Herbert, Wray. 1996. "The Moral Child. We're at Ground Zero in the Culture Wars: How to Raise Decent Kids when Traditional Ties to Church, School and Community Are Badly Frayed." *U.S. News and World Report* (June 3), 52–59.

Herder, Johann Gottfried. 1911. *Volkslieder*. 2 vols. 1778–79; rpt., Munich: Georg Mhller.

———. 1975. *Stimmen der Volker in Liedern*. Ed. Heinz Rolleke. 2 vols. 1778–79; rpt., Stuttgart: Reclam.

———. 1993. *Against Pure Reason: Writings on Religion, Language, and History*. Trans. and ed. Marcia Bunge. Minneapolis: Fortress Press.

Herman, Bernard L. 1987. *Architecture and Rural Life in Central Delaware, 1700–1900*. Knoxville: University of Tennessee Press.

Herskovits, Melville J. 1930. "Review of *Black Roadways* by Martha Beckwith." *Journal of American Folklore* 43:332–38.

———. 1941. *The Myth of the Negro Past*. New York: Harper & Bros.

———. 1946. "Folklore after a Hundred Years: A Problem of Redefinition." *Journal of American Folklore* 59:89–100.

———. 1949. "Folklore." In *Standard Dictionary of Folklore, Mythology, and Legend*, ed. Maria Leach, 400. New York: Funk and Wagnalls.

———. 1953. *Franz Boas: The Science of Man in the Making*. New York: Scribner's.

———. 1958. *The Myth of the Negro Past*. 1941; rpt., Boston: Beacon Press.

———. 1959. "Prepared Comments." *Journal of American Folklore* 72:216–20.

Herskovits, Melville J., and Frances S. Herskovits. 1958. *Dahomean Narrative*. Evanston: Northwestern University Press.

Hertzberg, Arthur. 1989. *The Jews in America: Four Centuries of an Uneasy Encounter*. New York: Touchstone.

Higginson, Thomas Wentworth. 1883. "An English Nation." *Harper's Magazine* 41:705–722.

Hijiya, James A. 1978. "Roots: Family and Ethnicity in the 1970s." *American Quarterly* 30:548–56.

Hines, Donald M. 1972. "The Development of Folklife Research in the United Kingdom." *Pennsylvania Folklife* 21(Spring):8–20.

Hinks, Roger. 1928. "The Superstition of the Antique." *Museum* 2(September):10.

Hinsley, Curtis M., Jr. 1981. *Savages and Scientists: The Smithsonian Institution and the Development of American Anthropology, 1846–1910*. Washington, D.C.: Smithsonian Institution Press.

Hirsch, E. D., Jr. 1987. *Cultural Literacy: What Every American Needs to Know*. Boston: Houghton Mifflin.

———, ed. 1989. *A First Dictionary of Cultural Literacy: What Our Children Need to Know*. Boston: Houghton Mifflin.

Hirsch, E. D., Jr., Joseph F. Kett, and James Trefil. 1988. *The Dictionary of Cultural Literacy*. Boston: Houghton Mifflin.

Hirsch, Jerrold. 1987. "Folklore in the Making: B. A. Botkin." *Journal of American Folklore* 100:3–38.

———. 1988. "Cultural Pluralism and Applied Folklore: The New Deal Precedent." In *The Conservation of Culture: Folklorists and the Public Sector*, ed. Burt Feintuch, 46–67. Lexington: University Press of Kentucky.

———. 1996. "Folk-Say." In *American Folklore: An Encyclopedia*, ed. Jan Harold Brunvand, 290–92. New York: Garland.

"Historical Societies." 1947. *Journal of American Folklore* 60:425.

Hobsbawm, Eric, and Terence Ranger, eds. 1983. *The Invention of Tradition*. Cambridge: Cambridge University Press.

Hoffman, Daniel. 1952. *Paul Bunyan: Last of the Frontier Demigods*. Philadelphia: Temple University Publications.

———. 1959. "Prepared Comments." *Journal of American Folklore* 72:223–32.

———. 1961. *Form and Fable in American Fiction*. New York: Oxford University Press.

Hoffman, Walter James. 1888. "Folk-Lore of the Pennsylvania Germans." *Journal of American Folklore* 1:125–35.

Hofstadter, Richard. 1989. *The American Political Tradition and the Men Who Made It.* 1948; rpt., New York: Vintage.

Hoggart, Richard. 1957. *The Uses of Literacy.* London: Chatto and Windus.

Hollinger, David A. 1975. "Ethnic Diversity, Cosmopolitanism and the Emergence of the American Liberal Intelligentsia." *American Quarterly* 27:133–51.

Hollis, Susan Tower, Linda Pershing, and M. Jane Young, eds. 1993. *Feminist Theory and the Study of Folklore.* Urbana: University of Illinois Press.

Holloway, Joseph E., ed. 1990. *Africanisms in American Culture.* Bloomington: Indiana University Press.

Holt, Thomas C. 1995. "DuBois, W. E. B." In *A Companion to American Thought,* ed. Richard Wightman Fox and James T. Kloppenberg, 187–90. Oxford, England: Blackwell.

Holtzberg-Call, Maggie. 1992. *The Lost World of the Craft Printer.* Urbana: University of Illinois Press.

Hom, Marlon K. 1992. *Songs of Gold Mountain: Cantonese Rhymes from San Francisco Chinatown.* Berkeley: University of California Press.

Honko, Lauri. 1983. "Research Traditions in Tradition Research." In *Trends in Nordic Tradition Research,* ed. Lauri Honko and Pekka Laaksonen, 13–22. Helsinki: Suomalaisen Kirjallisuuden Seura.

———. 1986. "Types of Comparison and Forms of Variation." *Journal of Folklore Research* 23:105–24.

———, ed. 1988. *Tradition and Cultural Identity.* Turku: Nordic Institute of Folklore.

Honko, Lauri, and Pekka Laaksonen, eds. 1983. *Trends in Nordic Tradition Research.* Helsinki: Suomalaisen Kirjallisuuden Seura.

Hopple, C. Lee. 1971–72. "Spatial Development of the Southeastern Pennsylvania Plain Dutch Community to 1970: Part I." *Pennsylvania Folklife* 21(2):18–40.

Hornbeck, Mark. 1996. "Rap Fairy Tales Top Wasteful State Spending List." *Detroit News* (February 21), D4.

Hostetler, John A. 1963. *Amish Society.* Baltimore: Johns Hopkins University Press.

Howe, Irving. 1976. *World of Our Fathers.* New York: Harcourt Brace Jovanovich.

Hubka, Thomas C. 1984. *Big House, Little House, Back House, Barn: The Connected Farm Buildings of New England.* Hanover, New Hampshire: University Press of New England.

Hufford, David. 1969. History and the Work of the Ethnic Culture Survey and the State Folklorist Program of the Pennsylvania Historical and Museum Commission. *Keystone Folklore Quarterly* 14:166–75.

———. 1989. "Customary Observances in Modern Medicine." *Western Folklore* 48:129–43.

Hufford, Mary. 1991. *American Folklife: A Commonwealth of Cultures.* Washington, D.C.: American Folklife Center, Library of Congress.

———. 1992. *Chaseworld: Foxhunting and Storytelling in New Jersey's Pine Barrens.* Philadelphia: University of Pennsylvania Press.

———, ed. 1994. *Conserving Culture: A New Discourse on Heritage.* Urbana: University of Illinois Press.

Hufford, Mary, Marjorie Hunt, and Steven Zeitlin. 1987. *The Grand Generation: Memory, Mastery, Legacy.* Washington, D.C.: Smithsonian Institution Traveling Exhibition Service and Office of Folklife Programs in association with University of Washington Press.

Huizer, Gerrit, and Bruce Mannheim. 1979. *The Politics of Anthropology: From Colonialism and Sexism toward a View from Below.* The Hague: Mouton.

Hultkrantz, Åke. 1960. *General Ethnological Concepts.* Vol. 1 of *International Dictionary of Regional European Ethnology and Folklore.* Copenhagen: Rosenkilde and Bagger.

Humphrey, Theodore C., and Lin T. Humphrey, eds. 1992. *"We Gather Together": Food and Festival in American Life*. 1988; rpt., Logan: Utah State University Press.

Hunt, Margaret, trans. and ed. 1884. *Grimm's Household Tales*, 2 vols. London: George Bell and Sons.

Hunter, James Davison. 1991. *Culture Wars: The Struggle to Define America*. New York: Basic Books.

———. 1994. *Before the Shooting Begins: Searching for Democracy in America's Culture War*. New York: Free Press.

Hurston, Zora Neale. 1931. "Hoodoo in America." *Journal of American Folklore* 44:317–417.

———. 1935. *Mules and Men*. Philadelphia: J. B. Lippincott.

———. 1938. *Tell My Horse: Voodoo and Life in Haiti and Jamaica*. Philadelphia: J. B. Lippincott.

Hustvedt, Sigurd Bernhard. 1930. *Ballad Books and Ballad Men*. Cambridge: Harvard University Press.

Hyatt, Marshall. 1990. *Franz Boas, Social Activist: The Dynamics of Ethnicity*. New York: Greenwood.

Hylton, Joseph Gordon. 1987. "American Civilization at Harvard, 1937–1987." Typescript, History of American Civilization Archives, Harvard University.

Hyman, Stanley Edgar. 1948. "Some Bankrupt Treasuries." *Kenyon Review* 10:484–500.

Hyman, Trina Schart. 1983. *Little Red Riding Hood by the Brothers Grimm*. New York: Holiday House.

Iida, Kimio. 1997. "Kyoto Plays Tradition Card to Lure Students Back." *Japan Times* (June 8), 3.

"In a Sign Language Four Sioux Indians Converse without the Use of Words." 1893. *Chicago Tribune* (July 13), 3.

Ingersoll, Bruce. 1995. "Old Oder: GOP's Plan to Curtail Government Benefits Bring No Pain to Amish." *Wall Street Journal* (December 22), A1.

Inglis, Fred. 1993. *Cultural Studies*. Oxford: Basil Blackwell.

Intervisual Communications. 1981. *Walt Disney's Snow White and the Seven Dwarfs*. New York: Windmill Books.

"Introducing Our Personality of the Week." 1936. *Lock Haven Express* (December 5), 2.

Isaac, Rhys. 1982. *The Transformation of Virginia, 1740–1790*. Chapel Hill: University of North Carolina Press.

Isbell, Robert. 1996. *Last Chivaree: The Hicks Family of Beech Mountain*. Chapel Hill: University of North Carolina Press.

Ives, Edward D. 1978. *Joe Scott, The Woodsman-Songmaker*. Urbana: University of Illinois Press.

———. 1988. *George Magoon and the Down East Game War: History, Folklore, and the Law*. Urbana: University of Illinois Press.

Jabbour, Alan. 1996a. "The American Folklife Center: A Twenty-Year Retrospective." *Folklife Center News* 18(1–2):3–19.

———. 1996b. "The American Folklife Center: A Twenty-Year Retrospective (Part 2)." *Folklife Center News* 18(3–4):3–23.

Jackson, Bruce, ed. 1966. *Folklore and Society: Essays in Honor of Benj. A. Botkin*. Hatboro, Pennsylvania: Folklore Associates.

———. 1984a. "Dorson's Farewell." *New York Folklore* 10:99–112.

———, ed. 1984b. *Teaching Folklore*. Buffalo, New York: Documentary Research.

————. 1986. "Ben Botkin." *New York Folklore* 12:23–32.

————. 1987. "Folklore and Feminism." Special issue of *Journal of American Folklore* 100, no. 398.

————. 1989. "Vietnam." Special issue of *Journal of American Folklore* 102, no. 406.

————. 1993. "The Folksong Revival." In *Transforming Tradition: Folk Music Revivals Examined,* ed. Neil V. Rosenberg, 73–83. Urbana: University of Illinois Press.

Jackson, Bruce, Judith McCulloh, and Marta Weigle, eds. 1984. *Folklore/Folklife.* Washington, D.C.: American Folklore Society.

Jackson, Bruce, Michael Taft, and Harvey S. Axlerod, comps. and eds. 1988. *The Centennial Index: One Hundred Years of the Journal of American Folklore.* Washington, D.C.: American Folklore Society.

Jacobeit, Wolfgang. 1991. "Concerning the Traditional Understanding of 'Folk Culture in the German Democratic Republic': A Scholarly-Historical Retrospective." *Asian Folklore Studies* 50:67–94.

Jacobs, Joseph. 1891. *Studies in Jewish Statistics: Social, Vital, and Anthropometric.* London: D. Nutt.

————. 1893. "The Folk." *Folklore* 4:233–38.

————. 1895. *English Fairy Tales.* New York: A. L. Burt.

————. 1919. *Jewish Contributions to Civilization: An Estimate.* Philadelphia: Jewish Publication Society.

————. 1967. *English Fairy Tales.* 1898; rpt., New York: Dover.

Jacobs, Melville. 1959a. *The Content and Style of an Oral Literature: Clackamas Chinook Myths and Tales.* Chicago: University of Chicago Press.

————. 1959b. "Folklore." In *The Anthropology of Franz Boas: Essays on the Centennial of His Birth,* ed. Walter Goldschmidt, 119–38. American Anthropological Association Memoirs, no. 89. San Francisco: American Anthropological Association and Howard Chandler.

————. 1966. "A Look Ahead in Oral Literature Research." *Journal of American Folklore* 79:413–27.

Jain, Ravindra K., ed. 1977. *Text and Context: The Social Anthropology of Tradition.* Philadelphia: Institute for the Study of Human Issues.

Jakobson, Roman, and Petr Bogatyrev. 1980. "Folklore as a Special Form of Creation." Trans. John M. O'Hara. *Folklore Forum* 13:1–21.

James, George Wharton. 1903. "Primitive Inventions." *Craftsman* 5:125–37.

Jansen, William Hugh. 1959a. "Discussion." *Journal of American Folklore* 72:236–37.

————. 1959b. "Prepared Comments." *Journal of American Folklore* 72:220–22.

Jennings, Karla. 1990. *The Devouring Fungus: Tales of the Computer Age.* New York: W. W. Norton.

Johnson, Abby Arthur. 1984. "The Big Old World of Harold Courlander." *Midwest Quarterly* 25:450–70.

Johnson, Charles S. 1923. "Romulus and Uncle Remus." *Opportunity* 1(July):195.

————. 1930. *The Negro in American Civilization: A Study of Negro Life and Race Relations in Light of Social Research.* New York: Henry Holt.

————. 1934. *Shadow of the Plantation.* Chicago: University of Chicago Press.

————. 1967. *Growing Up in the Black Belt: Negro Youth in the Rural South.* 1941; rpt., New York: Schocken.

Johnson, Geraldine Niva. 1985. *Weaving Rag Rugs: A Women's Craft in Western Maryland.* Knoxville: University of Tennessee Press.

Johnson, Jay, and William C. Ketchum, Jr. 1983. *American Folk Art of the Twentieth Century.* New York: Rizzoli.

Johnson, Warren. 1985. *The Future Is Not What It Used to Be: Returning to Traditional Values in an Age of Scarcity*. New York: Dodd, Mead.

Jones, Bessie, and Bess Lomax Hawes. 1987. *Step It Down: Games, Plays, Songs & Stories from the Afro-American Heritage*. Athens: University of Georgia Press.

Jones, Louis C. 1950. "Folk Culture and the Historical Society." *Minnesota History* 31:11–17.

———. 1956. "Three Eyes on the Past: A New Triangulation for Local Studies." *New York Folklore Quarterly* 12:31–3, 143–49.

———. 1959. "Discussion." *Journal of American Folklore* 72:235–36.

———. 1962. "The Little People." *New York Folklore Quarterly* 18:243–64.

———. 1975. *Outward Signs of Inner Beliefs: Symbols of American Patriotism*. Cooperstown: New York State Historical Association.

———. 1982. *Three Eyes on the Past: Exploring New York Folk Life*. Syracuse: Syracuse University Press.

Jones, Michael Owen. 1975. *The Hand Made Object and Its Maker*. Berkeley: University of California Press.

———. 1980a. "A Feeling for Form, as Illustrated by People at Work." In *Folklore on Two Continents: Essays in Honor of Linda Dégh*, ed. Nikolai Burlakoff and Carl Lindahl, 260–69. Bloomington, Indiana: Trickster Press.

———. 1980b. "L. A. Add-ons and Re-dos: Renovation in Folk Art and Architectural Design." In *Perspectives on American Folk Art*, ed. Ian M. G. Quimby and Scott T. Swank, 325–63. New York: W. W. Norton.

———. 1982. "Another America: Toward a Behavioral History Based on Folkloristics." *Western Folklore* 41:43–51.

———. 1987. *Exploring Folk Art: Twenty Years of Thought on Craft, Work, and Aesthetics*. Logan: Utah State University Press.

———. 1989. *Craftsman of the Cumberlands: Tradition and Creativity*. Lexington: University Press of Kentucky.

———, ed. 1990. "Emotions in Work." Special issue of *American Behavioral Scientist* 30(January–February).

———. 1991. "Why Folklore and Organization(s)?" *Western Folklore* 50:29–40.

———. 1994. "Applying Folklore Studies: An Introduction." In *Putting Folklore to Use*, ed. Michael Owen Jones, 1–41. Lexington: University Press of Kentucky.

———. 1996. "Organizational Folklore." In *American Folklore: An Encyclopedia*, ed. Jan Harold Brunvand, 531–33. New York: Garland.

Jones, Michael Owen, Bruce Giuliano, and Roberta Krell, eds. 1983. *Foodways and Eating Habits: Directions for Research*. Los Angeles: California Folklore Society.

Jones, Michael Owen, Michael Dane Moore, and Richard Christopher Snyder, eds. 1988. *Inside Organizations: Understanding the Human Dimension*. Newbury Park, California: Sage.

Jones, Steven Swann. 1979. "Slouching towards Ethnography: The Text/Context Controversy Reconsidered." *Western Folklore* 38:42–47.

———. 1983. "The Structure of Snow White." *Fabula* 24:56–71.

———. 1984. *Folklore and Literature in the United States: An Annotated Bibliography of Studies of Folklore in American Literature*. New York: Garland.

Jones, Suzi. 1976. "Regionalization: A Rhetorical Strategy." *Journal of the Folklore Institute* 13:105–20.

Jones, Tim. 1997. "Wheels of Change for the Amish: Modern Options Bring Horse-Drawn Buggies Clip-Clopping toward the 21st Century." *Chicago Tribune* (March 2) 12:1.

Jones-Jackson, Patricia. 1987. *When Roots Die: Endangered Traditions on the Sea Islands*. Athens: University of Georgia Press.

Jordan, Philip. 1938. "Humor of the Backwoods, 1820–1840." *Mississippi Valley Historical Review* 25:25–38.

———. 1946. "Toward a New Folklore." *Minnesota History* 27:273–80.

———. 1948. *The National Road.* Indianapolis: Bobbs-Merrill.

———. 1953. "The Folklorist as Social Historian." *Western Folklore* 12:194–201.

Jordan, Rosan A., and Susan J. Kalčik, eds. 1985. *Women's Folklore, Women's Culture.* Philadelphia: University of Pennsylvania Press.

Jordan, Terry G. 1985. *American Log Buildings: An Old World Heritage.* Chapel Hill: University of North Carolina Press.

Joselit, Jenna Weissman. 1994. *The Wonders of America: Reinventing Jewish Culture, 1880–1950.* New York: Hill and Wang.

Joyce, Rosemary O. 1989. *A Bearer of Tradition: Dwight Stump, Basketmaker.* Athens: University of Georgia Press.

Joyner, Charles. 1975. "A Model for the Analysis of Folklore Performance in Historical Context." *Journal of American Folklore* 88:254–65.

———. 1984. *Down by the Riverside: A South Carolina Slave Community.* Urbana: University of Illinois Press.

———. 1988. "Tradition, Creativity and the Appalachian Dulcimer." *International Folklore Review* 6:74–77.

Kallir, Jane. 1981. *The Folk Art Tradition: Naive Painting in Europe and the United States.* New York: Viking.

Kamenetsky, Christa. 1972. "Folklore as a Political Tool in Nazi Germany." *Journal of American Folklore* 85:221–38.

———. 1977. "Folktale and Ideology in the Third Reich." *Journal of American Folklore* 90:168–78.

———. 1984. *Children's Literature in Hitler's Germany.* Athens: Ohio University Press.

———. 1992. *The Brothers Grimm and Their Critics: Folktales and the Quest for Meaning.* Athens: Ohio University Press.

Kammen, Michael. 1972. *People of Paradox: An Inquiry Concerning the Origins of American Civilization.* New York: Knopf.

———. 1978. *A Season of Youth: The American Revolution and the Historical Imagination.* Ithaca: Cornell University Press.

———. 1991. *Mystic Chords of Memory: The Transformation of Tradition in American Culture.* New York: Alfred A. Knopf.

———. 1993. "The Problem of American Exceptionalism: A Reconsideration." *American Quarterly* 45:1–43.

Kaplan, Anne R. 1980. "The Folk Arts Foundation of America: A History." *Journal of the Folklore Institute* 17:56–75.

Kaplan, Anne R., Marjorie A. Hoover, and Willard B. Moore. 1986. *The Minnesota Ethnic Food Book.* St. Paul: Minnesota Historical Society Press.

Kashatus, William C. 1996. "Images of William Penn: An Evolving Portrait of Pennsylvania's Founding Father." In *An Image of Peace: The Penn Treaty Collection of Mr. and Mrs. Meyer P. Potamkin,* 7–19. Harrisburg: Pennsylvania Historical and Museum Commission.

Katz, Lilian G. 1991. "Are Fairy Tales Good for Kids?" *Parents* (November), 243.

Katz-Fishman, Walda, and Jerome Scott. 1994. "Diversity and Equality: Race and Class in America." *Sociological Forum* 9:569–81.

Kautsky, Karl. *Are the Jews a Race?* New York: International Publishers.

Keeling, Richard. 1991. *A Guide to Early Field Recordings (1900–1949) at the Lowie Museum of Anthropology*. Berkeley: University of California Press.

Kern, James R., and Minna M. Kern, eds. 1907. *German Stories Retold (Grimms Märchen)*. New York: American Book Company.

Kern, Stephen. 1983. *The Culture of Time and Space, 1880–1918*. Cambridge: Harvard University Press.

Kessler-Harris, Alice. 1992. "Cultural Locations: Positioning American Studies in the Great Debate." *American Quarterly* 44:299–312.

Ketner, Kenneth Laine. 1973. "The Role of Hypotheses in Folkloristics." *Journal of American Folklore* 86:114–30.

———. 1976. "Identity and Existence in the Study of Human Traditions." *Folklore* 87:192–200.

King, Lyndel. 1989. "Foreword." In *Circles of Tradition: Folk Arts in Minnesota*, ed. Willard B. Moore, vii–ix. St. Paul: Minnesota Historical Society Press.

Kingsley, John Sterling, ed. 1885. *The Standard Natural History*. Vol. 6. *The Natural History of Man*. Boston: S. E. Cassino.

Kirk, Russell, ed. 1982. *Portable Conservative Reader*. New York: Viking.

Kirkland, James; Holly F. Mathews; C. W. Sullivan III; and Karen Baldwin, eds. 1992. *Herbal and Magical Medicine: Traditional Healing Today*. Durham, North Carolina: Duke University Press.

Kirpatrick, Curry. 1987. "Me and My Good Friends: It Was Glitz Time in La La Land as Celebs Invaded the Forum to See and Be Seen." *Sports Illustrated* (June 15), 24–25.

Kirshenblatt-Gimblett, Barbara. 1988. "Mistaken Dichotomies." *Journal of American Folklore* 101:140–55.

———. 1989a. "Authoring Lives." *Journal of Folklore Research* 26:123–50.

———. 1989b. "Objects of Memory: Material Culture as Life Review." In *Folk Groups and Folklore Genres: A Reader*, ed. Elliott Oring, 329–38. Logan: Utah State University Press.

———. 1994. "On Difference." *Journal of American Folklore* 107:233–38.

———. 1996a. "From the Paperwork Empire to the Paperless Office: Testing the Limits of the 'Science of Tradition.'" In *Folklore Interpreted: Essays in Honor of Alan Dundes*, ed. Regina Bendix and Rosemary Levy Zumwalt, 69–92. New York: Garland.

———. 1996b. "Topic Drift: Negotiating the Gap between the Field and Our Name." *Journal of Folklore Research* 33:245–54.

Kitchener, Amy V. 1994. *The Holiday Yards of Florencio Morales*. Jackson: University Press of Mississippi.

Klein, Barbro. 1995. "Folklorists in the United States and the World Beyond." *American Folklore Society News* 24(1):12–15.

Klein, H. M. J. 1946. *History and Customs of the Amish People*. York, Pennsylvania: Maple Press.

Klöpper, Clemens. 1899. *Folklore in England and America*. Dresden: C. A. Koch.

Klymasz, Robert B. 1976. "Soviet Views of American Folklore and Folkloristics, 1950–1974." In *Folklore Today: A Festschrift for Richard M. Dorson*, ed. Linda Dégh, Henry Glassie, and Felix J. Oinas, 305–12. Bloomington, Indiana: Research Center for Language and Semiotic Studies, Indiana University.

Knapp, Mary, and Herbert Knapp. 1976. *One Potato, Two Potato: The Folklore of American Children*. New York: W. W. Norton.

Knapp, William I. 1898. "Address of Welcome on Behalf of the Chicago Folk-Lore Society." In *The International Folk-Lore Congress of the World's Columbian Exposition*, ed. Helen Wheeler Bassett and Frederick Starr, 24–25. Chicago: Charles H. Sergel.

Kniffen, Fred B. [1965] 1986. "Folk Housing: Key to Diffusion." In *Common Places: Readings in Vernacular Architecture*, ed. Dell Upton and John Michael Vlach, 3–26. Athens: University of North Carolina Press.

Knortz, Karl. 1882. *Aus der transatlantischen Gesellschaft: Nordamerikanische Kulturbilder.* Leipzig: Bernhard Schlicke.

———. 1906. *Was ist Volkskunde und wie studiert man dieselbe?* 3d ed. Jena: H. W. Schmnidts.

———. [1905] 1988. "Zur amerikanischen Volkskunde (American Folklore)." Trans. Helga B. Van Iten and James R. Dow. *Folklore Historian* 5:14–43.

Koch, John. 1995. "Multicultural Twist Works on Fairy Tales." *Boston Globe* (March 26), B26.

Kodish, Debora. 1986. *Good Friends and Bad Enemies: Robert Winslow Gordon and the Study of American Folksong.* Urbana: University of Illinois Press.

Koltyk, Jo Ann. 1993. "Telling Narratives through Home Videos: Hmong Refugees and Self-Documentation of Life in the Old and New Country." *Journal of American Folklore* 106:435–49.

Korson, George. 1964. *Minstrels of the Mine Patch: Songs and Stories of the Anthracite Industry.* 1938; rpt., Hatboro, Pennsylvania: Folklore Associates.

Kotkin, Amy J., and Steven J. Zeitlin. 1983. "In the Family Tradition." In *Handbook of American Folklore*, ed. Richard M. Dorson, 90–99. Bloomington: Indiana University Press.

Krappe, Alexander Haggerty. 1930. "'American' Folklore." In *Folk-Say*, ed. B. A. Botkin, 291–97. Norman: University of Oklahoma Press.

———. 1964. *The Science of Folklore.* 1930; rpt., New York: W. W. Norton.

Krasniewicz, Louise. 1986. "Growing Up Catholic and American: The Oral Tradition of Catholic School Students." *New York Folklore* 12:51–67.

Kraybill, Donald B. 1989. *The Riddle of Amish Culture.* Baltimore: Johns Hopkins University Press.

———, ed. 1993. *The Amish and the State.* Baltimore: Johns Hopkins University Press.

Kraybill, Donald B., and Steven Nolt. 1995. *Amish Enterprise: From Plows to Profits.* Baltimore: Johns Hopkins University Press.

Kraybill, Donald B., and Marc A. Olshan, eds. 1994. *The Amish Struggle with Modernity.* Hanover, New Hampshire: University Press of New England.

Krell, Roberta. 1980. "At a Children's Hospital: A Folklore Survey." In *Children's Folklore*, ed. Sylvia Ann Grider, 223–31. Los Angeles: California Folklore Society. Also published in *Western Folklore* 39(July 1980).

Kristeller, Paul Oskar. 1983. "'Creativity' and 'Tradition.'" *Journal of the History of Ideas* 44:105–14.

Krohn, Kaarle. 1971. *Folklore Methodology: Formulated by Julius Krohn and Expanded by Nordic Researchers.* Trans. Roger L. Welsch. 1926; rpt., Austin: University of Texas Press.

Kroll, Jack. 1977. "Fiddler's Reprise." *Newsweek* (January 10), 66.

Kuhns, Oscar. 1901. *The German and Swiss Settlements of Colonial Pennsylvania: A Study of the So-Called Pennsylvania Dutch.* New York: Henry Holt.

Kurian, George Thomas. 1984. *New Book of World Rankings.* 2d ed. New York: Facts on File.

Kurin, Richard. 1989. "Why We Do the Festival." In *1989 Festival of American Folklife*, ed. Peter Seitel, 8–21. Washington, D.C.: Smithsonian Institution.

———. 1990. "Folklife in Contemporary Multicultural Society." In *1990 Festival of American Folklife*, ed. Peter Seitel, 8–17. Washington, D.C.: Smithsonian Institution.

———. 1993. "Culture on the 1990s Agenda." In *1993 Festival of American Folklife*, ed. Peter Seitel, 9–14. Washington, D.C.: Smithsonian Institution.

———. 1996a. "Festival of American Folklife." In *American Folklore: An Encyclopedia*, ed. Jan Harold Brunvand, 252–53. New York: Garland.

———. 1996b. "Smithsonian Institution Center for Folklife Programs and Cultural Studies." In *American Folklore: An Encyclopedia*, ed. Jan Harold Brunvand, 672–73. New York: Garland.

La Belle, Thomas J., and Christopher R. Ward. 1994. *Multiculturalism and Education: Diversity and Its Impact on Schools and Society*. Albany: State University of New York Press.

Landis, H. K. 1939. "Local Folk Museums." *Chronicle of the Early American Industries Association* 2(April):71.

———. 1945. "Landis Valley Museum." *Chronicle of the Early American Industries Association* 3(September):43, 46, 49.

Lang, Andrew. 1885. *Custom and Myth*. New York: Harper.

———. 1901. *Magic and Religion*. New York: Longmans, Green.

———, ed. 1965. *The Green Fairy Book*. 1892; rpt., New York: Dover.

Langlois, Janet. 1978. "Belle Gunness, the Lady Bluebeard: Community Legend as Metaphor." *Journal of the Folklore Institute* 15:147–60.

Langstaff, John, and Carol Langstaff. 1973. *Shimmy Shimmy Coke-Ca-Pop! A Collection of City Children's Street Games and Rhymes*. Garden City, New York: Doubleday.

Lanier, Gabrielle M., and Bernard L. Herman. 1997. *Everyday Architecture of the Mid-Atlantic: Looking at Buildings and Landscape*. Baltimore: Johns Hopkins University Press.

Lankford, George, ed. 1987. *Native American Legends*. Little Rock: August House.

Lasch, Christopher. 1986. "'Traditional Values': Left, Right, and Wrong." *Harper's* (September), 13–16.

Lasswell, Harold D. 1949. "The Structure and Function of Communication in Society." In *Mass Communications*, ed. Wilbur Schramm, 102–15. Urbana: University of Illinois Press.

Latham, Jean Lee. 1962. *The Brave Little Tailor, Hansel and Gretel, Jack and the Beanstalk*. Indianapolis: Bobbs-Merrill.

Lauter, David. 1993. "Traditional Democratic Values Having a Rebirth." *Los Angeles Times* (August 7), A20.

Lawless, Elaine J. 1988. *Handmaidens of the Lord: Pentecostal Women Preachers and Traditional Religion*. Philadelphia: University of Pennsylvania Press.

Lawless, Ray M. 1960. *Folksingers and Folksongs in America*. New York: Duell, Sloan and Pearce.

Lawrence, William Witherle. 1911. *Medieval Story and the Beginnings of the Social Ideals of English-Speaking People*. New York: Columbia University Press.

———. 1928. *Beowulf and Epic Tradition*. Cambridge: Harvard University Press.

Laws, G. Malcolm. 1950. *Native American Balladry: A Descriptive Study and a Bibliographical Analysis*. Philadelphia: American Folklore Society.

———. 1964. *Native American Balladry*. Rev. ed., Philadelphia: American Folklore Society.

Leach, Edmund. 1976. *Culture and Communication*. Cambridge: Cambridge University Press.

Leach, MacEdward. 1949. "Folklore." In *Standard Dictionary of Folklore, Mythology, and Legend*, ed. Maria Leach, 401. New York: Funk and Wagnalls.

Leach, MacEdward, and Tristram P. Coffin, eds. 1961. *The Critics and the Ballad*. Carbondale: Southern Illinois University Press.

Leach, Maria, ed. 1949–50. *Funk and Wagnalls Standard Dictionary of Folklore, Mythology, and Legend.* 2 vols. New York: Funk and Wagnalls.

———. 1959. *The Thing at the Foot of the Bed.* New York: World.

Learned, Marion Dexter. 1903. "The Pennsylvania-German and His English and Scotch-Irish Neighbors." *Addresses at the Sixth Annual Meeting of the Lebanon County Historical Society* 2(11):317–29.

———. 1907. "An American Ethnographical Survey." *Americana Germanica* 9:30–53.

———. 1911. *The American Ethnographical Survey: Conestoga Expedition.* Philadelphia: Americana Germanica.

Lears, T. J. Jackson. 1981. *No Place of Grace: Antimodernism and the Transformation of American Culture, 1880–1920.* New York: Pantheon.

———. 1985. "The Concept of Cultural Hegemony: Problems and Possibilities." *American Historical Review* 90:567–93.

———. 1988. "Packaging the Folk: Tradition and Amnesia in American Advertising, 1880–1940." In *Folk Roots, New Roots: Folklore in American Life*, ed. Jane S. Becker and Barbara Franco, 103–40. Lexington, Massachusetts: Museum of Our National Heritage.

———. 1994. *Fables of Abundance: A Cultural History of Advertising in America.* New York: Basic Books.

Leary, James P. 1991. *Midwestern Folk Humor.* Little Rock: August House.

Lee, Dorothy Demetracopoulou. 1932. "A Study of Wintu Mythology." *Journal of American Folklore* 45:375–500.

———. 1933. "The Loon Woman Myth: A Study in Synthesis." *Journal of American Folklore* 46:101–28.

———. 1941. "Review of *Hawaiian Mythology* by Martha Beckwith." *American Anthropologist* 43:293–95.

———. 1942. "Greek Accounts of the Vrykolakas." *Journal of American Folklore* 55:126–32.

———. 1946. "Greek Tales of Nastradi Hodjas." *Folklore* 57:188–95.

———. 1947. "Greek Tales of Priest and Priestwife." *Journal of American Folklore* 60:163–67.

———. 1951. "Greek Personal Anecdotes of the Supernatural." *Journal of American Folklore* 64:307–12.

———. 1959. *Freedom and Culture.* Englewood Cliffs, New Jersey: Prentice-Hall.

———. 1976. *Valuing the Self: What We Can Learn from Other Cultures.* Prospect Heights, Illinois: Waveland Press.

Lee, Dorothy Demetracopoulou, and Cora Du Bois. 1931. *Wintu Myths.* Berkeley: University of California Publications in American Archaeology and Ethnology.

Lee, O-Young. 1984. *The Compact Culture: The Japanese Tradition of "Smaller Is Better."* Trans. Robert N. Avery. Tokyo: Kodansha International.

Leehrsen, Charles. 1984. "Boston Ends a Marathon." *Newsweek* (June 25), 75.

Lester, Julius. 1987. *The Tales of Uncle Remus: The Adventures of Brer Rabbit.* New York: Dial.

———. 1989. "The Storyteller's Voice: Reflections on the Rewriting of Uncle Remus." In *The Voice of the Narrator in Children's Literature: Insights from Writers and Critics*, ed. Charlotte F. Otten and Gary D. Schmidt, 69–73. New York: Greenwood.

Levin, Patricia. 1996. "Amish Tourism in Lancaster County—An Analysis." Paper delivered at the Pennsylvania-German Society Annual Meeting, Harrisburg, Pennsylvania.

Levine, Lawrence W. 1977. *Black Culture and Black Consciousness: Afro-American Folk Thought from Slavery to Freedom.* New York: Oxford University Press.

———. 1983. "How to Interpret American Folklore Historically." In *Handbook of American Folklore*, ed. Richard M. Dorson, 338–44. Bloomington: Indiana University Press.

————. 1992. "The Folklore of Industrial Society: Popular Culture and Its Audiences." *American Historical Review* 97:1369–99.

Levy, Dan. 1993. "Gays Mix It Up with Religious Fundamentalists." *San Francisco Chronicle* (November 9), A15.

Levy, Jerrold E., Raymond Neutra, and Dennis Parker. 1987. *Hand Trembling, Frenzy Witchcraft, and Moth Madness: A Study of Navajo Seizure Disorders.* Tucson: University of Arizona Press.

Lewis, Elaine Lambert. 1946. "New Jersey Folklore Society." *Journal of American Folklore* 59:72.

Lewis, George H. 1989. "The Maine Lobster as Regional Icon: Competing Images over Time and Social Class." *Food and Foodways* 3:303–16.

————, ed. 1993. *All That Glitters: Country Music in America.* Bowling Green, Ohio: Popular Press.

Lewis, R. W. B. 1955. *The American Adam: Innocence, Tragedy, and Tradition in the Nineteenth Century.* Chicago: University of Chicago Press.

Life Magazine. 1961. *The Life Treasury of American Folklore.* New York: Time.

Limón, J. E., and M. J. Young. 1986. "Frontiers, Settlements, and Development in Folklore Studies, 1972–1985." *Annual Review of Anthropology* 15:437–60.

Lind, William S., and William Marshner, eds. 1987. *Cultural Conservatism: Toward a New National Agenda.* Washington, D.C.: Free Congress Research and Education Foundation.

Lindahl, Carl, and Erika Brady, eds. 1980. *Folklore and Medieval Studies.* Bloomington, Indiana: Folklore Forum.

Lipman, Jean, Elizabeth Warren, and Robert Bishop. 1986. *Young America: A Folk-Art History.* New York: Hudson Hills Press in association with the Museum of American Folk Art.

Lipman, Jean, and Alice Winchester. 1974. *The Flowering of American Folk Art, 1776–1876.* New York: Viking Press.

Liss, Julia. 1995. "Boas, Franz." In *A Companion to American Thought,* ed. Richard Wightman Fox and James T. Kloppenberg, 81–83. Oxford: Basil Blackwell.

List, George. 1991. *Singing about It: Folk Song in Southern Indiana.* Bloomington: Indiana University Press.

Lloyd, Timothy C., and Patrick B. Mullen. 1990. *Lake Erie Fishermen: Work, Tradition, and Identity.* Urbana: University of Illinois Press.

Locke, Alain. [1925] 1994. "The New Negro." In *Within the Circle: An Anthology of African American Literary Criticism from the Harlem Renaissance to the Present,* ed. Angelyn Mitchell, 21–31. Durham: Duke University Press.

Lockwood, Yvonne. 1977. "The Sauna: An Expression of Finnish-American Identity." *Western Folklore* 36:71–84.

Loehr, Rodney C. 1951. "Some More Light on Paul Bunyan." *Journal of American Folklore* 64:405–7.

Lomax, Alan. 1976. "… And the Pursuit of Happiness." *1976 Festival of American Folklife,* ed. Bess Lomax Hawes and Susanne Roschwalb, 4–5. Washington, D.C.: Smithsonian Institution.

Lomax, John A., and Alan Lomax. 1938. *Cowboy Songs, and Other Frontier Ballads.* 1910; revised and enlarged edition, New York: Macmillan.

Loomis, Charles P., and J. Allan Beegle. 1951. *Rural Social Systems.* Englewood Cliffs, New Jersey: Prentice-Hall.

Loomis, Ormond H. 1983. *Cultural Conservation: The Protection of Cultural Heritage in the United States.* Washington, D.C.: Library of Congress.

Loomis, Roger Sherman, ed. 1927. *Medieval Studies in Memory of Gertrude Schoepperle Loomis*. New York: Columbia University Press.

Lord, Albert Bates. 1960. *The Singer of Tales*. Cambridge: Harvard University Press.

———. 1962. "Homer." In *Homer: A Collection of Critical Essays*, ed. George Steiner and Robert Fagles, 62–78. Englewood Cliffs, New Jersey: Prentice-Hall.

———. 1991. *Epic Singers and Oral Tradition*. Ithaca: Cornell University Press.

Louisiana Folklife Program. 1989. *Folklife in the Florida Parishes*. N.p.: Louisiana Folklife Program.

Lowe, Donald M. 1982. *History of Bourgeois Perception*. Chicago: University of Chicago Press.

Lowie, Robert. 1913. "Societies of the Crow, Hidatsa, and Mandan Indians." *American Museum of Natural History Anthropological Papers* 11:145–358.

Loza, Steven. 1992. *Barrio Rhythm: Mexican American Music in Los Angeles*. Urbana: University of Illinois Press.

Lubbock, John. 1978. *The Origin of Civilisation and the Primitive Condition of Man*. 1870; rpt., Chicago: University of Chicago Press.

Lund, Jens, ed. 1989. *Folk Arts of Washington State: A Survey of Contemporary Folk Arts and Artists in the State of Washington*. Tumwater: Washington State Folklife Council.

Luomala, Katharine. 1951. "Review of *The Kumulipo* by Martha Beckwith." *Journal of American Folklore* 65:429–32.

———. 1962. "Martha Warren Beckwith: A Commemorative Essay." *Journal of American Folklore* 75:341–53.

———. 1970. "Introduction." In *Hawaiian Mythology,* by Martha Beckwith, vii–xxix. 1940; rpt., Honolulu: University of Hawaii Press.

Lüthi, Max. 1970. *Once upon a Time: On the Nature of Fairy Tales*. Trans. Lee Chadeayne and Paul Gottwald. New York: Frederick Ungar.

———. 1982. *The European Folktale: Form and Nature*. Trans. John D. Niles. Philadelphia: Institute for the Study of Human Issues.

———. 1984. *The Fairytale as Art Form and Portrait of Man*. Trans. Jon Erickson. Bloomington: Indiana University Press.

Mabie, Hamilton, ed. 1905. *Fairy Tales Every Child Should Know*. New York: Doubleday, Page.

———, ed. 1909. *Fairy Tales from Grimm*. New York: Barse.

MacColl, W. D. [1913] 1970. "The International Exhibition of Modern Art." In *The Call of the Wild (1900–1916)*, ed. Roderick Nash, 179–84. New York: George Braziller.

MacDowell, Marsha, ed. 1987. *Folk Arts in Education: A Resource Handbook*. East Lansing: Michigan State University Museum.

———. 1997. *African-American Quiltmaking in Michigan*. East Lansing: Michigan State University Press.

MacDowell, Marsha, and Ruth D. Fitzgerald, eds. 1987. *Michigan Quilts: 150 Years of a Textile Tradition*. East Lansing: Michigan State University Museum.

MacGregor-Villarreal, Mary. 1989. "Brazilian Parallels to Dorson's 'Theory for American Folklore.'" *Western Folklore* 48:359–73.

Madden, Betty I. 1974. *Art, Crafts, and Architecture in Early Illinois*. Urbana: University of Illinois Press.

Maidment, Brian C. 1975. "Joseph Jacobs and English Folklore in the 1890s." In *Studies in the Cultural Life of the Jews in England*, ed. Dov Noy and Issachar Ben-Ami, 185–96. Jerusalem: Magnes Press.

Malinowski, Bronislaw. 1926. *Myth in Primitive Psychology*. New York: W. W. Norton.

———. 1944. *A Scientific Theory of Culture, and Other Essays*. Chapel Hill: University of North Carolina Press.

———. 1954. *Magic, Science and Religion*. 1948; rpt., Garden City: Doubleday.

———. 1961. *Argonauts of the Western Pacific: An Account of Native Enterprise and Adventure in the Archipelagoes of Melanesian New Guinea*. 1922; rpt., New York: E. P. Dutton.

Malone, Bill C. 1968. *Country Music, U.S.A.* Austin: University of Texas Press.

———. 1979. *Southern Music, American Music*. Lexington: University Press of Kentucky.

———. 1985. *Country Music, U.S.A.* Rev. ed., Austin: University of Texas Press.

Malpezzi, Frances, and William M. Clements. 1992. *Italian-American Folklore*. Little Rock: August House.

Mandel, Jerome, and Bruce Rosenberg, eds. 1970. *Medieval Literature and Folklore Studies: Essays in Honor of Francis Lee Utley*. New Brunswick: Rutgers University Press.

Manheim, Ralph, trans. 1988. *Dear Mili: An Old Tale by Wilhelm Grimm*. New York: Farrar, Straus and Giroux.

Mann, William Julius. 1880. *Die gute alte Zeit in Pennsylvanien*. Philadelphia: Kohler.

Maranda, Pierre, and Elli Köngäs Maranda, eds. 1971. *Structural Analysis of Oral Tradition*. Philadelphia: University of Pennsylvania Press.

Marković, Mihailo. 1979. "Praxis: Critical Social Philosophy in Yugoslavia." In *Praxis: Yugoslav Essays in the Philosophy and Methodology of the Social Sciences*, ed. Mihailo Marković and Gajo Petrović, xi–xxxvi. Boston: D. Reidel.

Marlow, Kristina. 1994. "For Politically Correct, Halloween Can Be Frightening." *Chicago Tribune* (September 30) 1:1.

Marmon, William. 1977. "Haley's Rx: Talk, Write, Reunite." *Time* (February 14), 72, 75.

Marsh, J. B. T. 1876. *The Story of the Jubilee Singers with Their Songs*. 5th ed. London: Hodder and Stoughton.

Marshall, Howard Wight. 1981a. *American Folk Architecture: A Selected Bibliography*. Washington, D.C.: American Folklife Center, Library of Congress.

———. 1981b. *Folk Architecture in Little Dixie: A Regional Culture in Missouri*. Columbia: University of Missouri Press.

———, ed. 1983. *Missouri Artist Jesse Howard, With a Contemplation on Idiosyncratic Art*. Columbia: Missouri Cultural Heritage Center.

———. 1995. *Paradise Valley, Nevada: The People and Buildings of an American Place*. Tucson: University of Arizona Press.

Marshall, Steve. 1996. "Boom Boxes in Amish Buggies Turn Off Town." *USA Today* (April 24), A2.

Martin, Charles E. 1984. *Hollybush: Folk Building and Social Change in an Appalachian Community*. Knoxville: University of Tennessee Press.

Martin, T. 1985. "K. C. Jones: Continuing the Celtics Winning Tradition." *Ebony* (April), 59–60.

Martz, Larry. 1986. "Trouble on the Far Right." *Newsweek* (April 14), 24–25.

Marx, Leo. 1964. *The Machine in the Garden: Technology and the Pastoral Ideal in America*. New York: Oxford University Press.

———. 1979. "Thoughts on the Origin and Character of the American Studies Movement." *American Quarterly* 31:398–406.

Mason, John Hope. 1988. "The Character of Creativity: Two Traditions." *History of European Ideas* 9:697–715.

Mason, Otis T. 1891. "The Natural History of Folklore." *Journal of American Folklore* 4:97–105.

————. 1894a. *Primitive Travel and Transportation.* Report of the U.S. National Museum, part 2, 237–593. Washington, D.C.: Government Printing Office.

————. 1894b. *Woman's Share in Primitive Culture.* New York: Appleton.

————. 1895. *The Origins of Invention: The Study of Industry among Primitive Peoples.* London: W. Scott.

Mast, Gerald. 1976. *A Short History of the Movies.* Indianapolis: Bobbs-Merrill.

Matthews, Washington. 1877. *Ethnography and Philology of the Hidatsa Indians.* U.S. Geological and Geographical Survey of the Rocky Mountain Region, Miscellaneous Publications, no. 7. Washington, D.C.

————. 1898. "The Rise of Empiricism." In *International Folk-Lore Congress,* ed. Helen Wheeler Bassett and Frederick Starr, 117–24. Chicago: Charles H. Sergel.

McCallum, Jack. 1987a. "Playing it Tough in the East." *Sports Illustrated* (June 1), 34–36.

————. 1987b. "Your Ball, L.A." *Sports Illustrated* (June 22), 14–21.

McCarl, Robert. 1985. *The District of Columbia Fire Fighters' Project: A Case Study in Occupational Folklife.* Washington, D.C.: Smithsonian Institution Press.

McCarthy, Tara. 1993. *Multicultural Fables and Fairy Tales: Stories and Activities to Promote Literacy and Cultural Awareness.* New York: Scholastic Professional Books.

McCarthy, William Bernard. 1978. "Creativity, Tradition, and History: The Ballad Repertoire of Agnes Lyle of Kilbarchan." Ph.D. diss., Indiana University.

McClain, Margy. 1988. *A Feeling for Life: Cultural Identity, Community and the Arts.* Chicago: Urban Traditions.

McClean, Paul. 1992. *Japan and America: How They Are Different,* with notes by Tohru Abe and Ikuko Kokubo. Tokyo: Asahi Press.

McCormick, Dell J. 1936. *Paul Bunyan Swings His Axe.* Caldwell, Idaho: Caxton.

————. 1939. *Tall Timber Tales: More Paul Bunyan Stories.* Caldwell, Idaho: Caxton.

McDonald, Barry. 1997. "Tradition as Personal Relationship." *Journal of American Folklore* 110:47–67.

McDonald, Forest. 1994. "What Makes Right? The Theme Is Freedom: Religion, Politics, and the American Tradition." *National Review* (October 24), 62–64.

McDowell, Tremaine. 1948a. *American Studies.* Minneapolis: University of Minnesota Press.

————. 1948b. "Folklore and American Studies." *American Heritage* 2:44–47.

McElvaine, Robert S. 1987. *The End of the Conservative Era: Liberalism after Reagan.* New York: Arbor House.

McFadden, Robert D. 1977. "Some Points of 'Roots' Questioned: Haley Stands by Book as Symbol." *New York Times* (April 10), 1, 29.

McGee, W. J. 1898. "Fifty Years of American Science." *Atlantic Monthly* 82:317–19.

McGlathery, James M., ed. 1988. *The Brothers Grimm and Folktale.* Urbana: University of Illinois Press.

————. 1991. *Fairy Tale Romance: The Grimms, Basile, and Perrault.* Urbana: University of Illinois Press.

————. 1993. *Grimms' Fairy Tales: A History of Criticism on a Popular Classic.* Columbia, South Carolina: Camden House.

McMahon, Felicia. 1990. "Inside Millie's Kitchen: Voices of the Adirondacks." *New York Folklore* 16:1–15.

McNeil, W. K. 1980. "A History of American Folklore Scholarship before 1908." Ph.D. diss., Indiana University.

————. 1985. "The Chicago Folklore Society and the International Folklore Congress of 1893." *Midwestern Journal of Language and Folklore* 11:5–19.

————, ed. 1987–88. *Southern Folk Ballads.* 2 vols. Little Rock: August House.

————, ed. 1989a. *Appalachian Images in Folk and Popular Culture.* Ann Arbor: UMI Research Press.

————. 1989b. *Ozark Mountain Humor.* Little Rock: August Houses.

————, comp. and ed. 1993. *Southern Mountain Folksongs: Traditional Songs from the Appalachians and the Ozarks.* Little Rock: August House.

————. 1995a. *Appalachian Images in Folk and Popular Culture.* 2d ed. Knoxville: University of Tennessee Press.

————. 1995b. *Ozark Country.* Jackson: University Press of Mississippi.

————. 1996a. "American Folklore Scholarship: The Early Years." In *American Folklore: An Encyclopedia,* ed. Jan Harold Brunvand, 17–23. New York: Garland.

————. 1996b. "Emrich, Duncan B. M. (1908–1977)." In *American Folklore: An Encyclopedia,* ed. Jan Harold Brunvand, 223. New York: Garland.

McNeil, W. K., and William M. Clements, eds. 1992. *An Arkansas Folklore Sourcebook.* Fayetteville: University of Arkansas Press.

Mead, George Herbert. 1964. *On Social Psychology.* Ed. Answelm Strauss. Chicago: University of Chicago Press.

Mead, Margaret. 1976. "Our 200th Birthday: What We Have to Celebrate." In *1976 Festival of American Folklife,* ed. Bess Lomax Hawes and Susanne Roschwalb, 5. Washington, D.C.: Smithsonian Institution.

Mechling, Jay, 1979. "If They Can Build a Square Tomato: Notes toward a Holistic Approach to Regional Studies." In *Prospects 4,* ed. Jack Salzman, 59–78. New York: Burt Franklin.

————. 1980. "The Magic of the Boy Scout Campfire." *Journal of American Folklore* 93:35–56.

————. 1981. "Male Gender Display at a Boy Scout Camp." In *Children and Their Organizations: Investigations in American Culture,* ed. R. Timothy Sieber and Andrew J. Gordon, 138–60. Boston: G. K. Hall.

————, ed. 1985. "William James and the Philosophical Foundations for the Study of Everyday Life." Special section, *Western Folklore* 44:301–32.

————. 1989a. "'Banana Cannon' and Other Folk Traditions between Human and Nonhuman Animals." *Western Folklore* 48:312–23.

————. 1989b. "The Collecting Self and American Youth Movements." In *Consuming Visions: Accumulation and Display of Goods in America, 1880–1920,* ed. Simon J. Bronner, 255–86. New York: W. W. Norton.

————. 1989c. "Mediating Structures and the Significance of University Folk." In *Folk Groups and Folklore Genres: A Reader,* ed. Elliott Oring, 339–49. Logan: Utah State University Press.

————. 1989d. "Richard M. Dorson and the Emergence of the New Class in American Folk Studies." *Journal of Folklore Research* 26:11–26.

————. 1993. "On Sharing Folklore and American Identity in a Multicultural Society." *Western Folklore* 52:271–90.

Mechling, Jay, Robert Merideth, and David Wilson. 1973. "American Culture Studies: The Discipline and the Curriculum." *American Quarterly* 25:363–89.

Medved, Michael. 1992. *Hollywood vs. America: Popular Culture and the War on Traditional Values.* New York: Harper Collins.

Meeker, Louis L. 1901. "Siouan Mythological Tales." *Journal of American Folklore* 14:161–64.

Meley, Patricia. 1989. "Paper Power: A Search for Meaning in the Folded Paper Toys of Pre-Adolescents." *Children's Folklore Review* 11:3–5.

Mercer, Henry C. [1897] 1987. "'Tools of the Nation Maker': Toward a Historical Interpretation of American Folklife." In *Folklife Studies from the Gilded Age: Object, Rite, and Custom in Victorian America*, ed. Simon J. Bronner, 279–91. Ann Arbor: UMI Research Press.

Merrill, Lynn L. 1989. *The Romance of Victorian Natural History*. New York: Oxford University Press.

Metcalf, Eugene W., Jr. 1983. "Black Art, Folk Art, and Social Control." *Winterthur Portfolio* 18:271–90.

———. 1986. "The Politics of the Past in American Folk Art History." In *Folk Art and Art Worlds*, ed. John Michael Vlach and Simon J. Bronner, 27–50. Ann Arbor: UMI Research Press.

Metcalf, Eugene W., Jr., and Claudine Weatherford. 1988. "Modernism, Edith Halpert, Holger Cahill, and the Fine Art Meaning of American Folk Art." In *Folk Roots, New Roots: Folklore in American Life*, ed. Jane S. Becker and Barbara Franco, 141–66. Lexington, Massachusetts: Museum of Our National Heritage.

Michaelis-Jena, Ruth. 1970. *The Brothers Grimm*. New York: Praeger.

Michelsen, Peter. 1966. *Dansk Folkemuseum and Frilandsmuseet: History and Activities*. Copenhagen: Nationalmuseet.

Mieder, Wolfgang. 1982. "Survival Forms of 'Little Red Riding Hood' in Modern Society." *International Folklore Review* 2:23–40.

———, ed. 1985. *Disenchantments: An Anthology of Modern Fairy Tale Poetry*. Hanover, New Hampshire: University Press of New England.

———. 1987. *Tradition and Innovation in Folk Literature*. Hanover, New Hampshire: University Press of New England.

———. 1989. *American Proverbs: A Study of Texts and Contexts*. Bern: Peter Lang.

———. 1991. *A Dictionary of American Proverbs*. New York: Oxford University Press.

———. 1992. "Paremiological Minimum and Cultural Literacy." In *Creativity and Tradition in Folklore: New Directions*, ed. Simon J. Bronner, 185–203. Logan: Utah State University Press.

———. 1993. *Proverbs Are Never Out of Season: Popular Wisdom in the Modern Age*. New York: Oxford University Press.

———. 1997. *The Politics of Proverbs: From Traditional Wisdom to Proverbial Stereotypes*. Madison: University of Wisconsin Press.

Miller, Bethene. 1942. *Paul Bunyan in the Army*. Portland, Oregon: Binsford and Morts.

Miller, Douglas T., and Marion Nowak. 1977. *The Fifties: The Way We Really Were*. Garden City: Doubleday.

Miller, John. 1992. *Deer Camp: Last Light in the Northeast Kingdom*. Cambridge: MIT Press.

Miller, Terry E. 1986. *Folk Music in America: A Reference Guide*. New York: Garland.

Mills, Gary B., and Elizabeth Shown Mills. 1981. "*Roots* and the New 'Faction.'" *Virginia Magazine of History and Biography* 89:3–26.

Minard, Rosemary, ed. 1975. *Womenfolk and Fairy Tales*. Boston: Houghton Mifflin.

Miner, Curtis. 1994. *Down at the Club: An Historical and Cultural Survey of Johnstown's Ethnic Clubs*. Johnstown, Pennsylvania: Johnstown Area Heritage Association.

Mintz, Jerome R. 1992. *Hasidic People: A Place in the New World*. Cambridge: Harvard University Press.

Mish, John L. 1949. "Folklore." In *Standard Dictionary of Folklore, Mythology, and Legend*, ed. Maria Leach, 401. New York: Funk and Wagnalls.

Mitchell, Arthur. 1881. *The Past in the Present: What Is Civilization?* New York: Harper and Brothers.

Mitchell, Brian. 1992. "'Political Correctness' vs. 'Traditional Values.'" *American Legion Magazine* (January), 22–24.

Mitchell, Roger E. 1992. "Tradition, Change, and Hmong Refugees." In *Creativity and Tradition in Folklore: New Directions*, ed. Simon J. Bronner, 263–75. Logan: Utah State University Press.

Mittelstadt, Mike. 1981. "SUNY Prof. Helps Others Explore 'Roots.'" *Vestal News* (May 14), 19.

"Modern-Day Amish Still Value Life's Simple Ways." 1991. *Detroit News* (July 24), B5.

Moerbeek, Kees. 1990. *Little Red Riding Hood.* Los Angeles: Intervisual Communications.

Montell, William Lynwood. 1983. *Don't Go up Kettle Creek: Verbal Legacy of the Upper Cumberland.* Knoxville: University of Tennessee Press.

Montenyohl, Eric L. 1989. "Richard M. Dorson and the Internationalization of American Folkloristics." *Western Folklore* 48:349–57.

Moonsammy, Rita Zorn, David Steven Cohen, and Lorraine E. Williams, eds. 1987. *Pinelands Folklife.* New Brunswick: Rutgers University Press.

Moore, Charles W., Kathryn Smith, and Peter Becker, eds. 1983. *Home Sweet Home: American Domestic Vernacular Architecture.* New York: Rizzoli.

Moore, David Chioni. 1994. "Routes: Alex Haley's *Roots* and the Rhetoric of Genealogy." *Transition* 64:4–21.

Moore, Pat. 1995. "Touring Amish Country: Travelers Take a Step Back in Time." *Chicago Tribune* (May 22), 8.

Moore, Willard B., ed. 1989. *Circles of Tradition: Folk Arts in Minnesota.* St. Paul: Minnesota Historical Society Press.

Morantz, Regina Markell. 1977. "The Scientist as Sex Crusader: Alfred C. Kinsey and American Culture." *American Quarterly* 29:563–89.

Morgan, John. 1990. *The Log House in East Tennessee.* Knoxville: University of Tennessee Press.

Morgan, Lewis Henry. 1974. *Ancient Society: Or Researches in the Lines of Human Progress from Savagery through Barbarism to Civilization.* 1877; rpt., Gloucester, Massachusetts: Peter Smith.

Morris, Elisabeth Woodbridge, ed. 1934. *Miss Wylie of Vassar.* New Haven: Yale University Press.

Morris, William, ed. 1976. *The American Heritage Dictionary of the English Language.* Boston: Houghton Mifflin.

Morrissette, Pat. 1932. "Paul Bunyan: An American Symbol." In *Folk-Say IV: The Land Is Ours*, ed. B. A. Botkin, 274–94. Norman: University of Oklahoma Press.

Moses, L. G. 1984. *The Indian Man: A Biography of James Mooney.* Urbana: University of Illinois Press.

Moss, Alfred A., Jr. 1981. *The American Negro Academy: Voice of the Talented Tenth.* Baton Rouge: Louisiana State University Press.

Moton, Robert. 1921. *Finding a Way Out: An Autobiography.* Garden City: Doubleday, Page.

———. 1929. *What the Negro Thinks.* Garden City: Doubleday, Page.

Muda, Tomohiro. 1997. "The Old in the New: Japan's Resilient Craftsmanship." *Pacific Friend* (March), 18–27.

Mullen, Patrick B. 1981. "A Traditional Storyteller in Changing Contexts." In *"And Other Neighborly Names": Social Process and Cultural Image in Texas Folklore*, ed. Richard Bauman and Roger D. Abrahams, 266–79. Austin: University of Texas Press.

———. 1988. *I Heard the Old Fishermen Say: Folklore of the Texas Gulf Coast.* 1978; rpt., Logan: Utah State University Press.

———. 1992. *Listening to Old Voices: Folklore, Life Stories, and the Elderly.* Urbana: University of Illinois Press.

———. 1996. "On Being a Folklorist in an English Department: Implications for Research." *Journal of Folklore Research* 33:48–55.

Murray, Daniel. 1904. "Color Problem in the United States." *Colored American* (December), 723–24.

Musäus, Johann Carl August. 1782–87. *Volksmärchen*. 5 vols. Gotha: Carl Wilhelm Ettinger.

Myerhoff, Barbara. 1978. *Number Our Days*. New York: Simon and Schuster.

———. 1992. *Remembered Lives: The Work of Ritual, Storytelling, and Growing Older*. Ann Arbor: University of Michigan Press.

Nabokov, Peter, and Robert Easton. 1989. *Native American Architecture*. New York: Oxford University Press.

Nash, Gary B. 1995a. "The History Standards Controversy and Social History." Supplement to *Journal of Social History* 29:39–49.

———. 1995b. "History Standards and Culture Wars." *Social Education* 59:5–7.

National Gallery of Art. 1987. *An American Sampler: Folk Art from the Shelburne Museum*. Washington, D.C.: National Gallery of Art.

Nelson, Marion, ed. 1994. *Material Culture and People's Art among the Norwegians in America*. Northfield, Minnesota: Norwegian-American Historical Association.

———. 1995. *Norwegian Folk Art: The Migration of a Tradition*. New York: Abbeville Press.

Nelson, Pamela B., ed. 1992. *Rites of Passage in America: Traditions of the Life Cycle*. Philadelphia: Balch Institute for Ethnic Studies.

Neustadt, Kathy. 1992. *Clambake: A History and Celebration of an American Tradition*. Amherst: University of Massachusetts Press.

Newall, Venetia. 1973. "The Jew as Witch Figure." In *The Witch Figure: Folklore Essays by a Group of Scholars in England Honouring the 75th Birthday of Katharine M. Briggs*, ed. Venetia Newall, 95–124. London: Routledge & Kegan Paul.

———. 1975. "The English Folklore Society under the Presidency of Haham Dr. Moses Gaster." In *Studies in the Cultural Life of the Jews in England*, ed. Dov Noy and Issachar Ben-Ami, 197–225. Jerusalem: Magnes Press, Hebrew University.

Newell, William Wells. 1888a. "English Folk-Tales in America." *Journal of American Folklore* 1:227–34.

———. 1888b. "Necessity of Collecting the Traditions of Native Races." *Journal of American Folklore* 1:162–63.

———. 1888c. "Notes and Queries." *Journal of American Folklore* 1:79–82.

———. 1888d. "On the Field and Work of a Journal of American Folklore." *Journal of American Folklore* 1:3–7.

———. 1889. "Editor's Note." *Journal of American Folklore* 2:1–2.

———. 1892. "Folk-Lore at the Columbian Exposition." *Journal of American Folklore* 5:239–40.

———. 1901. "Resignation." *Journal of American Folklore* 14:56.

———. 1992. *Games and Songs of American Children*. 1884; rpt., Baltimore: Clearfield.

Newman, Bruce. 1984a. "Super Star Wars: It's Magic Johnson against Larry Bird in the NBA Finals." *Sports Illustrated* (June 4), 34–43.

———. 1984b. "The Toasts of Both Coasts." *Sports Illustrated* (March 5), 12–15.

Nicolaisen, W. F. H. 1973. "Folklore and Geography: Towards an Atlas of American Folk Culture." *New York Folklore Quarterly* 29:3–20.

———. 1975. "Surveying and Mapping North American Culture." *Mid-South Folklore* 3:35–39.

———. 1983. "Folklore and … What?" *New York Folklore* 9:89–98.

———. 1984. "Names and Narratives." *Journal of American Folklore* 97:259–72.

————. 1990. "Why Tell Stories?" *Fabula* 31:5–10.

Nieto, Sonia. 1996. *Affirming Diversity: The Sociopolitical Context of Multicultural Education.* White Plains, New York: Longman.

Noble, Allen G., ed. 1992. *To Build in a New Land: Ethnic Landscapes in North America.* Baltimore: Johns Hopkins University Press.

Northall, G. F. 1892. *English Folk-Rhymes.* London: Kegan Paul, Trench, Trubner.

Noyes, Dorothy. 1989. *Uses of Tradition: Arts of Italian Americans in Philadelphia.* Philadelphia: Philadelphia Folklore Project, Samuel S. Fleisher Art Memorial.

Nugent, Frank S. 1938. "The Music Hall Presents Walt Disney's Delightful Fantasy, 'Snow White and the Seven Dwarfs'—Other New Films at Capitol and Criterion." *New York Times* (January 14), 21.

Nusz, Nancy J., ed. 1991. *Folklife in Education.* Special issue of *Southern Folklore* 48 (1).

O'Connor, Laura. 1995. "Slave Spirituals: Allegories of the Recovery from Pain." In *Folklore, Literature, and Cultural Theory: Collected Essays,* ed. Cathy Lynn Preston, 204–13. New York: Garland.

Ohrn, Steven, ed. 1984. *Passing Time and Traditions: Contemporary Iowa Folk Artists.* Ames: Iowa State University Press.

Oinas, Felix, ed. 1978. *Folklore, Nationalism, and Politics.* Columbus, Ohio: Slavica Press.

Old Penn Weekly Review. 1911. "Marion Dexter Learned, Ph.D., L.H.D." *Pennsylvania-German* 12:354–55.

Oliver, Paul. 1970. *Aspects of the Blues Tradition.* New York: Oak Publications.

————. 1984. *Songsters and Saints: Vocal Traditions on Race Records.* Cambridge: Cambridge University Press.

————. 1987. *Dwellings: The House across the World.* Austin: University of Texas Press.

————. 1989. "Handed-Down Architecture: Tradition and Transmission." In *Dwellings, Settlements and Tradition: Cross-Cultural Perspectives,* ed. Jean-Paul Bourdier and Nezar Alsayyad, 53–75. Lanham, Maryland: University Press of America.

————, ed. 1997. *Encyclopedia of Vernacular Architecture of the World.* Cambridge: Cambridge University Press.

Oliver, Paul, Ian Davis, and Ian Bentley. 1981. *Dunroamin: The Suburban Semi and Its Enemies.* London: Barrie & Jenkins.

Olrik, Axel. 1965. "Epic Laws of Folk Narrative." In *The Study of Folklore,* ed. Alan Dundes, 129–41. Englewood Cliffs, New Jersey: Prentice-Hall.

Olrik, M. Joergen. 1934. *Problems Relating Specifically to Ethnographical and Folk-Art Collections.* Paris: International Museums Office, League of Nations.

Opie, Peter, and Iona Opie. 1952. *Oxford Dictionary of Nursery Rhymes.* Oxford: Clarendon Press.

————. 1959. *The Lore and Language of Schoolchildren.* Oxford: Clarendon Press.

————. 1969. *Children's Games in Street and Playground.* Oxford: Oxford University Press.

————. 1985. *The Singing Game.* Oxford: Oxford University Press.

Oring, Elliott. 1976. "Three Functions of Folklore: Traditional Functionalism as Explanation in Folkloristics." *Journal of American Folklore* 89:67–80.

————. 1984a. "Dyadic Traditions." *Journal of Folklore Research* 21:19–28.

————, ed. 1984b. *Humor and the Individual.* Los Angeles: California Folklore Society.

————. 1986a. "Folk Narratives." In *Folk Groups and Folklore Genres,* ed. Elliott Oring, 121–46. Logan: Utah State University Press.

————. 1986b. "On the Concepts of Folklore." In *Folk Groups and Folklore Genres,* ed. Elliott Oring, 1–22. Logan: Utah State University Press.

———. 1992. *Jokes and Their Relations.* Lexington: University Press of Kentucky.

———. 1994. "The Arts, Artifacts, and Artifices of Identity." *Journal of American Folklore* 107:211–47.

———. 1996a. "Humor." In *American Folklore: An Encyclopedia,* ed. Jan Harold Brunvand, 374–76. New York: Garland.

———. 1996b. "Theorizing Trivia: A Thought Experiment." *Journal of Folklore Research* 33:241–44.

Otis, Charles P., ed. 1887. *Brüder Grimm, Kinder- und Hausmärchen.* New York: Henry Holt.

Owen, Mary Alicia. 1969. *Voodoo Tales, As Told among the Negroes of the Southwest.* 1893; rpt., New York: Negro Universities Press.

Page, Clarence. 1997. "Dershowitz's Lessons for Blacks." *Forward* (April 11), 7.

Page, Linda Garland, and Hilton Smith. 1993. *The Foxfire Book of Appalachian Toys and Games.* Chapel Hill: University of North Carolina Press.

Paredes, Américo. 1993. *Folklore and Culture on the Texas-Mexican Border.* Austin: University of Texas Press.

Paredes, Américo, and Ellen J. Stekert, eds. 1971. *The Urban Experience and Folk Tradition.* Austin: University of Texas Press.

Parillo, Vincent N. 1994. "Diversity in America: A Sociohistorical Analysis." *Sociological Forum* 9:523–45.

Parrington, Vernon Louis. 1930. *The Beginnings of Critical Realism in America, 1860–1920: Volume Three of Main Currents in American Thought.* New York: Harcourt, Brace, and World.

Parry, Milman. 1971. *The Making of Homeric Verse: The Collected Papers of Milman Parry,* ed. Adam Parry. Oxford: Clarendon Press.

Parsons, Elsie Clews. 1914. "Femininity and Conventionality." *American Academy of Political and Social Science* 56:47–53.

Parsons, William T. 1980–81. "Aldes un Neies/Old and New." *Pennsylvania Folklife* 30(2):94–95.

Patterson, Daniel W. 1979. *The Shaker Spiritual.* Princeton: Princeton University Press.

Patterson, Daniel W., James L. Peacock, and Ruel W. Tyson, Jr., eds. 1988. *Diversities of Gifts: Field Studies in Southern Religion.* Urbana: University of Illinois Press.

Patterson, Daniel W., and Charles G. Zug III, eds. 1990. *Arts in Earnest: North Carolina Folklife.* Durham, North Carolina: Duke University Press.

Peacock, James L. 1986. "The Creativity of Tradition in Indonesian Religion." *Journal of the History of Ideas* 44:105–13.

Pearson, Barry Lee. 1984. *"Sounds So Good to Me": The Bluesman's Story.* Philadelphia: University of Pennsylvania Press.

———. 1990. *Virginia Piedmont Blues: The Lives and Art of Two Virginia Bluesmen.* Philadelphia: University of Pennsylvania Press.

Peate, Iorwerth. 1960. "Review of *American Folklore* by Richard Dorson." *Gwerin* 3:61–62.

"Pennsylvania Dutch Seminars." 1952. *Pennsylvania Dutchman* 4, no. 3 (July): 1.

"Pennsylvania Dutch Seminars." 1953. *Pennsylvania Dutchman* 4, no. 15 (Easter): 1.

Pennsylvania Historical and Museum Commission. 1950. "The Pennsylvania Historical and Museum Commission, 1945–1950." Typescript, State Library of Pennsylvania, Harrisburg.

———. 1996. *An Image of Peace: The Penn Treaty Collection of Mr. and Mrs. Meyer P. Potamkin.* Harrisburg: Pennsylvania Historical and Museum Commission.

Pentikäinen, Juha. 1978. "Oral Transmission of Knowledge." In *Folklore in the Modern World*, ed. Richard M. Dorson, 237–52. The Hague: Mouton.

Peppard, Murray B. 1971. *Paths through the Forest: A Biography of the Brothers Grimm*. New York: Holt, Rinehart and Winston.

Perin, Constance. 1988. *Belonging in America: Reading between the Lines*. Madison: University of Wisconsin Press.

Perrault, Charles. 1697. *Contes de ma mère l'oye. Histoires ou contes du temps passé avec des moralités*. Paris: Claude Barbin.

Peters, Erskine. 1996. "Spirituals, African American." In *American Folklore: An Encyclopedia*, ed. Jan Harold Brunvand, 682–84. New York: Garland.

Peterson, Elizabeth. 1983. "American Sports and Folklore." In *Handbook of American Folklore*, ed. Richard M. Dorson, 257–64. Bloomington: Indiana University Press.

———, ed. 1996a. *The Changing Faces of Tradition: A Report on the Folk and Traditional Arts in the United States*. Washington, D.C.: National Endowment for the Arts.

———. 1996b. "Folk Arts Private Non-Profit Organizations." In *The Changing Faces of Tradition: A Report on the Folk and Traditional Arts in the United States*, ed. Elizabeth Peterson, 58–67. Washington, D.C.: National Endowment for the Arts.

Pfister, Joel. 1991. "The Americanization of Cultural Studies." *Yale Journal of Criticism* 4:199–229.

Philadelphia Branch of the American Folklore Society. [1893] 1987. "Hints for the Local Study of Folk-Lore in Philadelphia and Vicinity." In *Folklife Studies from the Gilded Age: Object, Rite, and Custom in Victorian America*, ed. Simon J. Bronner, 71–72. Ann Arbor: UMI Research Press.

Pike, Kenneth. 1967. *Language in Relation to a Unified Theory of the Structure of Human Behavior*. The Hague: Mouton.

Pitkin, Albert Hastings. 1918. *Early American Folk Pottery*. Hartford, Connecticut: Privately Published.

Pitts, Walter F. 1992. *Old Ship of Zion: The Afro-Baptist Ritual in the African Diaspora*. New York: Oxford University Press.

Pocius, Gerald L., ed. 1991. *Living in a Material World: Canadian and American Approaches to Material Culture*. St. John's, Newfoundland: Institute of Social and Economic Research.

———. 1995. "Art." *Journal of American Folklore* 108:413–31.

Pollard, Josephine. 1883. *Hours in Fairy Land*. New York: McLoughlin Bros.

Poole, Josephine. 1991. *Snow White*. New York: Alfred A. Knopf.

Popper, Karl. 1965. *Conjectures and Refutations: The Growth of Scientific Knowledge*. 2d ed. New York: Basic Books.

Porter, David, ed. 1997. *Internet Culture*. New York: Routledge.

Porter, Joseph C. 1986. *Paper Medicine Man: John Gregory Bourke and His American West*. Norman: University of Oklahoma Press.

Posen, I. Sheldon. 1986. *You Hear the Ice Talking: The Ways of People and Ice on Lake Champlain*. Plattsburgh, New York: Clinton-Essex-Franklin Library System.

Pound, Louise. 1922. *American Ballads and Songs*. New York: Charles Scribner's Sons.

———. 1987. *Nebraska Folklore*. 1959; rpt., Lincoln: University of Nebraska Press.

Preston, Cathy Lynn. 1994. "'Cinderella' as a Dirty Joke: Gender, Multivocality, and the Polysemic Text." *Western Folklore* 53:27–49.

———. 1996. "Cultural Studies." In *American Folklore: An Encyclopedia*, ed. Jan Harold Brunvand, 183–85. New York: Garland.

Preston, Michael J. 1994. "Traditional Humor from the Fax Machine." *Western Folklore* 53:147–70.

———. 1996a. "Computer Folklore." In *American Folklore: An Encyclopedia*, ed. Jan Harold Brunvand, 154–55. New York: Garland.

———. 1996b. "Xeroxlore." In *American Folklore: An Encyclopedia*, ed. Jan Harold Brunvand, 769–70. New York: Garland.

Price, Richard, and Sally Price. 1995. *On the Mall: Presenting Maroon Tradition-Bearers at the 1992 Festival of American Folklife*. Bloomington: Special Publications of the Folklore Institute, Indiana University.

Propp, Vladimir. 1968. *Morphology of the Folktale*. Trans. Laurence Scott and rev. Louis A. Wagner. 2d ed., Austin: University of Texas Press.

———. 1984. *Theory and History of Folklore*. Trans. Ariadna Y. Martin and Richard P. Martin. Minneapolis: University of Minnesota Press.

"Prosperity out of Fantasy." 1938. *New York Times* (May 2), 16.

Puckett, Newbell Niles. 1926. *Folk Beliefs of the Southern Negro*. Chapel Hill: University of North Carolina Press.

———. 1929. "Negro Life and Lore." *Saturday Review of Literature* 5 (November 2):339–40.

Pukui, Mary Wiggin. 1933. *Hawaiian Folk Tales*. 3d series. Poughkeepsie: Folklore Foundation.

Puschmann-Nalenz, Barbara. 1987. "Black Novel as History, History as Black Novel: Eine Hybrid Forme des modernen Romans." *Die Neueren-Sprachen* 86:217–32.

Quayle, Dan. 1992. "A Great Society Is Based on Values." *St. Louis Post-Dispatch* (May 24), B3.

———. 1994. *Standing Firm: A Vice-Presidential Memoir*. New York: Harper Collins.

———. 1995. "Multiculturalism Sounds Nice, But It Has Its Dangers." *USA Today* (November 7), A11.

Quimby, Ian M. G., and Scott T. Swank, eds. 1980. *Perspectives on American Folk Art*. New York: W. W. Norton.

Racine, Marty. 1995. "Amish Community Takes Visitors Back." *Houston Chronicle* (October 22), H1.

Radin, Max. 1935. "Tradition." In *Encyclopedia of the Social Sciences*, ed. E. R. A. Seligman, 15:62–67. New York: MacMillan.

Radin, Paul. 1970. "Introduction to the Torchbook Edition." In *The Origins of Culture*, by Edward Burnett Tylor, ix–xv. Gloucester, Massachusetts: Peter Smith.

Radner, Joan Newton, ed. 1993. *Feminist Messages: Coding in Women's Folk Culture*. Urbana: University of Illinois Press.

Ramsay, John M. 1996. "Berea College." In *American Folklore: An Encyclopedia*, ed. Jan Harold Brunvand, 80. New York: Garland.

Randolph, Vance. 1952. *Who Blowed Up the Church House? and Other Ozark Folk Tales*. New York: Columbia University Press.

———. 1955. *The Devil's Pretty Daughter, and Other Ozark Folk Tales*. New York: Columbia University Press.

———. 1958. *Sticks in the Knapsack, and Other Ozark Folk Tales*. New York: Columbia University Press.

———. 1964. *Ozark Magic and Folklore*. 1947; rpt., New York: Dover.

———. 1976. *Pissing in the Snow and Other Ozark Folktales*. Urbana: University of Illinois Press.

———. 1982. *Ozark Folksongs*. Ed. Norm Cohen. Urbana: University of Illinois Press.

———. 1987. *Ozark Folklore: An Annotated Bibliography*. 2 vols. Columbia: University of Missouri Press.

Raphael, Ray. 1988. *The Men from the Boys: Rites of Passage in Male America.* Lincoln: University of Nebraska.

Rapoport, Amos. 1989. "On the Attributes of 'Tradition.'" In *Dwellings, Settlements and Tradition: Cross-Cultural Perspectives,* ed. Jean-Paul Bourdier and Nezar Alsayyad, 77–105. Lanham, Maryland: University Press of America.

Rayfield, J. R. 1972. "What Is a Story?" *American Anthropologist* 74:1085–1106.

Redfield, Robert. 1950. *The Little Community.* Chicago: University of Chicago Press.

Reed, Henry M. 1987. *Decorated Furniture of the Mahantongo Valley.* Lewisburg, Pennsylvania: University of Pennsylvania Press for Center Gallery, Bucknell University.

Reichard, Gladys. 1943. "Franz Boas and Folklore." *Memoirs of the American Anthropological Association* 61:52–57.

"Report on Graduates and Ex-Students." 1894. *Southern Workman* 23(June):106.

Reuss, Richard, ed. 1975. *Roads into Folklore.* Bloomington, Indiana: Folklore Forum Bibliographic and Special Series, no. 14.

Rhoads, William B. 1985. "The Colonial Revival and the Americanization of Immigrants." In *The Colonial Revival in America,* ed. Alan Axelrod, 341–61. New York: W. W. Norton.

Richmond, W. Edson. 1981. "Richard Mercer Dorson, March 12, 1916–September 11, 1981." *Journal of the Folklore Institute* 18:95–96.

———. 1996a. "Child, Francis James (1825–1896)." In *American Folklore: An Encyclopedia,* ed. Jan Harold Brunvand, 136. New York: Garland.

———. 1996b. "Gummere, Francis Barton (1855–1919)." In *American Folklore: An Encyclopedia,* ed. Jan Harold Brunvand, 353. New York: Garland.

Riedl, Norbert. 1966. "Folklore and the Study of Material Aspects of Folk Culture." *Journal of American Folklore* 79:557–62.

Riesman, David. 1950. *The Lonely Crowd: A Study of the Changing American Character.* New Haven: Yale University Press.

Rieuwerts, Sigrid. 1996. "The Folk-Ballad: The Illegitimate Child of the Popular Ballad." *Journal of Folklore Research* 33:221–26.

Rikoon, J. Sanford. 1988. *Threshing in the Midwest, 1820–1940: A Study of Traditional Culture and Technological Change.* Bloomington: Indiana University Press.

Ring, Constance Varney, Samuel Bayard, and Tristram Coffin. 1953. "Mid-Hudson Song and Verse." *Journal of American Folklore* 66:43–68.

Rinzler, Ralph. 1976. "A Festival to Cherish Our Differences." In *1976 Festival of American Folklife,* ed. Bess Lomax Hawes and Susanne Roschwalb, 7. Washington, D.C.: Smithsonian Institution.

Riordan, James. 1985. *The Woman in the Moon, and Other Tales of Forgotten Heroines.* New York: Dial Books for Young Readers.

Ripley, S. Dillon. 1976. "In Celebration…." *1976 Festival of American Folklife,* ed. Bess Lomax Hawes and Susanne Roschwalb, 2–3. Washington, D.C.: Smithsonian Institution.

Robacker, Earl F. 1943. *Pennsylvania German Literature: Changing Trends from 1683 to 1942.* Philadelphia: University of Pennsylvania Press.

———. 1959. "The Rise of Interest in Folk Art." *Pennsylvania Folklife* 10(1):20–29.

Roberts, Helen H. 1925. "A Study of Folk Song Variants Based on Field Work in Jamaica." *Journal of American Folklore* 38:149–216.

———. 1928. "Lullabies in Jamaica." *Journal of American Folklore* 41:588–91.

Roberts, John W. 1989. *From Trickster to Badman: The Black Folk Hero in Slavery and Freedom.* Philadelphia: University of Pennsylvania Press.

Roberts, Leonard W. 1955. *South from Hell-fer-Sartin: Kentucky Mountain Folk Tales.* Lexington: University of Kentucky Press.

Roberts, Sam. 1995. *Who We Are: A Portrait of America Based on the Latest U.S. Census*. New York: Times Books.

Roberts, Steven V. 1990. "The Culture Wars of 1990." *U.S. News and World Report* (June 25), 22–24.

———. 1994. "America's New Crusade." *U.S. News and World Report* (August 1), 26–30.

Roberts, W. Sean. 1995. "Pennsylvania's Amish Add Small Business to Farming." *Christian Science Monitor* (November 9), 9.

Roberts, Warren E. 1984. *Log Buildings of Southern Indiana*. Bloomington, Indiana: Trickster Press.

———. 1988. *Viewpoints on Folklife: Looking at the Overlooked*. Ann Arbor: UMI Research Press.

Rocco, Emma Scogna. 1990. *Italian Wind Bands: A Surviving Tradition in the Milltowns of Pennsylvania*. New York: Garland.

Roemer, Danielle M. 1977. "A Social Interactional Analysis of Anglo Children's Folklore: Catches and Narratives." Ph.D. diss., University of Texas at Austin.

———. 1994. "Photocopy Lore and the Naturalization of the Corporate Body." *Journal of American Folklore* 107:121–38.

Rölleke, Heinz. 1988. "New Results of Research on *Grimms' Fairy Tales*." In *The Brothers Grimm and Folktale*, ed. James M. McGlathery, 101–11. Urbana: University of Illinois Press.

Roosevelt, Theodore. 1926a. *American Ideals, The Strenuous Life, Realizable Ideals*. New York: Charles Scribner's Sons.

———. 1926b. *Literary Essays*. New York: Charles Scribner's Sons.

Roseberry, William. 1992. "Multiculturalism and the Challenge of Anthropology." *Social Research* 59:841–58.

Rosenberg, Bruce A. 1988. *Can These Bones Live? The Art of the American Folk Preacher*. Rev. ed. Urbana: University of Illinois Press.

Rosenberg, Neil V., ed. 1993. *Transforming Tradition: Folk Music Revivals Examined*. Urbana: University of Illinois Press.

Rosenberger, Jesse Leonard. 1923. *The Pennsylvania Germans*. Chicago: University of Chicago Press.

———. 1929. *In Pennsylvania-German Land, 1928–29*. Chicago: University of Chicago Press.

Rosenzweig, Roy. 1997. "How Americans Use and Think about the Past: Implications for the Teaching of History." Paper delivered to the Japan American Studies Association Meeting, Aichi University of Education.

Roth, Michael. 1995. *The Ironist's Cage: Memory, Trauma, and the Construction of History*. New York: Columbia University Press.

Roth, Rodris. 1985. "The New England, or 'Old Tyme,' Kitchen Exhibit at Nineteenth-Century Fairs." In *The Colonial Revival in America*, ed. Alan Axelrod, 159–83. New York: W. W. Norton.

Rounds, Glen. 1936. *Ol' Paul, The Mighty Logger*. New York: Holiday House.

Rourke. Constance. 1931. *American Humor: A Study of the National Character*. New York: Harcourt, Brace.

———. 1942. *The Roots of American Culture and Other Essays*. New York: Harcourt, Brace, and World.

———. 1959. *American Humor: A Study of the National Character*. 1931; rpt., New York: Harcourt Brace Jovanovich.

Rowe, Karen E. 1979. "Feminism and Fairy Tales." *Women's Studies* 6:237–57.

Rubin, Joan Shelley. 1980. *Constance Rourke and American Culture.* Chapel Hill: University of North Carolina Press.

Rumford, Beatrix T. 1980. "Uncommon Art of the Common People: A Review of Trends in the Collecting and Exhibiting of American Folk Art." In *Perspectives on American Folk Art*, ed. Ian M. G. Quimby and Scott T. Swank, 13–53. New York: W. W. Norton.

Rumford, Beatrix T., and Carolyn J. Weekley. 1989. *Treasures of American Folk Art from the Abby Aldrich Rockefeller Folk Art Center.* Boston: Little, Brown.

Rutherford, Frank. 1971. *All the Way to Pennywell: Children's Rhymes of the North East.* Durham, England: University of Durham Institute of Education.

Rutherford, Susan D. 1983. "Funny in Deaf—Not in Hearing." *Journal of American Folklore* 96:310–22.

Ryan, Joanne. 1982. "Where Are the 'Folk' in Folk Art?" *Craft International* 1:8.

Rydell, Robert W. 1984. *All the World's a Fair: Visions of Empire at American International Expositions, 1876–1916.* Chicago: University of Chicago Press.

———. 1989. "The Culture of Imperial Abundance: World's Fairs in the Making of American Culture." In *Consuming Visions: Accumulation and Display of Goods in America, 1880–1920*, ed. Simon J. Bronner, 191–216. New York: W. W. Norton.

Safire, William. 1989. "Praxis Makes Perfect." *New York Times Magazine* (June 11), 20.

Saitsu, Yumiko. 1996. "Discourse That Creates *Minzoku Bunkazai* (Folk Cultural Properties)." *Machikaneyama Ronso* 30:47–62.

Sajna, Mike. 1990. *Buck Fever: The Deer Hunting Tradition in Pennsylvania.* Pittsburgh: University of Pittsburgh Press.

Sakaiya, Taichi. 1993. *What Is Japan? Contradictions and Transformations.* Trans. Steven Karpa. New York: Kodansha.

Sakane, Kahori. 1997. "Starting the Year with Tradition." *Daily Yomiuri* (January 15), 9.

Salzman, Jack, ed. 1986. *American Studies: An Annotated Bibliography.* 3 vols. London: Cambridge University Press.

Samuelson, Sue. 1983. "Notes on a Sociology of Folklore as a Science." *New York Folklore* 9:13–20.

Sandburg, Carl. 1927. *The American Songbag.* New York: Harcourt Brace.

———. 1936. *The People, Yes.* New York: Harcourt Brace.

Sanches, Mary, and Barbara Kirshenblatt-Gimblett. 1976. "Children's Traditional Speech Play and Child Language." In *Speech Play: Research and Resources for the Study of Linguistic Creativity*, ed. Barbara Kirshenblatt-Gimblett, 65–110. Philadelphia: University of Pennsylvania Press.

Sanderson, Stewart F., and E. Estyn Evans. 1970. "The Academic Status of Folklore in Britain." *Journal of the Folklore Institute* 7:101–9.

San Souci, Robert D. 1993. *Cut from the Same Cloth: American Women of Myth, Legend, and Tall Tale.* New York: Philomel.

Santino, Jack, ed. 1985. *Healing, Magic, and Religion.* Los Angeles: California Folklore Society.

———. 1992a. "The Folk *Assemblage* of Autumn: Tradition and Creativity in Halloween Folk Art." In *Folk Art and Art Worlds*, ed. John Michael Vlach and Simon J. Bronner, 151–69. 1986; rpt, Logan: Utah State University Press.

———. 1992b. "Yellow Ribbons and Seasonal Flags: The Folk Assemblage of War." *Journal of American Folklore* 105:19–33.

———. 1994a. *All around the Year: Holidays and Celebrations in American Life.* Urbana: University of Illinois Press.

————, ed. 1994b. *Halloween and Other Festivals of Death and Life.* Knoxville: University of Tennessee Press.

————. 1996. *New Old-Fashioned Ways: Holidays and Popular Culture.* Knoxville: University of Tennessee Press.

Santoli, Al. 1988. *New Americans: An Oral History.* New York: Ballantine Books.

Sayers, Stephen. 1986. "Folklore as Science." *Talking Folklore* 1:22–35.

Scarborough, William S. 1903. "The Educated Negro and His Mission." *American Negro Academy* 8:3.

Schamschula, Eleonore. 1996. *A Pioneer of American Folklore: Karl Knortz and His Collections.* Moscow, Idaho: University of Idaho Press.

Schantz, F. J. F. 1900. *The Domestic Life and Characteristics of the Pennsylvania-German Pioneer.* Lancaster: Pennsylvania German Society.

Schechter, Harold. 1988. *The Bosom Serpent: Folklore and Popular Art.* Iowa City: University of Iowa Press.

Scherbatskoy, Mary. 1976. *Five Children's Games and Cultural Activities from Chinese Tradition.* Washington, D.C.: Smithsonian Institution.

Scheub, Harold. 1977. "Performance of Oral Narrative." In *Frontiers of Folklore,* ed. William R. Bascom, 54–78. Boulder, Colorado: Westview Press.

Schickel, Richard. 1968. *The Disney Version: The Life, Times, Art and Commerce of Walt Disney.* New York: Avon.

Schlesinger, Arthur, Jr. 1992. *The Disuniting of America: Reflections on a Multicultural Society.* New York: W. W. Norton.

Schneider, Keith. 1986. "Working 80 acres, Amish Prosper amid Crisis." *New York Times* (August 28), A10.

Schoemaker, George H., ed. 1990. *The Emergence of Folklore in Everyday Life: A Fieldguide and Sourcebook.* Bloomington, Indiana: Trickster Press.

Schoepperle, Gertrude. 1920. "Review of *Celtic Mythology.*" *Journal of American Folklore* 33:170–72.

————. 1960. *Tristan and Isolt: A Study of the Sources of the Romance.* 1913; rpt., New York: B. Franklin.

Schreiner, Olive. 1911. *Women and Labor.* New York: Frederick A. Stokes.

Schultz, Franz, ed. 1924. *Die Märchen der Brüder Grimm in der Urform nach der Handschrift.* Offenbach am Main, Germany: Kingspor.

Scieszka, Jon. 1991. *The Frog Prince Continued.* New York: Viking.

Scott, Janny. 1997. "An Appomattox in the Culture Wars." *New York Times Weekly Review* (May 25), 1–4.

Sennett, Richard. 1974. *The Fall of Public Man: On the Social Psychology of Capitalism.* New York: Vintage.

Shaler, Nathaniel Southgate. 1884. "The Negro Problem." *Atlantic Monthly* 45:696–709.

————. 1886. "Race Prejudices." *Atlantic Monthly* 58:510–18.

————. 1890. "Science and the African Problem." *Atlantic Monthly* 66:36–45.

————. 1893. "European Peasants and Immigrants." *Atlantic Monthly* 71:646–55.

————. 1895. "Scientific Aspects of the Negro Question." *Public Opinion* 18:147.

————. 1900. "The Future of the Negro in the Southern States." *Popular Science Monthly* 57:147–56.

Sharp, Cecil, and Maud Karpeles. 1932. *English Folk Songs from the Southern Appalachians.* 2 vols. London: Oxford University Press.

Sharps, Ronald LaMarr. 1991. "Happy Days and Sorrow Songs: Interpretations of Negro Folklore by Black Intellectuals." Ph.D. diss., George Washington University.

Sharrow, Gregory, ed. 1992. *Many Cultures, One People: A Multicultural Handbook about Vermont for Teachers.* Middlebury: Vermont Folklife Center.

Shay, Frank. 1930. *Here's Audacity! American Legendary Heroes.* New York: Macaulay.

Sheehy, Collen Josephine. 1991. "The Flamingo in the Garden: Artifice, Aesthetics, and Popular Taste in American Yard Art." Ph.D. diss., University of Minnesota.

Shephard, Esther. 1924. *Paul Bunyan.* New York: Harcourt Brace.

Sherman, Josepha. 1992. *A Sampler of Jewish American Folklore.* Little Rock: August House.

Sherman, Sharon. 1995. *Chainsaw Sculptor: The Art of J. Chester "Skip" Armstrong.* Jackson: University Press of Mississippi.

Sherzer, Joel. 1976. "Play Languages: Implication for (Socio) Linguistics." In *Speech Play: Research and Resources for the Study of Linguistic Creativity*, ed. Barbara Kirshenblatt-Gimblett, 19–36. Philadelphia: University of Pennsylvania Press.

Shi, David E. 1985. *The Simple Life: Plain Living and High Thinking in American Culture.* New York: Oxford University Press.

Shils, Edward. 1971. "Tradition." *Comparative Studies in Society and History* 13:122–59.

———. 1981. *Tradition.* Chicago: University of Chicago Press.

Shiver, Sam M. 1941. "Finger Rhymes." *Southern Folklore Quarterly* 5:221–34.

Shoemaker, Alfred L. 1940. "Studies on the Pennsylvania German Dialect of the Amish Community in Arthur, Illinois." Ph.D. diss., University of Illinois.

———. 1949a. "Pennsylvania Dutch Folklore." *Pennsylvania Dutchman* (May 5), 1.

———. 1949b. "Stop Sneering." *Pennsylvania Dutchman* (May 5), 3.

———. 1951. *Traditional Rhymes and Jingles of the Pennsylvania Dutch.* Lancaster: Pennsylvania Dutch Folklore Center.

———. 1953. *Hex No!* Lancaster: Pennsylvania Dutch Folklore Center.

———. 1954. *The Pennsylvania Dutch Country.* Lancaster: Pennsylvania Dutch Folklore Center.

———, ed. 1955. *1955 Tourist Guide through the Dutch Country.* Lancaster: Pennsylvania Dutch Folklore Center.

———, ed. 1956. *1956 Tourist Guide through the Dutch Country.* Lancaster: Pennsylvania Dutch Folklore Center.

———. 1957. "The Pennsylvania Dutch Village." *Pennsylvania Folklife* 8, no. 3 (spring): 7.

———, ed. 1959a. *Amish and Pennsylvania Dutch Tourist Guide.* Kutztown: Pennsylvania Folklife Society.

———. 1959b. *Christmas in Pennsylvania: A Folk Cultural Study.* Kutztown: Pennsylvania Folklife Society.

———, ed. 1959c. *The Pennsylvania Barn.* Kutztown: Pennsylvania Folklife Society.

———. 1960. *Eastertide in Pennsylvania: A Folk Cultural Study.* Kutztown: Pennsylvania Folklife Society.

Shoemaker, Henry W. 1907. *Pennsylvania Mountain Stories.* Reading: Bright Printing.

———. 1912. *Tales of the Bald Eagle Mountains.* Reading: Bright Printing.

———. 1913. *Susquehanna Legends Collected in Central Pennsylvania.* Reading: Bright Printing.

———. 1914. *Black Forest Souvenirs, Collected in Northern Pennsylvania.* Legends of the West Branch of the Susquehanna. Reading: Bright-Faust.

———. 1916. *Juniata Memories: Legends Collected in Central Pennsylvania.* Philadelphia: J. J. McVey.

———. 1917a. *The Abuse of Wealth.* Address to Ministerial Association of Williamsport, Pennsylvania, April 16. Altoona: Altoona Tribune Press.

———. 1917b. *Pennsylvania Folk Lore: Its Origin and Preservation.* Altoona: Times Tribune.

———. 1922. "The Folk Lore and Legends of Clinton County." Address to Clinton County Historical Society, Lock Haven, Pennsylvania, March 15. Typescript, Annie Halenbake Ross Library, Lock Haven, Pennsylvania.

———. 1923. *True Stories of the Pennsylvania Mountains.* Altoona: Altoona Tribune Press.

———. 1924. *More Allegheny Episodes: Legends and Traditions, Old and New Gathered among the Pennsylvania Mountains.* Altoona: Mountain City Press.

———. 1931. *Mountain Minstrelsy of Pennsylvania.* Philadelphia: Newman McGirr.

———. 1939. *Conserving Pennsylvania's Historic Past.* Harrisburg: Pennsylvania Historical Commission.

———. 1943. "Pennsylvania Folklore Society." *Journal of American Folklore* 56:180–81.

Shorto, Russell. 1990. *Cinderella: The Untold Story.* New York: Birch Lane.

Showalter, Michael S. 1996. "An Image of Peace: Penn's Treaty with the Indians." In *An Image of Peace: The Penn Treaty Collection of Mr. and Mrs. Meyer P. Potamkin,* 20–34. Harrisburg: Pennsylvania Historical and Museum Commission.

Shuldiner, David P. 1997. *Folklore, Culture, and Aging: A Research Guide.* Westport, Connecticut: Greenwood Press.

Siefert, Marsha. 1989. "Style as Substance: Dorson as an Author of Folklore Scholarship." *Journal of Folklore Research* 26:61–72.

Sigler, Jay A., ed. 1969. *The Conservative Tradition in American Thought: An Anthology.* New York: Putnam.

Simpson, Jacqueline. 1989. "Folklore in *Folklore*: Trends Since 1959." *Folklore* 100:3–8.

Simpson, K. 1984. "When East Meets West." *Sport* (June), 54–59.

Singer, Isaac Bashevis. 1964. "Sholem Aleichem: Spokesman for a People." *New York Times* (September 20) 2:1.

Sink, Susan. 1983. *Traditional Crafts and Craftsmanship in America: A Selected Bibliography.* Washington, D.C.: American Folklife Center, Library of Congress.

Siporin, Steve. 1992. *American Folk Masters: The National Heritage Fellows.* New York: Harry N. Abrams.

Sitton, Thad. 1995. *Backwoodsmen: Stockmen and Hunters along a Big Thicket River Valley.* Norman: University of Oklahoma Press.

Sizemore, Jean. 1994. *Ozark Vernacular Houses: A Study of Rural Homeplaces in the Arkansas Ozarks, 1830–1930.* Fayetteville: University of Arkansas Press.

Skinner, Charles M. 1896. *Myths and Legends of Our Own Land.* Philadelphia: J. B. Lippincott.

———. 1903. *American Myths and Legends.* Philadelphia: J. B. Lippincott.

Skirbekk, Gunnar, ed. 1983. *Praxeology: An Anthology.* Bergen, Norway: Universitetsforlaget.

Sklar, Robert. 1971. "Cultural History and American Studies: Past, Present and Future." *American Studies: An International Newsletter* 10:3–9.

Slobin, Mark. 1982. *Tenement Songs: The Popular Music of the Jewish Immigrants.* Urbana: University of Illinois Press.

Smiley, Portia. 1919. "Folklore from Virginia, South Carolina, Georgia, Alabama, and Florida." *Journal of American Folklore* 32:357–83.

Smith, Craig. 1995. "Dan Quayle and Family Values: Epideictic Appeals in Political Campaigns." *Southern Communication Journal* 60:152–64.

Smith, Elmer Lewis. 1961. *The Amish Today: An Analysis of Their Beliefs, Behavior and Contemporary Problems.* Allentown: Pennsylvania German Folklore Society.

Smith, H. W. 1995. *The Myth of Japanese Homogeneity: Social-Ecological Diversity in Education and Socialization.* Comack, New York: Nova Science.

Smith, Henry Nash. 1950. *Virgin Land: The American West as Symbol and Myth.* Cambridge: Harvard University Press.

Smith, Joan. 1992. "Traditional Family Values." *San Francisco Chronicle* (June 14), D1.

Smith, Paul. 1985. *The Complete Book of Office Mis-Practice.* London: Routledge and Kegan Paul.

———. 1986. *Reproduction Is Fun: A Book of Photocopy Joke Sheets.* London: Routledge and Kegan Paul.

Smith, Robert J., and Jerry Stannard, eds. 1989. *The Folk: Identity, Landscapes and Lores.* University of Kansas Publications in Anthropology, no. 17. Lawrence: Department of Anthropology, University of Kansas.

Snyder, Louis L. 1959. "Nationalistic Aspects of the Grimm Brothers' Fairy Tales." *Journal of Social Psychology* 23:219–21.

Sobnosky, Matthew J. 1993. "Fighting the Culture War: Traditional Values and the Future of the Republican Party." *American Behavioral Scientist* 37:308–14.

Sollors, Werner. 1997. *Neither Black nor White Yet Both: Thematic Explorations of Interracial Literature.* New York: Oxford.

"Some Amish to Use Tractors: Those Opposed May Move." 1995. *New York Times* (April 16) 1:20.

Sommers, Laurie Kay. 1996. "Definitions of 'Folk' and 'Lore' in the Smithsonian Festival of American Folklife." *Journal of Folklore Research* 33:227–31.

Spencer, Anna Garlin. 1911. "The Primitive Working-Woman." *Forum* 46:546–48.

Spencer, Herbert. 1873. *The Study of Sociology.* New York: D. Appleton.

Spencer, Martin E. 1994. "Multiculturalism, 'Political Correctness,' and the Politics of Identity." *Sociological Forum* 9:547–67.

Spengler, Oswald. 1962. *The Decline of the West.* New York: Alfred A. Knopf.

Spier, Leslie. 1959. "Some Central Elements in the Legacy." In *The Anthropology of Franz Boas: Essays on the Centennial of His Birth,* ed. Walter Goldschmidt, 146–56. Memoir no. 89. San Francisco: American Anthropological Association and Howard Chandler.

Spiller, Robert. 1973. "Unity and Diversity in the Study of American Culture: The American Studies Association in Perspective." *American Quarterly* 25:611–18.

Spivak, Lawrence E., and Charles Angoff, eds. 1944. *The American Mercury Reader.* Philadelphia: Blakiston.

Spottswood, Richard K. 1990. *Ethnic Music on Records: A Discography of Ethnic Recordings Produced in the United States, 1893–1942.* 7 vols. Urbana: University of Illinois Press.

Spradley, James P., and Brenda J. Mann. 1975. *The Cocktail Waitress: Woman's Work in a Man's World.* New York: John Wiley and Sons.

Sprug, Joseph W. 1994. *Index to Fairy Tales, 1987–1992.* Metuchen, New Jersey: Scarecrow Press.

Stahl, Sandra Dolby. 1989. *Literary Folkloristics and the Personal Narrative.* Bloomington: Indiana University Press.

Stahr, J. S. 1910. "The Rev. Joseph Henry Dubbs, D.D., LL.D.: An Appreciation." *The Pennsylvania-German* 11:420–22.

Staub, Shalom. 1982. "The Work of the Office of State Folklife Programs." *Keystone Folklore,* n.s., 1:1–7.

———, ed. 1988. *Craft and Community: Traditional Arts in Contemporary Society.* Philadelphia: Balch Institute for Ethnic Studies and the Pennsylvania Heritage Affairs Commission.

Stearns, Sharon. 1946. *Snow White and the Seven Dwarfs.* Chicago: Wilcox and Follett.

Stein, Joseph. 1966. *Fiddler on the Roof: Based on Sholom Aleichem's Stories.* New York: Pocket Books.

Steinberg, Stephen. 1981. *The Ethnic Myth: Race, Ethnicity, and Class in America.* New York: Atheneum.

Steinfirst, Susan. 1992. *Folklore and Folklife: A Guide to English-Language Reference Sources.* 2 vols. New York: Garland.

Stekert, Ellen J. 1987. "Autobiography of a Woman Folklorist." *Journal of American Folklore* 100:578–85.

Stern, Stephen. 1989. "Dorson's Use and Adaptation of Prevailing Historical Models of American Folklore." *Journal of Folklore Research* 26:43–50.

———. 1991. "The Influence of Diversity on Folklore Studies in the Decades of the 1980s and '90s." *Western Folklore* 50:21–27.

Stern, Stephen, and John Allan Cicala, eds. 1991. *Creative Ethnicity: Symbols and Strategies of Contemporary Ethnic Life.* Logan: Utah State University Press.

Sternberg, Thomas. 1851. *The Dialect and Folk-Lore of Northamptonshire.* London: J. R. Smith.

Stevens, James. 1925. *Paul Bunyan.* New York: Alfred Knopf.

———. 1932. *The Saginaw Paul Bunyan.* New York: Alfred Knopf.

———. 1947. *Paul Bunyan's Bears.* Seattle: F. McCaffrey.

———. 1950. "Folklore and the Artist." *American Mercury* 70:343–49.

Stevens, Phillips, Jr., ed. 1984. "Folklore in Buffalo." Special issue of *New York Folklore* 10, nos. 3–4.

Stevens, Sylvester K. 1965. "An Historian Looks at Folklore." In *Two Penny Ballads and Four Dollar Whiskey: A Pennsylvania Folklore Miscellany,* ed. Kenneth S. Goldstein and Robert H. Byington, ix–xi. Hatboro, Pennsylvania: Folklore Associates.

Stevens, Sylvester K., and Donald H. Kent. 1947. *Conserving Pennsylvania's Historical Heritage.* Harrisburg: Publications of the Pennsylvania Historical and Museum Commission.

Stewart, Susan. 1991. *Crimes of Writing: Problems in the Containment of Representation.* New York: Oxford University Press.

St. George, Robert. 1995. "Folklore." In *A Companion to American Thought,* ed. Richard Wightman Fox and James T. Kloppenberg, 239–41. Oxford: Blackwell.

Stilgoe, John R. 1982. *Common Landscape of America, 1580 to 1845.* New Haven: Yale University Press.

Stillinger, Elizabeth. 1980. *The Antiquers.* New York: Alfred A. Knopf.

Stocking, George W., Jr. 1968. *Race, Culture, and Evolution: Essays in the History of Anthropology.* New York: Free Press.

———., ed. 1974. *A Franz Boas Reader: The Shaping of American Anthropology, 1883–1911.* Chicago: University of Chicago Press.

———. 1982. *Race, Culture, and Evolution: Essays in the History of Anthropology.* 1968; rpt., Chicago: University of Chicago Press.

———. 1987. *Victorian Anthropology.* New York: Free Press.

Stoeltje, Beverly J. 1988. "Introduction: Feminist Revisions." *Journal of Folklore Research* 25:141–54.

"The Stoll Report." 1997. *Forward* (March 28), 5.

Stone, Kay F. 1986. "Feminist Approaches to the Interpretation of Fairy Tales." In *Fairy Tales and Society: Illusion, Allusion, and Paradigm,* ed. Ruth B. Bottigheimer, 229–36. Philadelphia: University of Pennsylvania Press.

———. 1988. "Three Transformations of Snow White." In *The Brothers Grimm and Folktale,* ed. James M. McGlathery, 52–65. Urbana: University of Illinois Press.

Stoudt, John Baer. 1915. *The Folklore of the Pennsylvania-German.* Lancaster: Pennsylvania German Society.

Stoudt, John Joseph. 1973. *Sunbonnets and Shoofly Pies: A Pennsylvania Dutch Cultural History.* New York: Castle Books.

Stow, Charles Messer. 1927. "Primitive Art in America." *Antiquarian* 8(May):20–24.

Straparola, Giovanni Francesco. 1894. *The Nights of Straparola*. Trans. W. G. Waters. 2 vols. London: Lawrence and Bullen.

Strauss, Anselm. 1978. "A Social World Perspective." In *Studies in Symbolic Interaction*, ed. Norman K. Denzin, vol. 1, 119–28. Greenwich, Connecticut: JAI Press.

Studer, Norman. 1962. "The Place of Folklore in Education." *New York Folklore Quarterly* 18:3–12.

Sullivan, C. W., III. 1992. "Learning the Structure of Traditional Narrative." *Children's Folklore Review* 15:17–24.

Sumner, William Graham. 1906. *Folkways: A Study of the Sociological Importance of Usages, Manners, Customs, Mores and Morals*. Boston: Ginn.

Sundquist, Eric J. 1995. "The Literature of Expansion and Race." In *The Cambridge History of American Literature: Volume 2, 1820–1865*, ed. Sacvan Bercovitch, 125–328. Cambridge: Cambridge University Press.

Suro, Roberto. 1992. "Clinton and Gore Choose Postcard Setting to Extol Traditional American Values." *New York Times* (July 12) 1:19.

Sutton-Smith, Brian. 1972. *The Folkgames of Children*. Austin: University of Texas Press.

———. 1981. *The Folkstories of Children*. Philadelphia: University of Pennsylvania Press.

Sutton-Smith, Brian, and Donna Kelly-Byrne, eds. 1984. *The Masks of Play*. West Point, New York: Leisure Press.

Sutton-Smith, Brian, Jay Mechling, Thomas W. Johnson, and Felicia R. McMahon, eds. 1995. *Children's Folklore: A Source Book*. New York: Garland.

Swank, Scott T. 1983. *Arts of the Pennsylvania Germans*. New York: W. W. Norton.

Sweterlitsch, Richard. 1996. "Fakelore." In *American Folklore: An Encyclopedia*, ed. Jan Harold Brunvand, 242. New York: Garland.

Taft, Michael. 1994. "1988–1994 Supplement to *The Centennial Index*." *Journal of American Folklore* 107:479–536.

Tatar, Maria. 1987. *The Hard Facts of the Grimms' Fairy Tales*. Princeton: Princeton University Press.

———. 1988. "Beauties vs. Beasts in the Grimms' *Nursery and Household Tales*." In *The Brothers Grimm and Folktale*, ed. James M. McGlathery, 133–45. Urbana: University of Illinois Press.

———. 1992. *Off with Their Heads! Fairy Tales and the Culture of Childhood*. Princeton: Princeton University Press.

Tate, Cecil F. 1973. *The Search for a Method in American Studies*. Minneapolis: University of Minnesota Press.

Taubman, Howard. 1964. "For Better or for Worse." *New York Times* (October 4) 2:1.

Taylor, Archer. 1949. "Folklore." In *Standard Dictionary of Folklore, Mythology, and Legend*, ed. Maria Leach, 402–3. New York: Funk and Wagnalls.

———. 1951. *English Riddles from Oral Tradition*. Berkeley: University of California Press.

———. 1965. "Recent Developments in Folk Atlases." *Journal of the Folklore Institute* 2:220–24.

———. 1972. *Comparative Studies in Folklore: Asia-Europe-America*. Taipei, Taiwan: Orient Cultural Service.

———. 1985. *The Proverb and an Index to "The Proverb."* 1931; rpt., Bern: Peter Lang.

Taylor, David A., and John Alexander Williams, eds. 1992. *Old Ties, New Attachments: Italian-American Folklife in the West*. Washington, D.C.: American Folklife Center, Library of Congress.

Taylor, Lonn W. 1980. "Fachwerk and Brettstuhl: The Rejection of Traditional Folk Culture." In *Perspectives on American Folk Art*, ed. Ian M. G. Quimby and Scott T. Swank, 162–76. New York: W. W. Norton.

Teske, Robert Thomas. 1979. "Living Room Furnishings, Ethnic Identity, and Acculturation among Greek Philadelphians." *New York Folklore* 5:21–32.

———. 1980. *Votive Offerings among Greek-Philadelphians.* New York: Arno Press.

———. 1983. "What Is Folk Art? An Opinion on the Controversy." *El Palacio* 88:34–38.

———. 1988. "State Folk Art Exhibitions: Review and Preview." In *The Conservation of Culture: Folklorists and the Public Sector*, ed. Burt Feintuch, 109–17. Lexington: University Press of Kentucky.

———. 1994. *Passed to the Present: Folk Arts along Wisconsin's Ethnic Settlement Trail.* Cedarburg, Wisconsin: Cedarburg Cultural Center.

Thigpen, Kenneth A. 1980. *Folklore and the Ethnicity Factor in the Lives of Romanian-Americans.* New York: Arno Press.

Thomas, William I. 1899. "Sex in Primitive Industry." *American Journal of Sociology* 4:474–88.

Thompson, E. P. 1955. *William Morris: From Romantic to Revolutionary.* London: Lawrence and Wishart.

Thompson, Laurence C. 1978. "Melville Jacobs (1902–1971)." *American Anthropologist* 80:640–46.

Thompson, Michael, Richard Ellis, and Aaron Wildavsky. 1990. *Cultural Theory.* Boulder, Colorado: Westview Press.

Thompson, Stith. 1928. *The Types of the Folktale: A Classification and Bibliography.* Folklore Fellows Communications, no. 74. Helsinki: Suomalainen Tiedeakatemia.

———. 1949. "Folklore." In *Standard Dictionary of Folklore, Mythology, and Legend*, ed. Maria Leach, 403. New York: Funk and Wagnalls.

———. 1951. "Folklore at Midcentury." *Midwest Folklore* 1:5–12.

———, ed. 1953. *Four Symposia on Folklore.* Bloomington: Indiana University Press.

———. 1959. "Prepared Comments." *Journal of American Folklore* 72:232.

———. [1953] 1965. "The Star Husband Tale." In *The Study of Folklore*, ed. Alan Dundes, 414–74. Englewood Cliffs, New Jersey: Prentice-Hall.

———. 1975. *Motif-Index of Folk-Literature.* 6 vols. 1955; rev. and enlarged ed., Bloomington: Indiana University Press.

———. 1977. *The Folktale.* 1946; rpt., Berkeley: University of California Press.

———. 1996. *A Folklorist's Progress: Reflections of a Scholar's Life*, ed. John H. McDowell, Inta Gale Carpenter, Donald Braid, Erika Peterson-Veatch. Bloomington: Special Publications of the Folklore Institute, no. 5, Indiana University.

Thoms, William. 1858. *Choice Notes from "Notes and Queries": Folk Lore.* London: Bell and Daldy.

———. [1846] 1965. "Folklore." In *The Study of Folklore*, ed. Alan Dundes, 4–6. Englewood Cliffs, New Jersey: Prentice-Hall.

Thomsen, Fred. 1993. "Plowing It Back: Harold W. Thompson and the New York Folklore Society, 1945–1957." *New York Folklore Quarterly* 10:57–74.

Tichi, Cecilia. 1994. *High Lonesome: The American Culture of Country Music.* Chapel Hill: University of North Carolina Press.

Tidwell, James N., ed. 1956. *A Treasury of American Folk Humor.* New York: Crown.

Titon, Jeff Todd. 1977. *Early Downhome Blues: A Musical and Cultural Analysis.* Urbana: University of Illinois Press.

———. 1980. "The Life Story." *Journal of American Folklore* 93:276–92.

———. 1988. *Powerhouse for God: Speech, Chant, and Song in an Appalachian Baptist Church.* Austin: University of Texas Press.

———. 1993. "Reconstructing the Blues: Reflections on the 1960s Blues Revival." In *Transforming Tradition: Folk Music Revivals Examined,* ed. Neil V. Rosenberg, 220–40. Urbana: University of Illinois Press.

Toelken, Barre. 1979. *The Dynamics of Folklore.* Boston: Houghton Mifflin.

———. 1986. "The Folklore of Academe." In *The Study of American Folklore: An Introduction,* by Jan Harold Brunvand, 502–28. New York: W. W. Norton.

———. 1996. *The Dynamics of Folklore.* Rev. and expanded ed., Logan: Utah State University.

Tokofsky, Peter. 1996. "Folk-Lore and *Volks-Kunde*: Compounding Compounds." *Journal of Folklore Research* 33:207–11.

Tomasky, Michael. 1996. *Left for Dead: The Life, Death, and Possible Resurrection of Progressive Politics in America.* New York: Free Press.

Tomlan, Michael A. 1992. *Tinged with Gold: Hop Culture in the United States.* Athens: University of Georgia Press.

Trachtenberg, Alan. 1982. *The Incorporation of America: Culture and Society in the Gilded Age.* New York: Hill and Wang.

Treadwell, Margaret. 1930. "A Chinese Boy Who Could Not Learn to Tremble." *Journal of American Folklore* 43:119.

Trent, Robert F. 1977. *Hearts & Crowns: Folk Chairs of the Connecticut Coast.* New Haven: New Haven Colony Historical Society.

Truman, Ben C. 1893. *History of the World's Fair.* Chicago: Ben C. Truman.

Tuan, Yi-Fu. 1989. "Traditional: What Does it Mean?" In *Dwellings, Settlements and Tradition: Cross-Cultural Perspectives,* ed. Jean-Paul Bourdier and Nezar Alsayyad, 27–34. Lanham, Maryland: University Press of America.

Tucker, Elizabeth. 1977. "Tradition and Creativity in the Storytelling of Pre-Adolescent Girls." Ph.D. diss., Indiana University.

———. 1992. "'Texts, Lies and Videotape': Can Oral Tales Survive?" *Children's Folklore Review* 15:25–32.

Tullos, Allen. 1989. *Habits of Industry: White Culture and the Transformation of the Carolina Piedmont.* Chapel Hill: University of North Carolina Press.

Turner, Arlin, ed. 1958. *The Negro Question: A Selection of Writings on Civil Rights in the South.* Garden City: Doubleday.

Turner, Patricia A. 1992. "Ambivalent Patrons: The Role of Rumor and Contemporary Legends in African-American Consumer Decisions." *Journal of American Folklore* 105:403–23.

———. 1993. *I Heard It Through the Grapevine: Rumor in African-American Culture.* Berkeley: University of California Press.

Turner, Terence. 1993. "Anthropology and Multiculturalism: What is Anthropology that Multiculturalists Should Be Mindful of It?" *Cultural Anthropology* 8:411–29.

Turney, Ida. 1941. *Paul Bunyan, The Work Giant.* Portland, Oregon: Binford and Mort.

"A Twenty-Year Tradition: Female Cadets." 1994. *Atlanta Constitution* (September 16), F1.

Twain, Mark. [1889] 1979. *A Connecticut Yankee in King Arthur's Court,* ed. Bernard L. Stein. Berkeley: University of California Press.

Twining, Mary Arnold, ed. 1987. "The New Nomads: Art, Life, and Lore of Migrant Workers in New York State." Special issue of *New York Folklore* 13(1–2).

Tylor, Edward. 1970. *The Origins of Culture.* 1871; rpt., Gloucester, Massachusetts: Peter Smith.

Untermeyer, Louis. 1946. *The Wonderful Adventures of Paul Bunyan.* New York: Heritage Press.

Upton, Dell, ed. 1986. *America's Architectural Roots: Ethnic Groups that Built America.* Washington, D.C.: Preservation Press.

Upton, Dell, and John Michael Vlach, eds. 1986. *Common Places: Readings in American Vernacular Architecture.* Athens: University of Georgia Press.

Utley, Francis Lee. 1952. "Conflict and Promise in Folklore." *Journal of American Folklore* 65:111–19.

———. [1961] 1965. "Folk Literature: An Operational Definition." In *The Study of Folklore*, ed. Alan Dundes, 7–24. Englewood Cliffs, New Jersey: Prentice-Hall.

———. 1974. "The Migration of Folktales: Four Channels to the Americas." *Current Anthropology* 15:5–27.

Van Gennep, Arnold. 1985. *Folklore.* Trans. Austin Fife. 1924; rpt., Middletown, Pennsylvania: Folklore Historian.

Vance, Lee J. 1887. "Folk-Lore Studies." *Open Court* 1:612–13, 662–65.

———. 1893. "Folk-Lore Study in America." *Popular Science Monthly* 43:586–98.

———. 1896/1897. "The Study of Folk-Lore." *Forum* 22:249–56.

Van Dommelen, David B. 1985. "Allen Eaton: In Quest of Beauty." *American Craft* 45(June/July):35–39.

Varenne, Hervé, ed. 1986. *Symbolizing America.* Lincoln: University of Nebraska Press.

Veblen, Thorstein. 1899. "The Barbarian Status of Women." *American Journal of Sociology* 4:503–14.

Vecsey, George. 1987. "Facing the Legends." *New York Times* (June 11), D23.

Veigle, Anne. 1990. "Amish Adapt to Farming Drop, 'Reach Out' Into Outside World." *Washington Times* (October 26), C1.

Velkomer, Walter E., ed. 1969. *The Liberal Tradition in American Thought: An Anthology.* New York: Putnam.

Verney, K. J. 1996. "'Roads Not Taken': Booker T. Washington and Black Leadership in the United States, 1895–1915." *Borderlines: Studies in American Culture* 3:144–58.

Virtanen, Leea. 1978. *Children's Lore.* Helsinki: Finnish Literature Society.

Vlach, John Michael. 1978. *Afro-American Tradition in Decorative Arts.* Cleveland: Cleveland Museum of Arts.

———. 1980. "American Folk Art: Questions and Quandaries." *Winterthur Portfolio* 15:345–55.

———. 1985a. "The Concept of Community and Folklife Study." In *American Material Culture and Folklife*, ed. Simon J. Bronner, 63–75. Ann Arbor: UMI Research Press.

———. 1985b. "Holger Cahill as Folklorist." *Journal of American Folklore* 98:148–62.

———. 1988. *Plain Painters: Making Sense of American Folk Art.* Washington, D.C.: Smithsonian Institution Press.

———. 1991a. *By the Work of Their Hands: Studies in Afro-American Folklife.* Ann Arbor: UMI Research Press.

———. 1991b. "The Wrong Stuff." *New Art Examiner* (September):22–24.

———. 1992. *Charleston Blacksmith: The Work of Philip Simmons.* 1981; rpt., Columbia: University of South Carolina Press.

———. 1993. *Back of the Big House: The Architecture of Plantation Slavery.* Chapel Hill: University of North Carolina Press.

Vlach, John Michael, and Simon J. Bronner, eds. 1992. *Folk Art and Art Worlds.* 1986; rpt., Logan: Utah State University Press.

Voget, Fred. 1975. *A History of Ethnology.* New York: Holt, Rinehart and Winston.

Voigt, Vilmos. 1980. "Folklore and 'Folklorism' Today." In *Folklore Studies in the Twentieth Century*, ed. Venetia Newall, 419–24. Totowa, New Jersey: Rowman and Littlefield.

———. 1983. "Folklore Function in the Development of Creativity: An Overview of Hungarian Experiences and Some General Examples." *Ethnologia Europaea* 13:180–88.

von Sydow, C. W. 1948. *Selected Papers on Folklore.* Copenhagen: Rosenkilde and Bagger.

Wachs, Eleanor. 1988. *Crime-Victim Stories: New York City's Urban Folklore.* Bloomington: Indiana University Press.

Wadsworth, Wallace. 1926. *Paul Bunyan and His Great Blue Ox.* New York: Doubleday.

Wagner, Roy. 1981. *The Invention of Culture.* Rev. and expanded ed., Chicago: University of Chicago Press.

Walker, F. R. 1905. "Sioux Games." *Journal of American Folklore* 18:277–90.

———. 1917. "The Sun Dance and Other Ceremonies of the Oglala Division of the Teton Dakota." *American Museum of Natural History Anthropological Papers* 16:51–221.

Walls, Robert E. 1996. "Bunyan, Paul." In *American Folklore: An Encyclopedia*, ed. Jan Harold Brunvand, 105–7. New York: Garland.

Ward, Daniel Franklin, ed. 1984. *Personal Places: Perspectives on Informal Art Environments.* Bowling Green, Ohio: Bowling Green State University Popular Press.

Ward, Donald, ed. and trans. 1981. *The German Legends of the Brothers Grimm.* Philadelphia: Institute for the Study of Human Issues.

———. 1988. "New Misconceptions about Old Folktales: The Brothers Grimm." In *The Brothers Grimm and Folktale*, ed. James M. McGlathery, 91–100. Urbana: University of Illinois Press.

———. 1994. "The German Connection: The Brothers Grimm and the Study of 'Oral' Literature." *Western Folklore* 53:1–26.

Ward, Lester Frank. 1888. "Our Better Halves." *Forum* 6:266–75.

Washington, Georgia. 1895. "Notes from Alabama—Courtship Dialogue and Signs and Superstitions." *Southern Workman* 24:78–79.

Washington, William De Hertburn. 1911. *Progress and Prosperity.* New York: National Educational Publishing.

Warner, Marina. 1993. "Women Against Women in the Old Wives' Tale." In *Cinema and the Realms of Enchantment*, ed. Duncan Petrie, 63–84. London: British Film Institute.

Warren, Kenneth W. 1996. "African American Cultural Movements." In *Encyclopedia of the United States in the Twentieth Century*, ed. Stanley I. Kutler, vol. 4, 1593–1607. New York: Charles Scribner's Sons.

Warshaver, Gerald E. 1991. "On Postmodern Folklore." *Western Folklore* 50:219–29.

Watanabe, Teresa. 1997. "The Boom Brigade: Japanese Teen Queens Rule the Trend Market" (June 8), 9.

Waterman, Richard A. 1949–50. "Folklore." In *Standard Dictionary of Folklore*, ed. Maria Leach, vol. 1, 403. New York: Funk & Wagnalls.

Waters, Donald, ed. 1983. *Strange Ways and Sweet Dreams: Afro-American Folklore from the Hampton Institute.* Boston: G. K. Hall.

Waters, Harry F. 1977. "After Haley's Comet." *Newsweek* (February 14), 97–98.

Waters, Mary C. 1990. *Ethnic Options: Choosing Identities in America.* Berkeley: University of California Press.

Watson, John F. 1857. *Annals of Philadelphia and Pennsylvania in the Olden Time.* 2 vols. 1830; rpt., Philadelphia: Elijah Thomas.

Watson, Wilbur H., ed. 1984. *Black Folk Medicine: The Therapeutic Significance of Faith and Trust.* New Brunswick, New Jersey: Transaction Books.

Wattenberg, Ben J. 1995. *Values Matter Most: How Democrats or Republicans or a Third Party Can Win and Renew the American Way of Life.* Washington, D.C.: Regnery Publishing.

"Wearing Your Right to Free Speech." 1997. *Japan Times* (June 9), 9.

Weaver, William Woys. 1986. "The Pennsylvania German House: European Antecedents and New World Forms." *Winterthur Portfolio* 21(1986):243–64.

Webb, Bernida. 1993. "Multiculturalism Key in Children's Books." *Times-Picayune* (New Orleans) (June 27), B4.

Wehr, Julian. 1945. *Snow White.* New York: Dutton.

Weigle, Marta, and Peter White. 1988. *The Lore of New Mexico.* Albuquerque: University of New Mexico Press.

Weiner, Michael, ed. 1997. *Japan's Minorities: The Illusion of Homogeneity.* London: Routledge.

Weiser, Frederick. 1991. "Publications of the Pennsylvania German Society and Its Predecessors, 1891–1991." *Der Reggeboge : Journal of the Pennsylvania German Society* 25:1–32.

Weissman, Lael. 1991. "Herder, Folklore, and Modern Humanism." *Folklore Forum* 24:51–65.

Wells, William. 1873. "Folk-Life in German By-Ways." *Scribner's Monthly* 5:590–601.

Welsch, Roger L. 1966. "Nebraska Finger Games." *Western Folklore* 25:173–94.

———. 1968. *Sod Walls: The Story of the Nebraska Sod House.* Broken Bow, Nebraska: Purcells.

West, John O. 1988. *Mexican-American Folklore.* Little Rock: August House.

Westerman, William. 1996. "Politics and Folklore." In *American Folklore: An Encyclopedia,* ed. Jan Harold Brunvand, 570–74. New York: Garland.

Westin, Jeane E. 1977. *Finding Your Roots: How Every American Can Trace His Ancestors at Home and Abroad.* New York: St. Martin's.

Whisnant, David E. 1983. *All That Is Native and Fine: The Politics of Culture in an American Region.* Chapel Hill: University of North Carolina Press.

White, Jessie Braham. 1913. *Snow White and the Seven Dwarfs: A Fairy Tale Play Based on the Story of the Brothers Grimm.* New York: Dodd, Mead.

Whiting, Robert. 1989. *You Gotta Have Wa.* New York: Vintage.

"Why 'Roots' Hit Home." 1977. *Time* (February 14), 69–71.

Widner, Ronna Lee. 1986. "Lore for the Folk: Benjamin A. Botkin and the Development of Folklore Scholarship in America." *New York Folklore* 12:1–22.

Wiebe, Robert H. 1975. *The Segmented Society: An Introduction to the Meaning of America.* New York: Oxford University Press.

Wiggins, William H., Jr. 1987. *O Freedom! Afro-American Emancipation Celebrations.* Knoxville: University of Tennessee Press.

Wigginton, Eliot, ed. 1972. *The Foxfire Book.* Garden City, New York: Anchor Books.

———. 1974. "A Reply to 'The Lesson of Foxfire.'" *North Carolina Folklore Journal* 22:35–41.

———. 1978. "Comment." *North Carolina Folklore Journal* 26:14–17.

———. 1989. "Foxfire." In *Encyclopedia of Southern Culture,* ed. Charles Reagan Wilson and William Ferris, 284–85. Chapel Hill: University of North Carolina Press.

Wildhaber, Robert. 1972. "Folk Atlas Mapping." In *Folklore and Folklife: An Introduction,* ed. Richard M. Dorson, 479–96. Chicago: University of Chicago Press.

Wiley, Fletcher H. 1995. "Affirmative Action: An American Tradition." *Boston Globe* (April 2), 73.

Wilgus, D. K. 1959. *Anglo-American Folksong Scholarship.* New Brunswick, New Jersey: Rutgers University Press.

Will, George F. 1912. "Some Hidatsa and Mandan Tales." *Journal of American Folklore* 25:93–94.

Williams, Dick. 1992. "Press's Disdain for Dan Quayle is Self-Evident." *Atlanta Journal* (July 28), A8.

Williams, John Alexander. 1975. "Radicalism and Professionalism in Folklore Studies: A Comparative Perspective." *Journal of the Folklore Institute* 11:211–34.

Williams, Michael Ann. 1991. *Homeplace: The Social Use and Meaning of the Folk Dwelling in Southwestern North Carolina.* Athens: University of Georgia Press.

———. 1995. *Great Smoky Mountains Folklife.* Jackson: University Press of Mississippi.

Williams, Raymond. 1983. *Keywords: A Vocabulary of Culture and Society.* Rev. ed., New York: Oxford University Press.

Williams, Stacey. 1965. *Liner Notes to The Newport Folk Festival—1964, Evening Concerts.* Vol. 3. Vanguard VRS-9186.

Wilson, Charles Reagan, and William Ferris, eds. 1989. *Encyclopedia of Southern Culture.* Chapel Hill: University of North Carolina Press.

Wilson, Joe. 1996. "Blues and Bluegrass: Tough Arts of the Underclass." In *The Changing Faces of Tradition,* ed. Elizabeth Peterson, 82–89. Washington, D.C.: National Endowment for the Arts.

Wilson, Thomas. 1893. "Primitive Industry." *Smithsonian Institution Annual for 1892.* Washington, D.C.: Government Printing Office.

Wilson, William A. 1973. "Herder, Folklore and Romantic Nationalism." *Journal of Popular Culture* 6:819–35.

———. 1976. *Folklore and Nationalism in Modern Finland.* Bloomington: Indiana University Press.

———. 1982a. *On Being Human: The Folklore of Mormon Missionaries.* Logan: Utah State University Press.

———. 1982b. "On Being Human: The Folklore of Mormon Missionaries." *New York Folklore* 18:5–28.

———. 1982c. "Richard M. Dorson's Theory for American Folklore: A Finnish Analogue." *Western Folklore* 41:36–42.

———. 1989. "Richard M. Dorson as Romantic-Nationalist." *Journal of Folklore Research* 26:35–42.

———. 1991. "The 1990 Archer Taylor Memorial Lecture. Personal Narratives: The Family Novel." *Western Folklore* 50:127–50.

———. 1996. "Building Bridges: Folklore in the Academy." *Journal of Folklore Research* 33:7–14.

Winchester, Alice. 1974. "Introduction." In *The Flowering of American Folk Art, 1776–1876,* by Jean Lipman and Alice Winchester, 8–14. New York: Viking.

Winkler, Karen J. 1994. "Anthropologists Urged to Rethink Their Definitions of Culture." *Chronicle of Higher Education* (December 14), A18.

Winslow, David. 1972. "The Rural Square Dance in the Northeastern United States: A Continuity of Tradition." Ph.D. diss, University of Pennsylvania.

Winthrop, Robert H. 1991. *Dictionary of Concepts in Cultural Anthropology.* New York: Greenwood.

Wise, Gene. 1979. "'Paradigm Dramas' in American Studies: A Cultural and Institutional History of the Movement." *American Quarterly* 31:293–337.

Wissler, Clark. 1907. "Some Dakota Myths I–II." *Journal of American Folklore* 20:121–31, 195–206.

Wolf, Thomas. 1979. *Presenting Performances: A Handbook for Sponsors.* Cambridge: New England Foundation for the Arts.

Wolfe, Ruth. 1997. "Nina Fletcher Little: Bridging the Worlds of Antiques and Folk Art." *Folk Art* 22 (Summer):29-37.

Wolitz, Seth L. 1988. "The Americanization of Tevye or Boarding the Jewish *Mayflower*." *American Quarterly* 40:514–36.

Wollenweber, L. A. 1869. *Gemälde aus dem Pennsylvanischen Volksleben*. Philadelphia: Schäfer und Koradi.

———. 1974. *Mountain Mary: An Historical Tale of Early Pennsylvania*. Trans. and introduced by John Joseph Stoudt. 1880; rpt., York, Pennsylvania: Liberty Cap Books.

Workman, Mark E. 1989. "Folklore in the Wilderness: Folklore and Postmodernism." *Midwestern Folklore* 15:5–14.

"World's Wonder Toys at Brooklyn Museum." 1920. *Playthings* (May):105–10.

Wright, Gwendolyn. 1981. *Building the Dream: A Social History of Housing in America*. New York: Pantheon.

Writers' Program of the Works Projects Administration in the State of Pennsylvania. 1940. *Pennsylvania: A Guide to the Keystone State*. New York: Oxford University Press.

Wylie, Laura Johnson. 1916. *Social Studies in English Literature*. Boston: Houghton Mifflin.

Yoachum, Susan. 1993. "Powerhouse Behind Lobbying Effort for 'Traditional Values.'" *San Francisco Chronicle* (September 13):A7.

Yoder, Don, ed. 1949. "Dubbs Describes Our Dialect." *Pennsylvania Dutchman* 1(15):5.

———. 1951. "Let's Take Our Blinders Off!" *Pennsylvania Dutchman* 3(1):1, 5–6.

———. 1963. "The Folklife Studies Movement." *Pennsylvania Folklife* 13(3):43–56.

———. 1969. "Sectarian Costume Research in the United States." In *Forms on the Frontier: Folklife and Folk Arts in the United States*, ed. Austin and Alta Fife and Henry H. Glassie, 41–75. Logan: Utah State University Press.

———. 1971. "Pennsylvania German Folklore Research: A Historical Analysis." In *The German Language in America: A Symposium*, ed. Glenn G. Gilbert, 70–105. Austin: University of Texas Press.

———. 1972. "Folk Costume." In *Folklore and Folklife: An Introduction*, ed. Richard M. Dorson, 295–324. Chicago: University of Chicago Press.

———, ed. 1976a. *American Folklife*. Austin: University of Texas Press.

———. 1976b. "Folklife Studies in American Scholarship." In *American Folklife*, ed. Don Yoder, 3–18. Austin: University of Texas Press.

———. 1982. "Folklife in Pennsylvania: An Historical Survey." *Keystone Folklore*, n.s., 1:8–20.

———. 1983. "The Pennsylvania German Connection." *F&M Today* 12(November):8–12.

———. 1990. *Discovering American Folklife: Studies in Ethnic, Religious, and Regional Culture*. Ann Arbor, Michigan: UMI Research Press.

Yoder, Don, and Thomas E. Graves. 1989. *Hex Signs: Pennsylvania Dutch Barn Symbols and Their Meaning*. New York: E. P. Dutton.

Yoffie, Leah R. C. 1916. "Present-Day Survivals of Ancient Jewish Customs." *Journal of American Folklore* 29:412–17.

Yolen, Jane. 1981. *Sleeping Ugly*. New York: Coward, McCann and Geoghegan.

———. [1977] 1982. "America's Cinderella." In *Cinderella: A Folklore Casebook*, ed. Alan Dundes, 294–306. New York: Garland.

———. 1983. *Tales of Wonder*. New York: Schocken.

———. 1989. *The Faery Flag: Stories of Fantasy and the Supernatural*. New York: Orchard.

———. 1993. *Here There Be Dragons*. New York: Harcourt Brace.

Zaretzke, Kenneth. 1982. "The Idea of Tradition." *Intercollegiate Review* 17:85–98.

Zeitlin, Steven J., Amy J. Kotkin, and Holly Cutting Baker. 1982. *A Celebration of American Family Folklore: Tales and Traditions from the Smithsonian Collection.* New York: Pantheon Books.

Zelinsky, Wilbur. 1973. *The Cultural Geography of the United States.* Englewood Cliffs, New Jersey: Prentice-Hall.

———. 1977. "The Pennsylvania Town: An Overdue Geographical Account." *Geographical Review* 67:127–47.

Zemljanova, L. M. 1964. "The Struggle between the Reactionary and the Progressive Forces in Contemporary American Folkloristics." *Journal of the Folklore Institute* 1:130–44.

Ziegler, Samuel H. 1943. "Pennsylvania German Folklore Society." *Journal of American Folklore* 56:182–83.

Zipes, Jack. 1979. *Breaking the Magic Spell: Radical Theories of Folk and Fairy Tales.* Austin: University of Texas Press.

———, ed. 1986a. *Don't Bet on the Prince: Contemporary Feminist Fairy Tales in North America and England.* New York: Methuen.

———. 1986b. "The Grimms and the German Obsession with Fairy Tales." In *Fairy Tales and Society: Illusion, Allusion, and Paradigm,* ed. Ruth B. Bottigheimer, 271–86. Philadelphia: University of Pennsylvania Press.

———, trans. 1987. *The Complete Fairy Tales of the Brothers Grimm.* New York: Bantam.

———. 1988a. *The Brothers Grimm: From Enchanted Forests to the Modern World.* New York: Routledge.

———. 1988b. *Fairy Tales and the Art of Subversion: The Classical Genre for Children and the Process of Civilization.* New York: Methuen.

———. 1993. *The Trials and Tribulations of Little Red Riding Hood: Versions of the Tale in Sociocultural Context.* New York: Routledge.

———. 1994. *Fairy Tale as Myth/ Myth as Fairy Tale.* Lexington: University Press of Kentucky.

Zorn, Steven. 1992. *Classic American Folk Tales.* Philadelphia: Courage Books.

Zuckerman, Michael. 1982. "Introduction: Puritans, Cavaliers, and the Motley Middle." In *Friends and Neighbors: Group Life in America's First Plural Society,* ed. Michael Zuckerman, 3–25. Philadelphia: Temple University Press.

Zug, Charles G., III. 1986. *Turners and Burners: The Folk Potters of North Carolina.* Chapel Hill: University of North Carolina Press.

Zumwalt, Rosemary. 1988. *American Folklore Scholarship: A Dialogue of Dissent.* Bloomington: Indiana University Press.

———. 1992. *Wealth and Rebellion: Elsie Clews Parsons, Anthropologist and Folklorist.* Urbana: University of Illinois Press.

Index

Index   591

Bauman, Richard, 18, 155, 233, 410, 454–56, 460

Baver, Florence, 301, 302

Bayard, Samuel P., 151, 223, 264, 327, 328, 331, 335, 337–40

Beam, C. Richard, 302

Beard, Charles, 352

Beard, George M., 96

Beauty and the Beast, 192

Bechstein, Ludwig, 196

Becker, Howard S., 453

Beckwith, Martha Warren, birth of, 239; career of, 7, 238, 241, 243, 247–54, 262; contributions of, 237, 264, 265, 398, 423, 449, 450, 479; death of, 264; education of, 239, 241, 244; students of, 238; writings of, 22, 225, 238, 243–46, 254–57, 259, 260, 262, 264

Beecher, Henry Ward, 98

Ben-Amos, Dan, 18, 42, 46, 47, 177, 233, 401, 402, 454, 455

Benedict, Ruth, 132, 247, 248

Benet, Stephen Vincent, 367

Bennett, Gillian, 153, 183

Bennett, William J., 55, 68

Benton, Thomas Hart, 368

Bergen, Fanny D., 417

Berlin University, 218

Bernstein, Richard J., 469

Bettelheim, Bruno, 205

bicentennial celebration of American independence, 32, 33, 266

Billington, James, 308

Bird, George O., 300, 301

Blair, Walter, 394

Bluebeard, 192

Bly, Robert, 216, 217

Boas, Franz, career of, 129–35, 431; contributions of, 137, 149, 151, 177, 253, 372, 373, 394, 397; influence of, 17, 109, 232, 233; students of, 241, 244–48, 256, 261, 356; writings of, 22, 23, 45, 139, 152, 237

Boggs, Ralph Steele, 282, 283, 285

Bogguss, Suzie, 214

Bolte, Johannes, 230

Bontemps, Arna, 129

Boone and Crockett Club, 95, 323

Boone, Daniel, 323

Boorstin, Daniel, 351, 352, 375, 399

Botkin, Benjamin A., 29, 214, 254, 290, 326, 328, 340, 353, 358, 362–64, 367–69, 375–87, 390, 391, 398, 399, 402, 403, 407

Bottigheimer, Ruth B., 235

Bourke, John G., 74, 132

Bourland, C. B., 247

Bourne, Randolph, 3

Brendle, Thomas, 282, 301

Brentano, Clemens, 190–93

Brer Rabbit, 110–14, 375

Brinton, Daniel, 77, 79, 132, 415

Brooklyn Institute Museum, 77, 81

Brooks, Garth, 214

Brooks, Van Wyck, 30, 354

Brothers Grimm. *See* Grimm, Jacob and Wilhelm

Brown, Charles E., 371

Brown University, 73

Brunner, Hattie, 416

Brunvand, Jan Harold, 20, 179, 310, 360

Bucknell University, 285, 324

Buffington, Albert F., 285

Bunyan, Paul, 29, 337, 358, 364, 365–67, 369–72, 379, 381, 398

Burchenal, Elizabeth, 449

Bureau of American Ethnology (BAE), 74, 78, 99, 100, 130, 131

Burne, Charlotte Sophia, 16, 144, 149, 221

Bush, George, 55, 58, 59

Butcher, Philip, 106

Cable, George Washington, 103–9, 111, 118

Cadzow, Donald, 328, 330, 331, 336, 340

Cahill, Holger, 424–28, 432–36, 441, 443, 444

Caldwell, Erskine, 327

California Folklore Society, 66

Campbell, Åke, 299

Campbell, Marie, 229

Canby, Henry Seidel, 432

Cantwell, Robert, 25

Carlisle Indian School, 52

Carpenter, George R., 315

Cather, Katherine Dunlap, 205

Chamberlain, Alexander F., 84, 164, 165, 173

Chaplin, Charlie, 208

Chase, Mary Ellen, 426